THE HERB BOOK

John B. Lust, N.D., D.B.M.

BANTAM BOOKS

TORONTO • NEW YORK • LONDON • SYDNEY • AUCKLAND

RL 11, IL age 13 and up

THE HERB BOOK
*A Bantam Book / published by arrangement with
Benedict Lust Publications*

PRINTING HISTORY
Benedict Lust edition published May 1974
2nd printing . . . October 1974
Bantam edition / December 1974

2nd printing ...... February 1975	9th printing .... August 1978
3rd printing .... July 1975	10th printing .... April 1979
4th printing .... April 1976	11th printing ..... February 1980
5th printing .... September 1976	12th printing .... August 1980
6th printing .... January 1977	13th printing .... March 1980
7th printing .... November 1977	14th printing .... August 1981
8th printing .... July 1978	15th printing .... June 1982

16th printing . . . June 1983
Bantam UK edition / September 1986

ISBN 0-553-17273-5

Published simultaneously in the United States and Canada

Printed and bound in Great Britain by
Cox & Wyman Ltd., Reading

THE HERB BOOK

has been called "The Natural Remedy Bible" . . . Crammed full of case histories, herbal formulas, full, yet concise descriptions of herbs, their properties and uses, the majority of them illustrated, THE HERB BOOK explains in easy-to-understand language how you may use Nature's gentle medicines to build a livelier, healthier, happier life!

Jean Brown.
Please return is Book
Shelf when you have
finished reading.

I dedicate this book to my wife, Virginia.

To all those who helped me during the years
of preparation I extend my grateful acknowledgment
with special thanks to:

Willard R. Carter

Dr. Christian Fey

Gisela Harbs

Dr. Walter Kempner

Ann and Klaus Krause

Alfred Leo

Dr. G. Lorenz

Dr. Benedict Lust

Barbara Lust

Paul Lust

Herbert Nachman

Dr. Barbara Newborg

Ralph Pereida

Tobi Sanders

James "Bud" Smith

Elsie Wheeler

CONTENTS

	Page
PREFACE	ix
How to Use This Book	xi

PART 1
Herbs and History	3
The World of the Plant	10
What Is a Plant?	11
The Names of Plants	16
Glossary of Botanical Terms	18
Getting and Keeping Herbs	25
The Call of the Wild: Roughing It	25
The Herb Garden: Do It Yourself	26
The Herb Dealer: Path of Least Resistance	27
Drying Herbs	28
Storing Herbs	29
Commercial Sources of Herbs and Herb Products	30
How to Make and Use Herb Preparations	36
Glossary of Medicinal Effects and Herbs That Produce Them	48
Plants Applicable to Various Conditions and Body Organs	59

PART 2   A COMPENDIUM OF BOTANICAL MEDICINE
Introduction	84
Listing of Plants	87

Alphabetical List of Herbs: English Names 420

Alphabetical List of Herbs: Latin Botanical Names .. 444

PART 3
Introduction 453

Herbal Mixtures: Formulas for Health 454

Eat, Drink, and Be Healthy 493
    Protein 494
    Vitamins 496
    Minerals 501
    Fats and Carbohydrates 506
    Enzymes 507
    Hormones 508

Herbs and Spices: The Art of Seasoning 509

Plants Are for Drinking 520
    Herb Teas 520
    Coffee Substitutes 526
    Juices 527
    Alcoholic Beverages 528

Beauty from Plants: Some Natural Cosmetics 530

Scents—Common and Uncommon 537

Dyes in Living Color 542
    General Information About Dyeing 544
    List of Plant Dyes by Color 546
    List of Plant Dyes by Plant 549

A Plant Miscellany 565

Plants and Astrology 571

Legend and Lore 575

Bibliography and References 625

Index 634
    Comprehensive Botanical Index 603
    Plant Index 634
    General Index 646
    List of Plants by Botanical Name 617

PREFACE

A summer day dawns in the rolling foothills of New Jersey's Ramapo Mountains . . . lacy mist shimmers above a lake of polished silver . . . dew glistens with new light on thick meadow grass, plants, and bushes.

The only sounds are the protests of quail flushed from their nesting places—aroused by the presence of a big, kindly, white-haired man as he pushes through the rich undergrowth. He is tanned, his white linen shirt open at the neck; his khaki trousers and sandals are wet from the dew.

He seems in harmony with the natural beauty that surrounds him.

A young lad trails along at his heels. They pause at a patch of flowering shrubs, and the man bends down almost as if to introduce a distinctive plant to the boy. "Look here," he says, "this fragrant plant is American angelica. Tea made from it will quickly restore your appetite if you've lost it." The boy, intrigued by the man's knowledge of the plant and its effectiveness as a remedy, listens intently and files the information in his memory for future use.

The man was Dr. Benedict Lust, the father of naturopathy, and I was the lad. It was almost 40 years ago. If there was ever a point in time I could say was the genesis of this book, it was that beautiful summer morning in the Paradise Gardens of my uncle's Yungborn Health Resort.

During the years that followed, my studies in natural healing revealed to me the importance of herbal medicine. I was convinced that man's relationship with Nature was the key to a long, satisfying and sickness-free life. That conviction grew stronger and stronger as I studied the works of natural healing method pioneers and observed the results of these methods on patients. Most helpful were the various experiments and tests I conducted on myself, without experiencing the harmful side effects of chemical drugs. Invariably, the results were beneficial: the longer a treatment was followed and the more compatible it was with Nature, the greater were the benefits.

Practice and research have proved that trust in herbal medicine is justified. The modern doctor who is open to a more natural approach can make use of this trust for the successful treatment of his patients. But this book does not want to infringe on the domain of the doctor; rather, it would meet the doctor halfway by educating his patients in the use of remedies made from plants and by awakening in them the will to be cured.

We still clearly observe in sick animals the curative instinct that drives them to hunt out and eat a specific plant as a remedy. This same instinct in man is numbered by a hypnotizing barrage of advertising for chemical-drug medicines. Even so, in all of us there still survives an intuitive preference for the natural healing powers of Nature's life line, the great continuum of life that both contains and sustains us. In relying on these powers, we recollect the primal strength of Nature and renew our bond to the only true healing force in existence: Nature herself. By cooperating with the inherent restorative power of the living organism, we attune ourselves once again to the rhythm of Nature. We grasp the living spirit!

As you take hold of Nature's life line, I hope that this book—born on a summer day long past—may help to bring you the eternal season of good health.

Durham, North Carolina   John B. Lust
May, 1973

HOW TO
USE THIS BOOK

THE HERB BOOK, like Gaul in Caesar's time, is divided into three main parts:

PART 1 contains introductory historical information, the background information to help you understand and put to use the rest of the book, and preliminary reference lists of plants with their properties and applicability to various ailments.

PART 2 contains the compendium of "materia medica," the individual numbered listings of medicinal plants with their botanical descriptions and their uses. Indexes of the plants by common and botanical names follow the compendium.

PART 3 emphasizes the variety of uses available for the plants listed in Part 2, and for many others, including plant mixtures for medicinal uses, nutritious and culinary plants, cosmetic and aromatic uses, plant dyes, and miscellaneous uses. It ends with astrology, lore, and legend, reflecting the psychological role of plants in man's history.

When looking for information, the two places to begin are the front and the back: the Table of Contents and the General Index. In most cases, these will quickly get you to the appropriate page or section. For the following specific types of information, you might consult the indicated sections in the order given.

1. To find a remedy for a specific medical problem:
   Herbal Mixtures (Part 3)
   Plants Applicable to Various Conditions (Part 1)
   Corresponding Compendium Listings (Part 2)
   How to Make and Use Herb Preparations (Part 1)

2. To find plants that produce certain medicinal effects:
   Glossary of Medicinal Effects (Part 1)
   Corresponding Compendium Listings (Part 2)
   How to Make and Use Herb Preparations (Part 1)

3. To find general medicinal information on a specific plant:
   Compendium Indexes (Part 2)
   Appropriate Compendium Listing (Part 2)

4. To identify a plant by a common or botanical name:
   Comprehensive Botanical Index (Following Part 3)
   Compendium Indexes (Part 2)

But don't wait until you need help: get acquainted with **The Herb Book** by browsing through its pages at your leisure and it will become an old friend, ready to serve you whenever the need arises.

PART 1

HERBS
AND HISTORY

Herbalism—the knowledge and study of herbs—may not be a term in your active vocabulary, but it is a reality in your life. The mustard on your table and many of the spices on your kitchen shelf come from herbs; most of the vegetables in your salad are herbs; and, if you have a yard, many of the plants growing there (whether by your or their own design) are also herbs. And whether you are a beginner, whose concern with herbs has been confined to clearing dandelions and other "weeds" out of your lawn, or an old-timer whose fingers are practically rooted in your own herb garden, this book is intended to bring you pleasure and useful information.

To begin at the beginning, an herb is defined as a non-woody plant that dies down to the ground after flowering. But the term *herb* is often applied more generally to any plant, part or all of which has been used for such purposes as medical treatment, nutritional value, food seasoning, or coloring and dyeing of other substances. The wider definition is the one most applicable to this book.

Historically, the most important uses of herbs were medicinal. For most of his existence, man had various but limited resources for treating injuries and diseases. Separately and in combination he used any and all of the following: magic and sorcery, prayer, music, crude operations (amputation, bleeding, trepanning), psychotherapy, physical therapy (diet, rest, exercise, fresh air, water), and internal and external remedies prepared from plants, animals, and minerals. Of all these, plant remedies represent the most continuous and universal form of treatment: whatever else men may have done to themselves and to each other in the name of medicine at various times, plants were the basic source of therapeutic products for professional and

3

folk medicine from the earliest days until the twentieth century. In fact, folk medicine—the household use of simple herbal remedies—is based on word-of-mouth tradition that probably stretches in an unbroken line to prehistoric times.

Prehistoric man used plants to treat physical complaints, as he used them for food and shelter, long before written history began. He undoubtedly learned by instinct and by generations of trial and error that certain plants were useful for treating illness, just as he learned that some were good to eat and others could cause poisoning and death. In the written record, the study of herbs dates back over 5,000 years to the Sumerians, who described well-established medicinal uses for such plants as laurel, caraway, and thyme. The first known Chinese herb book (or herbal), dating from about 2700 B.C., lists 365 medicinal plants and their uses—including ma-huang, the shrub that introduced the drug ephedrine to modern medicine. The Egyptians of 1000 B.C. are known to have used garlic, opium, castor oil, coriander, mint, indigo, and other herbs for medicine, food, and dyes; and the Old Testament also mentions herb use and cultivation, including mandrake, vetch, caraway, wheat, barley, and rye.

The ancient Greeks and Romans valued plants for various uses: as medicines, symbols and magical charms, food seasonings, cosmetics, dyes, room scenters, and floor coverings. Most importantly, Greek and Roman medical practices, as preserved in the writings of Hippocrates and—especially—Galen, provided the patterns for later western medicine. Hippocrates advocated the use of a few simple herbal drugs—along with fresh air, rest, and proper diet—to help the body's own "life force" in eliminating the problem. Galen, on the other hand, believed that direct intervention with large doses of more or less complicated drug mixtures—including plant, animal, and mineral ingredients, often accompanied by some magical incantations—was necessary to correct bodily imbalances that caused disease. The first European treatise on the properties and uses of medicinal plants, *De Materia Medica*, was compiled by the Greek physician Dioscorides in the first century A.D.; his compendium of more than 500 plants remained an authoritative reference into the seventeenth century. Similarly important for herbalists and botanists of later centuries was the Greek book that founded the science of botany, Theophrastus' *Historia Plantarum,* written in the fourth century B.C.

The uses of plants for medicine and other purposes changed little during the Middle Ages. The early Christian church discouraged the formal practice of medicine, preferring faith healing; but many Greek and Roman writings on medicine, as on other subjects, were preserved by diligent hand copying of manuscripts in monasteries. The monasteries thus tended to become local centers of medical knowledge, and their herb gardens provided the raw materials for simple treatment of common disorders. At the same time, folk medicine in the home and village continued uninterrupted, supporting numerous wandering and settled herbalists. Among these were the "wise-women," who prescribed ancient, secret herbal remedies along with spells and enchantments and who were the targets of much of the witch hysteria of the later Middle Ages. Medical schools began to return in the eleventh century, teaching Galen's system. During the Middle Ages, then, an herb with a reputation for healing might find itself prescribed by a peasant grandmother, sold by a wandering herbalist, charmed as an ingredient in a magic potion or amulet by a wise-woman or a quack, or compounded into a complex and often vile mixture to be dispensed by a physician in the hope that it would drive out whatever possessed the victim. Above all, plants were burdened with a mass of both pagan and Christian superstition that often was more important than their actual properties.

The continuing importance of herbs for the centuries following the Middle Ages is indicated by the hundreds of herbals published after the invention of printing in the fifteenth century. Theophrastus' *Historia Plantarum* was one of the first books to be printed, and Dioscorides' *De Materia Medica* was not far behind. The fifteenth, sixteenth, and seventeenth centuries were the great age of herbals, many of them available for the first time in English and other languages rather than Latin or Greek. The first herbal to be published in English was the anonymous *Grete Herball* of 1526, but the two best-known herbals in English are *The Herball or General Historie of Plantes* (1597) by John Gerard and *The English Physician Enlarged* (1653) by Nicholas Culpeper. Gerard's text was basically a pirated translation of a book by the Belgian herbalist Dodoens, and his illustrations came from a German botanical work. The original edition contained many errors due to faulty matching of the two parts. Culpeper's blend of traditional medicine with astrology, magic, and folklore was ridiculed by the physicians of his day (mainly in retaliation for his making their Latin book of official medicines public by translating it into English); yet his book—like Gerard's and other herbals—enjoyed phenomenal popularity.

But the seventeenth century also saw the beginning of a slow erosion of the preeminent position held by plants as sources of therapeutic effects. The introduction by the physician Paracelsus of active chemical drugs (like arsenic, copper sulfate, iron, mercury, and sulfur), followed by the rapid development of chemistry and the other physical sciences in the eighteenth and nineteenth centuries, led inexorably to the dominance of chemotherapy—chemical medicine—as the orthodox system of the twentieth century.

The day-to-day reality, however, changed little before the twentieth century. Plants still provided the basic materials for medicine, dyeing, and perfume, as well as for most of the quack elixirs, pills, and other preparations that were in great vogue in both the eighteenth and nineteenth centuries. Well into the first half of the nineteenth century, herb women were still crying their wares in London for those who could not gather their own in the country. Folk medicine, as usual, continued to rely on the village herbalist and on the innumerable natural home remedies that have always been the province of grandmothers. Many such traditional remedies also immigrated into the United States, where they blended with the native lore learned from the Indians to produce American folk medicine. Native plants, in addition, provided Americans with new beverages and new colors for dyeing fabrics, many of which were exported back to the Old World.

Meanwhile, in both European and American professional medicine the change toward large-dose chemotherapy did not go unchallenged. In Europe, the system of homeopathic medicine was founded and successfully practiced in the nineteenth century by Samuel Hahnemann, who believed that symptoms—such as fever or boils—are the means by which the body acts to eliminate the cause of disease. Homeopathic treatment of ailments, therefore, is designed to reinforce symptoms instead of combating them, using microscopic doses of herbal drugs that, when given to a healthy person, produce symptoms like those of the ailments themselves. Homeopathy is grounded in the Hippocratic idea of eliminating disease by helping the body's natural recuperative powers, as is another system of European origin—naturopathy.

The German physician-priest Father Sebastian Kneipp, who combined herbs with his world-famous natural "water cure," directed Dr. Benedict Lust to take this method of healing to America in 1895. Dr. Lust opened the first health food store here in 1896 and named it the "Kneipp Store." Affiliated with it he had two *Yungborn Sanitariums,* one in Butler, New Jersey, the other in Tangerine, Florida. From this nucleus he provided true naturopathy to tens of thousands of natural-health seekers. His school, The American School of Naturopathy, granted degrees in this healing art. The organization flourished but as a rule met severe opposition from the organizations of orthodox medicine. His original books still command wide attention among the large numbers of people who are seeking a better way to control and build better health.

Both Kneipp's and Benedict Lust's books, which can be found in the Bibliography, have never lost their appeal and are currently the most popular of all the back-to-nature remedy books.

Naturopathy relies on simple herbal remedies—in conjunction with fasting, exercise, fresh air, sunshine, water, and diet—to help the body regain health naturally. Both homeopathy and naturopathy took hold in the United States late in the nineteenth century, along with several other, shorter lived medical movements oriented toward herbal and natural treatment. They did not prevent the triumph of chemotherapy, yet unorthodox medicine has survived because for many people it offers something that chemotherapy lacks: relative simplicity and treatment that is in harmony with life, not antagonistic to it.

The basic assumption behind natural healing is that man is part of a continuum of being. Since he is a living being, his physical (and mental) condition is linked especially to the properties and influences of natural organic substances. Many of these, in various quantities, are necessary to life itself; others are valuable, if not essential, for maintaining the body at its optimum state of health.

The philosophy of natural healing is that your body is capable of healing itself, once the proper conditions are provided. Natural healing remedies and diets, therefore, tend to be general rather than specifically oriented to a particular disease or illness. They are designed to neutralize or eliminate from your body the harmful substances that impair its power to heal itself. There is great variety, of course, in "the thousand natural shocks that flesh is heir to," and no universal formula works for all of them; but long experience has taught that nature also provides remedies specific enough to make possible an equally great variety of treatments.

The twentieth century has not been kind to old knowledge and traditions, including those of herbalism. In the rush for faster, more efficient, more convenient ways to do things, we have left old ways behind without hesitation. Through it all, a few voices have opposed the headlong rush from Nature, but with little success. "Progress" in our time is based on waste: throwing away things when they have been used or "made obsolete" by something newer and therefore better. Old herbal knowledge and ways have been largely replaced by "modern" ideas and techniques: natural remedies by synthetic drugs, natural foods by processed convenience products, plant dyes and colorings by chemical substitutes, common sense and self-reliance by deference to authority and lack of self-confidence.

But there is hope for herbalism and natural healing in the twentieth century. Everywhere a revival of interest and a new spirit of inquiry are evident. In the United States, herbalism, fasting, psychic healing, and acupuncture are serious topics of study; chiropractic and osteopathy have already earned their survival. In more tolerant Canada and Europe, homeopathy and naturopathy are firmly established forms of treatment. Medicine in the emerging nations includes both that imported from the "advanced" countries and that practiced for thousands of years by the medicine man; even in China traditional herbalism coexists successfully with western-style medicine. The debt to plants as the original sources of valuable modern medicines is today more readily acknowledged: quinine from cinchona bark, morphine from the opium poppy, digitalis from foxglove, the tranquilizer reserpine from rauwolfia, ephedrine from ma-huang, and many others. New plants are being seriously investigated for therapeutic properties.

As the excesses of the "modern" philosophy of waste

8

become apparent, we are looking back and finding that perhaps there is something worth saving in those "outdated" ideas after all. And from the vantage point of the late twentieth century, we have both the perspective and the resources to assess the true relationships—physical and psychological—of plants to man, to test for ourselves what remains valid today of the ancient claims and beliefs. The current revival of interest in the values, properties, and uses of nature's products gives hope that thousands of years of accumulated knowledge will not be completely buried in the stampede so dubiously named progress.

And what of the future? It is our fate to live in an age of complexity; as Matthew Arnold put it, we are

Wandering between two worlds, one dead,
The other powerless to be born.

The simple explanations of the past are museum pieces; the simple explanations of the future—if any—are at best gleams in the eyes of far-out philosophers. It is for us to provide the bridge by accepting the complexity of our existence and attempting to join its diverse elements into a new, comprehensive unity. Twentieth-century medicine, then, must be open to competing ideas, old or new, objectively testing them and selecting what is best in each for promoting the well-being of mankind. There is room for herbalism, chemotherapy, psychic healing, acupuncture, psychotherapy, homeopathy, surgery, hypnotism, diet therapy, manipulation, naturopathy, and much else: to find the proper place for each in one great system of medicine is the challenge and the promise of the future.

THE WORLD
OF THE PLANT

The smallest bacteria are spheres about a hundred-thousandth of an inch in diameter; the largest trees—the redwoods of California and Oregon—can reach heights of 340 feet. In terms of size, these are the endpoints of the plant kingdom; and in between fall more than 300,000 known species of bacteria, algae, mosses, fungi, herbs, shrubs, trees, and several other forms of plant life. Collectively, they form the basis of all life on earth, for no other living thing can survive without them. In addition to producing oxygen, they are the intermediaries that transform the simple elements and compounds of the soil and the air into the complex substances animals need for food. No matter what you eat—with a few exceptions, like salt—trace it back far enough along the "food chain" and you come to a plant. Plants, in fact, have justly been called the food factories of the world. (See Part 3 for the nutrients that plants provide.) At the same time, although some plants can cause illness, many provide us with a wealth of medicinal substances that help to restore health (see Part 2); and plants supply us, too, with wood, cloth, paper, color, fragrance, and beauty—to name just a few of their contributions. Considering our dependence on them, most of us know surprisingly little about plants. This discussion presents some basic facts about them, to provide you with a general frame of reference for a better understanding and appreciation of the remaining parts of the book.

The plants of primary interest to us are classified as *angiosperms* and *gymnosperms*. Angiosperms are the flowering plants, a group numbering over 200,000 species. The gymnosperms, represented by only some 500 species, are trees and shrubs, including the conifers. These two groups account for nearly all the plants considered in this book, the few exceptions being the ferns and seaweeds, club moss, ergot, and Irish moss. The description that follows applies specifically to the flowering plants, but much of it is true of the others also.

WHAT IS A PLANT?

Look in any dictionary and you will find a more or less involved definition of the word *plant*. But since no such definition can do justice to the diversity of the plant kingdom, it seems best to avoid that approach here and, proceeding on faith, to describe instead what we don't feel quite competent to define. This may not be the intellectually tidy way, but it's probably more informative.

To begin, then: the parts of a flowering plant are root, stem, leaf, flower, and fruit. Let's consider each in turn.

The Root

Roots are underground parts of plants (but not all underground parts are roots). They have two main functions: 1) they anchor the plant in the ground; 2) they absorb water and minerals from the soil. Many roots, like the carrot, also serve as food storage organs for their plants.

A *taproot* is a single main root with distinctly smaller branch roots. *Fibrous roots* are thin and all more or less the same size. The development of the root system depends both on the type of plant and on soil conditions, varying from the use of only a few inches of soil to 50-foot-deep forays in search of water. A single plant with a highly branching root system not untypically develops millions of roots totaling hundreds of miles in length and thousands of square feet in absorbent surface area.

The Stem

Some parts of herbaceous perennial plants that many people consider roots are actually underground portions of the plant's stem. These are classified as rootstocks (or rhizomes), stolons, corms, and bulbs.

A *rootstock* grows horizontally in the ground, sending down roots from its lower side and one or more erect stems (or sometimes leaves) from its upper side. One feature that distinguishes it from a true root is the presence of scaly leaves at regular intervals along its length. The rootstock lives from year to year, sending up new growth each season. Some rootstocks are thick and fleshy; others are long and thin. Some thin rootstocks develop locally thick parts for food storage; these are called *tubers* (the potato being the best-known example).

A *stolon* is much like a rootstock, but it grows along the surface of the ground, sending roots down and stems up at intervals. A *runner*, like that of the strawberry plant, is a type of stolon.

A *corm* is a short, thick, vertical underground stem that survives from one season to the next in a dormant state. The second season it produces one or more aerial stems and also one or more new corms. The new corms store food produced by the growing plant and then go through the next dormant period to produce their own plants and corms the following season. The "bulbs" of gladiolus are actually corms.

Bulbs are different from corms, although the latter are often called bulbs. A bulb consists of a short, erect stem enclosed by fleshy leaves (as in onions) or leaf bases (as in daffodils) that serve to store food between growing seasons. Some bulbs survive for several years; others are replaced by new bulbs each year.

The portion of the plant that everyone recognizes as the stem is more precisely called the *aerial stem*. Its main function is to bear leaves, the stem with its leaves being called the *shoot. Herbaceous stems* are those that contain no woody tissue; these usually die down at the end of the growing season, unlike their woody counterparts in trees and shrubs. *Erect stems* are those that grow more or less upward without special support; vines have stems that trail on the ground or climb by attaching themselves to other plants or objects. In addition to bearing leaves, the aerial stem performs the vital functions of transporting water and minerals up from the roots to the leaves and transporting manufactured food substances as they are distributed to all parts of the plant for use or storage.

The Leaf

Leaves come in all sizes and shapes (including some that look more like stems or like flowers), but the typical leaf has a flat *blade* and a stalk, or *petiole*, by which it is attached to the stem. Some leaves manage nicely without a petiole; these are called *sessile*. Leaves tend to grow in regular patterns on the stem; *opposite leaves* grow in pairs from opposite sides at the same point along the stem; *alternate leaves* grow on opposite sides but at different points on the stem; *whorled leaves* grow in groups of three or more around the stem at one point. *Radical leaves* grow directly from a non-aerial stem. *Simple leaves* have a one-piece blade; *compound leaves* consist of individual leaflets which grow either from a single point (*palmate leaf*) or oppositely along the leaf stalk (*pinnate leaf*). See the accompanying illustration and the definitions in the glossary of botanical terms for explanations of the various shapes and forms of leaves.

The primary function of the average green leaf is to carry on photosynthesis—the process by which plants use the energy of sunlight to combine simple substances absorbed from the soil and the air into complex food substances. In the process, plants use up carbon dioxide from the air and produce oxygen. At night the balance reverses, and plants use up oxygen just as we do; but overall the amount of oxygen produced is greater than that consumed (fortunately for us). The critical agent in photosynthesis is the green pigment chlorophyll: only green plant parts are photosynthetic. Green leaves contain various other pigments as well, but these show up only when the leaf dies and its chlorophyll breaks down. The yellow and red autumn colors of many trees are due to leaf pigments which are present but are masked by the chlorophyll while the leaves are alive.

The Flower

Perhaps when you read earlier that the function of the stem is to bear leaves, you thought, "What about the flowers?" True enough, the stem does bear flowers, but botanically flowers are merely specialized shoots—specialized for reproduction. The typical flower consists of several whorls (circular ranks) of parts set on a *receptacle*, the somewhat enlarged end of a stem or flower stalk. The outermost whorl is the *calyx*, a set of leaf-like parts (*sepals*) that protect the flower before it opens. The next whorl in is the *corolla*, consisting of modified, usually

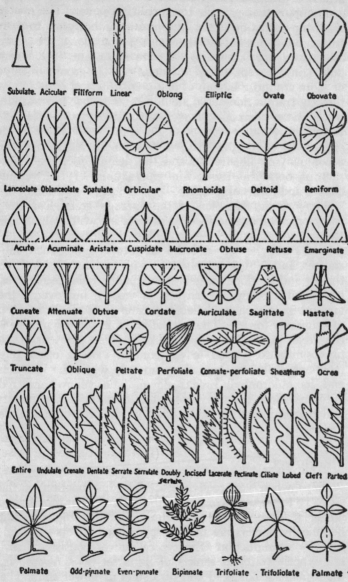

Fig. 1. Terms of vegetative structures.

white or brightly colored leaves called *petals*. One or more whorls of club-shaped *stamens* come next; these are the male organs that provide the fertilizing pollen. The center of all this attention is the female organ, the *pistil*, consisting of one or more *carpels*. A carpel is made up of a bulbous *ovary* which contains the seeds-to-be (*ovules*), and a stalk (the *style*), part of which (the *stigma*) is rough or sticky to capture pollen for fertilization.

Flowers that have the complete set of parts—sepals, petals, stamens, and one or more pistils—are *complete;* those that are missing one or more parts are *incomplete. Perfect flowers* have both stamens and pistils; *imperfect flowers* have only one or the other (a few have neither), being *staminate* (male) if they have stamens, *pistillate* (female) if they have pistils. Some plants bear both staminate and pistillate flowers on the same plant; others have the two kinds on different plants. The tranfer of pollen from stamen to pistil—the pollination necessary for seed to form—is accomplished in various ways, depending on the plant and physical circumstances. The usual ways are by direct contact between stamen and stigma, by insects, or by wind.

Flowers can occur alone or in various kinds of clusters (inflorescences). See the accompanying illustration and the definitions in the glossary of botanical terms for details.

The Fruit

In botany, *fruit* has a much broader and yet more definite meaning than in popular usage: it is the ripened ovary or ovaries—sometimes with associated other parts—of a flower or flower cluster. *True* or *simple fruits* develop from ovaries only; *accessory fruits* (like strawberries or rose hips) develop from ovaries and one or more other parts of the flower. With few exceptions—seedless grapes and pineapples, for example—a fruit forms only after pollination.

Botanically, nuts, beans, corn grains, tomatoes, and dandelion "seeds" are just as much fruits as are blueberries, oranges, cherries, and peaches. You may be surprised to find, though, that tomatoes, cucumbers, and oranges are berries; walnuts and almonds are drupes like cherries and peaches; and peanuts are legumes like peas and beans. Fascinating though it is, a full explanation of the various types of fruit would require greater detail than is possible here; the glossary of botanical terms contains basic definitions for most of them.

The basic function of fruit is to provide for the dispersal of seed at the proper time, but the fruit also serves to protect the seeds as they mature. Considering that seeds range in size from barely visible (orchid) to over a foot in diameter (double coconut), you should not be surprised to find considerable variety in the dispersal mechanisms that different plants have developed. Some fruits split open spontaneously while still on the plant to scatter seeds onto the ground or into the wind; others drop from the plant intact but have wings or feathered tufts attached to help them ride the wind. And some maverick plants—collectively called tumbleweeds—abandon themselves to the wind entirely and scatter seeds as they roll along the ground. Some seeds are spread mainly by birds and other animals, which eat the fruit but excrete the undigested seeds. Prickly fruits often hitch a ride on passing animals or people who carry them elsewhere; others can float on water until they are washed up on a new shoreline. There are still other ways, but these are enough to suggest the boundless ingenuity of Nature in providing for the propagation of each species.

THE NAMES OF PLANTS

If botanists had to rely on the common names of plants in their work, they would spend most of their time trying to figure out which plant was meant by a given name. One man's *redroot* would be another man's *green amaranth*, and which of many plants was meant by *healall* would be anybody's guess. The problem would be compounded when botanists speaking different languages tried to communicate, or when one of the many plants without common names was being considered.

The *binomial system*, using a pair of Latin or latinized words to identify each species, solves the problem by providing a nearly unambiguous way to name plants (and animals too), independent of popular names and language differences. The first and second parts of the binomial, or botanical name, identify the genus and species of the plant, the species being the smallest group that can be consistently identified as distinct from other groups. The genus includes various species that show certain common elements. There are further levels of classification above genus, but these need not concern us here.

The genus name is always capitalized; the species name is usually not capitalized but may be (optionally) for some plants. The two names are usually derived from an historical name for the plant, a physical characteristic, a use to which the plant has been put, a geographical location, or the name of a botanist being honored. Some examples:

Common Name	Genus	Species
Dandelion	*Taraxacum* (from an Arabian name for the plant)	*officinale* (medicinal)
Houseleek	*Sempervivum* (Latin for "live forever")	*tectorum* (pertaining to houses or roofs)
American Ginseng	*Panax* (from the Greek root of "panacea")	*quinquefolius* (five-leaved)
Lobelia	*Lobelia* (after the botanist de Lobel)	*inflata* (swollen, referring to the calyx)

There are some species that include plants with significant enough variations to be categorized. These are accommodated by adding another term to the binomial; for example, a particular variety or subspecies of sweet fern (a shrub rather than a real fern) is designated *Comptonia peregrina* var. *asplenifolia* (or just *Comptonia peregrina asplenifolia*) because its leaves resemble the fronds of asplenium ferns.

Even the binomial system is not foolproof, however. Authorities sometimes disagree on the relationships among plants, so that several botanical names can become attached to one plant. To handle this problem without having to resolve it, botanists generally add to the botanical name they use an abbreviation of its author's name. Thus, *Bellis perennis* L. indicates that Linnaeus, the Swedish botanist and naturalist who originated the binomial system, assigned this binomial to the wild daisy.

GLOSSARY OF BOTANICAL TERMS

The technical terms of botany are often difficult and obscure, but they represent an indispensable, precise shorthand when describing the physical attributes of plants. Without them, many more words would be needed to ensure a complete and accurate description. The following glossary defines the technical terms used in this book, as well as some others commonly encountered in books about plants.

Achene—a small, dry fruit that contains one loose seed and that does not split open spontaneously (e.g., sunflower "seed")

Acuminate—tapering gradually to a point at the apex

Acute—coming sharply to a point at the apex

Alternate—arranged singly at different points along a stem or axis

Annual—completing the cycle from seed to death in one year or season

Apex—the tip

Appressed—pressed flat or close up against something

Aril—an outer covering or appendage of some seeds

Ascending—rising upward gradually from a prostrate base

Awn—a bristle characteristic of the spikelets in some grasses

Axil—the angle formed by a stem with a branch, leaf stalk, or flower stalk growing from it

Axillary—growing from an axil

Axis—the main stem of a plant, or a central line of symmetry, development, or growth

Berry—a stoneless, pulpy fruit containing one or more embedded seeds (e.g., grape)

Biennial—completing the cycle from seed to death in two years or seasons

Bilabiate—two-lipped

Bipinnate—pinnate, with pinnate leaflets

Blade—the broad, thin part of a leaf or petal

Bloom—a powdery, whitish coating on leaves, stems, or fruit

Bract—a small, sometimes scale-like leaf, usually associated with flower clusters

Bud—a protuberance on a stem, from which a flower, leaf, or shoot develops

Bulb—a thick, rounded, underground organ consisting of layered, fleshy leaves and membranes

Calyx—the outer part of a flower, usually consisting of green, leafy sepals

Capsule—a dry, many-seeded, spontaneously splitting fruit that arises from a compound pistil

Carpel—the wall of a simple pistil, or part of the wall of a compound pistil

Catkin—a spikelike flower cluster that bears scaly bracts and petalless, unisexual flowers

Cauline—relating to or growing on a stem

Clasping—partly or completely surrounding the stem

Claw—the narrow, curved base of a petal or sepal in some flowers

Compound—made up of two or more definable parts

Compound pistil—a pistil made up of two or more partially or completely united carpels

Cone—a rounded, more or less elongated cluster of fruits or flowers covered with scales or bracts

Cordate—heart-shaped, with the point at the apex

Corm—a bulblike but solid, fleshy underground stem base

Corolla—the petals of a flower, which may be separate or joined in varying degrees

Corymb—a generally flat-topped flower cluster with pedicels varying in length, the outer flowers opening first

Creeper—a shoot that grows along the ground, rooting all along its length

Crenate—having rounded teeth along the margin

Culm—the hollow stem of grasses and bamboos

Cyme—a branching, relatively flat-topped flower cluster whose central or terminal flower opens first, forcing development of further flowers from lateral buds

Deciduous—falling off each season (as leaves); bearing deciduous parts (as trees)

Decompound—having divisions that are also compound

Decumbent—lying on the ground but having an ascending tip

Decurrent—descriptive of leaves whose edges run down onto the stem

Dentate—sharply toothed, with the teeth pointing straight out from the margin

Digitate—compound, with the elements growing from a single point

Dilated—expanded, broadened, flaring

Disk flower—one of the tubular flowers or florets in the center of the flower head of a composite flower such as the daisy (see also *ray flower*)

Dissected—cut into fine segments

Double—descriptive of flowers that have more petals than normal

Doubly serrate—serrate, with small teeth on the margins of the larger ones

Drupe—a fleshy fruit containing a single seed in a hard "stone" (e.g., peach)

Entire—having no teeth or indentations

Evergreen—retaining green foliage for more than one season

Filiform—threadlike

Floret—a small flower in a flower head or other cluster

Frond—the leaf of a fern

Fruit—the seed-bearing part of a plant

Funnelform—descriptive of a flower whose corolla tube widens gradually and uniformly from the base

Glabrous—not hairy

Glandular—having glands, which secrete sticky substances

Glaucous—covered with bloom

Globose—approximately spherical

Grain—achene-like fruit, but with the seed not loose

Head—a flower spike or raceme shortened to form a compact, flattened to globose cluster

Herb—a plant that has no woody tissue and that dies down to the ground at the end of a growing season

Herbaceous—herblike; not woody

Hesperidium—a partitioned berry with a leathery, removable rind (e.g., orange)

Hoary—closely covered with short and fine whitish hairs

Incised—sharply and irregularly slashed or cut

Indigenous—native; naturally occurring

Inflorescence—technically, the way flowers are arranged in a cluster; generally, a flower cluster

Internode—the part of a stem or branch between nodes

Interrupted—descriptive of a structure, the pattern or sequence of whose elements is broken by the insertion of other elements

Lanceolate—widening to a maximum near the base and tapering to a point at the apex

Lateral—occurring on or growing from the side (compare *terminal*)

Leaf—a vegetative organ which, when complete, consists of a flat blade, a petiole or stalk, and (usually two) small leafy appendages at the base of the petiole

Leaflet—a division or part of a compound leaf

Legume—a one-celled fruit that splits along two sutures or seams (e.g., pea)

Linear—long and narrow, with nearly parallel sides

Lip—one of the parts in a corolla or calyx divided into two unequal parts

Lobe—a part or division, especially when rounded, of an organ

Lyrate—lobed to resemble a lyre, with the terminal lobe largest and the lower lobes smaller

Node—the place where a leaf grows or can grow

Nut—a hard-walled, one-seeded fruit that does not split spontaneously (e.g., hazelnut)

Ob- —a prefix that indicates reversal of the usual orientation (e.g., *oblanceolate* means widening gradually from the pointed base to a maximum near the apex, which may be more or less rounded)

Oblong—longer than wide and rounded at the ends, with nearly parallel sides for much of the length

Obtuse—rounded or blunt

Opposite—growing two to a node on opposite sides

Orbicular—circular or approximately round

Oval—broadly elliptical

Ovate—shaped like an egg, with the narrow end at the apex

Ovoid—ovate

Palmate—compounded, divided, lobed, or ribbed so that the divisions or ribs spread out like fingers from a single point

Panicle—a raceme compounded by branching

Papilionaceous—descriptive of a flower whose petals are arranged to resemble a butterfly

Pedicel—the stalk of one flower in a cluster

Peduncle—the stalk of a flower cluster or of a solitary flower

Peltate—having a stalk attached at or near the middle

Perennial—living through three or more seasons

Persistent—remaining on the plant; not falling off readily

Petal—one unit of the corolla

Petiole—the stalk of a leaf

Pinna (plural *pinnae*)—a leaflet or primary division of a pinnately compound leaf

Pinnate—having leaflets arranged in opposite rows along the petiole

Pinnatifid—split about halfway to the midrib, such that the divisions are pinnately arranged

Pinnule—one of the divisions of a pinnate leaflet in a bi-pinnate leaf

Pistil—the female reproduction organ of a flower

Pod—generally, a dry fruit that splits open

Pome—a fleshy fruit with a central seed-bearing core (e.g., apple)

Procumbent—growing along the ground without rooting, and having ascending tips

Prostrate—growing flat along the ground

Pubescent—covered with down or soft, short hairs

Punctate—having translucent spots or depressions

Raceme—an elongated flower cluster in which flowers grow on pedicels along part of the length of the peduncle

Radical—growing from or pertaining to a root; growing from a non-aerial stem

Ray flower—one of the flattened, petal-like outer flowers or florets ringing the disk in the heads of some composite flowers, such as the daisy (see also *disk flower*)

Receptacle—the end of the stem or stalk on which the flower parts are borne

Rhizome—an underground portion of a stem, producing shoots on top and roots beneath; different from a root in that it has buds, nodes, and scaly leaves; rootstock

Rootstock—rhizome

Rosette—a circular or spiral arrangement of leaves growing from a center or crown

Runner—a thin stem or shoot growing along the ground and producing roots at the nodes

Sagittate—resembling an arrowhead in shape

Samara—a winged fruit that does not split spontaneously (e.g., maple)

Scale—a small, usually dry leaf that is closely pressed against another organ

Scape—a leafless flower stalk that grows from the ground

Sepal—a leaf or division of the calyx

Serrate—saw-toothed, with the teeth pointing toward the apex

Sessile—having no stalk

Sheath—an expanded or tubular structure that partially encloses a stem or other organ

Shoot—a stem or branch and its leaves, especially when young

Shrub—a woody plant that produces no trunk but branches from the base

Simple—not compounded (leaves) or branched (stems, flower clusters)

Smooth—not rough (compare *glabrous*)

Solitary—not growing as part of a cluster or group

Spadix—a fleshy spike

Spathe—one or two bracts enclosing a flower cluster (especially a spadix)

Spatulate—shaped like a spoon, with a narrow end at the base

Spike—a flower cluster in which sessile flowers grow along part of the length of the peduncle

Spikelet—a small spike, particularly one of the few-flowered spikes making up the inflorescence of a grass

Spore—a one-celled reproductive body produced by relatively primitive plants

Spur—a slender, hollow projection from a petal or sepal

Stamen—the male or pollen-bearing organ of a flower

Strobile—a cone or conelike structure

Style—the slender, elongated part of a pistil

Suture—a natural seam or groove along which a fruit splits

Taproot—a single main root that grows vertically into the ground

Terminal—occurring at or growing from the end opposite the base (compare *lateral*)

Ternate—occurring in threes or divided into three parts

Trifoliate—having three leaves

Trifoliolate—having three leaflets

Tripinnate—descriptive of a pinnate leaf having pinnate leaflets with pinnate pinnules

Tuber—a thick, fleshy part, usually of a rootstock

Umbel—a more or less flat-topped flower cluster in which the pedicels (rays) arise from a common point. In compound umbels, each primary ray terminates in a secondary umbel

Valve—one of the parts into which a capsule divides when splitting

Whorl—a circular arrangement of three or more leaves, flowers, or other parts at the same point or level

GETTING
AND KEEPING
HERBS

It has been said that nature provides a remedy for every disease. That may be true, but getting at the remedy can be another matter. You have, basically, three (legal) possibilities: collect herbs in the wild, grow them yourself, or buy them. Each has advantages and drawbacks.

THE CALL OF THE WILD: Roughing It

Collecting your herbs in the wild is probably the cheapest way to get your remedies, but it also involves considerable effort. In the United States and other countries, many wild plants growing on public lands are protected by law, so that collecting them in quantity becomes impractical. With the permission of the owner, you can gather plants growing on private property; but most owners are reluctant to let strangers wander around their land. Even if you get permission, you never know what may have been sprayed on the plants you find, whether on private or public land. And finally, wild specimens of many of the plants you may want will be rare or nonexistent in your area or even in your part of the world.

Let's suppose, though, that these obstacles are not insurmountable and that you have access to at least some herbs useful for medicinal or other purposes. (Look around a little, and you may be surprised at what you find. Euell Gibbons—the famous expert on wild plants—one October found a dozen edible and medicinal plants in the neglected, block-long median of a San Francisco street.) A few general guidelines will help you get the most out of your natural resources. First of all, pick a warm, dry, sunny day—just the sort of day you want to be outdoors anyway. After a rain, let two or three sunny days pass before venturing out. (Actually, this may be the best time, since rain helps wash off externally applied pesticides.) Gather your plants as early in the day as possible, but not before the dew has dried. Choose only healthy plants that show no damage from pests or disease. Both roots and bark (meaning the living inner bark) are best for gathering in spring or fall, i.e., before or after flowering. Collect bark only from small branches that can be cut off the tree or shrub; don't damage large limbs or the trunk. Plants in flower are the ones to choose when the whole plant, the leaves, or, of course, the flowers are to be collected. Gather seeds and fruit when they are ripe (unless unripe ones are specified for use).

Proper identification of plants is obviously vital. Even with accurate descriptions and pictures, it is often possible to mistake one plant for another, including poisonous for nonpoisonous ones. If you do gather wild plants for remedies, learn the positive identification of those you will be seeking, preferably from someone already familiar with them. If you don't have a guide, try to find an herbarium with actual specimens at a museum or university; or study as many plant identification books as you can find, especially any that specialize in the flora of your area. *Never use any plant that you have not positively identified.*

THE HERB GARDEN: Do It Yourself

If the problems of going out to find wild plants seem too great for you, you can always take another approach: bring the plants to you. This other way of getting fresh herbs—growing your own in an herb garden—can be as simple or as complex as you like. Your herb garden can vary from a few flowerpots on a windowsill or balcony to a full-blown, yard-size garden with perhaps dozens of common and uncommon plants growing in patterned arrangements. Even a small garden can be invaluable:

according to Sebastian Kneipp, sage, wormwood, and yellow gentian together make an entire garden pharmacy. Some herbal authorities insist that cultivated plants are less effective medicinally than their wild cousins, but the matter is not so simple. The health and vigor of a plant (and therefore its potency) depend on soil quality and environmental conditions. The knowledgeable and conscientious organic gardener can provide the best combination of soil type, moisture, and sun or shade for each plant in his garden, so that it rivals all but the most fortunate of wild specimens. This is not the place to go into detail, however; there are a number of excellent books available that present complete information about growing herbs for anyone from the apartment dweller to the country squire. See the Bibliography for some of these; your library, bookstore, or health food store may have others.

THE HERB DEALER: Path of Least Resistance

The easiest—although generally the most expensive—way of getting your herbs is from an herb dealer. As a group, herb dealers offer a number of advantages: a wide selection, including many otherwise unobtainable foreign and exotic plants; the confidence that you are getting the plant you want, although some rare and expensive herbs in the trade may be adulterated with cheaper plants; and convenience. Almost any herb you may want is available in some form from a commercial source somewhere. You can get seeds or live plants to use fresh or to grow; you can get dried plants, plant parts, or plant mixtures, often with a choice of cut, powdered, or whole forms; you can get preparations in capsule, tablet, or liquid forms; and you can get plant oils, resins, and gums, not to mention the numerous derived plant products like soaps, cosmetics, and perfumes. No one dealer offers everything, of course: some try to offer as big a selection as possible, but most specialize to a greater or lesser degree.

The first place to look for an herb dealer is in the yellow pages of your own telephone book, under the headings Herbs, Health Food Products, Perfumers' Raw Materials and Supplies, Pharmacies (look for ones that list botanicals), Seeds and Bulbs, and Spices. If you have a local herb dealer, he probably has or can get almost anything you want; and you have the advantage of knowing with whom you are dealing. For those who are not so fortunate, the list of sources for herbs and herb products beginning on page 30 should be helpful. Each listing includes the general products handled by the dealer, but you should get current, detailed information by writing before ordering anything. These dealers will take mail orders, and many will send catalogs or useful information. Some of their publications, in fact, are so interesting and enticing, your biggest problem may be to resist buying everything in sight!

DRYING HERBS

Whether you collect wild plants or grow your own, you will want to dry some of them for later use. But drying often decreases the effectiveness of the desirable properties. To conserve these as much as possible, you must be careful to dry your plants in the shade, to avoid temperature extremes, and to disturb them as little as possible during the drying process.

The two best ways to dry herbs are: 1) spreading them out in a thin layer on a clean surface or on paper, and 2) hanging them up in bundles. Either way, use a dry, well-ventilated place where no moisture or direct sunlight can affect the plants. Select only the best fresh greens, and be careful to handle and bruise them as little as possible to avoid unsightly discoloration in the dried product. For plants and leaves, temperatures should be no higher than 85 to 95 degrees Fahrenheit, for roots, not over 115 degrees. Small roots can be dried whole; large ones should be cut into two or more pieces lengthwise and hung up to dry threaded on a string. To dry bulbs, remove the outer coat, slice, and dry with heat not over 100 degrees. To dry bark, scrape off the outer bark, peel the layers of inner bark, and dry in sunlight (except wild black cherry, which should be dried in shade). Plants are dry when the stems are brittle and break readily. For storage, the leaves are usually removed from the stems and stalks, which in most cases have little value in themselves.

STORING HERBS

The two greatest enemies to preserving the effectiveness of dried herbs are light and oxygen. Use airtight jars made of dark glass (or airtight tins) and keep them in a cool, dry place. Because a loss of potency with time is inevitable, do not keep dried herbs for more than a year. (Bark can often be kept longer but loses effectiveness after about three years.) Renew your stock whenever fresh herbs are again available. In case stored herbs are exposed to moisture, they can be dried again at warm room temperature.

COMMERCIAL SOURCES OF HERBS AND HERB PRODUCTS

CALIFORNIA

Berkeley Health Foods
2311 Shattuck Avenue
Berkeley, California 94704
(Herb teas, minerals,
   vitamins)

Lhasa Karnak Herb Co.
2482 Telegraph Avenue
Berkeley, California 94704
(Herbs, teas, spices)

Vetterle & Reinelt
Capitola, California 95010
(Plants, seeds, garden books
   and products)

Clyde Robin
P.O. Box 2091
Castro Valley, California
   94546
(Native plants, rare plants,
   seeds)

Mrs. M. C. White
67616 Hacienda Drive
Desert Hot Springs, California
   92240
(*Aloe vera* plants, citrus
   fruits, vegetables)

Mail Box Seeds
Shirley Morgan
2042 Encinal Avenue
Alameda, California 94501
(Seeds)

Steve Mohorko Co.
16803 Ceres Avenue
Fontana, California 92335
(Herbs, seeds, spices)

Herbs of Mexico
3859 Whittier Blvd.
Los Angeles, California 90023
(Herbs from all over the
   world)

CALIFORNIA (cont.)

Organic Foods and Gardens
2655 Commerce Way
Los Angeles, California 90040

Star Herb Company
352 Miller Avenue
Mill Valley, California 94941
(Importers and Distributors of
   Botanicals and Ginseng)

The Ransom Seed Co.
c/o Campbell
Devon Lane
Newport Beach, California
   92660
(Berries, flowers, seeds, trees)

W. Atlee Burpee Co.
6350 Rutland
Riverside, California 92502
(Seeds, books)

Golden Gate Herbs
Box 810
Occidental, California
   95465
(Medicinal herbs)

Nature's Herb Company
281 Ellis Street
San Francisco, California
   94102
(Herbs, herbal preparations)

Kitazawa Seed Co.
356 W. Taylor Street
San Jose, California 95110
(Seeds for oriental plants)

The Herb Store
P.O. Box 5756
Sherman Oaks, California 91403

Vita Green Farms
P.O. Box 878
Vista, California 92083
(Seeds, vegetables)

CALIFORNIA (cont.)

Tillotson's Roses
341 Brown's Valley Road
Watsonville, California 95076
("Roses of Yesterday and
Today," their catalogue and
reference book on old roses;
cost $1.00, refundable on
first order)

CONNECTICUT

Capriland's Herb Farm
Silver Street
Coventry, Connecticut 06238
(Herbs)

Herb's Herbs
P.O. Box 577
New Canaan, Connecticut
06840
(Herbs, spices, herbal foot
baths and skin ointments)

DELAWARE

Bunting's Nurseries, Inc.
Selbyville, Delaware 19975
(Berries, evergreens, flowers,
fruits, nuts)

GEORGIA

Thomasville Nurseries, Inc.
Thomasville, Georgia 31792
(Specialty flowers and shrubs)

IDAHO

Lewiston Health Food
Center
861 Main
Lewiston, Idaho 83501
(Herbs, health foods,
vitamins, books)

ILLINOIS

Everett L. Anderson
Route 2
McLeansboro, Illinois 62859
(Herb Dealer; enclose self-
addressed envelope with all
inquiries)

ILLINOIS (cont.)

Kramer's Health Food Store
29 East Adams Street
Chicago, Illinois 60603
(Herbs, dietary foods)

Dr. Michael's Herb Products
5109 North Western Avenue
Chicago, Illinois 60625

Jewel Tea Co., Inc.
1955 W. North Avenue
Melrose Park, Illinois 60160
(Teas, general merchandise)

R. H. Shumway Seedsman
628 Cedar
Rockford, Illinois 61101
(Seeds, garden supplies)

INDIANA

Indiana Botanic Gardens, Inc.
Hammond, Indiana 46325
(Herbs, herb preparations,
gums, oils, resins)

Moses J. Troyer
Lone Organic Farm
Route 1, Box 58
Millersburg, Indiana 46543
(Herbs)

KANSAS

Tropical Paradise Greenhouse
8825 W. 79th Street
Overland Park, Kansas 66204
(Wildflowers, hothouse
plants)

KENTUCKY

Dandelions Unlimited
38 West 6th Street
Covington, Kentucky 41011
(Dandelion and slippery elm
preparations)

Ferry-Morse Seed Co.
Box 200
Fulton, Kentucky 42041
(Herbs, citrus fruits, flowers,
seeds)

KENTUCKY (cont.)

L. S. Dinkelspiel Co.
229 E. Market Street
Louisville, Kentucky 40202

F. C. Taylor Fur Co.
227 E. Market Street
Louisville, Kentucky 40202

MAINE

Conley's Garden Center
Boothbay Harbor, Maine
  04538
(Wildflowers, ferns, garden
  plants)

MARYLAND

Carroll Gardens
P.O. Box 310
East Main Street
Westminster, Maryland 21157
(Herbs, garden plants)

MASSACHUSETTS

Blackthorn Gardens
48 Quincy Street
Holbrook, Massachusetts
  02343
(Herbs, wild and garden
  flowers)

Leslie's Wildflower Nursery
30 Summer Street
Methuen, Massachusetts
  01844
(Wildflowers, ferns, garden
  flowers, seeds)

MICHIGAN

International Growers
  Exchange
Box 397
Farmington, Michigan 48024
(Worldwide rare plants)

Burgess Seed and Plant Co.
67 E. Battle Creek Street
Galesburg, Michigan 49053
(Seeds, garden supplies)

MINNESOTA

International House
75 W. Island Avenue, Box D
Minneapolis, Minnesota 55401
(Exotic plants and accessories)

MISSOURI

Clearwater Farms
Des Arc, Missouri 63636
(Ginseng seed)

Geological Botany Co.
622 W. 67th Street
Kansas City, Missouri 64113
(Botanical products)

MONTANA

Lady Bug Natural Products
P.O. Box 873
Shelby, Montana 59474

St. Louis Commission Co.
4157 N. Kingshighway
St. Louis, Missouri 63115

NEW JERSEY

Plant Oddities
Box 127
Basking Ridge, New Jersey
  07920
(Unusual nursery stock)

Wunderlich-Diez Company
State Highway 17
Hasbrouk Heights, New Jersey

Le Jardin du Gourmet
Box 245
Ramsey, New Jersey 07446
(Herbs, spices, seeds)

Rocky Hollow Herb Farm
Lake Wallkill Road
Sussex, New Jersey 07461
(Herbs)

NEW YORK

Aphrodisia,
28 Carmine Street
New York, New York 10014
(Herbs, oils, spices, books)

NEW YORK (cont.)

Caswell-Massey Company, Ltd.
320 W. 13th Street
New York, New York 10010
(Herb and natural soaps;
  ingredients for aromatic
  uses of herbs)

Herbs and Spices by Panacea
323 Third Avenue
New York, New York 10010

Kalustyan Orient Export
  Trading Corp.
123 Lexington Avenue
New York, New York 10016
(Herbs, spices, grains)

Kiehl Pharmacy
109 Third Avenue
New York, New York 10003
(Herbs, spices, drugs,
  vitamins)

S. B. Penick & Co.
100 Church Street
New York, New York 10007
(Distributors in Bulk of
  Imported Botanicals)

H. Roth & Son
1577 First Avenue
New York, New York 10028
(Herbs, spices)

Schapira Coffee Co.
117 West 10th Street
New York, New York 10011
(Rare teas, coffees)

H. L. Wild
510 E. 11th Street
New York, New York 10009
(Lumber, woods for furniture)

Nelson's Natural Foods
1558 Central Park Avenue
Yonkers, New York 10710

NORTH CAROLINA

Gardens of the Blue Ridge
Ashford, North Carolina 28603
(Wildflowers, garden plants)

NORTH CAROLINA (cont.)

Wilcox Drug Co., Inc.
P.O. Box 391
Boone, North Carolina 28607

Three Laurels
Marshall, North Carolina
  28753
(Wildflowers, garden plants)

OHIO

Frank Lemaster & Co.
Route 1
Londonderry, Ohio 45647

OREGON

Nichols Garden Nursery
1190 North Pacific Highway
Albany, Oregon 97321
(Herbs, spices, seeds, plants)

The Fishers
Route 2, Box 205
Monmouth, Oregon 97862
(Herbs)

PENNSYLVANIA

Andrew Gallant
Route 2
Albion, Pennsylvania 16401
(Garlic seed)

Natural Development Co.
Bainbridge, Pennsylvania
  17502
(Edible seeds and grains)

Hershey Estates
Hershey, Pennsylvania 17033
(Soaps, cosmetics)

Tatra Herb Company
222 Grove Street
Morrisville, Pennsylvania
  19067
(Herbs)

PENNSYLVANIA (cont.)

Haussman's Pharmacy
6th and Girard Avenue
Philadelphia, Pennsylvania
    19127
(Herbs, mixtures, oil, gums,
    cosmetics)

Penn Herb Company
603 N. 2nd Street
Philadelphia, Pennsylvania
    19123
(Herbs, books)

Edward's Health Center
480 Station Road
Quakerstown,
    Pennsylvana 18951

RHODE ISLAND

Greene Herb Gardens
Greene, Rhode Island 02827
(Fresh and dried herbs, teas,
    seeds)

Meadowbrook Herb Garden
Route 138
Wyoming, Rhode Island
    02898
(Herbs, herb products, spices,
    cosmetics)

TENNESSEE

Blue Ridge Ginseng
McDonald, Tennessee 37353
(Ginseng seed)

Savage Farm Nursery
Box 125
McMinnville, Tennessee
    37110
(Wildflowers, garden plants)

TEXAS

Plimmers Enterprises
P.O. Box 701
Alpine, Texas 79830
(Herbs, nuts)

TEXAS (cont.)

Arrowhead Mills
Box 866
Hereford, Texas 79045
(Grains)

VERMONT

Putney Nursery, Inc.
Box 13
Putney, Vermont 05346
(Wildflowers)

Vermont Country Store
Weston, Vermont 05161
(Herbs, spices, condiments,
    grains)

WASHINGTON

Cedarbrook Herb Farm
Route 1, Box 1047
Sequim, Washington 98382
(Herb plants)

WISCONSIN

Northwestern Processing
    Company
217 North Broadway
Milwaukee, Wisconsin 53202
(Herbs, teas, coffees, spices,
    nuts)

Woodland Acres Nursery
Route 2
Crivitz, Wisconsin 54114
(Wildflowers, ferns, seeds)

Olds Seed Co.
Box 1069
Madison, Wisconsin 53701
(Seeds)

CANADA

Botanical Herbs and Health
    Products
P.O. Box 88 Station "N"
Montreal, Quebec, Canada

Murchie's
1008 Robson Street
Vancouver 105, B.C., Canada
(Teas, coffees, spices)

34

CANADA (cont.)

Rolly's Health Food Store
634 Yonge Street
Toronto, Ontario, Canada
(Medicinal herbs, health
foods, vitamins)

Dominion Herb Distributors,
Inc.
61 St. Catherine Street West
Montreal 129, Quebec,
Canada
(Herbs, gums, seeds)

World-Wide Herb Ltd.
11 St. Catherine Street East
Montreal 129, Quebec,
Canada
(Herbs)

SCOTLAND

D. Napier & Sons
17, 18 Bristo Place and
1 Teviot Place
Edinburgh EH1, Scotland
(Herbs, preparations, herb
products)

FRANCE

Peking-Konsgze
7, Ave du General Mangin
Paris, France

Compagnie du Sud
3 Rue des Precheurs
Paris, France

Hannibal
280 Rue St. Honore
Paris, France

HOW TO
MAKE AND USE
HERB PREPARATIONS

Since the effectiveness and the value of most herbs are greatest when the plants are fresh, the best preparations are usually those you make yourself from freshly gathered herbs. And what a satisfying feeling to be able to identify your remedy in the field and to extract nature's healing elements and put them to use, all through your own efforts! (Some plants, however, should be used only dried or in professional preparations to avoid or minimize detrimental effects. Such requirements are indicated in the listing in Part 2.) Next best are preparations made from herbs which have been well preserved by proper drying and storage (see pages 28-29).

But even the best plant materials can be ruined if you use the wrong kind of process in preparing your remedies. The choice depends primarily on the identity of the plant, the plant parts being used, the elements to be extracted (if any), the form in which the remedy will be taken or applied, and the effect to be achieved. Although most of the descriptions in Part 2 include individual instructions for preparing remedies, there are standard methods that you can use in many cases. Wherever the description in Part 2 includes no method of preparation (except in the case of poisonous plants), you can use the methods described in this section. A little experimentation will soon indicate the adjustments that need to be made to suit your needs or someone else's.

Don't be impatient, though, if you don't get immediate results from these preparations. Herbs are not one-shot wonder drugs in the modern sense; rather, their effectiveness is based on gradual action to restore the natural balance of bodily functions that constitutes health. Very few plant remedies produce lasting beneficial effects after only one or a few doses; most treatments involve taking the remedy daily for at least several weeks. Their effectiveness is also greatly helped or hindered by your overall life style, especially your diet. A healthful diet and sufficient exercise to keep your body in good condition are valuable both for preventing much illness and for helping to overcome it when it does strike.

The only prepared remedies that can be kept for any length of time are ointments and those made with alcohol. The alcohol will preserve the latter, and a little gum benzoin or tincture or benzoin (a drop per ounce of fat) will preserve salves or ointments made with a perishable base. Make infusions, decoctions, cold extracts, juice, poultices, and fomentations fresh each time. Whenever you do store any plant preparations, sterilize the containers before putting the preparations in them.

The following types of preparations are those most commonly and conveniently used in herbal medicine. The doses given are for average adult use and must be adjusted for age and condition. For children and weak or elderly people (or when using very potent plants), use one-third to two-thirds the adult dose.

INFUSION

An infusion is a beverage made like tea, by combining boiling water with the plants (usually the green parts or the flowers) and steeping to extract their active ingredients. The relatively short exposure to heat in this method of preparation minimizes the loss of volatile elements. The usual amounts are about ½ to 1 oz. to a pint of water. Most often the water is poured over the plants, but some recipes require that the plants be added to boiling water, the pot then being immediately removed from the heat. Use an enamel, porcelain, or glass pot to steep the plants for about 10 minutes; then cover the pot with a tight-fitting lid to minimize evaporation. For drinking, strain the infusion into a cup or glass. Sometimes sugar or honey is added to improve the taste. For most purposes, take the infusion lukewarm or cool; but to induce sweating and to break up a cold or a cough, take it hot. Most herb teas are taken over a period of time in small, regular doses ranging from a teaspoon to a mouthful. The cumulative daily dose usually ranges from 1 to 4 cups, depending on the severity of the problem and the potency of the plant.

DECOCTION

When you want to extract primarily the mineral salts and bitter principles of plants, rather than vitamins and volatile ingredients, decoction is your method of preparation. Hard materials, such as roots, wood, bark, and seeds, also generally require boiling to extract their active ingredients. Boil about a half ounce plant parts per cup of water in an enamelled or nonmetallic pot. Green plant parts can be added to cold water, brought to a boil, and boiled for 3 to 4 minutes; or they can be added to boiling water and then boiled for the same time. The mixture then steeps with a cover on the pot for 2 to 3 minutes. Hard materials need boiling for about 10 minutes and longer steeping to extract their ingredients. Strain out the plant parts before drinking or using the decoction. Directions for taking decoctions are the same as for infusions.

COLD EXTRACT

Preparation with cold water will effectively preserve the most volatile ingredients and extract only minor amounts of mineral salts and bitter principles. Add about double the amount of plant material used for an infusion to cold water in an enamelled or nonmetallic pot. Let the mixture stand for 8 to 12 hours, strain, and the drink is ready. Directions for taking are the same as for infusions.

JUICE

Chop fresh plants or plant parts up into small pieces and press to squeeze out the juice. Add a little water to the pressed material and press again to get the rest. This is a good method for extracting water-soluble constituents, especially those sensitive to heat. It is excellent for getting vitamins and minerals from the plant; but the juice must be taken within a short time after pressing, since the vitamin content declines rapidly and fermentation sets in.

POWDER

Grind dried plant parts with a mortar and pestle or other implements until you have a powder. Powder can be taken with water, milk, or soup; sprinkled on food; or swallowed in gelatin capsules. A No. 0 capsule holds about 10 grains; No. 00 holds about 15 grains. The most common dose for powders is the amount that you can pick up on the tip of a dinner knife.

SYRUP

A basic syrup to which you can add medicinal ingredients can be made by simply boiling 3 lb. raw or brown sugar in a pint of water until it reaches the right consistency. Or you can boil the plant materials in honey or store-bought syrup and then strain through cheesecloth. Syrup is especially useful for administering medicines to children.

TINCTURE

Combine 1 to 4 oz. powdered herb (the amount depending on the plant's potency) with 8 to 12 oz. alcohol. Add water to make a 50% alcohol solution (you have to know what percent alcohol you started with). Let stand for two weeks, shaking once or twice a day; then strain and pour the liquid into a bottle suitable for storage. Like other alcoholic extracts, tinctures will keep for a long time. Homeopaths use very dilute tinctures as their basic medicinal preparations.

ESSENCE

Dissolve an ounce of the herb's essential oil in a pint of alcohol. This is a good way to preserve the volatile essential oils of many plants, which are generally not soluble in water.

OINTMENT

Mix well one part of the remedy in powdered form with four parts hot petroleum jelly, lard, or similar substance. For purists, an old method is to boil the ingredients in water until the desired properties are extracted. Strain the liquid, add the decoction to olive or other vegetable oil, and simmer until the water has completely evaporated. Add beeswax as needed to get a firm consistency. Melt the mixture by heating slowly, and stir until completely blended. As pointed out above, a little gum benzoin or a drop of tincture of benzoin per ounce of fat (when a perishable fat is used as a base) will help to preserve the ointment.

POULTICE

The poultice (or cataplasm) is used to apply a remedy to a skin area with moist heat. To prepare, bruise or crush the medicinal parts of the plant to a pulpy mass and heat. If using dried plants (or if needed even with fresh plants), moisten the materials by mixing with a hot, soft, adhesive substance, such as moist flower or corn meal, or a mixture of bread and milk. Apply directly to the skin. A good way is to spread the paste or pulp on a wet, hot cloth, apply, and wrap the cloth around to help retain moisture and heat. Moisten the cloth with hot water periodically as necessary. Where irritant plants are involved (as in a mustard "plaster"), keep the paste between two pieces of cloth to prevent direct contact with the skin; after removing the poultice, wash the area well with water or herb tea (especially camomile or mugwort) to remove any residue that may have gotten on the skin. You can use a poultice to soothe, to irritate, or to draw impurities from the body, depending on which plant or plants you use.

FOMENTATION

Soak a cloth or towel in an infusion or decoction, wring out the excess, and apply as hot as possible to the affected area. A fomentation has about the same applications as a poultice but is generally less active in its effect.

COLD COMPRESS

Soak a cloth or towel in an infusion or decoction that has been cooled, wring out the excess, and apply to the affected area. Leave on until it is warmed by body heat, usually 15 to 20 minutes. Repeat application with a fresh cool compress. Continue until relieved.

HYDROTHERAPY: The Herb Bath

Hydrotherapy—the use of water for treatment of illness—is particularly popular in Europe, where health spas have elaborate facilities for all types of "water cures." Often these include the use of mineral water or of mineral and herbal bath additives to enhance the natural healing power of the water or to produce particular effects on the body. But you don't have to go to a European health resort to take healing baths: with a few simple supplies, you can enjoy their benefits right at home.

Full or partial herb baths come in all shapes and sizes, from the bathtub to the eye cup. Basically, they are baths to which plant decoctions or infusions have been added. Depending on the plants used and the temperature, such baths can calm or stimulate the mind and body; open or close pores; relieve inflammation, itching, or pain; and exert various other beneficial effects.

To make a decoction for adding to a full bath, anywhere

from a few ounces to several pounds of plant parts may be tied or sewn into a linen or other cloth bag and then boiled in a quart or more of water. For partial baths, the only difference is that smaller quantities (usually about a third as much as for a full bath) are used. When taking the bath, you can also put the bag into the water to extract more of the properties, and you can use it as an herbal "washcloth" to give yourself a brisk rubdown.

The Full Bath

Warm baths (90 to 95°F) are calming and soothing to the nerves. They can also be helpful for bladder and urinary problems, mild colds, and low fevers. Both hot (100 to 113°F) and cold (55 to 65°F) shock the system, causing increased heart action (with the cold bath the heart slows down after the initial shock). The hot bath followed by being bundled in blankets will cause profuse sweating and can thus be helpful for colds and fevers as well as for eliminating body wastes retained because of improper kidney function. With addition of the proper herbs, of course, you can create a bath for practically any purpose you want: to soften, moisturize, or scent the skin, to remove excess oil, to relieve itching, to stimulate or relax, to tighten or tone the skin, to ease muscular aches, and many more. Choose your plant additives by the properties described in Part 2 and experiment.

The Half Bath

The half bath is halfway between the full bath and the sitzbath: you sit in water up to the navel with the legs and feet under water but the upper body out of the water. A cold half bath of 5 to 15 seconds (once a day) can be helpful for headache, insomnia, nervous problems, overactive thyroid, flatulence, and constipation. The warm half bath (about 95°F for 10 minutes) can be used for low blood pressure and for menopausal problems. The warm half bath often includes a vigorous brushing of the skin and may be ended with a brief spray of cold water on the back.

The Sitzbath

The sitzbath, which is not too distantly related to the sitz-mark so well known in skiing, involves sitting in a relatively small amount of water. There are, especially in Europe, bathtubs made especially for sitzbaths, but any tub large enough to sit in will do. To take a sitzbath, put enough warm or hot herbal bath water in the tub so that it reaches your navel when you sit in it. Prop your feet up on a hassock set beside the tub and then wrap yourself with large towels or blankets so that you are completely covered from the neck down. If you are using a bathtub, put in about 4 inches of water, keep your knees up, and splash the water onto your abdomen. Stay in the tub for 10 to 20 minutes, then rinse with a short cold bath or shower. (Hardy souls take cold sitzbaths too, but these last no more than a few minutes at a time.) Sitzbaths are beneficial for the genito-urinary tract, the lower abdominal area, and the rectum. They can be helpful for inflammations, pelvic congestion, cramps, hemorrhoids, menstrual problems, and kidney and intestinal pains.

The Footbath

A footbath is a simple matter of putting the feet and calves into a deep pot or tub filled with the herbal bath water. For chronically cold feet, a hot footbath of about 15 minutes makes a good treatment; it has also been recommended for bladder, kidney, throat, and ear inflammations. Cold footbaths (lasting until the cold becomes uncomfortable or the feet feel warm) have been touted for tired feet, constipation, insomnia, headache, nosebleed, and colds. (One man made the papers not long ago by claiming that he cured his colds by immersing his big toe in ice water for one minute.) Alternating between hot and cold (1 to 2 minutes in the hot herbal bath, a half minute in cold water, alternating for 15 minutes and ending with the cold) is said to promote circulation in the legs, help prevent varicose veins, and even be good for weak menstrual flow. It is also said to be helpful for insomnia, headache, high blood pressure, and chronically cold feet.

The Eye Bath

Two basic methods of treating eye problems (sore eyes, inflammations, etc.) with herb decoctions or infusions are available. One is to use an eye cup—a small cup shaped to fit over the eye. The other method—suitable especially for treating both eyes at the same time—is to use a bowl or basin holding enough of the preparation to immerse the face in. With either method, the bath consists of three or four applications, during each of which you open and close your eyes several times while in contact with the liquid.

The Vapor Bath

Vapor baths are particularly suited to providing medication by inhalation, but they can also be helpful in external applications. For an inhalant vapor bath, you need a chair, a pot containing a steaming herb infusion or decoction, something to set the pot on, and enough blankets to enclose you and the whole works completely. Arrange the chair and the pot so that you can hold your head over the pot to inhale the vapors. Have someone drape blankets all around so that you and the pot are entirely enclosed. With your head over the pot, breathe the vapor for 15 to 30 minutes. This is sometimes followed by a cold sitz- or half bath lasting only a few seconds and then by 1 or 2 hours in bed, warmly wrapped in blankets like a mummy. This vapor bath treatment is good for colds, sinus and respiratory problems, and middle ear inflammations.

The sauna provides the ideal external vapor bath, but those of us who don't happen to have one handy can improvise with a cane chair (or a chair that has holes in the seat), two pots with steaming herb infusion or decoction, a wooden grate, and enough blankets to enclose everything, including a person from the neck or waist down. Place one pot under the chair, the other in front of the chair so that you can comfortably rest your feet on the wooden grate when it is placed on top of the pot. Sit on the chair, put your feet on the grate, and have someone enclose you and the pots completely. You need to be enclosed only from the waist down, but it may be easier to make a good seal at the neck. This vapor bath lasts about

20 or 30 minutes, perhaps followed by a cold half bath of a few seconds. The final part of the treatment is bed, as with the inhalant vapor bath. The external vapor bath is good for kidney and intestinal pains, and for prostate problems. If you have cystitis or prostatitis, omit the cold half bath.

Other Baths

The baths described are not the only ones possible, of course. You can easily adapt these techniques to treat any part of the body locally by immersion or vapor. Also, you can get the benefit of different temperatures by changing the temperature during the bath: add hot water to increase, cold water to decrease. In either case, though, the total amount of water in the bath should stay the same, so that as much must be removed as is added.

Some Useful Bath Formulas

(Unless specified otherwise, amounts are for a full bath; for partial baths use a third as much.)

1. To make a good eyewash, dissolve ½ tsp. aloes and 1 tsp. boric acid in 1 cup water.

2. Steep 2 oz. balm leaves in 1 qt. boiling-hot water for 15 minutes. Add to bath water for nervous tension, insomnia, and other nervous problems.

3. Boil 1 lb. dried English walnut leaves in 1½ qt. water for 45 minutes. Add the decoction to bath water for rheumatism, gout, skin problems, glandular swellings, and sweaty feet.

4. Add 7 oz. European angelica roots to 2 qt. cold water; bring to a boil, then let steep for 5 minutes. Good for the nerves and for skin problems.

5. Add 3 to 4 oz. fragrant valerian root to 1 qt. cold water; let soak for 10 to 12 hours, then bring to a boil and boil briefly. Add to bath water for insomnia and nervous problems.

6. Steep 3 to 4 oz. German camomile flowers in 1 qt. boiling-hot water for 1 hour. Add to bath water for

skin problems, wounds, and varicose ulcers. For hemorrhoids, make a vapor bath by putting 1 or 2 handfuls camomile flowers and 3 qt. boiling-hot water in a pail. Sit on the pail so that the top is closed off. See also German camomile entry in Part 2.

7. For an eyewash, steep 1 tsp. goldenseal, ½ tsp. myrrh, and 2 heaping tsp. boric acid in 1 pint boiling-hot water. Add 1 tsp. of the infusion to ½ cup water and use.

8. Boil 2 to 2½ lb. chopped horse chestnuts in water. Add the decoction to bath water for leg ulcers, varicose veins, hemorrhoids, neuralgia, and sunburn.

9. Steep ½ lb. juniper berries or 1 lb. fresh shoots in boiling-hot water. Add the infusion to a full bath for rheumatic and skin problems.

10. Boil 1 lb. male fern rootstock in water. Add the decoction to a footbath for varicose veins.

11. Steep 3 to 4 oz. mother of thyme in 1 pint boiling-hot water for 10 minutes. Add the infusion to bath water for nervous exhaustion.

12. Put ½ lb. ground mustard in a cloth bag and boil in water. Add the decoction to a hot footbath for colds, flu, and respiratory problems.

13. Put 1 to 2 lb. oat straw in 3 to 5 qt. cold water; bring to a boil and boil for 30 minutes. Add the decoction to bath water for rheumatic problems.

14. Boil 1 lb. oak bark in 5 qt. water for 2 hours. Add the decoction to bath water for skin problems, varicose ulcers, and chilblains. Use as a 20-minute daily sitzbath for hemorrhoids.

15. Steep 2 oz. rosemary leaves in 1 pint boiling-hot water for 10 minutes. Add the infusion to bath water to stimulate circulation, digestion, and general metabolic activity.

16. Boil 1 lb. fresh shave grass thoroughly in 3 qt. water. Add the decoction to bath water to stimulate circulation and for wounds, varicose ulcers, and skin problems.

17. Add 2 to 3½ lb. young twigs or young green cones from the spruce tree to 4 gallons cold water. Let stand

for 12 to 24 hours, and then boil in the same water for 2 hours. Add the decoction to bath water for rheumatic, digestive, and nervous problems. It also makes a good room freshener when used in a humidifier.

18. Add 1 lb. chopped sweet flag root to 5 qt. cold water. Let stand for 2 hours, then bring quickly to a boil and steep for 5 minutes. Add the liquid to the bath water to stimulate circulation and for chilblains, low blood pressure, and general tiredness.

19. Steep 3 to 4 oz. thyme in 1 pint boiling-hot water for 10 minutes. Add the infusion to bath water for rheumatic and asthmatic problems, cramps, bronchitis, bruises, swellings, and sprains.

20. Add 1 lb. wheat bran and 1 lb. rye bran to 2½ qt. cold water. Bring to a boil and boil for a short time. Add the decoction to bath water for skin problems; keep the bath water at about 95°F.

GLOSSARY OF MEDICINAL EFFECTS AND HERBS THAT PRODUCE THEM

All the following terms are commonly found in standard reference works on herbal medicine. A few are not used in this book, but they are included here for reference and information. Examples of herbs having these properties are listed by their Part 2 Compendium numbers.

ABORTIFACIENT: An agent that induces or causes premature expulsion of a fetus.
> 094, 112, 138, 186, 191, 218, 287, 288, 330, 331, 335, 367, 368, 414, 449

ACRID: Having a hot, biting taste or causing heat and irritation when applied to the skin.
> 061, 078, 079, 080, 093, 157, 228, 308, 309, 393, 428, 475

ADJUVANT: An herb added to a mixture to aid the effect of the principal ingredient.
> 001, 005, 006, 021, 082, 083, 085, 086, 092, 102, 109, 157, 165, 169, 173, 215, 234, 253, 283, 284, 285, 286, 434, 438, 442, 493

ALTERATIVE: An agent which produces gradual beneficial change in the body, usually by improving nutrition, without having any marked specific effect and without causing sensible evacuation.
> 017, 046, 048, 050, 054, 061, 065, 077, 096, 127, 129, 164, 165, 176, 180, 212, 230, 267, 277, 278, 280, 337, 341, 343, 344, 345, 351, 358, 379, 400, 401, 418, 422, 423, 424, 427, 458, 461, 462, 463, 465, 481, 483, 500, 501, 508, 511

ANALGESIC: A drug which relieves or diminishes pain; anodyne.

084, 274, 275, 324, 354, 355, 486, 487, 488, 489, 490

ANAPHRODISIAC: An agent which reduces sexual desire or potency.

(See also Erotomania—page 66)
488

ANESTHETIC: An agent that deadens sensation.

005, 084, 267, 336, 497

ANODYNE: An agent that soothes or relieves pain.

078, 079, 080, 082, 083, 084, 090, 093, 102, 107, 113,
194, 215, 233, 251, 252, 283, 285, 286, 292, 299, 302,
311, 324, 351, 358, 360, 392, 401, 478, 486, 487, 488,
493, 494

ANTHELMINTIC: An agent that destroys or expels intestinal worms; vermicide; vermifuge.

041, 044, 060, 088, 134, 148, 149, 163, 168, 185, 242,
245, 246, 297, 320, 340, 349, 352, 359, 362, 363, 390,
448, 449, 452, 457, 461, 465, 495, 496, 497

ANTIBIOTIC: An agent that destroys or arrests the growth of micro-organisms.

084, 224, 441

ANTICOAGULANT: An agent that prevents clotting in a liquid, as in blood.

509, 510

ANTIEMETIC: An agent that counteracts nausea and relieves vomiting.

(See also Nausea, Vomiting—page 75)
102, 104, 224, 370

ANTIHYDROTIC: An agent which reduces or suppresses perspiration.

(See also Night Sweats—page 76)
393

ANTILITHIC: An agent which reduces or suppresses urinary calculi (stones) and acts to dissolve those already present.

032, 033, 043, 044, 066, 070, 095, 115, 128, 144, 163,
175, 179, 209, 237, 274, 295, 339, 341, 347, 364, 367,
368, 369, 376, 412, 470, 493, 512

ANTIPERIODIC: An agent which counteracts periodic or intermittent diseases (such as malaria).

018, 019, 020, 040, 062, 063, 104, 139, 163, 176, 227, 263, 398

ANTIPHLOGISTIC: An agent which reduces inflammation. (See also Inflammation—page 72)
083, 177, 454

ANTIPYRETIC: An agent which prevents or reduces fever. (See also Febrifuge)

ANTISCORBUTIC: A source of vitamin C for curing or preventing scurvy.

ANTISCROFULOUS: Counteracting scrofula.
002, 095, 223, 341, 372, 387, 399, 400, 455, 466, 471, 483, 500, 501

ANTISEPTIC: An agent for destroying or inhibiting pathogenic or putrefactive bacteria.
003, 012, 042, 046, 102, 114, 129, 139, 156, 176, 180, 183, 224, 248, 304, 305, 306, 319, 320, 397, 401, 446, 454, 473, 481, 486, 487, 488, 489, 497

ANTISPASMODIC: An agent that relieves or checks spasms or cramps.
021, 028, 031, 036, 039, 053, 058, 078, 079, 080, 081, 082, 083, 084, 085, 090, 093, 099, 109, 111, 113, 122, 124, 137, 146, 152, 153, 162, 168, 181, 182, 194, 199, 227, 233, 248, 251, 252, 254, 255, 258, 268, 269, 271, 278, 283, 284, 285, 286, 299, 307, 318, 320, 326, 328, 332, 338, 339, 365, 366, 387, 392, 393, 396, 416, 417, 441, 452, 453, 458, 478, 480, 485, 493, 497, 499, 509, 510, 513

ANTITUSSIVE: An agent that relieves coughing. (See also Cough—page 64)

APERIENT: A mild stimulant for the bowels; a gentle purgative.
027, 063, 064, 077, 081, 115, 119, 128, 131, 164, 347, 376, 380, 457, 491

APHRODISIAC: An agent for arousing or increasing sexual desire or potency.
024, 087, 094, 102, 109, 141, 147, 166, 170, 232, 233, 251, 260, 272, 276, 283, 320, 344, 359, 364, 392, 402, 403, 404, 441, 466, 470

APPETIZER: An agent that excites the appetite. (See also Appetite, Lack of—page 60)
004, 018, 019, 031, 035, 040, 073, 084, 085, 086, 092,

094, 097, 098, 104, 109, 122, 140, 169, 170, 179, 215,
230, 249, 278, 281, 303, 304, 313, 347, 378, 392, 445,
466, 477

AROMATIC: A substance having an agreeable odor and stimulating qualities.

005, 018, 020, 021, 028, 070, 082, 083, 085, 090, 109,
114, 122, 146, 166, 169, 173, 215, 234, 235, 248, 268,
269, 272, 283, 284, 285, 286, 289, 290, 291, 313, 323,
330, 331, 387, 390, 393, 394, 401, 402, 403, 434, 442,
445, 471, 480, 493, 497, 498

ASTRINGENT: An agent that contracts organic tissue, reducing secretions or discharges.

012, 014, 017, 033, 035, 038, 040, 041, 042, 043, 044,
046, 048, 049, 050, 051, 052, 053, 058, 066, 099, 100,
101, 104, 106, 107, 127, 135, 141, 142, 143, 144, 145,
173, 175, 176, 178, 179, 191, 193, 195, 198, 203, 209,
212, 217, 219, 220, 221, 222, 223, 236, 237, 238, 240,
243, 247, 250, 251, 259, 261, 262, 263, 265, 266, 270,
272, 274, 278, 293, 294, 295, 305, 308, 310, 314, 317,
319, 334, 335, 337, 338, 339, 341, 342, 343, 344, 345,
347, 349, 352, 359, 361, 364, 365, 370, 371, 373, 377,
378, 379, 380, 384, 388, 393, 396, 397, 398, 399, 402,
411, 415, 419, 421, 425, 433, 436, 439, 440, 443, 446,
447, 454, 464, 466, 467, 471, 473, 476, 481, 484, 486,
487, 488, 489, 490, 492, 499, 500, 501, 512

BALSAM: 1) A soothing or healing agent. 2) A resinous substance obtained from the exudations of various trees and used in medicinal preparations.

353, 354, 355, 446

BITTER: Characterized by a bitter principle which acts on the mucous membranes of the mouth and stomach to increase appetite and promote digestion.

019, 049, 050, 051, 212, 230, 257, 281, 282, 361

BITTER TONIC:

015, 073, 076, 082, 104, 177, 279, 359, 363, 435, 455,
459, 499, 511

CALMATIVE: An agent that has a mild sedative or tranquilizing effect.

028, 037, 039, 083, 122, 162, 194, 225, 232, 251, 268,
269, 293, 307, 426, 493

CARDIAC: An agent that stimulates or otherwise affects the heart.

053, 161, 182, 186, 188, 254, 288, 289, 293, 336, 371, 462, 493, 497

CARMINATIVE: An agent for expelling gas from the intestines.

005, 018, 019, 020, 021, 028, 031, 041, 066, 070, 083, 085, 086, 087, 088, 090, 094, 096, 109, 114, 122, 146, 153, 155, 162, 168, 169, 173, 223, 234, 247, 248, 260, 268, 269, 271, 278, 283, 284, 285, 286, 289, 290, 291, 305, 313, 320, 321, 322, 326, 330, 338, 339, 346, 390, 400, 402, 434, 442, 445, 452, 453, 479, 480, 490, 497

CATHARTIC: An agent that acts to empty the bowels; laxative.

026, 045, 054, 061, 063, 073, 089, 123, 130, 188, 212, 231, 267, 277, 297, 351, 405, 407, 408, 409, 411, 437, 465, 482, 512

CAUSTIC: A corrosive substance capable of burning or eating away tissues.

(See also Acrid)

CHOLAGOGUE: An agent for increasing the flow of bile into the intestines.

024, 054, 077, 081, 091, 097, 119, 133, 134, 140, 148, 165, 168, 183, 184, 192, 248, 255, 278, 279, 283, 285, 286, 295, 296, 319, 365, 374, 387, 409, 418, 457, 497, 500, 501, 502, 503, 504, 505

COAGULANT: An agent that induces clotting in a liquid, as in blood.

178, 237, 243, 244, 343, 344, 345, 413, 414, 425

COUNTERIRRITANT: An agent for producing irritation in one part of the body to counteract irritation or inflammation in another part.

(See also Irritant)

DEMULCENT: A substance that soothes irritated tissue, particularly mucous membrane.

001, 006, 013, 030, 096, 104, 107, 135, 136, 157, 159, 170, 178, 181, 201, 214, 224, 226, 229, 253, 261, 265, 266, 299, 319, 324, 343, 344, 345, 372, 473, 478, 491

DEODORANT: An herb that has the effect of destroying or masking odors.

139, 191, 260, 452, 453, 486, 487, 488, 489, 492

DEPRESSANT: An agent which lessens nervous or functional activity; opposite of stimulant.

016

DEPURATIVE: An agent that cleanses and purifies the system, particularly the blood.

058, 064, 077, 113, 119, 120, 129, 137, 165, 192, 213, 236, 308, 309, 360, 375, 400, 401, 406, 413, 421, 469, 477, 483, 484, 491, 494, 500, 501, 512, 513

DETERGENT: An agent that cleanses wounds and sores of diseased or dead matter.

DIAPHORETIC: An agent that promotes perspiration; sudorific.

016, 018, 019, 020, 023, 025, 027, 028, 036, 039, 043, 046, 047, 060, 062, 063, 064, 065, 070, 077, 078, 079, 080, 081, 083, 087, 090, 093, 106, 108, 113, 116, 123, 130, 131, 132, 140, 143, 144, 145, 156, 167, 169, 172, 173, 180, 183, 191, 192, 216, 225, 238, 255, 256, 258, 263, 268, 269, 270, 274, 278, 281, 282, 289, 307, 312, 324, 327, 328, 330, 338, 339, 341, 346, 347, 356, 358, 366, 367, 374, 375, 391, 395, 400, 401, 407, 423, 424, 426, 445, 451, 452, 460, 470, 475, 479, 480, 485, 486, 487, 488, 489, 493

DIGESTIVE: An agent that promotes or aids digestion.
(See also Indigestion—page 71)

021, 040, 087, 092, 095, 097, 098, 129, 140, 168, 179, 247, 296, 303, 304, 325, 478

DISINFECTANT: An agent that cleanses infection by destroying or inhibiting the activity of disease-producing micro-organisms.
(See also Antiseptic)

DIURETIC: An agent that increases the secretion and expulsion of urine.

003, 004, 012, 013, 018, 020, 023, 024, 026, 027, 032, 033, 036, 039, 041, 043, 044, 045, 048, 053, 055, 056, 057, 059, 060, 061, 066, 067, 070, 075, 077, 078, 079, 080, 087, 088, 093, 094, 095, 097, 106, 110, 113, 114, 115, 116, 119, 120, 122, 128, 130, 131, 132, 133, 134, 135, 136, 141, 144, 146, 158, 163, 164, 165, 168, 172, 173, 175, 176, 179, 180, 183, 185, 186, 187, 188, 191, 192, 193, 196, 204, 209, 210, 213, 214, 215, 216, 218, 219, 225, 226, 234, 237, 238, 240, 245, 248, 249, 253, 254, 255, 258, 260, 261, 262, 270, 272, 274, 277, 280, 284, 288, 289, 295, 299, 308, 311, 320, 323, 324, 326, 327, 329, 332, 338, 339, 341, 342, 344, 346, 347, 356, 360, 364, 365, 367, 374, 375, 376, 377, 388, 391, 395, 397, 400, 401, 402, 405, 406, 408, 412, 413, 414, 416,

417, 418, 421, 422, 424, 433, 437, 438, 440, 450, 455,
458, 460, 462, 469, 470, 475, 477, 483, 484, 485, 486,
487, 488, 489, 490, 491, 493, 494, 499, 506, 507, 509,
510, 511, 512

EMETIC: An agent that causes vomiting.
002, 016, 026, 049, 050, 051, 054, 059, 062, 063, 087,
123, 124, 125, 131, 140, 167, 188, 189, 192, 211, 258,
277, 280, 287, 311, 336, 337, 359, 379, 395, 405, 407,
417, 419, 428, 429, 430, 431, 432, 437, 458, 470, 481,
485

EMMENAGOGUE: An agent that promotes menstrual flow.
015, 020, 028, 046, 047, 053, 059, 060, 067, 085, 097,
112, 138, 141, 159, 163, 188, 203, 223, 225, 260, 262,
293, 326, 330, 359, 367, 387, 390, 392, 440, 445, 449,
450, 451, 494

EMOLLIENT: An agent used externally to soften and soothe.
002, 006, 007, 013, 023, 104, 107, 136, 157, 159, 201,
206, 207, 208, 214, 255, 256, 261, 265, 266, 319, 491,
509, 510

ERRHINE: An agent that promotes sneezing and nasal
discharges.
026, 105, 114, 169, 248, 294, 471, 479

EUPHORIANT, EUPHORIGEN: An agent that induces an abnormal sense of vigor and buoyancy.
084, 313

EXANTHEMATOUS: Relating to skin diseases or eruptions.
(See also Skin—page 77)
034, 137, 158

EXPECTORANT: An agent that promotes the discharge of
mucus from the respiratory passages.
016, 017, 018, 020, 021, 023, 025, 035, 041, 046, 051,
053, 058, 059, 062, 085, 095, 096, 105, 107, 113, 114,
123, 134, 139, 145, 146, 147, 153, 163, 167, 168, 181,
183, 187, 192, 193, 209, 216, 217, 223, 228, 251, 253,
258, 260, 261, 264, 265, 266, 268, 269, 270, 281, 282,
299, 306, 310, 320, 324, 326, 329, 343, 344, 345, 346,
354, 356, 360, 374, 392, 396, 397, 398, 399, 402, 403,
407, 417, 418, 422, 423, 426, 441, 442, 446, 452, 453,
458, 462, 469, 470, 472, 477, 478, 479, 485, 509, 510,
513, 514

FEBRIFUGE: An agent that reduces or eliminates fever.
015, 016, 045, 047, 059, 063, 064, 067, 073, 087, 104,

108, 117, 120, 127, 140, 143, 145, 156, 163, 164, 168, 184, 209, 212, 215, 225, 243, 263, 292, 319, 335, 353, 363, 440, 445, 486, 487, 488, 489, 497, 498, 502, 503, 504, 505, 513

GALACTAGOGUE: An agent that encourages or increases the secretion of milk.
031, 064, 085, 122, 141, 146, 172, 224, 281, 282, 308

HALLUCINOGEN: An agent that induces hallucinations.
(See also Boredom—page 62)
084, 313, 336, 405

HEMOSTATIC: An agent that stops bleeding.
(See also Styptic)
049, 050, 051, 103, 107, 138, 178, 237, 278, 308, 343, 344, 345, 413, 439, 454, 492

HEPATIC: A drug that acts on the liver.
(See also Liver—page 73)
027, 054

HYDRAGOGUE: A purgative that produces abundant watery discharge.
(See also Purgative)

HYPNOTIC: An agent that promotes or produces sleep.
(See also Insomnia—page 72)
111, 162, 215, 233, 252, 450

IRRITANT: An agent that causes inflammation or abnormal sensitivity in living tissue.
089, 092, 113, 124, 188, 196, 197, 218, 228, 234, 238, 239, 240, 303, 304, 327, 358, 390, 441, 449, 451, 452, 453, 460, 475, 479, 490, 494

LAXATIVE: An agent promoting evacuation of the bowels; a mild purgative.
003, 022, 027, 096, 125, 153, 157, 165, 167, 173, 245, 253, 254, 276, 319, 324, 329, 348, 349, 351, 370, 408, 421, 448, 462, 465, 478, 483, 511

MUCILAGINOUS: Characterized by a gummy or gelatinous consistency.
013, 112, 136, 142, 147, 150, 151, 159, 201, 202, 207, 208, 229, 255, 256, 324

NARCOTIC: A drug which relieves pain and induces sleep when used in medicinal doses; in large doses narcotics produce convulsions, coma, or death.
016, 039, 093, 194, 233, 252, 312, 336, 340, 417, 435

NAUSEANT: An agent that produces an inclination to vomit.

NEPHRITIC: A medicine applicable to diseases of the kidney.

(See also Kidneys—page 73)

NERVINE: An agent that has a calming or soothing effect on the nerves; formerly, any agent that acts on the nervous system.

(See also Nervous Conditions—page 75)

152, 162, 199, 227, 258, 287, 318, 374, 396, 398, 508

OXYTOCIC: An agent that stimulates contraction of the uterine muscle and so facilitates or speeds up childbirth.

047, 060, 084, 112, 138, 335

PECTORAL: A remedy for pulmonary or other chest diseases.

(See also Lungs—page 74)

006, 064, 068, 069, 143, 179, 196, 302

POISON: A substance which has a harmful or destructive effect when in contact with living tissue.

PURGATIVE: An agent that produces a vigorous emptying of the bowels.

007, 026, 045, 065, 068, 069, 074, 075, 076, 087, 089, 093, 118, 125, 128, 130, 131, 132, 133, 148, 155, 159, 184, 186, 189, 192, 210, 231, 236, 246, 267, 280, 296, 304, 311, 312, 347, 359, 374, 378, 418, 428, 429, 430, 431, 432, 469, 478, 481, 514

REFRIGERANT: An agent that lowers abnormal body heat.

012, 027, 029, 107, 117, 204, 222, 250, 264, 283, 285, 286, 371, 440, 448, 502, 503, 504, 505

RESTORATIVE: An agent that restores consciousness or normal physiological activity.

040, 064, 147, 150, 152, 153, 154, 162, 170, 171, 179, 229, 310, 317, 318, 366, 457, 480, 484, 502, 503

RUBEFACIENT: A gentle local irritant that produces reddening of the skin.

078, 079, 080, 113, 188, 218, 234, 238, 240, 277, 290, 327, 453

SEDATIVE: A soothing agent that reduces nervousness, distress, or irritation.

043, 053, 059, 094, 108, 153, 156, 177, 182, 215, 227, 248, 251, 252, 292, 294, 310, 328, 329, 330, 332, 334, 392, 416, 445, 452, 476, 492, 508

SIALAGOGUE: An agent that stimulates the secretion of saliva.

061, 092, 117, 140, 169, 250, 358, 407, 412, 470

SPECIFIC: An agent which cures or alleviates a particular condition or disease.

STIMULANT: An agent that excites or quickens the activity of physiological processes.

005, 018, 019, 020, 021, 023, 047, 059, 070, 082, 086, 088, 092, 095, 114, 123, 127, 128, 130, 134, 139, 141, 146, 155, 169, 170, 173, 179, 180, 185, 211, 213, 216, 223, 225, 235, 241, 248, 260, 263, 271, 272, 276, 277, 284, 288, 290, 291, 313, 318, 321, 342, 354, 358, 366, 374, 387, 390, 397, 401, 402, 407, 423, 424, 434, 457, 459, 460, 469, 470, 480, 490, 497

STOMACHIC: An agent that strengthens, stimulates, or tones the stomach.

018, 021, 028, 031, 082, 085, 086, 109, 114, 117, 119, 122, 146, 162, 165, 170, 187, 199, 218, 223, 234, 247, 248, 256, 260, 268, 269, 283, 284, 285, 286, 293, 305, 320, 321, 323, 325, 339, 347, 348, 353, 363, 380, 387, 390, 402, 406, 422, 434, 442, 445, 450, 467, 469, 476, 494, 497, 498, 501, 502, 503, 504, 505, 506, 507

STYPTIC: An agent that contracts tissues; astringent; specifically, a hemostatic agent that stops bleeding by contracting the blood vessels.

040, 048, 058, 219, 259, 272, 377, 399, 414, 425, 499

SUDORIFIC: An agent that promotes or increases perspiration.

(See also Diaphoretic)

TAENIACIDE: A substance that kills tapeworms.

(See also Vermifuge)

TONIC: An agent that strengthens or invigorates organs or the entire organism.

004, 017, 018, 021, 033, 040, 046, 052, 059, 062, 063, 064, 066, 092, 093, 097, 104, 110, 119, 120, 127, 134, 140, 141, 150, 151, 155, 163, 164, 165, 173, 179, 212, 215, 216, 223, 224, 227, 234, 235, 241, 243, 248, 263, 264, 268, 269, 272, 276, 278, 283, 285, 286, 307, 308, 314, 317, 320, 321, 335, 337, 342, 353, 364, 366, 373, 378, 379, 384, 395, 400, 403, 406, 416, 419, 422, 433, 438, 440, 443, 449, 453, 457, 458, 461, 462, 465, 466,

467, 471, 478, 483, 484, 486, 487, 488, 489, 491, 492, 500, 501, 502, 504, 505, 513

VASOCONSTRICTOR: An agent that narrows the blood vessels, thus raising blood pressure.
(See also Blood Pressure, Low—page 62)
128, 138, 183, 414, 439

VASODILATOR: An agent that widens the blood vessels, thus lowering blood pressure.
(See also Blood Pressure, High—page 61)
182, 288, 439

VERMICIDE: An agent that destroys intestinal worms.
(See also Anthelmintic)

VERMIFUGE: An agent that causes the expulsion of intestinal worms.
015, 045, 062, 118, 143, 186, 189, 212, 325, 408, 499

VESICANT: An agent that produces blisters.
023, 025, 234, 245, 303, 460

VULNERARY: A healing application for wounds.
(See also Wounds—page 81)
007, 023, 036, 041, 062, 081, 103, 107, 135, 141, 145, 222, 237, 245, 299, 324, 325, 356, 396, 413, 436, 438, 447, 499, 507, 510

PLANTS APPLICABLE TO VARIOUS CONDITIONS AND BODY ORGANS

This listing is compiled from several sources of reference information on herbal medicine. The fact that a plant appears under a given heading means that some part or a preparation derived from some part of the plant has been used at one time or another to treat the condition or affect the bodily part involved. Not all of these uses are described specifically in Part 2 of this book; many are included here for completeness and for reference purposes. This listing is therefore not to be construed as a self-sufficient guide to herbal treatment: it is only a guide or point of departure. Your first step after consulting this list is to refer to the descriptions in Part 2 for detailed information. If you then should need still more information, some of the reference works listed in the Bibliography may provide further answers.

ACNE
Burdock
Echinacea
English walnut
Fragrant valerian
Kidney bean
Wild strawberry

ALCOHOLISM
Cannabis
Cayenne
Feverfew
Fringe tree
Goldenseal
Mother of thyme
Nerve root
Passion flower
Quassia

ALCOHOLISM
(cont.)
Red currant
Yellow jessamine

ALLERGY
Cubeb
Ma-huang
Papaya
Red eyebright
Skunk cabbage

AMENORRHEA:
see Menstruation,
Tardy

ANEMIA
Alfalfa
Artichoke

ANEMIA (cont.)
Barberry
Brooklime
Burnet saxifrage
Chive
Comfrey
Dandelion
Dwarf nettle
Elecampane
European angelica
European vervain
Fenugreek
Fumitory
Gentian (all)
Ground ivy
Iceland moss
Lad's love
Milfoil

ANEMIA (cont.)
Mother of thyme
Nettle
Peruvian bark
Quassia
St. Benedict thistle
St. Johnswort
Spinach
Sweet flag
Watercress
Wild Oregon grape

ANURIA: see
Urination,
Incomplete

APPETITE,
LACK OF
Alder buckthorn
Alfalfa
Allspice
Alpine cranberry
American centaury
Anise
Arnica
Artichoke
Bear's garlic
Bennet
Bitter milkwort
Black mustard
Black pepper
Blackthorn
Buck bean
Burnet saxifrage
Camomile (both)
Caraway
Cardamom
Cayenne
Celery
Chicory
Chive
Colombo
Coriander
Dandelion
Dill
English walnut
European angelica
European centaury
Galangal
Garden thyme
Garlic
Gentian (all)
Ginseng
Goldenseal
Greater pimpernel

APPETITE,
LACK OF (cont.)
Hops
Horseradish
Iceland moss
Imperial masterwort
Ironweed
Juniper
Lad's love
Lady's mantle
Leek
Madder
Milfoil
Milk thistle
Mint (all)
Mugwort
Parsley
Pitcher plant
Plum
Privet
Purple goatsbeard
Red currant
Rhubarb
Rosemary
Rough avens
Saffron
St. Benedict thistle
Savory
Silvery lady's mantle
Speedwell
Star anise
Sweet cicely
Sweet flag
Sweet marjoram
Tarragon
Turkey corn
Turtlebloom
Virginia snakeroot
Wafer ash
Water avens
Watercress
White mustard
Wild angelica
Wild clover
Wild hyssop
Wild marjoram
Winter savory
Wood sorrel
Wormwood
Yellow goatsbeard

ARTERIO-
SCLEROSIS
Arnica
Artichoke

ARTERIO-
SCLEROSIS
(cont.)
Bear's garlic
Black currant
Chervil
European mistletoe
Garlic
Hawthorn
Hedge garlic
Nutmeg
Olive
Onion
Pansy
Rue
Shave grass
Shepherd's purse
Watercress
Witch grass

ARTHRITIS
Alder buckthorn
Alfalfa
Black currant
Black elder
Black poplar
Buck bean
Burdock
Buttercup (all)
Cayenne
Chickweed
Comfrey
Dropwort
European aspen
European centaury
European goldenrod
Garden violet
Horseradish
Juniper
Lady's thumb
Life everlasting
Marsh tea
Meadow saffron
Meadowsweet
Monkshood
Mountain holly
Pokeweed
Red bryony
Restharrow
St. Benedict thistle
Sassafras
Shave grass
White melilot
Willow (all)
Wintergreen
Witch grass

ARTHRITIS (cont.)
Wormwood
Yellow melilot
Yew

ASTHMA
Almond
Althea
Arum
Asefetida
Balm
Balm of Gilead
Betony
Black cohosh
Blue vervain
Boneset
Burdock
Cannabis
Celandine
Coltsfoot
Comfrey
Common mullein
Cubeb
Dwarf nettle
Elecampane
Eucalyptus
European centaury
Fragrant valerian
Garden thyme
German camomile
Ground ivy
Gum plant
Hedge garlic
Horehound
Horseradish
Hyssop
Indian turnip
Jimson weed
Lettuce (both)
Lobelia
Lovage
Marsh hibiscus
Masterwort
Milkweed
Mullein
Myrrh
Nettle
New Jersey tea
Orange mullein
Parsley
Peony
Pleurisy root
Prickly ash
Quaking aspen

ASTHMA (cont.)
Saw palmetto
Skunk cabbage
Speedwell
Spikenard (both)
Sumbul
Sundew
Tacamahac
Watercress
Wild black cherry
Wild marjoram
Yerba santa

BACKACHE
(*Indicates those
for external
application.)
Alpine cranberry
American
spikenard
Barberry
Bearberry
Betony
Black cohosh
Black elder
*Black mustard
*Blue gentian
Buchu (all)
*Buckhorn brake
*Cayenne
Dwarf nettle
German camomile
Horsemint
Life everlasting
Nettle
*Oat
Pennyroyal (both)
Prickly ash
Tansy
*Twin leaf
*White mustard

BAD BREATH: see
Halitosis

BEDWETTING
Balm
Bearberry
Betony
Bistort
Black alder
Buchu
Cubeb
Fennel
Hollyhock
Hops

BEDWETTING
(cont.)
Indian corn
Lady's mantle
Mallow (both)
Milfoil
Milkweed
Oat
Pansy
Plantain (all)
Red alder
Restharrow
St. Johnswort
Shave grass
Silverweed
Smooth alder
Sticklewort
Willow (all)

BLEEDING,
EXTERNAL:
see Wounds

BLEEDING,
INTERNAL:
see Hemorrhage,
Internal

BLOOD,
VOMITING:
see Hemorrhage,
Internal

BLOOD PRESSURE,
HIGH
American sanicle
Barberry
Bear's garlic
Black cohosh
Blue cohosh
Blue vervain
Boneset
Chervil
Cleavers
Ergot
European mistletoe
Garden violet
Garlic
Hawthorn
Onion
Parsley
Rue
Scotch broom
Skullcap
Storksbill
Wild black cherry

BLOOD PRESSURE, LOW
Anise
Balm
Cat's foot
Dyer's broom
Hawthorn
Heather
Lavender
Ma-huang
Milfoil
Motherwort
Rosemary
Shepherd's purse
Storksbill

BOREDOM
Belladonna
Cannabis
Ergot
Horse chestnut
Indian black drink
Jimson weed
Mulberry (both)
Nerve root
Nutmeg
Peyote
Prickly lettuce
Scotch broom
Wormwood

BRONCHITIS
Althea
Anise
Arum
Asafetida
Asarum
Barley
Bearberry
Betony
Bilberry
Bitter milkwort
Black cohosh
Black elder
Black poplar
Blind nettle
Borage
Buttercup (all)
Catnip
Celery
Chickweed
Coltsfoot
Comfrey
Common mullein
Cowslip
Cubeb

BRONCHITIS
(cont.)
Cypress spurge
Dandelion
Elecampane
Eucalyptus
European angelica
European aspen
European sanicle
European seneka
Fennel
Garden raspberry
Garden thyme
Garden violet
Goldenseal
Greater pimpernel
Ground ivy
Heather
Hemp nettle
Hepatica (both)
Horehound
Horse chestnut
Iceland moss
Irish moss
Jimson weed
Knotgrass
Lad's love
Licorice
Lovage
Low mallow
Lungwort
Marsh hibiscus
Mother of thyme
Mountain holly
Mouse ear
Mullein
Nasturtium
New Jersey tea
Norway spruce
Onion
Orange
Orange mullein
Orris root
Pansy
Pasque flower
Peach tree
Plantain (all)
Pleurisy root
Primrose
Radish
Saffron
Sage
St. Johnswort
Sandalwood
Savory

BRONCHITIS
(cont.)
Saw palmetto
Senega snakeroot
Skunk cabbage
Slippery elm
Speedwell
Spruce
Star anise
Sumbul
Sundew
Sweet cicely
Sweet marjoram
Watercress
Water eryngo
White melilot
White mustard
White pond lily
Wild marjoram
Winter savory
Yellow melilot
Yerba santa

BRUISES
Aloe
American elder
Arnica
Balm of Gilead
Bittersweet
    nightshade
Birch
Black elder
Buckhorn brake
Burnet saxifrage
Calendula
Celery
Cinnamon fern
Comfrey
Corkwood
Dwarf nettle
English oak
European sanicle
Fenugreek
Figwort
Flax
Flower-of-an-hour
Garden thyme
Garden violet
Hemp agrimony
Herb Robert
Hound's-tongue
Hyssop
Laurel
Life everlasting
Lobelia

BRUISES (cont.)
Low cudweed
Mother of thyme
Mugwort
Nettle
Okra
Olive
Pearly everlasting
Pennyroyal (both)
Primrose
Quaking aspen
Rattlesnake plantain
St. Johnswort
Shinleaf
Solomon's seal
  (both)
Stone root
Tacamahac
Tansy
White pond lily
Willow (all)
Wintergreen
Witch hazel
Wormwood
Yerba santa

BURNS
Aloe
American elder
Basswood
Bennet
Bittersweet
  nightshade
Burdock
Calendula
Chickweed
Coltsfoot
Comfrey
Common plantain
Cucumber
Gum plant
Hound's-tongue
Houseleek
Lady's mantle
Olive
Poplar (all)
Pumpkin
Quaking aspen
St. Johnswort
Sweet flag
Wild daisy
Willow (all)
Witch hazel

CALLOUSES: see
  Corns, Callouses

CHILBLAINS
Barberry
Bennet
Calendula
English oak
English walnut
European angelica
European mistletoe
Hawthorn
Hedge garlic
Horseradish
Lady's mantle
Milfoil
Mugwort
Oat
Onion
Sage
St. Benedict thistle
Shepherd's purse
Turnip
Watercress

CHILDBIRTH,
  EASING
Althea
American spikenard
Bennet
Birthwort
Black cohosh
Blind nettle
Blue cohosh
Cannabis
Columbine
Comfrey
Common groundsel
Cotton
European ragwort
Flax
Garden raspberry
Garden violet
Goat's rue
Horehound
Iceland moss
Lady's mantle
Pansy
Primrose
Ragwort
Shepherd's purse
Silverweed
Spikenard (both)
Squaw vine
Wild red raspberry
Wormwood

COLDS
Althea

COLDS (cont.)
American angelica
American elder
American ivy
American spikenard
Balm
Basswood
Betony
Bilberry
Birch
Black elder
Bloodroot
Blue vervain
Boneset
Butternut
Camomile (both)
Catnip
Coltsfoot
Cyclamen
Everlasting (all)
Feverfew
Fig
Fragrant valerian
Galangal
Garden thyme
Ginger
Ginseng
Gray goldenrod
Ground ivy
Guaiac
Gum plant
Hedge mustard
Hollyhock
Horehound
Hyssop
Laurel
Lemon
Licorice
Lobelia
Ma-huang
Marsh hibiscus
Masterwort
Milfoil
Nasturtium
Pennyroyal (both)
Peppermint
Pleurisy root
Prickly ash
Rose
Safflower
Sage
St. Benedict thistle
Sarsaparilla
Savory
Saw palmetto

COLDS (cont.)
Senega snakeroot
Smartweed
Soapwort
Sticklewort
Sweet goldenrod
Water eryngo
Water smartweed
White pine
Wild bergamot
Wild black cherry
Wild daisy
Wild ginger
Wild sarsaparilla
Wintergreen
Witch grass
Wormwood
Yellow parilla
Yerba santa

COLIC: see
Carminative and
Antispasmodic
(in the Glossary
of Medicinal
Effects)

CONSTIPATION
Agave
Alder buckthorn
Aloe
American mountain
ash
Asparagus
Basil
Bird's tongue
Black elder
Black root
Blackthorn
Blue flag
Boneset
Boxwood
Bryony (both)
Buck bean
Burdock
Butternut
Cabbage rose
Calendula
Cascara sagrada
Castor bean
Celandine
Chickweed
Chicory
Common buckthorn
Common plum
Cucumber

CONSTIPATION
(cont.)
Cypress spurge
Dogbane
Dog's mercury
Dyer's broom
European centaury
Female fern
Feverfew
Fig
Flax
Fringe tree
Fumitory
Goldenseal
Hedge bindweed
Hedge hyssop
Hemp agrimony
Hyssop
Jalap
Kidney vetch
Larkspur
Licorice
Mallow (both)
Mandrake
Mercury herb
Mezereon
Mugwort
Mulberry (both)
Olive
Peach tree
Pokeweed
Pride of China
Primrose
Purging flax
Radish
Red elder
Red sedge
Restharrow
Rhubarb
Rowan
St. Benedict thistle
Scotch broom
Senega snakeroot
Senna (all)
Shepherd's purse
Soapwort
Sorrel
Spurge (all)
Sticklewort
Tamarind
Turtlebloom
Wahoo
Water dock
White holly
White mustard

CONSTIPATION
(cont.)
Wild clover
Wild daisy
Wild indigo
Wild jalap
Wild Oregon grape
Wild plum
Wormwood
Yellow dock
Yellow toadflax

CONSUMPTION:
see Lungs

CORNS,
CALLOUSES
Bittersweet
nightshade
Celandine
Dandelion
Garlic
Houseleek
Lemon
Onion
Roman camomile
Wintergreen

COUGH
Acacia
Almond
Althea
American ivy
American spikenard
Asafetida
Balm of Gilead
Basswood
Bilberry
Birthroot
Bitter milkwort
Black cohosh
Black elder
Bloodroot
Blue vervain
Borage
Buckhorn brake
Cannabis
Celandine
Cinnamon fern
Coltsfoot
Comfrey
Corkwood
Cotton
Cubeb
Elecampane
English ivy

64

COUGH (cont.)
European sanicle
European seneka
Evening primrose
Female fern
Flax
Flowering spurge
Flower-of-an-hour
Garden raspberry
Garden thyme
Garden violet
Ginseng
Heather
Hedge mustard
Horehound
Horseradish
Hound's-tongue
Hyssop
Iceland moss
Irish moss
Jimson weed
Lad's love
Lemon
Lettuce (both)
Licorice
Lobelia
Lovage
Lungwort
Maidenhair
Mallow (both)
Marsh hibiscus
Marsh tea
Milfoil
Mother of thyme
Mullein (all)
Myrrh
Norway spruce
Okra
Onion
Orris root
Pansy
Parsley
Pearly everlasting
Plantain (all)
Pleurisy root
Quaking aspen
Radish
Rosemary
Rough avens
Saffron
Senega snakeroot
Skunk cabbage
Slippery elm
Smartweed
Sundew

COUGH (cont.)
Sweet gum
Tacamahac
Water avens
Water smartweed
White pine
Wild black cherry
Wild clover
Wild marjoram
Wild sarsaparilla
Yerba santa
Yew

CRAMPS
Anise
Balm
Bear's garlic
Belladonna
Betony
Black elder
Blind nettle
Blue cohosh
Burnet saxifrage
Buttercup (all)
Calendula
Camomile (both)
Cannabis
Caraway
Cayenne
Celandine
Coral root
Coriander
Cowslip
Dill
European angelica
Fennel
Fragrant valerian
Fraxinella
Garden thyme
Garlic
Henbane
Imperial masterwort
Lady's mantle
Lavender
Masterwort
Milfoil
Mother of thyme
Motherwort
Nerve root
Pasque flower
Peppermint
Radish
Ragged cup
Rose
Rosemary

CRAMPS (cont.)
Rue
Savory
Silverweed
Sweet marjoram
Twin leaf
Water mint
Wild angelica
Wild daisy
Wild marjoram
Wild yam
Winter savory
Woodruff
Wormwood

See also: ANTI-
    SPASMODIC
    (in the Glossary
    of Medicinal
    Effects)

CUTS: see Wounds

CYSTITIS: see
    Genito-Urinary
    Ailments

DANDRUFF
Agave
Camomile (both)
English elm
English ivy
English walnut
Figwort
Olive
Quassia
Rosemary
Willow (all)

DIABETES
    (*Diabetes
    mellitus*)
Artichoke
Bilberry
Blue cohosh
Chicory
Common lettuce
Dandelion
Dwarf nettle
Elecampane
European centaury
European Solomon's
    seal
Fenugreek
Flax

DIABETES (cont.)
Goat's rue
Juniper
Kidney bean
Milfoil
Nettle
Onion
Queen of the
  meadow
Saw palmetto
Spotted cranebill
Sumac
Wild red raspberry
Wintergreen

DIARRHEA
Acacia
Alpine cranberry
Amaranth
American mountain
  ash
Apple
Barberry
Basil
Bear's garlic
Beechdrops
Bennet
Betony
Bilberry
Bistort
Bitter milkwort
Black alder
Blackberry
Black birch
Black cohosh
Black currant
Black walnut
Brier hip
Calendula
Carrot
Catnip
Cinnamon fern
Colombo
Coltsfoot
Columbine
Comfrey
Dropwort
Eglantine
Eur. five-finger
  grass
European goldenrod
European vervain
Five-finger grass
Garden thyme
Garlic
Great burnet

DIARRHEA (cont.)
Ground ivy
Herb Robert
Horse chestnut
Horsemint
Horseweed
Hound's-tongue
Hyssop
Iceland moss
Knotgrass
Lady's mantle
Lady's thumb
Larch
Life everlasting
Lion's foot
Loosestrife
Lungwort
Madder
Magnolia
Matico
Meadowsweet
Motherwort
Mouse ear
Pansy
Pearly everlasting
Peppermint
Periwinkle (both)
Pilewort
Plantain (all)
Pomegranate
Privet
Radish
Red alder
Rhatany
Rhubarb
Rock-rose
Rough avens
Rowan
Sage
Savory
Silverweed
Slippery elm
Smooth alder
Spotted cranebill
Sticklewort
Sumac
Sweet fern
Sweet gum
Tormentil
Virginia mouse-ear
Water avens
Wax myrtle
White pond lily
Wild black cherry
Wild red raspberry

DIARRHEA (cont.)
Wild strawberry
Winter savory
Witch grass
Witch hazel
Woundwort

DIZZINESS
Balm
Bearded darnel
Betony
Catnip
Hawthorn
Indian pipe
Lavender
Lemon
Motherwort
Peppermint
Rose
Rue
Sage
Shepherd's purse

DOUCHE: see
  Vaginal Douche

DRINKING: see
  Alcoholism

DYSMENORRHEA:
  see Menstruation,
  Difficult

DYSPEPSIA: see
  Indigestion

ECZEMA: see Skin

EMPHYSEMA: see
  Lungs

EROTOMANIA
Belladonna
Black willow
Coriander
Cucumber
Fragrant valerian
Hops
Life everlasting
Mouse ear
Pearly everlasting
Prickly lettuce
Sage
Skullcap
Star grass
Wild marjoram

ERYSIPELAS: see
  Skin

EYES
Althea
American angelica
Borage
Calendula
Carrot
Celandine
Cornflower
Dandelion
Dropwort
European sanicle
Fennel
French rose
German camomile
Goldenseal
Herb Robert
Jasmine
Marsh hibiscus
Meadowsweet
Oat
Parsley
Plantain (all)
Red eyebright
Rose of China
Rue
Sarsaparilla
Sassafras
Savory
Slippery elm
Speedwell
Squaw vine
Sticklewort
Sycamore maple
White melilot
White pond lily
White willow
Wintergreen
Witch hazel
Woodruff
Yellow dock
Yellow melilot

FEVER
American angelica
American sanicle
Apple tree
Balm of Gilead
Basil
Bennet
Birch (both)
Bird's tongue
Black currant
Black elder
Black poplar
Blackthorn
Blue vervain

FEVER (cont.)
Boneset
Borage
Brier hip
Buck bean
Burnet saxifrage
Buttercup (all)
Butternut
Calendula
Carline thistle
Catnip
Colombo
Coral root
Cowslip
Dandelion
Desert tea
Dogbane
Dogwood
Dropwort
Echinacea
English ivy
English oak
Eucalyptus
European angelica
European centaury
European linden
Feverweed
Fraxinella
Fringe tree
Garden violet
Ginseng
Goat's rue
Hemp agrimony
Horehound
Indian pipe
Lad's love
Life everlasting
Lobelia
Magnolia
Ma-huang
Mandrake
Marsh tea
Masterwort
Meadowsweet
Milfoil
Mountain holly
Olive
Pasque flower
Passion flower
Pearly everlasting
Pennyroyal (both)
Peruvian bark
Pilewort.
Quaking aspen
Quassia

FEVER (cont.)
Ragged cup
Red elder
Sage
St. Benedict thistle
Sandalwood
Sarsaparilla
Sassafras
Sticklewort
Strawberry-bush
Sumac
Tacamahac
Tormentil
Wahoo
Water eryngo
White oak
Wild angelica
Wild bergamot
Wild marjoram
Willow (all)
Wintergreen
Wormwood
Yellow parilla
Yerba santa

FLATULENCE:
see Carminative
(in the Glossary
of Medicinal
Effects)

FLU: see Influenza

FRIGIDITY: see
Impotence,
Frigidity

GALL BLADDER
Artichoke
Barberry
Burdock
Cat's foot
Celandine
Chicory
Club moss
Dandelion
Elecampane
European centaury
Female fern
Fumitory
Garlic
Gentian (all)
Hemp agrimony
Hepatica (both)
Lavender
Milfoil

GALL BLADDER
(cont.)
Milk thistle
Mouse ear
Mugwort
Oat
Onion
Peppermint
Radish
Red pimpernel
Rosemary
St. Benedict thistle
Sticklewort
Wild daisy
Witch grass
Wormwood
Yellow toadflax

GALLSTONES
Alder buckthorn
Artichoke
Barberry
Cascara sagrada
Chicory
Dandelion
Dogbane
Dropwort
European vervain
Flax
Fringe tree
Hyssop
Mandrake
Meadowsweet
Milk thistle
Milkweed
Parsley
Restharrow
Sticklewort
Willow (all)
Woodruff

GAS, INTESTINAL:
see Carminative
(in the Glossary
of Medicinal
Effects)

GASTRITIS: see
Stomach

**GASTRO-
ENTERITIS**
Althea
Arum
Balm
Basil

**GASTRO-
ENTERITIS**
(cont.)
Bear's garlic
Bilberry
Bistort
Black currant
Blind nettle
Blue flag
Borage
Buck bean
Carrot
Chicory
Cleavers
Coltsfoot
Common mullein
Elecampane
English oak
English walnut
European centaury
Eur. five-finger grass
Garden thyme
Garlic
German camomile
Hemp nettle
Herb Robert
Hyssop
Iceland moss
Imperial masterwort
Knotgrass
Lad's love
Licorice
Loosestrife
Mallow (both)
Marsh hibiscus
Milfoil
Mother of thyme
Mouse ear
Mullein
Oat
Orange mullein
Peppermint
Plantain (all)
Red eyebright
Red sedge
Rhatany
Rough avens
Sage
St. Benedict thistle
St. Johnswort
Savory
Silverweed
Silvery lady's mantle
Sweet flag
Sweet marjoram

**GASTRO-
ENTERITIS**
(cont.)
Water avens
Water mint
White melilot
Wild angelica
Wild strawberry
Winter savory
Witch grass
Wood sorrel
Yellow bedstraw
Yellow melilot

**GENITO-URINARY
AILMENTS**
(Those marked
with * disinfect
the urine—useful
for venereal
diseases.)
*Agave
*Alpine cranberry
American angelica
American sanicle
*Bearberry
Birch (both)
Birthroot
Blackthorn
Black willow
*Blazing star (all)
Blind nettle
Blue cohosh
*Buchu
*Burdock
*Cannabis
Celery
Cleavers
Comfrey
Common plantain
*Cubeb
Desert tea
*Echinacea
*Goldenseal
*Guaiac
Heather
Hemlock spruce
Hepatica (both)
Horseweed
Indian corn
*Juniper
Mandrake
Milfoil
*Nasturtium
New Jersey tea

68

GENITO-URINARY AILMENTS (cont.)

Parsley
*Pipsissewa
Prickly ash
Queen of the meadow
*Rock-rose
*Sandalwood
*Sassafras
Saw palmetto
Scurvy grass
Shave grass
Slippery elm
Speedwell
Spotted cranebill
Squaw vine
Sumac
Water eryngo
White pond lily
Wild Oregon grape
*Wintergreen
Witch grass
Witch hazel
Yellow dock
*Yerba santa

GIDDINESS: see Dizziness

GONORRHEA: see Genito-Urinary Ailments

GOUT
Alpine cranberry
Balm of Gilead
Betony
Birch (both)
Bittersweet nightshade
Black mustard
Buck bean
Burdock
Celery
Comfrey
Dropwort
Dwarf nettle
English walnut
Gentian (all)
Guaiac
Hedge garlic
Hedge hyssop
Herb Robert

GOUT (cont.)
Horseradish
Imperial masterwort
Jimson weed
Marsh tea
Meadow saffron
Meadowsweet
Monkshood
Mountain holly
Nettle
Oat
Pennyroyal (both)
Quaking aspen
St. Johnswort
Sarsaparilla
Sassafras
Speedwell
Tacamahac
Watercress
White mustard
Willow (all)
Witch grass
Yellow parilla
Yerba maté

GRIPPE: see Influenza

GUMS
(Mostly as a mouthwash. For bleeding, see also HEMORRHAGE; for inflammation, see also INFLAMMATION.)
Barberry
Bennet
Bistort
Blackberry
Black currant
Comfrey
Dogwood
Echinacea
English walnut
Goldenseal
Myrrh
Periwinkle (both)
Pokeweed
Rhatany
Shave grass
Spotted cranebill
Watercress
Willow (all)
Witch hazel

HAIR, LOSS OF
(Massage with alcoholic extract is especially effective. These are not for baldness; it's too late by then.)
Agave
Arnica
Black elder
Burdock
Calendula
Dropwort
Dwarf nettle
Juniper
Lad's love
Lavender
Maidenhair
Meadowsweet
Milfoil
Nasturtium
Nettle
Rosemary
Sage
Soapwort
Sweet flag
Watercress
White birch
White onion
White willow

HALITOSIS
American senna
Apple
Bennet
Caraway
Dill
Echinacea
European linden
Goldenseal
Musk-mallow
Myrrh
Rosemary

HARDENING OF THE ARTERIES: see Arteriosclerosis

HAY FEVER: see Allergy

HEADACHE
(* for migraine)
American elder
*Balm
*Basil

69

HEADACHE
(cont.)
Birch (both)
*Black elder
Blue vervain
*Buck bean
Camomile (both)
*Cannabis
Catnip
*Cleavers
*Dropwort
*Dwarf nettle
*Ergot
European angelica
*European centaury
*European mistletoe
*European vervain
*Fennel
Feverfew
*Fragrant valerian
Fringe tree
Garden thyme
Ginger
Ground ivy
Henna
*Hops
Indian turnip
Kola tree
*Lady's mantle
*Lavender
Lily of the valley
Low cudweed
Ma-huang
*Meadowsweet
*Mugwort
*Nettle
New Jersey tea
Pennyroyal (both)
*Peppermint
*Primrose
Radish
Red eyebright
Rose
*Rosemary
Sage
*St. Benedict thistle
Savory
*Shepherd's purse
*Speedwell
*Sticklewort
Virgin's bower
White melilot
Wild bergamot
Willow (all)
Wintergreen
Winter savory

HEADACHE
(cont.)
*Woodruff
*Wormwood
Yellow melilot
*Yerba maté
Yerba santa

HEART
American angelica
American mistletoe
Arnica
Balm
Barberry
Bearsfoot
Bear's garlic
Bennet
Betony
Bistort
Black hellebore
Bloodroot
Blue cohosh
Blue vervain
Borage
Buttercup (all)
Calendula
Cayenne
Cowslip
Cucumber
European mistletoe
Foxglove
Fragrant valerian
Garden violet
Garlic
Green hellebore
Hawthorn
Horse chestnut
Kola tree
Lady's mantle
Lily of the valley
Mexican tea
Milfoil
Motherwort
Mugwort
Oat
Onion
Pasque flower
Primrose
Rosemary
Rue
Saffron
St. Johnswort
Shepherd's purse
Silverweed
Strawberry-bush
Virginia snakeroot

HEART (cont.)
Wahoo
Woodruff
Wormseed

HEMORRHAGE,
EXTERNAL: see
Wounds

HEMORRHAGE,
INTERNAL
(* Indicates
those suitable for
douche or enema;
† indicates those
to snuff for nose-
bleed.)
Amaranth
American
mistletoe
Arnica
Birthroot
*Bistort
Black alder
Black mullein
Cabbage rose
†Club moss
Comfrey
†Desert tea
Dwarf nettle
English oak
Ergot
Eur. five-finger
grass
European
goldenrod
Five-finger grass
Ginseng (both)
†*Goldenseal
Great burnet
Hemlock spruce
Hepatica (both)
*Horseweed
Knotgrass
Lady's mantle
Lemon
Life everlasting
Loosestrife
Milfoil
†Mouse ear
Nettle
Pearly everlasting
Periwinkle (both)
Plantain (all)

70

HEMORRHAGE, INTERNAL
(cont.)
Red alder
Rhatany
St. Johnswort
Sanicle (both)
Shave grass
Shepherd's purse
Silvery lady's mantle
Smooth alder
Sorrel
†*Spotted cranebill
Storksbill
*Sumac
Tormentil
Water mint
†*Wax myrtle
†*White oak
Willow (all)
*Witch hazel
Woundwort

HEMORRHOIDS
Alder buckthorn
Aloe
Amaranth
Birch (both)
Black mullein
Burdock
Burnet saxifrage
Common plantain
Dwarf nettle
German camomile
Goldenseal
Horse chestnut
Horseweed
Houseleek
Lemon
Lungwort
Milfoil
Nettle
Oak (all)
Pilewort
Pokeweed
Poplar (all)
Smartweed
Solomon's seal (both)
Turtlebloom
Water smartweed
Wild black cherry
Witch hazel
Yellow toadflax

HIVES: see Skin

HOARSENESS
(Usually as a gargle)
Althea
American mountain ash
Blackberry
Black currant
Coltsfoot
Comfrey
Common mullein
Female fern
Garden raspberry
Goldenseal
Hedge garlic
Hedge mustard
Iceland moss
Lobelia
Lungwort
Maidenhair
Mallow (both)
Marsh hibiscus
Marsh tea
Mullein
Okra
Onion
Orange mullein
Plantain (all)
Rowan
Sage
Skunk cabbage
Slippery elm
Wild black cherry

HYPERACIDITY: see Stomach

IMPOTENCE, FRIGIDITY
Asiatic ginseng
Carline thistle
Celery
Common lettuce
Common plantain
English walnut
Fenugreek
Jasmine
Lovage
Mexican damiana
Onion
Saffron
Savory
Saw palmetto
Water eryngo

INDIGESTION
American angelica
American centaury
Anise
Artichoke
Balm
Barberry
Birch (both)
Black mustard
Buck bean
Camomile (both)
Caraway
Carline thistle
Carrot
Cascara sagrada
Cayenne
Colombo
Comfrey
Coriander
Cornflower
Cubeb
Dandelion
Dill
Dogbane
Elecampane
Eucalyptus
European angelica
European centaury
European linden
European sanicle
Fennel
Feverfew
Fragrant valerian
Fringe tree
Fumitory
Garlic
Gentian (all)
Goldenseal
Goldthread
Hops
Horsemint
Horseradish
Hyssop
Iceland moss
Imperial masterwort
Ironweed
Juniper
Laurel
Lavender
Lovage
Magnolia
Masterwort
Milfoil
Milk thistle
Mother of thyme

INDIGESTION
(cont.)

Mugwort
Nutmeg
Oat
Orange
Oswego tea
Papaya
Parsley
Peppermint
Peruvian bark
Purple goatsbeard
Quassia
Red eyebright
Red pimpernel
Rhubarb
Rosemary
Saffron
Sage
St. Benedict thistle
Sallow
Sandalwood
Savory
Star anise
Strawberry-bush
Sweet cicely
Sweet flag
Sweet marjoram
Turkey corn
Turtlebloom
Virginia snakeroot
Wahoo
White mustard
Wild bergamot
Wild black cherry
Wild ginger
Winterberry
Winter savory
Wormwood
Yellow goatsbeard

INFLAMMATION

American elder
Arnica
Balm of Gilead
Borage
Bryony (both)
Burnet saxifrage
Cannabis
Chicory
Coltsfoot
Comfrey
Common mullein
Cucumber
Echinacea
Fenugreek

INFLAMMATION
(cont.)

German camomile
Ginseng (both)
Goldenseal
Greater pimpernel
Gumplant
Hedge bindweed
Lobelia
Monkshood
Mugwort
Mullein
Nasturtium
Orange mullein
Pokeweed
Quaking aspen
Sandalwood
Sarsaparilla
Slippery elm
Solomon's seal
   (both)
Tacamahac
Tansy
White pond lily
Willow (all)
Wintergreen
Witch hazel

INFLUENZA

Birch (both)
Boneset
Borage
Brier hip
Burnet saxifrage
Butternut
Calendula
Coltsfoot
Dropwort
English ivy
European angelica
Garden thyme
Garden violet
Lady's mantle
Lavender
Mallow (both)
Meadowsweet
Mountain holly
Mouse ear
Norway spruce
Pansy
Pleurisy root
Primrose
Rosemary
Sage
Sticklewort

INSECT BITES

Aloe
Balm
Basil
Betony
Birthroot
Bistort
Black cohosh
Borage
Calendula
Coltsfoot
Comfrey
Echinacea
Fennel
Gentian (all)
Goldenrod (all)
Hound's-tongue
Houseleek
Leek
Lion's foot
Marsh tea
Mint (all)
Olive
Parsley
Pennyroyal (both)
Plantain (all)
Shinleaf
Skullcap
Wild hyssop
Witch hazel
Yerba santa

INSOMNIA

Anise
Balm
Bearded darnel
Blind nettle
Blue vervain
Brier hip
Cannabis
Catnip
Cleavers
Coral root
Damask rose
Dandelion
Dill
European linden
Fragrant valerian
Garden violet
German camomile
Hawthorn
Heather
Hops
Lettuce (both)
Life everlasting
Mother of thyme

INSOMNIA (cont.)
Nerve root
Orange
Passion flower
Pearly everlasting
Primrose
Rosemary
Skullcap
Squaw vine
Sweet marjoram
White birch
White melilot
Wild marjoram
Woodruff
Yellow melilot

ITCHING:
see Skin

JAUNDICE:
see Liver

KIDNEYS
Alfalfa
Aloe
American sanicle
Birthroot
Black cohosh
Black currant
Black elder
Bloodroot
Brier hip
Burnet saxifrage
Carline thistle
Celery
Cucumber
Desert tea
Dogbane
Dropwort
Dwarf nettle
European goldenrod
Fraxinella
Fringe tree
Heather
Hemlock spruce
Hepatica (both)
Horseradish
Indian corn
Juniper
Kidney bean
Madder
Mallow (both)
Meadowsweet
Milkwort
Mouse ear
Oat
Parsley

KIDNEYS (cont.)
Peony
Pipsissewa
Pokeweed
Queen of the
    meadow
Red pimpernel
Restharrow
Sassafras
Seven barks
Shave grass
Turkey corn
Watercress
Water smartweed
White birch
White oak
Wild daisy
Wild Oregon grape
Witch grass

LACTATION
    (To promote the
    flow of milk.
    Those marked
    with * will stop
    it.)
Anise
Basil
Bitter milkwort
*Black walnut
Borage
Burnet saxifrage
Caraway
Dill
Dwarf nettle
*English walnut
European angelica
European seneka
European vervain
Fennel
Fraxinella
Goat's rue
Hops
Iceland moss
Lavender
Parsley
*Sage
Wild raspberry

LEUCORRHEA
Althea
Alum
Amaranth
Balm
Bearberry
Bistort

LEUCORRHEA
    (cont.)
Black walnut
Blind nettle
Blue cohosh
Buchu (all)
Comfrey
Common groundsel
Cubeb
English walnut
European centaury
European ragwort
Fenugreek
Fraxinella
German camomile
Goldenseal
Horehound
Juniper
Lady's mantle
Life everlasting
Magnolia
Milfoil
Pearly everlasting
Plantain (all)
Ragwort
Sage
St. Benedict thistle
St. Johnswort
Shave grass
Silverweed
Slippery elm
Squaw vine
Sticklewort
Sumac
Tansy
Tormentil
Wax myrtle
White oak
White pond lily
Wild daisy
Wild Oregon grape
Wintergreen
Wormwood

LIVER
Alder buckthorn
American angelica
Artichoke
Barberry
Black cohosh
Black root
Bloodroot
Blue flag

73

LIVER (cont.)
Burdock
Butternut
Cascara sagrada
Cat's foot
Celandine
Chicory
Clubmoss
Dandelion
Elecampane
English oak
European centaury
European ragwort
Evening primrose
Female fern
Fringe tree
Fumitory
Garlic
Gentian (all)
Hemp agrimony
Hepatica (both)
Lavender
Mandrake
Milk thistle
Mouse ear
Mugwort
New Jersey tea
Oat
Onion
Orris root
Peppermint
Pokeweed
Prickly ash
Radish
Ragged cup
Red pimpernel
Rosemary
St. Benedict thistle
Sandalwood
Sticklewort
Turtlebloom
Wahoo
White birch
White oak
Wild daisy
Wild Oregon grape
Witch grass
Wood sorrel
Wormwood
Woundwort
Yellow bedstraw
Yew

LUMBAGO: see
Backache

LUNGS
(* Indicates
those suitable for
supplementary
followup treat-
ment of tuber-
culosis.)
*Agave
*American sanicle
Bear's garlic
*Betony
*Birthroot
Bitter milkwort
*Blue vervain
Celery
*Chickweed
*Colombo
*Comfrey
Cubeb
*Dwarf nettle
Eucalyptus
European seneka
*Fenugreek
Flax
*Ground ivy
*Hemp nettle
*Iceland moss
*Irish moss
*Kidney bean
*Knotgrass
*Lad's love
Lady's thumb
Life everlasting
*Lungwort
*Milfoil
*New Jersey tea
Pansy
Pearly everlasting
*Pennyroyal (both)
*Plantain (all)
Pleurisy root
*Redroot
*Red sedge
*Sage
*Shave grass
*Skunk cabbage
*Slippery elm
Strawberry-bush
Wahoo
*Watercress
*Wax myrtle
*Wild black cherry
*Yerba santa
Yew

MENOPAUSE
Balm
Bearded darnel
Birthwort
Blind nettle
Chervil
European mistletoe
Fragrant valerian
Great burnet
Hawthorn
Hops
Lady's mantle
Milfoil
Motherwort
Mugwort
Rosemary
Rue
Shepherd's purse
Silverweed
Silvery lady's
mantle
White melilot
Woodruff
Wormwood
Yellow melilot

MENORRHAGIA:
see Menstruation,
Excessive

**MENSTRUATION,
DIFFICULT**
Balm
Belladonna
Black cohosh
Buttercup (all)
Calendula
Carline thistle
Common groundsel
Cowslip
Elecampane
Eur. five-finger
grass
European ragwort
German camomile
Hops
Lady's mantle
Milfoil
Monkshood
Mother of thyme
Mugwort
Parsley
Pasque flower
Ragwort
Saffron
Sage

74

MENSTRUATION, DIFFICULT (cont.)
Shepherd's purse
Silverweed
Silvery lady's mantle
Storksbill
Wild marjoram
Woodruff
Wormwood

MENSTRUATION, EXCESSIVE
Amaranth
American sanicle
Birthroot
Bistort
Burnet saxifrage
Comfrey
Common groundsel
Cotton
Ergot
European ragwort
Goldenseal
Great burnet
Horseweed
Knotgrass
Milfoil
Periwinkle (both)
Ragwort
Shave grass
Shepherd's purse
Smartweed
Sorrel
Star grass
Storksbill
Tansy
Wax myrtle
Wild strawberry
Witch hazel

MENSTRUATION, TARDY
Alder buckthorn
Blind nettle
Birthroot
Birthwort
Carrot
Celery
Common groundsel
Cotton
Damask rose
European ragwort
Fraxinella
German camomile
Ginger

MENSTRUATION, TARDY (cont.)
Lady's mantle
Larch
Lovage
Milfoil
Parsley
Pennyroyal (both)
Peppermint
Pride of China
Ragwort
Rosemary
Rose of China
Sage
Silvery lady's mantle
Star grass
Sweet marjoram
Tansy
Tarragon
Thuja
Watercress
White mustard
Wild ginger

METRORRHAGIA: see Hemorrhage, Internal

MIGRAINE: see Headache

MORNING SICKNESS: see Nausea, Vomiting

MOUTH, INFLAMMATION IN: see Stomatitis

MILK: See Lactation

NAUSEA, VOMITING (* Indicates not to be taken during pregnancy.)
Anise
Asparagus
Balm
Balm of Gilead
Barley
Basil
Blue flag
Calendula
Caraway

NAUSEA, VOMITING (cont.)
Clove
Colombo
European linden
Fragrant valerian
Gentian (all)
German camomile
Ginger
Ginseng (both)
Goldenseal
Hops
Horsemint
Kidney vetch
Lavender
Oswego tea
Peach tree
*Pennyroyal (both)
Peppermint
Quaking aspen
Rough avens
Sage
Savory
Spearmint
Star anise
Sweet marjoram
Tacamahac
Water avens
Wild clover
Wild red raspberry
Wild yam
Winter savory
Woodruff
Yellow melilot

NERVOUS CONDITIONS
Almond
American sanicle
Asafetida
Balm
Betony
Blue vervain
Borage
Catnip
Celery
Corydalis
European linden
Fragrant valerian
Garden violet
German camomile
Hawthorn
Henbane
Hops
Indian pipe
Jasmine

NERVOUS
CONDITIONS
(cont.)
Lavender
Lettuce (both)
Life everlasting
Motherwort
Mountain laurel
Musk-mallow
Nerve root
New Jersey tea
Olive
Orange (both)
Pansy
Passion flower
Peach tree
Pearly everlasting
Peppermint
Periwinkle (both)
Queen of the
meadow
Red pimpernel
Rosemary
Sage
St. Johnswort
Savory
Skullcap
Skunk cabbage
Spruce
Squaw vine
Thyme
Twin leaf
Wild clover
Wild marjoram
Wild yam
Witch hazel
Woodruff
Yellow jessamine

NEURALGIA
Allspice
Black elder
Blue cohosh
Buttercup (all)
Cannabis
Celery
Cowslip
German camomile
Henbane
Horse chestnut
Hound's-tongue
Kola tree
Monkshood
Mountain laurel
Pasque flower

NEURALGIA
(cont.)
Queen of the
meadow
Skullcap
Solomon's seal
(both)
Twin leaf
Wild marjoram
Wild yam
Willow (all)
Woodruff
Wormwood
Yellow jessamine
Yerba maté

NIGHT SWEATS
Balm
English walnut
European linden
French rose
Hops
Hyssop
Nettle
Sage
Wild strawberry

NOSEBLEED: see
Hemorrhage,
Internal

OBESITY
Alder buckthorn
Apple
Balm
Black currant
Black elder
Celery
Chickweed
Cleavers
Common buckthorn
Dwarf nettle
Dropwort
European centaury
European goldenrod
Fennel
Fig tree
Ground ivy
Hops
Irish moss
Meadowsweet
Nettle
Restharrow
St. Johnswort
Sassafras
Scurvy grass

OBESITY (cont.)
Shave grass
Watercress
White birch
White melilot
Willow (all)
Yellow melilot

PERSPIRATION:
see Antihydrotic
(in the Glossary
of Medicinal
Effects)

PILES: see
Hemorrhoids

PIMPLES: see
Acne

PODAGRA: see
Gout

POSTNASAL DRIP:
see Sinus

PROSTATE
Blind nettle
Buchu
Carline thistle
Club moss
Dwarf nettle
European goldenrod
Garlic
Goldenseal
Horse chestnut
Indian corn
Lady's mantle
Larkspur
Nettle
Parsley
Pipsissewa
Poplar (all)
Rosemary
Saw palmetto
Speedwell
Thuja
White pond lily
Wintergreen
Witch grass

RASH: see Skin

RESTLESSNESS:
see Nervous
Conditions

RHEUMATISM

Alfalfa
Allspice
Alpine cranberry
Apple
Arum
Asparagus
Barberry
Birch (both)
Bird's tongue
Birthwort
Bittersweet
  nightshade
Black cohosh
Black currant
Black elder
Black mustard
Blue cohosh
Blue flag
Borage
Boxwood
Brier hip
Bryony (both)
Buchu (all)
Buck bean
Burdock
Burnet saxifrage
Buttercup (all)
Carline thistle
Cayenne
Celery
Colombo
Columbine
Comfrey
Coriander
Cowslip
Dandelion
Dropwort
Dwarf nettle
Dyer's broom
English walnut
European linden
Feverfew
Garden thyme
Guaiac
Heather
Hedge garlic
Hemp agrimony
Henbane
Horsemint
Horseradish
Horseweed
Imperial masterwort
Indian turnip
Juniper
Kidney bean

RHEUMATISM (cont.)

Laurel
Male fern
Marsh tea
Meadow saffron
Meadowsweet
Monkshood
Mother of thyme
Mountain holly
Nettle
Oat
Pansy
Pasque flower
Pipsissewa
Pokeweed
Poplar (all)
Prickly ash
Quassia
Red sedge
Rosemary
Rowan
Rue
Sarsaparilla
Sassafras
Scurvy grass
Skullcap
Skunk cabbage
Sticklewort
Sweet flag
Watercress
White melilot
White mustard
Wild clover
Wild Oregon grape
Willow (all)
Wintergreen
Witch grass
Wormwood
Yellow melilot
Yellow parilla
Yerba santa
Yew

SCIATICA

Black elder
Buttercup (all)
Fenugreek
Ground ivy
Kidney bean
Life everlasting
Monkshood
Mustard (both)
Yellow jessamine
Yellow toadflax

SEXUAL DESIRE, EXCESSIVE:
see Erotomania

SEXUAL DESIRE, IMPAIRED:
see Impotence, Frigidity

SHINGLES: see
Skin

SINUS

Blue flag
Coltsfoot
Common mullein
Eucalyptus
Fennel
Garlic
Goldenseal
Ground ivy
Gum plant
Hyssop
Leek
Mullein
Orange mullein
Wax myrtle

SKIN

Adder's tongue
American elder
American sanicle
Arum
Barberry
Basswood
Bearded darnel
Bearsfoot
Beechdrops
Bilberry
Birch (both)
Birthwort
Bittersweet
  nightshade
Black alder
Black hellebore
Black nightshade
Blackthorn
Black walnut
Bloodroot
Buck bean
Buttercup (all)
Calendula
Carline thistle
Celandine
Celery
Chervil
Chickweed
Chicory

SKIN (cont.)

Cleavers
Comfrey
Common lettuce
Common mullein
Coral root
Cucumber
Cypress spurge
Dwarf nettle
Dyer's broom
Echinacea
English elm
English ivy
English walnut
European centaury
European goldenrod
European sanicle
European vervain
Evening primrose
Figwort
Fumitory
Garden violet
Goldenseal
Green hellebore
Guaiac
Heather
Hedge hyssop
Henna
Herb Robert
Horehound
Houseleek
Juniper
Kidney bean
Knotgrass
Lady's thumb
Laurel
Lemon
Life everlasting
Madder
Magnolia
Ma-huang
Marsh tea
Mezereon
Mountain laurel
Mullein
Musk-mallow
Nettle
New Jersey tea
Oak (all)
Oat
Olive
Orange mullein
Pansy
Papaya
Pearly everlasting
Pennyroyal (both)

SKIN (cont.)

Peppermint
Periwinkle (both)
Pokeweed
Pomegranate
Prickly ash
Primrose
Privet
Rattlesnake plantain
Red elder
Red pimpernel
Red sedge
Rose
St. Benedict thistle
Sandalwood
Sarsaparilla
Sassafras
Shave grass
Silverweed
Slippery elm
Smartweed
Smooth alder
Soapwort
Sorrel
Speedwell
Spikenard (both)
Stillingia
Sweet fern
Sweet gum
Sycamore maple
Thuja
Turkey corn
Virginia snakeroot
Watercress
Water dock
Water smartweed
White pond lily
Wild clover
Wild indigo
Wild jalap
Wild Oregon grape
Wild strawberry
Willow (all)
Winterberry
Wintergreen
Witch grass
Witch hazel
Wood sorrel
Wormwood
Yellow bedstraw
Yellow dock
Yellow parilla
Yellow toadflax

SLEEPLESSNESS:
see Insomnia

SMOKING, TO STOP (* Indicates a tobacco substitute.)

American angelica
Black cohosh
Blue cohosh
Blue vervain
Catnip
*Coltsfoot
Echinacea
Fragrant valerian
Hedge hyssop
Kola tree
Magnolia
Motherwort
Nerve root
Peppermint
Quassia
Skullcap
Slippery elm
Sweet flag

SORE THROAT (* Indicates those especially suitable for gargle.)

Acacia
*Althea
*Amaranth
*American mountain ash
*American sanicle
*Arum
*Balm of Gilead
*Barberry
Basswood
*Bistort
*Black alder
Black currant
Black elder
Blackthorn
Blazing star (all)
Brier hip
Buck bean
Burdock
*Burnet saxifrage
Carline thistle
Columbine
*Comfrey
Corkwood
*English oak
English walnut

SORE THROAT
(cont.)
* *Eur. five-finger grass
* *European sanicle
* *Fenugreek
* *Five-finger grass
* Flower-of-an-hour
* Galangal
* Ginger
* *Goldenseal
* *Goldthread
* *Greater pimpernel
* Ground ivy
* Groundsel
* *Hemlock spruce
* *Henna
* Hollyhock
* Horehound
* *Hyssop
* Juniper
* Lemon
* Life everlasting
* Lovage
* Low cudweed
* *Mallow (both)
* *Marsh hibiscus
* *Mouse ear
* Myrrh
* *New Jersey tea
* Orris root
* Pearly everlasting
* *Peruvian bark
* *Pomegranate
* *Privet
* *Quaking aspen
* Red alder
* *Red currant
* Restharrow
* *Rock-rose
* Rose
* *Rowan
* *Sage
* *Savory
* Shave grass
* Shinleaf
* *Silverweed
* Slippery elm
* Smooth alder
* Speedwell
* Spotted cranebill
* *Sticklewort
* *Sumac
* *Tacamahac
* *Tormentil

SORE THROAT
(cont.)
* *Twin leaf
* *Wax myrtle
* *White oak
* *White pond lily
* Wild bergamot
* Wild ginger
* Wild plum
* Wild strawberry
* *Wintergreen
* *Winter savory
* *Witch hazel
* *Woundwort

STOMACH
(* Indicates
those helpful for
ulcers.)
* *Alfalfa
* Allspice
* *Althea
* *Amaranth
* *American angelica
* *American sanicle
* Anise
* *Arum
* *Balm
* *Balm of Gilead
* Basil
* Bearded darnel
* Bennet
* *Bistort
* Bitter milkwort
* Black mustard
* Black pepper
* Buck bean
* *Burdock
* Burnet saxifrage
* *Calendula
* Camomile (both)
* Caraway
* Carline thistle
* Catnip
* Cayenne
* *Chickweed
* Chicory
* Clove
* Colombo
* *Comfrey
* Coriander
* Cornflower
* *Dwarf nettle
* *Elecampane
* *European angelica

STOMACH (cont.)
* European centaury
* Fennel
* *Fenugreek
* Flax
* Fragrant valerian
* Galangal
* Garden thyme
* *Garlic
* Gentian (all)
* Ginger
* *Goldthread
* Hedge mustard
* *Hops
* Horehound
* Horse chestnut
* Hyssop
* *Iceland moss
* Imperial masterwort
* Juniper
* *Knotgrass
* Lad's love
* Lavender
* *Licorice
* Lovage
* *Low cudweed
* *Marsh hibiscus
* Milfoil
* Milkweed
* Mother of thyme
* Musk-mallow
* *Nettle
* Nutmeg
* *Okra
* *Onion
* Orange (both)
* Papaya
* *Pennyroyal (both)
* Peruvian bark
* *Plantain (all)
* *Prickly ash
* *Quaking aspen
* Quassia
* *Ragged cup
* *Sage
* Savory
* Scurvy grass
* *Shave grass
* *Silverweed
* Speedwell
* Star anise
* Sticklewort
* Sweet flag
* Sweet marjoram

STOMACH (cont.)
*Tacamahac
Tansy
Tarragon
*Twin leaf
*Virgin's bower
Wafer ash
Water dock
White melilot
White mustard
Wild ginger
Wild marjoram
*Wild strawberry
Willow (all)
Winter savory
Witch grass
Wood sorrel
Wormwood
Yellow melilot

STOMATITIS
Bilberry
Bistort
Black currant
Blackthorn
English walnut
Garden thyme
Herb Robert
Hollyhock
Matico
Myrrh
New Jersey tea
Sage
White pond lily

STRANGURY: see
Urination,
Incomplete

SYPHILIS: see
Genito-Urinary
Ailments

TENSION: see
Nervous
Conditions

TETTERS: see
Skin

TONSILLITIS
(Mostly as gargles)
American hellebore
Betony
Bistort
Black walnut
Common mullein
Echinacea

TONSILLITIS
(cont.)
Goldenseal
Lemon
Mallow (both)
Mullein
New Jersey tea
Orange mullein
Peppermint
Pokeweed
Rowan
Sage
Slippery elm
Stone root
Tansy
White pine
Willow (all)
Witch hazel
Yellow jessamine

TOOTHACHE
Balm
Burnet saxifrage
Clove
Common plantain
German camomile
Hops
Mullein
Myrrh
Pennyroyal
Periwinkle (both)
Prickly ash
Rose
Sassafras
Savory
Scotch broom
Smartweed
Sweet marjoram
Tansy
Water smartweed
Wild marjoram

TUBERCULOSIS:
see Lungs

UPSET STOMACH:
see Indigestion

URINATION,
INCOMPLETE
American elder
Arnica
Asarum
Asparagus
Barberry
Bennet

URINATION,
INCOMPLETE
(cont.)
Birch (both)
Black currant
Black elder
Blackthorn
Brier hip
Brooklime
Buchu (all)
Burnet saxifrage
Buttercup (all)
Carline thistle
Carrot
Celery
Chervil
Chickweed
Chicory
Club moss
Cowslip
Cubeb
Dandelion
Dropwort
Dwarf elder
Elecampane
European angelica
European linden
European linden
European vervain
Garden violet
Greater pimpernel
Guinea sorrel
Hepatica (both)
Horsemint
Horseradish
Horseweed
Indian corn
Jimson weed
Juniper
Kidney bean
Larch
Leek
Licorice
Lovage
Low cudweed
Lungwort
Marsh tea
Matico
Meadowsweet
Onion
Orris root
Pansy
Parsley
Pasque flower
Peach tree

80

URINATION,
  INCOMPLETE
  (cont.)
Pipsissewa
Purple goatsbeard
Queen of the
  meadow
Radish
Red elder
Red eyebright
Restharrow
Water eryngo
White holly
White weed
Willow (all)
Witch grass
Yellow goatsbeard
Yellow toadflax

VAGINAL
  DOUCHE
Acacia
Althea
Amaranth
Barberry
Birthroot
Black walnut
Blind nettle
Blue cohosh
Calendula
Common plantain
Fenugreek
French rose
Goldenseal
Hemlock spruce
Hollyhock
Indian pipe
Lady's mantle
Magnolia
Marsh hibiscus
Milfoil
Myrrh
Oak (all)
Pomegranate
Privet
Shave grass
Shinleaf
Silvery lady's
  mantle
Slippery elm
Spotted cranebill
Sumac
Wax myrtle
White pond lily
Wintergreen
Witch hazel

VARICOSE VEINS
Barberry
Bear's garlic
Bennet
Bistort
Blind nettle
Brier hip
Burnet saxifrage
Calendula
European mistletoe
Great burnet
Hawthorn
Horse chestnut
Red oak
Sassafras
Shave grass
Shepherd's purse
Sticklewort
Sweet marjoram
Wax myrtle
White melilot
White oak
Witch hazel
Yellow melilot

VENEREAL
  DISEASE: see
  Genito-Urinary
  Ailments

VERTIGO: see
  Dizziness

VIRILITY: see
  Impotence,
  Frigidity

VOMITING: see
  Nausea, Vomiting

WARTS
Alder buckthorn
Bulbous buttercup
Calendula
Celandine
Dandelion
Fig tree
Garlic
Houseleek
Lemon
Mandrake
Marsh crowfoot
Milkweed
Mullein
Spurge (all)
Sundew
Thuja

WARTS (cont.)
White weed
Wild sage

WORMS
Aloe
American senna
Bennet
Bird's tongue
Black birch
Blue vervain
Buck bean
Butternut
Carrot
Catnip
Cyclamen
Elecampane
English walnut
Female fern
Fraxinella
Garden thyme
Garlic
Goat's rue
Houseleek
Jalap
Kousso
Lad's love
Larch
Larkspur
Life everlasting
Male fern
Mexican tea
Mother of thyme
Mugwort
Mulberry (both)
Onion
Papaya
Pinkroot
Pomegranate
Pride of China
Pumpkin
Quassia
Tamarind
Tansy
Tarragon
Turtlebloom
White oak
Wild plum
Wormseed
Wormwood
Woundwort

WOUNDS
Aloe
Althea
Amaranth

American elder
Arnica
Beechdrops
Betony
Birthwort
Bistort
Blackberry
Blue vervain
Buttercup (all)
Calendula
Camomile (both)
Carline thistle
Cleavers
Club moss
Comfrey
Cowslip
Cyclamen
Dandelion
Echinacea
English elm
Eucalyptus
European goldenrod
European linden

European sanicle
European vervain
Figwort
Flax
Gentian (all)
Goldenseal
Hemp agrimony
Horseweed
Houseleek
Kidney vetch
Lady's mantle
Larch
Lemon
Lungwort
Onion
Pansy
Papaya
Pasque flower
Peach tree
Pearly everlasting
Plantain (all)
Poplar (all)

Prickly ash
St. Johnswort
Shave grass
Silvery lady's
  mantle
Slippery elm
Solomon's seal
  (both)
Stone root
Sweet gum
Sycamore maple
White melilot
White pine
White pond lily
White weed
Wild daisy
Wild indigo
Willow (all)
Woundwort
Yellow bedstraw
Yellow melilot
Yerba santa

PART 2

A COMPENDIUM OF
BOTANICAL MEDICINE

INTRODUCTION

Of the more than 300,000 known species of plants, about 2,000 have been or are used for medicinal purposes. Some have been traditional remedies for thousands of years; others had their day (or their century) and then fell out of favor. But while some rose and others fell, the primacy of plants in general as the sources of medicine was unchallenged—until the twentieth century. This century has seen the advanced nations of the world indulge themselves in a technological binge that has brought us instant coffee, instant houses, and—yes—instant medicine. The average modern patient visits a doctor expecting to be given a pill or a shot, or even an operation, that will "take care of it" immediately.

As we assess the present global hangover that marks the end of the binge, perhaps we can gain a new perspective and reintegrate our fragmented reality, taking the best from both past and present. The compendium of plants and their medicinal uses presented in this part of the book contains much of the learned and folk wisdom of the past, but often as verified or modified by modern discoveries. In the course of hundreds and thousands of years, herbal medicine and natural healing have accumulated a considerable burden of erroneous and half-true beliefs that make it easy, particularly in the United States, for their detractors to equate serious practitioners with hawkers of snake oil and elixirs of life. But true natural medicine has nothing to fear from objective scientific analysis; indeed, in Europe modern research in herbal medicine and natural healing—vital elements of the European medical profession—is routinely carried on, both to dispose of old myths (or verify them) and to discover still new ways to use the healing powers of plants. A similar approach, taken seriously, could bring a sorely lacking balance to American medicine and innumerable benefits to the American public.

The plant listings that follow are written and organized to be as useful as possible. A typical entry presents the following information:

Primary Name. This is usually one of the names by which the plant is most commonly or most widely known. Many such common names, however, apply to whole groups of related or similar plants, so that they are not generally adequate to identify the specific plant involved. Some listings, in fact, are grouped under such a general name; the specific plant names are then given first under "Common Name(s)."

Botanical Name. This is the binomial designation (see "The World of the Plant" in Part 1) that provides the most positive identification of the plant. For reasons discussed earlier, these may not always agree with the binomials given for the same plants in other sources. Botanical reference works such as those in the Bibliography generally list synonymous binomials; check these in the library to make the correlations.

Common Name(s). These are other names by which the plant is known; they may be as common as the primary name or may be limited to certain geographical areas. The names are generally listed alphabetically; but for plants grouped under a common primary name, the alphabetical list follows a more specific common name for each individual species.

Medicinal Part(s). This specifies which part or parts of the plant are used medicinally. The term *herb* here means the aboveground part of the plant, excluding perhaps the toughest parts of the stem or branches. *Plant* means the whole plant, roots and all. *Bark* refers to the inner, living bark.

Description. The physical appearance, habitat, and other characteristics of the plant are described in detail. "The World of the Plant" (Part 1) will help you to understand the unavoidable technical terminology. These descriptions, along with the illustrations, will be useful especially to those who go out to "stalk the wild herbs," whether in the countryside, in a vacant lot, or even in a nursery. But keep in mind their limitations: individual plants, for example, can vary considerably in physical appearance and in flowering times. And if you have stumbled on what all the evidence says is a brier hip patch somewhere in California, don't let all that vitamin C go to waste just because the description says the plant grows in the eastern United States. Plants have a way of getting around and taking up residence in odd places without consulting the botanists who try to keep track of them.

Properties and Uses. First comes an alphabetical list of the main categories of medicinal activity that the plant is known for. (See the "Glossary of Medicinal Effects" in Part 1 for definitions.) Then follows a description of the ways that the plant or its parts have been used medicinally. This will not necessarily include all the uses indicated by the category list, but the listed uses that are not described will generally be self-evident.

It will be obvious from this part of each entry that many

plants have similar or identical properties. This happens because —unlike the high-powered, specific drugs of modern medicine —most plant medicines act on the body with active ingredients that are relatively limited in number but that are organically balanced to cooperate with the natural restorative processes of the body. Although the proportions of various ingredients can vary widely (either in different plants or in different medicinal proparations of the same plant), so that some plants do have more or less specific activity, the basic principle is that of promoting the gradual and natural return of the body to health. In practice, of course, having many plants with similar properties has the advantage that wherever you live and whatever time of year it is, you can probably find a green-growing remedy for what ails you.

Preparation and Dosage. The most common forms of medicinal preparations are indicated, with directions for making and taking them. (See also "How to Make and Use Herb Preparations" in Part 1.) It is important to keep in mind here that most of these dosages are typical values only. They provide, for the average adult, a reasonable level of treatment; but individual requirements may vary widely, depending on age, sex, body build, general level of health, severity or complexity of the condition being treated, and other factors. Be prepared to modify— or even discontinue—dosages as the individual case dictates. Where a range of dosages is given, begin with the lowest and go higher if necessary (remember, though, that most plant medicines act gradually, not drastically). Unless specified otherwise, average doses for children and weak or elderly people are from one-third to two-thirds of the average adult doses. Where no directions for use are included (except in the case of poisonous plants), try the standard methods described in "How to Make and Use Herb Preparations." A cup in this section means an 8-ounce measuring cup.

Just a quick look through Part 2 will make plain that *The Herb Book* is not just about herbs, as defined by botanists; it includes trees, shrubs, seaweeds, and a few other types of plants as well. But *herb* in the title is not a botanical word: basically it can be defined as "a plant that is useful to man." (Similarly, a plant is called a *weed* by those who consider it useless or undesirable.) With that expanded definition in hand, you can proceed through the book with an easy mind. Certainly, it is no matter to lose sleep over; if you do, check under "Insomnia" in the reference list of ailments in Part 1 for herbs that may help.

ACACIA
(Acacia senegal)

Common Names: Cape gum, Egyptian thorn, gum arabic tree.

Medicinal Part: Gum.

Description: Acacia is a small, spiny, leguminous tree or shrub which grows in sandy soil, mostly in tropical Africa. After the rainy season ends, the stem begins to exude gum, which is collected from December to June for marketing as gum arabic. The acacia has alternate, bipinnate leaves and axillary racemes of yellow flowers arranged in globose heads. The fruit is an oblong pod.

Properties and Uses: Demulcent. Gum arabic's main effect is to form a protective, soothing coating over inflammations in the respiratory, alimentary, and urinary tracts. In conjunction with various astringents, it is helpful for coughs, sore throat, and catarrh, as well as in cases of diarrhea and dysentery. The sweetened mucilage has sometimes been used to treat the early stages of typhoid fever. The mucilage also makes a good vehicle for other medicines, in addition to having nutritional value in its own right.

Preparation and Dosage: Gum arabic is usually dissolved in water to make a mucilage.

Mucilage: A dose is from 1 to 4 tsp.

Syrup: Mix 1 part mucilage with 3 parts of a syrup. A dose is from 1 to 4 tsp.

002   ADDER'S TONGUE

(Erythronium americanum)

Common Names: Dog-tooth violet, erythronium, lamb's tongue, rattlesnake violet, snake leaf, yellow erythronium, yellow snakeleaf, yellow snowdrop.

Medicinal Parts: Bulb, leaves.

Description: Adder's tongue is a perennial plant that grows in thin woods or open areas with rich soil all over the United States. Its bulbous root is light brown on the outside and white inside. It grows two lanceolate, pale green leaves with purplish or brownish spots; and one drooping, yellow flower appears in April or May.

Properties and Uses: Emetic, anti-scrofulous, emollient. Internally the plant is taken in the form of an infusion. For scrofula and other skin problems, make the plant into a poultice for external application and take the infusion at the same time. If you prefer, mix the expressed juice with cider for internal use —it probably tastes better.

Preparation and Dosage: The plant must be used fresh.

Infusion: Use 1 tsp. leaves or 2 tsp. root with 1 cup boiling water.

Daily dose is 1 cup.

Poultice: Use crushed leaves, or simmer the root in milk to get the proper consistency.

003

AGAVE
(Agave americana)

Common Names: American agave, American century, century plant, flowering aloe, spiked aloe.

Medicinal Part: The plant.

Description: Agave is a perennial plant which grows in the arid and semiarid regions of tropical America, and in some parts of Europe. (The agave plants found in the U.S. are related species.) The broad-linear, fibrous leaves grow upward from next to the ground to form a massive rosette. They are gray and smooth on both sides and have prickly edges. After 10 years or more, the plant produces a flower stalk 20 to 40 feet tall which bears large yellowish-green flowers on many horizontal branches. The fruit is a three-celled capsule. After flowering and fruiting, the plant dies.

Properties and Uses: Antiseptic, diuretic, laxative. The sap of agave has disinfectant properties and can be taken to check the growth of putrefactive bacteria in the stomach and intestines. It can also be used as a laxative and as a disinfectant diuretic (useful for syphilis). It has been recommended at times for pulmonary tuberculosis, diseased liver, and jaundice. Water in which agave fiber has been soaked for a day can be used as a scalp disinfectant and tonic in cases of falling hair.

Preparation and Dosage:

Decoction: Boil 1 tbsp. plant in 1 pint water.

Powder: Take ½ tsp., three times a day.

004

ALFALFA
(Medicago sativa)

Common Names: Buffalo herb, lucerne, purple medic.

Medicinal Part: Leaves.

Description: Alfalfa is a perennial plant found on the borders of fields, in low valleys, and widely cultivated. The erect, smooth stem grows from an elongated taproot to a height of 12 to 18 inches and bears pinnately trifoliate leaves with oblong-obovate or linear-oblong leaflets. The blue or purplish flowers grow in racemes from June to August, producing finally the characteristic spirally coiled seed pods.

Properties and Uses: Appetizer, diuretic, tonic. Alfalfa tea is commonly used as a beverage, but it can also be used medicinally. Take it every day to improve your appetite, relieve urinary and bowel problems, eliminate retained water, and even help cure peptic ulcers.

005 ALLSPICE

(Pimenta officinalis)

Common Names: Clove pepper, Jamaica pepper, pimento.

Medicinal Part: Fruit.

Description: Allspice is the dried berry of the pimento, an evergreen tree growing as high as 40 feet in the West Indies, South America, Central America, and Mexico. It bears opposite, leathery, oblong to oblong-lanceolate leaves whose pinnately arranged veins show prominently on the underside. Small white flowers grow in many-flowered cymes in the upper leaf axils from June to August. The fruit is a fleshy, sweet berry which is purplish-black when ripe. The berries used for allspice, however, are collected when they have reached full size but are not yet ripe. The name comes from the berry's taste, which has been described as a combination of cloves, juniper berries, cinnamon, and pepper.

Properties and Uses: Aromatic, carminative, stimulant. Pimento water and oil of pimento are useful in cases of flatulent indigestion or simple flatulence; the oil has also been recommended for hysterical paroxysms. Taken with laxatives, the oil lessens the tendency to gripe; the water also makes a good vehicle for less palatable medicines. As an ointment or a bath additive, allspice is said to have some anesthetic effects. Allspice makes a stimulating plaster for rheumatism and neuralgia.

Preparation and Dosage:

Pimento Water: Combine 5 parts crushed berries with 200 parts water and distill down to half the original volume. A dose is from 1 to 2 fluid ounces.

Oil: A dose is from 2 to 5 drops. For flatulence, take 2 or 3 drops on sugar.

Powder: A dose is from 10 to 30 grains.

Plaster: Boil crushed berries in water until the mixture is thick enough to spread on a linen cloth.

006 ALMOND

(Prunus amygdalus)

Common Names: Greek nuts, Jordan almond.

Medicinal Part: Kernels.

Description: The almond tree is cultivated, especially in California, southern Europe, and the Mediterranean countries. It usually grows from 10 to 20 feet high and has lanceolate, finely serrate leaves on thorny branches. The large flowers usually occur in pairs and are soft rose to whitish in color.

Properties and Uses: Demulcent, emollient, pectoral. For a good, cleansing facial scrub, include ground almonds in your preparation. Their emollient properties also make them suitable as ingredients in cosmetics. The oil derived from a bitter variety of almond has sedative properties and is sometimes used in cough remedies. The oil from a sweet variety makes a soothing ingredient in internal medications and can also be used externally as an emollient. Almond butter makes a rich protein substitute for peanut butter, usually well tolerated by diabetics.

007, ALOE

(Aloe vera)

Common Names: Barbados aloe, Curacao aloe.

Medicinal Part: Leaves.

Description: The aloe is a perennial plant found wild in East and South Africa and also cultivated in the West Indies and other tropical areas. It has also been reported in the Zapata area of Texas. The strong, fibrous root produces a rosette of fleshy basal leaves as in the agave but considerably smaller. The narrow-lanceolate leaves are 1 to 2 feet long and whitish-green on both sides, and they bear spiny teeth on the margins. The yellow to purplish, drooping flowers, which are evident most of the year, grow in a long raceme at the top of a flower stalk up to 4½ feet high. The fruit is a triangular capsule containing numerous seeds.

Properties and Uses: Emollient, purgative, vulnerary. Aloes is the dried juice of the aloe plant. Because of its nauseating taste, it is generally used in powder or pill form when taken for a purgative. It also tends to gripe and cause a constipative reaction, so that it should be combined with a carminative for best results. The fresh leaves of the aloe can be split to expose the gelatinous juice and then rubbed on the skin for sunburn and other minor burns, wrinkles, insect bites, skin irritations, and minor cuts and scratches. The fresh juice is also said to help heal wounds by preventing or drawing out infection. A tea made from the dried juice makes a good wash for wounds and for the eyes.

Preparation and Dosage:

Powder: A dose is from 1 to 5 grains.

Fluid Extract: A dose is from 5 to 30 drops.

Wash: Dissolve ½ tsp. aloes in 1 cup water. If desired, add 1 tsp. boric acid as a preservative and to help in healing.

NOTE: Several other aloes are also used medicinally, including

008   ALOE LATIFOLIA

Found in South Africa. Some natives use the leaf pulp to treat inflamed boils and sores; others use the leaf pulp and the plant's yellow juice to cure ringworm.

009   ALOE PERRYI

Bombay aloe; Turkey aloe, Zanzibar aloe; found on the island of Socotra near the entrance of the Gulf of Aden. This is used like Barbados aloe, although considered by some to be less powerful.

010   ALOE SAPONARIA

Found in South Africa. Natives use the leaf pulp and yellow juice for ringworm.

011   ALOE TENUIOR

Found in South Africa. Natives use a decoction of the root for tapeworm.

012 ALPINE CRANBERRY

(Vaccinium vitis idaea)

Common Names: Cowberry, red bilberry, whortleberry.

Medicinal Parts: Leaves, berries.

Description: Alpine cranberry is a small evergreen plant that grows in European coniferous forests with dry soil and also in mountain marshes. It grows from a creeping rootstock to a height of 4 to 10 inches. The leaves are alternate, obovate, pale green with brown spots underneath, and have rolled edges. Its reddish-white, bell-shaped flowers grow in a terminal cluster from May to August. The fruit is a red berry.

Properties and Uses: Leaves: antiseptic, astringent, diuretic. Berries: astringent, refrigerant. An infusion of leaves is useful for bladder problems because of its disinfectant action, which is similar to that of bearberry. Alpine cranberry can be substituted for bearberry, using double the amount of leaves (and it tastes much better). A decoction of the leaves can also be used for gout and rheumatism. The berries taste good, are refreshing, arouse the appetite, and are helpful in curbing diarrhea. They are good sources of vitamin C.

Preparation and Dosage: Gather leaves after the berries are ripe.

Infusion: Use 1 tbsp. leaves with ½ cup boiling water.

Cold Extract: Use 1 tbsp. leaves with ½ cup cold water; let stand for 10 hrs.

Decoction: Use 1 heaping tsp. dried leaves to ½ cup water. Take unsweetened, a mouthful at a time.

013 ALTHEA

(Althaea officinalis)

Common Names: Marshmallow, mortification root, sweet weed, wymote.

Medicinal Parts: Root, leaves, flowers.

Description: Althea is a perennial plant, 2 to 4 feet high, that is cultivated but also occurs wild in damp meadows and wet places. The rootstock is white and tastes sweet and mucilaginous when chewed. It sends up several unbranched, woolly stems with serrate, pubescent leaves. The axillary flowers are from 1 to 2 inches across and may be light red to white or purple in color.

Properties and Uses: Demulcent, emollient, diuretic. Althea's particular excellence is soothing irritated tissue. Externally, use it as a poultice for irritations, burns, carbuncles and furuncles, and wounds. An infusion of the leaves or flowers serves as a soothing gargle. A decoction of the root makes a good vaginal douche or a soothing eyewash. Use the cold extract of the root or the whole plant as a tea that is good for coughs, whooping cough, bronchitis, and lung catarrh. For bronchial asthma, sweenten with honey and take a mouthful at a time. The tea also helps in many digestive and urinary problems and can be taken for ulcers and colitis.

Preparation and Dosage: The leaves develop their mucilaginous content after flowering. Gather the root in spring or fall and peel before using. Since the infusion and decoction tend to be gelatinous, use the cold extract method to make the tea.

Cold Extract: Use 1 to 2 tbsp. root or plant with 1 cup cold water. Let stand for 8 hours, then strain. Take 1 cup a day, cold or slightly warmed up.

Infusion: Use 2 tbsp. flowers or leaves to 1 cup boiling water; steep for 5 minutes.

Decoction: Use 1 tsp. root to 1 cup boiling water. Simmer until the desired consistency is obtained.

Tincture: A dose of the tincture is 20 to 40 drops.

Poultice: Mix grated root with honey to obtain a thick mash. Spread on a linen cloth and apply. Renew every 2 to 3 hours.

014   AMARANTH

(Amaranthus hypochondriacus)

Common Names: Lady bleeding,
lovely bleeding, pilewort, prince's
feather, red cockscomb, spleen
amaranth.

Medicinal Part: Leaves.

Description: Amaranth is an annual herb that is cultivated and
occurs wild mainly in the central
states of the U.S. Its stout, upright
stem grows 3 or 4 feet high and
bears alternate, oblong-lanceolate,
pointed, green leaves that have a
red-purplish spot. Its flowers appear in August and grow in clusters.

Properties and Uses: Astringent. As an astringent, amaranth is
good taken internally for diarrhea, dysentery, hemorrhage from
the bowels, and excessive menstruation. It can also be used as a
douche for leucorrhea, as a wash for skin problems, and as a
gargle for mouth and throat irritations.

Preparation and Dosage: Make amaranth as an infusion or decoction.

Infusion or Decoction: Use 1 tsp. leaves with 1 cup water. Take
cold, 1 to 2 cups a day.

Tincture: A dose of the tincture is ½ to 1 tsp.

015   AMERICAN CENTAURY

(Sabatia angularis)

Common Names: Bitterbloom, bitter clover, eyebright, red centaury, rose pink, wild succory.

Medicinal Part: The herb.

Description: American centaury is a biennial plant, 1 to 2 feet
high, that grows in most parts of the U.S. on damp, rich soils.
The yellow, fibrous root sends up a branched, erect, quadrangular, smooth stem. The leaves are opposite, smooth, and entire,
their bases clasping. A terminal umbel consists of many rose- or
carnation-colored flowers that appear from June to September.
The seeds are borne in short, wheat-like husks.

Properties and Uses: Bitter tonic, emmenagogue, febrifuge, vermifuge. The warm infusion is particularly good as a bitter tonic
for indigestion (dyspepsia) and during convalescence, when the

appetite suffers. The other categories indicate older uses and may be more or less effective.

Preparation and Dosage: Gather the plant when in flower.

Infusion: Use 1 tsp. chopped herb with 1 cup boiling water; steep for ½ hour. Take 1 tbsp. every few hours or as needed.

Tincture: Take 15 to 40 drops every 3 to 4 hours.

016 AMERICAN HELLEBORE

(*Veratrum viride*)

Common Names: American white hellebore, bugbane, devil's bite, earth gall, green hellebore, Indian poke, itchweed, swamp hellebore, tickleweed, white hellebore.

Medicinal Part: Rootstock.

Description: American hellebore is a perennial plant whose branched stem may grow from 2 to 8 feet tall. It is found in swamps, moist meadows, and low grounds from Canada to Georgia, as far west as Minnesota, and in the mountains of the Pacific Coast states. The rootstock is thick and fleshy and has many large whitish roots. It has a strong, unpleasant smell when fresh and a sweetish-bitter, somewhat acrid taste. The leaves are alternate, changing from oval near the bottom to lanceolate or linear at the top. A more or less drooping panicle of green flowers appears from June to August.

Properties and Uses: Diaphoretic, emetic, expectorant, febrifuge, narcotic. American hellebore acts as a cardiac depressant. Deaths are recorded from overdoses of the drug. Sometimes the leaves are gathered and cooked as a vegetable by mistake, with severe skin reactions and poisoning as a result.

Preparation and Dosage: Too dangerous to be used without medical supervision.

017 AMERICAN IVY

(*Parthenocissus quinquefolia*)

Common Names: American woodbine, creeper, false grapes, five leaves, Virginia creeper, wild woodbine, wild woodvine, woodbine, woody climber.

Medicinal Parts: Bark, twigs.

Description: American ivy is a woody vine that can be found in almost all parts of the United States. It supports itself on trees, walls, fences, and other surfaces with tendrils whose tiny discs stick tenaciously. The leaves are digitate, consisting of five toothed, pointed, smooth leaflets. The inconspicuous flowers are greenish or white, and in autumn the plant bears clusters of small, dark blue berries.

Properties and Uses: Alterative, astringent, expectorant, tonic. The bark and twigs are usually made into a syrup for use in coughs and colds, but a decoction can also be used.

Preparation and Dosage: Collect bark in the fall, after the berries have ripened.

Decoction: Use 1 tsp. chopped or granulated twigs or bark with 1 cup water. Take cold, 1 cup during the day, a mouthful at a time.

Tincture: A dose is 5 to 20 drops.

018 ANGELICA

(a) (Angelica archangelica)

Common Names: European angelica, garden angelica.

Medicinal Parts: Rootstock, roots, seeds.

Description: European angelica is a biennial or perennial plant that is found in well-watered mountain ravines, on riverbanks, in damp meadows, and in coastal areas of northern Europe and Asia; it is also cultivated. The stem is round, grooved, hollow, branched near the top, tinged with blue, and 3 to 7 feet high. It grows from a brown to red-brown rootstock that has a spicy, agreeable odor and a taste that is sweet at first, then bitter and sharp. The leaves grow from dilated sheaths that surround the stem, the lower ones large and bi- or tri-pinnate, the upper ones small and pinnate. The plant bears greenish-white flowers in large, terminal, compound umbels, from which comes a honey-like odor. The flowering time is June to August. The fruit is elliptic-oblong, strongly compressed, and composed of two yellow winged seeds.

Properties and Uses: Appetizer, carminative, expectorant, stimulant, stomachic, tonic. The seeds are also said to be diaphoretic and diuretic. Take angelica tea or tincture to stimulate appetite, to relieve flatulence and muscle spasms, and to stimulate kidney action. It is useful for all sorts of stomach and intestinal difficulties, including ulcers and vomiting with stomach cramps. It can also be used for intermittent fever, nervous headache, colic, and general weakness. However, used in large doses, angelica can have untoward effects on blood pressure, heart action, and respiration. Externally, angelica salve can be used as a beneficial skin lotion and also to help relieve rheumatic pains. As a bath additive, angelica is said to be good for the nerves. A decoction of the root can be applied to the skin for scabies or itching and also to wounds. As a compress it can be used for gout.

Preparation and Dosage: The rootstock and roots are gathered in the second year.

Infusion: Use 1 tsp. crushed seeds with ½ cup boiling water. Take as needed.

Decoction: Use 1 tsp. root and rootstock with ¾ cup cold water. Bring to a boil, then let steep 5 minutes. Take the ¾ cup in two equal parts during the day.

Bath Additive: Use a decoction from 7 oz. of root and rootstock.

Cold Extract: Use 1 tsp. dried root and rootstock with ¾ cup water. Let stand 8–10 hours, then strain. Take 1 to 1½ cups a day.

Powder: Take ¼ to ½ tsp. three times a day.

019 ANGELICA (cont.)

(b) (Angelica sylvestris)

Common Names: Wild angelica, European wild angelica, goutweed.

Medicinal Parts: Rootstock, roots.

Description: Wild angelica is similar in size, habitat, and general features to *A. archangelica.* The rootstock, however, is thick and gray on the outside, the leaves are more sharply toothed, and the flowers are pure white and smaller.

Properties and Uses: Appetizer, bitter, carminative, diaphoretic, stimulant. Use wild angelica much the same as garden angelica. Its primary usefulness is for colic, cramps, and mild stomach upsets. CAUTION: Wild angelica can be confused with European water hemlock, which is poisonous.

Preparation and Dosage: Gather the rootstock and roots in the spring.

Decoction: Use 2 tsp. dried rootstock and root with 1 cup water. Boil 5 to 10 minutes. Take one cup a day.

Powder: Take ¼ to ½ tsp. three times a day.

ANGELICA (cont.)

(c) (Angelica atropurpurea)

Common Names: American angelica, angelica, archangel, belly-ache root, high angelica, masterwort, purple angelica, wild archangel.

Medicinal Parts: Rootstock, roots, seed.

Description: American angelica also generally resembles A. archangelica and is found in fields and damp places in Canada and the northeastern and north central states of the U.S. The rootstock is purple, the leaves are ternately compound, and the flowers are white to greenish-white, appearing from May to August. The whole plant has a powerful but not disagreeable odor when fresh.

Properties and Uses: Aromatic, carminative, diaphoretic, diuretic, emmenagogue, expectorant, stimulant. Use American angelica much as you would its European relatives. Its most common use is for heartburn and flatulent colic.

Preparation and Dosage: See A. archangelica.

---

021 **ANISE**

(Pimpinella anisum)

Common Names: Anise plant, aniseed, common anise.

Medicinal Part: Seed.

Description: Anise is an annual plant that occurs wild but is widely cultivated. The spindle-shaped, thin, woody root sends up a round, grooved, branched stem up to 1½ feet high. The lowest leaves are round-cordate and long-petioled, the middle leaves are pinnate, and those at the top are incised into narrow lobes. The small, white flowers appear in  compound umbels during July and August. The downy, brown, ovate fruit is about ⅛ inch long and ripens during August and September. The whole plant has a fragrant odor, and the seeds taste sweet when chewed.

Properties and Uses: Antispasmodic, aromatic, carminative, digestive, expectorant, stimulant, stomachic, tonic. Anise promotes digestion, improves appetite, alleviates cramps and nausea, and relieves flatulence and, especially in infants, colic.

Anise water promotes milk production in nursing mothers, and during the 2 a.m. feeding you can also use it as a soothing eye-wash. Anise is also said to promote the onset of menstruation when taken as an infusion. Anise oil helps relieve cramping and spasms and is good as a stomach tonic. For insomnia, take a few seeds in a glass of hot milk before going to bed. Anise can also be made into a salve to use for scabies or lice. A tea made from equal parts of anise, caraway, and fennel makes an excellent intestinal purifier. Because of its sweetness, anise is a good additive to improve the flavor of other medicines.

Preparation and Dosage: Alcohol extracts the medicinal properties of anise more effectively than water.

Infusion: Use 1 tsp. crushed seed to ½ or 1 cup boiling water. Steep 10 minutes and strain. Take 1 to 1½ cups during the day, a mouthful at a time.

Decoction: For colic, boil 1 tbsp. seed in ½ pint milk for 10 minutes; strain and drink hot.

Tincture: To prepare, add 2 oz. seed to ½ qt. brandy. Add some clean lemon peels and let stand in a sunny place for 20 days, then strain. Take 1 tsp. at a time.

Anise Water: Boil ½ tsp. seed in a half pint water, then strain.

022   APPLE TREE

(Pyrus malus)

Medicinal Part: Fruit.

Description: Apples are common enough not to need description.

Properties and Uses: Peeled and grated apple is excellent for illnesses involving diarrhea. A fasting diet of one or two days with only grated apple allowed is effective. Unripe apples are better for this than ripe ones. If, on the other hand, you need a mild laxative, eat some apples whole. Apple peels can be dried and made into a tea that is recommended for rheumatic illness. Apple wine is an ancient cure-all that was mentioned by Galen in the second century A.D. Use only wine that is at least two years old.

Preparation and Dosage:

Infusion: Use 1 to 2 tsp. dried apple peels with 1 cup simmering water. Take from 1 to 3 cups a day.

CAUTION: Apple seeds eaten alone in large quantities can be poisonous. A case is recorded of a man who saved the seeds until he had a cupful. He ate them all at once, and they killed him. On the other hand, a great Professor Emeritus of Medicine* once told me that the best advice he could give to a lay person was, "Do what you did in Paradise, eat an apple a day and get some physical exercise." His experience has proven we suffer from ill health because we overeat. The Paradise Diet is the way to regenerate your body and find heaven on earth. (Read *Rational Fasting by Arnold Ehret,* $1.35 +25¢ for postage, published by Beneficial Books, P.O. Box 404, New York, N.Y. 10016.)

* Dr. Walter Kempner, Professor of Medicine, Duke University.

023 ARNICA

(Arnica montana)

Common Names: Arnica flowers, arnica root, common arnica, leopardsbane, mountain arnica, mountain tobacco, wolfsbane.

Medicinal Parts: Flowers, rootstock.

Description: Arnica is a perennial plant that is generally found in mountainous areas of Canada, the northern U.S., and Europe. The horizontal, dark brown, branched rootstock sends up a slightly hairy, simple or lightly branched stem that reaches a height of 1 to 2 feet. The basal leaves are oblong-ovate and short-petioled; the upper leaves are smaller and sessile. Each plant has one to nine large, yellow, daisy-like flowerheads whose rays are notched on the outer tips. The flowers appear from June to August.

Properties and Uses: Diaphoretic, diuretic, emollient, expectorant, stimulant, vulnerary. Arnica is primarily for external use. Used as tincture or salve, it helps to promote the healing of wounds, bruises, and irritation. However, only very dilute solutions of tincture should be used, since the tincture can cause blistering and inflammation when applied. Arnica is also sometimes used as a poultice, and a tea made from the flowers for a compress on the stomach to relieve abdominal pains. The dilute tincture can be helpful in inflammation of the mouth and throat, and some doctors use it for internal bleeding and as a cardiac agent. Except in emergencies, arnica should not be used for any purpose without medical direction.

Preparation and Dosage: Use professionally prepared remedies whenever possible.

Infusion: Use 1 tsp. dried flowers with ½ cup boiling water. Take in three equal portions during the day for diaphoretic, diuretic, and expectorant action.

External Wash: Steep 2 heaping tsp. flowers in 1 cup boiling water. Use cold.

Tincture: Use a dilute solution of 1 to 2 tbsp. to a cup of water.

Ointment: Heat 1 oz. flowers in 1 oz. olive oil or lard in a water bath (as in a double boiler) for a few hours. Strain through several layers of cheesecloth.

024 ARTICHOKE

(Cynara scolymus)

Common Names: Garden artichoke, globe artichoke.

Medicinal Parts: Flower heads, leaves, root.

Description: Artichoke is a perennial plant which grows in the Mediterranean area and the Canary Islands and is widely cultivated elsewhere as a food plant. Its tuberous root produces a stem from 3 to 5 feet high, with alternate, thistle-like leaves that are grayish-green above and a woolly white underneath. The blue flowers are enveloped in the familiar globular heads of purplish-green, spiny scales which terminate the main branches. Artichokes destined for the dinner table are flower heads that were picked before maturity. Flowering time varies from spring to mid-summer, depending on the warmth of the climate.

Properties and Uses: Cholagogue, diuretic. The flower heads are commonly eaten as a vegetable, but extracts of the leaves and root are said to be helpful in preventing arteriosclerosis and have also been used for jaundice, dyspepsia, liver insufficiency, chronic albuminuria, and postoperative anemia. In some countries, the artichoke is considered an aphrodisiac.

ARUM

(Arum maculatum)

Common Names: Cocky baby, cuckoopint, cypress powder, dragon root, gaglee, ladysmock, Portland arrowroot, starchwort.

Medicinal Part: Rootstock.

Description: Arum is a perennial plant that grows in moist, shady places, along hedges, among bushes, and in deciduous forests. Its tuberous rootstock is poison when fresh but edible when dried or sufficiently cooked. It is about the size of a walnut and is brown outside, white inside. Arum's arrowhead-shaped leaves are also poisonous when eaten. Its flowers, which bloom in May and June, trap insects which the plant digests for food.

Properties and Uses: Acrid (fresh), diaphoretic, expectorant. Arum is generally used mixed with honey or syrup for internal use and as an ointment for external use. Internally, it can be used for bronchitis, asthma, chronic catarrh, flatulence, and rheumatic problems. For sore throat, gargle the decoction by itself. A 1:1 mixture of arum and sweet flag in powder form is sometimes recommended as a stomachic. An ointment made with arum is useful for sores and ringworm, and for swellings simmer arum with cumin in wine or oil to make a plaster. In any case, only the dried root should be used.

026 ASARUM

(Asarum europaeum)

Common Names: Asarabacca, European snakeroot, hazelwort, public house plant, wild nard.

Medicinal Parts: Rootstock, leaves.

Description: Asarum is a perennial plant that grows in European woods. It is a low plant with a horizontal, creeping rootstock and prostrate stem. Two long-petioled, upright, shiny, dark green leaves grow from each bud on the stem, rising from 2 to 4 inches above the ground. The large, solitary flowers appear from March to May and are characterized by a green-brown color on the outside, reddish-black on the inside.

Properties and Uses: Rootstock: diuretic, emetic, purgative. Leaves: cathartic, emetic, errhine. The basic use for asarum is as an emetic. As an errhine, it can be mixed with lance-leaf plantain to eliminate mucus from the nose and respiratory passages. Asarum is too dangerous to use without medical direction.

027 ASPARAGUS

(Asparagus officinalis)

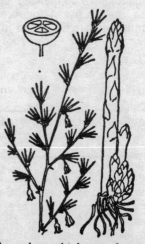

Common Name: Sparrow grass.

Medicinal Parts: Young shoots, seed.

Description: Asparagus is a perennial plant that is generally cultivated for food but may be found wild around gardens and in waste places. The short, horizontal rootstock has long, thick roots and sends up the young shoots that we eat as vegetables. If allowed to mature, these become branched stems that reach 5 feet in height. What look like leaves on the stem and branches are actually filiform branches which are clustered in the axils of the scaly, inconspicuous leaves. In May and June the plant bears small, solitary, pendulous, bell-shaped, greenish-white flowers. The fruit is a red berry, about ⅓ inch in diameter, containing black seeds and ripening in August.

Properties and Uses: Aperient, diaphoretic, diuretic. Asparagus acts to increase cellular activity in the kidneys and therefore increases the rate of urine production (it is not to be used when the kidneys are inflamed). It may also encourage evacuation of the bowels by increasing fecal bulk with undigested fiber. Asparagus has also been recommended for gouty and rheumatic problems (except podagra). The powdered seed can be used to relieve nausea and calm the stomach.

028 BALM

(Melissa officinalis)

Common Names: Balm mint, bee balm, blue balm, cure-all, dropsy plant, garden balm, lemon balm, melissa, sweet balm.

Medicinal Parts: Herb, leaves.

Description: Balm is a perennial plant that is common in the Mediterranean area and the Near East but is also naturalized in some places in the U.S. Mostly it is cultivated as a culinary herb, but it grows wild in fields and gardens and along roadsides. The stem is upright, hairy, quadrangular, and branched and grows as high as 3 feet. The leaves are opposite, ovate, long-petioled, somewhat hairy, bluntly serrate, and acuminate. The bilabiate flowers grow in axillary clusters and may vary in color from pale yellow to rose colored or blue-white. The flowering time is July and August. When bruised, the whole plant smells like lemon.

Properties and Uses: Antispasmodic, calmative, carminative, diaphoretic, emmenagogue, stomachic. Balm is a remedy for common female complaints and is useful for all sorts of nervous problems, hysteria, melancholy, and insomnia. Use balm tea to relieve cramps, dyspepsia, flatulence, colic, chronic bronchial catarrh, and some forms of asthma. Try it also for migraine and toothache, and, during pregnancy, for headaches and dizziness. The warm infusion has diaphoretic effects. An infusion of the leaves added to bath water is also said to promote the onset of menstruation. Use the crushed leaves as a poultice for sores, tumors, milk-knots, and insect bites. Balm is also used in herb pillows because of its agreeable odor.

Preparation and Dosage: Collect the plant before or after flowering. The fresh plant is more effective than the dried.

Infusion: Use 2 tsp. chopped herb or leaves to 1 cup boiling water. Drink warm, as required.

Cold Extract: Use 2 tbsp. per cup of cold water; let stand 8 hours.

Tincture: The dose is ½ to 1 tsp.

Powder: Take 10 to 40 grains at a time.

029   BARBERRY

(Berberis vulgaris)

Common Names: European barberry, jaundice berry, pepperidge, pepperidge bush, sowberry.

Medicinal Parts: Bark of the root, berries.

Description: Barberry is a deciduous shrub that grows in hard, gravelly soil in the northeastern states and sometimes in rich soils in the western states. The root is yellow on the outside and its bark has a bitter taste. The stems, growing from 3 to 8 feet high, are reddish when young but turn dirty gray when older. The leaves are obovate to oval and have a soft, bristly point. The small, yellow flowers appear from April to June and hang from the branches in clusters. The bright red, oblong berries, ripening in August and September, have an agreeable acid taste and should be eaten only when ripe.

Properties and Uses: Root: hepatic, laxative. Berries: laxative, refrigerant. The bark of the root contains an alkaloid that promotes the secretion of bile and is therefore indicated for various liver ailments. It also tends to dilate the blood vessels, thereby lowering blood pressure. A teaspoon of the root will purge the bowels, or use an infusion of the berries with wine for the same purpose. A decoction of either berries or root bark makes a good mouthwash or gargle for mouth and throat irritations. The fresh juice of the fruit is also said to strengthen the gums and relieve pyorrhea when brushed on or applied directly to the gums.

Preparation and Dosage: Gather the root in spring or fall. Use only ripe berries.

Decoction: Use ½ to 1 tsp. root bark with 1 cup water. Boil

briefly, then steep for 5 minutes. Take ½ to 1 cup during the day, a mouthful at a time.

Tincture: Take 3 to 7 drops, 3 or 4 times a day, in water.

030 BARLEY

(Hordeum vulgare)

Common Names: Pearl barley (hulled grain), Scotch barley.

Medicinal Part: Grain.

Description: Barley is an annual plant that is widely cultivated as a food grain. Its stout, simple stem (or culm) is hollow and jointed and grows from 1½ to 3 feet high. The narrow, tapering leaves ascend the stem in two ranks, the third leaf over the first; and their bases form loose sheaths around the stem. The flowers grow in bristly-bearded terminal spikes, producing eventually the elliptic, furrowed barley grains.

Properties and Uses: Demulcent. When hulled barley (pearl barley) is cooked, a mucilaginous substance is obtained which makes a good source of nutrition for those with throat or stomach problems. Mixing barley water with milk makes a soothing preparation for stomach and intestinal irritation. Barley has also been recommended for feverish conditions. The demulcent properties of cooked barley make it useful as an external application for sores and tumors.

Preparation and Dosage:

Decoction: Wash 2 oz. barley with cold water and boil in 1 cup water for a few minutes. Discard this water and boil the barley in 4 pints of water until the total volume is 2 pints. Strain and use as required.

Barley Water: Wash pearl barley in cold water. Boil 1 part pearl barley in 9 parts water for 20 minutes and strain. A dose is from 1 to 4 oz.

BASIL

(Ocimum basilicum)

Common Names: Common basil, St. Josephwort, sweet basil.

Medicinal Part: The herb.

Description: Basil is an annual plant found wild in the tropical and sub-tropical regions of the world; elsewhere it is cultivated as a kitchen herb. Its thin, branching root produces bushy stems growing from 1 to 2 feet high and bearing opposite, ovate, entire or toothed leaves which are often purplish-hued. The two-lipped flowers, varying in color from white to red, sometimes with a tinge of purple, grow in racemes from June to September. The plant is very aromatic.

Properties and Uses: Antispasmodic, appetizer, carminative, galactagogue, stomachic. Basil's usefulness is generally associated with the stomach and its related organs. It can be used for stomach cramps, gastric catarrh, vomiting, intestinal catarrh, constipation, and enteritis. As an antispasmodic, it has sometimes been used for whooping cough. Basil has also been recommended for headache. Some of its other uses are indicated by the categories above.

Preparation and Dosage:

Infusion: Steep 1 tsp. dried herb in ½ cup water. Take 1 to 1½ cups a day, a mouthful at a time. Can be sweetened with honey if taken for a cough.

BEAN

(*Phaseolus vulgaris*)

Common Names: Kidney bean, common bean, green bean, navy bean, pinto bean, snap bean, string bean, wax bean.

Medicinal Parts: Pods, beans.

Description: The kidney bean is an annual, twining plant which probably originated in South America and which is still the predominant bean cultivated in the Americas. Its leaves are alternate, each leaf consisting of three broad-ovate to rhombic-ovate, entire, pointed leaflets. The white, yellow, or purplish flowers grow in sparse, axillary clusters. The fruit is a green or yellow pod; the color of the seeds, or beans, depends on the variety. Diverse as they are, all the beans named above are varieties of the kidney bean. The dry beans are picked when mature, the others at various stages of immaturity.

Properties and Uses: Diuretic. Bean pods are effective in lowering blood sugar levels and can be used (with the concurrence of a physician) for mild cases of diabetes. A bean pod diet for this purpose would mean eating 9 to 16 pounds of pods per week (they can be cooked like vegetables). The pods are most effective before the beans are ripe, and fresh pods are more effective than dried. Dried pods are particularly to be used in conjunction or rotation with other efficacious herbs, such as bilberry, milfoil, dandelion, and juniper. These can be taken, alone or mixed, as a tea. Bean pod tea is also useful for dropsy, sciatica, chronic rheumatism, kidney and bladder problems, uric acid accumulations, and loss of albumin in the urine during pregnancy. Prolonged use of the decoction made from the beans is recommended for difficult cases of acne. Bean meal can also be applied directly to the skin for moist eczema, eruptions, and itching. Wash the skin every 2 to 3 hours with German camomile tea and apply new meal.

Preparation and Dosage:

Decoction: Use anywhere from 2 tbsp. to 3 handfuls dried, small-cut pods with 1 qt. water. Boil for 3 hours. Take ½ to ¾ qt. a day.

BEARBERRY

(Arctostaphylos uva-ursi)

Common Names: Arberry, bear's grape, kinnikinnick, mealberry, mountain box, mountain cranberry, red bearberry, sagackhomi, sandberry, upland cranberry, uva ursi.

Medicinal Part: Leaves.

Description: Bearberry is a small, evergreen shrub found in the northern U.S. and in Europe, especially in dry, sandy or gravelly soils. A single long, fibrous main root sends out several prostrate or buried stems from which grow erect, branching stems 4 to 6 inches high. The bark is dark brown or somewhat reddish. The leaves are entire, oval or obovate, rounded at the apex, often puberulent, ½ to 1 inch long, and slightly rolled down at the edges. The white or pink flowers grow in sparse terminal clusters. The fruit is a bright red or pink berry containing several one-seeded nutlets.

Properties and Uses: Astringent, diuretic, tonic. Bearberry helps to reduce accumulations of uric acid and to relieve the pain of bladder stones and gravel. Use it to alleviate chronic cystitis; it usually will change the color of urine but this need not cause alarm. The tea or tincture can also be used for bronchitis, nephritis, and kidney stones. It may also help where bedwetting is a problem. CAUTION: Excessive use of bearberry can lead to stomach distress, and prolonged use can produce chronic poisoning.

Preparation and Dosage: Fall is the best time to pick the leaves.

Infusion: Soak the leaves in alcohol or brandy, then add 1 tsp. soaked leaves to 1 cup boiling water. Drink 2 to 3 cups a day, cold. You can also let the leaves soak in brandy for a whole week before making the infusion with water and add a teaspoon of the brandy to each cup of infusion.

Tincture: Take 10 to 20 drops in water, 3 to 4 times a day.

034   BEARDED
DARNEL
(Lolium temulentum)

Common Names: Cheat, tare.

Medicinal Part: Seed.

Description: Bearded darnel is an annual plant that occurs as a hated weed in grain fields, waste places, moist farm fields, and along roadsides. The stiff, round, hollow stalk grows to a height of 1 to 3 feet and bears long, linear, flat leaves that are rolled up when young. The flowers grow in a terminal spike consisting of 5- to 7-flowered spikelets, each of which is embraced along almost its full length by a bract. Long, stiff bristles point upward from the flowers. The seed is small, yellow-brown to orange-brown, ovate, and somewhat compressed.

Properties and Uses: Bearded darnel is sometimes used by doctors to treat dizziness, insomnia, blood congestion, and stomach problems. It may also be used for skin problems like herpes, scurf, and sores. It is poisonous in large quantities and is not to be used without medical direction. Nonpoisonous remedies are available for all its uses, both internal and external.

035   BEAR'S GARLIC

(Allium ursinum)

Common Names: Ransoms, ramsons.

Medicinal Part: The whole plant.

Description: Bear's garlic is a perennial plant that grows in moist woods, woody ravines, and shady places, congregating in large patches of growth. An onion-like root sends a somewhat angular stem to a height of 6 to 16 inches and also sprouts two large, petioled, shiny, lanceolate leaves. From April to June the pure white flowers appear, growing in an umbel and characterized by a garlicky smell. The plant's black seeds are spread mostly by ants (who perhaps don't have too good a sense of smell).

Properties and Uses: Astringent, expectorant. Bear's garlic is said to be helpful in arteriosclerosis, including advanced conditions, for liver problems, and for pinworms. It is also good for diarrhea, colic, and lack of appetite. It has been used to treat gastro-intestinal catarrh with both diarrhea and constipation, as well as emphysema with bronchitis. It has been found to effect a slow, long-lasting lowering of blood pressure. In general, it can be used like garlic.

Preparation and Dosage: Bear's garlic must be used fresh (the bulb can be dried but not the rest of the plant). It is best to use it as a salad green, as a vegetable, or in soup.

036   **BEDSTRAW**

(a) (Galium aparine)

Common Names: Cleavers, coachweed, cleaverwort, goose grass, gosling weed, hedge-burs, loveman, stick-a-back, sweethearts.

Medicinal Part: The herb.

Description: Cleavers is an annual plant found in moist or grassy places and along riverbanks and fences in Canada, the eastern half of the U.S., and the Pacific coast. A slender taproot produces the weak, square, procumbent or climbing, prickly stem that grows from 2 to 6 feet long. The rough, oblong-lanceolate to almost linear leaves occur in whorls of 6 or 8 around the stem. The small, white or greenish-white flowers grow in cymes on long, axillary peduncles from May to September. The fruit consists of two joined, bristly, globular, one-seeded carpels.

Properties and Uses: Antispasmodic, diaphoretic, diuretic, vulnerary. The predominant uses for cleavers are external, although the tea has been recommended for stomach and intestinal catarrh and for irritations of mucous membranes, including those of the urinary tract. The juice of the fresh plant or a tea made from the dried plant is popular for skin problems. The juice or tea is applied daily and allowed to dry (before each application, wash the affected area with rectified alcohol, burning the cloth each time). If preferred, make a salve for the skin by mixing the fresh juice with butter (renew every 3 hours and burn the cloth used to apply it). Applying the crushed fresh leaves directly is also said to be helpful for skin problems and for stopping bleeding. Cleavers is popularly used in Europe for healing wounds and sores.

Preparation and Dosage: Use the juice of the fresh plant or dry the plant immediately to keep for later use.

Infusion: Steep 1 oz. dried herb in 1 pint warm (not boiling) water for 2 hours. Take 2 to 8 tbsp., three or four times a day.

Tincture: Take 20 to 30 drops in water, as required.

037 BEDSTRAW (cont.)

(b) (Galium verum)

Common Names: Yellow bedstraw, cheese rennet, curdwort, lady's bedstraw, maid's hair, yellow cleavers.

Medicinal Part: The herb.

Description: Yellow bedstraw is found in dry fields of the northeastern U.S. and in pastures and meadows in Europe. The slender, square, smooth stem grows from 6 inches to 3 feet high and bears linear, bristle-tipped leaves in whorls of 6 or 8. From May to September, tiny yellow flowers appear in dense panicles.

Properties and Uses: Yellow bedstraw is used essentially like cleavers (see above), its activity being perhaps somewhat stronger. In addition, yellow bedstraw tea has been recommended for epilepsy and dropsy, and as a calmative.

Preparation and Dosage:

Infusion: Steep 1 tbsp. dried herb in ½ cup water. Take 1 cup a day, freshly made each time.

Juice: Take 1 tsp. in ½ cup hot water over the course of a day.

038 BEECHDROPS

(Epifagus virginiana)

Common Names: Cancer root, pinedrops.

Medicinal Part: The plant.

Description: This native North American plant grows as a parasite on the roots of beech trees. It has a scaly, tuberous root and a branching, slender, leafless stem that reaches a height of 12 to 18 inches. The entire plant is a dull red color.

Properties and Uses: Astringent. Beechdrops is used externally for wounds, bruises, cuts, skin irritation, and other conditions where an astringent is called for.

039 BELLADONNA

(Atropa belladonna)

Common Names: Black cherry, deadly nightshade, dwale, poison black cherry.

Medicinal Parts: Leaves, tops, berries.

Description: Belladonna is a perennial plant found occasionally in waste places in the eastern states of the U.S., more commonly in European pastures, mountain forests, ruins, and waste places. A thick, creeping, whitish, fleshy rootstock sends up an erect, leafy stem that usually splits into three branches and attains a height of up to 5 feet. The dull green, ovate leaves grow in pairs, one leaf being half as large as the other. Belladonna flowers are solitary, axillary, bell-shaped, and dull brown to dark purple in color. The fruit is a sweet-tasting, black, shiny berry about the size of a cherry.

Properties and Uses: Antispasmodic, calmative, diaphoretic, diuretic, narcotic. The narcotic action of belladonna can produce paralysis by affecting the central nervous system. Not to be used without medical direction.

BENNET

(Geum urbanum)

Common Names: Blessed herb, European avens, star of the earth, yellow avens.

Medicinal Parts: Rootstock, flowering herb.

Description: Bennet is a perennial plant that grows around hedges, fences, walls, and in deciduous forests, preferring shady places. The rootstock is 1 to 3 inches long, finger-thick, yellow to brown outside, pinkish or pink-violet inside. The erect, hairy stem is red at the bottom and grows to a height of 1 to 2 feet. The lower leaves are lyrate and pinnate, the upper ternate or trifid; the leaflets broadly ovate and serrate. From June to August, the plant bears bright yellow, star-shaped, drooping flowers.

Properties and Uses: Astringent, styptic, tonic. As an astringent, bennet is useful for diarrhea; and it also makes a good gargle for gum problems and halitosis. It promotes appetite and acts as a tonic during convalescence. A wine extract of the root promotes digestion in older people and can also be used for chronic bronchial catarrh and for intermittent fever.

Preparation and Dosage:

Decoction: Use 1 tsp. dried root or herb with 1 cup water. Take 1 cup a day.

Tincture (from root): Take 10 drops, 3 times a day.

Powder: Take ¼ to ½ tsp., 3 times a day.

BETONY

(Stachys officinalis)

Common Names: Lousewort, purple betony, wood betony.

Medicinal Parts: Flowering herb.

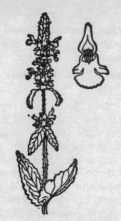

Description: Betony is a perennial plant found in old European gardens, damp or dry meadows, on sunny slopes, and along forest paths. The hairy, unbranched or slightly branched, quadrangular stem grows to a height of 6 to 24 inches. The leaves are opposite, more or less hairy on both sides, the lower leaves oblong-cordate, the upper more lanceolate. Spicate whorls of red-purple flowers appear from June to August.

Properties and Uses: Anthelmintic, astringent, carminative, diuretic, expectorant, vulnerary. Betony is recommended for asthma and bronchitis, as well as for heartburn. The infusion is also popularly used for neurasthenia, bladder and kidney problems, spitting blood, and excessive sweating; regular use is recommended for varicose veins. A strong decoction is said to be effective against worms. The juice of the plant can be used to heal cuts, external ulcers, and old sores. If you have a sprain, don't throw away the leaves boiled to make a decoction: make them into a poultice to put on the injured part. Finally, taking ½ to 1 cup of the infusion a day is recommended for children who, for no apparent reason, fail to thrive.

Preparation and Dosage:

Infusion: Use 1 to 2 tsp. per cup of water; take 1 to 2 cups during the day, a mouthful at a time.

Decoction: Use 2 tsp. with ½ cup water; sweeten to taste. Take ½ cup per day, a mouthful at a time.

---

042 BILBERRY

(Vaccinium myrtillus)

Common Names: Black whortleberry, blueberry, burren myrtle, dyeberry, huckleberry, hurtleberry, whinberry, whortleberry, wineberry.

Medicinal Parts: Leaves, berries.

Description: Bilberry is a shrubby perennial plant that grows in the sandy areas of the northern U.S. and in the woods and forest meadows of Europe. The angular, green, branched stem grows from a creeping rootstock to a height of 1 to 1½ feet. The leaves are alternate, obovate to ovate, weakly serrate, dark green and shiny on top, and ½ to 1 inch long. The reddish pink or red and white, solitary, axillary flowers have a pitcher-shaped corolla and appear in May and June. The fruit is a blue-black (may be red in some areas), 5-seeded berry. Although often called huckleberry, the bilberry is more nearly related to the cranberry.

Properties and Uses: Antiseptic, astringent. In case of diarrhea, use the leaf as an effective remedy. Fresh berries require some experimentation, because they can produce diarrhea in some people and stop it in others. They work well mixed with grated apple. The dried berries are definitely astringent and can be taken alone or mixed with apple powder. The berries have the advantage of passing through the stomach without affecting it, then beginning to work in the small intestine. A concentrated decoction of the berries is also said to be good for typhoid fever. Fresh or well-preserved berry juice makes a good mouth-wash or gargle for respiratory catarrhal problems. For inflamed gums or for leucoplasia (an inflammation of the tongue which produces white patches), keep a mouthful of the juice in the mouth for a while. Eating the fresh berries has also been ob-served to regulate bowel action, stimulate appetite, end intes-tinal putrefaction (which produces gas and flatulence), and expel ascarids. Leaf teas can also be used for coughs, vomiting, stomach cramps, and catarrhal enteritis. Use them in addition as a gargle for stomatitis and as a wash for skin problems and burns. CAUTION: Leaves can produce symptoms of poisoning if used over long periods.

Preparation and Dosage: Gather the leaves when the plant is fully developed but before the berries are ripe.

Infusion: Use 2 to 3 tsp. leaves with 1 cup water. Take 1 cup a day.

Decoction: Use 1 tsp. dried berries with 1 cup water. Take 1 to 2 cups a day, cold.

Cold Extract: Use ⅓ oz. dried berries with 1 cup water; let stand for 8 hours.

Tincture: Take 15 to 40 drops in water, 3 or more times a day as needed.

043   BIRCH

(a) (Betula alba)

Common Names: White birch, canoe birch, paper birch.

Medicinal Parts: Young leaves, bark.

Description: White birch is a tree found growing to a height of 65 feet in the northern U.S., Canada, and northern Europe. It has white bark which can be peeled off in horizontal strips. Its leaves are cordate, bright green above and lighter beneath, serrate, and glabrous or minutely hairy. The flowers are borne in male and female catkins, the female developing into seed cones.

Properties and Uses: Astringent, diuretic, diaphoretic. The leaf tea made by infusion is said to eliminate gravel and dissolve kidney stones when taken daily for a time, 1 to 1½ cups a day. It can also be used as a wash or bath additive for skin problems. A decoction of the leaves is sometimes recommended for baldness (or try the fresh expressed juice). If you have trouble sleeping, try the decoction before going to bed as a mild sedative. For chronic or severe skin problems, use a decoction of birch bark as a wash or bath additive. The inner bark contains an oil which is sometimes substituted for wintergreen in liniment.

Preparation and Dosage: The leaves must be used fresh.

Infusion: Use 1 tbsp. leaves with ½ cup hot water.

Decoction: Use 1 tbsp. leaves with ½ cup water. Boil briefly, let stand for 2 hours, then add ½ tsp. bicarbonate of soda. Take up to 1 cup a day.

Expressed Juice: Take 1 tsp. at a time, as required.

044 BIRCH (cont.)

(b) (Betula lenta)

Common Names: Black birch, cherry birch, mahogany birch, mountain mahogany, spice birch, sweet birch.

Medicinal Parts: Leaves, bark.

Description: Black birch is a tree that grows 60 to 80 feet high and can be found from Maine to Georgia and west to Michigan. The bark is brown when the tree is young, dark gray later, and is horizontally striped. On old trees the bark is more irregularly broken. The ovate, pointed leaves occur alternately in pairs and are finely serrate. The flowers grow in male catkins about 3 inches long and female catkins about 1 inch long, the male appearing in the fall and the female the following spring.

Properties and Uses: Anthelmintic, astringent, diuretic. Use leaf tea for urinary problems and to expel intestinal worms. A tea made from the inner bark makes a good mouthwash, and taken internally is good for diarrhea, rheumatism, and boils. An oil similar to oil of wintergreen can be distilled from the inner bark and twigs.

Preparation and Dosage:

Decoction: Use 1 tsp. inner bark or leaves with 1 cup water. Take 1 to 2 cups a day.

Tincture: A dose is ¼ to ½ tsp.

045   BIRD'S TONGUE
(Fraxinus excelsior)

Common Name: European ash.

Medicinal Parts: Bark, leaves.

Description: Bird's tongue is a European tree, 100 to 130 feet high, commonly planted in parks and along streets and found wild in woods and along river- and stream-banks. The leaves are opposite and odd pinnate, consisting of seven ovate, acute leaflets. The small flowers appear before or with the leaves in spring and are borne in small, crowded panicles. The fruit is a one-seeded, flat samara that is winged at the top.

Properties and Uses: Bark: diuretic, febrifuge. Leaves: cathartic. The bark is primarily used to reduce fever, but it is also sometimes effective to expel intestinal worms. The leaf tea is popular in Europe as a mild purgative and is often used for rheumatism.

Preparation and Dosage: Use the bark of young branches and twigs.

Infusion: Use 1 to 2 tsp. leaves to ½ cup hot water. Steep 2 to 3 minutes, then strain. Take 1 to 1½ cups a day, unsweetened, a mouthful at a time.

Decoction: Use 1 tsp. bark to ½ cup water. Boil briefly, steep for 2 to 3 minutes. Take ½ to 1 cup a day, unsweetened, a mouthful at a time. (Improve the taste by adding some peppermint or sweet marjoram, if desired.)

046

BIRTHROOT

(Trillium pendulum)

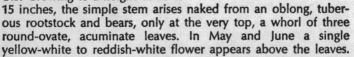

Common Names: Bethroot, coughroot, ground lily, Indian balm, Indian shamrock, jew's-harp plant, lamb's quarter, milk ipecac, nodding wakerobin, pariswort, rattlesnake root, snakebite, three-leaved nightshade, trillium, wake-robin.

Medicinal Part: Rootstock.

Description: Birthroot is an herbaceous perennial plant found in rich soils and shady woods of the central and western states of the U.S. Growing to a height of 10 to 15 inches, the simple stem arises naked from an oblong, tuberous rootstock and bears, only at the very top, a whorl of three round-ovate, acuminate leaves. In May and June a single yellow-white to reddish-white flower appears above the leaves.

Properties and Uses: Antiseptic, astringent, diaphoretic, emmenagogue, expectorant, tonic. Birthroot can be used for coughs, bronchial problems, hemorrhage from the lungs, pulmonary consumption, and, especially when boiled in milk, for diarrhea. It is also useful, both internally and externally, for female problems. As a poultice or a salve, it makes effective application for insect bites and stings.

Preparation and Dosage:

Decoction: Use 1 tsp. root with 1 cup water (or milk). Drink either hot or cold just before going to bed. Take 1 to 2 cups a day.

Tincture: Take ¼ to ½ tsp. at a time.

047

BIRTHWORT

(Aristolochia clematitis)

Common Names: Aristolochia root, upright birthwort.

Medicinal Parts: Rootstock, flowering herb.

Description: Birthwort is a perennial plant found growing around fences, thickets, field edges, and vineyards. The erect, yellow-green, somewhat sinuous stem grows to a height of 1 to 3 feet from a long, thin rootstock. The dark green leaves are kidney-shaped and short-petioled. The flowers occur in axillary clusters and feature a yellowish-green, curved, tubular calyx. Flowering time is May and June.

Properties and Uses: Diaphoretic, emmenagogue, febrifuge, oxytocic, stimulant. Birthwort is a remedy that goes back to the ancient Egyptians, who used it for snakebite. Early writings also indicate that it has long been used to promote uterine contractions during childbirth. Birthwort has also been effective against abdominal complaints and menstrual problems. The decoction can be used externally for wounds and also for leg ulcers. CAUTION: Birthwort contains a substance that acts similar to the poisonous alkaloid colchicine. Use with care, preferably under medical direction.

Preparation and Dosage: When the plant is in flower, use the entire plant, including the rootstock; otherwise use the rootstock alone.

Decoction: Use 2 tbsp. fresh plant (or rootstock) with 1 cup water. Boil for 10 minutes, then strain. Dosage as directed by a doctor.

Cold Extract: Use 2 tsp. plant or rootstock with 1 cup cold water. Let stand for 6 to 8 hours. Dosage as directed by a doctor.

048 · BISTORT

(Polygonum bistorta)

Common Names: Dragonwort, easter giant, patience dock, red legs, snakeweed, sweet dock.

Medicinal Part: Rootstock.

Description: Bistort is a mountain perennial that is found at higher elevations west of the Rocky Mountains and in Europe, in damp soil such as wet meadows and streambanks. The rootstock is thick, knobby, twisted into an S or double-S shape, up to 3 feet long, black on the outside and red on the inside, and ringed with old leaf scars. The basal leaves are bluish-green, long-petioled, and oblong-lanceolate. The few leaves on the simple, glabrous stem are lanceolate to linear, short-petioled to sessile, and have a dry leaf sheath at the base. The red to rose-colored flowers are borne in a dense, spike-like raceme, appearing from May to August.

Properties and Uses: Alterative, astringent, diuretic. Bistort is an excellent remedy for diarrhea, even for bloody diarrhea and dysentery. The decoction can also be used as a mouthwash for gum problems and for inflammations of the mouth (stomatitis), and as a wash for external sores and hemorrhage (or use the rootstock to make a poultice). When directly applied to a wound, the powder will stop the bleeding.

Preparation and Dosage:

Decoction: Use about 2 tsp. rootstock with 1 cup of water. Boil for 5 to 10 minutes. Take 1 cup a day.

049   BLACK ALDER

(a) (*Alnus glutinosa*)

Common Names: European alder, owler.

Medicinal Parts: Bark, leaves.

Description: Black alder takes the form of a deciduous tree up to 80 feet high, growing in Europe, Asia, North Africa, and locally in North America. It is found in cooler regions, forming dense stands around swamps and along streams and rivers. The alternate leaves of black alder are round-obovate, usually doubly serrate, scalloped, and have a tuft of down on the underside. The flowers are segregated by sex into separate catkins, the reddish-purple female ones developing into hard cones that contain the seeds. Two to eight catkins will occur in a cluster on a forked peduncle.

Properties and Uses: Astringent, bitter, emetic, hemostatic. Fresh alder bark will cause vomiting, so use dried bark for other than emetic purposes. A decoction of the bark makes a good gargle for sore throat and pharyngitis. The powdered bark and the leaves have been used as an internal astringent and tonic, and the bark also as an internal and external hemostatic against hemorrhage. Boiling the inner bark in vinegar produces a useful external wash for lice and for skin problems such as scabies and scabs. You can even use the liquid to clean your teeth.

Preparation and Dosage:

Decoction: Boil 1 tsp. bark or leaves in 1 cup water. For internal use, take 1 to 2 cups a day, in mouthful doses.

Tincture: A dose is from ½ to 1 tsp.

Powder: A dose is from 8 to 12 grains.

050 RED ALDER
(b) (Alnus rubra)

Common Name: Oregon alder.

Medicinal Parts: Bark, leaves.

Description: Red alder grows as a shrub or tree. It has elliptic-ovate leaves that are dark green on top and rusty-haired underneath. It is found in evergreen and redwood forests from Northern California to Alaska.

Properties and Uses: Astringent, bitter, emetic, hemostatic. Similar to black alder.

Preparation and Dosage: Same as for black alder.

051 SMOOTH ALDER
(c) (Alnus serrulata)

Common Name: Hazel alder.

Medicinal Parts: Bark, leaves.

Description: Smooth alder is a shrub or tree with blackish bark that is lightly speckled with small, grayish to orange lenticels. Its leaves are elliptic to obovate, finely serrate and usually fine-haired underneath. It can be found from Nova Scotia to Oklahoma, Florida, and Louisiana.

Properties and Uses: Astringent, bitter, emetic, hemostatic. Similar to black alder.

Preparation and Dosage: Same as for black alder.

052 BLACKBERRY
(Rubus villosus)

Common Names: Bramble, cloudberry, dewberry, goutberry, high blackberry, thimbleberry.

Medicinal Parts: Roots, leaves.

Description: Blackberry is a trailing perennial plant that grows in dry or sandy soil in the northeastern and middle states of the U.S. and is cultivated elsewhere. The slender branches feature sharp, recurved prickles. The leaves are finely hairy or almost glabrous and pinnate with 3 to 5 leaflets. The leaflets are ovate and doubly serrate. The upper leaves are sometimes simple and palmately lobed. The white, five-petaled flowers appear from June to September. The fruit is an aggregate of black drupelets collectively called the blackberry.

Properties and Uses: Astringent, tonic. Blackberry leaves and roots are a long-standing home remedy for diarrhea. Prolonged use of the tea is also beneficial for enteritis, chronic appendicitis, and leucorrhea. It is said to have expectorant properties as well. A tea made from the dried root can be used for dropsy. The chewing of the leaves for bleeding gums goes back to the time of Christ.

Preparation and Dosage:

Infusion: Use 2 tsp. dried leaves to ½ cup water. Take ½ to 1 cup a day.

Decoction: Use 1 tsp. root or leaves to 1 cup water. Take 1 to 2 cups a day, cold.

Tincture (of root): Take 15 to 40 drops in water, as needed.

053 BLACK COHOSH

(Cimicifuga racemosa)

Common Names: Black snakeroot, bugbane, bugwort, cimicifuga, rattleroot, rattleweed, richweed, squawroot.

Medicinal Part: Rootstock.

Description: Black cohosh is a native North American perennial plant found on hillsides and in woods at higher elevations from Maine and Ontario to Wisconsin, Georgia, and Missouri. The large, creeping, knotty rootstock, scarred with the remains of old growth, produces a stem up to 9 feet high. The leaves are ternate, then pinnate and sometimes even further divided; the leaflets are ovate or oblong and are irregularly toothed and cut. Small, white, fetid flowers grow in long racemes from May to August.

Properties and Uses: Antispasmodic, astringent, diuretic, emmenagogue, expectorant, sedative. Black cohosh is said to be a potent remedy for hysteria and for spasmodic problems such as whooping cough, consumption, and chorea (St. Vitus' Dance). It has a sedative effect on the nervous system, but it also acts as a cardiac stimulant. The infusion and decoction have been used for rheumatism and chronic bronchitis, and as emetics. American Indians used black cohosh to treat female complaints as well as for rheumatism. Small doses are helpful for diarrhea in children. CAUTION: Large doses can cause symptoms of poisoning.

Preparation and Dosage: Collect the rootstock in the fall, after the leaves have died down and the fruit has appeared.

Decoction: Boil 2 tsp. rootstock in 1 pint water. Take 2 to 3 tbsp., six times a day, cold.

Tincture: A dose is from 10 to 60 drops.

Fluid Extract: A dose is from 5 to 30 drops.

054 BLACK ROOT

(Varonicastrum virginicum)

Common Names: Beaumont root, Bowman's root, Culver's physic, Culver's root, hini, leptandra, oxadoddy, physic root, purple leptandra, tall speedwell, tall veronica, whorlywort.

Medicinal Part: Root.

Description: Black root is a perennial plant native to the U.S., growing in moist soil and swamps from New England to Minnesota and south to Kansas. The slender, simple stem grows to a height of 2 to 5 feet from a horizontal, woody rootstock. The lanceolate, finely serrate leaves grow in whorls of four to seven; and the numerous white flowers grow in panicled spikes. The fruit is an oblong-ovate, flattened, many-seeded capsule.

Properties and Uses: Cathartic, cholagogue, emetic, hepatic. Used cautiously, an infusion of the dried root can be useful for conditions resulting from sluggish activity of the liver. The root contains leptandrin, a violent emetic and cathartic.

Preparation and Dosage: Not recommended for use without medical direction.

Infusion: Use 1 tsp. dried root to 1 cup boiling water. Steep for 30 minutes. Take in three equal parts, before each meal.

Tincture: Take 2 to 4 drops in water.

055 BLAZING STAR

(a) (Liatris spicata)

Common Names: Marsh blazing star, colic root, dense button-snakeroot, devil's bit, devil's bite, gayfeather.

Medicinal Part: Root.

Description: Marsh blazing star is a glabrous perennial plant which is found in damp meadows, on the borders of marshes, and in other damp soils from Massachusetts to Florida and Louisiana, and westward to Ontario, South Dakota, and Arizona. The tuberous root produces a stem up to 6 feet high, with alternate, linear, dotted leaves, the lower of which are up to one foot long. Dense spikes of small flower heads made up of blue-purple florets bloom from August to October.

Properties and Uses: Diuretic. A decoction of marsh blazing star root has been used as a gargle for sore throat, and also as an effective remedy for gonorrhea.

Preparation and Dosage:

Decoction: Boil 1 heaping tsp. root in 1 cup water. Take 2 oz., three or four times a day.

Tincture: A dose is from ½ to 1 tsp.

056 BLAZING STAR (cont.)

(b) (Liatris squarrosa)

Common Names: Scaly blazing star, blazing star root, rattle-snake-master.

Medicinal Part: Root.

Description: Scaly blazing star is a native North American perennial plant found in dry, open woods, clearings, and fields from Ontario to Pennsylvania and Florida, and westward to South Dakota, Nebraska, and Texas. It resembles the marsh blazing star but is much smaller, the stem growing only as high as 2 feet and the leaves to 6 inches long. The flower spike is also smaller and appears from June to September.

Properties and Uses: Diuretic. Scaly blazing star is used like marsh blazing star. It is also reputed to be helpful for snakebite, the bruised root being applied to the wound externally (after making incisions through the bites and sucking out as much poison as possible) and a decoction in milk being given internally.

Preparation and Dosage: Same as for marsh blazing star. For snakebite, substitute milk for water.

057. BLAZING STAR (cont.)

(c) (Liatris scariosa)

Common Names: Tall blazing star, blue blazing star, gayfeather, large button-snakeroot.

Medicinal Part: Root.

Description: Tall blazing star is a finely hairy or glabrous perennial plant found in dry woods and fields and along roadsides from Maine and Ontario south to Florida and west to Manitoba, South Dakota, and Texas. The tuberous root produces a stem up to 3 feet high with alternate leaves, the lower broad-lanceolate and long-petioled, the upper much smaller, dotted, and sessile. Hemispherical flower heads, consisting of blue-purple florets, grow in interrupted racemes from August to October.

Properties and Uses: Same as for scaly blazing star.

Preparation and Dosage: Same as for scaly blazing star.

058 BLIND NETTLE

(Lamium album)

Common Names: Dead nettle, nettle flowers, stingless nettle, white archangel, white nettle.

Medicinal Parts: Plant, flowers.

Description: Blind nettle is a perennial plant found in the gardens and waste grounds of New England, and in Europe along roadsides, hedges, fences, walls, railroad embankments, and thickets. The rootstock is horizontal, creeping, and widely branched. The hollow, quadrangular stem is hairy, little-branched, and green or sometimes violet-hued. The leaves are opposite, petioled, ovate and cordate, hairy on both sides, and serrate. White, bilabiate flowers appear from April to October.

Properties and Uses: Antispasmodic, astringent, expectorant, styptic. An infusion made from the plant is helpful for leucorrhea, irregular menstrual periods, and weak menstrual flow. It can also be taken for stomach and intestinal problems and used as a vaginal douche. As a bath additive, the infusion is said to be good for uterine cramps and also for boils and tumors. Similarly, try a poultice of boiled leaves and flowers for tumors, boils, sores, varicose veins, and gouty pains. A tea (or tincture) made from the flowers is often used for insomnia. Finally, as part of a spring tonic diet, use the young leaves to make salad.

Preparation and Dosage: Gather the plant in dry, sunny weather.

Infusion: Use 2 tsp. plant or flowers with 1 cup water. Take 1 to 1½ cups a day, unsweetened, a mouthful at a time.

Powder: Take ¼ to ½ tsp., three times a day.

059　　BLOODROOT

(Sanguinaria canadensis)

Common Names: Indian paint, Indian plant, Indian red paint, pauson, red paint root, red puccoon, red root, sanguinaria, tetterwort.

Medicinal Part: Rootstock.

Description: Bloodroot is a small perennial plant, about 6 inches high, found in shaded, rich soils in the northeastern states of the U.S. The finger-thick rootstock contains a red juice when fresh; when dried it is yellow inside and brown outside. The leaves are basal, each coming from a bud on the rootstock; they are cordate or reniform in shape, palmately veined and lobed. The naked flower stem is shorter than the footstalk of a leaf and bears a white flower with 8 to 12 petals arranged in two or more whorls.

Properties and Uses: Diuretic, emetic, emmenagogue, expectorant, febrifuge, sedative, stimulant, tonic. Bloodroot is used in very small doses, primarily as an expectorant. It can also be used externally for sores, eczema, and other skin problems. Large doses are sedative, and an overdose can be fatal.

Preparation and Dosage: Do not use without medical supervision.

060 BLUE COHOSH
(Caulophyllum thalictroides)

Common Names: Beechdrops, blueberry, blue ginseng, papoose root, squaw root, yellow ginseng.

Medicinal Part: Rootstock.

Description: Blue cohosh is a perennial plant found in eastern North America, near running streams, around swamps, and in other moist places. The round, simple, erect stem grows from a knotty rootstock and bears a large, sessile, tri-pinnate leaf whose leaflets are oval, petioled, and irregularly lobed. The 6-petaled, yellow-green flowers are borne in a raceme or panicle. The fruit is a pea-sized, dark blue berry borne on a fleshy stalk.

Properties and Uses: Anthelmintic, diaphoretic, diuretic, emmenagogue, oxytocic. Blue cohosh is used to regulate menstrual flow, particularly for suppressed menstruation. The Indians used it to induce labor, also for children's colic and for cramps. Normally, it should be given in combination with other herbs indicated for the condition involved. Blue cohosh can be very irritating to mucous surfaces and can cause dermatitis on contact. Children have been poisoned by the berries.

Preparation and Dosage: Blue cohosh should be used with medical supervision.

Infusion: Use 1 oz. rootstock with 1 pint boiling water; steep for a half hour. Take 2 tbsp. every 2 to 3 hours, in hot water.

Tincture: Take 5 to 10 drops at a time.

061 BLUE FLAG
(Iris versicolor)

Common Names: Flag lily, fleur-de-lis, flower-de-luce, iris, liver lily, poison flag, snake lily, water flag, wild iris.

Medicinal Part: Rootstock.

Description: Blue flag is a wetlands perennial plant native to eastern North America and exported from here to Europe. Its stout stem grows from a thick, cylindrical, creeping rootstock and bears two ranks of swordshaped long, narrow leaves. Each stem has 2 or 3 large, blue or purplish flowers featuring three petallike, spreading or recurved sepals below and three petals, smaller than the sepals, above.

Properties and Uses: Cathartic, diuretic, sialagogue. Blue flag is said to be good for chronic vomiting, heartburn, chronic gastritis and enteritis, liver and gallbladder ailments, and catarrhal sinus problems. It is highly recommended for migraine, especially when caused by stomach disorders. The Indians also used blue flag for dropsy. The bruised fresh leaves are also sometimes used externally for burns and sores. CAUTION: Blue flag contains an acrid, resinous substance that acts on the gastrointestinal tract, the liver, and the pancreas. It may also cause dermatitis in some people.

Preparation and Dosage: Gather the root in the fall.

Infusion: Use 1 tsp. rootstock with 1 pint boiling water. Take 2 to 3 tbsp., six times a day, cold.

Cold Extract: Use 1 tsp. dried and powdered root with 1 cup cold water. Let stand for 8 hours, then strain. Take ½ to 1 cup a day, a mouthful at a time, slightly warm.

Tincture: Take 10 to 25 drops in water, three times a day.

062 BLUE VERVAIN
(Verbena hastata)

Common Names: American vervain, false vervain, Indian hyssop, purvain, Simpler's joy, traveler's joy, vervain, wild hyssop.

Medicinal Parts: Rootstock, herb.

Description: Blue vervain is a bristly perennial native to the northern U.S. and Canada and also to be found in England. The quadrangular stem reaches a height of 2 to 5 feet and bears leaves that are oblong-lanceolate, gradually acuminate, serrate, and 3 to 6 inches long. Some of the lower leaves are hastately lobed at the base, making good on the botanical name. The small, deep blue or purplish-blue flowers are sessile in dense spikes, 2 to 3 inches long, which are arranged in a panicle. The fruit consists of four nutlets which ripen soon after the plant flowers.

Properties and Uses: Antiperiodic, diaphoretic, emetic, expectorant, tonic, vermifuge, vulnerary. Blue vervain has been called a natural tranquilizer and is used as an antiperiodic for nervous problems. The warm tea, taken often, is recommended for fevers and colds, especially for getting rid of congestion in throat and chest. It can also be used for insomnia and other nervous conditions and is often effective for eliminating intestinal worms. Taken cold, the infusion acts as a tonic. Externally, blue vervain tea heals sores and wounds.

Preparation and Dosage:

Infusion: Use 2 tsp. rootstock or herb with 1 pint boiling water. For a tonic, take 2 to 3 tsp., six times a day, cold.

Tincture: Take 10 to 20 drops at a time.

063 BONESET

(Eupatorium perfoliatum)

Common Names: Agueweed, crosswort, eupatorium, feverwort, Indian sage, sweating plant, teasel, thoroughwort, vegetable antimony, wood boneset.

Medicinal Part: Herb.

Description: Boneset is an indigenous perennial plant found in swampy areas and along streambanks in eastern North America. The rough, hairy stem grows to a height of 1 to 5 feet from a horizontal, crooked rootstock. The leaves are rough, serrate, and taper to a long point. Terminal corymbs of numerous, white flowers appear in August and September. The fruit is a tufted achene. The plant has only a weak odor but a very bitter taste.

Properties and Uses: Aperient, cathartic, diaphoretic, emetic, febrifuge, tonic. The effect of boneset depends on the form it is taken in. Taken cold, the infusion has tonic and mildly laxative effects. Taken warm, it is diaphoretic and emetic and can be used to break up a common cold, for intermittent fever, and for the flu. The hot infusion is both emetic and cathartic.

Preparation and Dosage:

Infusion: Use 1 level tsp. herb with 1 cup boiling water; steep for 30 minutes and strain. As a tonic, take cold, 1 tsp. three to six times a day.

Tincture: Take 10 to 40 drops at a time.

BORAGE

(Borago officinalis)

Common Names: Bugloss, burrage, common bugloss.

Medicinal Parts: Herb, flowers.

Description: Borage is an annual plant that grows wild in the Mediterranean countries and is cultivated elsewhere. The hollow, bristly, branched and spreading stem grows up to 2 feet tall. The leaves are bristly, oval or oblong-lanceolate, the basal ones forming a rosette and the others growing alternately on the stem and branches. The blue or purplish, star-shaped flowers grow in loose racemes from June to August.

Properties and Uses: Aperient, diaphoretic, febrifuge, galactagogue, pectoral, tonic. Borage is said to be good for reducing fever and for restoring vitality during convalescence from illness. Its diaphoretic action is also credited with some antidotal effect against poisons. It also seems to have some calmative properties that make it useful for nervous conditions. Borage has even been recommended for pleurisy and peritonitis for its calmative and anti-inflammatory action. The leaves and seeds stimulate the flow of milk in nursing mothers. The fresh herb has also been made into an eyewash and used as a poultice for inflammations, but contact with the fresh leaves may cause dermatitis in sensitive persons.

Preparation and Dosage: Prolonged use of borage is not advisable.

Infusion: Use 1 tsp. dried flowers or 2 to 3 tsp. dried leaves with ½ cup water; steep for 5 minutes and strain.

065   **BOXWOOD**

(Buxus sempervirens)

Common Names: Box, bush tree.

Medicinal Parts: Bark, leaves.

Description: Boxwood is a small evergreen tree or shrub found along the Atlantic coast, especially as an ornamental and hedge plant, and in dry hills and sandy soil in Europe. It may be from 3 to 25 feet high, is heavily branched, with angular or winged, slightly hairy twigs. The leaves are opposite, leathery, simple, oval to oblong-lanceolate, dark green above and pale beneath. The pale yellow flowers grow in axillary clusters, and the fruit is a globular capsule containing six glossy black seeds.

Properties and Uses: Diaphoretic, purgative. Boxwood is said to be an excellent purgative. CAUTION: Animals have died from eating the leaves.

066   **BRIER HIP**

(Rosa canina)

Common Names: Brier rose, dogberry, dog rose, eglantine gall, hep tree, hip fruit, hip rose, hip tree, hop fruit, hogseed, sweet brier, wild brier, witches' brier.

Medicinal Part: Fruit.

Description: Brier hip is a bushy shrub that grows in open fields and thickets and on dry banks from Nova Scotia to Virginia and Tennessee. It is naturalized from Europe, where it is found around the edges of woods, hedges, garden fences, and on sloping ground. Varying in height from 2 to 13 feet, its numerous stems are covered with sharp spines and prickles. The leaves are odd-pinnate, usually consisting of 5 to 7 leaflets that are opposite, ovate, acute, serrate, and hairy beneath. The flowers are red, pale red, or nearly white and appear from May to July. The oblong, scarlet to orange-red fruit, or hip, contains many one-seeded achenes and ripens in the fall.

Properties and Uses: Astringent, carminative, diuretic, tonic. Brier hips are particularly beneficial for the digestive apparatus and produce a diuretic effect without irritating the kidneys. Where there is a tendency toward kidney stones or gravel, use brier hips as a preventive or arrestant. They are also recommended for kidney or bladder inflammation. By eliminating uric acid accumulations, brier hips also help in gouty and rheumatic complaints. A decoction of crushed achenes is also sometimes used for fever and as a beverage tea.

Preparation and Dosage:

Infusion: Use 1 to 2 tsp. hips (without seeds) with 1 cup boiling water.

Decoction: Use ½ to 1 tsp. powdered achenes with 1 cup water. Boil until ½ cup of liquid remains. Drink in the course of the day.

067 BROOKLIME

(Veronica beccabunga)

Common Names: Beccabunga, mouth-smart, neckweed, speedwell, water pimpernel, water purslain.

Medicinal Part: The herb.

Description: Brookline is a succulent perennial plant found growing in wet places, as in streams and ditches. Its round stem grows 1 to 1½ feet high from a creeping, jointed rootstock. The leaves are glabrous, ovate or broadly elliptical, and finely serrate. The small blue flowers grow in axillary spikes from May to August.

Properties and Uses: Diuretic, emmenagogue, febrifuge. The fresh juice of the herb is mildly diuretic. In older herbals, it is also recommended for intestinal disorders and anemia. Once prized, it is little used today.

Preparation and Dosage:

Juice: Take 1 tsp. to 3 tbsp., three times a day. Take in milk if the stomach is sensitive.

068 BRYONY

(a) (Bryonia alba)

Common Names: White bryony, tetterberry, wild bryony, wild hops, wild vine, wood vine.

Medicinal Part: Rootstock.

Description: White bryony is a perennial climbing plant cultivated in the U.S. and Europe, and occasionally found wild in moist areas and vineyards of Europe. The prickly stem grows to a length of 10 feet and climbs using spiral tendrils that grow opposite to the leaves. The rootstock is dirty white, spindle-shaped, and fleshy and contains a milky juice. The leaves are cordate, five-lobed, and rough. Small, greenish-white or yellowish flowers grow in axillary corymbs from June to August. The fruit is a black, pea-sized berry.

Properties and Uses: Pectoral, purgative. White bryony is a powerful purgative. In some places in Germany, the rootstock is hollowed out and filled with beer. After 1 or 2 days, the beer is taken, a teaspoon at a time, for constipation. The dried root is also sometimes used for chest problems, such as whooping cough. CAUTION: The rootstock is poisonous in large doses. The berries are very poisonous: 40 of them will kill an adult, 15 a child.

Preparation and Dosage: Except in an emergency, do not use white bryony without medical direction.

Infusion: Use 1 tsp. granulated rootstock with 1 pint boiling water. Take 1 tsp. every 1 or 2 hours, or as required.

Tincture: A dose is 5 to 10 drops.

069 BRYONY (cont.)

(b) (Bryonia dioica)

Common Names: Red bryony, devil's turnip, wild hops, wild vine, wild white vine.

Medicinal Part: Rootstock.

Description: Red bryony is very similar to white bryony. The large, white rootstock can grow to the size of a person's head. The leaves are cordate-palmate, and the fruit is a red berry.

Properties and Uses: Same as white bryony. The same danger of poisoning exists from the rootstock and berries. In addition, red bryony contains a dangerously poisonous resin.

Preparation and Dosage: As in white bryony, with the same cautions.

070 BUCHU

(Barosma betulina)

Common Names: Bookoo, bucco, bucku, oval buchu, short buchu.

Medicinal Part: Leaves.

Description: Buchu is a small shrub, 2 to 3 feet high, which grows principally in South Africa. Its opposite, glossy, pale-green leaves are obovate or ovate in outline and have strongly curved tips and serrate margins. The five-petaled flowers are whitish to pink; the fruit is an ovate capsule.

Properties and Uses: Aromatic, carminative, diaphoretic, diuretic, stimulant. Used by the Hottentots long before any white men came to South Africa, buchu finds its primary application in urinary disorders. A strong tea of the dried leaves is helpful for painful urination and for inflammation, gravel, and catarrh of the bladder. It can also be taken for leucorrhea. In South Africa, an infusion of buchu leaves in brandy is drunk as a stomachic and stimulant tonic.

Preparation and Dosage:

Infusion: Steep 1 tbsp. leaves in 1 cup water for 30 minutes. Take 3 to 4 tbsp., three or four times a day.

Tincture: Take 10 to 20 drops in water, three times a day.

SHORT BUCHU
(Barosma crenulata)

Another form and source of buchu from South Africa.

072

LONG BUCHU
(Barosma serratifolia)

Still another South African buchu. Same properties as above.

073   BUCK BEAN
(Menyanthes trifoliata)

Common Names: Bean trefoil, bogbean, bog myrtle, brook bean, marsh clover, marsh trefoil, moonflower, trefoil, water shamrock.

Medicinal Part: Leaves.

Description: Buck bean is a perennial water plant, found on the shorelines and in the ditches and marshy meadows of Pacific North America, Canada, Alaska, and Eurasia. The eastern and north central states of the U.S. have a smaller variety. The black, branching, jointed rootstock sends up a flower stem dilated at the base, as well as the dark green, ternate leaves with obovate, sessile leaflets. The racemed flowers are white inside, rose-colored outside.

Properties and Uses: Bitter tonic, cathartic, febrifuge. Use buck bean tea to relieve fever and migraine headache, or for indigestion and to promote appetite. Externally, buck bean can be used for ulcerous sores and for herpes.

Preparation and Dosage:

Infusion: Use 1 tbsp. dried leaves with 1 cup water. Steep for 15 minutes, and take 1 cup a day, unsweetened, a mouthful at a time. To stimulate appetite, take ½ cup about 30 minutes before eating.

Cold Extract: Use 2 tsp. leaves to 1 cup water. Let stand for 8 hours.

Powder: Take ½ to 1 tsp., three times a day.

074   BUCKTHORN

(a) (Rhamnus frangula)

Common Names: Alder buck-thorn, alder dogwood, arrow-wood, black alder dogwood, black alder tree, black dogwood, Euro-pean black alder, European buck-thorn, Persian berries.

Medicinal Part: Bark.

Description: Buckthorn as a shrub may grow to 20 feet high, as a tree to 25 feet, in swamps and damp places of the northern and north-eastern U.S. as well as Europe. The spreading, thornless branches have green bark when young, turning to brownish-gray when older. The light olive-green leaves are alter-nate, obovate, slightly toothed or entire, and glabrous. The five-petaled, green flowers grow in axillary clusters, 2 to 6 flowers per axil. The fruit is a three-seeded berry-like drupe that turns from green through red to purplish-black and has a greenish-brown pulp.

Properties and Uses: Purgative. The purgative action of buck-thorn is said to be similar to that of rhubarb. It works without irritating the system and can be used for all conditions causing or associated with constipation, including liver and gallbladder problems. It produces no constipative backlash after purgation as some other remedies do, neither does it become less effec-tive with repeated use. Buckthorn should not be used during pregnancy, however. With medical approval, a mixture of equal parts buckthorn, senna leaves, milfoil, and witch-grass root may be used during this time. Buckthorn tea is also said to be good for lead colic, obesity, dropsy, and hemorrhoids. CAUTION: Fresh bark and unripe fruit can cause symptoms of poisoning. Storage for a year or heating to 212°F will render the bark safe.

Preparation and Dosage: The best bark is from branches that are 3 to 4 years old. Age the bark for at least a year before using; after three years it begins to weaken.

Decoction: Use 1 tsp. bark with ½ cup cold water. Bring to a boil. Drink before going to bed. Use no more than ½ oz. of bark per day.

Cold Extract: Use 1 tsp. bark with ½ cup cold water. Let stand for 12 hours. Drink in the evening.

Tincture: A dose is from 5 to 20 drops.

075

BUCKTHORN (cont.)

(b) (Rhamnus cathartica)

Common Names: Common buckthorn, purging buckthorn, way-thorn.

Medicinal Part: Fruit.

Description: Common buckthorn is a deciduous shrub found in Europe, Asia, and the eastern U.S., often as a hedge plant. In the wild, it may grow 12 feet high or more, in thickets, among hedges, and along the edges of woods. Its branchlets are usually tipped with sharp spines; and its ovate or elliptic, crenate-serrate leaves grow in opposite pairs on the stems and branches. During May and June, small, greenish or yellowish flowers appear in 2- to 5-flowered axillary clusters. The fruit is a black, fleshy berry-like drupe.

Properties and Uses: Diuretic, purgative. The dried, ripe berries of the common buckthorn have been used as a purgative since the 9th century. The dried berries can be eaten or an infusion made from them for a purgative effect. Fresh berries can be made into a syrup. CAUTION: Excessive doses of the berries can produce poisoning.

Preparation and Dosage:

Berries: Adults take 1/10 to 2/10 oz. dried berries; children take half as much.

Syrup: Boil fresh berry juice with sugar to get a syrupy consistency. Adults take 1 to 2 tbsp., children ½ tsp. at a time.

BUCKTHORN (cont.)

(c) (Rhamnus purshiana)

Common Names: Cascara sagrada, California buckthorn, cascara, sacred bark.

Medicinal Part: Bark.

Description: Cascara sagrada is a deciduous tree native to the mountainous areas of North America from British Columbia to Montana and northern California. The tree grows from 15 to 25 feet high, and its reddish-brown bark is often covered with a gray lichen. The alternate, dark green, elliptic to oblong-ovate leaves are finely and irregularly toothed or nearly entire. They are rounded at the base and may be obtuse or acute at the apex. Small, greenish flowers grow in finely hairy umbels, producing eventually black, pea-sized drupes.

Properties and Uses: Bitter tonic, purgative. Cascara sagrada bark is one of the best and commonest plant laxatives. An extract of the bark is still prescribed and marketed under various brand names. It encourages peristalsis by irritating the bowels, but it is also useful for chronic constipation since it has a lasting tonic effect on relaxed bowels. Cascara sagrada has also been used for gallstones and liver ailments and for chronic dyspepsia.

Preparation and Dosage: Bark must be at least a year old before being used.

Infusion: Steep 1 tsp. bark in 1 cup water for 1 hour. Take 1 to 2 cups a day, before meals or on an empty stomach.

Tincture: Take 40 to 60 drops with water, morning and evening, as required.

077   BURDOCK

(*Arctium lappa*)

Common Names: Bardana, burr seed, clotbur, cocklebur, grass burdock, hardock, hareburr, hurrburr, turkey burrseed.

Medicinal Parts: Root, seed, leaves.

Description: Burdock is a biennial plant found in the northern U.S. and in Europe, along fences, walls, and roadsides, in waste places, and around populated areas. The root is long, fleshy, gray-brown outside, and whitish inside. In its second year, the plant grows a furrowed, reddish, pithy stem with woolly branches. During the first year burdock has only basal leaves. Both basal and stem leaves are oblong-cordate to cordate, green and hairy on top and downy gray beneath. The purple flowers appear in loose corymbose clusters from July to September.

Properties and Uses: Aperient, cholagogue, diaphoretic, diuretic. The decoction or infusion of burdock root is aperient, but not for all individuals; for some it may even be constipative. Both the tea and the tincture can be used for stomach ailments. Burdock is also said to neutralize and eliminate poisons in the system. The leaves are not generally used but do contain a substance that stimulates the secretion of bile. If they are to be used for liver problems, use fresh leaves only. A decoction of leaves also makes a good wash for sores and may be helpful for acne. The fresh, bruised leaves are sometimes used as a remedy for poison oak or poison ivy. The seeds contain an oil that is used medicinally, but only with medical supervision.

Preparation and Dosage: Collect the root in the spring or fall of the second year, i.e., when the plant has a stem. The root may be used fresh or dried.

Decoction: Use 1 tsp. root with 1 cup cold water. Let stand for 5 hours, then bring to a boil. Take 1 cup a day.

Tincture: Take 10 to 25 drops, in water, camomile tea, or regular tea, three or four times a day.

Juice: Grate the fresh root and add half again as much water. Squeeze out the liquid. Drink 1 cup a day, a mouthful at a time.

078   BUTTERCUP

(a) *(Ranunculus acris)*

Common Names: Tall field buttercup, bachelor's buttons, blisterweed, burrwort, crowfoot buttercup, globe amaranth, gold cup, meadowbloom, meadow crowfoot, tall crowfoot, yellows, yellowweed.

Medicinal Part: Fresh plant.

Description: Tall field buttercup is a perennial plant found in the eastern U.S. and from western British Columbia south to Oregon. The simple stem grows 1 to 3 feet high and bears palmately compound, sharply incised, downy leaves on long petioles which are dilated at the base (some of the upper leaves may be nearly sessile). The shiny yellow flowers for which the plant is named appear from May to September.

Properties and Uses: Acrid, anodyne, antispasmodic, diaphoretic, rubefacient. Tall field buttercup is used like the pasque flower. Only the fresh plant is poisonous and effective medicinally. A homeopathic extract of the fresh plant is used for skin diseases, rheumatism, sciatica, arthritis, and rhinitis.

Preparation and Dosage: Do not use without medical supervision.

BUTTERCUP
(cont.)

(b) (*Ranunculus bulbosus*)

Common Names: Bulbous buttercup, acrid crowfoot, crowfoot,
crowfoot buttercup, cuckoo buds,
frogwort, king's cup, meadowbloom, pilewort, St. Anthony's
turnip.

Medicinal Part: Fresh plant.

Description: Bulbous buttercup is
a perennial plant found in fields,
pastures, and dry meadows of the
northeastern U.S. and some Pacific
coastal areas. The hairy stem grows
6 to 18 inches high above the
ground and swells out into a solid, fleshy bulb, or corm, under
the ground. Small, fibrous roots grow from the bottom of the
bulb. The long-petioled basal leaves are three-parted, with the
leaflets three-lobed. The upper leaves are pinnate, with narrow
leaflets. Several golden-yellow flowers appear on each stem
from May to July.

Properties and Uses: See tall field buttercup, part (a). The juice
of the bulb is sometimes used to remove warts.

Preparation and Dosage: Do not use without medical supervision.

080

BUTTERCUP
(cont.)

(c) (*Ranunculus sceleratus*)

Common Names: Marsh crowfoot,
celery-leaved buttercup, cursed
crowfoot, water crowfoot.

Medicinal Part: Fresh plant.

Description: Marsh crowfoot occurs as an annual or biennial plant,
growing in wet, marshy places in
the northern U.S., the western
coastal states, and Canada. The
fibrous root sends a stiff, hollow,
glabrous, branched stem to a
height of 6 to 18 inches. The leaves
are thick, light green, shiny, and

palmately lobed. Pale yellow flowers appear between May and November.

Properties and Uses: See tall field buttercup, part (a). Marsh crowfoot is the most active of the three buttercup species: mere contact with the skin can cause irritation and blistering.

Preparation and Dosage: Do not use without medical supervision.

081 CALENDULA
(Calendula officinalis)

Common Names: Garden marigold, holigold, marigold, Mary bud, pot marigold.

Medicinal Parts: Leaves, flowers.

Description: Calendula is an annual garden plant with an angular, branched, hairy stem 1 to 2 feet high. The leaves are alternate, sessile, spatulate or oblanceolate, dentate with widely spaced teeth, and hairy. From June to October the plant bears large, yellow or orange, terminal flower heads.

Properties and Uses: Antispasmodic, aperient, cholagogue, diaphoretic, vulnerary. An infusion of the flowers (either the rayflowers alone or the whole head) can be used for such gastrointestinal problems as ulcers, stomach cramps, colitis, and diarrhea. It is also useful taken internally for fever, boils, abscesses, and to prevent recurrent vomiting. The fresh juice of the herb or flowers can substitute for the infusion. For external use, a very good salve for wounds can be made from the dried flowers or leaves, from the juice pressed out of the fresh flowers, or from the tincture. The salve or dilute tincture is also good for bruises, sprains, pulled muscles, sores, and boils. To get rid of warts, rub on the fresh juice. The tincture is often used internally for gastritis and for menstrual difficulties.

Preparation and Dosage:

Infusion: Use 1 to 2 tsp. fresh or dried flowers with ½ cup water; steep for 5 to 10 minutes and strain. Take 1 tbsp. every hour.

Juice: Take 1 tsp. at a time, always freshly pressed.

Tincture: To make, soak a handful of flowers in ½ qt. rectified alcohol or whiskey for 5 to 6 weeks. A dose is 5 to 20 drops.

Salve: Boil 1 oz. dried flowers or leaves, or 1 tsp. fresh juice, with 1 oz. of lard.

082 CAMOMILE

(a) (Anthemis nobilis)

Common Names: Roman camomile, chamomile, garden camomile, ground apple, low camomile, whig plant.

Medicinal Part: Flowers.

Description: Roman camomile is a low European perennial found in dry fields and around gardens and cultivated grounds. The stem is procumbent; the leaves alternate, bipinnate, finely dissected, and downy to glabrous. The solitary, terminal flowerheads, rising 8 to 12 inches above the ground, consist of prominent yellow disk flowers and silver-white ray flowers. The flowering time is June and July.

Properties and Uses: Anodyne, antispasmodic, aromatic, bitter tonic, stimulant stomachic. Camomile tea is good for flatulent colic, dyspepsia, and for fever and restlessness in children. It also makes a good wash for open sores and wounds. Camomile oil can be taken internally for colic, spasms, and stomach cramps. The flowers can also be made into a rubbing oil for swellings, callouses, and painful joints.

Preparation and Dosage:

Infusion: Use 1 tbsp. flowers with 1 cup water; steep for a half hour. For children, give 1 tsp. every half hour.

Tincture: Take 10 to 20 drops in water, three or four times a day.

Oil: Take 6 drops on a sugar cube.

Rubbing Oil: Steep 1 oz. fresh or dried flowers in olive oil for 24 hours or more. Strain before using.

083 CAMOMILE (cont.)

(b) (Matricaria chamomilla)

Common Names: German camomile, chamomilla, wild camomile.

Medicinal Part: Flowers.

Description: German camomile is a Southern European annual plant found wild along roadsides, in fields, and cultivated in gardens. The round, downy, hollow, furrowed stem may be procumbent or rise upright to a height of 16 inches. The leaves are pale green, bipinnate, sharply incised, and sessile. The flower heads are like those of Roman camomile, and the white ray-flowers are often bent down to make the disk-flowers even more prominent.

Properties and Uses: Anodyne, antiphlogistic, antispasmodic, calmative, carminative, diaphoretic, tonic. German camomile tea is valuable in many nervous conditions, insomnia, neuralgia, lumbago, rheumatic problems, and rashes. It also tends to reduce inflammation and to facilitate bowel movement without acting directly as a purgative. Use it as a wash or compress for skin problems and inflammations, including inflammations of mucous tissue. Keeping a mouthful in the mouth for a time will temporarily relieve toothache. To help asthma in children or to relieve the symptoms of a cold, try a vapor bath of the tea. German camomile can also be used as a relaxing, antispasmodic, anodyne bath additive. Use it for a sitz bath to help hemorrhoids, or as a foot- or hand-bath for sweaty feet or hands. For hemorrhoids and for wounds, the flowers are also made into a salve.

Preparation and Dosage:

Infusion: Use 2 tsp. dried (or fresh) flowers with ½ cup boiling water. Take a mouthful at a time. Or add 2 tbsp. flowers to 2 cups cold water and heat to just short of boiling.

Bath Additive: Use 1 lb. flowers with 5 qt. cold water. Bring to a boil, then steep covered for 10 minutes. Strain and add to bathwater. A less effective way is to hang a linen bag containing the flowers in the tub. Use proportionately smaller amounts for partial baths.

084   CANNABIS

(Cannabis sativa)

Common Names: Marijuana, pot, bhang, grass, Indian hemp, marihuana, weed.

Medicinal Part: Flowering tops.

Description: Cannabis is an herbaceous annual plant found growing wild and also cultivated in warm climates. It can be found to some extent everywhere in the U.S., especially in the central and midwestern states. The rough, angular, branched stems reach a height of 3 to 10 feet and bear opposite (or alternate near the top), palmate leaves with 5 to 7 narrow, lanceolate, coarsely serrate, pointed leaflets. The flowers are small and green, the male growing on one plant in axillary panicles, the female on another in spike-like clusters from August to October. The fruit is a small, ash-colored achene.

Properties and Uses: Although the current interest in cannabis centers on its euphorigenic properties, the plant has in the past also shown much promise as a medicinal agent. One researcher's catalog of past uses includes: analgesic-hypnotic, topical anesthetic, antiasthmatic, antibiotic, antiepileptic and antispasmodic, antidepressant and tranquilizer, antitussive, appetite stimulant, oxytocic, preventive and anodyne for neuralgia (including migraine), aid to psychotherapy, and agent to ease withdrawal from alcohol and opiates. Restrictions placed on cannabis in the U.S. since 1937 have practically eliminated its use as a medicinal agent, and even research into its properties was practically nonexistent until the last few years. Its medical history suggests that cannabis has only low toxicity (no confirmed deaths have been attributed to cannabis poisoning), but it also indicates that cannabis drugs are unstable and of variable potency. The euphorigenic substances of cannabis, isomers of tetrahydrocannabinol (THC), are found particularly in resins contained in the upper leaves and the bracts of the female flowers.

Preparation and Dosage: Not recommended for use without medical direction. Plants grown in dry, sandy soil are the most active medicinally. See further information in Part 3, "Legend and Lore."

085   CARAWAY

(Carum carvi)

Medicinal Part: Seed.

Description: Caraway is a biennial or perennial plant cultivated and found wild in the northern and northwestern U.S., Europe, and Asia. The hollow, furrowed, angular, branched stem grows in the second year from a white, carrot-shaped root. The leaves are bi- or tripinnate and deeply incised, the upper ones on a sheath-like petiole. The small white or yellow flowers appear in May and June, forming a compound umbel with

rays of unequal length. The fruit is dark brown, oblong, flattened, and two-seeded.

Properties and Uses: Antispasmodic, appetizer, carminative, emmenagogue, expectorant, galactagogue, stomachic. Like a number of other common kitchen spices, caraway has a beneficial effect on the appetite and digestion. It also promotes the onset of menstruation, relieves uterine cramps, promotes the secretion of milk, and is mildly expectorant. Use caraway for flatulent colic, particularly in infants, and also as a stomach settler after taking nauseous medicines.

Preparation and Dosage: The seeds may be chewed as is or the following preparations used:

Infusion: Use 3 tsp. crushed seeds with ½ cup water.

Decoction: Use 1 tsp. seeds to ½ cup water. Boil briefly, steep covered for 10 minutes and strain. Take 1 to 1½ cups a day, a mouthful at a time. Or boil 3 tsp. seeds in ½ cup milk for a short time, then steep for 10 minutes.

Oil: Take 3 to 4 drops of caraway oil, three times a day.

Powder: Take ¼ to ½ tsp., two to three times a day.

086   CARDAMOM

(Elettaria cardamomum)

Common Names: Bastard cardamom, cardamom seeds, cardamon, Malabar cardamom.

Medicinal Part: Seed.

Description: Cardamom is a perennial plant found commonly in southern India but also cultivated in other tropical areas. The simple, erect stems grow to a height of 6 to 10 feet from a thumb-thick, creeping rootstock. The leaves are lanceolate, dark green and glabrous above, lighter and silky beneath. The small, yellowish flowers grow in loose racemes on prostrate flower stems. The fruit is a three-celled capsule holding up to 18 seeds.

Properties and Uses: Appetizer, carminative, stimulant, stomachic. Cardamom seeds are useful for flatulence, but they are usually used as adjuvants with other remedies. They are also used as a spice in cooking and as a flavoring in other medicines.

087 CARLINE THISTLE

(Carlina acaulis)

Common Names: Dwarf carline, ground thistle, southernwood root.

Medicinal Part: Rootstock.

Description: Carline thistle is a European perennial plant found generally on slopes and in pastures, preferring limestone soils. The finger-thick rootstock is brown on the outside, lighter and fissured on the inside, and has an unpleasant, pungent odor when fresh but an aromatic odor when dried. The lanceolate, sharply incised leaves, similar to dandelion leaves, are radially arranged in a circle on the ground. A single, large, stemless flower, with a creamy-white center and silvery-white, petal-like bracts, sits immediately on top of the rosette of leaves.

Properties and Uses: Carminative, diaphoretic, digestive, diuretic, febrifuge; in large doses emetic, purgative. Carline thistle is recommended in some herbals for kidney and stomach problems, dropsy, impotence, and fever related to gastric problems. Its present use is mostly external. The rootstock applied externally is said to remove scars, and a decoction of it prepared with white wine or wine vinegar is used for washing wounds and for skin problems.

Preparation and Dosage:

Infusion: Use 6 tsp. rootstock with 1 cup water. Take 1 to 2 cups a day.

Decoction: Use 1 tsp. rootstock to ½ cup of water; boil briefly. Take 1 to 1½ cups a day, a mouthful at a time.

Tincture: Take 10 drops on a sugar cube or in water, three times a day.

Powder: Take ¼ to ½ tsp. in water, two or three times a day.

CARROT
(Daucus carota)

Common Names: Beesnest plant, bird's-nest root, Queen Anne's lace.

Medicinal Parts: Root (cultivated), seed (wild).

Description: Carrot is an annual or biennial plant widely cultivated and also found wild in farmlands, pastures, and meadows. The wild carrot has a tough, white, inedible root. The stem of the carrot plant is hairy and branched, the leaves bipinnate and cut into fine divisions. The lacy, white flowers appear in a concave umbel from June to September.

Properties and Uses: Anthelmintic, carminative, diuretic, stimulant. Carrot soup makes an effective remedy for diarrhea and is easily digestible for those suffering from stomach and intestinal problems. Carrot is also useful for preventing putrefaction in the intestine and for gastro-intestinal catarrh. The carrot's content of potassium salts accounts for its diuretic action, and it contains an essential oil that is effective against roundworms as well (eat 2 to 3 raw carrots a day for several days). Take carrot juice for stomach acidity and heartburn. And of course everyone knows that carrots are good for the eyes: specifically, their carotene content provides the material for the body to make vitamin A, which is important for proper vision, especially night vision. An infusion or decoction of the seeds of wild carrot can be used for flatulence, as a diuretic, and to promote the onset of menstruation.

Preparation and Dosage:

Infusion or Decoction: Use 1 tbsp. wild carrot seeds with 1 cup water. Take 1 cup a day.

Juice: Take 1 to 2 cups a day, or eat 10 to 12 oz. of freshly grated carrot for breakfast. An electric juicer makes fresh carrot juice easily available.

Soup: Boil 1 pound peeled, grated carrot in ¾ cup water until thick. Strain through a sieve. Then add 1 quart of meat broth.

089 **CASTOR BEAN**

(Ricinus communis)

Common Names: Bofareira, castor-oil plant, Mexico seed, oil plant, palma Christi.

Medicinal Part: Seed.

Description: Castor bean is an herbaceous annual plant that is found mostly cultivated in temperate climates, where it grows from 3 to 10 feet high. It is often grown in the northern U.S. as an ornamental plant. The stout stem bears alternate, peltate, palmately lobed leaves that may be from 4 inches to 2½ feet broad. A terminal raceme of flowers appears in later summer. The fruit is a spiny capsule which splits into three one-seeded parts, the seeds being smooth, glossy, black or mottled with gray or brown.

Properties and Uses: Cathartic. The oil pressed out of the seeds is one of the most commonly used purgatives. CAUTION: The entire plant, including the seeds, contains an irritant substance that poisons the blood. The oil is safe because the poison remains in the seed.

090 **CATNIP**

(Nepeta cataria)

Common Names: Catmint, catnep, catrup, catswort, field balm.

Medicinal Part: The herb.

Description: Catnip is a perennial herb of the mint family. Its erect, square, branching stem is hairy and grows from 3 to 5 feet high. The oblong or cordate, pointed leaves have scalloped edges and gray or whitish hairs on the lower side. The bilabiate flowers are white with purple spots and grow in spikes from June to September.

Properties and Uses: Anodyne, antispasmodic, aromatic, carminative, diaphoretic. Make catnip tea for upset stomach, colic, spasms, flatulency, and acid. It can also be used for an enema. Popular uses in Europe are for chronic bronchitis and for diarrhea.

Preparation and Dosage:

Infusion: Use 1 tsp. herb with 1 cup boiling water. Steep only: do not allow to boil. Take 1 to 2 cups a day.

Tincture: Take ½ to 1 tsp. at a time.

091 CAT'S FOOT

(Antennaria dioica)

Common Name: Mountain everlasting.

Medicinal Part: The flowering herb.

Description: Cat's foot is a small perennial plant found growing in large patches in the mountains of the Pacific coast states and in both mountains and flatlands of Europe. Its woolly stem rises 3 to 8 inches above the ground and bears linear-oblanceolate leaves, whereas the basal leaves are spatulate. The flowers grow in cymose clusters, the white male flowers having a filiform corolla, the rose-colored female flowers a tubular, 5-toothed corolla. Flowering time is from May to August.

Properties and Uses: Cholagogue. Cat's foot is useful for chronic problems with the biliary passages. It is also said to stimulate the flow of gastric juices and pancreatic secretions, and to raise blood pressure. It is sometimes recommended for dysentery, but better remedies are available.

Preparation and Dosage:

Infusion: Use 1 tsp. fresh or dried flowering herb with ½ cup boiling water; steep for 10 minutes. Take ½ to 1 cup a day.

092 CAYENNE

(Capsicum frutescens)

Common Names: Africa pepper, American pepper, bird pepper, capsicum, chili pepper, cockspur pepper, goat's pepper, pod pepper, red pepper, Spanish pepper, Zanzibar pepper.

Medicinal Part: Fruit.

Description: Cayenne is a perennial plant in its native tropical America but is annual when cultivated outside tropical zones. Growing to a height of 3 feet or more, its glabrous stem is woody at the bottom and branched near the top. The leaves are ovate to lanceolate, entire, and petioled. The drooping, white to yellow flowers grow alone or in pairs or threes between April and September. The ripe fruit, or pepper, is a manyseeded pod with a leathery outside in various shades of red or yellow.

Properties and Uses: Appetizer, digestive, irritant, sialagogue, stimulant, tonic. In powder or tablet form, capsicum is used as a general stimulant and to build up resistance at the beginning of a cold. It can also be taken as an infusion for stomach and bowel pains or cramps. Small quantities of the fresh fruit or the powder will stimulate appetite. For external use, cayenne is made into plasters or liniment or the tincture is applied to increase blood flow to areas afflicted with rheumatism, arthritis, pleuritis, or pericarditis. CAUTION: Prolonged application to the skin can cause dermatitis and raise blisters. Excessive consumption can cause gastroenteritis and kidney damage.

Preparation and Dosage:

Infusion: Use ½ to 1 tsp. pepper per cup of boiling water. Take warm, 1 tbsp. at a time.

Powder: For acute conditions, take 3 to 10 grains, for chronic conditions 1 to 3 grains.

093   **CELANDINE**

(Chelidonium majus)

Common Names: Chelidonium, garden celandine, great celandine, tetterwort.

Medicinal Parts: Rootstock, herb.

Description: Celandine is a biennial or perennial plant widespread in damp, rich soil in the northeastern U.S. and along fences, roads, hedges, as well as in waste places, in Europe. The finger-thick, cylindrical rootstock is red-brown on the outside, orange-yellow inside, and contains a milky juice. The hollow stem is round, smooth, and swollen at the joints. The leaves are alternate, pinnate or pinnatifid, with ovate, mildly and irregularly lobed leaflets. The bright yellow flowers have four petals, are ½ to ¾ inch across, and grow in a sparse umbel from April to September. The entire plant contains a bitter, orange-yellow juice that turns red when exposed to air.

Properties and Uses: Anodyne, antispasmodic, caustic, diaphoretic, diuretic, hydragogue, narcotic, purgative. Taken internally, celandine has a special effect on the digestive system (stomach, gallbladder, liver), and its antispasmodic properties make it useful for asthmatic symptoms. As a hydragogue it is used for dropsical conditions. Externally, made into an ointment or a poultice, celandine can be used for skin diseases like herpes, eczema, and ringworm. The juice has some antiseptic properties and has long been used to remove warts. Mix with vinegar when using the juice on the skin. CAUTION: The juice can produce poisoning by congesting the lungs and liver and by narcotic action on the nervous system. Skin poisoning has also resulted from handling the crushed plant.

Preparation and Dosage: Gather the rootstock in spring, before plant flowers. Use with extreme caution, preferably with medical direction. The dried plant is less active than the fresh.

Infusion: Use 1 level tsp. rootstock or herb with 1 cup boiling water; steep for 30 minutes. Drink cold, ½ cup a day.

Tincture: A dose is 10 to 15 drops.

Juice: For warts, dab no more than 2 or 3 warts at a time with fresh juice, two or three times a day.

094   CELERY

(Apium graveolens)

Common Names: Garden celery, wild celery.

Medicinal Parts: Root, leaves, seed.

Description: Celery is a widely cultivated, biennial plant which also grows wild in salty soils of North and South America, Europe, and Africa. The fleshy, bulbous root sends up, in the second year, an angular, furrowed, branched stem from 1 to 3 feet high. Celery leaves are opposite, dark green, shiny, and pinnate, the leaflets wedge-shaped, incised, coarsely toothed. The white to gray-white flowers bloom in paniculate compound umbels from July to November. The fruit is a small, ribbed, elliptic-ovate seed.

Properties and Uses: Plant: appetizer, diuretic, emmenagogue. Seeds: carminative, sedative. The expressed juice of the plant, particularly the fleshy petioles, is the most effective form of medicine. It can be used for dropsy, rheumatic tendencies, gout, tendencies toward overweight, flatulence, chronic pulmonary catarrh, lack of appetite, and deficiency diseases. It is a strong diuretic which is not to be used when acute kidney problems exist (moderate use is allowable when kidney problems are chronic). Celery also promotes the onset of menstruation; take it only in moderate amounts during pregnancy. As a salad vegetable or made into a tea, celery can be helpful also in clearing up skin problems. A decoction of the seeds can be used for bronchitis, rheumatism, and as a sedative for nervousness. A yellowish oil extracted from the root can restore sexual potency impaired by illness.

Preparation and Dosage:

Decoction: Use ½ tsp. seeds with ½ cup of water; boil briefly and strain.

Juice: Take 1 tbsp., two or three times a day, an hour before meals. An electric vegetable juicer makes fresh celery juice easy to extract. Mixes well with carrot and apple juice. Due to its high sodium content, use less than you do of the carrots and apples, if blood pressure is high.

Oil: Take 6 to 8 drops in water, two times a day.

095   CHERVIL

(Anthriscus cerefolium)

Medicinal Part: Flowering herb.

Description: Chervil is an annual plant cultivated in many places as a kitchen spice. The round, finely grooved, branched stem grows 12 to 26 inches high from a thin, whitish root. The leaves are opposite, light green, and bipinnate, the lower leaves petioled, the upper sessile on stem sheaths. The small, white flowers grow in compound umbels from May to July. The elongated, segmented seeds ripen in August and September.

Properties and Uses: Digestive, diuretic, expectorant, stimulant. The juice pressed out of the fresh flowering herb is popularly used for various purposes, including scrofula, eczema, gout stones, abscesses, dropsy, and women's abdominal complaints. The infusion is popularly used in Europe to lower blood pressure.

Preparation and Dosage:

Infusion: Use 1 tsp. fresh or dry herb with ½ cup water. Take ½ to 1 cup a day, unsweetened, a mouthful at a time.

CHICKWEED

(Stellaria media)

Common Names: Adder's mouth, Indian chickweed, satin flower, starwort, stitchwort, tongue-grass, winterweed.

Medicinal Part: The herb.

Description: Chickweed is an annual or biennial weed found in abundance all over the world in gardens, fields, lawns, waste places, and along roadsides. The usually creeping, brittle stems grow from 4 to 12 inches long and bear opposite, entire, ovate leaves. The small, white flowers can be found blooming all year long in terminal, leafy cymes or solitary in the leaf axils.

Properties and Uses: Carminative, demulcent, expectorant, laxative. For serious constipation, take a decoction of chickweed as described below. For other internal uses indicated by its categories, chickweed is not one of the more valuable plants. The fresh leaves can be crushed and applied directly or made into an ointment with lard or vaseline for bruises, irritations, and other skin problems. Chickweed can also be used as a vegetable, like spinach.

Preparation and Dosage: Chickweed can be used fresh or dried.

Infusion: Steep 1 tbsp. herb in ½ cup water. Take ½ to 1 cup a day.

Decoction: Boil 3 heaping tbsp. herb in 1 qt. water until a pint of liquid remains. For constipation, take a cupful warm every 3 hours, or more often, until the bowels move.

Juice: Take 1 tsp. to 1 tbsp., three times a day.

097 CHICORY

(Cichorium intybus)

Common Names: Succory, wild chicory, wild succory.

Medicinal Parts: Rootstock, flowering herb.

Description: Chicory is a perennial plant that is commonly cultivated and also found wild in the U.S. and Europe. The rootstock is light yellow outside, white inside, and, like the rest of the plant, contains a bitter, milky juice. The stiff, angular, branching stem bears lanceolate leaves that are coarsely toothed near the bottom of the

plant but entire higher up. The light-blue to violet-blue, axillary or terminal flowerheads feature rays that are toothed at the ends. Flowering time is from July to September or October.

Properties and Uses: Appetizer, cholagogue, digestive, diuretic, tonic. Chicory is often recommended for jaundice and for spleen problems. The juice of the leaves and a tea made from the flowering plant promote the production of bile, the release of gallstones, and the elimination of excessive internal mucus. They are also useful for gastritis, lack of appetite, and digestive difficulties. A decoction of the rootstock is said to be beneficial to the glandular organs of the digestive system. For painful inflammations, try applying the boiled leaves and flowers wrapped in a cloth.

Preparation and Dosage: Gather the rootstock from March to May.

Decoction: Use 1 tsp. rootstock or herb per ½ cup of cold water; bring to a boil and strain. Take 1 to 1½ cups a day, a mouthful at a time.

Juice: Take 1 tbsp. in milk or water, three times a day.

098   CHIVE

(Allium schoenoprasum)

Medicinal Part: Leaves.

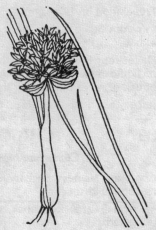

Description: Chive is a widespread perennial plant, both cultivated and wild. It grows to a height of 8 to 12 inches from a small, elongated, bulbous root. The leaves are hollow, cylindrical, closed at the top and dilated to surround the stem at the bottom. The otherwise naked stem bears a terminal globose cluster of reddish-blue or purple flowers in June and July. The fruit is a three-sided black seed.

Properties and Uses: Appetizer, digestive. Chives help to stimulate appetite and to promote the digestive processes. The plant also contains iron and arsenic (in harmless amounts) and may therefore be helpful for anemia.

Preparation and Dosage: Always use fresh, and avoid subjecting to heat (such as boiling with soup). The common method of chopping it fresh and sprinkling it over food just prior to serving is best.

099 CINQUEFOIL

(a) (Potentilla anserina)

Common Names: Silverweed, crampweed, goosegrass, goose tansy, moor grass, silver cinquefoil.

Medicinal Part: The herb.

Description: Silverweed is a low perennial plant, varieties of which are found in dry fields, meadows, and pastures and also in marshy places all over North America and Europe. Its rootstock sends out slender, rooting runners and also produces a rosette of basal, pinnate leaves consisting of 13 to 21 oblong, serrate leaflets that are dark green on top and covered with silvery hairs beneath. The bright-yellow flowers grow singly on long peduncles from May to September.

Properties and Uses: Antispasmodic, astringent. Silverweed tea (made with water or milk) is an excellent remedy for diarrhea and is even said to be good for dysentery. As an antispasmodic, it can also be used to relieve cramps; but it is generally mixed with balm leaves and German camomile flowers to make a tea for that purpose. The tea is also useful as an external astringent for skin problems, mouth and throat sores, and similar complaints.

Preparation and Dosage:

Decoction: Boil 2 tsp. herb in 1 cup water or milk.

Mixed Tea: Mix equal parts of silverweed, balm leaves, and German camomile flowers. Steep 1 tsp. of the mixture in ½ cup water. Sweeten with honey. Take 1 to 1½ cups a day, a mouthful at a time.

CINQUEFOIL
(cont.)

(b) (Potentilla canadensis)

Common Names: Five-finger grass,
cinquefoil, finger leaf, five fingers.

Medicinal Parts: Root, leaves.

Description: Five-finger grass is a
perennial plant found mostly in
dry soils from Quebec to Georgia
and west to Minnesota and Oklahoma. Its procumbent stem bears
petioled leaves palmately divided
into five sharp-toothed, obovate
to oblanceolate leaflets. Solitary
yellow flowers grow on long peduncles from the axils of the
leaves from April to August.

Properties and Uses: Astringent. Like silverweed, five-finger
grass makes a good gargle and mouthwash and a good remedy
for diarrhea. The powdered root or bark of the root can be
used, as well as the leaves. The root bark has also been recommended for stopping nosebleed and other internal bleeding.

Preparation and Dosage:

Infusion: Steep 2 or 3 tsp. leaves in 1 cup water. Take 1 cup a
day.

Decoction: Boil 1 oz. root bark in 1½ cups of water until 1 cup
of liquid remains. Take ¼ cup, two or three times a day.

Powdered Root: Take ¼ to ½ tsp. at a time.

Tincture: A dose is from 20 to 40 drops.

101 CINQUEFOIL (cont.)

(c) (Potentilla reptans)

Common Name: European five-finger grass.

Description: European five-finger grass is very similar in appearance to *P. canadensis* (above) and can be used for the same
medicinal purposes.

102 CLOVE

(Caryophyllus aromaticus or Syzygium aromaticum)

Medicinal Part: Flower buds.

Description: The clove is an evergreen tree, 15 to 30 feet tall, native to the Spice Islands and the Philippines but also grown in Sumatra, Jamaica, the West Indies, Brazil, and other tropical areas. It has opposite, ovate leaves more than 5 inches long; and its flowers, when allowed to develop, are red and white, bell-shaped, and grow in terminal clusters. The familiar clove used in the kitchen is the dried flower bud. The fruit is a one- or two-seeded berry.

Properties and Uses: Anodyne, antiemetic, antiseptic. Clove oil will stop the pain of a toothache when dropped into a cavity. A few drops of the oil in water will stop vomiting, and clove tea will relieve nausea. Eating cloves is said to be aphrodisiac.

103 CLUB MOSS

(Lycopodium clavatum)

Common Names: Foxtail, lycopod, staghorn, vegetable sulfur, wolf claw.

Medicinal Part: Spores.

Description: Club moss is a low perennial plant found in dry, coniferous forests and acid soils all over the world. The creeping, slender stem roots all along its length and sends up branches bearing small, stiff, linear, green leaves tipped with a white bristle. The yellow spores are borne on one or two club-like spikes growing on a long footstalk from the end of a branch.

Properties and Uses: Hemostatic, vulnerary. American Indians, as well as Europeans, have used club moss spores as a powder to stop nosebleed and bleeding from wounds. The powder has also been used to absorb fluids from damaged tissue in various injuries. At one time, it served to coat pills to prevent them from sticking to each other when packed together. CAUTION: The plant itself is poisonous, but the spores are not.

104 COLOMBO

(Cocculus palmatus)

Common Names: Calumbo, colomba, colomba root, foreign colombo, kalumb.

Medicinal Part: Rootstock.

Description: Colombo is a climbing perennial plant found in the forests of southeastern Africa. The thick, brown rootstock sends up one or two round and hairy stems which are simple in the male plant and branched in the female. The leaves are alternate, cordate, and three- to nine-lobed.

Properties and Uses: Antiemetic, febrifuge, tonic. Colombo makes a good remedy for vomiting and nausea, especially during pregnancy. It is also useful for remittent and intermittent fevers, for chronic diarrhea, and for colon problems. As a bitter tonic, it serves to improve appetite and is helpful for dyspepsia.

Preparation and Dosage: Keep the rootstock in slices until ready to use, then pulverize it.

Infusion: Use 1 level tsp. rootstock with 1 cup boiling water; steep for 30 minutes and strain. Take 1 tsp., three to six times a day.

Tincture: Take 5 to 10 drops at a time.

105 COLTSFOOT

(Tussilago farfara)

Common Names: British tobacco, bullsfoot, butterbur, coughwort, flower velure, foal's-foot, horsefoot, horsehoof.

Medicinal Parts: Leaves, flowers.

Description: Coltsfoot is a perennial plant found in the U.S., Europe, and the East Indies in wet areas such as streambanks, in pastures, and on ridges or embankments, preferring loamy and limestone soils. The creeping rootstock sends up first the downy white, scaly flower stems topped by large yellow flowers, then the cordate, dentate leaves from whose shape the plant gets its name. The leaves stand on long footstalks and are glabrous above and downy white beneath.

Properties and Uses: Astringent, demulcent, emollient, expectorant. Coltsfoot is one of the time-tried remedies for respiratory problems. Use it for coughs, colds, hoarseness, bronchitis, bronchial asthma, pleurisy, and throat catarrh. For chronic bronchitis, shortness of breath, and dry cough, try smoking the leaves. Coltsfoot can also be used for diarrhea. The crushed leaves or a decoction can be applied externally for insect bites, inflammations, general swellings, burns, erysipelas, leg ulcers, and phlebitis.

Preparation and Dosage: Collect the flowers as soon as they open, the leaves when they reach full size.

Infusion: Use 1 to 3 tsp. leaves or flowers with 1 cup water; steep for 30 minutes and strain. Sweeten with honey and take warm.

Juice: Take 1 to 2 tbsp., three times a day.

Tincture: Take 1 to 2 tsp. at a time.

106   COLUMBINE

(Aquilegia vulgaris)

Common Name: Garden columbine.

Medicinal Part: The plant.

Description: Columbine is a perennial, herbaceous plant that has come from Europe to be naturalized in the eastern U.S. Its prominently branching stem is sparsely hairy and grows from 1 to 2½ feet high. Both the basal and lower stem leaves are shaggy-haired underneath and biternate, with the leaflets or ultimate segments broadly wedge-shaped. The nodding blue, purple, or white flowers grow at the ends of the branches during the summer. Their five petals have characteristic nectar-containing, backward-projecting spurs about ¾ inch long.

Properties and Uses: Astringent, diuretic, diaphoretic. A decoction of columbine root can be taken to help stop diarrhea. The flowers taken with wine promote perspiration, and the seeds with wine have been said to speed the delivery of a child. Columbine leaves have sometimes been used in lotions to soothe sores in the mouth and throat. A lotion made from the fresh root can be rubbed into the affected area to relieve rheumatic aches and pains.

Preparation and Dosage:

Infusion: Steep 1 tsp. plant parts in 1 cup water. Take 1 tbsp., three to six times a day.

Tincture: A dose is from 5 to 10 drops.

107 COMFREY

(Symphytum officinale)

Common Names: Blackwort, bruisewort, gum plant, healing herb, knitback, salsify, slippery root, wallwort.

Medicinal Part: Rootstock.

Description: Comfrey is a perennial plant common in moist meadows and other moist places in the U.S. and Europe. The rootstock is black outside, fleshy and whitish inside, and contains a glutinous juice. The angular, hairy stem bears bristly, oblong lanceolate leaves, some petioled, some sessile. There are also tongue-shaped basal leaves that generally lie on the ground. The whitish or pale purple flowers have a tubular corolla resembling the finger of a glove and grow in forked scorpioid racemes from May to August.

Properties and Uses: Anodyne, astringent, demulcent, emollient, expectorant, hemostatic, refrigerant, vulnerary. A decoction of the rootstock makes a good gargle and mouthwash for throat inflammations, hoarseness, and bleeding gums. Drink it to take care of most digestive and stomach problems, for intestinal difficulties, for excessive menstrual flow, and to stop spitting blood. Powdered rootstock can also be taken internally for bloody urine (hematuria), leucorrhea, diarrhea, gastro-intestinal ulcers, dysentery, and persistent coughs. Externally, use the powder as a hemostatic agent, and make a poultice for wounds, bruises, sores, and insect bites. The hot pulp of the rootstock makes a good external application for bronchitis, pleurisy, and for the pain and inflammation of pulled tendons. Add the rootstock to your bath water regularly for a more youthful skin.

Preparation and Dosage:

Decoction: Boil 2 tsp. rootstock in 1 cup water or wine. Take a wineglassful or a teacupful two to three times a day.

Infusion: Use 2 tsp. rootstock per ½ cup water. Take 1 to 2 cups a day, warm, a mouthful at a time.

Tincture: Take ½ to 1 tsp. at a time.

Cold Extract Tea: Use 3 heaping tsp. fresh or dried rootstock with 1 cup water; let stand for 10 hours and strain. Bring the soaked rootstock to a boil in ½ cup water, then strain. Mix this with the cold extract and drink a mouthful at a time over the course of the day.

Pulp: Stir fresh, chopped rootstock into a little hot water to form a thick mash. Spread on a linen cloth and apply. Renew every 2 to 4 hours.

108   CORAL ROOT

(Corallorhiza odontorhiza)

Common Names: Chickentoes, crawley, dragon's claw, fever root, scaly dragon's claw, turkey claw.

Medicinal Part: Rootstock.

Description: Coral root is a native American, perennial plant that grows around the roots of trees in dry woodlands from Maine to Minnesota and south to Georgia, Alabama, Mississippi, and Missouri. The dark brown, branched, toothed, coral-like underground rootstocks send up simple scapes with sheaths instead of leaves and with terminal racemes of 3 to 20 flowers. The hood-like flowers are reddish or purplish on the outside, paler and flecked with purple lines on the inside. One petal forms a white lip with purple spots and a purple rim. Flowering time is August to October.

Properties and Uses: Diaphoretic, febrifuge, sedative. Coral root is an effective remedy for fevers, cramps, and skin diseases. Because of its relative scarcity, it is often combined with other herbs. The tea can be used internally or externally. For insomnia, take the tea before going to bed.

Preparation and Dosage:

Infusion: Steep 1 tsp. rootstock in 1 cup water. Take hot or cold, 1 to 2 cups a day.

Tincture: Take 10 to 20 drops at a time.

CORIANDER

(Coriandrum sativum)

Medicinal Part: Seed.

Description: Coriander is a small annual plant that has been cultivated for thousands of years and is still grown in North and South America, Europe, and the Mediterranean area. The round, finely grooved stem grows 1 to 2 feet high from a thin, spindle-shaped root. The leaves are pinnately decompound, the lower ones cleft and lobed, the upper finely dissected. From June to August the white to reddish flowers appear flat, compound umbels of 3 to 5 rays. The brownish, globose seeds have a disagreeable smell until they ripen, when they take on their spicy aroma.

Properties and Uses: Antispasmodic, appetizer, aromatic, carminative, stomachic. In addition to the indicated uses, coriander can be applied externally for rheumatism and painful joints. Coriander also improves the flavor of other medicinal preparations. At one time it was considered to have aphrodisiac effects.

Preparation and Dosage:

Infusion: Steep 2 tsp. dried seeds in 1 cup water. Take 1 cup a day.

Powder: Take ¼ to ½ tsp. at a time.

110　CORNFLOWER

(Centaurea cyanus)

Common Names: Bachelor's button, bluebonnet, bluebottle, blue centaury, cyani.

Medicinal Part: Flower.

Description: Cornflower is an annual herb native to Europe but also found cultivated in the U.S. The thin, stiff, branched stem grows to a height of 12 to 24 inches and bears narrow, lanceolate leaves, pinnate and lobed near the base and nearly filiform near the top. The large, blue flowers (white or rose-colored in some varieties) appear from June to August.

Properties and Uses: Diuretic, tonic. The cornflower is commonly used for dyspepsia and often appears in mixed teas recommended for cosmetic purposes. Sometimes the flowers are made into an eyewash or eyedrops and made into compresses for use on the eyes.

111　CORYDALIS

(Corydalis cava)

Common Name: Early fumitory.

Medicinal Part: Rootstock.

Description: Corydalis is a perennial plant found in the deciduous forests, thickets and hedges of Europe. The erect stem grows 6 to 12 inches high and bears soft, bluish-green, pinnately decompound and incised leaves. In April and May it is topped by a raceme of purple-red or rose-colored, sometimes white, flowers with corollas spurred at the base.

Properties and Uses: Antispasmodic, hypnotic. The high alkaloid content of corydalis makes it an effective remedy, when properly used, for palsy, trembling hands, and general excitement. One of its alkaloids that works on the nervous system is an ingredient in medications used for Parkinson's disease. Once upon a time, corydalis was used to expel worms.

Preparation and Dosage: Do not use without medical supervision.

112 COTTON
(Gossypium spp.)

Medicinal Parts: Bark of the root, seeds.

Description: Cotton is a biennial or triennial plant cultivated in many parts of the world, in the United States principally in the southern states. The round, hairy, branching stem grows from a spindle-shaped root and bears hoary, palmate leaves with five pointed lobes. The flowers have five yellow petals, each with a purple spot near the bottom. The fruit is a three- or five-celled capsule, each cell containing a seed buried in cotton fiber.

Properties and Uses: Root: abortifacient, emmenagogue, oxytocic. Seed: mucilaginous. A fluid extract or a decoction made from the bark of the root was once used as a substitute for ergot to promote menstruation, to induce uterine contractions during childbirth, and to effect abortion. The seeds have been used as a soothing remedy for coughs.

Preparation and Dosage: Do not use without medical supervision.

113 COWSLIP
(Caltha palustris)

Common Names: American cowslip, marsh marigold, meadow bouts, palsywort, water dragon.

Medicinal Part: The herb.

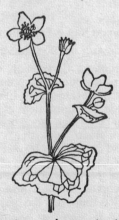

Description: Cowslip is a perennial plant that grows in marshes and along streambanks and pond edges in the northeastern U.S. and in Europe. The hollow, furrowed, glabrous stem grows 1 or 2 feet high and bears one or more kidney-shaped, dark green, shiny, crenate leaves. Bright yellow sepals make up for the lack of petals in the flowers which grow in cymose clusters in April and May.

Properties and Uses: Anodyne, antispasmodic, diaphoretic, diuretic, expectorant, rubefacient. Cowslip can be used like the pasque flower, but its action is somewhat weaker. The plant is sometimes eaten in the springtime as greens or pot-herbs.

CAUTION: Cowslip contains irritant acrid elements. Use only after cooking or drying.

Preparation and Dosage: Use for medicinal purposes with medical direction only.

114 CUBEB

(Piper cubeba)

Common Names: Java pepper, tailed cubebs, tailed pepper.

Medicinal Part: Unripe fruit.

Description: Cubeb is a perennial vine or shrub that grows in the forests of Penang, Sumatra, New Guinea, and the neighboring islands. The round branches of the creeping or climbing stem are ash-gray and take root at the joints. The leaves are smooth, oblong-ovate, and pointed. The flowers grow in smooth, scaly spikes, developing into a cluster of berries. Cubebs are the dried, unripe berries, which look like black pepper.

Properties and Uses: Antiseptic, carminative, diuretic, expectorant, stimulant, stomachic. Cubeb is helpful for indigestion, catarrh, bronchitis, coughs, and lung problems. Cubeb cigarettes are said to relieve hay fever, asthma, and pharyngitis. Cubeb oil is useful for urinary ailments and acts as an antiseptic against gonorrhea.

Preparation and Dosage:

Infusion: Steep 1 tsp. cubebs in 1 cup water. Take hot or cold, a mouthful three times a day or ½ cup when going to bed.

Oil: A dose is 5 to 15 drops.

Powder: A dose is ½ to 2 tsp.

115 CUCUMBER
(Cucumis sativus)

Medicinal Part: Fruit.

Description: The cucumber plant is a fleshy, bristly, creeping or climbing vine that attaches itself to objects by means of tendrils. The leaves are mostly long-petioled, cordate, and incised to make five points. The flowers are golden-yellow and bell-shaped.

Properties and Uses: Aperient, diuretic. Cucumber's ability to eliminate water from the body makes it important for those with heart and kidney problems. It also helps to dissolve uric acid accumulations such as kidney and bladder stones. Cucumber salad is good for chronic constipation; cucumber juice has beneficial effects on the intestines, lungs, kidneys, and skin. For skin problems and for cosmetic purposes, rub the juice into the skin. Apply it also to inflammations, bed sores, and burns.

Preparation and Dosage: The most effective cucumbers are those that are fully ripe, as indicated by a beginning yellow color.

Juice: Mix with apple, celery, or carrot juice to improve the taste. Take as required. Easily prepared in an electric vegetable juicer.

116 CURRANT
(a) (Ribes nigrum)

Common Names: Black currant, quinsy berry.

Medicinal Parts: Leaves, fruit.

Description: Black currant is a bush, growing to a height of 6 or 7 feet in moist soils and shallow marshes; it is also cultivated. The leaves are alternate, palmately 3- to 5-lobed, doubly serrate, and more or less cordate. Drooping racemes of greenish-white or greenish-yellow flowers appear in April and May. The fruit is a berry that is dark brown at first, turning black when ripe.

Properties and Uses: Diaphoretic, diuretic. The leaf tea stimulates the kidneys and is good for gouty and rheumatic problems, as well as for arteriosclerosis. Drunk cold, it is also useful for hoarseness and other throat ailments. Both the leaf tea and the expressed juice of the berries can be used for whooping cough in children. The berries or their juice is also beneficial for kidney problems and colic pains. Use an infusion of the dried berries as a gargle for inflammation in the mouth and throat and as a mouthwash for bleeding gums.

Preparation and Dosage: Collect the leaves after flowering, the berries when ripe. Do not use leaves that have a fungus on the lower side. Use only the leaf blades, not the petioles.

Infusion: Use 1 tsp. dried leaves to ½ cup water. Parboil and steep for 5 minutes. Take 1 to 1½ cups a day, unsweetened, a mouthful at a time. For whooping cough only, sweeten with honey.

Infusion: Use 1 to 2 tsp. dried berries to 1 cup boiling water to make a gargle or mouthwash.

Berry Juice: Take 1 tbsp. several times a day, or as needed.

117 CURRANT (cont.)

(b) (Ribes rubrum)

Common Names: Red currant, garden currant, garnetberry, raisin tree, wineberry.

Medicinal Part: Fruit.

Description: Red currant is a low shrub that grows wild in northern Europe and in the Himalayas and is commonly cultivated for its fruit elsewhere. The stems, which grow from 3 to 6 feet high, have thin, dry, peeling bark; the young growth is finely hairy. The leaves are alternate, triangular-ovate, dentate and cut, and hairy along the veins on the lower side. Yellow-green flowers grow in drooping racemes during April and May. The shiny red (white in some varieties), translucent, veined berries ripen in early and mid-summer.

Properties and Uses: Febrifuge, refrigerant, sialagogue, stomachic. Fresh red currant berries or berry juice promotes appetite and can also be taken for upset stomach. When the berries are eaten whole, the indigestible seeds provide bulk to help regulate activity of the bowels. Currant juice also makes a good mouthwash and gargle for sores in the mouth and throat. As a drink, it refreshes and cools a patient suffering from feverish thirst. Some people find the juice thinned with water to be a good substitute for alcohol.

118 CYCLAMEN

(Cyclamen europaeum)

Common Names: Groundbread, sowbread, swinebread.

Medicinal Part: Rootstock.

Description: Cyclamen is a low European perennial plant, found in the Mediterranean area, the Alps, and other mountain forests. The bulbous rootstock sends up long-petioled, leathery, cordate, palmately veined leaves that are dark gray-green with lighter spots on top and reddish underneath. From June to September the drooping flowers, varying from white through pink to red-violet, appear on naked reddish stems which roll up at seeding time so that the seeds ripen under the protection of the leaves.

Properties and Uses: Drastic purgative. In popular use by Europeans, a decoction of the dried bulb is used for dropsy, mucous congestion, colds, flatulence, and intestinal worms and the powder to help heal purulent wounds. CAUTION: Even small doses of cyclamen are poisonous to humans. Pliny the Elder reports its use as a poison for arrowheads.

Preparation and Dosage: Do not use without medical supervision.

119 DANDELION

(Taraxacum officinale)

Common Names: Blowball, cankerwort, lion's tooth, priest's crown, puffball, swine snout, white endive, wild endive.

Medicinal Part: Plant.

Description: The dandelion is a perennial plant found, to the dismay of many, almost everywhere. The oblong or spatulate, irregularly dentate or pinnatifid leaves grow in a rosette from the milky taproot, which also sends up one or more naked flower stems, each terminating in a single yellow flower. The familiar puffball that succeeds the flower is a globular cluster of achenes, each of which is fitted with a parachute-like tuft.

Properties and Uses: Aperient, cholagogue, diuretic, stomachic, tonic. Dandelion has two particularly important uses: to promote the formation of bile and to remove excess water from the body in edemous conditions resulting from liver problems. The root especially affects all forms of secretion and excretion from the body. By acting to remove poisons from the body, it acts as a tonic and stimulant as well. The fresh juice is most effective, but dandelion is also prepared as a tea. Lukewarm dandelion tea has been recommended for dyspepsia with constipation, fever, insomnia, and hypochondria. An infusion of the fresh root is said to be good for gallstones, jaundice, and other liver problems. Dandelion leaves are popular and healthful as salad greens, especially in springtime. For chronic rheumatism, gout, and stiff joints, follow an eight-week dandelion cure as described below.

Preparation and Dosage: Use the whole plant before it flowers, the leaves during flowering, and the root alone in the fall.

Infusion: Steep 2 tsp. plant or root in 1 cup boiling water. Take ½ to 1 cup a day, lukewarm or cold.

Decoction: Use 4 oz. fresh plant with 2 pints water; boil down gently to 1 pint and strain. Take 3 tbsp., six times a day.

Cold Extract: Use 2 tsp. plant with 1 cup water; let stand for 8 hours.

Juice: For a spring tonic, take 1 tsp. juice pressed from the leaves in milk, one to three times a day. An electric vegetable juicer is helpful.

Dandelion Cure: Use 2 tsp. fresh root and leaves with ½ cup water; boil briefly and then steep for 15 minutes. Take ½ cup, morning and evening. In addition, take daily 1 to 2 glasses of water with 3 tbsp. juice (pressed from root and leaves) per glass. Use dandelion leaves in salad.

120   DESERT TEA

(Ephedra spp.)

Common Names: Brigham Young weed, desert herb, ephedra, Mormon tea, squaw tea, teamster's tea.

Medicinal Part: The herb.

Description: Desert tea is a broom-like shrub which somewhat resembles shave grass. Its various species can be found in the arid areas of the Northern Hemisphere, including the deserts of the southwestern U.S. The jointed, grooved, green stems and branches of some species reach heights of up to 7 feet, but most are smaller. Two or three scalelike leaves, more or less persistent depending on the species, grow at each joint in the stem and branches. Male and female cones appear on different plants, the male featuring prominent yellow pollen sacs.

Properties and Uses: Diuretic, febrifuge, tonic. Although most commonly taken as a pleasant beverage, desert tea has also been used as a remedy for kidney and bladder problems. Natives of the American Southwest drink a decoction several times a day to relieve kidney pain or to treat a fever. American Indians used it, both internally and externally, to treat syphilis and mucous discharges. Early pioneers considered desert tea a good "blood purifier."

Preparation and Dosage:

Decoction: To use as a diuretic, take a glassful of the cold decoction every morning.

121   MA-HUANG

(Ephedra sinica)

is a Chinese species of ephedra which has been used there for over 2,000 years to treat headache, colds, fevers, and skin eruptions. It contains a potent alkaloid, ephedrine, which is present only minutely in other species. Used medicinally for colds, asthma, and hay fever.

122   **DILL**

(Anethum graveolens)

Common Names: Dilly, garden dill.

Medicinal Part: Fruit.

Description: Dill is an annual plant widely cultivated as a spice but also found growing wild in North and South America and in Europe. The hollow, finely grooved stem grows 1 to 3 feet high and is striped dark green and white with bluish spots. The leaves are bluish-green, bipinnate with filiform leaflets; the base dilates into a sheath surrounding the stem. Flat, compound umbels of yellow flowers appear from July to September, producing eventually the oval, ribbed dill seeds.

Properties and Uses: Antispasmodic, calmative, carminative, diuretic, galactagogue, stomachic. Dill tea, made with water or white wine, is a popular remedy for upset stomach. Dill also helps stimulate appetite, and a decoction of the seed may be helpful for insomnia as well as for pains due to flatulence. Nursing mothers can use dill to promote the flow of milk, particularly in combination with anise, coriander, fennel, and caraway. Try chewing the seeds to clear up halitosis.

Preparation and Dosage:

Infusion: Steep 2 tsp. seeds in 1 cup water for 10 to 15 minutes. Take ½ cup at a time, 1 to 2 cups a day.

123   **DOGBANE**

(Apocynum androsaemifolium)

Common Names: Bitterroot, catchfly, flytrap, honeybloom, milk ipecac, milkweed, mountain hemp, spreading dogbane, wallflower, wandering milkweed, western wallflower.

Medicinal Part: Rootstock.

Description: Dogbane is a native perennial plant found in both the Atlantic and Pacific coastal states, in dry, sandy soils and around the edges of forests. A large, horizontal, milky rootstock sends up a glabrous stem with tough, fibrous bark to a height of 1 to 4 feet. The leaves are opposite, roundish to oblong-ovate or ovate, dark green above, lighter and hairy beneath, and grow on short, reddish petioles. The nodding flowers grow in terminal cymes and are pink outside, pink and white striped inside.

Flowering time is May to August. The fruit is a pair of long, slender pods. All parts of the plant contain a milky juice.

Properties and Uses: Cathartic, diaphoretic, emetic, expectorant, stimulant. Dogbane has been used to relieve dyspepsia, constipation, fever, gallstones, and dropsy. Given in large doses, it is cathartic and emetic. When used, it is generally combined with less harsh medications suitable for the intended purpose. CAUTION: Eating the leaves has killed livestock.

Preparation and Dosage: Not recommended for use without medical direction.

Infusion: Steep 1 tsp. rootstock in 1 pint boiling water. Take cold, 2 to 3 tsp. six times a day.

Tincture: Take 5 to 10 drops in water before meals.

124 DOG POISON

(*Aethusa cynapium*)

Common Names: Fool's-cicely, fool's-parsley, small hemlock.

Medicinal Part: The herb.

Description: Dog poison is an annual plant found growing in waste places and gardens, and along hedges and fences, in the northeastern U.S., eastern Canada, and Europe. The white, spindle-shaped root produces a round, slender, glabrous, blue-flecked, branched stem, 1 to 3 feet high, with alternate, tripinnate leaves, the leaflets incised, dark green above and shiny yellow-green beneath. White flowers appear in compound umbels from June to September.

Properties and Uses: Antispasmodic, emetic, irritant. Dog poison is now used only in homeopathic preparations for spasms and for nervous stomach problems. CAUTION: Eating the leaves or roots (mistaken for parsley or radishes) can be fatal. Dog poison looks similar to parsley but can be distinguished by the shiny, yellow-green underside of the leaves (not shiny in parsley) and the white flowers (yellow-green in parsley).

Preparation and Dosage: Do not use without medical direction.

125 DOG'S MERCURY

(Mercurialis perennis)

Common Names: Dog's cole, perennial mercury.

Medicinal Part: The herb.

Description: Dog's mercury is a perennial plant found in waste places in the eastern U.S., having been naturalized from Europe, where it grows especially in shady mountain woods. The round, furrowed, glabrous, branched stem bears opposite, dark green, ovate, serrate, hairy leaves. The flowers are light green and axillary, the male in spikes, the female solitary or in twos and threes. Flowering time is April and May.

Properties and Uses: Emetic, purgative. The fresh plant is sometimes used as a laxative. A homeopathic tincture is used for rheumatism and stomach problems. CAUTION: The fresh plant is poisonous, and the poison is believed to be cumulative in effect. Thorough drying or boiling seems to destroy the poisonous activity.

Preparation and Dosage: Do not use without medical direction.

126 MERCURY HERB

(Mercurialis annua)

is an annual species of mercury with a square stem and light green leaves. It is used like dog's mercury and is similarly poisonous.

127 DOGWOOD

(Cornus florida)

Common Names: Boxwood, budwood, cornelian tree, dogtree, false box, Florida cornel, Florida dogwood, flowering cornel, flowering dogwood, green ozier, Virginia dogwood.

Medicinal Part: Bark.

Description: Dogwood is a native American tree, growing to 40 feet high and found from Maine to Florida and west to Minnesota, Kansas, and Texas. The bark is brown and rough, the leaves opposite, ovate, pointed, and darker green above than beneath. The flowers are small and greenish-yellow but are obscured by the large, white or pink bracts so that the whole looks like a large white or pink flower. The fruit is a glossy, red berry.

Properties and Uses: Astringent, febrifuge, stimulant, tonic. Dogwood bark is best used as an ointment for ague and similar complaints. It was sometimes used as a substitute when Peruvian bark could not be obtained.

Preparation and Dosage: Use only dried dogwood bark.

Infusion: Steep 1 tbsp. bark in 1 pint water for 30 minutes and strain. Take ½ cup every 2 or 3 hours, or as needed.

Tincture: Take 20 to 40 drops in water, as needed.

128 DYER'S BROOM

(Genista tinctoria)

Common Names: Dyer's greenweed, dyer's whin, furze, green broom, greenweed, waxen woad, woad waxen, wood waxen.

Medicinal Part: Flowering twigs.

Description: Dyer's broom is a perennial herbaceous shrub which is found in dry uplands from Maine to Massachusetts and in eastern New York, as well as in meadows, pastures, and woods in Europe. Growing to a height of 1 to 2 feet, the stems are woody, slightly hairy, and branched. The alternate, nearly sessile leaves are glabrous and lanceolate. Golden-yellow flowers grow in narrow panicles from June to August. The fruit is a long, shiny pod shaped like a green-bean pod.

Properties and Uses: Aperient, diuretic, stimulant, vasoconstrictor. Dyer's broom tea acts as a mild purgative and has also been recommended for gravel and stones. It stimulates the central nervous system, its action being comparable to that of nicotine. Dyer's broom also raises blood pressure by constricting the blood vessels and should therefore not be used by persons with high blood pressure. The tincture or extract can be used externally for herpes or tetters.

Preparation and Dosage:

Infusion: Steep 2 tsp. flowering twigs in ½ cup water. Take no more than 1 cup a day.

ECHINACEA

(Echinacea angustifolia)

Common Names: Kansas nigger-head, narrow-leaved purple cone-flower, Sampson root.

Medicinal Part: Rootstock.

Description: This native herbaceous perennial plant grows from the prairie states northward to Pennsylvania. The stout, bristly stem bears hairy, linear-lanceolate leaves, tapering at both ends, the lower on long petioles, the upper sessile. The distinctive flower features 12 to 20 large, spreading, dull-purple rays and a conical disk made up of numerous purple, tubular florets. Flowering time is June to October.

Properties and Uses: Antiseptic, depurative, digestive. Echinacea is one of the "blood-purifying" plants used for conditions such as eczema, acne, and boils thought to indicate contaminants in the blood. It also promotes proper digestion and can be tried for fever. Used externally in combination with myrrh, it is said to be good for typhoid fever. The rootstock may also help to dispel flatulence.

Preparation and Dosage: Do not use the rootstock once it has lost its odor.

Decoction: Use 1 tsp. rootstock with 1 cup water. Take 1 tbsp., three to six times a day.

Tincture: Take 15 to 30 drops in water every 1 to 3 hours, as indicated.

ELDER

(a) (Sambucus canadensis)

Common Names: American elder, black elder, common elder, elderberry, rob elder, sweet elder.

Medicinal Parts: Root, bark, leaf buds, leaves, flowers.

Description: American elder is a native American shrub, growing 5 to 12 feet high in damp areas and waste places, particularly in the central and eastern states of the U.S. The stems are covered with rough, yellowish-gray bark and bear opposite, pinnate leaves with lance-ovate, serrate leaflets. Numerous small, white flowers appear in flat cymes from May to July. The fruit is a dark purple berry.

Properties and Uses: Cathartic, diaphoretic, diuretic, purgative, stimulant. A tea made from the root acts as a diuretic and a hydragogue cathartic. Some Indians used root-bark tea for headache, mucous congestion, and to promote labor in childbirth. An infusion of leaves and flowers or a decoction of bark serves as an antiseptic wash for skin problems, wounds, and inflammations. Flower tea taken warm is said to stimulate and to induce sweating; it can also be taken for headaches due to colds and for rheumatism. Taken cold, it has diuretic properties. An infusion of the leaf buds is strongly purgative. Fresh berry juice, evaporated into a syrup, is moderately purgative. It also makes a good ointment for burns when mixed with lard or a creamy base. The dried berries can be made into a tea useful for diarrhea and cholera. CAUTION: All parts of the fresh plant can cause poisoning. Children have been poisoned by chewing or sucking on the bark. Cooked berries are safe and are commonly used in pies and jam.

Preparation and Dosage:

Infusion: Use 1 tsp. plant parts with 1 cup water.

Tincture: Take 20 to 40 drops in water, three or four times a day.

(b) (Sambucus nigra)

Common Names: Black elder, black-berried European elder, boor tree, bountry, elder, ellanwood, ellhorn, European elder, German elder.

Medicinal Parts: Root, bark, young shoots, leaves, flowers, fruit.

Description: Black elder may take the form of a shrub or small tree, 10 to 30 feet high. It is found in Europe, in moist, shady places and among underbrush, also cultivated. The bark is light brown near the bottom of the stem, gray-white higher up, somewhat torn and stippled with warts. The leaves are opposite, odd-pinnate; the leaflets ovate, acuminate, finely serrate, dark green. In June and July black elder sports cymes of white to yellow-white flowers, which develop into berries that turn from green through red-brown to shiny black.

Properties and Uses: Bark and root: diuretic, emetic, purgative. Leaves and shoots: diuretic. Flowers: diaphoretic. Fruit: aperient. Both the bark of young branches and the root (the inner bark of which is used) are purgative and diuretic in proper dosage. In large doses they are emetic and strongly purgative and can cause inflammation in the gastrointestinal tract. A tea made from the leaves and young shoots increases the production of urine and helps to eliminate excess water from the body. In proper dosage, black elder remedies can be used for urinary problems, kidney problems, dropsy, edema, rheumatic ailments, and constipation. The tea of the flowers promotes perspiration and is used particularly for colds and for rheumatic complaints. The berries are not to be eaten raw and the fresh juice is not to be used (unless you like diarrhea and vomiting). Cook the berries lightly, whether for eating or for juice. They can be made into a jam which is mildly laxative and suitable for irritated or inflamed intestines and for small children. For neuralgia, sciatica, or lumbago, follow a juice cure regimen, taking about 2 tbsp. of warm or cold juice two times a day until results are obtained.

Preparation and Dosage: The bark (and root bark) must be used fresh. Be sure to cook berries lightly before using.

Infusion: Use 2 tbsp. flowers to 1 cup boiling water. Take up to 3 cups a day, preferably hot.

Infusion: Use 1 level tsp. bark or root bark to ½ cup boiling water. Take no more than 1 cup a day, a mouthful at a time.

Cold Extract: Use 1 tbsp. leaves to 1 cup cold water. Let stand for 8 to 10 hours.

132   ELDER (cont.)

(c) (Sambucus racemosa)

Common Name: Red elder.

Medicinal Parts: Root, fruit.

Description: Red elder is a shrub found commonly in mountain forests and clearings in Europe and western Asia, but also in the northern U.S. and Canada. Light-brown stems and branches grow as high as 15 feet and bear opposite, odd-pinnate leaves with five to seven oval or ovate, serrate, pointed leaflets. A dense terminal panicle of yellow-green or yellowish white flowers appears during April and May. The fruit is a three-seeded red berry about a quarter inch in diameter.

Properties and Uses: Diaphoretic, diuretic, purgative. The root is the primary medicinal part, being useful mainly as a purgative and diuretic. The seedless berries can be made into a nutritious jam. CAUTION: The seeds inside the berries are poisonous.

Preparation and Dosage:

Decoction: Boil 1 tsp. root in 1 cup water for a short time. Take 1 cup a day.

133   ELDER (cont.)

(d) (Sambucus ebulus)

Common Names: Dwarf elder, blood elder, danewort, walewort, wild elder.

Medicinal Part: Rootstock.

Description: Dwarf elder is a perennial, herbaceous shrub that grows in small clusters in the eastern and central states of the U.S. and in Europe. A creeping rootstock produces erect, stiff, grooved stems with odd-pinnate leaves, the leaflets lanceolate, acuminate, and serrate. The white flowers are tinged with reddish-purple and grow in cymes from June to August. The fruit is a shiny, black, four-seeded berry.

Properties and Uses: Cholagogue, diuretic, purgative. Much used in earlier times, dwarf elder has lost favor in medical circles but is still used in homeopathy and in popular practice. In Europe, its diuretic and laxative properties are used in home remedies. An ointment made from the tincture or from an infusion of the rootstock has been used for burns. CAUTION: The berries are poisonous.

Preparation and Dosage:

Infusion: Steep 1 tsp. rootstock in 1 cup boiling water. Take cold, 1 to 2 cups a day, a mouthful at a time.

Tincture: Take 3 to 15 drops, three times a day.

134   ELECAMPANE

(Inula helenium)

Common Names: Elfdock, elfwort, horse-elder, horseheal, scabwort.

Medicinal Part: Rootstock.

Description: Elecampane is a perennial plant that is cultivated and also grows wild along roadsides and in fields and waste places eastward from Minnesota and Missouri and northward from North Carolina. The fibrous, top-shaped rootstock is brown outside and white inside. The stout, round stem is coarse and woolly, 3 to 6 feet high, and bears large, alternate, ovate, serrate, olive-colored leaves with white veins. The large, yellow flower heads are solitary or grow in paniculate clusters from July to September. The fruit is a brown, quadrangular achene.

Properties and Uses: Anthelmintic, cholagogue, diuretic, expectorant, stimulant, tonic. Elecampane tea is much used to quiet coughing, to stimulate digestion and to tone the stomach; for bronchitis, urinary and respiratory tract inflammation, and menstrual problems. Elecampane oil is used for respiratory and intestinal catarrh, chronic diarrhea, chronic bronchitis, and whooping cough. The decoction or tincture is used for worms, and externally as a wash or fomentation for skin problems such as scabies and itches.

Preparation and Dosage: Gather the rootstock in the fall of the second year.

Infusion: Use 1 heaping tsp. rootstock with 1 cup water. Take 1 to 2 cups a day. If desired, sweeten with honey, 1 tsp. honey to

½ cup tea. (A maceration in red wine is also used in place of the tea.)

Fluid Extract: Take 20 to 40 drops, three or more times a day.

Tincture: Take ½ to 1 tsp. at a time.

135   ELM

(a) (Ulmus campestris)

Common Names: English elm, common elm, European elm.

Medicinal Part: Bark, leaves.

Description: English elm is a large tree found primarily in England, Europe, and Asia Minor. The stem is covered with rough, thick bark; and the short, horizontal or ascending branches bear alternate, ovate, crenate, rough leaves. Red flowers appear in catkins in early spring, before the leaves.

Properties and Uses: Astringent, demulcent, diuretic, vulnerary. The bark of young branches can be used as a decoction or tincture for herpes, scurf, itch, and other skin problems. Soaking bark and bruised leaves in vinegar also makes a useful wash for the skin. The leaves have sometimes been used to help heal wounds.

Preparation and Dosage:

Decoction: Use 4 oz. of fresh inner bark or bark of young branches with 4 pints water. Boil down to 2 pints. Take ¼ cup, two to three times a day.

136   ELM (cont.)

(b) (Ulmus fulva)

Common Names: Slippery elm, American elm, Indian elm, moose elm, red elm, rock elm, sweet elm, winged elm.

Medicinal Part: The inner bark.

Description: Slippery elm is an American deciduous tree found planted along streets and growing in forests from Quebec to Florida, the Dakotas, and Texas. Growing to a height of 50 feet and more, its stem is covered with dark-brown, rough, furrowed outer bark; the inner bark is whitish and aromatic. Its alternate, obovate-oblong leaves are doubly serrate, very rough on top, and downy underneath. The small flowers grow in dense axillary clusters during March and April.

Properties and Uses: Demulcent, diuretic, emollient. The inner bark of slippery elm is noted primarily for its soothing properties. Internally it is helpful where inflammatory irritation exists, as in sore throat, diarrhea, dysentery, and many urinary problems. Externally it is applied as a poultice to irritated and inflamed skin and to wounds. It has also been used to make rectal and vaginal suppositories, enemas, and a vaginal douche.

Preparation and Dosage:

Infusion: Steep 2 oz. or more of inner bark in 1 qt. water for an hour or longer. Take 1 tsp. every 30 minutes. Sweeten with honey or syrup if desired.

Decoction: Add 1 heaping tbsp. inner bark to 1 pint boiling-hot water and let stand for 1 hour. Bring to a boil and simmer for a few minutes. Then let stand for another hour, boil and simmer again.

NOTE: Due to its depletion from Dutch Elm Disease, the American elm should be protected against widespread use of its bark. The bark cannot be used without disfiguring or killing a noble tree.

137 ENGLISH IVY
(Hedera helix)

Common Names: Gum ivy, true ivy.

Medicinal Part: Leaves.

Description: English ivy is a climbing evergreen vine common in the temperate climates of Europe and Asia and also introduced into the U.S. The woody stem, growing to a length of over 50 feet, bears air roots along its length which enable the plant to cling to smooth surfaces. The leathery, glossy, dark-green leaves are variously three- to seven-lobed. The small, green or yellowish-green flowers appear in umbels from August to October. The fruit is a black berry, which ripens in winter.

Properties and Uses: Antispasmodic, exanthematous. English ivy is primarily for external use as a wash for sores, burns, cuts, dandruff, and other skin problems. CAUTION: The leaves may cause dermatitis in sensitive people. A cold extract may be tried as a remedy for bilious complaints and chronic catarrhal problems. Small doses are said to dilate the blood vessels and large doses to constrict them. CAUTION: English ivy is also said to break down red blood corpuscles by releasing their hemoglobin.

Preparation and Dosage: The whole plant, including the berries, is poisonous. Use should be under medical supervision.

Cold Extract: Use 1 tsp. leaves with 1 cup cold water; let stand for 8 hours. Take 1 cup in the course of the day.

138 ERGOT

(Claviceps purpurea)

Common Names: Cockspur rye, hornseed, mother of rye, smut rye, spurred rye.

Medicinal Part: Dried sclerotia.

Description: Ergot is a fungus which replaces the seeds of the rye plant (*Secale cornatum*). It takes the form of black or purplish-black, crooked grains or "spurs," about ¾ to 1½ inches long and 1/10 to 2/10 inch thick. It has a nauseous odor and a disagreeable taste.

Properties and Uses: Abortifacient, emmenagogue, hemostatic, oxytocic, vasoconstrictor. Medicinal preparations made from ergot are useful in contracting the uterine muscles, particularly after delivery to prevent hemorrhage, and have also been used for menstrual difficulties. One ergot derivative, ergotamine tartrate, helps to relieve migraine and cluster headaches by constricting the swollen blood vessels causing the pain. Ergot is also a source of LSD.

Preparation and Dosage: Do not use without medical direction.

139 EUCALYPTUS

(Eucalyptus globulus)

Common Name: Blue gum.

Medicinal Part: Leaves.

Description: Eucalyptus is a tall, evergreen tree native to Australia and Tasmania. Among its various species, the blue gum is the one commonly grown in the U.S., being found in California, Florida, and parts of the South. The trunk, which grows to 300 feet high or more, is covered with peeling, papery bark. The leaves on the young plant, up to 5 years old, are opposite, sessile, soft, oblong, pointed, and a hoary blue color. The mature leaves are alternate, petioled, leathery, and shaped like a scimitar. The flowers are solitary, axillary, and white, with no petals and a woody calyx. The fruit is a hard, four-celled, many-seeded capsule enclosed in the calyx cup.

Properties and Uses: Antiseptic, deodorant, expectorant, stimulant. Most eucalyptus medications are made from the greenish-yellow oil obtained from the mature leaves. The oil, or lozenges and cough drops made from it, is useful for lung diseases, colds, and sore throat. It can also be used as a vapor bath for asthma and other respiratory ailments, and as an antiseptic bath additive. Its expectorant properties are useful for bronchitis. The oil is also said to be useful for pyorrhea and for burns, to prevent infection. A cold extract made from the leaves is helpful for indigestion and for intermittent fever. Externally, the antiseptic and deodorant qualities of the oil make it suitable for use on purulent wounds and ulcers.

Preparation and Dosage:

Oil: Boil mature leaves in water and condense the vapor to recover the oil.

140   EUROPEAN CENTAURY

(Centaurium umbellatum or Erythraea centaurium)

Common Names: Bitter herb, common centaury, lesser centaury, centaury.

Medicinal Part: Flowering herb.

Description: European centaury is an annual or biennial plant found all over Europe in damp meadows, forest clearings, and sandy soils. The stem is 6 to 18 inches high, quadrangular to hexagonal, hollow when older, and branched near the top. The basal leaves are ovate and grow in a rosette; the stem leaves are opposite, sessile, and ovate-oblong. The rose-red, funnel-shaped flowers grow in cymes from June to September.

Properties and Uses: Appetizer, cholagogue, diaphoretic, digestive, emetic, febrifuge, tonic. European centaury is one of the traditional panaceas, having been recommended and used for practically everything except diarrhea. It stimulates the activity of the salivary, stomach, and intestinal glands, thereby relieving constipation and gas and promoting proper digestion. This activity probably accounts for many of its other beneficial effects. The tea is commonly taken for heartburn, colic, suppressed menstruation, and anemia. Taken over a long period, it tends to help in taking off weight. A strong decoction is said to be emetic, a strong infusion diaphoretic, and a light infusion tonic. Externally, a lotion made from European centaury removes skin blemishes like freckles and spots. In general, use it much like yellow gentian. It is particularly recommended for people who lead sedentary lives and who don't get much outdoor exercise.

Preparation and Dosage:

Infusion: Use 2 tsp. herb with 1 cup water.

Cold Extract: Use 1 tsp. herb with ½ cup cold water; let stand for 8 to 10 hours. Take ½ cup, spread over the day. Do not take it immediately after a meal.

Powder: Take ¼ to ½ tsp. about 30 minutes before each meal.

141   EUROPEAN VERVAIN

(Verbena officinalis)

Common Names: Enchanter's plant, herb of the cross, holy herb, Juno's tears, pigeon's grass, pigeonweed, simpler's joy, vervain.

Medicinal Part: The whole plant.

Description: European vervain is an annual or perennial native of the Mediterranean region which has escaped from cultivation in the U.S. and established itself in most of the country, particularly along roadsides. The whitish, branched, spindle-shaped root or rootstock sends up a stiff, quadrangular stem branched near the top. The leaves are opposite, oblong to lanceolate, entire and sessile at the top, deeply cleft and petioled at the bottom. The white or purplish flowers grow in slender spikes from June to October.

Properties and Uses: Astringent, diuretic, emmenagogue, galactagogue, stimulant, tonic, vulnerary. In addition to the normal uses indicated by the categories, the decoction is said to be good for eczema and other skin conditions. It has also been used for whooping cough, dropsy, jaundice, and kidney and liver problems. An infusion or decoction is used to help heal wounds. European vervain is considered by some to be an aphrodisiac, and it is said to secure the favor of the ladies.

Preparation and Dosage:

Cold Extract: Use 1 tbsp. of the plant with 1 cup water; let stand for 8 to 10 hours. Take 1 cup a day.

Powder: Take ¼ to ½ tsp. three times a day.

Tincture: Take 20 to 40 drops in water, as needed.

142 EVENING PRIMROSE

(Oenothera biennis)

Common Names: Common evening primrose, fever plant, field primrose, king's cureall, night willow-herb, scabish, scurvish, tree primrose, primrose.

Medicinal Part: The plant.

Description: Evening primrose is a coarse, annual or biennial plant found in dry meadows and waste places and along roadsides east of the Rockies to the Atlantic. The stem is erect, stout, and soft-hairy, with alternate, rough-hairy, lanceolate, taper-pointed leaves about 3 to 6 inches long. The yellow, lemon-scented flowers, 1 to 2½ inches across, open at dusk and grow in spikes from June to October. The fruit is an oblong, hairy capsule.

Properties and Uses: Astringent, mucilaginous. Use evening primrose as a soothing remedy for coughs associated with colds. It has also been used for mental depression, its effectiveness perhaps due to a stimulating effect on the liver, spleen, and digestive apparatus. It can also be made into an ointment useful for rashes and other skin irritations. The entire plant is edible.

Preparation and Dosage:

Infusion: Use 1 tsp. of the plant with 1 cup of water. Take 1 cup a day, a mouthful at a time.

Tincture: Take 5 to 40 drops, as needed.

143 EVERLASTING

(a) (Gnaphalium polycephalum)

Common Names: Life everlasting, chafe weed, common everlasting, field balsam, Indian posy, old field balsam, sweet balsam, sweet-scented life everlasting, white balsam.

Medicinal Part: The herb.

Description: Life everlasting is a fragrant, herbaceous annual plant found in dry fields, open pine woods, and clearings in the Atlantic coastal states and west to Kansas and Texas. The erect, branched, white-woolly stem grows 1 to 3 feet high and bears alternate, sessile, lanceolate leaves that have wavy margins and are dark green above and white-woolly beneath. Yellow flower heads grow in several terminal panicled clusters from July into September.

Properties and Uses: Astringent, diaphoretic, febrifuge, pectoral, vermifuge. An infusion of life everlasting, taken as a tea, is useful for lung problems, leucorrhea, and intestinal problems, including hemorrhage. The cold infusion is said to help expel intestinal worms. A homeopathic tincture has been used for sciatica, lumbago, and some kinds of arthritis. The fresh juice is reputed to calm excessive sexual desire. Externally, life everlasting makes a good fomentation for bruises. The dried flowers are sometimes used like hops to make a calming herb pillow. The plant may also have some anodyne properties. As a mouthwash and gargle, the infusion is good for sores in the mouth and throat.

Preparation and Dosage: The fresh herb can be chewed or the leaves applied for external problems.

Infusion: Steep 1 tsp. leaves and flowers in 1 cup boiling-hot water. Take 1 to 2 cups a day.

144   EVERLASTING (cont.)

(b) (Gnaphalium uliginosum)

Common Names: Low cudweed, dysentery weed, everlasting, marsh cudweed, mouse ear, wartwort.

Medicinal Part: The herb.

Description: Low cudweed is a low-spreading, densely white-woolly plant that grows in damp soil in the northern half of the U.S. and in Canada. The branching, creeping stem bears sessile, linear to spatulate, pointed leaves that resemble a mouse's ear. The brownish-white flower heads grow in head-shaped clusters that terminate the branches. Flowering time is July to September.

Properties and Uses: Astringent, diaphoretic, diuretic. Low cudweed is used primarily for its diuretic properties and as a mouthwash and gargle for mouth and throat problems. American Indians smoked it like tobacco to cure headache.

Preparation and Dosage:

Infusion: For internal use, steep 1 oz. herb in 1 pint boiling-hot water. Take 3 to 4 tbsp. at a time.

(c) (*Anaphalis margaritacea*)

Common Names: Pearly everlasting, cottonweed, cudweed, Indian posy, ladies' tobacco, large-flowered everlasting.

Medicinal Part: The herb.

Description: Pearly everlasting is a perennial plant found in dry hills and in clearings in Alaska, Canada, and the northern U.S. from Pennsylvania across to northern California. Several erect stems grow from the base to a height of 1 to 2 feet. The leaves are alternate, sessile, linear-lanceolate, green above and woolly beneath, with rolled-back edges. The white or yellow flowers grow in many globular flower heads arranged in compound corymbs, appearing from July to September.

Properties and Uses: Astringent, diaphoretic, expectorant, febrifuge, vulnerary. Pearly everlasting has basically the same properties as life everlasting. The name ladies' tobacco suggests that it has also been used in place of tobacco; and its categories indicate usefulness for colds, coughs, and fever.

Preparation and Dosage: As in life everlasting above.

146   FENNEL

(*Foeniculum vulgare*)

Common Names: Large fennel, sweet fennel, wild fennel.

Medicinal Parts: Root, seed.

Description: Fennel is a biennial or perennial plant that grows wild in the Mediterranean area and in Asia Minor but is commonly cultivated (and sometimes found wild) in the U.S. and Europe. The long, carrot-shaped root produces a stout, pithy, finely grooved stem with fine bluish stripes. The leaves are decompound, dissected into numerous filiform segments, the upper leaves on broad sheaths that surround the stem. Large, compound umbels of yellow flowers appear from July to October. The fruit consists of two joined carpels, together taking an oblong form with prominent ribs.

Properties and Uses: Antispasmodic, aromatic, carminative, diuretic, expectorant, galactagogue, stimulant, stomachic. The seeds are usually used, but both seed and root are excellent stomach and intestinal remedies. Fennel helps to arouse appetite; relieve colic, abdominal cramps, and flatulence; and expel mucous accumulations. For flatulence, take fennel oil with sugar or as a saturated solution in water. Add it also to gargles for coughing and hoarseness. To stimulate the flow of milk in nursing mothers, use the tincture or boil the seed in barley water. Externally, rub the oil on affected parts to relieve rheumatic pains, and use a decoction of the seeds as an eyewash for irritation and eyestrain.

Preparation and Dosage: Gather the root in the spring.

Infusion: Steep 1 tbsp. freshly crushed seeds in 1 cup water for 5 minutes. Sweeten with honey to taste.

Decoction: Boil ½ tsp. seed in water. Strain. Use as an eyewash, three times a day.

Milk Decoction: Boil 1 tsp. seed in ½ cup milk for 5 to 10 minutes. Take for colic.

Tincture: Take 10 to 30 drops in water, as required.

Fennel-honey: Add 1 to 3 drops fennel oil to 1 tbsp. honey and mix. Take a teaspoon at a time. A natural cough remedy.

147   FENUGREEK

(Trigonella foenum-graecum)

Medicinal Part: Seed.

Description: Fenugreek is an annual plant widely cultivated for both medicinal and culinary uses. A long taproot sends up a round stem with few branches. The leaves are trifoliate, on hairy petioles, with obovate leaflets. In June and July, axillary, sessile, yellowish flowers appear. The fruit is a 16-seeded, compressed, malodorous legume.

Properties and Uses: Expectorant, mucilaginous, restorative. Fenugreek is one of the oldest medicinal plants, dating back to the ancient Egyptians and Hippocrates. Large amounts of the decoction are given to strengthen those suffering from tuberculosis or recovering from an illness. It can also be taken for bronchitis or fevers and gargled for sore throat. Fenugreek has at times been, and sometimes still is, considered an aphrodisiac. Make a poultice of pulverized seeds for gouty pains, neuralgia, sciatica, swollen glands, wounds, furuncles, fistulas, tumors, sores, and skin irritations.

Preparation and Dosage:

Decoction: Use 2 tsp. seed with 1 cup cold water; let stand for 5 hours. Then heat and boil for 1 minute. Take 2 to 3 cups a day. Improve the taste with peppermint oil, lemon extract, honey, or sugar.

148   FERN

(a) (Polypodium vulgare)

Common Names: Female fern, brake fern, brake rock, brakeroot, common polypody, fern brake, fern root, rock brake, rock polypod, stone brake.

Medicinal Part: Rootstock.

Description: Female fern is a perennial plant found all over the U.S., growing in shady areas, among rocks, and on decaying tree stumps. The creeping rootstock, brown and irregular in shape, shows its history in two rows of leaf scars. The leaves, or fronds, are green, glabrous, and pinnatifid almost to the midrib, the pinnae being lanceolate or oblong-lanceolate. On the undersides of the pinnae, accumulations of spore-cases take the form of golden dots arranged in a row on each side of the midveins.

Properties and Uses: Anthelmintic, cholagogue, demulcent, purgative. In popular usage, the infusion of female fern is used for coughs, hoarseness, and respiratory problems. It can also be used to wash external wounds. A strong decoction makes a good purgative and anthelmintic (especially for tenia worms), or use a mixed tea (see below) as a purgative and an alcoholic extract for worms. Female fern has also been recommended in herbals for fever, jaundice, and lack of appetite.

Preparation and Dosage: Use the rootstock either immediately after gathering or well dried.

Decoction: Boil the rootstock in water until a syrupy consistency is achieved. Take 2 to 8 tbsp., three or four times a day.

Mixed Tea: Use 3 tsp. rootstock with ½ cup cold water; let stand for 8 hours and strain. Take the strained-out rootstock and add to boiling-hot water; let steep for 1 hour and strain. Mix the two liquids and take the mixture in the course of a day, a mouthful at a time.

FERN (cont.)

(b) (Dryopteris filixmas)

Common Names: Male fern, aspidium, bear's paw root, knotty brake, sweet brake.

Medicinal Part: Rootstock.

Description: Male fern is a perennial plant found in woods, ravines, and on rocky slopes all over the world. The dark brown, scaly rootstock produces a tuft of fronds which are curled spirally when new but open and mature to a height of 9 to 24 inches. The fronds are broadly oblong-lanceolate to oblong and pinnate, the lanceolate-acuminate to oblong-lanceolate pinnae themselves pinnatifid or lobed more than halfway to the midrib. Spore clusters appear as two rows of yellow dots on the bottom of each lobe from July to September.

Properties and Uses: Anthelmintic. Male fern is an ancient tapeworm remedy, dating back to the Greeks and Romans, but it must be used with great care. Leaving a male fern medication in the body too long can cause poisoning, so that one to two hours after taking it a purgative must be used to remove both the worms and the remaining active ingredients. No alcohol may be taken while male fern is being used. CAUTION: Improper dosages taken internally can lead to blindness and death. For external use, a decoction of the rootstock can be added to a footbath for varicose veins. In European folk medicine, a popular belief is that sewing the fronds into a linen bag and applying to affected parts will help rheumatism. At least, it does no harm.

Preparation and Dosage: Since proper preparation and dosage are essential, use male fern for tapeworm only under medical supervision. Collect the rootstock in the fall.

Decoction: Boil 1 lb. rootstock in water and add the liquid to a footbath.

150 FERN (cont.)

(c) (Osmunda regalis)

Common Names: Buckhorn brake, bog onion, buckhorn, buckhorn male fern, fern brake, flowering brake, flowering fern, hartshorn bush, herb Christopher, king's fern, royal flowering fern, St. Christopher's herb, water fern.

Medicinal Part: Rootstock.

Description: Buckhorn brake is a perennial plant which grows in meadows and other moist areas, mostly in Europe, Great Britain, and Africa; a variety without hairs on the fruiting parts of the fronds grows in eastern North America. The large, scaly rootstock is covered with matted fibers and often rises like a trunk up to a foot out of the ground. The pale green, bipinnate fronds have brown stalks and are ovate in outline; the oblong-elliptic pinnules are finely toothed. Sterile fronds are leafy only; fertile ones are topped by a tripinnate panicle of fertile pinnae which turn brownish in maturity and bear green spores. The fruiting axis bears black hairs. Fruiting time is from April to June.

Properties and Uses: Mucilaginous, tonic. A decoction of buckhorn brake is useful for clearing internal obstructions, for soothing coughs, and for jaundice if taken early. It has also been used as a tonic for convalescents. The mucilage makes a good ointment for sprains, bruises, and wounds; mixed with brandy it was once popular as a rub for backache.

Preparation and Dosage: Collect rootstocks in late spring or late summer, and dry carefully.

Infusion or Decoction: Use 1 heaping tsp. cut-up rootstock with 1 cup water; for infusion, steep for 30 minutes. Take 1 tbsp. per hour, or as required. To get a more gelatinous consistency, use more of the rootstock.

Tincture: A dose is from 20 to 40 drops.

151 CINNAMON-COLORED FERN or CINNAMON FERN
(Osmunda cinnamomea)

NOTE: Cinnamon-colored fern or cinnamon fern (*Osmunda cinnamomea*) is a native North American fern which grows from Newfoundland to Minnesota and Florida and west to New

Mexico, from Mexico into South America, and also in Asia. Its pinnate sterile fronds, lanceolate to oblong-lanceolate in outline, grow on the outside, reaching 2 to 5 feet in height. The bipinnate fertile fronds, 1 to 3 feet high, grow in the center, their pinnae contracted and bearing cinnamon-brown spore cases. This fern can be used like buckhorn brake, although it is said to be less effective. It can be boiled in milk to produce mucilage which is helpful for diarrhea.

152 FERULA

(a) (Ferula sumbul)

Common Names: Sumbul, musk root.

Medicinal Parts: Rootstock and roots.

Description: Sumbul is a perennial herb native to central and western Asia. Its thick, brown, spongy rootstock produces a stem with alternate, pinnately decompound leaves with thread-like segments. The small, yellow flowers grow in compound, many-rayed umbels.

Properties and Uses: Antispasmodic, nervine. Sumbul's anti-spasmodic properties have made it useful for asthma and bron-chitis. It has also been used in the past for hysteria, for hypo-chondria, and for general debility (neurasthenia). The rootstock's musky odor makes it a good substitute for musk oil.

Preparation and Dosage:

Infusion: Steep 1 tsp. rootstock and roots in 1 pint water. Take in mouthful doses, two or three times a day.

Tincture: A dose is from 2 to 5 drops.

153 FERULA (cont.)

(b) (Ferula foetida)

Common Names: Asafetida, devil's dung, food of the gods.

Medicinal Part: Juice.

Description: Asafetida is the gummy dried juice of a large Asiatic perennial plant found in Turkestan, Afghanistan, and Iran. Its large, bristly, fleshy root produces a stem from 6 to 10 feet high, with alternate, pinnately decompound leaves on wide, sheathing petioles. The pale greenish-yellow flowers grow at the top of the stem in clusters of compound, many-rayed umbels.

Properties and Uses: Antispasmodic, carminative, expectorant, laxative, sedative. Asafetida acts as a local stimulant to mucous membrane, particularly that of the alimentary canal. It has been found useful for whooping cough, asthma, and bronchitis, as well as for croup and flatulent colic in infants. It was formerly used as a sedative for hysteria, infantile convulsions, and spasmodic nervous conditions.

Preparation and Dosage: In June the roots of four-year-old plants which have not flowered are cut to collect the milky juice. This dries to a brownish, gummy substance which is divided into lumps or powdered.

Powder: Because of its nauseating taste, asafetida is usually taken in 3-grain pills.

Tincture: A dose is ½ to 1 tsp.

NOTE: Asafetida is also derived from another species of ferula, *Ferula assa-foetida*, which grows in Iran and West Afghanistan.

155   FEVERFEW
(Chrysanthemum parthenium)

Common Names: Featherfew, febrifuge plant.

Medicinal Part: The herb.

Description: Feverfew is a perennial plant that is cultivated but is occasionally found wild in waste places and along roadsides and wood-borders from Quebec to Ohio and south to Maryland and Missouri, also in California. The round, leafy, branching stem bears alternate, bipinnate leaves with ovate, hoary-green leaflets. The flowers have yellow disks and from 10 to 20 white, toothed rays. They make their appearance in corymbose heads in June and July.

Properties and Uses: Carminative, emmenagogue, purgative, stimulant, tonic. Once in popular use, feverfew has fallen into considerable disuse; even its name no longer seems to fit. It is also hard to find, even at herbal outlets. If you are lucky enough to get it, try the warm infusion for colic, flatulence, eructations, indigestion, colds, and alcoholic d.t.'s. A cold extract has a tonic effect. The flowers in particular show a purgative action.

Preparation and Dosage:

Infusion: Use 1 heaping tsp. of the herb with 1 cup water. Take 1 to 2 cups a day, in tablespoon doses.

Tincture: Take 10 to 30 drops in water every 2 to 3 hours, as indicated. For d.t.'s, take 15 to 40 drops, as often as required.

156   FEVERWEED

(Gerardia pedicularia)

Common Names: American foxglove, bushy gerardia, false foxglove, fern-leaved false foxglove, lousewort.

Medicinal Part: The herb.

Description: Feverweed is a sticky and hairy, annual or perennial plant that grows in dry woods and thickets from Maine to Florida and west to Ontario, Minnesota, and Missouri. The numerous stems are 1 to 4 feet high and bear opposite, fernlike leaves, 1 to 3 inches long, which are pinnately lobed and deeply serrate. The large, yellow, bell-shaped flowers grow in loose terminal racemes in August and September.

Properties and Uses: Antiseptic, diaphoretic, febrifuge, sedative. A warm infusion of feverweed is particularly effective in producing perspiration and is said to be highly effective against ephemeral fever.

Preparation and Dosage:

Infusion: Use 1 tsp. herb with 1 cup water. Take 1 cup a day.

Tincture: Take 5 to 20 drops at a time.

157   FIG TREE

(Ficus carica)

Common Name: Common fig.

Medicinal Part: Fruit.

Description: The deciduous fig tree is a native of the Mediterranean region and is cultivated elsewhere for its fruit. Its wood is soft, and with its many branches it reaches a height of up to 30 feet. The alternate, long-petioled leaves are usually deeply three- to five-lobed and are broad-ovate to nearly orbicular in outline. The thick, palmately ribbed leaf blade is rough on top and finely hairy underneath. The genus *Ficus* is unique in bearing its flowers inside a nearly closed receptacle or branch which ripens into the fleshy, pear-shaped fruit we call the fig (it is technically called a syconium). The receptacle usually contains both male and female flowers, the male at one end of an internal cavity, the female at the other end. Pollination is accomplished by specialized insects which crawl inside through a small opening at the top. Ripe figs vary in color from greenish-yellow to purple, depending on the variety.

Properties and Uses: Demulcent, emollient, laxative. For internal use, the fig has mildly laxative properties and is often used in combination with senna and carminative herbs. When you have a cold, a decoction of figs acts as a demulcent to soothe the mucous membranes of the respiratory passages. The fresh fig, roasted and cut in half, makes a good emollient poultice for boils and small tumors. The stems and leaves contain an acrid milky juice that can be used to remove warts.

158 FIGWORT

(Scrophularia nodosa)

Common Names: Carpenter's square, figwort root, heal-all, kernelwort, knotty-rooted figwort, scrofula plant.

Medicinal Part: The plant.

Description: Figwort is a perennial plant, growing 2 to 4 feet high in rich woodlands and thickets from Maine to Georgia and Tennessee, and west to South Dakota and Kansas. The knobby rootstock is brown outside, whitish and fibrous inside. The erect, quadrangular, glabrous stem bears opposite, ovate to lanceolate, serrate leaves with an offensive odor. Small, globular, dark purple flowers appear in terminal panicles from June to October.

Properties and Uses: Diuretic, exanthematous. Figwort is essentially a skin medication used for eczema, scabies, scurf, tumors, rashes, etc. It can also be made into an ointment or fomentation for use on scratches, bruises, and minor wounds.

Preparation and Dosage:

Infusion: Use 1 heaping tsp. of the plant with 1 cup water. Take 1 to 2 cups a day.

Tincture: Take ½ to 1 tsp. at a time. Also may be used externally.

159   FLAX

(Linum usitatissimum)

Common Names: Common flax, flax seed, linseed, lint bells, winterlien.

Medicinal Part: Seed.

Description: Flax is an annual plant widely cultivated in the U.S. (mostly the northwestern states), Canada, and Europe but also found wild along roadsides and railroad lines and in waste places. The erect, slender, glabrous stem has few branches and bears alternate, sessile, simple, entire, lanceolate to oblong leaves. Each branch has one or two blue or violet-blue, five-petaled flowers from June to August. The fruit is an 8- to 10-seeded capsule; the seeds are smooth, flattened, shiny, and light brown.

Properties and Uses: Demulcent, emollient, purgative. A decoction of the seeds can be used for coughs, catarrh, lung and chest problems, and digestive and urinary disorders. To eliminate gallstones, take 1½ to 2 tbsp. linseed oil and lie down on your left side for a half hour. The gallstones will pass into the intestines and be eliminated from there. Eating the seeds intact is useful for constipation. The seeds swell up in the intestines, encouraging elimination by increasing the volume of fecal matter. For emollient uses and for rheumatic complaints, make a linseed poultice as described below.

Preparation and Dosage: Use only ripe seeds. CAUTION: Immature seed pods can cause poisoning.

Decoction: Use 1 tbsp. seed with 1 qt. water. Boil until ½ qt. liquid remains. Take in the course of a day.

Poultice: Cook seeds until they are soft (or use pulverized seed). Put them immediately into a linen bag and apply as hot as can be tolerated.

Seeds: For constipation, take 1 to 2 tbsp. whole seeds, washing them down with lots of water. If necessary, follow with stewed prunes.

160   PURGING FLAX or FAIRY FLAX
(Linum catharticum)

NOTE: Another flax plant, purging flax or fairy flax (*Linum catharticum*), is common in European meadows and pastures. It has opposite leaves and white flowers. In small quantities the plant has purgative properties; in large quantities it is emetic. An infusion of the dried herb is used. CAUTION: Large quantities of purging flax can cause fatal poisoning.

161 FOXGLOVE

(Digitalis purpurea)

Common Names: Digitalis, American foxglove, dead men's bells, dog's finger, fairy fingers, fairy gloves, finger flower, folks' glove, lion's mouth, ladies' glove, purple foxglove.

Medicinal Part: Leaves.

Description: Foxglove is a biennial plant cultivated as an ornamental in the U.S. but also found wild in pastures and burned-over areas on the Pacific coast from British Columbia to northern California. The stem is stout, succulent, simple, and downy, growing to a height of 2 to 5 feet. The leaves are alternate, oblong-lanceolate, crenate, and downy, the lower petioled, the upper sessile. From June to September one-sided racemes of bell-shaped flowers appear, which are rose-colored to purple on the outside and whitish with red spots on the inside.

Properties and Uses: Cardiac. Foxglove contains glycosides which are extracted from the second year's growth of leaves to make the heart drug digitalis. Even touching the plant with bare skin has been known to cause rashes, headache, and nausea.

Preparation and Dosage: Poison. Do not use without medical direction.

162 FRAGRANT VALERIAN

(Valeriana officinalis)

Common Names: Valerian, all-heal, English valerian, German valerian, great wild valerian, heliotrope, setwall, vandal root, Vermont valerian, wild valerian.

Medicinal Part: Rootstock.

Description: Fragrant valerian is a perennial plant, about 2 to 4 feet high, which has escaped from cultivation to inhabit roadsides and thickets from New England south to New Jersey and west to Ohio. It is also very common all over

Europe. The yellow-brown, tuberous rootstock produces a hollow, angular, furrowed stem with opposite, pinnate leaves which have from 7 to 25 lanceolate, sharply serrate leaflets. The rose-colored to reddish, sometimes white, flowers are small and fragrant, appearing in compact terminal cymes from June to August.

Properties and Uses: Antispasmodic, calmative, carminative, hypnotic, nervine, stomachic. Fragrant valerian is useful for all sorts of nervous conditions, migraine, and insomnia. It is also helpful for hysteria, neurasthenia, fatigue, and stomach cramps that cause vomiting. CAUTION: Large doses or extended use may produce symptoms of poisoning. Take the tea twice daily for no more than two to three weeks at a time. Fragrant valerian tea can also be used as an enema for pinworms, and externally as a wash for sores and pimples (for these take the tea internally at the same time).

Preparation and Dosage: Use only the fresh rootstock.

Infusion: Steep 1 tsp. rootstock in 1 pint boiling water. Take cold, 1 cup in the course of the day, or when going to bed.

Cold Extract: Use 2 tsp. rootstock with 1 cup water; let stand for 24 hours and strain. Take ½ to 1 cup when going to bed.

Tincture: Take 20 drops on sugar or in water, three times a day.

163   FRAXINELLA

(Dictamnus albus)

Common Names: Bastard dittany, burning bush, dittany, false dittany, gas plant, diptam.

Medicinal Parts: Rootstock, herb, seed.

Description: Fraxinella is a perennial plant introduced from Europe and sometimes cultivated as a garden ornamental in the northern U.S. The knobby, cylindrical, whitish rootstock sends up several round, downy, green-and-purple stems with alternate, odd-pinnate leaves. The leaflets are ovate-lanceolate, serrate, and covered with glandular dots. A long raceme of large, rose-colored (sometimes white or red-purple) flowers with darker veins appears in June and July. The fruit is a five-parted capsule. The entire plant has a lemon-like smell. Some of the plant's names refer to its production of a flammable substance in the summer which ignites with a flash over the whole plant but without harming it.

Properties and Uses: Anthelmintic, diuretic, emmenagogue, expectorant, febrifuge, tonic. A decoction of the rootstock is popularly used for intermittent fever and for stomach cramps, as well as for other uses indicated by the categories. A decoction of the rootstock and the seed is used for kidney and bladder stones, to promote the onset of menstruation, and for leucorrhea, cramps, and hysteria. An infusion of the flowering tops is also said to be diuretic and good for gravel. A tincture made from the leaves and the flowers is used in a liniment for rheumatic pains. Perhaps the plant would even make a good natural flashbulb, at least in summer. CAUTION: Contact with the plant may cause dermatitis where the skin is subsequently exposed to sunlight.

Preparation and Dosage:

Infusion or Decoction: Use 1 tbsp. rootstock, herb, or seed with 1 cup water. Take 1 cup a day, a mouthful at a time.

164 FRINGE TREE

(Chionanthus virginicus)

Common Names: Gray beard tree, old man's beard, poison ash, snowflower, white fringe.

Medicinal Part: Bark.

Description: Fringe tree grows from 8 to 25 feet high, in the middle and southern U.S. and in New England. It is cultivated in parks and gardens and also occurs wild along riverbanks and on higher ground. The leaves are opposite, smooth, and oblong to oval in shape. In May and June, when the leaves are only partially developed, the fragrant white flowers, from whose fringe-like petals the tree derives its name, appear in dense panicles. The fruit is an oval, purple drupe.

Properties and Uses: Aperient, diuretic, febrifuge, tonic. A preparation of fringe-tree bark abates fever, is good for acute dyspepsia, and has a beneficial effect on the kidneys and the liver, including acute or chronic liver inflammation and cirrhosis of the liver. The bark can also be made into a poultice for external use on wounds and skin irritations.

Preparation and Dosage:

Decoction: Boil 1 tsp. bark in 1 cup water. Take 1 cup a day.

Tincture: Take 7 to 10 drops in water, as indicated.

FUMITORY

(Fumaria officinalis)

Common Names: Earth smoke, hedge fumitory.

Medicinal Part: The flowering herb.

Description: Fumitory is an annual plant found practically everywhere on earth, mostly around areas where other plants are cultivated. The sub-erect, hollow stem is angular, smooth, and bluish hued. The leaves are alternate, gray-green, and bi- or tripinnate with small, narrow divisions. The small flowers vary from reddish-purple to yellowish-white, have a reddish-black spot at the tip, and grow in loose racemes from May to September.

Properties and Uses: Cholagogue, diuretic, laxative, stomachic, tonic. Fumitory is used internally primarily for liver and gall-bladder problems. Larger doses act as a laxative and diuretic, but excessive doses can cause diarrhea and stomachache. For chronic constipation, use fumitory in combination with other appropriate herbs. Take fumitory also for scabies and other skin problems.

Preparation and Dosage: Use the dried herb.

Infusion: Steep 1 heaping tsp. herb in 1 cup water. Take cold, a wineglassful every 4 hours.

Cold Extract: Use 1 tsp. herb with ½ cup cold water. Let stand for 8 to 10 hours. Take ½ to 1 cup a day.

Tincture: Take ½ to 1 tsp. at a time.

166 GALANGAL
(*Alpinia galanga*)

Common Names: Catarrh root, galanga, large galangal.

Medicinal Part: Rootstock.

Description: Galangal is a perennial plant, varieties of which are found wild and cultivated in China, Southeast Asia, Indonesia, and Iran. The creeping rootstock is cylindrical and branched, ringed with the leaf sheaths of the past, rust brown or red outside, and gray-white and mealy inside. Its odor and taste are reminiscent of its relative, ginger. Aside from the basal leaves, procumbent stems also bear linear-lanceolate leaves as well as white flowers growing in racemes. During flowering, the plant reaches a height of 3 to 5 feet.

Properties and Uses: Galangal is used like ginger. Lovers of the Middle Ages (not middle-aged lovers) used it as an aphrodisiac.

Preparation and Dosage: See ginger.

167. GARDEN VIOLET
(*Viola odorata*)

Common Name: Sweet violet.

Medicinal Part: The whole plant.

Description: Garden violet is a small, European, perennial plant that is commonly cultivated and also grows wild in meadows, thickets, hedges, and along roadsides and the edges of woods. The creeping rootstock sends out runners along the ground which also take root. The leaves are basal, petioled, and cordate. The spurred, violet, sometimes white or rose-colored, flowers grow on long peduncles from March to May.

Properties and Uses: Diaphoretic, emetic, expectorant, laxative. Garden violet is primarily an herb for respiratory problems. A tea made from the leaves is excellent as a soothing gargle, as well as for headache. A decoction of the rootstock makes a particularly good expectorant. For inflamed mucous tissue in the mouth, rinse with a tea made from the rootstock or the whole plant. A tea or syrup made from the plant, especially the rootstock and the flowers, is a soothing remedy for coughs and whooping cough. Use it also as a calming agent for insomnia and hysterical or nervous problems. The flowers and the seeds can be used as a mild laxative. In large doses, the rootstock is emetic.

Preparation and Dosage: Collect the rootstock in the fall.

Infusion: Steep 1 tsp. mixed plant parts in ½ cup water and strain.

Decoction: Boil 1 tbsp. rootstock or plant parts in ½ cup water. Soaking for a few hours before boiling is said to strengthen the activity.

Syrup: Pour 1 qt. boiling-hot water over an equal volume of compressed flowers; let stand for 10 hours and strain. Heat the resulting liquid to simmering and pour over a new batch of flowers. Let stand and strain as before. Repeat the procedure several more times (the more the better). Heat the final liquid, let cool, and add honey until a syrupy consistency is obtained.

168 GARLIC

(*Allium sativum*)

Common Name: Clove garlic.

Medicinal Part: The bulb.

Description: Garlic is a perennial plant that is widely cultivated as one of the most common kitchen herbs. The garlic bulb is compound, consisting of individual bulbs, or cloves, enclosed together in a white skin. The stem is simple, smooth, and round and is surrounded at the bottom by tubular leaf sheaths from which grow the long, flat, linear leaves. The stem is topped by a rounded umbel of small, white, usually sterile flowers, among which grow 20 to 30 small bulbs. The entire umbel is at first enclosed in a teardrop-shaped leaf (pointing upward) which eventually falls off.

Properties and Uses: Anthelmintic, antispasmodic, carminative, cholagogue, digestive, diuretic, expectorant, febrifuge. Garlic stimulates the activity of the digestive organs and therefore relieves various problems associated with poor digestion. As an expectorant, it is useful for chronic stomach and intestinal catarrh, as well as for chronic bronchitis. Garlic also regularizes the action of the liver and gallbladder. It is helpful for all intestinal infections, such as dysentery, cholera, typhoid and paratyphoid fever, and for problems due to putrefactive intestinal bacteria. The tincture of garlic lowers blood pressure and helps to counteract arteriosclerosis. Its beneficial effect on blood circulation and heart action can bring relief for many common body complaints. A cold extract of garlic can be used as an enema for intestinal worms, particularly pinworms. The problem with garlic is that when you use it you inherit the smell along with the benefits.

Preparation and Dosage: Gather bulbs in the fall.

Juice: Take ½ tsp. of the juice pressed from the bulb, thinned with water, 2 or 3 times a day.

Cold Extract: Let several cloves of garlic stand in ½ cup water for 6 to 8 hours.

Cloves: For coughs, take grated garlic mixed with honey.

Tincture: Let ½ lb. peeled cloves soak in 1 qt. brandy for 14 days at a temperature of 85°F in a bottle with an airtight seal. Shake several times a day. Strain when the time is up to get a tincture which will keep for about a year. Take 5 to 25 drops, several times a day, as needed.

169   GINGER

(Zingiber officinale)

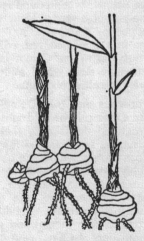

Common Names: African ginger, black ginger, race ginger.

Medicinal Part: Rootstock.

Description: Ginger is a perennial plant indigenous to tropical Asia and cultivated in other tropical areas, especially Jamaica. The aromatic, knotty rootstock is thick, fibrous, and whitish or buff-colored. It produces a simple, leafy stem covered with the leaf sheaths of the lanceolate-oblong to linear leaves. The plant reaches a height of 3 to 4 feet, the leaves growing 6 to 12 inches long. The sterile flowers are white with purple streaks and grow in spikes.

Properties and Uses: Adjuvant, appetizer, carminative, diaphoretic, sialagogue, stimulant. Ginger tea or tincture, taken hot, promotes cleansing of the system through perspiration and is also said to be useful for suppressed menstruation. Take it to clear up flatulent colic or combine it with laxative herbs to make them more palatable or milder in action. Try it at the onset of a cold to ease the effects of the usual symptoms. Finally, to stimulate the flow of saliva and to soothe a sore throat, chew the rootstock as is.

Preparation and Dosage:

Infusion: Mix ½ tsp. powdered rootstock with 1 tsp. (or more) honey. Add 1 cup boiling-hot water. If desired, add an ounce of brandy or other liquor.

Tincture: Take 15 or more drops at a time, warm.

170 GINSENG

(a) (Panax schin-seng)

Common Names: Asiatic ginseng, Chinese ginseng, wonder-of-the-world.

Medicinal Part: Root.

Description: Asiatic ginseng is a small perennial plant which grows in the damp woodlands of Manchuria and is cultivated primarily in Korea. The aromatic root commonly grows to a length of 2 feet or more and is often divided at the end. The simple, glabrous stem bears near the top a whorl of three or five palmately compound leaves consisting of five oblong-ovate, finely double-serrate leaflets. From June to August the plant is topped by a solitary simple umbel of greenish-yellow flowers. The fruit is a small, red, edible, drupelike berry. Ginseng's high reputation in the Orient ensures that the wild plant remains extremely rare; world trade in ginseng consists almost exclusively of cultivated plants.

Properties and Uses: Demulcent, panacea, stimulant, stomachic. The Chinese have held ginseng root in almost religious esteem (grounded, in fact, in their most basic notions of man and existence) as a panacea for all ailments for thousands of years, those roots resembling a human being in shape being the most highly prized. It is considered especially valuable for feverish and inflammatory illnesses, for hemorrhage, and for blood diseases. Women also take it for everything from normalizing menstruation to easing childbirth. In a general way, it is said to promote both mental and physical vigor; and, considering the population of China, who can quarrel with its reputation as an aphrodisiac? In the more prosaic western view, ginseng does promote appetite and may be helpful for digestive disturbances. It is mildly stimulating to the central nervous system and to various glands, accounting perhaps for its reputation as a rejuvenator. As a demulcent, it is helpful for coughs, colds, and various chest problems.

Preparation and Dosage: The root is collected after flowering. Use only thoroughly dried root. Make it into a tea according to your taste and use as needed.

171   GINSENG (cont.)

(b) (Panax quinquefolius)

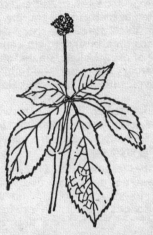

Common Names: American ginseng, five-fingers, five-leafed ginseng, redberry.

Medicinal Part: Root.

Description: American ginseng is a perennial plant which was at one time found wild in the rich, cool woodlands of eastern North America. Popular demand for the roots wiped out the wild supply, and ginseng is now found here only under cultivation (mainly in Wisconsin). American ginseng is similar in appearance to Asiatic ginseng, but its root is spindle-shaped or forked and its leaflets are oblong-obovate in shape and have coarsely serrate or dentate margins.

Properties and Uses: Analysis shows that American ginseng and Asiatic ginseng have essentially the same constituents; and, interestingly, the bulk of the American crop has traditionally been exported to Europe and Asia to supplement the supply from the Orient. Like its cultivated Oriental counterpart, however, it is not considered as efficacious as the wild plant. American Indians in some areas used a decoction of ginseng root to relieve nausea and vomiting. Several tribes used it as an ingredient in love potions and charms.

Preparation and Dosage: Same as Asiatic ginseng.

172 GOAT'S RUE
(Galega officinalis)

Medicinal Part: The herb.

Description: Goat's rue is a perennial plant found wild in southern
Europe and western Asia and cultivated in both Europe and the U.S.
The thick, spreading root system
sends up a bushy growth consisting of many hollow, striated stems
bearing alternate, odd-pinnate
leaves with six to eight pairs of
ovate, entire leaflets which tend to
fold together. The lilac to white
flowers appear in spikes from June
to September. Seeds are borne in
long, erect pods.

Properties and Uses: Diaphoretic, diuretic, galactagogue. Goat's
rue is not commonly used today. In the past it has been used
for fevers and worms, and was believed to cure bites from
poisonous animals. An extract of the dried plant is sometimes
used to stimulate the flow of milk in nursing mothers. The
seeds apparently lower blood sugar levels and may be useful
for diabetes. CAUTION: Sheep have been poisoned by the
fresh plant.

Preparation and Dosage: Use under medical direction.

173 GOLDENROD
(a) (Solidago odora)

Common Names: Sweet goldenrod, anise-scented goldenrod,
blue mountain tea, bohea-tea, common goldenrod, wound
weed.

Medicinal Part: Leaves.

Description: The creeping rootstock of this perennial plant produces a slender, simple stem growing to a height of 2 to 4 feet.
The leaves are sessile, thin, entire, lanceolate, and covered with
transparent dots. The golden-yellow flowers appear in terminal
panicled racemes from July to September. Sweet goldenrod can
be found in dry, sandy soils in the eastern half of the U.S.

Properties and Uses: Astringent, carminative, diaphoretic, diuretic, stimulant. Warm sweet goldenrod tea has diaphoretic
properties; taken cold it stimulates the system and helps to
dispel flatulence. A tea made from the dried leaves and flowers
is an aromatic beverage and can be used to improve the taste

of other medicinal preparations. American Indians applied a lotion made from goldenrod flowers to beestings.

Preparation and Dosage:

Infusion: Steep 1 tsp. leaves in 1 cup water. Take 1 to 2 cups a day, warm or cold.

174 GRAY GOLDENROD
(Solidago nemoralis)

NOTE: Gray goldenrod *(Solidago nemoralis)*, also called dyer's weed, field goldenrod, and yellow goldenrod, is also used medicinally, especially as a carminative and diaphoretic. Its color is a grayish-green or olive-green; its stem is hairy; and its rough leaves are spatulate, varying from large, toothed, and petioled below to smaller, entire, and clasping higher up. The yellow flowers grow in a large, terminal, one-sided panicle.

175 GOLDENROD (cont.)
(b) (Solidago virgaurea)

Common Name: European gold-enrod.

Medicinal Parts: Flowering tops, leaves.

Description: European goldenrod is a perennial plant which grows to a height of up to 3 feet in dry meadows and woods, and in sandy, sunny places in Europe and northern and western Asia. The short rootstock with many fibrous roots produces a hairy, round, striped stem with alternate, oblong-lanceolate, weakly serrate leaves, the lower ones having dilated petioles, the upper nearly sessile. The yellow flowers appear in terminal racemes or panicled racemes from July to October.

Properties and Uses: Astringent, diuretic. European goldenrod has been used, in the form of tea, tincture, or alcoholic extract, for chronic nephritis and arthritis, menorrhagia, whooping cough, and chronic eczema. It is said to be useful for kidney problems, especially when indicated by dark, cloudy urine, and for clearing up kidney and bladder stones. Its astringent action makes it useful against diarrhea and internal hemorrhage.

Crushed fresh leaves can be used for wounds, sores, and insect bites.

Preparation and Dosage:

Infusion: Steep 1 oz. flowering tops in 1 pint water.

Decoction: Use 1 tbsp. tops with ½ cup water; boil for a short time, then steep for a few minutes. Take 1 cup a day, freshly made each time.

Powder: Take ⅓ to 1 tsp. in honey, three times a day.

Tincture: Take ½ tsp., two or three times a day.

176   GOLDENSEAL

(Hydrastis canadensis)

Common Names: Eye balm, eye root, ground raspberry, Indian plant, jaundice root, orangeroot, tumeric root, yellow puccoon, yellowroot.

Medicinal Part: Rootstock.

Description: Goldenseal is a small, perennial plant, usually cultivated but also found wild in rich, shady woods and damp meadows from Connecticut to Minnesota and southward. A thick, knotty, yellow rootstock sends up a hairy stem, about a foot high, with two palmately five-lobed, serrate leaves near the top. The stem is topped by a small, solitary, apetalous flower whose greenish-white sepals fall away when the flower opens. The fruit resembles a raspberry and consists of fused, two-seeded drupes.

Properties and Uses: Antiperiodic, antiseptic, astringent, diuretic, laxative, tonic. Goldenseal has been a popular remedy for both internal and external uses. Its acts particularly on mucous membranes and can be used for all catarrhal conditions. The infusion makes a good vaginal douche and an antiseptic mouthwash. Apply the tea with a toothbrush for sore gums or pyorrhea. Use it also as an external wash for skin diseases, sores, erysipelas, or ringworm (sprinkle powdered rootstock on after washing with tea). Snuff the powder up the nostrils for nasal congestión or catarrh. Goldenseal also has been popular for home use as a laxative and for stomach ailments. Small doses taken frequently will help relieve nausea during pregnancy. To make a soothing eyewash, mix goldenseal with boric acid (see below).

Preparation and Dosage: CAUTION: Eating the fresh plant produces ulcerations and inflammation of mucous tissue.

Infusion: Add 1 tsp. powdered rootstock to 1 pint boiling-hot water; let stand until cold. Take 1 to 2 tsp. three to six times a day.

Eyewash: Add 1 tsp. rootstock and 1 tsp. boric acid to 1 pint boiling-hot water; stir, let cool, and pour off the liquid. Add 1 tsp. of the liquid to ½ cup water to make an eyewash.

177   GOLDTHREAD

(Coptis trifolia)

Common Names: Cankerroot, mouthroot, yellowroot.

Medicinal Part: Rootstock.

Description: Goldthread is a low perennial plant found in mossy woods and swamps from Labrador south to Maryland and west to Minnesota, Iowa, and Tennessee. From a slender, golden, creeping rootstock arise the basal, long-petioled, trifoliate, evergreen leaves and the naked scapes, 3 to 6 inches high, which terminate in a small, white flower. Flowering time is May to August. The fruit is an oblong capsule.

Properties and Uses: Bitter tonic, antiphlogistic, sedative. Goldthread has been used internally as a bitter tonic, particularly for dyspepsia. Its main use has been as a wash or gargle for sores and ulcerations in the mouth, throat, and even stomach. It has also been a popular folk remedy for inflammations of mucous membranes in the mouth and around the eyes.

Preparation and Dosage: Collect the rootstock in the fall.

Decoction: Boil 1 tsp. rootstock in 1 cup water. Take 1 tbsp., three to six times a day; or use as wash or gargle.

Tincture: Take 5 to 10 drops at a time.

178   GREAT BURNET

(Sanguisorba officinalis)

Common Names: Italian burnet, Italian pimpernel.

Medicinal Part: The plant.

Description: Great burnet is a perennial plant that grows in old gardens, damp meadows, peat bogs, and coastal areas of the U.S. and Europe. The stems bear pinnate leaves, with roundish to ovate, serrate leaflets. Long, naked peduncles topped by dense spikes of purplish flowers enable the plant to reach a height of 2 to 3 feet. Flowering time is July to September.

Properties and Uses: Astringent, hemostatic. The two main uses for great burnet are to stop diarrhea and to coagulate blood so as to end hemorrhaging. The plant has also been recommended at times for inflammation of the veins (phlebitis) and for varicose veins. A decoction of the root has been used for menopausal problems.

Preparation and Dosage:

Decoction: Use 1 to 2 tsp. dried plant with 1 cup water. Boil for 2 to 5 minutes and strain. Take 1 cup in the course of a day, a mouthful at a time.

Cold Extract: Use 2 tsp. plant with 1 cup cold water. Let stand for 8 hours. Take 1 cup a day, as with the decoction.

Expressed Juice: Take 5 to 6 tbsp. fresh juice daily.

Tincture: Take 30 to 50 drops at a time.

179   GROUND IVY

(Nepeta hederacea)

Common Names: Alehoof, cat's-foot, cat's-paw, creeping Charlie, gill-over-the-ground, gillrun, hay maids, hedge maids, turnhoof.

Medicinal Parts: Flowering herb, leaves.

Description: Ground ivy is a creeping, perennial plant found in moist soils of the eastern states and the Pacific coast, as well as in Europe. The four-sided, finely haired, procumbent stem, from a few inches to 2 feet long, grows roots from the nodes along its length. The leaves are opposite, hairy, crenate, from reniform to cordate but nearly round. The bluish-purple, two-lipped flowers grow in axillary whorls of six from April to July.

Properties and Uses: Appetizer, astringent, digestive, diuretic, pectoral, stimulant, tonic. Ground ivy is helpful in relieving diarrhea and inflammation of mucous membranes, as in colds, sore throat, and bronchitis. Snuffing the fresh juice up the nose often helps nasal congestion and headache. It has been used for problems caused by hypoacidity, for catarrhal enteritis, and for liver ailments. Ground ivy has also been beneficial in cases of neurasthenia and morbid hysteria; and, made into a bath additive, it is said to be good for sciatica, gout, gravel, and stones. The fresh juice may be given to small children, a few drops at a time, for tummyache. To stimulate appetite and promote digestion, use a decoction of the dried herb. CAUTION: In very large quantities ground ivy can be poisonous.

Preparation and Dosage:

Infusion: Steep 1 tsp. fresh herb or leaves in ½ cup water. Take ½ to 1 cup a day.

Juice: Take 1 tsp., three times a day.

Tincture: Take ¼ to ½ tsp. at a time.

180 GUAIAC

(Guaiacum officinale)

Common Names: Guaiacum, guayacan, lignum vitae, pockwood.

Medicinal Part: Resin.

Description: Guaiac is the resin from a tree that grows in the West Indies, Mexico, Central America, and northern South America. The crooked trunk grows 30 to 40 feet high and provides lignum vitae, the olive-brown, heavy, very hard wood which contains the oily resin.

Properties and Uses: Antiseptic, diaphoretic, diuretic, stimulant. Guaiac has found application in cases of gout, catarrh, syphilis, rheumatism, and skin diseases. Take a decoction of the wood and keep warm to induce perspiration or keep cool for diuretic action.

Preparation and Dosage:

Decoction: Boil 1 tsp. granulated wood in 1 cup water. Take 1 tbsp., three to six times a day.

Resin: Take 2 to 5 grains at a time.

181 GUM PLANT
(*Grindelia robusta*)

Common Names: August flower, gumweed, resin-weed.

Medicinal Parts: Leaves, flowering tops.

Description: Gum plant is a bushy perennial native to, but not plentiful in, the coastal areas of California. Several stems grow together to a height of 1 to 2 feet and bear alternate, oblong to ovate or lanceolate, sharply serrate or denticulate (the uppermost may be entire), leathery leaves. Two to five yellow flower heads grow in a terminal cyme from August to September.

Properties and Uses: Antispasmodic, demulcent, expectorant. Used in small doses, gum plant is helpful for colds, nasal congestion, bronchial irritation, and for the spasms of whooping cough and asthma. Externally, the tea can be used as a wash for burns, rashes, blisters, and inflammations; a fluid extract, diluted with 6 to 10 parts water, can be applied to skin irritation caused by poison ivy (soak a clean bandage, keep it moist, and change often). CAUTION: Gum plant tends to take up selenium* compounds from the soil and store them. Large doses can be poisonous; smaller doses may cause slowing of the heartbeat.

Preparation and Dosage: Use dried plant parts only.

Infusion: Steep 1 tsp. dried leaves or flowering tops in 1 cup boiling-hot water. Take 1 cup a day.

Tincture: Take 5 to 30 drops, as required.

* A sulphur-like non-metallic element.

182 HAWTHORN
(*Crataegus oxyacantha*)

Common Names: English hawthorn, May bush, May tree, quickset, thorn-apple tree, whitethorn.

Medicinal Parts: Flowers, fruit.

Description: The hawthorn grows as either a shrub or a tree in England and continental Europe; in England it is widely grown as a hedge plant. Its trunk or stems have hard wood, smooth and ash-gray bark, and thorny branches. The small, shiny leaves are dark green on top, light bluish-green underneath, and have three irregularly toothed lobes. The white flowers have round petals and grow in terminal corymbs during May and June. The fruit, or haw, is a 2- to 3-seeded, fleshy pome, scarlet on the outside, yellowish and pulpy on the inside.

Properties and Uses: Antispasmodic, cardiac, sedative, vasodilator. Hawthorn normalizes blood pressure by regulating heart action; extended use will usually lower blood pressure. It is good for heart muscle weakened by age, for inflammation of the heart muscle (myocarditis), for arteriosclerosis, and for nervous heart problems. Executives under strain from pressures of the job can benefit from hawthorn tea. The tea is also a good remedy for other nervous conditions, particularly insomnia.

Preparation and Dosage:

Infusion: Steep 1 tsp. flowers in ½ cup water. Take 1 to 1½ cups a day, a mouthful at a time. Sweeten with honey if desired.

Decoction: Use 1 tsp. crushed fruit with ½ cup cold water. Let stand for 7 or 8 hours, then bring quickly to a boil and strain. Take 1 to 1½ cups a day, a mouthful at a time, sweetened with honey if desired.

Tincture: Use concentrated preparations under medical direction.

183   HEATHER

(Calluna vulgaris)

Common Names: Common heather, ling, Scotch heather.

Medicinal Part: Flowering shoots.

Description: Heather is an evergreen shrub, rare in the U.S. but commonly found on poor soils and marshy grounds in Great Britain and Europe. The prostrate, grayish, hairy stem grows up to 3 feet long and sends up branches 1 to 1½ feet high. The dull green, sometimes gray, small, linear-lanceolate leaves grow in two overlapping rows. Branching spikes of light violet, bell-shaped flowers appear in August and September.

Properties and Uses: Antiseptic, cholagogue, diaphoretic, diuretic, expectorant, vasoconstrictor. Some people find heather useful for insomnia, and it has also been recommended for gouty and rheumatic pains, stomachache, coughs, and facial skin problems. Heather contains compounds that act to constrict the blood vessels, strengthen the heart, and moderately raise blood pressure. They also stimulate the flow of bile and of urine.

Preparation and Dosage: Heather may be used fresh or dried.

Infusion: For insomnia, steep 1 tsp. shoots in ½ cup water. Sweeten with 1 tsp. honey.

Decoction: Boil 4 tsp. shoots in 1 cup water for a short time only. Take ½ cup a day.

184   HEDGE BINDWEED

(Convolvulus sepium)

Common Names: Devil's vine, great bindweed, hedge lily, lady's nightcap, Rutland beauty, trailing bindweed.

Medicinal Parts: Flowering plant, rootstock.

Description: Hedge bindweed is a perennial herbaceous vine found in waste places, thickets, and cultivated ground in the eastern half of the U.S. and also in all of Europe. The trailing or twining stem is glabrous, angular, and from 3 to 10 feet long, growing from a creeping rootstock. The leaves are alternate, sagittate, on slender petioles. The flaring, funnel-shaped flowers are white or pink with white stripes and grow solitary on long, quadrangular peduncles from the leaf axils from June into October.

Properties and Uses: Cholagogue, febrifuge, purgative. Hedge bindweed is used primarily as a purgative, but it also helps reduce inflammation of mucous membranes. The powdered rootstock or a decoction made from the plant is commonly used. The fresh juice should be taken only in small quantities; in large quantities it produces constipation. Like all strong purgatives, hedge bindweed is not for extended use.

Preparation and Dosage:

Decoction: Boil 1 tsp. flowering plant in 1 cup water. Take 1 tbsp. at a time, as needed.

Juice: Take ½ tsp., one or two times a day.

Powdered Rootstock: Take 1 level tsp., one or two times a day.

185   **HEDGE GARLIC**

(Sisymbrium alliaria)

Common Name: Jack-by-the-hedge.

Medicinal Part: The plant.

Description: Hedge garlic is a European, annual or biennial plant found along roadsides, hedges, walls, fences and among bushes. The blue-green, usually simple stem grows up to 3 feet high and is mostly glabrous but thinly hairy at the bottom. The leaves are glabrous and coarsely serrate, the basal reniform, the stem leaves cordate to almost triangular. When bruised, they smell like garlic. The small, white flowers grow in a broad raceme from April to June.

Properties and Uses: Hedge garlic is used in basically the same ways as mustard and garlic (which see). In addition, it is popularly used as a springtime-cure diuretic for rheumatism, gout, and asthma. In the past it has been praised as a stimulant and an anthelmintic. CAUTION: As with mustard, skin irritation can result from use of the plant as poultice or plaster.

186   **HEDGE HYSSOP**

(Gratiola officinalis)

Medicinal Part: The herb.

Description: Hedge hyssop is a European perennial herb which grows to a height of about 1 foot in low, wet places. The branched, hollow, quadrangular stem grows from a thin, creeping rootstock and bears opposite, sessile, lanceolate, shallow-toothed leaves. The solitary, axillary flowers have a tubular corolla that is rose-colored or reddish with yellow streaks. Flowering time is June to August. NOTE: Related American species are annuals and have flowers whose corollas have yellow tubes and white lips.

Properties and Uses: Cardiac, diuretic, purgative, vermifuge.

Hedge hyssop is potent medicine and should be used only in the form of prepared extracts and tinctures to minimize the danger of poisoning. Large doses of the plant produce numerous and dangerous effects. The tincture is said to help in the effort to stop smoking. It can also be taken for gout, mild dropsy, chronic eczema, and persistent itching skin.

Preparation and Dosage: Use only under medical supervision.

187 HEDGE MUSTARD

(Sisymbrium officinale)

Common Names: English watercress, erysimum, thalictroc.

Medicinal Part: The plant.

Description: Hedge mustard is a common, much-hated, annual weed found in fields and waste places all over North America (except the extreme north) and Europe. Growing from 1 to 4 feet tall, the purple-hued, branching stem bears light green, lyrately pinnatifid or pinnate leaves with dentate or coarsely toothed segments. The small, yellow flowers grow in terminal racemes from April to as late as November. Beneath the flower clusters, linear or oblong seed pods develop, closely pressed to the axis in a long, slender raceme. The seeds resemble those of mustard.

Properties and Uses: Diuretic, expectorant, stomachic. Hedgemustard tea is popularly used in Europe for colds, coughs, hoarseness, chest congestion, laryngitis, bronchial catarrh, and the like, particularly as part of a springtime cure.

Preparation and Dosage:

Infusion: Steep 1 tsp. of the plant in ½ cup water for 4 to 5 minutes. Take 1½ to 2 cups a day, a mouthful at a time. For catarrhal problems, sweeten with honey if desired.

188 HELLEBORE

(a) (Helleborus niger)

Common Names: Black hellebore, Christmas rose.

Medicinal Part: Rootstock.

Description: Black hellebore is a perennial plant cultivated and found wild around the edges of forests in the subalpine and southern parts of Europe. It has also been introduced into the U.S. as a garden plant. The simple stem grows as high as 1 foot and bears a few small leaflets. The basal leaves growing from the rootstock are dark green, leathery, petioled, palmately 7- to 9-parted. The large, white, showy flowers appear from December to March.

Properties and Uses: Cardiac, cathartic, diuretic, emetic, emmenagogue, irritant, rubefacient. Black hellebore is used variously to stimulate the heart, and to treat depression, mania, epilepsy, and skin problems. The leaves and rootstock contain a variety of glycosides similar in activity to digitalis. Contact with the bruised herb may also cause dermatitis.

Preparation and Dosage: Black hellebore is not for use without medical direction under any circumstances.

189 HELLEBORE (cont.)

(b) (Helleborus foetidus)

Common Names: Bearsfoot, fetid hellebore, oxheal, stinking hellebore.

Medicinal Parts: Rootstock, herb.

Description: Bearsfoot is a European perennial that grows on the dry, rocky slopes of the Alps. Its stem is branched and bears leaves that grow from pale green sheaths. The greenish and bell-shaped flowers appear from March to May.

Properties and Uses: Emetic, purgative, vermifuge. Bearsfoot is said to be most active of the hellebores, having basically the same properties as black hellebore. It is rarely used.

Preparation and Dosage: Bearsfoot is not for use without medical direction under any circumstances.

190 HELLEBORE (cont.)

(c) (Helleborus viridis)

Common Names: Green hellebore, winter hellebore.

Medicinal Part: Rootstock.

Description: Green hellebore is a European perennial found mostly in alpine forests. It is similar to black hellebore, but its stem is branched, each branch bearing one flower in conjunction with a palmately compound leaf. The flowers appear in March and April.

Properties and Uses: Green hellebore is used like black hellebore, but it is more potent. Obviously, the same cautions apply.

Preparation and Dosage: Green hellebore is not for use without medical direction under any circumstances.

191   HEMLOCK SPRUCE

(Tsuga canadensis)

Common Names: Canada-pitch tree, hemlock gum tree, hemlock pitch tree, hemlock tree, weeping spruce.

Medicinal Part: Bark.

Description: Hemlock spruce is a North American evergreen tree, growing 50 to 100 feet high in mountain ravines and woods and in swampy areas. The bark is a dull brownish-gray on the outside and red underneath and is made up of large, rough scales. The leaves are short and needle-like, and both male and female flowers grow in catkins. The woody seed cones are less than an inch long.

Properties and Uses: Astringent, diaphoretic, diuretic. A tea of the inner bark or the young twigs is helpful in kidney and bladder problems and makes a good enema for diarrhea. Use it also to wash external sores and ulcers and as a gargle or mouthwash for mouth and throat problems. Put powdered bark in the shoes for tender or sweaty feet or for foot odor.

Preparation and Dosage:

Infusion: For internal use, steep 1 tsp. inner bark or twigs in 1 cup boiling-hot water.

Decoction: For external use, simmer 1 tsp. bark or twigs in 1 cup water for 10 minutes.

192 HEMP AGRIMONY

(Eupatorium cannabinum)

Common Names: Sweet-smelling trefoil, water maudlin.

Medicinal Part: The plant.

Description: Hemp agrimony is a European perennial plant which grows along shorelines, in ditches, and in other moist places. The reddish, bluntly angular stem is somewhat bristly and branched at the top. The short-petioled leaves are opposite, dark green on top, gray-green below, and palmately three- to five-parted, with lanceolate, serrate leaflets. The reddish flowers grow in compound terminal cymes from July to September.

Properties and Uses: Cholagogue, diaphoretic, diuretic, emetic, expectorant, purgative. An infusion of the leaves is helpful for liver problems and is also recommended for rheumatism. A decoction of the rootstock is used as an expectorant; in large doses it acts as a laxative and emetic. Hemp agrimony can also be applied externally to wounds, bruises, sores, swellings, etc.

Preparation and Dosage:

Infusion: Steep 2 tsp. leaves or herb in 1 cup water. Take 1 cup a day.

Cold Extract: Soak 1 tbsp. leaves or herb in 1 cup cold water for 8 to 10 hours. Take 1 cup a day.

193 HEMP NETTLE

(Galeopsis tetrahit)

Common Names: Bastard hemp, bee-nettle, dog-nettle, hemp dead nettle.

Medicinal Part: The herb.

Description: Hemp nettle is an annual weed found in gardens and waste places all over Canada, in Alaska, and from the Great Lakes south to West Virginia. The square, branching stem is swollen at the joints and covered with bristly, downward-pointing hairs. The opposite, ovate, coarsely toothed leaves are from 2 to 5 inches long and bristly on both sides. Dense, whorled, terminal or axillary clusters of pale magenta, two-lipped flowers with bell-shaped, spiny calyxes appear from June to October.

Properties and Uses: Astringent, diuretic, expectorant. Hemp nettle is particularly good for clearing up bronchial congestion and phlegm and is commonly used for coughs. It seems to have a beneficial effect on the blood and has been recommended for anemia and other blood disorders. Europeans also use it as a home remedy for spleen problems and tuberculosis.

Preparation and Dosage: Use the dried herb.

Infusion: Steep 2 tsp. dried herb in ½ cup water for 5 to 10 minutes. Take 1 to 1½ cups a day.

Decoction: Boil 2 to 4 tsp. dried herb in 1 cup water for 10 minutes. Take 1 cup a day.

194   HENBANE

(Hyoscyamus niger)

Common Names: Black henbane, devil's eye, fetid nightshade, hen-bell, hog bean, Jupiter's bean, poison tobacco, stinking nightshade.

Medicinal Part: The herb.

Description: Henbane is a biennial plant found growing in dry, sandy soils, waste grounds and grave-yards and around the foundations of neglected houses in the northern states of the U.S., and in Canada and Europe. The brown, spindle-shaped rootstock produces, in the second year, a dirty-green stem covered with sticky hairs and bearing alternate, sticky, oblong-lanceolate, sessile leaves. The funnel-shaped flowers are dull yellow or beige, with purple veins and bases, and grow in one-sided, leafy spikes from July to September. The plant has a fetid odor.

Properties and Uses: Anodyne, antispasmodic, calmative, narcotic. Because of the danger of poisoning, henbane is used primarily for external applications. An oil obtained from the leaves is made into anodyne lotions and used for earache and rheumatism. A decoction or tincture is sometimes taken for nervousness and irritability or to relieve pain. Once upon a time, henbane was believed to have aphrodisiac properties and was a main ingredient in love potions. Hamlet's father was murdered by pouring a distillation of henbane in his ear (perhaps he had complained of earache). CAUTION: The whole plant is poisonous. Children have been poisoned by eating the seeds or seed pods.

Preparation and Dosage: Use only under medical direction.

195 HENNA
(Lawsonia inermis)

Common Names: Alcanna, Egyptian privet, Jamaica mignonette, mignonette tree, reseda.

Medicinal Part: Leaves.

Description: Henna is a small shrub that grows in Arabia, North Africa, Iran, and the East Indies. The grayish-green leaves are elliptical and from 1 to 2 inches long. Fragrant red flowers, highly prized by Egyptian ladies, grow in large panicles.

Properties and Uses: Astringent. A decoction made from the leaves is useful as a gargle and, taken internally or used externally, for skin problems. It is also sometimes taken as a headache remedy.

196 HEPATICA
(Hepatica triloba)

Common Names: Liverleaf, liverwort, round-lobed hepatica.

Medicinal Parts: Leaves, flowers.

Description: Hepatica is a small perennial plant found in woodlands of the eastern U.S., westward to Iowa and Missouri, and in Canada and Europe. The much-branched rootstock produces a rosette of three-lobed, long-petioled leaves which are green on top and reddish-purple beneath. The leaves last through the winter, the new leaves appearing after the plant flowers. The light blue, sometimes reddish-blue or white, flowers grow on hairy scapes from December to May.

Properties and Uses: Diuretic, pectoral. Hepatica tea has been used for bronchitis, liver congestion, gallbladder problems, and kidney and bladder ailments. It is also said to stop gastric hemorrhage and vomiting of blood. The fresh plant is irritating to the skin and should not be used on wounds. CAUTION: Large doses can produce symptoms of poisoning.

Preparation and Dosage:

Cold Extract: Use 2 tsp. fresh leaves or 4 tsp. dried leaves and flowers with 1 cup cold water. Let stand for 8 hours and strain. Take 1 cup a day.

Tincture: Add a handful of the dried herb to ½ to ¾ qt. whiskey. Let stand at room temperature for about 3 weeks, then strain. Take 10 to 15 drops on a sugar cube, three times a day, for liver, gallbladder, and kidney problems.

197   SHARP-LOBED HEPATICA, or HEART LIVERLEAF
(Hepatica acutiloba)

NOTE: The other species of North American hepatica is sharp-lobed hepatica, or heart liverleaf (*Hepatica acutiloba*). It is similar to round-leaved hepatica, except that its leaves have pointed lobes and that it flowers in March and April. Medicinally, both plants are equivalent.

198   HERB ROBERT
(Geranium robertianum)

Common Names: Dragon's blood, storkbill, wild crane's-bill.

Medicinal Part: The herb.

Description: Herb Robert is a disagreeable-smelling annual plant which grows in rocky woods from Nova Scotia south to Pennsylvania and west to Manitoba and Missouri; it is also common in Europe, Asia, and North Africa. The reddish stem is glandular-hairy, thick, juicy, and forked. The opposite, palmate leaves with pinnate or pinnatifid leaflets are deep green, often tinged with red. The purplish-red or rose-colored flowers grow in pairs from May to October. The petals have long claws which suggest the long bill of a stork or crane.

Properties and Uses: Astringent. Internal use of herb Robert is recommended for diarrhea, gastritis, enteritis, gout, and hemor-

224

rhage. A hot poultice of boiled leaves is said to be good for bladder pains, fistulas, bruises, erysipelas, and persistent skin problems. The green, crushed herb can also be applied to relieve pain and inflammations. Use the tea also as a rinse for inflammations in the mouth, and the dilute tea as an eyewash.

Preparation and Dosage: Remove any developing fruit before using.

Infusion: Steep 1 level tbsp. dried herb in 1 cup water for a short time. Take 1 cup a day.

Cold Extract: Use 2 tsp. dried herb with 1 cup cold water. Let stand for 8 to 10 hours in a covered pot.

HIBISCUS

The name Hibiscus refers actually to a genus including about 200 species of plants, a number of which have medicinal uses. The hibiscus best known for medicinal properties is

199 MUSK-MALLOW
(Hibiscus abelmoschus)

Common Names: Musk seed plant, rose mallow, Syrian mallow, target-leaved hibiscus, water mallow.

Medicinal Part: Seeds.

Description: Musk-mallow is an annual or biennial plant which grows wild in Egypt, India, and the East and West Indies; it is also cultivated elsewhere. The stem, growing from 2 to 6 feet high, bears alternate leaves which are usually sharply lobed and irregularly toothed but sometimes only shallowly lobed and like maple leaves. Both sides are thinly hairy. The large, axillary flowers are yellow and have red centers. An oblong, pointed, hairy capsule up to 3 inches long contains the kidney-shaped, grayish-brown, musk-odored seeds.

Properties and Uses: Antispasmodic, nervine, stomachic. An emulsion made from the seeds is said to be useful for spasmodic problems; an emulsion made with milk can be used for itchy skin. In Egypt, the seeds are chewed to relieve stomach problems, to soothe the nerves, and to "sweeten" the breath. Egyptians also consider the seeds to have aphrodisiac powers.

NOTE: Other species of hibiscus with medicinal uses are

200   HIBISCUS BANCROFTIANUS

Hibiscus bancroftianus—an herbaceous plant of the West Indies which is used like althea.

201   HIBISCUS ESCULENTUS

Hibiscus esculentus—okra, gumbo; found in tropics of the Old World. Both roots and fruit are used as demulcents, the leaves as emollient poultices.

202   HIBISCUS PALUSTRIS

Hibiscus palustris—marsh hibiscus; found in the swamps of the eastern U.S. Used like althea.

203   HIBISCUS ROSA-SINENSIS

Hibiscus rosa-sinensis—rose of China, Chinese hibiscus. Grown mostly for ornament, this shrub or small tree also has astringent and demulcent properties. A decoction of roots is used as an eyewash in Malaya; the bark is used in Asia as an emmenagogue; the flowers are said to be astringent.

204   HIBISCUS SABDARIFFA

Hibiscus sabdariffa—Guinea sorrel, Jamaica sorrel, roselle; a tall annual plant found in tropics of the Old World. The herb is useful as a diuretic and refrigerant.

205   HIBISCUS SAGITTIFOLIUS

Hibiscus sagittifolius—a perennial herb found in Indochina. The root is said to be highly effective against excessive mucous discharge (blenorrhagia).

206   HIBISCUS SURATTENSIS

Hibiscus surattensis—a trailing shrub found in the tropical countries of Asia and Africa. It is used to soothe coughs and as an emollient.

207   HIBISCUS TILIACEUS

Hibiscus tiliaceus—corkwood, Cuban bast, mahoe; a shrub or tree found in tropical countries. The inner bark has mucilaginous and emollient properties.

Hibiscus trionum—flower-of-an-hour, Venice mallow; originally from central Africa, now found as a weed in North America. The plant has mucilaginous and emollient properties.

209   HOLLY

(a) (Ilex aquifolium)

Common Names: Mountain holly, English holly, European holly.

Medicinal Part: Leaves.

Description: Mountain holly is an evergreen tree or shrub which grows wild and cultivated in Europe and is cultivated in the U.S. for Christmas decorations. As a tree, it grows as high as 30 feet; as a shrub it reaches about 15 feet. It has smooth bark and green branches, which bear alternate, dark green, shiny, leathery or waxy, spiny leaves. During May and June, small white flowers appear in umbellate clusters, developing on the female plants into pea-sized, red, berry-like drupes which remain through the winter.

Properties and Uses: Astringent, diuretic, expectorant, febrifuge. Although little used today, mountain holly has been used in the past for gout, stones, and urinary problems, for chronic bronchitis, rheumatism, and arthritis. CAUTION: The berries are mildly poisonous and are dangerous to small children.

Preparation and Dosage:

Decoction: Boil 1 to 2 tbsp. dried leaves in 1 cup water. Take 1 cup a day.

210   HOLLY (cont.)

(b) (Ilex opaca)

Common Names: White holly, American holly.

Medicinal Part: Leaves.

Description: White holly is a native North American evergreen tree or shrub found along the Atlantic coast and from Florida west to Missouri and Texas. Its bark is smooth and grayish-brown; the dark green leaves are alternate, elliptical, and spiny. White flowers grow in axillary clusters, those on the female plants developing into scarlet, berry-like drupes that remain through the winter. Flowering time is May and June.

Properties and Uses: Diuretic, purgative. White holly seems to have been used in the past primarily as a means of cleansing the system by promoting the proper elimination of waste products from the body. CAUTION: The berries are mildly poisonous and are dangerous to small children.

211   HOLLY (cont.)

(c) (Ilex vomitoria)

Common Names: Indian black drink, black drink plant, emetic holly, yaupon holly.

Medicinal Part: Leaves.

Description: Indian black drink is a small evergreen tree or shrub which grows in sandy woods and clearings from Florida to Texas, and north into Virginia and Arkansas. Its bark is close and whitish-gray; the leaves are alternate, leathery, lance-oval or elliptic, and crenate. The nearly sessile, white flowers grow in axillary clusters from May to June, those on the female plants developing into red, berry-like drupes.

Properties and Uses: Emetic, stimulant. American Indians smoked the leaves or toasted them in a clay pot and then made an infusion of them that was drunk for various ceremonial purposes, including purification by vomiting. If not made into a strong tea, dried leaves make a good beverage whose caffeine content is mildly stimulating. CAUTION: The berries are mildly poisonous and are dangerous to small children.

212   HOLLY (cont.)

(d) (Ilex verticillata)

Common Names: Winterberry, black-alder, brook alder, false alder, feverbush, striped alder.

Medicinal Parts: Bark, fruit.

Description: Winterberry is a deciduous shrub, 6 to 8 feet high, common in the swamps of eastern North America and in England. The stems have bluish-gray bark and alternate branches. The leaves are elliptic-ovate or -obovate, olive-green, glabrous on top and downy beneath. The plant bears small white flowers from May to July, after which come the pea-sized, glossy, red berries that remain on the stems and branches into winter.

Properties and Uses: Bark: Astringent, bitter, febrifuge, tonic. Berries: cathartic, vermifuge. The bark is sometimes mixed with goldenseal to make an infusion for dyspepsia. A decoction of bark is also good for external use as a wash for skin irritations and eruptions. Mixed with cedar apples, the berries have been used to make a medicine for worms. CAUTION: The berries in sufficient quantity can cause poisoning.

Preparation and Dosage:

Infusion or Decoction: Use 1 tsp. root (or berries) to 1 cup water. Take 1 to 2 cups a day, cold.

Infusion for Dyspepsia: Use 2 tsp. powdered bark and 1 tsp. powdered goldenseal with 1 pint boiling water. Take 3 to 4 tbsp. at a time, cold, every 1½ hours.

213   HOLLY (cont.)

(e) (Ilex paraguariensis)

Common Names: Yerba maté, maté, Paraguay tea, yerba.

Medicinal Parts: Leaves, twigs.

Description: Yerba maté is an evergreen shrub or small tree up to 20 feet high, which grows in southern Brazil, Paraguay, and Argentina. Its alternate, elliptic-obovate leaves have a narrowed base and a rounded or bluntly pointed tip; their margins are crenate-serrate. The axillary flowers are whitish and inconspicuous. The fruit is a rounded, reddish berry-like drupe up to ¼ inch in diameter.

Properties and Uses: Depurative, diuretic, stimulant. Maté, the tea made from the plant, is the South American equivalent to coffee in the United States. Charles Darwin called it "the ideal stimulant," and it has been praised as being beneficial for headache, migraine, neuralgia, and insomnia, in addition to its ability to relieve fatigue and stimulate mental and physical energy. It has also been called an excellent "blood purifier." Its stimulant principle is caffeine, but it contains less than coffee or regular tea. Maté may be the answer for the coffee addict who wants to get rid of his coffee nerves without breaking the habit.

214 HOLLYHOCK

(Althaea rosea)

Common Names: Althea rose, malva flowers, rose mallow.

Medicinal Part: Flowers.

Description: Hollyhock is a tall plant indigenous to India and southern Europe but widely cultivated as a garden plant for its flowers. The tall, hairy, unbranched stem bears both leaves and flowers along its length, the large flowers coming in many different colors and having either one or two sets of petals. Flowering time is from July to September.

Properties and Uses: Demulcent, diuretic, emollient. Tea made from hollyhock flowers helps to soothe inflammation in the mouth and throat. A fomentation or vapor bath of the tea may be helpful for earache. Hollyhock flowers are used as an emollient ingredient in various cosmetics.

215 HOPS

(Humulus lupulus)

Medicinal Part: Fruit.

Description: The hop vine is a perennial climbing plant found wild in many places in the world but mostly cultivated in the U.S. Many angular, rough stems grow up to 20 feet long from a branched rootstock. The leaves are rough, opposite, cordate, serrate, and three to five-lobed. The flowers are yellowish-green, the male arranged in hanging panicles, the female in catkins. The name *hops* usually refers to the scaly, conelike fruit that develops from the female flowers.

Properties and Uses: Anodyne, diuretic, febrifuge, hypnotic, sedative, tonic. Hops are most commonly used for their calming effect on the nervous system. Hop tea is recommended for nervous diarrhea, insomnia, and restlessness. It will also help to stimulate appetite, dispel flatulence, and relieve intestinal cramps. It can be usefully combined with fragrant valerian (for antispasmodic properties) for coughs and nervous spasmodic conditions. The cold tea, taken an hour before meals, is particularly good for digestion. Hops also have diuretic properties and can be taken for various problems with water retention and excess uric acid. However, excessive doses or prolonged use can have detrimental effects and should be avoided. A hop pillow is a popular method of overcoming insomnia.

Preparation and Dosage: Hops lose their effectiveness rapidly when stored.

Infusion: Steep 1 tsp. hops in ½ cup water.

Hop Pillow: Sprinkle hops with alcohol and fill a small bag or pillowcase with them.

216   HOREHOUND

(Marrubium vulgare)

Common Names: Hoarhound, marrubium, white horehound.

Medicinal Part: The herb.

Description: Horehound is a perennial plant found in waste places, in upland fields and pastures, and along roadsides in coastal areas of the U.S., Canada, Mexico, and Europe. A fibrous, spindle-shaped rootstock sends up numerous bushy, square, downy stems. The leaves are opposite, petioled, usually wrinkled, roundish-ovate, rough on top, and wooly underneath. The small, white, two-lipped flowers feature a spiny calyx and grow in axillary whorls from June to September.

Properties and Uses: Diaphoretic, diuretic, expectorant, stimulant, tonic. Horehound is above all a remedy for coughing and bronchial problems generally. As an expectorant, it can be taken as a tea, a syrup, or a dilute alcoholic extract for acute and chronic bronchitis, as well as for coughs and hoarseness. Horehound has also been given for typhoid fever and paratyphoid fever. It is said to restore the normal balance of secretions by various organs and glands. Try it also for nervous heart conditions, to calm heart action. Taken warm, the infusion is diaphoretic and diuretic; taken cold, it makes a good stomach tonic. Externally, either the tea or the crushed leaves can be applied for temporary or persistent skin problems.

Preparation and Dosage:

Infusion: Steep 1 tsp. herb in ½ cup water. Take 1 to 1½ cups a day, a mouthful at a time. Sweeten with honey if taken for lung or heart problems.

Syrup: Add a pound of sugar to 1 pint of the infusion.

Juice: Take 1 tsp. fresh juice, two times a day.

Tincture: Take 5 to 40 drops in hot water, as needed.

217   HORSE CHESTNUT

(Aesculus hippocastanum)

Common Names: Buckeye, Spanish chestnut.

Medicinal Parts: Leaves, bark, fruit.

Description: The horse chestnut is a deciduous tree native to southeastern Europe but commonly cultivated in the U.S. and Canada, as well as in Europe and England. The tree grows from 50 to 80 feet high and bears palmately compound leaves with 5 to 7 wedge-shaped, serrate, pointed leaflets. White, red, or yellow flowers appear in panicles from May to June. The fruit is a prickly, green, globular capsule which contains from 1 to 6 shiny, brown seeds.

Properties and Uses: Astringent, expectorant. Horse chestnut has shown good results when used for varicose veins, leg ulcers, hemorrhoids, recurrent neuralgia, and sunburn. The bark is useful for diarrhea and the fruit for bronchitis and respiratory catarrh. In European folk medicine, carrying the fruit in one's pocket is believed to be good for preventing and curing arthritis. CAUTION: The leaves, seeds, and green capsule shells sometimes cause poisoning if taken in sufficient amounts. Roasting the seeds seems to destroy the poison in them.

Preparation and Dosage:

Infusion: Steep 1 tsp. bark (from branches) in 1 cup water.

Powder: Take ½ tsp. for diarrhea, varicose veins, and hemorrhoids. For catarrh, take ¼ to ½ tsp., two times a day.

Bath Additive: Boil 2 to 2½ pounds chopped fruit in water and add the resulting liquid to bath water.

218   HORSERADISH

(Armoracia lapathifolia)

Medicinal Part: Root.

Description: Horseradish is a perennial plant native to southeastern Europe and western Asia, and occasionally found wild but usually cultivated in other parts of the world. The long, white, cylindrical or tapering root produces a 2- to 3-foot-high stem in the second year. The large basal leaves are lanceolate with scalloped edges; the stem leaves are much smaller, sessile, lanceolate, and serrate to entire. A panicle of numerous white flowers appears during June and July.

Properties and Uses: Diuretic, rubefacient, stomachic. The diuretic properties of fresh horseradish make it useful for gouty and rheumatic problems and also for bladder infections. For the latter, take 3 to 4 tbsp. a day of grated horseradish with wine vinegar and some grape sugar (dextrose). For colitis and intestinal problems due to putrefaction, 15 to 20 drops of juice taken three times a day between meals will help. For catarrhal lung problems, coughs, and asthma, take horseradish combined with honey and raw sugar. Externally, horseradish is used as an irritant to stimulate blood flow; it can also be made into a poultice for rheumatism and into a bath additive for chilblains. CAUTION: Do not take large quantities of horseradish at one time. Stop taking it if diarrhea or night sweating occurs.

Preparation and Dosage: Only undried horseradish is effective. The root can be preserved fresh for months in a refrigerator or packed in damp sand and kept in a cool place.

Vinegar: Cover finely grated horseradish with vinegar and let stand for 10 days. Take 1 tsp., two or three times a day, well diluted with water. This can also be applied externally.

Poultice: Spread fresh, grated root on a linen cloth. Lay on the affected area, with cloth against the skin, until a burning sensation is felt.

Syrup: Steep 1 tsp. root in ½ cup boiling-hot water in a covered pot for 2 hours. Strain and add sugar until a syrupy consistency is reached.

NOTE: Horseradish taken in any form can be made more palatable with sugar or honey.

219 HORSEWEED

(Erigeron canadensis or
Conyza canadensis)

Common Names: Pride weed, bitterweed, bloodstaunch, butterweed, Canada fleabane, colt's tail, mare's tail.

Medicinal Part: Leaves or plant.

Description: Horseweed is a native North American annual plant found also in South America and Europe. It generally inhabits waste places, roadsides, fields, and meadows all over North America except the extreme northern parts. The grooved, bristly, and hairy stem bears alternate, entire or serrate leaves that are oblanceolate and petioled near the bottom of the plant, narrow and sessile near the top. Numerous small, green and white flower heads appear in panicled terminal clusters from June to November.

Properties and Uses: Astringent, diuretic, styptic. Horseweed's astringent and styptic properties make it particularly suitable for diarrhea, dysentery, internal hemorrhage, and hemorrhoids. American Indians boiled the root to make a tea for menstrual irregularities. As a diuretic, it has also been recommended for bladder problems and rheumatism.

Preparation and Dosage:

Infusion: Steep 1 level tsp. leaves or plant in 1 cup water for 30 minutes. Take 1 to 2 cups a day.

Enema: Steep 1 tsp. leaves or plant in 1 qt. boiling-hot water for 20 minutes. Use hot (110–112°).

220 HOUND'S-TONGUE

(Cynoglossum officinale)

Common Names: Dog-bur, dog's tongue, gypsy flower, sheep-lice, woolmat.

Medicinal Parts: Root, herb.

Description: Hound's-tongue is a biennial weed found in waste places, in sandy, rocky soil, and along roadsides in the states north and east from Montana and Kansas, as well as in Europe. The erect stem, 1 to 3 feet high, bears alternate, sessile, lanceolate leaves that are downy on both sides. The basal leaves are similar but have petioles and are shaped somewhat like a dog's tongue. The reddish-purple flowers have funnel-shaped corollas and grow in curving racemes from May to September. The bruised plant has a disagreeable, mousy odor.

Properties and Uses: Astringent. Hound's-tongue is primarily used for diarrhea. It has also been used externally for burns, bruises, and difficult wounds, but its effectiveness has been questioned. The bruised herb can be used as first aid for insect bites. CAUTION: Hound's-tongue is weakly poisonous and should be taken with care. It may also cause dermatitis in susceptible individuals.

Preparation and Dosage: Use the dried root or herb. Gather the root in spring, the herb in early summer.

Infusion: Steep 1 tsp. dried root or herb in 1 cup water. Take in the course of a day.

221 VIRGINIA MOUSE-EAR
(Cynoglossum morrisoni)

NOTE: Virginia mouse-ear *(Cynoglossum morrisoni)* is a related annual plant similar in appearance to hound's-tongue but with white or light blue flowers. The root is an effective astringent.

222 HOUSELEEK
(Sempervivum tectorum)

Common Names: Aaron's rod, bullock's eye, hens and chickens, Jupiter's eye, Jupiter's beard, liveforever, thunder plant.

Medicinal Part: Leaves.

Description: Houseleek is a perennial European plant that is found cultivated and also growing wild in dry, stony soils, on walls, and even on the roofs of houses. The fibrous rootstock produces a thick rosette of fleshy, spinypointed leaves and an erect, round stem covered with small, scalelike leaves. The stem is topped by a cluster of starlike, rose-colored flowers during July and August.

Properties and Uses: Astringent, refrigerant, vulnerary. The fresh, bruised leaves make a cooling application for the forehead during feverish illnesses and can also be used for burns, insect bites, and other skin problems. The juice pressed from the leaves (or the leaves themselves, sliced in half) has been used for warts, freckles, and other skin blemishes. An infusion of the leaves can be taken internally, or a decoction used externally, for shingles, skin problems in general, hemorrhoids, worms, and uterine neuralgia.

Preparation and Dosage: Use only fresh leaves.

Infus.on or Decoction: Use 1 tsp. leaves with 1 cup water. Take 1 cup a day.

Tincture: Take 5 to 20 drops at a time (can also be applied to warts and skin blemishes).

223 HYSSOP

(Hyssopus officinalis)

Medicinal Part: The herb.

Description: Hyssop is a bushy, evergreen plant introduced into the warmer parts of the U.S. from southern Europe. Once widely cultivated for medicinal uses, it is now grown mostly as an ornamental shrub. The plant consists of several square, branched, downy stems which are woody at the bottom and bear opposite, sessile, glabrous to hairy, linear-lanceolate leaves. The rose-colored to bluish-purple flowers grow in successive axillary whorls at the tops of the branches and stems from June to October.

Properties and Uses: Astringent, carminative, emmenagogue, expectorant, stimulant, stomachic, tonic. Hyssop is used in essentially the same way as sage, with which it is sometimes combined to make a gargle for sore throat. Hyssop tea can be used for poor digestion, breast and lung problems, coughs due to colds, nose and throat infections, mucous congestion in the intestines, flatulence, scrofula, dropsy, and jaundice. The decoction is said to help relieve inflammations, and it can also be used as a wash for burns, bruises, and skin irritations, and as a gargle for sore throat or chronic catarrh. Apply the crushed leaves directly to bruises or to wounds to cure infection and promote healing.

Preparation and Dosage: Do not use continuously for extended periods.

Infusion: Steep 1 tsp. dried herbs in ½ cup water. Take ½ to 1½ cups a day, a mouthful at a time. For breast and lung problems, sweeten with honey if desired.

Decoction: Use 1 tsp. herb with 1 cup water. Take 1 to 2 cups a day.

Poultice: Soak the fresh herb in boiling water for 15 minutes and place on a cloth for application.

224 ICELAND MOSS

(Cetraria islandica)

Common Name: Eryngo-leaved liverwort.

Medicinal Part: The plant.

Description: Iceland moss is a foliaceous lichen found in cool, damp places in Europe, Great Britain, Iceland, and the northern parts of North America and Asia. The thallus, or body of the plant, is branched and erect or spreading, reaching a height of 2 to 3 inches. It varies in color from olive-green to grayish-white and is sometimes flecked with red.

Properties and Uses: Anti-emetic, demulcent, galactagogue, tonic. Iceland moss tea can be used for respiratory catarrh, gastroenteritis, anemia, and regulation of gastric acid. It also serves to stimulate the flow of milk but should not be used if the breasts or nipples are inflamed. It is useful too for coughs, hoarseness, and bronchitis. Iceland moss is sometimes given for tuberculosis, since it acts to dissolve mucous congestion and also hinders the growth of the tubercle bacillus. The plant makes a nourishing food, but it must be boiled for a long time to make it palatable. CAUTION: Use in excessive doses or for prolonged periods can cause gastrointestinal irritation and liver problems.

Preparation and Dosage: Gather Iceland moss in dry weather from May to September.

Decoction: Boil 1 tsp. plant in ½ cup water for an extended period, adding more water if necessary. Take 1 to 2 cups a day.

Double Tea: Add 1 tsp. plant to ½ cup cold water and let stand overnight, then warm slightly and strain. Put the soaked plant in cold water and let stand all day; in the evening, bring quickly to a boil and strain. Drink each tea, a mouthful at a time, after it is made.

225 IMPERIAL MASTERWORT

(Imperatoria ostruthium)

Common Name: Masterwort.

Medicinal Part: Rootstock.

Description: Imperial masterwort is a perennial plant that is cultivated and also found wild in European mountain meadows.

The ringed rootstock is dirty yellow to brown outside, white and milky inside. It produces an erect, glabrous, hollow stem bearing leathery, alternate leaves which are ternately or biternately divided into ovate, serrate segments. The petioles are dilated at the base. Flat, compound umbels of white flowers grow from the leaf axils during July and August.

Properties and Uses: Calmative, diaphoretic, diuretic, emmenagogue, febrifuge, stimulant. A weak decoction of imperial masterwort is good for catarrhal problems, digestive difficulties and lack of appetite, uterine cramps, menstrual problems, mucous congestion, gout, and rheumatism. Old herbals praise it also for effectiveness against bronchitis and fever.

Preparation and Dosage: The rootstock can be used fresh or dried.

Infusion: Steep 1 to 2 tsp. rootstock in 1 cup water for 10 minutes; take 1 cup a day.

Decoction: Use 1 tsp. rootstock with ½ cup water; boil lightly and steep about 3 minutes, then strain. Take ½ to 1½ cups a day, a mouthful at a time, unsweetened.

Powder: Take ⅔ tsp., three times a day.

226 INDIAN CORN

(Zea mays)

Common Names: Corn, maize.

Medicinal Part: Styles (corn silk).

Description: Corn is familiar enough not to need description.

Properties and Uses: Demulcent, diuretic. Corn silk makes a good diuretic preparation, which is sometimes helpful in such urinary problems as cystitis, pyelitis, and oliguria and also in edemous conditions. If kept too long without being completely dried, however, corn silk takes on purgative properties. For those who want to lose weight, corn silk makes an effective and harmless dieting food. The tea can also be used as a non-irritating enema.

Preparation and Dosage: Corn silk can be used fresh or dried.

Infusion: Steep 1 tsp. corn silk in ½ cup boiling-hot water for a few minutes and strain. Take 1 tbsp. every 2 or 3 hours, warm or lukewarm.

Tincture: Take 15 to 30 drops in water, three or four times a day.

227   INDIAN PIPE

(Monotropa uniflora)

Common Names: Birdnest, convulsion-root, corpse plant, fairy smoke, fit plant, ghost flower, pipe plant.

Medicinal Part: Root.

Description: Indian pipe is a unique perennial plant found in dark, rich woodlands in the temperate and warmer parts of North America. A mass of dark, brittle, saprophytic roots produces the ivory-white, waxy stem growing 4 to 10 inches high and covered with scaly bracts. The stem is topped by a single, nodding, white, pipe-bowl-shaped flower which turns black when bruised.

Properties and Uses: Antispasmodic, nervine, sedative, tonic. Indian pipe root makes a good remedy for spasms, fainting spells, and various nervous conditions and may be helpful in remittent and intermittent fever. Mixed with fennel seed, it makes a good eyewash and vaginal douche.

Preparation and Dosage:

Infusion: Use 1 tsp. Indian pipe root and 1 tsp. fennel seed with 1 pint boiling water. Steep for 20 minutes and strain.

228   INDIAN TURNIP

(Arisaema triphyllum)

Common Names: Bog-onion, dragonroot, jack-in-the-pulpit, wakerobin, wild turnip.

Medicinal Part: Rootstock (corm).

Description: Indian turnip is a perennial plant that grows mainly in moist woods in the states east from Louisiana, Kansas, and Minnesota. The rootstock is a turnip-shaped, dark, rough, acrid corm, from which grows a single flower-stalk sheathed at the bottom by the footstalks of the plant's two leaves. The leaves are ternately divided, the leaflets ovate or oblong-ovate, and pointed. The greenish-yellow flowers grow in a thick, fleshy spike which is hooded by a green and purplish-brown bract called a spathe. Flowering time is from April to June.

Properties and Uses: Acrid, expectorant. Indian turnip was used in American medicine during the nineteenth century for asthma, rheumatism, and whooping cough. Since the fresh root is dangerously irritating to mucous tissue and the dried root is inactive, the roots were used partially dried. Among American Indians, the Pawnee applied the powdered root to the head to cure headache, and the Hopis drank it in water to induce temporary or permanent sterility. Thorough drying, boiling, or heating makes the root edible.

Preparation and Dosage: The fresh or partially dried root is too dangerous for use without medical supervision.

229 IRISH MOSS

(Chondrus crispus)

Common Names: Carrageen, pearl moss.

Medicinal Part: The plant.

Description: Irish moss is a seaweed that grows among submerged rocks off the coast of France and, naturally, Ireland. The plant consists of a greenish frond that turns purple when dried.

Properties and Uses: Demulcent, mucilaginous. Among the people who live where it grows, Irish moss is considered an excellent remedy for tuberculosis, coughs, bronchitis, and intestinal problems. It also makes a nourishing food for those recovering from tuberculosis and other illnesses. Medicinally, it is generally used in the form of a decoction.

Preparation and Dosage: The plant is used dried.

Decoction: Use 1 tsp. plant with 1 cup water. Take 1 to 2 cups a day.

230 IRONWEED

(Vernonia fasciculata)

Medicinal Part: Rootstock.

Description: Ironweed is a coarse, perennial plant found in woods, on prairies, and along river- and streambanks in states west of Ohio. The simple, glabrous stem grows 2 to 10 feet high and bears alternate, ascending, purplish-green, linear or oblong-lanceolate leaves. The reddish-purple or purple flowers grow in dense cymes of short-peduncled heads from July to September.

Properties and Uses: Bitter tonic. The rootstock of ironweed is taken in the form of a powder or a decoction primarily to stimulate appetite and promote digestion.

Decoction: Use 1 tsp. rootstock with 1 cup water. Take 1 to 2 cups a day, ½ to 1 hour before meals.

231 JALAP
(Ipomoea jalapa)

Medicinal Part: Root.

Description: Jalap is an annual, herbaceous vine found in one area of Mexico near Xalapa. The tuberous root produces several brownish, twining stems which bear petioled, cordate leaves with a soft point. The purple flowers have a long, funnel-shaped corolla.

Properties and Uses: Cathartic. Jalap is used as a purgative for complete and rapid emptying of the bowels. It should not be used when intestinal irritation is present.

Preparation and Dosage:

Decoction: Use 1 tsp. root with 1 cup water. Take 1 cup a day, a mouthful at a time.

232 JASMINE
(Jasminum officinale)

Medicinal Part: Flowers.

Description: Jasmine is a vinelike plant indigenous to the warm parts of the eastern hemisphere and now cultivated also in gardens in the southern U.S. Jasmine has opposite, dark green, pinnate leaves and sweet-smelling white flowers.

Properties and Uses: Calmative. According to old herbals, jasmine flowers calm the nerves. However, others suggest that the scent arouses erotic interests, and a few drops of jasmine oil (if you can afford it) massaged on the body with some almond oil may help overcome frigidity. In India, jasmine is used as a remedy for snakebite, and the leaves are used for eye problems.

Preparation and Dosage:

Infusion: Steep 1 to 2 tsp. jasmine flowers in 1 cup water. Take 1 cup a day.

233 JIMSON WEED
(Datura stramonium)

Common Names: Devil's apple, devil's trumpet, Jamestown weed, mad-apple, nightshade, Peru-apple, stinkweed, stinkwort, stramonium, thorn-apple.

Medicinal Parts: Leaves, seed.

Description: Jimson weed is a fetid, annual plant found in waste places, pastures, gardens, and roadsides all over North and South America and in many other parts of the world. A large, whitish root produces the round, glabrous, yellowish-green, branching stem which grows from 1 to 5 feet high. The leaves are alternate, dark green above and lighter beneath, ovate, and irregularly incised and toothed. Large, white, funnel-shaped flowers grow on short peduncles in the axils of the branches from June to September. The fruit is an ovate, prickly capsule containing many black seeds.

Properties and Uses: Anodyne, antispasmodic, hypnotic, narcotic. Jimson weed is a dangerous plant in inexperienced hands, and an overdose is likely to be fatal. A tincture is sometimes given for spasmodic coughing, chronic laryngitis, and asthma. The leaves have been made into cigarettes for smokers with asthma and other respiratory problems. In South America, jimson weed is believed to have aphrodisiac powers.

Preparation and Dosage: Do not use without medical supervision.

JUNIPER

(Juniperus communis)
(Prickly juniper,
Juniperus oxycedrus)

Medicinal Parts: Berries, new twigs.

Description: Juniper is an evergreen shrub found in dry, rocky soil in North America from the Arctic circle to Mexico, as well as in Europe and Asia. The plant usually grows from 2 to 6 feet high, but may reach a height of 25 feet. The bark is chocolate-brown tinged with red. The needle-shaped leaves have white stripes on top and are a shiny yellow-green beneath. They occur on the branches in whorled groups of three. Yellow male flowers occur in whorls on one plant, green female flowers consisting of three contiguous, upright seed buds on another plant. Flowering time is April to June. The fruit is a berry-like cone which is green the first year and ripens to a bluish-black or dark purple color in the second year.

Properties and Uses: Antiseptic, carminative, diuretic, rubefacient, stomachic, tonic. Juniper is normally taken internally by eating the berries or making a tea from them. It is useful for digestive problems resulting from an underproduction of hydrochloric acid, and is also helpful for gastrointestinal infections, inflammations, and cramps. In large doses, or with prolonged use it can irritate the kidneys and urinary passages; therefore it is not recommended for those with kidney problems or with kid problems (i.e., pregnant women). The berries have also been recommended for eliminating excess water and for gouty and rheumatic pains. As a spice, they are often used to enhance flavor, stimulate appetite, and counteract flatulence. Juniper oil, derived from the berries, penetrates the skin readily and is good for bone-joint problems; but the pure oil is irritating and, in large quantities, can cause inflammation and blisters. Breathed in a vapor bath, it is useful for bronchitis and infection in the lungs. Juniper tar, or oil of cade, is produced by destructive distillation of the wood of another species *(Juniperus oxycedrus)* and is used for skin problems and for loss of hair.

Preparation and Dosage:

Infusion: Steep 1 tsp. crushed berries in ½ cup water for 5 to 10 minutes in a covered pot and strain. Take ½ to 1 cup a day, a mouthful at a time. If desired, sweeten with 1 tsp. honey (or raw sugar) unless used for gastrointestinal problems.

Jam or Syrup: Adults take 1 tbsp., two times a day, in water, tea, or milk. Children take 1 tsp., three times a day. Take an hour before meals as an appetizer.

Dried Berries: Chew a few a day.

235   KHUS-KHUS

(Vetiveria zizanioides)

Common Name: Vetiver.

Medicinal Part: Root.

Description: Khus-khus is a tall perennial grass which grows in large clumps in tropical and subtropical Asia and the East Indies; it is also cultivated in the southeastern U.S. The erect stem, growing up to 7 or 8 feet high, bears long, narrow, glabrous leaves that are rough on both sides and somewhat stiff. The flowers grow in paired spikelets in a narrow panicle from 6 to 12 inches long.

Properties and Uses: Aromatic, stimulant, tonic. Most of the uses for the aromatic roots of khus-khus are nonmedical (see Part 3), but a tea made from the roots can be taken as a generally stimulating and tonic drink.

236   KIDNEY VETCH

(Anthyllis vulneraria)

Common Names: Ladies' fingers, lamb's toes, staunchwort, woundwort.

Medicinal Part: Flowering tops.

Description: Kidney vetch is a European perennial plant found in limestone soils, dry meadows, hills, and railroad embankments. The procumbent or erect stem grows from a strong taproot to a length of 8 to 16 inches. The basal leaves are petioled and simple or pinnate; the stem leaves are odd-pinnate, the leaflets lanceolate with the odd leaflet larger than the others. The yellow flowers are arranged in ovoid or subglobose, clover-like heads, appearing from May to September.

Properties and Uses: Astringent. A warm infusion of kidney vetch can be used to wash wounds, which are then covered with a poultice which is renewed every hour. The tea is often given to children as a mild purgative, and it sometimes helps to allay vomiting in children.

Preparation and Dosage: Kidney vetch can be used fresh or dried.

Infusion: Steep 1 tsp. flower heads in ½ cup water. Take 1 cup a day, sweetened with honey.

237   KNOTWEED

(a) (Polygonum aviculare)

Common Names: Knotgrass, beggarweed, bird knotgrass, birdweed, cow grass, common knotweed, crawlgrass, doorweed, ninety-knot, pigweed.

Medicinal Part: Flowering herb.

Description: Knotgrass is an annual plant found in waste places and cultivated soils all over the world. The creeping, prostrate stem bears alternate, sessile, lanceolate leaves that narrow at the base, which is covered by brownish, sheathing, knotlike stipules. The axillary flowers, growing all along the stem, are green and white or green with pink or purple margins. Flowering time is from June to October.

Properties and Uses: Astringent, diuretic, hemostatic, vulnerary. Knotgrass is recommended for diarrhea, dysentery, and enteritis. It is also said to be good for bronchitis, jaundice, and lung problems. As a blood coagulant, it is useful for all forms of internal bleeding, including stomach ulcers. Knotgrass has been successfully used for cholera infantum, a serious condition with simultaneous vomiting and diarrhea in infants. Taken regularly, the tea or the tincture dissolves gravel and stones.

Preparation and Dosage:

Infusion: Steep 4 tsp. flowering herb in 1 cup water for 5 minutes. Take 1 to 1½ cups a day, a mouthful at a time, as needed.

Decoction: Use 4 tsp. flowering herb with 1 cup water. Take a mouthful at a time, as needed. For stomach and intestinal problems, take 1 to 1½ cups a day; for lung problems 1½ cups a day.

Tincture: Take 10 to 20 drops knotgrass with 5 to 20 drops shave grass in water, three or more times a day.

(b) (Polygonum hydropiper and Polygonum punctatum)

Common Names: (P. hydropiper): Smartweed, water pepper. *(P. punctatum):* Water smartweed.

Medicinal Part: The herb.

Description: These two very similar plants are both annuals which grow to a height of 1 or 2 feet. Smartweed is found in damp soils, mostly in the central and northeastern states; water smartweed inhabits wet places, swamps, and shorelines all over North America. The erect, reddish or greenish stems bear alternate, lanceolate, acrid leaves with bristly margins in the case of smartweed and dry, brown margins in water smartweed. Small, green flowers margined with white, pink, or yellow grow in slender, drooping racemes from July to September.

Properties and Uses: Astringent, diaphoretic, diuretic, rubefacient. A cold extract of the smartweeds can be taken for coughs and colds and can be applied externally for skin problems. The fresh, crushed herb is a good substitute for a mustard plaster as a rubefacient and to relieve the pain of tumors. A strong decoction has been used for hemorrhoids and scabies and as a gargle for toothache and problems in the larynx. The fresh juice, pure or thinned with water, is effective in drawing pus out of sores.

Preparation and Dosage: CAUTION: The acrid juice can cause both internal and external inflammation. Professionally made preparations should be used, and with medical supervision.

KNOTWEED
(cont.)

(c) (Polygonum persicaria)

Common Names: Lady's thumb, doorweed, heartease, heartweed, pinkweed, redleg, spotted knotweed.

Medicinal Part: The herb.

Description: Lady's thumb is an annual plant that grows in waste places and damp soils all over the world. The erect, smooth, glabrous, branching stem grows 1½ to 2 feet high and bears alternate, lanceolate, somewhat rough leaves that have a dark, triangular mark near the center. Dense, cylindrical spikes of greenish, magenta, or pink flowers appear from June to October.

Properties and Uses: Astringent, diuretic, rubefacient. In European folk medicine, lady's thumb is used for arthritis, lung problems, diarrhea, jaundice, and chronic eczema. The juice is sometimes applied to wounds, bruises, and cuts; but it is irritating to sensitive tissue and must be used with care.

Preparation and Dosage:

Infusion: Steep 1 tsp. herb in 1 cup water. Take 1 to 2 cups a day.

241 KOLA TREE
(Cola acuminata)

Common Names: Caffeine nut, kola nut, guru nut.

Medicinal Part: Seed.

Description: The kola tree grows wild in West Africa and is cultivated in tropical South America and in the West Indies. The fruit is a yellowish-brown, woody pod that contains several large, flattened, white or red nuts.

Properties and Uses: Stimulant, tonic. Kola nuts contain more caffeine than coffee berries and are taken as a stimulant to prevent fatigue. They also act as a tonic agent for the heart and are sometimes useful in relieving pains of neuralgia and headache.

Preparation and Dosage:

Infusion: Steep 1 tsp. kola nuts in 1 cup water. Take 1 cup a day.

Powder: The powder can be taken conveniently in size 00 gelatin capsules, one or two at a time as needed.

242 KOUSSO

(Hagenia abyssinica)

Medicinal Part: Flowers.

Description: Don't go out looking for a kousso tree unless you happen to be visiting the tablelands of northeastern Ethiopia. The flowers are small and greenish-purple.

Properties and Uses: Anthelmintic. Taken in proper doses, kousso flowers have no effect except to eliminate tapeworms. Excessive doses may cause nausea or vomiting.

Preparation and Dosage: Kousso flowers are obtained in powder form.

Infusion: Add ½ oz. powder to 1 cup warm water. If the worms have not been expelled after 4 hours, take 1 tbsp. castor oil.

243 LADY'S MANTLE

(Alchemilla vulgaris)

Medicinal Part: The herb.

Description: Lady's mantle is a perennial plant found in damp places and in dry, shady woods in eastern North America, Greenland, Europe, and northern Asia. The stem, 4 to 18 inches high, is at first green or blue-green, turning later to reddish or brownish, and it may be hairy or glabrous, depending on the location. The mostly basal, rounded leaves are palmately 7- to 9-lobed and finely toothed. The small, green flowers grow in loose panicles from May to October.

Properties and Uses: Astringent, febrifuge, tonic. Lady's mantle is taken internally for lack of appetite, rheumatism, stomach ailments, diarrhea, enteritis, and menstrual problems. It also tends to coagulate blood and is useful for internal bleeding and as a mouth rinse after having teeth pulled. Externally, lady's mantle makes a good douche for leucorrhea, and a wash or poultice for wounds.

Preparation and Dosage: Gather the plant after the dew has dried, from June to August.

Infusion: Steep 4 tsp. dried herb or leaves in 1 cup water for 10 minutes. Take 1 to 1½ cups a day. For external uses, double the amount of herb or leaves.

244   SILVERY LADY'S MANTLE
(Alchemilla alpina)

NOTE: Silvery lady's mantle (*Alchemilla alpina*), a species found at higher elevations, can be used like lady's mantle and also for flatulence and gas problems. Make a decoction by boiling 1 tbsp. fresh or dried herb in 1 cup water for 5 minutes. Take 1 cup a day.

245   LARCH

(Larix europaea)

Common Names: Common larch, European larch.

Medicinal Parts: Bark, resin, young shoots, needles.

Description: The common larch is a European tree found in mountainous areas and in coniferous forests; in America it is often planted as an ornamental tree. The larch bears light green needles in clusters of 15 to 20 (fewer on young shoots) and is unusual among members of the pine family in shedding its needles every year. The red or reddish-brown flowers, which emerge in spring before the leaves, are borne in catkins. The scaly cones are bright red when young, turning to dark red and finally to chestnut-brown when mature. The cones stay on the tree after the needles have fallen.

Properties and Uses: Anthelmintic, diuretic, laxative, vulnerary. A cold extract of larch bark has diuretic properties, and the powdered bark can be used on purulent and difficult wounds to promote their healing. A light decoction of fresh needles and young shoots can be added to bath water to make a stimulating bath. Boring into the tree releases resin from which "Venice turpentine" is obtained. In European folk medicine, Venice turpentine is used for innumerable internal and external ailments. Internally, doses of 5 to 8 drops are taken for tapeworm, bloody diarrhea, and for suppressed menstruation. Externally, it is applied to wounds, sores, and skin problems. In either case, it is important to use only small amounts, since even moderate amounts can cause kidney damage internally and swelling and blisters externally.

Preparation and Dosage:

Compress: Soak a cloth in hot water and wring out. Moisten with a small amount of Venice turpentine and apply to the affected part. Remove after 30 minutes and do not repeat until the next day.

Venice Turpentine: For internal use, mix 5 to 8 drops with honey.

246   LARKSPUR

(*Delphinium consolida*)

Common Names: Branching larkspur, knight's spur, lark heel, lark's claw, staggerweed, stavesacre.

Medicinal Part: Flowering plant.

Description: Larkspur is an annual plant found in rich or dry woods and on rocky slopes throughout the U.S. but most commonly in the western states; it is also common in Europe. A slender taproot produces the leafy, branching stem which reaches a height of 2 to 4 feet and bears both petioled and sessile, finely divided leaves. The blue or purple flowers feature a spur projecting backward from the upper part and grow in terminal racemes from June to August.

Properties and Uses: Anthelmintic, purgative. Because of its relatively weak action, larkspur is not much used medicinally today. Poisoning is possible if large quantities are consumed; the seeds and the young plants are dangerous.

Preparation and Dosage: Gather the flowering plant before seed formation.

Infusion: Steep 1 tsp. dried plant in 1 cup water for 5 minutes. Take 1 cup a day.

247 LAUREL

(*Laurus nobilis*)

Common Names: Bay, bay laurel, bay tree, Grecian laurel, Indian bay, Roman laurel, sweet bay.

Medicinal Parts: Leaves, fruit.

Description: Laurel is an evergreen bush or tree found both wild and cultivated around the Mediterranean Sea. Bay leaves are leathery, lanceolate, and pointed at both ends. Whitish flowers grow in axillary clusters during April and May, developing later into black, egg-shaped berries.

Properties and Uses: Astringent, carminative, digestive, stomachic. Bay oil, pressed from the berries and leaves, can be used in salves and liniment for rheumatism, bruises, and skin problems. Both fruit and leaves also stimulate the digestive apparatus. A decoction of fruit or leaves, made into a paste with honey or syrup, can be applied to the chest for colds and other chest problems.

248 LAVENDER

(*Lavandula vera or L. officinalis*)

Medicinal Parts: Flowers, leaves.

Description: Lavender is a Mediterranean shrub which is cultivated for its aromatic flowers in the U.S. and Europe. The stems, growing 1 or 2 feet high, are gray-green and angular, with flaking bark. The gray-green leaves are opposite, sessile, downy, and lanceolate to oblong-linear. The lilac-colored, tubular flowers are arranged in successive whorls up the stem. Flowering time is July to September.

Properties and Uses: Antispasmodic, carminative, cholagogue, diuretic, sedative, stimulant, stomachic, tonic. Lavender is normally taken or used in the form of an oil derived from the flowers by distillation with water. It is used for flatulence, migraine headache, fainting, and dizziness. It also has some antiseptic properties and is useful against putrefactive bacteria in the intestines. Lavender oil also makes a stimulating, tonic embrocation. In the absence of the oil, an infusion of the leaves can be used instead; and a decoction of the leaves is a useful remedy for stomach problems, nausea and vomiting.

Preparation and Dosage: Gather the leaves before flowering.

Infusion: Steep 1 tsp. leaves in ½ cup water. Take ½ to 1 cup a day.

Oil: Take 5 drops on a sugar cube, two times a day.

249   LEEK

(Allium porrum)

Medicinal Parts: Bulb, lower stem, leaves.

Description: Leek is an annual, or sometimes perennial, plant that is generally found in cultivation. Its linear leaves dilate at the bottom into leaf sheaths that surround the stem. The round stem grows from a slightly bulging bulb and is topped by a globular, umbellate cluster of white to light red flowers, with some small bulbs growing among the blossoms. Flowering time is June and July.

Properties and Uses: Leek has about the same properties as garlic, but to a lesser degree. It also stimulates appetite and helps to relieve congestion in the respiratory passages. Leek makes a good, non-irritating diuretic. The crushed leaves can be used externally to ease the sting of insect bites.

Preparation and Dosage: Eat leeks lightly steamed or fresh as a salad.

250   LEMON

(Citrus limon)

Medicinal Part: Fruit.

Description: Lemons grow on trees, particularly in California and Florida. The rest is equally well known.

Properties and Uses: Astringent, refrigerant. Lemon juice is a popular home remedy for numerous ailments, particularly colds, coughs, and sore throat. It is sometimes taken too for headaches and rheumatism. Externally, lemon juice can be used on sunburn, warts, and corns, and it is currently enjoying a revival of interest as a hair rinse and facial astringent. Lemon's vitamin C and astringency also make lemon powder useful to stop bleeding in wounds.

Preparation and Dosage: Take lemon juice straight or diluted with water, as needed, preferably unsweetened. For coughs and colds, add honey (and some liquor, if you are inclined that way). For a cold, take a hot bath and go to bed. Before falling asleep, have a cup of hot lemon juice (1 lemon) and water in which you have dissolved a tablespoon of honey and two tablespoonsful of liquor. You'll wake the next morning with your cold gone—or at least considerably better. For persistent coughing—take a teaspoon of honey with fresh lemon juice squeezed over it. Hold in your mouth and swallow slowly. Unlike drug cough medicines, you can use this as frequently as you like. The juice of a lemon mixed with a pint of warm water can be used as a retention enema for acute hemorrhoids; retain for 5 minutes. Lemon juice in hot water is said to relieve stomach distress and dizziness. The juice of a lemon in a glass of warm water upon arising is a good habit to promote regularity.

251   LETTUCE

(a) (Lactuca sativa)

Common Name: Common lettuce, garden lettuce.

Medicinal Parts: Juice, leaves.

Description: Everyone is familiar with common lettuce as it is available in the supermarket, but this is the plant picked before it is fully grown. When allowed to mature, lettuce develops a tall stem with alternate leaves and panicled heads of yellow flowers. Flowering time is June to August.

Properties and Uses: Anodyne, antispasmodic, expectorant, sedative. When allowed to go to seed, garden lettuce and several other varieties contain a milky juice that has narcotic effects. In common lettuce, it is a harmless substance which can be used as a calming agent for insomnia and various nervous conditions. It is also helpful for coughs, asthma, and cramps. Although salad lettuce is picked before the juice develops, eating a few leaves before going to bed may be helpful for insomnia. A decoction of the leaves also makes a good skin wash.

Preparation and Dosage: Since lettuce loses its medicinal value rapidly after being picked, use it as fresh as possible.

LETTUCE (cont.)

(b) (*Lactuca virosa*)

Common Names: Prickly lettuce, acrid lettuce, poison lettuce, wild lettuce.

Medicinal Parts: Juice, leaves.

Description: Prickly lettuce is a biennial plant that grows a leafy, round stem from 2 to 7 feet high in its second year. The leaves are alternate, dentate, and oblong or oblong-lanceolate. Yellow flower heads grow in an open panicle. The whole plant is filled with milky juice.

Properties and Uses: Anodyne, antispasmodic, hypnotic, narcotic, sedative. The milky juice, known as lactucarium when dried, was once commonly used to induce sleep and to treat nervous disorders, and sometimes for whooping cough and bronchial problems. American Indian women took a tea made from the leaves to stimulate the flow of milk. Some medical people believe that the effects produced by lettuce are psychological and result from the similarities of appearance and taste between the juice of lettuce and that of the opium poppy.

Preparation and Dosage: Prickly lettuce is much more potent than garden lettuce. Do not use without medical supervision.

253 LICORICE

(*Glycyrrhiza glabra*)

Common Names: Licorice root, sweet licorice, sweet wood.

Medicinal Part: Rootstock.

Description: Licorice is a perennial plant found wild in southern and central Europe and parts of Asia, and cultivated elsewhere. The woody rootstock is wrinkled and brown on the outside, yellow on the inside, and tastes sweet. The stem, which is round on the lower part and angular higher up, bears alternate, odd-pinnate leaves with 3 to 7 pairs of ovate, dark green leaflets. Axillary racemes of yellowish or purplish flowers appear from June to August, depending on location.

Properties and Uses: Demulcent, diuretic, expectorant, laxative. Licorice is primarily used in medicine for bronchial problems, coughs, hoarseness, mucous congestion, etc. It can also be taken for stomach problems, such as peptic ulcers, and for bladder and kidney ailments. A strong decoction makes a good laxative for children and may also help to reduce fever. Add licorice to other medicines to make them more palatable.

Preparation and Dosage:

Infusion or Decoction: Use 1 tsp. rootstock with 1 cup water. Take 1 cup a day.

254   LILY OF THE VALLEY

(Convallaria majalis)

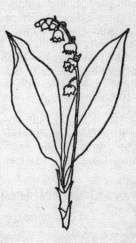

Common Names: May lily, May bells.

Medicinal Part: The plant.

Description: Lily of the valley is a perennial plant native to Eurasia but commonly grown in gardens in the U.S. and Canada, from where it sometimes escapes into the neighboring countryside. A slender, creeping rootstock produces two oblong-elliptic, pointed, basal leaves up to 1 foot long. Their bases sheathe the bottom of the flower stalk, which bears at the top a one-sided raceme of white, bell-shaped flowers. Flowering time is from early spring into June.

Properties and Uses: Antispasmodic, cardiac, diuretic, laxative. Lily of the valley is sometimes given for neurasthenia, apoplexy, epilepsy, and dropsy. It can also be made into an ointment for headache and for rheumatic or gouty pains. In homeopathy, it is used as a cardiac drug. CAUTION: Lily of the valley contains glycosides that act somewhat like digitalis and can produce irregular heartbeat and upset stomach.

Preparation and Dosage: Do not use without medical supervision.

255   LINDEN

(a) (Tilia europaea)

Common Names: European linden, European lime tree.

Medicinal Parts: Flowers, inner bark.

Description: European linden is a deciduous tree which grows to a height of 100 feet. It is found in the forests and on the mountain slopes of Europe and is commonly planted along streets there. Linden leaves are cordate, serrate, and somewhat unsymmetrical; the underside may be glabrous or hairy and is bluish-green in color. Greenish-yellow or yellow-brown flowers grow in erect cymes during June and July.

Properties and Uses: Flowers: antispasmodic, diaphoretic, diuretic. Bark: Cholagogue, emollient. An infusion of fresh linden flowers is useful for colds, sore throat, and influenza, and also for mild bladder and kidney problems; but it is not to be used for long periods or heart damage may result. The infusion can also be used as a mouthwash and gargle. For external use, beat the inner bark until its mucilaginous content can be squeezed out and apply this to wounds, sores, and skin problems and blemishes. In the past, the charcoal from linden wood was sometimes used externally for wounds and internally for halitosis, spasmodic cough, night sweats, and fever.

Preparation and Dosage:

Infusion: Steep 1 tsp. fresh flowers in ½ cup water for 10 minutes. Take 1½ cups a day.

Tincture: Take 15 to 40 drops, as indicated.

256   LINDEN (cont.)

(b) *(Tilia americana)*

Common Names: Basswood, American linden, bast tree, lime tree, spoonwood, wycopy.

Medicinal Parts: Flowers, leaves, bark.

Description: The basswood tree grows in the eastern U.S. and in Canada, reaching a height of up to 120 feet. The brownish-gray bark is perpendicularly, but not deeply, fissured. The cordate, serrate leaves are from 4 to 7 inches long; the flowers are fragrant and yellow or white.

Properties and Uses: Flowers and leaves: diaphoretic, stomachic. Bark: emollient. Basswood flowers and leaves are a traditional home remedy for colds, coughs, and sore throats. The inner bark, as in the European linden, contains mucilaginous materials and makes a soothing application for skin irritations and burns.

Preparation and Dosage:

Infusion: Steep 1 tsp. flowers or leaves in 1 cup water. Take 1 to 2 cups a day.

LION'S FOOT

(Prenanthes alba)

Common Names: Canker root, cankerweed, rattlesnake root, white cankerweed, white lettuce.

Medicinal Part: The plant.

Description: Lion's foot is a perennial plant indigenous to the rich woods of the eastern third of the U.S. and Canada. The smooth, purple-tinged stem grows to a height of 2 to 4 feet and contains a milky juice. The leaves are smooth, thick, and deep green, the basal triangular in shape, the stem ones lanceolate. All are deeply and irregularly toothed. Numerous fragrant, pendant flower heads grow in broad, terminal panicles or axillary clusters during August and September. The florets are cream-colored and tinged with lilac.

Properties and Uses: Astringent, bitter. A decoction of the root is helpful against diarrhea and dysentery. In the past, drinking the milky juice was believed to be useful for snakebite. A poultice of the leaves can be used as first aid for snake and insect bites.

Preparation and Dosage:

Decoction: Use 1 tsp. root with 1 cup water. Take 1 cup a day.

258 LOBELIA

(Lobelia inflata)

Common Names: Bladderpod, emetic herb, emetic weed, gagroot, Indian tobacco, vomitroot, vomitwort, wild tobacco.

Medicinal Part: The plant.

Description: Lobelia is an indigenous North American annual or biennial plant found in pastures, meadows, and cultivated fields of the eastern U.S., as far west as Arkansas and Nebraska. Related species are found in other parts of the country. The erect, angular stem, growing from 6 inches to 3 feet high, is hairy and contains a milky sap. The thin, light green leaves are alternate, hairy, ovate, and bluntly serrate. Numerous small, two-lipped, blue flowers grow in spike-like racemes from July to November. The fruit is a two-celled capsule filled with small, brown seeds.

Properties and Uses: Antispasmodic, diaphoretic, diuretic, emetic, expectorant, nervine. In the past, lobelia was used particularly for its antispasmodic qualities to treat asthma and whooping cough, and also to induce vomiting. Externally, the plant can be made into a poultice for bruises, insect bites, sprains, felons, ringworm, erysipelas, and poison ivy irritation. CAUTION: Although some herbal practitioners have sworn by lobelia as a harmless but effective panacea for what ails man, overdoses of homemade medicinal preparations have resulted in poisoning.

Preparation and Dosage: Use professionally prepared medications under medical supervision only.

259   LOOSESTRIFE

(Lythrum salicaria)

Common Names: Long purples, milk willow-herb, purple loosestrife, purple willow-herb, rainbow weed, soldiers, spiked loosestrife, spiked willow-herb, willow sage.

Medicinal Part: The herb.

Description: Loosestrife is a bushy, perennial plant which has settled in swamps, marshes, and moist places in the eastern U.S. after being introduced from Europe. The square, hairy stem grows 2 to 4 feet high and bears opposite, lanceolate, downy leaves. Purple six-petaled flowers grow in dense terminal spikes from June to August.

Properties and Uses: Astringent, styptic. Loosestrife is effective against diarrhea, including simple diarrhea and that associated with serious illnesses such as dysentery and typhoid fever. The infusion or fluid extract is also used for gastroenteritis and is particularly useful for diarrhea in infants. Loosestrife helps to stop internal bleeding, and it works without producing constipation.

Preparation and Dosage:

Infusion: Steep 1 oz. fresh herb in 1 cup water.

Decoction: Boil 1 oz. herb in 1 pint water until 1 cup liquid remains. Take 4 tbsp., three times a day.

Fluid Extract: Usual dose for infants is 10 to 15 drops; for adults, 1 tsp.

LOVAGE

(Levisticum officinale)

Common Names: European lovage, lavose, sea parsley.

Medicinal Part: Rootstock.

Description: Lovage is a European perennial plant found wild in southern Europe and Asia Minor but widely cultivated all over the continent. The short, thick rootstock produces a round, hollow stem 3 to 6 feet high and branched near the top. The leaves vary from long-petioled and decompound, with incised, ovate leaflets, to sessile and simple near the top. The small, pale yellow flowers grow in compound umbels from June to August. The whole plant has a strong, aromatic odor.

Properties and Uses: Carminative, diuretic, emmenagogue, expectorant, stimulant, stomachic. Lovage is mostly used for its diuretic properties in cases of water retention and urinary difficulties. In excessive doses, however, it can cause kidney damage; and it should not be used by those with kidney problems. Lovage also makes a good remedy for digestive difficulties, gastric catarrh, and flatulence. Skin problems will sometimes respond to a decoction added to bath water. Lovage promotes the onset of menstruation and should not be used by pregnant women.

Preparation and Dosage: The rootstock can be used fresh or dried.

Infusion: 1 tsp. fresh or dried root to 1 cup water. Take 1 to 1½ cups a day.

Decoction: Boil 1½ to 2 oz. rootstock in 4 to 6 qt. water for use as bath additive.

Powder: Take ¼ to ½ tsp., three times a day, as indicated.

LUNGWORT

(Pulmonaria officinalis)

Common Names: Jerusalem cowslip, Jerusalem sage, maple lungwort, spotted comfrey, spotted lungwort.

Medicinal Part: Flowering herb.

Description: Lungwort is a perennial plant that grows in shady areas in Europe and in the northern parts of the U.S.; it is also cultivated in gardens. The horizontal, creeping rootstock produces several bristly stems with alternate, ovate, dark green leaves which are petioled at the bottom of the plant and become sessile near the top. The funnel-shaped flowers grow in terminal clusters from March to May. They turn from rose-colored to blue, both colors being found on the plant at the same time.

Properties and Uses: Astringent, demulcent, emollient, expectorant. Lungwort tea is used for diarrhea, hemorrhoids, respiratory problems, coughs, and hoarseness. It also has mildly diuretic properties. The decoction may be beneficial for mild lung problems. Externally, the plant is used for all kinds of wounds.

Preparation and Dosage:

Infusion: Steep 2 tbsp. herb in 1 cup water. Take 1 cup a day.

Decoction: Use the same quantities, but boil for a few minutes. Take 1 cup a day.

Juice: Take 1 tsp., three times a day, with honey.

Powder: Take 1 tsp., three times a day, in milk.

262 **MADDER**

(Rubia tinctorum)

Medicinal Part: Rootstock.

Description: Madder is a European herbaceous perennial plant which grows in the Mediterranean area. A cylindrical, reddish-brown, creeping rootstock up to 3 feet long produces several angular prostrate or climbing stems which bear lanceolate leaves in whorls of 4 to 6. The flowers are small and yellow-green.

Properties and Uses: Astringent, diuretic, emmenagogue. Madder is useful for all problems with the urinary tract, particularly where the urine becomes alkaline. As a treatment supporting other measures, it has been used for rickets, slow-healing broken bones, inflammations, lack of appetite, diarrhea, and hectic fever. Externally, a decoction of madder can be used for skin problems, especially tubercular conditions of skin and mucous tissue.

Preparation and Dosage: The rootstock is collected when it is 3 to 6 years old.

Infusion: 1 tsp. fresh or dried root to 1 cup water. Take 1 to 1½ cups a day.

Decoction: Boil 1½ to 2 oz. rootstock in 4 to 6 qt. water for use as bath additive.

263   MAGNOLIA

(Magnolia glauca)

Common Names: Beaver tree, holly bay, Indian bark, red bay, red laurel, swamp laurel, swamp sassafras, sweet magnolia, white bay.

Medicinal Part: Bark.

Description: Magnolia is an ever-green tree found in the Atlantic and Gulf coast states. It has smooth, ash-colored bark and soft, leathery leaves which are alternate, elliptical, glossy bright green on top, and pale underneath. The large, distinctive flowers are cream-colored and appear from May to August.

Properties and Uses: Astringent, diaphoretic, febrifuge, stimulant, tonic. Magnolia bark is good for dyspepsia, dysentery, intermittent fever, erysipelas, and other skin diseases. It can also be made into a douche for leucorrhea. Some people have been cured of the tobacco habit by drinking magnolia bark tea. Magnolia bark can also be substituted for Peruvian bark as a safer remedy.

Preparation and Dosage: Gather the bark in spring and summer. Decoction: Use 1 tsp. bark with 1 cup water. Take 1 cup a day. For external use, simmer 1 tbsp. bark in 1 pint water for 10 minutes.

MAIDENHAIR

(Adiantum pedatum)

Common Names: Five-finger fern, maiden fern, rock fern.

Medicinal Part: Leaves.

Description: Maidenhair is a delicate perennial fern found in moist, cool places in North America and Asia. The creeping rootstock produces leaves from 1 to 2½ feet high, growing on dark, polished stalks which are forked at the top. Each fork bears 3 to 8 long-oblong pinnae, or leaflets, which are themselves divided into smaller, oblong segments, or pinnules, which are incised on the upper margin but entire on the lower side.

Properties and Uses: Expectorant, refrigerant, tonic. A decoction made from the leaves helps to clear up coughs and congestion due to colds, as well as hoarseness and catarrhal problems. Maidenhair is sometimes a constituent in hair rinses, and related species of the fern have been used since antiquity as a hair tonic.

Preparation and Dosage:

Decoction: 1 tsp. fresh leaves or 2 tsp. dried leaves with 1 cup water. Take 1 to 2 cups a day.

265 MALLOW

(a) (Malva sylvestris)

Common Names: High mallow, cheeseflower, common mallow, country mallow.

Medicinal Part: The herb.

Description: High mallow is an annual or perennial plant found in waste places, rubbish dumps, fields, and along fences and roadsides (as well as cultivated) in Europe and sparingly in the U.S., Canada, and Mexico. The tapering, whitish root produces a round stem, 2 to 3 feet high, with alternate, light green, downy leaves which are 5- to 7-lobed. The pink or purple axillary flowers have five narrow petals and appear from May to October.

Properties and Uses: Astringent, demulcent, emollient, expectorant. High mallow makes a good demulcent tea for coughs, hoarseness, bronchitis, inflammation of the larynx and tonsils, and irritation of the respiratory passages. It can also be taken for laryngitis, emphysema, and lung catarrh, and for catarrhal gastritis and enteritis. Externally, a decoction can be used to wash wounds and sores. Make a poultice of the herb to soothe irritations and inflammations. A warm enema made from the leaves is helpful for intestinal inflammation.

Preparation and Dosage: Use the fresh plant only.

Infusion: Add 1 to 2 tsp. herb to ½ cup cold water. Let stand for 8 hours, then warm up to lukewarm. (Do not boil or steep the herb in boiling-hot water.)

Decoction: For external use, boil 1 tbsp. herb in ½ cup water for a short time.

266 MALLOW (cont.)

(b) (Malva rotundifolia)

Common Names: Low mallow, blue mallow, cheese plant, cheeses, dwarf mallow.

Medicinal Part: The herb.

Description: Low mallow is an annual or perennial plant found along roadsides and fences, in waste places, and also cultivated throughout North America (except the extreme north). The creeping, branching stem grows from 6 to 24 inches long and bears downy, rounded, crenate, slightly 5- to 7-lobed leaves on long petioles. The axillary, purplish-pink, trumpet-shaped flowers appear from May to November.

Properties and Uses: Same as high mallow, above.

Preparation and Dosage: Same as high mallow, above.

MANDRAKE

(Podophyllum peltatum)
(European mandrake, Mandragora officinarum)

Common Names: American mandrake, duck's foot, ground lemon, hog apple, Indian apple, May apple, raccoon berry, wild lemon, wild mandrake.

Medicinal Part: Rootstock.

Description: Mandrake is a perennial plant that forms dense copses in open woodlands of eastern North America, as far west as Minnesota and Texas. The dark brown, fibrous, jointed rootstock produces a simple, round stem which forks at the top into two petioles, each supporting a large, round, palmately 5- to 9-lobed, yellowish-green leaf. A solitary, waxy-white or cream-colored flower grows on a short peduncle from the fork in the stem during May or June. Some plants, growing from different rootstocks, are non-flowering. These have only a single leaf on an unforked stem.

Properties and Uses: Cathartic. The American Indians used mandrake root as a cathartic, and sometimes to commit suicide. In any case, it is unquestionably an energetic purgative, but an overdose is likely to be fatal. Some Indians used the crushed rootstock on warts, but susceptible individuals trying it may end up with dermatitis. If used during pregnancy, mandrake may cause birth defects in the child.

Preparation and Dosage: Recommended for use under medical supervision only.

NOTE: The European mandrake (*Mandragora officinarum*), also called mandragora or Satan's apple, is not related to the American plant. It is native to the countries surrounding the Mediterranean and has been used there for thousands of years. Its large, brown root, growing 3 or 4 feet deep into the ground, often divides and branches and sometimes resembles a human figure. It produces little or no stem; its basal, ovate leaves stand erect at first but tend to lie spread on the ground when mature. The greenish-yellow or purple, bell-shaped flowers grow on stalks 3 to 4 inches high. The fruit is a large, fleshy, yellow to orange-colored berry. Mandrake root was used in ancient times as an anesthetic for surgery, as a "sleeping pill" when in pain, but also as a remedy for melancholy. The fresh root is strongly emetic and purgative; the dried root bark also has emetic properties. Mandrake's use today is limited to homeopathic preparations for hay fever, colic, asthma, and coughs. In some areas, mandrake root is believed helpful in promoting conception. Like the American plant, European mandrake is poisonous.

268　MARJORAM
(a) (*Origanum vulgare*)

Common Names: Wild marjoram, mountain mint, oregano, winter marjoram, wintersweet.

Medicinal Part: The herb.

Description: Wild marjoram is a perennial plant that grows wild in the Mediterranean region and in Asia and is cultivated in the U.S. Its creeping rootstock produces a square, downy, purplish stem with opposite, ovate leaves that are dotted with small depressions. Purple, two-lipped flowers grow in terminal clusters from July to October.

Properties and Uses: Antispasmodic, calmative, carminative, diaphoretic, expectorant, stomachic, tonic. An infusion of the fresh herb has beneficial effects on upset stomach and indigestion, headache, colic, and nervous complaints, as well as on coughs, whooping cough, and other respiratory ailments. It also helps to relieve abdominal cramps in women and will regulate the menstrual cycle when taken three or four days before the regular time. An infusion of the flowers is said to prevent seasickness and to have a calming effect. Wild marjoram oil is also used externally in liniments and lotions and will ease toothache when dropped into a hollow tooth. The tea makes a calming and tonic bath additive. The bruised leaves made into a sleep pillow may be helpful for insomnia.

Preparation and Dosage:

Infusion: Steep 2 to 3 tsp. herb in 1 cup water. Take 1 to 2 cups a day.

MARJORAM
(cont.)

(b) (Majorana hortensis)

Common Names: Sweet marjoram, knotted marjoram.

Medicinal Part: The herb.

Description: Sweet marjoram occurs in both annual and perennial varieties, growing wild in the Mediterranean area and in Asia; it is cultivated in the U.S. The square, branched stem is downy with gray hair and bears small, petioled, opposite, elliptical leaves, also with gray down. The pale red or white flowers grow in small clusters from July to September.

Properties and Uses: As in wild marjoram. Sweet marjoram is particularly helpful for gastritis, and a weak tea is good for colic in children. Use the oil of sweet marjoram externally as a lotion for varicose veins, gout, rheumatism, and stiff joints. The plant is also sometimes made into an herb pillow for rheumatic pains.

Preparation and Dosage:

Infusion: Steep 2 tsp. fresh herb in 1 cup water. Take ½ to 1 cup a day, as needed.

Juice: Take 1 tbsp., three times a day.

Lotion: Put the fresh herb in olive oil and let stand in the sun for 2 to 3 weeks.

MARSH TEA

(Ledum palustre)

Common Names: Marsh cistus, moth herb, narrow-leaved Labrador tea, swamp tea, wild rosemary.

Medicinal Part: The herb.

Description: Marsh tea is an evergreen shrub that is found particularly in peat bogs and moist places in the northern areas of North America, Europe, and Asia. It is sometimes cultivated as an ornamental. The rust-colored, woolly branches bear alternate, leathery, linear leaves that are green and glabrous on top and covered with rust-colored down beneath. Terminal umbels of white, or sometimes rose-colored, flowers appear from May to July.

Properties and Uses: Astringent, diaphoretic, diuretic, expectorant. Used externally, marsh tea makes a good remedy for all kinds of skin problems. Internally, it stimulates the nerves and the stomach. Because of its diaphoretic and diuretic properties, an infusion or cold extract can be used for rheumatism, gout, and arthritis. A syrup made from marsh tea is sometimes used for coughs and hoarseness. CAUTION: Excessive doses can cause poisoning.

Preparation and Dosage:

Infusion: Steep 1 tbsp. dried leaves or herb in ½ cup water. Take ½ cup a day.

Cold Extract: Soak 1 tbsp. dried leaves or herb in ½ cup cold water for 10 hours. Take ½ cup a day.

271. MASTERWORT

(Heracleum lanatum)

Common Names: Cow cabbage, cow parsnip, hogweed, madnep, woolly parsnip, youthwort.

Medicinal Parts: Rootstock, seed.

Description: Masterwort is a large perennial plant found on wet ground in Canada and the northern half of the U.S. The large, fleshy rootstock produces a stout, grooved, woolly stem, often 2 inches thick at the base and 3 to 8 feet high. The thin, hairy leaves are ternately compound and have broad, irregularly toothed leaflets. Large, compound umbels of dull white or purplish flowers appear during June and July.

Properties and Uses: Antispasmodic, carminative, stimulant. A decoction of masterwort rootstock or seed can be taken for colds, asthma, dyspepsia, colic, cramps, and spasmodic problems. It can also be used as an external wash for wounds, sores, and ulcers. CAUTION: The fresh foliage can produce dermatitis in susceptible individuals. Cattle are reported to have been killed from eating the foliage.

272. MATICO

(Piper angustifolium)

Medicinal Part: Leaves.

Description: Matico is a tall shrub found in Peru. Dried matico leaves are available from herb dealers.

Properties and Uses: Astringent, diuretic, stimulant, styptic, tonic. Matico leaves are used internally for diarrhea and for respiratory complaints. Externally, the powdered leaves can be put on wounds and cuts to stop bleeding; they can also be made into an astringent mouthwash. Peruvians have faith in matico as an aphrodisiac.

Preparation and Dosage:

Infusion: Use 1 tsp. leaves with 1 cup water. Take 1 to 2 cups a day.

MEADOW SAFFRON

(*Colchicum autumnale*)

Common Names: Autumn crocus, colchicum, naked ladies, upstart.

Medicinal Parts: Bulb, seeds.

Description: Meadow saffron is a perennial plant common in damp meadows of Europe, England, and Africa and cultivated in the U.S. and Canada. The large bulb is dark brown on the outside and contains a white, acrid juice. It produces several lilac or purple, crocus-like flowers in the fall, followed by smooth, narrow, dark green, basal leaves and long-elliptic seed capsules the next spring.

Properties and Uses: Meadow saffron contains the poisonous alkaloid colchicine, which is used medicinally for gout and arthritis. The whole plant is poisonous, and small amounts of the bulb or seeds can cause death. Not for home use under any circumstances.

274 MEADOWSWEET

(*Filipendula ulmaria*)

Common Names: Bridewort, doll-off, meadsweet, meadow queen, meadow-wort, pride of the meadow, queen of the meadow.

Medicinal Part: The plant.

Description: Meadowsweet is a perennial plant very common in European damp meadows; it can also be found in the eastern U.S. and Canada, as far west as Ohio. A creeping rootstock sends up a reddish, angular stem, branched near the top and bearing alternate, pinnate leaves, the leaflets entire or irregularly cleft, serrate, and downy white beneath. The terminal leaflet is 3- to 5-lobed and doubly serrate. Small, yellowish-white or reddish flowers grow in panicled cymes from June to August.

Properties and Uses: Astringent, diaphoretic, diuretic. Meadowsweet contains salicylic acid, which makes it useful for influenza, problems in the respiratory tract, gout, rheumatism, arthritis, and fever. Meadowsweet tea is also recommended for dropsy and other problems with water retention, and for bladder and kidney ailments. As an astringent, it can also be taken for diarrhea. Externally, the decoction can serve as a wash for wounds or sore eyes.

Preparation and Dosage:

Infusion: Steep 2 tbsp. herb in 1 cup water. Take 1 cup a day.

Decoction: Boil 2 tbsp. plant or dried rootstock in 1 cup water. Take 1 cup a day. Or soak the dried rootstock in cold water for 6 hours, bring to a boil and steep for 1 or 2 minutes.

Powder: Take ¼ to ½ tsp., three times a day.

Juice: Take 1 tbsp. a day, in water.

275   DROPWART or GOATSBEARD
(Filipendula hexapetala)

NOTE: Dropwort or goatsbeard (*Filipendula hexapetala*) is a related European and Asian plant with a tuberous rootstock and fernlike leaves. Medicinally it is equivalent to meadowsweet.

276   MEXICAN DAMIANA
(Turnera aphrodisiaca)

Common Name: Damiana.

Medicinal Part: Leaves.

Description: Mexican damiana is a small shrub which grows in dry places in Texas, Baja California, and northern Mexico. The obovate, toothed, light green damiana leaves are available from herb dealers.

Properties and Uses: Laxative, stimulant, tonic. Damiana seems to be considered as something of a natural "upper," to be taken for nervous and sexual debility. In particular, it is reputed to have aphrodisiac properties. It is usually taken in a 1:1 mixture with saw palmetto berries.

Preparation and Dosage:

Infusion: Steep 1 tsp. leaves in 1 cup water. Take 1 to 2 cups a day.

Fluid Extract: Take 15 drops to 1 tsp., three times a day, before meals.

Powder: Take 3 to 6 grains, three times a day, before meals.

277 MEZEREON

(Daphne mezereum)

Common Names: Daphne, spurge flax, spurge laurel, spurge olive, wild pepper.

Medicinal Part: Bark.

Description: Mezereon is a small, European and Asian shrub that has escaped from cultivation to grow wild in thickets and open woods in the northeastern states of the U.S. and eastern Canada. The stems have tough, leathery, gray-brown bark and bear alternate, smooth, lanceolate leaves. The rose-purple flowers appear on the branches in lateral clusters from February to April, before the leaves appear. The fruit is a red berry.

Properties and Uses: Cathartic, diuretic, emetic, rubefacient, stimulant. Mezereon was once used as a purgative, emetic, and rubefacient but is little used today. Homeopathists still use medications made from the bark for skin problems and for respiratory and digestive ailments. CAUTION: The entire plant is poisonous, and three or four berries can kill a person. People have even been poisoned by eating birds that had eaten the berries.

Preparation and Dosage: Do not use without medical supervision under any circumstances.

278 MILFOIL

(Achillea millefolium)

Common Names: Noble yarrow, nosebleed, sanguinary, soldier's woundwort, thousandleaf, yarrow.

Medicinal Part: The herb.

Description: Milfoil is a perennial plant found all over the world in waste places, fields, pastures, meadows, and along railroad embankments and roadsides. The light brown, creeping rootstock produces a round, smooth, pithy stem that branches near the top and may be glabrous or hairy. The alternate leaves are linear-lanceolate in outline and are pinnately divided into many small segments, the leaflets themselves sharply cleft. The flower heads have white rays and yellow (turning to brown) disks and are arranged in convex or flat compound corymbs. Flowering time is from June to November.

Properties and Uses: Antispasmodic, astringent, carminative, cholagogue, diaphoretic, hemostatic, tonic. Milfoil tea has a long history of use for lack of appetite, stomach cramps, flatulence, gastritis, enteritis, gallbladder and liver problems, and internal hemorrhage, particularly in the lungs. It appears to be especially effective in stimulating the flow of bile. Fresh milfoil juice acts as a general tonic and prophylactic by building up the blood. At the same time, it is good for various forms of internal bleeding, as evidenced by nosebleed, coughing or spitting blood, rectal or hemorrhoidal bleeding, bloody urine, and excessive menstrual flow. It can also be taken internally or used as a douche for leucorrhea. The decoction makes a good wash for all kinds of wounds and sores, for chapped hands, and (as may be needed) for sore nipples. CAUTION: Extended use of milfoil may make the skin sensitive to light.

Preparation and Dosage:

Infusion: Use 1 tbsp. dried herb with 1 cup water. Parboil and steep for 5 minutes. Take 1 cup a day.

Decoction: For external use, boil 2 tbsp. dried herb in 1 cup water.

Juice: Take 1 tsp. juice in 2 tsp. cold water, one to four times a day.

279   MILK THISTLE

(Carduus marianus)

Common Names: Holy thistle, Marythistle, St. Mary's thistle.

Medicinal Parts: Leaves, seeds.

Description: Milk thistle is a stout, annual or biennial plant found in dry, rocky soils in southern and western Europe and in some parts of the U.S. The branched, shining-brown stem grows 1 to 3 feet high and bears alternate, dark green, shiny leaves with spiny, scalloped edges and white spots along the veins. The upper leaves clasp the stem. Large, solitary, purple flower heads subtended by spiny bracts appear from June to August.

Properties and Uses: Leaves: bitter tonic. Seeds: cholagogue. Use the leaves for common stomach problems like lack of appetite and dyspepsia. The seeds are good for liver, gallbladder, and spleen problems, and for jaundice and gallstone colic.

Preparation and Dosage:

Infusion: Steep 1 tsp. seeds in ½ cup water. Take 1 to 1½ cups a day, a mouthful at a time.

Powder: Take 1 tsp. powdered seeds with water, four or five times a day.

Tincture: Take 15 to 25 drops, four or five times a day.

280 MILKWEED

(Asclepias syriaca)

Common Names: Common milkweed, common silkweed, cottonweed, silkweed, silky swallowwort, swallow-wort, Virginia silk.

Medicinal Part: Rootstock.

Description: Milkweed is a common perennial plant in fields and waste places of eastern North America, as far west as Kansas and Saskatchewan. The simple, erect stem grows 3 to 6 feet high and bears opposite, oblong-ovate to oblong, short-petioled leaves. Terminal or lateral umbels of small, dull purple flowers appear from June to August.

Properties and Uses: Diuretic, emetic, purgative. Milkweed is useful for kidney problems, dropsy, water retention, asthma, stomach ailments, and gallstones. Some American Indians rubbed the juice on warts; others drank an infusion of the rootstock to produce temporary sterility. CAUTION: Milkweed is poisonous in large quantities, especially for children.

Preparation and Dosage:

Infusion: For gallstones, mix equal parts milkweed and althea. Steep 1 tsp. in 1 cup boiling-hot water. Take 3 cups over the course of a day, one of them hot on retiring.

MILKWORT

(a) (Polygala amara)

Common Names: Bitter milkwort, dwarf milkwort, European bitter polygala, European Senega snakeroot, evergreen snake-root, flowering wintergreen, fringed polygala, little pollom.

Medicinal Part: The plant.

Description: Bitter milkwort is a European perennial plant that grows in the dry parts of wet meadows and in sunny, rocky places, preferring limestone soils. The usually simple stem, only 4 to 6 inches high, rises from a rosette of obovate basal leaves and itself bears alternate, oblong-ovate leaves. Terminal racemes of blue, sometimes rose-colored or white, flowers appear from April to June.

Properties and Uses: Bitter, diaphoretic, expectorant, galacta-gogue. Bitter milkwort is commonly used for coughs, chronic bronchitis, and other chronic lung problems. The bitter con-stituents also are useful to arouse a sluggish appetite. Extended use of the rootstock is said to be useful in relieving chronic diarrhea. Nursing mothers whose baby's appetite exceeds the supply of milk available may find bitter milkwort helpful for increasing the milk flow.

Preparation and Dosage: Plants growing in dry areas are most efficacious.

Infusion: Use 1 tsp. of the plant with 1 cup boiling water. Take 1 cup a day.

Decoction: Use 4 tbsp. leaves with ¾ cup water. Boil for an extended time. Take 1 tbsp. every 3 hours.

Powder: Take ¼ to ½ tsp. at a time.

MILKWORT (cont.)

(b) (Polygala vulgaris)

Common Names: European seneka, European milkwort, gang flower, Rogation flower, senega snakeroot.

Medicinal Part: Rootstock.

Description: This perennial relative of bitter milkwort is very similar to it in appearance, but it is usually found in grassy areas such as parks, pastures, and forest meadows. European seneka is not found in the U.S.

Properties and Uses: Like bitter milkwort, but not as potent. The powdered root has been used for pleurisy and a decoction for dropsy.

Preparation and Dosage:

Decoction: Use 1 oz. rootstock with 1 pint water; boil down to ¾ pint. For dropsy, take 3 tsp. every hour.

283 MINT

(a) (Mentha piperita)

Common Names: Peppermint, brandy mint, lamb mint.

Medicinal Part: Leaves.

Description: Peppermint is a hybrid perennial plant which is mostly cultivated but also found wild in moist soil in the eastern U.S. and in Europe. The erect, square, branching stem is tinged with reddish-purple and has opposite, dark green, ovate to lanceolate, serrate leaves. Axillary and terminal spikes of small, purple flowers appear from July through September. The whole plant has the characteristic smell of menthol.

Properties and Uses: Anodyne, antispasmodic, carminative, cholagogue, refrigerant, stomachic, tonic. Peppermint tea or oil can be taken for nervousness, insomnia, cramps, coughs, migraine, poor digestion, heartburn, nausea, abdominal pains, and various problems such as headache and vomiting due to nervous causes. Peppermint tea also makes a good substitute for coffee or tea. In large quantities, peppermint is said to be aphrodisiac. Externally, the leaves make a cooling and slightly anodyne application. They can also be made into a salve or a bath additive for itching skin conditions.

Preparation and Dosage: Collect the leaves on a hot, sunny day, preferably just before flowering time.

Infusion: Steep 2 to 3 tsp. leaves in 1 cup water. Take 1½ to 2 cups a day, but for no more than 8 to 12 days consecutively. After that time, wait at least a week before resuming, or heart problems may result.

Oil: Take 3 to 4 drops on a sugar cube with hot tea. For gas pains, take 1 or 2 drops in half a glass of water.

Tincture: Take 10 to 50 drops, depending on age and the severity of the problem.

(b) (Mentha spicata)

Common Names: Spearmint, lamb mint, mint, Our Lady's mint, sage of Bethlehem.

Medicinal Part: The herb.

Description: Spearmint is a perennial plant found in wet and moist soils in temperate climates over most of the world. The leafy, glabrous, square stems are about 2 feet high and bear sessile or short-petioled, oblong or ovate-lanceolate, unevenly serrate leaves. The stem is topped by slender, interrupted, leafless spikes of pale purple flowers which appear from July to September.

Properties and Uses: Antispasmodic, carminative, diuretic, stimulant, stomachic. Spearmint shares many of the uses described under peppermint, above. It is also often given for common women's complaints and for suppressed or painful urination. An infusion of spearmint combined with horehound is sometimes given to children for fever.

Preparation and Dosage:

Infusion: Steep 1 tsp. herb in 1 cup water for 30 minutes. Take frequently, a tablespoon at a time.

Oil: Take 2 to 4 drops on a sugar cube.

Tincture: Take 10 to 50 drops, according to age and condition.

MINT (cont.)

(c) (Mentha crispa)

Common Names: Curled mint, crisped-leaved mint, cross mint.

Medicinal Part: The herb.

Description: Curled mint is a perennial plant that is cultivated in North America and Europe. Its weak, square, branching stem grows from 1½ to 3 feet high and bears ovate, acute leaves with scalloped, incised margins. The lower leaves are petioled, the upper sessile. Red-lilac to light violet flowers grow in dense, terminal, whorled spikes.

Properties and Uses: Same as peppermint.

Preparation and Dosage: Same as peppermint.

MINT (cont.)

(d) (Mentha aquatica)

Common Name: Water mint.

Medicinal Part: Leaves.

Description: Water mint is a perennial plant found in wet and damp places in the northern hemisphere. The square, purplish stem grows about 2½ feet high and bears opposite, petioled, ovate, serrate leaves often tinged with purple. Red to light violet flowers grow in a rounded, whorled spike at the top of the stem from July to October.

Properties and Uses: Same as peppermint. A decoction made with vinegar has been helpful in stopping the vomiting of blood.

Preparation and Dosage: Same as peppermint.

287 MISTLETOE

(a) (Phoradendron flavescens)

Common Names: American mistletoe, birdlime, golden bough.

Medicinal Part: Leaves.

Description: American mistletoe is an evergreen, semiparasitic shrub which grows on various kinds of trees in the eastern, southern, and western United States. The branching, woody stem is swollen at the nodes and bears opposite, leathery, yellowish-green, obovate to elliptic leaves which are hairy when young but glabrous at maturity. The flowers grow in jointed spikes, developing into mucilaginous, white berries.

Properties and Uses: Emetic, nervine. In the past, American mistletoe was used for cholera, epilepsy, convulsions, hysteria, delirium, heart problems, and nervous debility. American Indians used it to cause abortion. An extract of the plant is known to increase uterine contractions and raise blood pressure when injected into the blood. The plant has also been used medicinally to stop bleeding after parturition. CAUTION: The berries are poisonous, and children's deaths have been attributed to eating them.

Preparation and Dosage: Do not use without medical supervision.

288 MISTLETOE (cont.)

(b) (Viscum album)

Common Names: European mistletoe, all-heal, birdlime, devil's fuge.

Medicinal Parts: Plant, berries.

Description: European mistletoe is an evergreen, semiparasitic plant found on the branches of deciduous trees in Europe and northern Asia. Roots growing from the yellow-green, forked stem penetrate through the bark into the wood of the host. The leaves are opposite, leathery, yellow-green, and narrowly obovate. Pale yellow or green flowers appear from March to May, the female developing into sticky white berries which ripen from September to November.

Properties and Uses: Cardiac, diuretic, stimulant, vasodilator. European mistletoe acts on the circulatory system, first raising blood pressure and then lowering it below the initial level and speeding up the pulse. At times in the past, it has been used for arteriosclerosis. It also stimulates glandular activity related to digestion, relieving many diverse problems traceable to faulty digestive processes. The tea can be used as a wash for chilblains and leg ulcers and made into a compress for varicose veins. CAUTION: Large doses have a detrimental effect on heart action. Also, eating the berries can be dangerous, especially for children.

Preparation and Dosage: Use with care, preferably under medical direction.

Cold Extract: 1. Soak 1 tsp. young twigs in 1 cup of cold water for 24 hours. Take 1 cup a day, in three equal parts morning, noon, and night. 2. Soak 6 tsp. leaves in 1½ cups cold water for 6 to 8 hours. Take 1½ cups in the course of a day, a mouthful at a time.

Juice: Wet the leaves and young twigs. When the water has been absorbed, press to extract the juice. Take 2 to 4 tsp. a day.

289 MONARDA

(a) (Monarda punctata)

Common Name: Horsemint.

Medicinal Parts: Leaves, flowering tops.

Description: Horsemint is a native perennial plant found mainly in the eastern and central United States. The branched, round stem bears opposite, lanceolate, downy leaves dotted with small depressions. The two-lipped flowers are yellowish with red spots and grow in successive axillary whorls subtended by large bracts.

Properties and Uses: Cardiac, carminative, diaphoretic, diuretic. Horsemint tea can be taken for flatulent colic, suppressed urine, diarrhea, rheumatism, and digestive or other stomach problems such as nausea and vomiting. American Indians used the plant for fever, chill, and inflammations. One tribe drank a cold extract to relieve backache, and another to stimulate heart action. The oil derived from the leaves promotes sweating when rubbed on.

Preparation and Dosage:

Infusion: Steep 1 tsp. leaves or tops in 1 cup water. Take 1 to 2 cups a day.

MONARDA
(cont.)

(b) (Monarda didyma)

Common Names: Oswego tea, bee balm, blue balm, high balm, low balm, mountain balm, mountain mint.

Medicinal Parts: Leaves, flowers.

Description: Oswego tea is a perennial plant found in moist soils from Georgia and Tennessee northward and as far west as Michigan and Ontario; it is also cultivated in gardens. The quadrangular, hairy stem bears opposite, deep green, ovate, serrate leaves from 3 to 6 inches long. The scarlet, two-lipped flowers grow in solitary terminal heads from July to September.

Properties and Uses: Carminative, rubefacient, stimulant. Oswego tea has been used mainly as a stomach preparation, to relieve nausea, vomiting, and flatulence.

Preparation and Dosage: Same as horsemint, above.

MONARDA
(cont.)

(c) (Monarda fistulosa)

Common Name: Wild bergamot.

Medicinal Part: Leaves.

Description: Wild bergamot is a perennial plant which inhabits dry hills and thickets in the eastern U.S. as far west as South Dakota and Nebraska; it is also cultivated for its aromatic oil. Its slender, square, hairy, branching stem grows 2 to 3 feet high and bears deep green, ovate-lanceolate, serrate leaves that are hairy on the lower side. The two-lipped, purple to rose-colored flowers have a hairy tuft on the upper lip. They appear in a terminal, solitary head from June to September.

Properties and Uses: Carminative, stimulant. Medical uses of wild bergamot have been mainly to relieve flatulence and to stimulate the system. American Indians, however, took wild bergamot tea for mild fever, headache, colds, and sore throat. One tribe inhaled the extracted oil for bronchial problems. Some tribes applied the oil or the boiled leaves to dry up pimples.

Preparation and Dosage: See horsemint, above.

292　MONKSHOOD

(Aconitum napellus)

Common Names: Aconite, friar's cap, mousebane, wolfsbane.

Medicinal Parts: Leaves, root.

Description: Monkshood is a European perennial plant that is also cultivated in gardens in the U.S. and Canada. The tuberous root produces an erect, simple, glabrous or slightly hairy stem with alternate, palmately 5- to 7-lobed leaves that are dark green on top and paler beneath. The hood-like, blue-purple flowers grow in long, irregular racemes from June to August.

Properties and Uses: Anodyne, febrifuge, sedative. Monkshood preparations are sometimes used for the pains of neuralgia, sciatica, and arthritis, as well as for gout, rheumatism, measles, nervous fever, and chronic skin problems. CAUTION: Monkshood is among the most poisonous of plants. Small doses can cause painful death in a few hours.

Preparation and Dosage: Do not use without medical direction under any circumstances.

NOTE: Various species of monkshood grow wild in North America, particularly in mountainous regions. These are similarly poisonous.

293 MOTHERWORT

(Leonurus cardiaca)

Common Names: Lion's ear, lion's tail, Roman motherwort, throw-wort.

Medicinal Parts: Flowering tops, leaves.

Description: Motherwort is a perennial plant found mainly in the northern part of the U.S. and all over Europe, in waste places, vineyards, and along fences and paths. The rootstock produces several square, hollow, grooved stems, often tinged with red-violet. The opposite, downy leaves are 3- to 7-lobed and sharply incised. Axillary whorls of bristly, red-purple, pink or white flowers appear from June to September.

Properties and Uses: Astringent, calmative, cardiac, emmenagogue, stomachic. Motherwort is most commonly used for nervous heart problems and for stomach gas and cramps. It has also been given for menopausal problems, shortness of breath, goiter, and congestion of respiratory passages. Motherwort has been of benefit too in cases of neuritis, neuralgia, and rheumatism. In general, it can be used like fragrant valerian. CAUTION: Contact with the plant may cause dermatitis in susceptible individuals.

Preparation and Dosage:

Infusion: Steep 1 tsp. tops or leaves in ½ cup water. Take 1 cup a day, unsweetened, a mouthful at a time.

Decoction: Boil 1 tsp. tops or leaves in 1 pint water until 1 cup liquid remains. Take ⅓ cup morning, noon, evening.

Cold Extract: Soak 2 tsp. tops or leaves in 1 cup cold water for 8 to 10 hours. Take 1 cup a day.

Tincture: Take 9 to 15 drops in water, three or more times a day as needed.

294 MOUNTAIN LAUREL

(Kalmia latifolia)

Common Names: Calico bush, lambkill, laurel, mountain ivy, rose laurel, sheep laurel, spoonwood.

Medicinal Part: Leaves.

Description: Mountain laurel is an evergreen shrub which grows

In moist places and on mountain tops from eastern Canada southward in the Appalachians and sometimes in lower coastal areas. Making a growth up to 35 feet high, the rough, branched stems bear alternate, leathery, ovate-lanceolate leaves that are pointed on both ends and are dark green above, lighter beneath. Numerous rose-colored to white flowers grow in terminal corymbs during June and July.

Properties and Uses: Astringent, sedative. In proper doses, mountain laurel has sedative properties and has also been used to ease the pain of neuralgia. For external use, it can be made into an ointment for skin problems. American Indians drank a decoction of the leaves to commit suicide. CAUTION: The leaves, twigs, flowers, and pollen grains contain a toxic substance which can cause death if taken in sufficient doses. Children have been poisoned by making tea from the leaves or sucking on the flowers.

Preparation and Dosage: Recommended for use under medical supervision.

Infusion: Steep 1 tsp. leaves in 1 pint water. Take 1 tbsp., two to four times a day.

295 MOUSE EAR

(Hieracium pilosella)

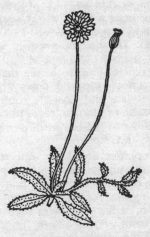

Common Names: Felon herb, hawkweed, mouse bloodwort, mouse-ear, hawkweed, pilosella.

Medicinal Part: The herb.

Description: Mouse ear is a small perennial plant found in dry soil on lawns, fields, pastures, hilly areas, and waste places from Ontario south to New York and Pennsylvania, and west to Michigan and Ohio. Creeping, leafy runners propagate the plant so that it forms dense, weedy patches. The bristly, spatulate leaves, forming a basal rosette, are green on top and downy-white beneath. Solitary (sometimes 2 to 4) yellow flowerheads rise from 4 to 15 inches above the ground on bristly scapes and are subtended by hairy, pointed bracts. Flowering time is from May to September.

Properties and Uses: Astringent, cholagogue, diuretic. Mouse ear makes a suitable remedy for diarrhea and can be used as a gargle for throat problems. As a powder, sniff it into the nose to stop nosebleed. The decoction has been recommended for liver and spleen problems, dropsy, and bladder stones. Taken over a long period, it is reputed to be helpful for cataracts, but this claim has been disputed.

Preparation and Dosage: Gather the plant when it is flowering.

Infusion: Steep 1 to 2 tsp. in 1 cup water. Take 1 cup a day.

Decoction: Boil 1 to 2 tsp. herb in 1 cup water until ½ cup liquid remains. Take ½ cup a day.

296   MUGWORT

(Artemisia vulgaris)

Common Names: Common mugwort, felon herb, sailor's tobacco.

Medicinal Parts: Rootstock, herb.

Description: Mugwort is a perennial plant that can be found in waste places, ditches, bushy areas, and along roadsides and fences in Europe, Asia, and North and South America. In the U.S., it grows in the eastern states as far south as Georgia and as far west as Michigan. The downy, grooved stems grow from 1 to 5 feet tall and bear alternate, pinnate leaves that are green on top and downy beneath. The leaflets are linear to spatulate and coarsely toothed. In addition, there is a basal rosette of pinnate leaves that survive the winter. Small, greenish-yellow to red-brown flower heads grow in panicled spikes from July to October.

Properties and Uses: Appetizer, digestive, cholagogue, purgative. Mugwort promotes the appetite and proper digestion by its beneficial effect on bile production, and it acts as a mild purgative. A decoction is sometimes used to regulate menstruation. It has also been used as a bath additive for gout, rheumatism, and tired legs. The fresh juice is helpful in relieving the itching of poison oak irritation. CAUTION: Excessive doses can lead to symptoms of poisoning, but nothing is to be feared from normal use.

Preparation and Dosage: Collect the herb when in flower, the rootstock in the fall.

Infusion: Steep 1 tbsp. dried herb in ½ cup water. Take during the day, a mouthful at a time.

Powder: Take ½ tsp. powdered rootstock with water, two times a day.

297 MULBERRY

(Morus rubra)

Common Name: Red mulberry.

Medicinal Part: Bark.

Description: Red mulberry is a tree, growing to 60 or 70 feet high, which is found from Massachusetts to Florida and west to Kansas and Nebraska. The alternate, serrate leaves are cordate, rough on top and soft or hairy beneath, and palmately lobed to simple. The purplish-red fruit, not a true berry, is made up of many small drupes.

Properties and Uses: Anthelmintic, cathartic. The bark of mulberry root is a traditional European remedy for tapeworms; it is used as a decoction. Mulberry bark has also long been used as a laxative preparation for home use. The axis of the red mulberry leaf contains a milky juice that was used by some American Indians to cure ringworm on the scalp. CAUTION: The milky juice and the unripe fruit cause hallucinations, nervous stimulation, and stomach upset.

Preparation and Dosage:

Powder: Take ½ tsp. powdered root bark with water for a laxative.

298 BLACK MULBERRY
(Morus nigra)

NOTE: Black mulberry (*Morus nigra*), is a European and Asian tree which is also cultivated in the U.S., particularly in the South and in California. It grows to 30 feet high and bears purple to black fruit. Medicinally, its bark is equivalent to that of red mulberry.

299 MULLEIN
(a) (Verbascum thapsus)

Common Names: Aaron's rod, blanket-leaf, candlewick, flannel-flower, feltwort, great mullein, hedge-taper, Jacob's staff, mullein dock, old man's flannel, shepherd's club, velvet dock, velvet plant.

Medicinal Parts: Leaves, flowers.

Description: Mullein is a tall biennial plant which grows in clearings, fields, pastures, and waste places from the Atlantic coast west to South Dakota and Kansas. The tall, stout, simple or branched stem bears alternate, thick, felt-like, light green leaves, whose stems are winged by decurrent bases. There is also a basal rosette of larger, obovate-lanceolate or -oblong leaves. Yellow, sessile flowers grow in cylindrical spikes, 1 to 3 inches long, from June to September.

Properties and Uses: Anodyne, antispasmodic, demulcent, diuretic, expectorant, vulnerary. Mullein tea makes a good remedy for coughs, hoarseness, bronchitis, bronchial catarrh, and whooping cough. It can also be used for gastrointestinal catarrh and cramps in the digestive tract. The flower tea will help relieve pain and induce sleep. For external use on inflammations or painful skin conditions, use the tea or a fomentation of the leaves boiled or steeped in hot vinegar and water. For nasal congestion or other respiratory problems, breathe the vapor from hot water with a handful of flowers added. The crushed fresh flowers are also said to remove warts. A poultice of leaves or the powder of dried leaves can be used for difficult wounds and sores.

Preparation and Dosage:

Infusion: Steep 1 tsp. leaves or flowers in 1 cup water. Take 1 to 2 cups a day.

Tincture: Take 15 to 40 drops in warm water, every 2 to 4 hours.

300

COMMON MULLEIN
(Verbascum thapsiforme)

301

ORANGE MULLEIN
(Verbascum phlomoides)

NOTE: Two old-world species of mullein, common mullein (*Verbascum thapsiforme*) and orange mullein (*Verbascum phlomoides*) are equivalent to *V. thapsus* for medicinal uses.

302

MULLEIN (cont.)
(b) (Verbascum nigrum)

Common Name: Black mullein.

Medicinal Part: Leaves.

Description: Black mullein is a biennial European plant growing along highways and hedges and reaching a height of 4 to 6 feet. Its basal leaves are about a foot long and 3 to 4 inches broad, pointed, and covered with down. The round, hoary stem has alternate leaves whose stems are winged by their decurrent bases. In July, the plant features a dense, long spike of yellow flowers.

Properties and Uses: Anodyne, pectoral. Black mullein is useful for coughs, spitting blood, and other chest ailments, as well as for griping and colic. Externally, a fomentation of black mullein is good for the pains and swelling of hemorrhoids.

303   MUSTARD

(a) (Brassica nigra)

Common Name: Black mustard.

Medicinal Part: Seed.

Description: Black mustard is an annual plant widely cultivated and also found wild in many parts of the world, including the fields and waste places of North America, except the far northern parts. The branching, angular stem grows 2 to 7 feet tall and bears alternate leaves, the lower ones lyrately pinnatifid and somewhat bristly, the upper glabrous, entire, and lanceolate. Yellow flowers grow in terminal racemes from June into November. The black seeds develop in bulgy, cylindrical pods which are closely pressed to the stem.

Properties and Uses: Appetizer, digestive, irritant. Black mustard is generally used externally as an irritant to encourage blood flow toward the surface in cases of rheumatism, sciatica, peritonitis, neuralgia, and various internal inflammations. Black mustard can be taken internally in very small amounts to promote appetite and stimulate the flow of gastric juices. CAUTION: Large amounts or prolonged use of black mustard, internally or externally, can cause serious irritation and inflammation; never let undiluted mustard oil contact the skin. Mustard oil can be mixed with rectified alcohol (1 part oil to 40 parts alcohol) and used as a lotion for gouty pains, lumbago, and rheumatism. A black mustard footbath for clearing blood congestion from the head, warming up cold feet, and lowering a fever in the early stages can be made by steeping 3 to 4 ounces mustard powder in a bag in warm water for 5 minutes. To make a stimulating bath for the whole body, add to the bath water 2 quarts cold water in which 7 to 9 ounces mustard powder has been steeped.

Preparation and Dosage:

Plaster: Mix mustard powder with cold water to make a thick paste, then spread the paste on a linen cloth. Put a layer of gauze over the affected area and then lay on the mustard cloth. The skin will begin to burn. Leave the mustard on until the burning becomes too uncomfortable. Thoroughly clean any remaining mustard paste from the skin. Powder the skin with rice flour and wrap the area with dry cotton. The skin should be back to normal in a few days. Do not use on sensitive areas. For persons with sensitive skin, mix the mustard powder with rye flour to reduce its effect.

304 MUSTARD (cont.)

(b) (Brassica hirta)

Common Name: White mustard.

Medicinal Part: Seed.

Description: White mustard, like black mustard, is widely cultivated and also found wild as a weed in fields and waste places of all North America (except the extreme north) and many other parts of the world. The branched, angular, bristly-haired stem may grow as high as 4 feet and bears leaves varying from pinnate with a large terminal lobe near the bottom of the plant to simple, irregularly round-lobed, oblong-ovate leaves on the stem. Yellow flowers grow in a slender terminal raceme from June to August. The white to yellowish seeds grow in pods which are tipped with a long beak and which stand out from the stem.

Properties and Uses: White mustard is used essentially like black mustard. In addition to the illnesses listed there, white mustard can be used for such problems as bronchitis and pleurisy. It is also said to have some antiseptic action. The whole seeds are sometimes taken as a purgative.

Preparation and Dosage: Same as black mustard. To avoid blistering, mix with egg whites instead of water.

305 MYRRH

(Commiphora myrrha)

Common Name: Gum myrrh tree.

Medicinal Part: Resin.

Description: Myrrh is the aromatic, gummy substance exuded by certain trees and shrubs growing in eastern Africa and Arabia. It can also be found in herb dealers' stocks.

Properties and Uses: Antiseptic, astringent, carminative, stomachic. Myrrh makes a good gargle and mouthwash for sores in the mouth and throat, sore teeth and gums, coughs, asthma, and other chest problems. It can also be taken internally for bad breath and for loose teeth and weak gums. Its disinfectant properties make myrrh suitable as a wash for sores and wounds and also as a douche. Add myrrh powder to the sore or wound after washing for continued disinfectant activity.

Preparation and Dosage:

Infusion: Steep 1 tsp. myrrh in 1 pint boiling-hot water for a few minutes and strain. For bad breath, add 1 tsp. goldenseal. Take 1 tsp., five or six times a day.

Gargle: Steep 1 tsp. myrrh and 1 tsp. boric acid in 1 pint boiling-hot water. Let stand 30 minutes and strain.

Tincture: Take 2 to 5 drops at a time, as needed.

306 NASTURTIUM

(*Tropaeolum majus*)

Common Names: Indian cress, large Indian cress.

Medicinal Parts: Flowers, leaves, seeds.

Description: Nasturtium is an annual plant native to South America but cultivated in gardens all over the world. The trailing or climbing stem grows 5 to 10 feet long and bears small, almost round, radially veined leaves. Red, orange, or yellow flowers, larger than the leaves, bloom from June to October.

Properties and Uses: Antiseptic, expectorant. Nasturtium is useful in breaking up congestion in the respiratory passages and chest during colds. The juice or tea can also be used as an internal or external disinfectant. Nasturtium is said to have a beneficial effect on the blood by promoting the formation of blood cells.

Preparation and Dosage:

Juice: Take ½ tsp. of the fresh juice, three times a day.

NERVE ROOT

(Cypripedium pubescens)

Common Names: American valerian, bleeding heart, lady's slipper, moccasin flower, monkey flower, Noah's ark, slipper root, Venus shoe, yellow lady's slipper, yellows.

Medicinal Part: Rootstock.

Description: Nerve root is a perennial plant native to the woods and meadows of North America, from Canada southward to North Dakota, Nebraska, and Georgia. The fleshy rootstock produces several round, glandular-hairy, leafy stems with alternate, sessile, sheathing, lanceolate leaves which are marked with several nerves. The characteristic flowers, with the lower lip forming an inflated sac suggesting the shape of a moccasin, are golden-yellow and lined with purple. Flowering time is from May to July.

Properties and Uses: Antispasmodic, diaphoretic, tonic. A tea made from the rootstock of nerve root makes a good tranquilizer for nervous headache, general nervousness, insomnia, hysteria, and delirium tremens. It can also be helpful against cramps and muscle spasms. Taken in large doses, the rootstock may cause hallucinations. CAUTION: The fresh plant can cause severe dermatitis after contact.

Preparation and Dosage: Gather the rootstock in the fall.

Infusion: Steep 5 tbsp. ground rootstock in 1 pint water for 1 hour. Take 1 tbsp. per hour, as needed. Or use 1 tsp. rootstock with 1 pint water and take 1 cup a day.

Tincture: Take 5 to 30 drops, as needed.

NETTLE

(Urtica dioica)

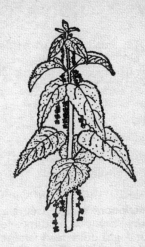

Common Names: Common nettle, common stinging nettle, great stinging nettle, stinging nettle.

Medicinal Part: The plant.

Description: Stinging nettle is a perennial plant found all over the world. In the U.S. it grows in waste places and gardens and along roadsides, fences, and walls in the states northward from Colorado, Missouri, and South Carolina. The square, bristly stem grows from 2 to 7 feet high and bears opposite, cordate, deeply serrate, pointed leaves which are downy underneath. The small, greenish flowers grow in axillary clusters from July to September.

Properties and Uses: Astringent, diuretic, galactagogue, hemostatic, tonic. The fresh juice or an infusion of the nettle plant has been used to stimulate the digestive system and to promote milk flow in nursing mothers. As an astringent it is also used for blood in the urine, hemorrhoids, and excessive menstrual flow. Nettle is a helpful remedy for ailments of the urinary tract and is said to reduce susceptibility to rheumatic problems and colds. A decoction of the plant is good for diarrhea. A decoction of the root is recommended for external use on the scalp for loss of hair. The fresh leaves have sometimes been used as a rubefacient, but severe irritation and blistering can result. Nettle can also be eaten as a vegetable, but old plants must be thoroughly cooked to be safe. Young plants in the spring can be used for salad or as a vegetable. CAUTION: Do not eat old plants uncooked; they can produce kidney damage and symptoms of poisoning. The bristly hairs of the nettle plant act like a hypodermic, injecting an irritant substance under the skin when touched: handle with care!

Preparation and Dosage:

Infusion: Steep 2 to 3 tbsp. leaves or plant in 1 cup water for 10 minutes.

Juice: Mix with an equal amount of water and take 1 tsp. at a time.

Scalp Wash: Boil 3 to 4 oz. chopped leaves in 2 cups water and 2 cups vinegar for a short time.

NOTE: Small or dwarf nettle *(Urtica urens)* is a smaller species of nettle with elliptic or ovate, coarsely serrate leaves and flowers in axillary, oblong, dense, short spikes. Medicinally, it is equivalent to *U. dioica.*

310 NEW JERSEY TEA

(Ceanothus americanus)

Common Names: Jersey tea, mountain-sweet, red root, Walpole tea, wild snowball.

Medicinal Part: Bark of the root.

Description: New Jersey tea is a small, deciduous shrub common in dry woods at low elevations all across the U.S. The large root is red inside and is covered with brownish or reddish bark. The round, slender, reddish stems bear alternate, ovate or oblong-ovate, finely serrate leaves which are dull green on top and finely hairy beneath. Small white flowers grow in long-stalked clusters which form large panicles at the ends of the branches from June to August.

Properties and Uses: Astringent, expectorant, sedative. New Jersey tea root-bark has been recommended for various chest problems, including chronic bronchitis, nervous asthma, whooping cough, and consumption. It has also been used as a gargle for inflammations and irritations in the mouth and throat, particularly for swollen tonsils. American Indians used a tea made from the whole plant for skin problems (including skin cancer and venereal sores). The tea may help raise a patient's spirits when despondency sets in during illness.

Preparation and Dosage:

Infusion: Steep 1 tsp. root-bark in 1 cup water. Take 1 to 2 cups a day.

Tincture: Take 10 to 20 drops in water, three or four times a day.

NIGHTSHADE

(a) (Solanum dulcamara)

Common Names: Bittersweet nightshade, bittersweet, bittersweet herb, bittersweet stems, bittersweet twigs, blue nightshade, felonwort, fever twig, garden nightshade, nightshade, nightshade vine, scarlet berry, staff vine, violet bloom, woody, woody nightshade.

Medicinal Parts: Bark of the root, twigs.

Description: Bittersweet nightshade is a perennial woody vine found in moist areas, around houses, and among hedges and thickets in the eastern and north-central states, the Pacific coast, and in Europe. The shrubby, thumb-thick, ashy-green, somewhat angular, climbing stem can reach a length of up to 10 feet. The dark green (or purplish when young) leaves are alternate and variable in shape (may be cordate, lanceolate-ovate, or hastate). The purple, star-shaped flowers appear in paniculate clusters on short lateral or terminal peduncles from May to August. The fruit is a scarlet, bitter berry that hangs on the vine for months after the leaves have fallen.

Properties and Uses: Anodyne, diuretic, emetic, herpatic, purgative. Although bittersweet nightshade is a relatively weak poison, it is used almost exclusively for external problems. Use it as a poultice for gout, herpes, furuncles, and felons. Combined with camomile it makes a good ointment for swellings, bruises, sprains, and corns. For skin diseases and sores, combine with yellow dock.

Preparation and Dosage: Bittersweet nightshade should not be taken internally without medical supervision.

NIGHTSHADE (cont.)

(b) (Solanum nigrum)

Common Names: Black nightshade, deadly nightshade, garden nightshade, poisonberry.

Medicinal Parts: Leaves, herb.

Description: Black nightshade is an annual plant found in gardens and along old walls and fences in various parts of the U.S. and southern Canada. Its erect, angular, branching stem grows

1 to 2 feet high and may be glabrous or covered with inward-bent hairs. The leaves are alternate, dark green, ovate, and wavy-toothed or nearly entire. Drooping, lateral, umbel-like clusters of white or pale violet flowers appear from July to October. The fruit is a many-seeded, pea-sized, purple or black berry.

Properties and Uses: Diaphoretic, narcotic, purgative. Taken internally in very small amounts, the leaves strongly promote perspiration and purge the bowels the next day. The juice of the fresh herb is sometimes used for fever and to allay pain. In large doses, black nightshade can cause serious, but usually not fatal, poisoning. Externally, the juice or an ointment prepared from the leaves can be used for skin problems and tumors. The berries are poisonous, but boiling apparently destroys the toxic substances and makes them usable for preserves, jams, and pies.

Preparation and Dosage: Take black nightshade internally only under medical supervision.

313 NUTMEG

(Myristica fragrans)

Medicinal Part: Seed.

Description: Nutmeg is a tropical evergreen tree native to Indonesia and cultivated in the West Indies, South Africa, the Molucca Islands, and other tropical areas. The brown, wrinkled, oval fruit contains a kernel which is covered by a bright red membrane. The membrane provides the spice mace, and the kernel the spice nutmeg.

Properties and Uses: Aromatic, carminative, hallucinogenic, stimulant. In small quantities, nutmeg acts on the stomach to improve appetite and digestion. Nutmeg oil is sometimes used to dispel flatulence. Nutmeg is also a mild hallucinogenic drug, somewhat like marijuana. In addition to hallucinations and elation, however, eating nutmegs produces stomach pain, double vision, delirium, and other symptoms of poisoning. CAUTION: Eating as few as two nutmegs can cause death.

OAK

(a) (Quercus alba)

Common Name: White oak.

Medicinal Part: Bark.

Description: White oak is a native
North American tree which grows
from Canada southward to the
Gulf of Mexico, as far west as
Texas. Usually 60 to 100 feet high,
it may grow as tall as 150 feet with
a trunk diameter up to 8 feet.
White oak bark is pale gray, and
the leaves have rounded or finger-
shaped lobes.

Properties and Uses: Astringent,
tonic. An infusion of white oak bark can be used internally or
externally (as enema or douche) for hemorrhoids and other
rectal problems, menstrual problems and blood in the urine.
Used internally and externally at the same time, white oak bark
makes a good medication for varicose veins. The tea has also
been used to stop internal hemorrhage, reduce fever, and wash
sores and skin irritations. For mouth and throat irritations, use it
as a gargle or mouthwash.

Preparation and Dosage:

Infusion: Steep 1 tbsp. bark in 1 pint water, simmering for 10
minutes. Take up to 3 cups a day.

Enema or Douche: Steep 1 heaping tbsp. in 1 qt. water for 30
minutes and strain.

315   **RED OAK**
(Quercus rubra)

316   **BLACK OAK**
(Quercus tinctoria)

NOTE: The barks of red oak (*Quercus rubra*) and black oak
(*Quercus tinctoria*) can be substituted for white oak bark for
external uses.

317   **OAK (cont.)**
(b) (Quercus robur)

Common Name: English oak.

Medicinal Part: Bark.

Description: English oak is a European species of oak which is very similar to white oak. The tree grows to 115 feet high and has round-lobed leaves like those of white oak.

Properties and Uses: Astringent, tonic. English oak bark is used essentially the same ways as white oak bark: as an internal or external astringent. The tea has also been recommended as a tonic after overexertion. Acorns are sometimes used as a coffee substitute.

Preparation and Dosage:

Decoction: Boil 1 tsp. bark in ½ cup water. Take 1 cup a day.

Wash: Boil ½ to 2 pounds bark in 2 qt. water until 1 qt. liquid remains.

318 OAT

(Avena sativa)

Medicinal Parts: Grain, straw.

Description: Oat is an annual grass which is widely cultivated for its edible grain. A fibrous root produces a hollow, jointed stem from 2 to 4 feet high with more or less rough, pale green, narrow, flat leaves. The flowers are arranged in a loose terminal panicle from 6 to 12 inches long which consists of (usually) two-flowered spikelets from ¾ to 1 inch long. The hairy, grooved grain is narrow, with almost parallel sides.

Properties and Uses: Antispasmodic, nervine, stimulant. Oats are used primarily for their nutritional value; they are of particular benefit in special diets for convalescents or for those with certain illnesses, including gastroenteritis and dyspepsia. Oat extract and tincture are useful as nerve and uterine tonics. A tea made from oat straw has been recommended for chest problems. In Europe, oat straw is used for various baths, which, when taken regularly, are helpful for a number of ailments:

Full Bath: Good for rheumatic problems, lumbago, paralysis, liver ailments and gout, kidney, and gravel problems.

Sitzbath: Good for bladder and abdominal problems, intestinal colic, and bedwetting.

Footbath: Good for tired or chronically cold feet.

Local Wash: Good for skin diseases, flaky skin, frostbite, chilblains, wounds, and eye problems.

Preparation and Dosage:

Decoction: Boil small pieces of oat straw in water for 1 hour. Strain and add a little honey.

Tincture: Take 10 to 20 drops, three times a day.

Fluid Extract: A dose is 10 to 30 drops, taken in hot water. When taking a dose before going to bed, take in cold water to avoid the risk of sleeplessness.

Bath: Boil 1 to 2 lb. straw in 3 qt. water for 30 minutes. Add to bath water.

319 OLIVE
(Olea europaea)

Medicinal Parts: Leaves, bark, fruit.

Description: The olive tree is an evergreen, native to the Mediterranean area but widely grown in tropical areas and warm climates. The hard, yellow wood of the gnarled trunk is covered by gray-green bark; the branches extend to a height of 25 feet or more. The opposite, leathery leaves are elliptic, oblong, or lanceolate in shape; they are dark green on top and have silvery scales underneath. The fragrant white flowers grow in axillary panicles that are shorter than the leaves. The fruit is an oblong or nearly round drupe which is shiny black when ripe.

Properties and Uses: Leaves: antiseptic, astringent, febrifuge, tranquilizer. Oil: cholagogue, demulcent, emollient, laxative. A decoction of the leaves or inner bark of the tree is effective against fever; an infusion of the leaves has a tranquilizing effect helpful for nervous tension. Olive oil taken internally increases the secretion of bile and acts as a laxative by encouraging muscular contraction in the bowels. It is also soothing to mucous membrane and is said to dissolve cholesterol. Olive oil is useful externally for burns, bruises, insect bites, sprains, and intense itching (pruritus). With alcohol it makes a good hair tonic, and with oil of rosemary a good treatment for dandruff. One of its most common uses is as a base for liniments and ointments.

Preparation and Dosage:

Infusion: Steep 1 to 2 tsp. leaves in 1 cup water for 10 minutes. A dose is 2 tsp.

Decoction: Boil 2 handfuls leaves or bark in 1 qt. water until 1 cup liquid remains.

Oil: As a laxative, take 1 to 2 fl. oz.; as a cholagogue, take 1 to 2 tsp. at a time.

ONION

(Allium cepa)

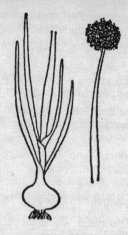

Medicinal Part: The bulb.

Description: Onion is a biennial or perennial plant which is mostly cultivated but also found wild in numerous varieties. The bulb itself is an underground part of the stem, the above-ground part of which is hollow and blue-green. The leaves are the same color and hollow, but shorter than the stem. They dilate to surround the stem at the bottom. Greenish-white flowers grow in a rounded, umbellate cluster from June to August, producing tiny bulbs as fruit.

Properties and Uses: Anthelmintic, antiseptic, antispasmodic, carminative, diuretic, expectorant, stomachic, tonic. Onion juice (or a decoction or extract) is used most often as a diuretic or expectorant agent, but it has also been used for ages for the other purposes indicated by the categories. As an antiseptic, onion helps to end putrefactive and fermentation processes in the gastrointestinal tract. It is also said to strengthen the heart (it tends to lower blood pressure) and to help restore sexual potency which has been impaired by illness or mental stress. Half an onion cut small and eaten with bread will relieve gas pains and heartburn. Onion juice mixed with honey is good for hoarseness and coughs. Externally, onion juice can be applied to suppurating wounds.

Preparation and Dosage:

Juice: Take 1 tsp., three or four times a day.

Cold Extract: Soak a chopped onion in 1 cup water for 24 hours and strain. Take ½ cup a day.

Decoction: Boil a medium-size, chopped onion in a little more than a cup of water until 1 cup liquid remains. Take 1 tbsp., several times a day for several days.

ORANGE

(Citrus aurantium)

Common Names: Bitter orange, Seville orange, sour orange.

Medicinal Parts: Flowers, rind of the fruit.

Description: The orange is an evergreen tree which originated in Asia but has become established elsewhere (as in Florida) and is commonly cultivated. The stem is covered with a smooth, grayish-brown bark; with its branches, it reaches a height of 20 to 30 feet. Long spines appear beside the buds. The alternate, ovate-oblong leaves are glossy and dotted with glands; their petioles are broadly winged, their margins are sinuate or crenately toothed. One or more fragrant, white, five-petaled flowers grow in the leaf axils. The fruit is the familiar orange (technically an hesperidium), with segmented sour pulp inside a roughish rind. This species is not eaten fresh but is made into marmalade.

Properties and Uses: Carminative, stimulant, stomachic, tonic. The dried rind of the bitter orange is helpful in cases of dyspepsia. The oil derived from the fresh rind can be used to dispel flatulence; it also makes a pleasant and nonirritating remedy for chronic bronchitis. An infusion of dried flowers acts as a mild nervous stimulant, but the oil obtained by distillation of the flowers has hypnotic properties when inhaled.

322 SWEET ORANGE
(Citrus sinensis)

NOTE: The sweet orange (*Citrus sinensis*), which is grown for eating, differs from the bitter orange in having narrowly winged petioles and few or no spines. The fruit is usually smaller and, of course, has a sweet taste. Medicinally it can be used like bitter orange, but it is less effective except as a carminative.

323 ORRIS ROOT
(Iris florentina)

Common Name: Florentine iris.

Medicinal Part: Rootstock.

Description: Orris root is the rootstock of Florentine iris, which grows in the Mediterranean countries. Commercial production of orris root is centered in Florence, Italy. Florentine iris has the typical erect, basal, sword-like leaves. The flowers are white with blue veins, the outer divisions fringed with yellow. Flowering time is from March through July.

Properties and Uses: Diuretic, stomachic. Orris root is a good diuretic which is useful for dropsy and other water retention problems. It is also used sometimes for bronchitis, coughs, and sore throat; for colic; and for congestion in the liver.

PANSY

(Viola tricolor)

Common Names: Garden violet, heartsease, Johnny Jumper, step-mother.

Medicinal Part: The plant.

Description: The pansy is an annual plant that is widely cultivated as a garden ornamental but is also found wild in fields and meadows and along the edges of forests in North America, northern Asia, and Europe. The angular, soft, hollow stem bears alternate, ovate to lanceolate, toothed leaves. The solitary, axillary flowers may be yellow, blue, violet, or two-colored, the flowering time being from March to October.

Properties and Uses: Anodyne, demulcent, diaphoretic, diuretic, expectorant, laxative, vulnerary. An infusion of pansy is useful for skin eruptions in children, for diarrhea, and for urinary problems. In popular usage, it also serves for jaundice, gout, rheumatic problems, arteriosclerosis, bedwetting, nervous complaints and hysteria and cramps in children. Its content of mucilage and salicylic acid makes it suitable too for chest and lung inflammations. The dried and powdered plant can be strewn into wounds or made into a salve with honey for external use. CAUTION: Excessive doses or prolonged, continuous use can lead to skin problems.

Preparation and Dosage:

Infusion: Steep 1 to 2 tsp. plant in ½ cup water. Take 1 cup a day, a mouthful at a time.

Cold Extract: Soak 2 to 4 tsp. plant in 1 cup cold water for 8 hours. Take 1 cup a day, a mouthful at a time.

325

PAPAYA

(Carica papaya)

Common Names: Custard apple, melon tree, pawpaw.

Medicinal Parts: Fruit, leaves.

Description: The papaya tree is found growing to a height of up to 25 feet in tropical America. The palmlike trunks have soft wood and sometimes divide into several erect stems, each with a head of large, palmately lobed leaves that are nearly orbicular in outline. The lobes themselves are pinnately lobed. The hollow petioles are two feet long or more. Male and female flowers are usually on separate trees: slender racemes of funnel-shaped, yellow male flowers become up to 3 feet long; the female flowers have five yellow, twisted petals and grow singly or in sparse corymbs. The fruit is a large, oblong or nearly spherical, fleshy berry with a yellow or orange rind like a gourd. It may be from 3 to 20 inches long and weigh up to 12 pounds or more.

Properties and Uses: Digestive, stomachic, vermifuge, vulnerary. Papaya is probably best known for its ability to aid digestion, an ability which is due to its content of papain, an enzyme similar to pepsin (which is produced by the gastric juices of the stomach). This protein-digesting enzyme makes papaya helpful for dyspepsia and other digestive difficulties. Either the fresh milky juice of the unripe fruit or the brownish powder to which it dries can be used. This juice has also been used to remove freckles, and internally it acts as an effective vermifuge. Papaya leaves are sometimes used to dress festering wounds. Improper protein breakdown in the system often leads to allergies. Papaya is effective in relieving allergies by its ability to denaturize proteins.

326   PARSLEY

(Petroselinum sativum)

Common Names: Common parsley, garden parsley, rock parsley.

Medicinal Parts: Plant, seeds.

Description: Parsley is a biennial or perennial herb which is found in cultivation everywhere. A thin, white, spindle-shaped root produces the erect, grooved, glabrous, angular stem. The lower leaves are bi- or tri-ternately divided or incised, the upper three-cleft to entire. All are shiny and dark green. The white or greenish-yellow flowers appear in compound umbels from June to August. The seeds are ovate and grayish-brown.

Properties and Uses: Antispasmodic, carminative, diuretic, emmenagogue, expectorant. Parsley tea, particularly that made from the seeds and the leaves, and also the fresh juice are used for dropsy, jaundice, asthma, coughs, and suppressed or difficult menstruation. The juice has also been used successfully to treat conjunctivitis and inflammation of the eyelids (blepharitis). It is important to take the proper dosage, and parsley is not to be used at all if kidney inflammation exists. Weak or sensitive persons can be helped by cooking a few slices of parsley root in their soup. An infusion of the herb is said to be effective against gallstones. The bruised leaves have been recommended for external application to contusions. A tea made from crushed seeds kills scalp vermin.

Preparation and Dosage:

Infusion: Steep 1 tbsp. leaves in 1 cup water for 20 minutes.

Decoction: Boil 1 level tsp. crushed seeds in ½ cup water. Take ½ to 1 cup a day.

327 PASQUE FLOWER

(Anemone patens)

Common Names: Easter flower, meadow anemone, wild crocus, wind flower.

Medicinal Part: The plant.

Description: Pasque flower is a perennial plant found on dry prairies from Illinois and Wisconsin to Texas, and westward and northwestward. The stem grows from 6 to 16 inches high and bears alternate, palmately dissected leaves with narrow, linear lobes. A solitary, terminal, erect flower features 5 or 6 petal-like, purplish-blue to whitish sepals, blooming in March and April.

Properties and Uses: Diaphoretic, diuretic, rubefacient. The fresh plant is the most active, but it is also highly irritating both externally and internally. The dried, powdered plant is sometimes used to promote the healing of wounds. CAUTION: Pasque flower contains alkaloids that cause depression, nervousness, and stomach upset, and which may be fatal if consumed in large quantities.

Preparation and Dosage: Do not use without medical supervision.

328 PASSION FLOWER

(Passiflora incarnata)

Common Names: Maypops, passion vine, purple passion flower.

Medicinal Parts: Plant, flower.

Description: Passion flower is a woody, hairy, climbing vine which grows wild in the southern U.S., from ·Virginia and Florida westward to Missouri and Texas. It is also cultivated in cooler climates. The stems, from 10 to 30 feet long, climb by means of axillary tendrils. The alternate, serrate leaves are palmately 3- to 5-lobed. Solitary, axillary, white flowers with a purple, blue, or pink calyx crown bloom from May to July. The fruit is an edible, many-seeded berry (maypop) almost as large as a chicken egg.

Properties and Uses: Antispasmodic, diaphoretic, sedative. Passion flower is most commonly used for nervous conditions such as insomnia, restlessness, hysteria, and nervous headache. Normally, however, it is used as part of a prolonged treatment and in the form of professionally prepared medications.

Preparation and Dosage: Use professionally prepared medications.

Tincture: Take 15 to 60 drops in water, as needed. For restlessness in children, give 3 to 10 drops in water every 30 minutes until results are obtained.

329 PEACH TREE

(Prunus persica)

Medicinal Part: Leaves.

Description: The peach tree is a well-known fruit tree widely cultivated in temperate and warm regions all over the world. In the U.S., California is the predominant peach-producing state. The tree may grow as high as 20 to 25 feet, but orchard trees are usually kept shorter. The leaves are thin, serrate, and oblong-elliptic to -lanceolate. The flowers are a delicate pink.

Properties and Uses: Diuretic, expectorant, laxative, sedative. Peach leaves will stimulate the flow of urine, and their mildly sedative properties may be helpful for various nervous conditions. As an expectorant, they can be used for chronic bronchitis and chest congestion. Peach leaves also help to relieve vomiting and morning sickness during pregnancy, but their dosage must be regulated to avoid excessive laxative action. Powdered dried leaves have sometimes been used to help heal sores and wounds.

Preparation and Dosage:

Infusion: Steep 1 level tsp. leaves in 1 cup water. Take 2 to 3 cups in the course of a day, as needed, with the first cup before breakfast.

Tincture: For nausea, take 2 to 15 drops in water, 30 minutes before meals or as needed.

330 PENNYROYAL

(Hedeoma pulegioides)

Common Names: American pennyroyal, mock pennyroyal, mosquito plant, squaw balm, squawmint, tickweed.

Medicinal Part: The herb.

Description: The American species of pennyroyal is an annual plant found in dry fields and open woods along the Atlantic coast and west to Minnesota and Nebraska. The erect, square, branching stem grows from 6 to 18 inches high and bears small, opposite, thin, ovate leaves which are sparingly toothed. Axillary clusters of small, tubular, lavender or purplish flowers appear from June to October. The whole plant has a pleasant, aromatic odor.

Properties and Uses: Carminative, diaphoretic, emmenagogue, sedative. Pennyroyal was commonly used in nineteenth-century medicine to induce perspiration at the beginning of a cold and to promote menstruation. It was taken also with brewer's yeast to induce abortion. It is helpful against nausea and nervous conditions but should not be taken during pregnancy. American Indians used pennyroyal tea for headache and for menstrual cramps and pain. The tea also makes a good external wash for skin eruptions, rashes, and itching.

Preparation and Dosage:

Infusion: Use 1 tsp. herb with 1 cup water. Take 1 to 2 cups a day.

Tincture: Take 20 to 60 drops at a time, as needed. For children, give small, frequent doses.

331 EUROPEAN PENNYROYAL

(Mentha pulegium)

NOTE: European pennyroyal (*Mentha pulegium*), or true pennyroyal, is similar to the American species in odor and uses.

332   **PEONY**

(Paeonia officinalis)

Common Name: Common peony.

Medicinal Part: Rootstock.

Description: The peony is a perennial plant which grows wild in southern Europe and is cultivated as a garden flower elsewhere. The thick, knobby rootstock produces a green, juicy stem from 2 to 3 feet high. The leaves are ternate or bi-ternate, with large, ovate-lanceolate leaflets. The large, solitary, red or purplish-red flowers resemble roses and bloom from May to August.

Properties and Uses: Antispasmodic, diuretic, sedative. In Europe, peony root is an old remedy for jaundice and for kidney and bladder problems. An extract made by steeping the root in wine was generally used. A decoction of the root has also been used for gout, asthma with cramps, and (in very small doses) eclampsia. CAUTION: The entire plant is poisonous, the flowers especially so. A tea made from flowers can be fatal.

Preparation and Dosage: Do not use without medical supervision.

333

334   **PERIWINKLE**

(Vinca major, Vinca minor)

Common Names: V. *major:* great periwinkle. V. *minor:* early-flowering periwinkle, lesser periwinkle.

Medicinal Part: The herb.

Description: Periwinkle is a prostrate, creeping plant that grows wild in Great Britain and Europe and is also cultivated there and in the U.S. The stem bears opposite, dark green, shiny leaves at the joints. During March and April a pale blue flower grows from each stem joint on a long, hollow stalk.

Properties and Uses: Astringent, sedative. Periwinkle makes a good remedy for diarrhea, excessive menstruation and hemorrhage. To stop bleeding in the mouth and nose and also to help toothache, chew the herb. Periwinkle tea can be used for nervous conditions, hysteria, and fits.

PERUVIAN BARK

(Cinchona spp.)

Common Names: Cinchona, Jesuits' bark.

Medicinal Part: Bark.

Description: Various species of the evergreen cinchona tree, native to Peru and Ecuador, are now grown more widely in tropical America, in India, and in the Orient. The branches bear opposite, elliptic-obovate leaves and fragrant, rose- or purple-colored flowers resembling lilac blossoms. Cinchona bark, varying in color with each species, can be removed from the tree in strips without harming the tree.

Properties and Uses: Astringent, febrifuge, oxytocic, tonic. Probably the greatest value of Peruvian bark lies in its quinine content, which makes it effective against malarial infection. But small doses are also good for fever and for indigestion. It makes a good mouthwash and gargle for mouth and throat problems. Because of its effect of stimulating uterine contractions, Peruvian bark should not be used during pregnancy (unless, of course, uterine contractions are desired to aid in a tardy delivery).

Preparation and Dosage: Use in small doses only, preferably with medical direction.

Infusion: Steep 1 tsp. bark in 1 cup water. Take ½ cup a day, no more than 1 to 2 cups total.

Tincture: Take 5 to 30 drops at a time.

336 PEYOTE

(Lophophora williamsii)

Common Names: Devil's root, dumpling cactus, mescal button, pellote, sacred mushroom.

Medicinal Part: The plant.

Description: Peyote is a succulent, spineless cactus which grows in the arid regions of southern Texas, Mexico, and Central America. A thick taproot produces the globular or top-shaped, dull bluish-green plant, which is 2 or 3 inches across and features from seven to thirteen vertical, more or less distinct ribs. One or more pale pink to white, funnelform flowers grow in the middle of the top, surrounded by long hair. The pinkish to red fruit is club-shaped and contains black seeds.

Properties and Uses: Cardiac, emetic, hallucinogenic, narcotic. The primary use for peyote is to induce visions in a ritualistic or religious context, particularly in American Indian tradition and, formally, in the Native American Church. The hallucinogenic constituent of peyote is mescaline, an alkaloid which also acts to stimulate the heart and the respiratory system but has narcotic effects in higher doses. Mescal buttons are sun-dried pieces of the plant; four to five buttons (215 to 230 grains) are enough to induce visions. A session with peyote produces a loss of the sense of time, partial anesthesia, relaxation of the muscles, dilation of the pupils, and often nausea and vomiting. One Indian tribe used the root to treat scalp diseases and as a hair tonic. CAUTION: Use with extreme care, and only under supervision of someone familiar with it.

337 PILEWORT

(Erechtites hieracifolia)

Common Name: Fireweed.

Medicinal Part: The plant.

Description: Pilewort is a native North American annual plant found in fields, woods, waste places, and burned-over areas from the Atlantic coast westward to Saskatchewan, Nebraska, Texas, and Mexico. The thick, succulent, grooved stem grows from 1 to 8 feet high and bears alternate, lanceolate, acute, irregularly dentate leaves that are petioled near the bottom of the plant and clasping near the top. Whitish, brush-shaped flower heads grow in loose terminal clusters from July to October. The plant has a disagreeable odor and taste.

Properties and Uses: Astringent, emetic, tonic. Pilewort can be used for diarrhea and for fever. It is said to be very effective against hemorrhoids. In large doses it produces vomiting.

Preparation and Dosage:

Infusion: Steep 1 heaping tsp. of the plant in 1 cup water. Take 1 to 2 cups a day.

Tincture: Take ½ to 1 tsp. at a time.

338 PIMPERNEL

(a) (Pimpinella magna)

Common Names: Greater pimpernel, false pimpernel, pimpinella.

Medicinal Part: Rootstock.

Description: Greater pimpernel is a European perennial plant which grows along the edges of woods, in marshy meadows, and in other wet places. Reaching a height of up to 3 feet, the stem bears alternate, odd-pinnate leaves on long petioles dilated at the base. The leaflets are ovate and coarsely toothed, the terminal leaflet more or less three-lobed. The small, purple or bluish flowers grow in compound umbels from June to September.

Properties and Uses: Antispasmodic, astringent, carminative, diaphoretic, diuretic. A decoction of greater pimpernel root makes a good gargle for inflammations of the throat. It can also be used for colds, bronchitis, and inflammation of the larynx. It is sometimes given for children's diseases which involve phlegmatic congestion, such as scarlet fever, measles, and German measles. Greater pimpernel has been used for all sorts of catarrhal problems and for nervous heart palpitations. Digestive problems and flatulence will often respond to it, and the fresh rootstock acts to relieve diarrhea. The tincture can be taken for heartburn.

Preparation and Dosage:

Cold Extract: Soak 2 tsp. dried rootstock in 1 cup cold water for 10 hours.

Infusion: Steep the rootstock used to make the cold extract in boiling-hot water and add the resulting tea to the cold extract. Take 1 to 2 cups a day, sweetened with honey if desired.

Decoction: Boil 2 tbsp. dried rootstock in 1 cup water. Use as a gargle.

Tincture: A dose is 10 drops, taken on a sugar cube.

339 PIMPERNEL (cont.)

(b) (Pimpinella saxifraga)

Common Names: Burnet saxifrage, pimpernel, pimpinella, saxifrage, small pimpernel.

Medicinal Part: Rootstock.

Description: Burnet saxifrage is a European perennial plant found on slopes and pastures, among bushes, and along the edges of woods, shorelines, and roadsides. A gnarled, twisted rootstock produces a round, finely grooved, branched stem with alternate, pinnate leaves. The leaflets are variable in shape, ranging from ovate to oblong-lanceolate, and from coarsely toothed to ternately incised. White or yellow-white flowers grow in compound umbels from July to October.

Properties and Uses: Antispasmodic, astringent, carminative, diaphoretic, diuretic, stomachic. Burnet saxifrage can be used like greater pimpernel. In addition, the powdered rootstock can be used for articular rheumatism, gout, bladder stones, and kidney inflammation. The infusion taken cold is said to be a good remedy for sour stomach. The seed of burnet saxifrage, like that of anise, stimulates milk flow in nursing mothers.

Preparation and Dosage: Same as greater pimpernel. In addition:

Powder: Take ½ tsp. in water, three times a day.

340   PINKROOT

(Spigelia marilandica)

Common Names: Carolina pink, Indian pink, star bloom, worm grass.

Medicinal Part: Rootstock.

Description: Pinkroot is an herbaceous perennial plant native to the rich woodlands of the eastern U.S. from New Jersey to Florida. The small, fibrous, yellow rootstock produces a smooth, erect, purplish stem with opposite, sessile, entire, lanceolate leaves about 2 to 4 inches long. The club-shaped flowers are red on the outside and yellow on the inside, growing in a short, one-sided spike from May to July.

Properties and Uses: Anthelmintic, narcotic. The effectiveness of pinkroot against worms was known by the American Indians, from whom its use was learned by the medical profession. Given in proper dosage and followed by a strong laxative, it was found to be highly effective for both children and adults. A decoction of the fresh rootstock was generally preferred, but the dried powdered rootstock was also commonly used. CAUTION: Pinkroot may produce side-effects such as rapid heartbeat, dizziness, and sluggishness. An overdose can be fatal.

Preparation and Dosage: Not recommended for use without medical supervision.

Powder: For adults, 4 to 8 grams each morning and evening for several days. Then take a strong laxative to remove the worms.

Mixture: To moderate the undesirable effects of pinkroot mix equal parts pinkroot, aniseed, male fern, senna leaves, and turtlebloom. Steep 1 tsp. of the mixture in 1 cup boiling-hot water. Take 1 cup at a time (children 1 tbsp.), as indicated, until results are obtained.

341 PIPSISSEWA

(Chimaphila umbellata)

Common Names: Bitter wintergreen, ground holly, king's cure, prince's pine, rheumatism weed, wintergreen.

Medicinal Part: The plant.

Description: Pipsissewa is a perennial, evergreen plant which favors the dry wood of the northern temperate areas of the world. It is found everywhere in the U.S. except the southernmost states of the east. A creeping, white rootstock produces several angular stems growing to about a foot high. The leathery, bright green leaves grow in whorls and are oblanceolate to oblong with sharply serrate margins. Terminal corymbs of waxy, white or pinkish flowers with purple centers appear from May to August.

Properties and Uses: Astringent, diaphoretic, diuretic. Pipsissewa is particularly noted for producing diuretic action without irritant side-effects. Prolonged use of the leaf tea is said to dissolve bladder stones. It has also been recommended for scrofula and rheumatic problems. With medical supervision, it can be used for dropsy, albuminuria, hematuria, chronic kidney problems, and gonorrhea. Externally, a tea or poultice made from the plant can be applied to ulcerous sores, tumors, blisters, and swellings.

Preparation and Dosage:

Infusion: Steep 1 tsp. leaves (or plant) in ½ cup water. Take in the course of a day, a mouthful at a time, unsweetened.

Tincture: Take 2 to 15 drops, as needed.

342 PITCHER PLANT

(Sarracenia purpurea)

Common Names: Eve's cup, flytrap, huntsman's cup, smallpox plant, watercup.

Medicinal Part: Rootstock.

Description: Pitcher plant is a native North American perennial plant found in swamps and wet areas from Maryland to Minnesota and in Canada. A horizontal, round rootstock produces the basal, pitcherlike, purple-veined leaves which are topped by an arching hood and are hairy and sticky on the inside (to trap insects, which the plant consumes). A solitary, large, red or purple flower nods on a naked flower stalk 1 to 2 feet high during May and June.

Properties and Uses: Astringent, diuretic, stimulant, tonic. Pitcher plant has sometimes been used for the purposes indicated by its categories, particularly as a tonic to stimulate appetite and digestion. Its most interesting use was that of some American Indians, who used an infusion of the rootstock against smallpox, both to provide immunity and to lessen the severity of the disease. A considerable controversy over its effectiveness resulted in its rejection by the medical profession in the nineteenth century, but the evidence was not conclusive on either side.

343 PLANTAIN

(a) (Plantago lanceolata)

Common Names: Lance-leaf plantain, buckhorn, chimney-sweeps, English plantain, headsman, ribgrass, ribwort, ripplegrass, snake plantain, soldier's herb.

Medicinal Part: The plant.

Description: Lance-leaf plantain is a perennial plant that inhabits meadows, roadsides, agricultural lands, and dooryards in the eastern and Pacific coastal states of the U.S., and in Canada and Europe. The erect, hairy, lanceolate leaves grow from the rootstock on margined petioles in a basal rosette. Several grooved flower stalks may grow from 6 to 30 inches high, tipped by a short spike of tiny white flowers whose brownish sepals and bracts give the spike its predominantly dark color. Flowering time is from April to November.

Properties and Uses: Astringent, demulcent, expectorant, hemostatic. Lance-leaf plantain is a useful remedy for cough irritations and hoarseness and for gastritis and enteritis. It is good for all respiratory problems, especially those involving mucous congestion. A decoction of the dried leaves promotes the coagulation of blood. The fresh juice, pressed from the whole plant, is helpful for chronic catarrhal problems, gastro-intestinal ailments, and worms. Externally, the fresh leaves are crushed for application to wounds, sores, cuts, scratches, insect bites, and even hemorrhoids.

Preparation and Dosage:

Infusion: Steep 1 tbsp. leaves in ½ cup water for 5 minutes. Take 1 cup a day.

Decoction: Boil 2 oz. dried leaves in ½ qt. water. Helps coagulate blood.

Juice: Take 1 tbsp. in water or milk or mixed with 1 tbsp. honey, three times a day.

Ointment: For hemorrhoids, boil 2 oz. of the plant in 1 pint soybean or peanut oil.

344 PLANTAIN (cont.)

(b) (Plantago major)

Common Names: Common plantain, broad-leaved plantain, dooryard plantain, greater plantain, round-leaved plantain, way bread, white man's foot.

Medicinal Part: The plant.

Description: Common plantain is a perennial plant that is, appropriately enough, common in waste places, lawns, dooryards, and roadsides all over North America (except the extreme north) and Europe. Its leaves are broadly ovate, entire or toothed, and characterized by a thick, channeled footstalk. The flower stalks grow from 6 to 18 inches high and are tipped with long, slender spikes of greenish-white flowers whose color is again overshadowed by brownish sepals and bracts. Flowering time is from May to October.

Properties and Uses: Astringent, demulcent, diuretic, expectorant, hemostatic. Common plantain can be used the same way as lance-leaf plantain. In addition, the juice or infusion can be taken for bladder problems and for gastrointestinal ulcers. A decoction can also be used externally for various skin problems, including ringworm, and also as a douche for leucorrhea. Chewing on the rootstock will give temporary relief from toothache. Finally, common plantain is sometimes recommended to increase virility (this use was probably suggested by the suggestive flower spike).

Preparation and Dosage:

Infusion: Steep 1 tsp. fresh or dried leaves in ½ cup water. Take 1 to 1½ cups a day, a mouthful at a time, unsweetened.

Juice: Take 2 to 3 tsp. a day in milk or soup.

(c) (Plantago media)

Common Names: Hoary plantain, gray ribwort, woolly plantain.

Medicinal Part: The plant.

Description: Hoary plantain is a perennial plant favoring the same habitats as the foregoing plantains, but it is geographically limited to the northeastern U.S. and some local areas in the western states. Its leaves are shorter than those of lance-leaf plantain, more ovate, and they are covered with white hairs. The fragrant white flowers grow in short, dense spikes from 1 to 3 inches long. Flowering time is May to September.

Properties and Uses: Same as lance-leaf plantain.

Preparation and Dosage: Same as lance-leaf plantain.

346   PLEURISY ROOT

(Asclepias tuberosa)

Common Names: Butterfly weed, Canada root, flux root, orange swallow-wort, tuber root, white root, wind root.

Medicinal Part: Root.

Description: Pleurisy root is a native North American perennial plant found in dry fields and sandy soils along the east coast and westward to Minnesota, Arizona, and northern Mexico. The fleshy, white root produces several stout, round, hairy stems from 1 to 3 feet high. The alternate, sessile leaves are lanceolate to oblong, a darker green above than beneath. Bright orange flowers grow in terminal, flat-topped umbels from June to September, later producing long, edible seed pods.

Properties and Uses: Carminative, diaphoretic, diuretic, expectorant. Pleurisy root was widely used as an expectorant in the late nineteenth century. It has been recommended for colds, flu, and bronchial and pulmonary problems. Sometimes it was given with cayenne at the beginning of a cold (see below). American Indians chewed the dried root or made a tea by boiling the root as a remedy for bronchitis, pneumonia, and dysentery. CAUTION: Animals have been poisoned by feeding on the leaves and stems. The fresh root may also produce undesirable symptoms.

Preparation and Dosage: Use the root dried or cooked.

Decoction: Boil 1 tsp. root in 1 cup water. Take 1 to 2 cups a day.

Tincture: Take 5 to 40 drops every 3 hours, depending on age and condition. At the beginning of a cold, take 5 to 15 drops in hot water and 3 grains cayenne every hour until you feel warm throughout. For children, the dose is 1 to 5 drops.

(a) (Prunus spinosa)

Common Names: Blackthorn, sloe, wild plum.

Medicinal Parts: Flowers, fruit, bark of the root.

Description: Blackthorn is a Eurasian tree or shrub, 10 to 15 feet high, commonly cultivated for ornamental purposes. It grows wild in clearings, among hedges, and along the edges of woods. The branches are very thorny and are covered with velvety hair when young. The small, alternate leaves are usually obtuse and range from obovate to ovate in shape. They are closely serrate and somewhat hairy on the veins beneath. In March and April, the small, white flowers grow profusely alone or in pairs along the branches. The harsh, astringent fruit is round, blue to black, and about ½ inch in diameter. It ripens in October.

Properties and Uses: Aperient, astringent, diaphoretic, diuretic, stomachic. A tea made from blackthorn flowers is a harmless and reliable purgative. It also has beneficial effects on the stomach and helps to stimulate appetite. In addition, it has been recommended for mild bladder problems, skin problems, catarrh, stomach cramps, dropsy, and stone formation. Try the juice of the fresh berries for inflammations in the mouth and throat. A jam made from the fruit makes a more palatable laxative than the fruit itself, and is especially suitable for children. A decoction of the root bark is said to be helpful for fever.

Preparation and Dosage: The fruit is more palatable if gathered after going through two or three night frosts.

Infusion: Steep 2 tsp. flowers (leaves may also be included) in ½ cup water. Take ½ cup in the morning, ½ cup in the evening, freshly made each time. Sweeten with honey if desired.

(b) (Prunus domestica)

Common Names: Common plum, European plum.

Medicinal Part: Fruit.

Description: Cultivated varieties of plum are grown in orchards in areas of temperate climate, mostly in the northern hemisphere. The thornless trees grow from 10 to 35 feet high and bear alternate, large, dull-green leaves which are wrinkled and coarsely serrate. They vary in shape from ovate to obovate and may be short-pointed to obtuse. About May the white or cream-colored flowers grow singly, in pairs, or in clusters on spurs along the branches. The fruit varies in size, color, and shape, depending on the variety.

Properties and Uses: Laxative, stomachic. Plums and prunes are well known for their laxative effect, but they also help to promote appetite and digestion. However, eaten in excessive quantities, fresh plums can produce stomach cramps and diarrhea. For a cold in its early stages, try 1 or 2 liqueur glasses of plum brandy in hot herb tea.

Preparation and Dosage: Plums may be eaten fresh or dried (prunes), made into jam, or taken as juice.

Prunes: For laxative effect, soak 5 to 10 prunes in water overnight, then eat them in the morning before breakfast.

349 PLUM (cont.)

(c) (Prunus americana)

Common Name: Wild plum.

Medicinal Parts: Fruit, bark.

Description: The native North American wild plum tree grows most commonly in thickets from southern New England southward and westward to Florida, Texas, Colorado, and Montana. The tree grows 20 to 30 feet high and has thorny branches with alternate, obovate to oblong-ovate, acuminate leaves with sharply serrate margins and hairy veins. The white flowers appear before the leaves, growing in small, umbel-like clusters. The fruit is usually small and hard, but sometimes large and tasty, and is generally yellow or red, ripening from August to October.

Properties and Uses: Anthelmintic, astringent, laxative. The wild plum shares the laxative properties of its relatives. In addition, American Indians gargled the decoction of the scraped inner bark for sores in the mouth and throat. One tribe drank a tea made from the root bark to expel worms.

POISON HEMLOCK

(Conium maculatum)

Common Names: Cicuta, hemlock, poison parsley, poison root, poison snakeweed, spotted cowbane, spotted hemlock, spotted parsley, water hemlock, water parsley, winter fern.

Medicinal Part: The herb.

Description: Poison hemlock is a biennial plant found in waste places and moist soils in the eastern U.S. and on the Pacific coast. A white or yellowish-white taproot produces a smooth, hollow, spotted stem with alternate, pinnately decompound leaves, the leaflets finely cut. Large, compound umbels of small, white flowers appear from June to August. The seeds are gray-green to grayish-brown, broadly ovate, ribbed, and somewhat compressed. When bruised, the fresh plant has a disagreeable mousy odor.

Properties and Uses: Poison hemlock is a dangerously poisonous plant, which has sometimes been used for sedation and to kill pain. In classical times, it was a standard method of executing convicted criminals, Socrates being the best-known of its victims. Poisoning has occurred when the seeds were mistaken for anise, the leaves for parsley, and the root for parsnip. Even blowing a whistle made from the hollow stem has caused poisoning.

Preparation and Dosage: Do not use poison hemlock under any circumstances without medical direction.

351 POKEWEED

(Phytolacca americana)

Common Names: Coakum, ink-berry, pigeonberry, poke, poke-root, red weed, scoke.

Medicinal Parts: Root, leaves, fruit.

Description: Pokeweed is a perennial plant native to North America and other parts of the world. In the U.S., it is found in damp soils and along the edges of woods from Maine to Florida and Texas. The large, fleshy root is covered with a thin, brown bark. It produces stems that are green when young and purplish later, reaching a height of 4 to 12 feet, a diameter of 1 inch. The alternate, simple, entire leaves are oblong- or ovate-lanceolate and acute or acuminate. Numerous small white or greenish-white flowers grow in peduncled racemes during July and August, followed by clusters of round, purple berries which contain a crimson juice.

Properties and Uses: Anodyne, cathartic. Pokeweed has been most commonly used for its laxative properties. The dried root has found application in relieving pain, reducing inflammation, treating rheumatism and arthritis, and combating skin parasites and diseases. The juice of the fruit has been used variously to treat cancer, hemorrhoids, and tremors. The sprouts of the young plants are sometimes eaten as pot-herbs after being boiled in two changes of water. CAUTION: The fresh or insufficiently cooked plant is poisonous, particularly the root. The seeds in the berries are also poisonous and are particularly hazardous for children.

Preparation and Dosage: Use the dried root or leaves. Use the berries without seeds.

Infusion or Decoction: Use 1 tbsp. root or leaves with 1 pint water. Take 1 tsp. at a time, as needed.

Tincture: A dose is 2 to 5 drops.

352 POMEGRANATE

(Punica granatum)

Medicinal Parts: Seeds, rind of the fruit.

Description: The pomegranate grows wild as a shrub in its native southern Asia and in hot areas of the world. Under cultivation, it is trained to a tree up to 20 feet high, being grown in Asia, the Mediterranean region, South America, and the southern states of the U.S. It is also grown in greenhouses in cooler climates. The slender, often spiny-tipped branches bear opposite, oblong or oval-lanceolate, shiny leaves about 1 to 2 inches long. One to five large, red or orange-red flowers grow together on the tips of axillary shoots. The brownish-yellow to red fruit, about the size of an orange, is a thick-skinned, several-celled, many-seeded berry; each seed is surrounded by red, acid pulp.

Properties and Uses: Anthelmintic, astringent. Pomegranate seeds have been used as a remedy for tapeworm since the time of the ancient Greeks. Its high tannin content makes the rind of the fruit an excellent astringent for internal and external use: for skin problems, as a gargle for throat and mouth irritation, as a vaginal douche, and for diarrhea. CAUTION: Large doses of the rind can cause cramps, vomiting, and other unpleasant effects.

353 POPLAR

(a) (Populus tremuloides)

Common Names: Quaking aspen, American aspen, aspen poplar, trembling poplar.

Medicinal Parts: Bark, buds.

Description: Quaking aspen is a small, deciduous tree found generally in mountainous, wooded areas of North America. Although usually 30 to 40 feet high, the quaking aspen sometimes reaches 100 feet. The bark is whitish and smooth on young trees, turning brownish and rough, especially near the base, on older trees. The alternate, ovate to orbicular, finely toothed leaves grow on very thin petioles which allow free movement in the wind, so that the tree appears to be "quaking." Male and female flowers grow in separate, slender catkins.

Properties and Uses: Balsamic, febrifuge, stomachic, tonic. The slightly sticky winter buds of quaking aspen can be made into a tea for internal or external use, or into a soothing salve. Drink the tea for coughs or gargle with it for sore throat. Use it externally as a wash for inflammations, cuts, scratches, wounds, and burns. Boil the buds in olive oil or lard to make a salve for the same external applications. Quaking aspen bark is highly esteemed by some for effectiveness against fever, and it is also said to relieve problems resulting from poor digestion.

POPLAR (cont.)

(b) (Populus candicans)

Common Names: Balm of Gilead, balsam poplar.

Medicinal Part: Buds.

Description: Balm of Gilead is a large, deciduous tree found on streambanks and planted along roadsides in the eastern U.S., over much of Canada, and into Alaska. It may grow as high as 100 feet but is usually smaller. Its winter buds are large, resinous and aromatic; the young twigs are sparsely hairy. The alternate, broadly ovate to deltoid leaves are dark green on top and whitish underneath, sometimes hairy on the lower veins. The male and female flowers occur on separate, scaly catkins.

Properties and Uses: Balsamic, expectorant, stimulant. Balm of Gilead buds are used and prepared like the buds of quaking aspen (see above). They can also be made into an inhalant to relieve congestion in the respiratory passages. Their salicin content may make them useful for the minor pains and aches that aspirin generally relieves.

Preparation and Dosage: Same as for quaking aspen.

355 **TACAMAHAC**

(Populus balsamifera)

NOTE: The buds of tacamahac (*Populus balsamifera*) can be used in place of balm of Gilead buds and are said by some to be superior. It is found along streams and lakes from Alaska through Canada into the northern U.S. Tacamahac grows up to 100 feet tall and has thick, ovate to ovate-lanceolate leaves with fine teeth and white undersides.

POPLAR (cont.)

(c) (Populus nigra)

Common Name: Black poplar.

Medicinal Part: Buds.

Description: Black poplar is a medium- to large-size tree found wild in the moist woods of Eurasia and also cultivated in some areas of the U.S. and Europe. The tree has gray bark, its branches are horizontal or bent toward the ground. Its alternate, triangular to ovate-triangular leaves are green on both sides and have margins with small, coarse teeth. The male and female flowers grow on separate, scaly catkins during March.

Properties and Uses: Diaphoretic, diuretic, expectorant, vulnerary. Black poplar buds are most commonly made into a salve for external use on wounds and hemorrhoids. They are also sometimes used in cosmetics for skin care. Internally the buds have been prescribed for urinary problems, bronchitis, arthritis and rheumatism.

Preparation and Dosage: Same as for quaking aspen.

357 **EUROPEAN ASPEN**
(Populus tremula)

NOTE: European aspen (*Populus tremula*) is another European poplar that can be used interchangeably with black poplar. It is a smaller tree found in light woods. Its leaves are orbicular or round-oval, green on top and grayish-green underneath. The leaves tremble in the wind like those of quaking aspen.

358   PRICKLY ASH

(Zanthoxylum americanum)

Common Names: Toothache bush, toothache tree, yellow wood.

Medicinal Parts: Bark, fruit.

Description: Prickly ash is a native North American shrub or tree, growing from 10 to 25 feet high in damp soils from Canada to Virginia and Nebraska. As the name indicates, the branchlets bear prickles up to ½ inch long. The leaves are alternate and odd-pinnate, with 5 to 11 ovate or elliptic leaflets that are softly hairy beneath. Small, yellowish-green flowers grow in axillary clusters during April and May, before the leaves appear. The fruit is a small, berry-like capsule containing one or more shiny black seeds.

Properties and Uses: Anodyne, diaphoretic, irritant, stimulant. Prickly ash bark was a toothache remedy for both Indians and white men in earlier times. It is not clear whether relief was due to an actual effect on the pain or to the distraction of attention caused by irritation produced by the bark. Some Indians also boiled the inner bark to make a wash for itching skin. Both the bark and the fruit have been used to treat rheumatism. Prickly ash is also said to be good for stomach problems, such as flatulence and poor digestion.

Preparation and Dosage:

Infusion or Decoction: Use 1 tsp. dried bark or berries with 1 cup water. Take 1 cup a day.

Tincture: A dose is 5 to 20 drops.

359 PRIDE OF CHINA

(Melia azedarach)

Common Names: Azedarach, Africa lilac, bead tree, China-berry, China-tree, hagbush, hop-tree, pride of India, pride tree.

Medicinal Parts: Root bark, fruit.

Description: Pride of China is a deciduous tree native to southwestern Asia but widely cultivated and naturalized in the West Indies and the southern U.S. Growing to 40 feet high or more, the thick trunk has spreading branches and is covered with furrowed bark. The alternate, bipinnate leaves are from 1 to 3 feet long and have numerous pointed, sharply serrate or lobed leaflets that range in shape from ovate and elliptic to lanceolate. The purplish, fragrant flowers grow in long-peduncled panicles, blooming in early spring. The fruit is a nearly round, yellow drupe from ½ to ¾ inch across.

Properties and Uses: Anthelmintic, astringent, bitter tonic, emetic, emmenagogue, purgative. A decoction of the root bark acts as a purgative and emetic, especially in large doses; it is also said to promote the onset of menstruation. The bark of the tree is bitter and astringent, and has been commonly used in India as a tonic. The seeds and oil of the fruit promote the elimination of intestinal worms. The tree also exudes a gum which has been considered by some to have aphrodisiac powers.

360 PRIMROSE

(Primula officinalis)

Common Names: Butter rose, English cowslip.

Medicinal Parts: Flowers, herb, rootstock.

Description: The primrose is a perennial plant common in Great Britain and continental Europe, in dry meadows, lightly wooded areas, underbrush, hedges, and along forest edges. The short, brown rootstock produces a rosette of downy, ovate to ovate-oblong leaves with undulating, crenate margins. The leaves contract at the base into winged petioles. A flower stalk, or scape, grows from 4 to 9 inches high, bearing a 5- to 12-flowered umbel of yellow, funnel-shaped flowers during April and May.

Properties and Uses: Anodyne, diuretic, expectorant. An infusion of primrose flowers is said to be helpful for ordinary and migraine headaches, insomnia, nervous conditions, and general weakness. A tea made from the flowering plant has been recommended for articular rheumatism. The rootstock makes a particularly good expectorant, a decoction being useful for catarrh, mucous congestion, coughs, bronchitis, and lung problems. In Europe, the primrose is considered a "blood purifier" useful for rheumatic, gouty and various other conditions attributed to contaminated blood. An ointment made of the leaves and flowers can be used for skin problems and blemishes. CAUTION: Some people are allergic to primroses and should, naturally, avoid medications made from them.

Preparation and Dosage:

Infusion: Steep 2 tsp. flowers (or herb and flowers) in ½ cup water. Take 1 cup a day. Make fresh each time.

Decoction: Boil 2 tsp. rootstock in 1 cup water.

Tincture: Take 5 to 20 drops, three or four times a day, as needed.

361 PRIVET

(Ligustrum vulgare)

Common Names: Prim, primwort, privy.

Medicinal Parts: Leaves, bark.

Description: Privet is a deciduous shrub which grows wild in southern Europe, northern Africa, and western Asia and is commonly cultivated as a hedge plant in parks and gardens in North America. Reaching a height of up to 15 feet in the natural state, the stems bear dark green, opposite, oblong-ovate to lanceolate leaves 1 or 2 inches long and about half as wide. The small, white, funnelform flowers grow in dense, pyramidal panicles during June and July. The fruit is a shiny black berry.

Properties and Uses: Astringent, bitter. A decoction of privet leaves or bark is helpful for diarrhea and other conditions for which an astringent is normally used. It also serves well as a mouthwash or gargle, a wash for skin problems, and a vaginal douche. Its bitter properties also make privet tea useful for improving appetite and digestion. CAUTION: The berries are poisonous; children have died from eating them.

Preparation and Dosage:

Decoction: Boil 1 tsp. leaves or bark in 1 cup water. Take 1 to 2 cups a day.

362 PUMPKIN

(Cucurbita pepo)

Common Name: Field pumpkin.

Medicinal Part: Seeds.

Description: The pumpkin is a large, annual, creeping plant which is widely cultivated in warm and temperate climates for its fruit. The stem, which may reach a length of 30 feet, has branched tendrils and bears alternate, stiff-haired, triangular or ovate-triangular leaves that may be sharply or weakly lobed. The leaves are larger than a hand and have irregularly sharp-serrate margins. Solitary, yellow, funnel-shaped flowers with pointed lobes grow on angular peduncles that expand where the flower attaches. Flowering time is from June to August. The fruit is the familiar large, orange, furrowed pumpkin which contains numerous white, elliptic seeds.

Properties and Uses: Anthelmintic. Large amounts of pumpkin seeds make a safe anthelmintic for children and adults. Pumpkin seed oil is also useful for healing wounds, especially burns, and for chapped skin.

Preparation and Dosage:

Seeds: To use for worms, crush 7 to 14 oz. seeds for children, up to 25 oz. for adults, and stir into fruit juice to make a mash to be eaten. Two or three hours later, take castor oil to drive out the worms. Take care, especially with tapeworm, that the entire worm is expelled.

363 QUASSIA

(Picraena excelsa)

Common Names: Bitter ash, bitter wood.

Medicinal Part: Wood.

Description: The quassia tree, a native of tropical America and the West Indies, grows from 50 to 100 feet high. It has smooth, gray bark and alternate, odd-pinnate leaves with oblong, pointed leaflets. Its small flowers are yellowish or greenish, its fruit is a small rupe about the size of a pea.

Properties and Uses: Anthelmintic, febrifuge, stomachic, bitter tonic. An infusion of quassia wood has been used to treat fever, rheumatism, and dyspepsia. Taken internally it kills round-worms, and as enema it kills pinworms. The tea is also said to destroy appetite for alcohol. Water left standing overnight in a cup made of quassia wood becomes a weak infusion suitable as a bitter tonic for the stomach. An infusion also serves as a scalp rinse to counteract dandruff.

Preparation and Dosage:

Infusion: Steep 1 tsp. quassia wood in 1 cup water. Take 1 cup a day.

Tincture: A dose is from 2 to 5 drops.

364   QUEEN OF THE MEADOW

(Eupatorium purpureum)

Common Names: Gravelroot, joe-pye weed, kidney root, purple boneset, trumpet weed.

Medicinal Parts: Rootstock, flowering herb.

Description: Queen of the meadow is a native North American perennial plant found in moist woods or meadows in southern Canada and from Maine to Florida and Texas. The woody, fibrous rootstock produces one or more hollow stems, from 3 to 10 feet high and marked with purple where the leaves attach. The elliptic-lanceolate, coarsely serrate leaves grow in whorls of 4 to 6. Flower heads of 6 or 7 flowers, varying from purple to whitish, grow in loose terminal clusters from August to September.

Properties and Uses: Astringent, diuretic, tonic. Queen of the meadow's role in American medicine has been mostly that of the diuretic, useful for kidney problems, urinary difficulties and gravel, dropsy, rheumatism, and neuralgia. The rootstock has some astringent properties and can be used for conditions where an astringent is helpful. One American Indian tribe con-sidered the plant useful as an aphrodisiac. A New England Indian named Joe Pye became famous by curing typhus with "joe-pye weed."

Preparation and Dosage:

Infusion: Steep 1 oz. rootstock in 1 pint water for 30 minutes. Take 1 oz. every three hours, or as needed.

Infusion: Steep 1 tsp. flowers or herb in 1 cup water. Take 1 to 2 cups a day.

Tincture: A dose is from 8 to 15 drops.

365. RADISH

(Raphanus sativus)

Common Names: Common radish, garden radish.

Medicinal Part: Root.

Description: Radish is an annual or biennial plant that is widely cultivated as a salad vegetable. The fleshy root, coming in various colors and shapes, produces an erect, hollow stem from 8 inches to 3 feet high. The alternate leaves are lyrately divided, with a large terminal segment. They may be glabrous or covered with sharp hairs. The white or lilac-colored flowers have violet veins and grow in branched racemes. Flowering time depends on the manner of cultivation.

Properties and Uses: Antispasmodic, astringent, cholagogue, diuretic. The juice pressed from grated, fresh radish is an old European home remedy for coughs, rheumatism, and gallbladder problems. For the latter, however, it must be taken as a "cure" lasting at least three weeks. Otherwise, radish has been used for chronic bronchitis, flatulence, diarrhea, headache, and insomnia. Radish is not recommended for use when the stomach or intestines are inflamed.

Preparation and Dosage: Radishes which have not developed flower stems are preferred.

Juice: Mix equal parts radish juice and honey. Take 1 tbsp. three times a day.

Juice Cure: Start by taking 3 to 4 oz. juice (by weight) before breakfast each day. Gradually increase the amount to 14 oz. a day. Depending on results, after 1 to 3 weeks, reduce the quantity to 3 or 4 oz. again until a complete cure is effected.

366. RAGGED CUP

(Silphium perfoliatum)

Common Names: Compass plant, cup plant, Indian cup, Indian gum, prairie dock, ragged cup, rosin weed.

Medicinal Parts: Rootstock, gum.

Description: Ragged cup is a perennial plant which grows in rich soils from Ontario to Georgia and Louisiana, and westward to South Dakota and Nebraska. The horizontal, pitted rootstock sends up a square, glabrous stem from 4 to 8 feet high. The large, opposite, ovate leaves are coarsely toothed, the lower ones narrowing to margined petioles, the upper clasping the stem with the bases of each pair of leaves united. The yellowish flowers grow in sunflower-like heads on long, forked, axillary peduncles. Flowering time is from July to September. The plant contains a resinous sap.

Properties and Uses: Antispasmodic, diaphoretic, stimulant, tonic. The gum, or resinous sap, of ragged cup has been used in medicine for its antispasmodic and stimulant properties. The rootstock can be considered as a general medical agent helpful for fevers, ulcers, liver and spleen problems, and physical debility.

Preparation and Dosage:

Infusion: Steep 1 tsp. rootstock in 1 cup water. Take 1 cup a day.

Powder: A dose of powdered rootstock is 20 grains.

Tincture: A dose is from 5 to 20 drops.

367. RAGWORT

(Senecio aureus)

Common Names: Cocash weed, coughweed, golden ragwort, grundy swallow, life root, squaw weed.

Medicinal Part: The plant.

Description: Ragwort is a native perennial plant found in marshes, along stream-banks, and in other wet areas from Newfoundland to Florida and westward to Wisconsin and Texas. The erect, grooved, brown-streaked stem grows from 1 to 2 feet high and bears alternate, oblong or lanceolate, pinnatifid or lyrate leaves. There are also coarsely toothed basal leaves which are cordate-ovate or reniform, long-petioled and sometimes purplish underneath. Flower heads with golden-yellow rays and brownish disks grow in terminal corymbs from May to July.

Properties and Uses: Diaphoretic, diuretic, emmenagogue. Ragwort has been used primarily in connection with female complaints, such as leucorrhea or suppressed menstruation. American Indians used it to speed childbirth and also to induce abortion. It has also been recommended for gravel and other problems of the urinary tract. CAUTION: Ragwort contains toxic alkaloids which are known to be poisonous to livestock.

368   **COMMON GROUNDSEL**
(Senecio vulgaris)

369   **EUROPEAN RAGWORT**
(Senecio jacoboea)

NOTE: Two related plants—common groundsel (*Senecio vulgaris*) and European ragwort (*Senecio jacoboea*)—have similar medicinal properties and are also said to affect the liver (not necessarily favorably). Common groundsel is a widespread weed that can be found in gardens, fields, and waste places all over the world. European ragwort is now a naturalized citizen of eastern Canada, the northeastern U.S. and individual localities elsewhere. The medicinal use of these plants without medical direction is not advisable.

370   RASPBERRY
(a) (Rubus strigosus)

Common Name: Wild red raspberry.

Medicinal Parts: Leaves, fruit.

Description: Wild red raspberry is a native shrubby plant widespread in thickets and untended fields over North America. A durable root produces the prickly, biennial stem with alternate, pinnate leaves consisting of three to five narrow, oblong-ovate, acuminate leaflets. The white, cup-shaped flowers appear in spring and summer of the second year. The red edible fruit, made up of cohering drupelets, ripens during the summer.

Properties and Uses: Antiemetic, astringent, laxative. Raspberry leaf tea has found many uses in and out of medicine, including that of a beverage tea. It makes a good remedy for diarrhea; when combined with cream it will relieve nausea and vomiting. It was also once taken by pregnant women to prevent miscarriage, increase milk, and reduce labor pains. Fresh raspberries are mildly laxative.

Preparation and Dosage:

Infusion: Steep 1 oz. leaves in 2 cups water for 15 minutes. Take 2 cups a day.

(b) (Rubus idaeus)

Common Names: Garden raspberry, European red raspberry.

Medicinal Parts: Leaves, fruit.

Description: Garden raspberry is a shrubby plant that is widely cultivated for its fruit but which also grows wild in and around forests in Europe. Growing as high as 6½ feet, the biennial stems have few or no prickles and bear alternate, pinnate leaves with three to seven serrate, broad-ovate to oblong-ovate, cordate leaflets which are usually downy white underneath. Clusters of one to six white flowers appear in the upper axils during spring and summer of the second year, producing the familiar red fruit which ripens later during the summer.

Properties and Uses: Astringent, cardiac, refrigerant. As with its wild cousin above, garden raspberry makes a leaf tea that is good for diarrhea and which can also be drunk as a beverage. As an astringent, it is also sometimes used as a gargle, a mouthwash, or an external wash for sores, wounds, skin rashes, etc. Fresh raspberry juice, mixed with a little honey, makes an excellent refrigerant beverage to be taken in the heat of a fever. Made into a syrup or taken with wine vinegar, the juice is said to have beneficial effects on the heart.

Preparation and Dosage:

Infusion: Steep 1 to 2 tbsp. leaves in ½ cup water. Take 1 cup a day.

Syrup: Cook 7 parts fresh juice with 10 parts sugar until the desired consistency is obtained.

Vinegar: Mix 1 part raspberry syrup with 2 parts wine vinegar.

372 **RATTLESNAKE PLANTAIN**

(Goodyera pubescens)

Common Names: Adder's violet, downy rattlesnake plantain, net-leaf plantain, networt, rattlesnake weed, scrofula weed, spotted plantain, water plantain.

Medicinal Parts: Leaves, rootstock.

Description: Rattlesnake plantain is a perennial plant native to evergreen woods and rich soils of the eastern U.S. The fleshy, creeping rootstock produces dark green, basal, ovate leaves with networks of white veins. A glandular-hairy flower stalk with leaf-like, lanceolate scales bears a spike-like raceme of white or greenish-white flowers from July to September.

Properties and Uses: Demulcent. The fresh leaves and rootstock of rattlesnake plantain make a helpful external application for scrofulous sores, skin rashes, bruises, and insect bites. If desired, they can be soaked in milk and then made into a poultice.

373 RED EYEBRIGHT

(Euphrasia officinalis)

Common Names: Euphrasy, eye-bright.

Medicinal Part: The herb.

Description: Red eyebright is a small, downy, annual herb very common in meadows, pastures, and other grassy areas of Europe and western Asia and probably naturalized locally in various places in the U.S. Its square, leafy stem grows up to 12 inches high and bears opposite, stiff, ovate leaves. The two-lipped, red or purple and white flowers grow in axillary leafy spikes from June to September.

Properties and Uses: Astringent, tonic. As the name suggests, red eyebright has been used to treat eye inflammations, eyestrain, and other eye ailments. A weak infusion of the fresh herb is used for these purposes, either as an eyewash or as fomentation. In addition, an infusion or poultice of red eyebright has been used for symptoms associated with colds, such as coughs, sore throat, nasal congestion, and catarrh. In Europe it has sometimes been taken for hay fever.

Preparation and Dosage: Make preparations fresh each time.

Infusion: Steep 1 heaping tsp. fresh herb in boiling-hot water for a few minutes. Take 1 to 2 cups a day.

Decoction: Boil 1 tsp. dried herb in 1 cup water for 5 minutes.

Tincture: Take 15 to 40 drops every three or four hours, as needed.

(Anagallis arvensis)

Common Names: Poor man's weatherglass, red chickweed, scarlet pimpernel.

Medicinal Part: The plant.

Description: Red pimpernel is a low annual plant found particularly in cultivated and loamy soils all over North America, especially in coastal states, as well as in Europe and Asia. The square, procumbent or ascending stems reach a length of about 12 inches. The sessile, ovate leaves grow in opposite pairs or in threes, are blue-green on top, and have brown or black spots on the underside. Starlike, axillary, red (sometimes blue or white) flowers bloom from June to October. Their characteristic of closing when bad weather impends accounts for the plant's "weatherglass" name.

Properties and Uses: Cholagogue, diaphoretic, diuretic, expectorant, nervine, purgative, stimulant. In moderate doses, red pimpernel causes sweating and increased kidney activity. In large doses, it acts on the central nervous system and the brain, producing trembling along with watery stools and copious urine. In skilled hands, it can be useful for various nervous conditions, liver problems, and dyspepsia. A tincture of the plant is sometimes used for skin problems and external sores. CAUTION: Improper doses can cause disagreeable internal effects. Also, the fresh leaves can cause dermatitis.

Preparation and Dosage: Do not use without medical direction.

375   RED SEDGE

(Carex arenaria)

Common Names: German sarsaparilla, red couchgrass, sand
sedge, sea sedge.

Medicinal Parts: Rootstock and
roots.

Description: Red sedge is a small,
perennial herb found on riverbanks, wet embankments, shorelines, and other sandy soils from
France to northern Europe. The
creeping rootstock grows to
lengths of over 30 feet but is very
thin. It produces stiff, grooved,
triangular flower stalks sheathed

with linear leaves which separate from the stalk near the bottom
or at various points along its length. Small terminal spikes of
tiny, green, inconspicuous flowers appear during May and June.

Properties and Uses: Diaphoretic, diuretic. Red sedge root has
sometimes been used to stimulate stomach and intestinal glands,
for gastro-intestinal catarrh, colic, chronic constipation, and also
for coughs and hoarseness. In mild cases of tuberculosis, the
rootstock's silicic acid content may be useful in stabilizing
scarred tissue. For various skin problems, take red sedge as a
diaphoretic tea. CAUTION: Do not use when acute kidney inflammation is present.

Preparation and Dosage:

Decoction: Boil 2 tbsp. rootstock and roots in 1 cup water.
Take 1 cup a day, warm.

Cold Extract: Soak 2 tsp. rootstock and roots in 1 cup cold
water for 8 hours. Take 1 cup a day.

RESTHARROW

(Ononis spinosa)

Common Names: Cammock, petty whin, stayplough.

Medicinal Part: Roots.

Description: Restharrow is a shrubby perennial plant fairly common in dry meadows, pastures, fallow land, and limestone soils in Europe and sometimes cultivated as a garden plant in the U.S. The plant's deep, sinuous roots produce spiny, much-branched stems which are woody at the base and which grow from 1 to 2 feet high. The alternate leaves are simple near the top and pinnate near the bottom, with three serrate, oblong leaflets. The rose-colored or white, papilionaceous (butterfly-shaped) flowers grow singly or in twos and threes in the leaf axils from June to August. The fruit is an ovate, hairy pod.

Properties and Uses: Aperient, diuretic. Restharrow is known primarily for its diuretic properties, which are effective but act without negative side-effects. It is good for edema and water retention, particularly for those who tend to accumulate uric acid and are thus susceptible to gravel and stones. Restharrow has also been recommended for urinary catarrh, kidney inflammations, and rheumatism. A decoction of the roots can be used externally for eczema, itching, and other skin problems.

Preparation and Dosage:

Infusion: Steep 3 to 4 tbsp. roots in 1 cup water for 5 minutes while stirring. Take 1 to 1½ cups a day, warm.

Decoction: Soak 2 tsp. roots in ½ cup cold water for 8 hours, then bring rapidly to a boil.

377 **RHATANY**

(Krameria triandra)

Common Name: Peruvian rhatany.

Medicinal Part: Root.

Description: Rhatany is a shrubby, leguminous, perennial plant that you are not likely to encounter unless you are wandering in the dry, gravelly hills of Peru. The long, horizontal root produces a procumbent, branching stem with alternate, hoary, oblong to obovate leaves. Red flowers grow on short stalks and bloom all year.

Properties and Uses: Astringent, diuretic, styptic. Rhatany root is a strong astringent which can be used for diarrhea and all other cases where astringent action is called for. Its styptic property also makes it useful to stop internal and external bleeding. In addition, rhatany root has been recommended (but to be used with care) for typhoid fever and for conditions involving inflammations of the alimentary system (e.g., enteritis, gastritis, proctitis).

Preparation and Dosage:

Infusion: Steep 1 tsp. root in 1 cup water. Take 1 cup a day.

Powder: Run water through powdered root until a red solution is obtained.

Tincture: A dose is from 5 to 20 drops.

378 RHUBARB

(Rheum palmatum)

Common Names: Chinese rhubarb, turkey rhubarb.

Medicinal Part: Rootstock.

Description: This species of rhubarb is a perennial herb which resembles the common garden rhubarb but which is cultivated outside its native Tibet and China mainly for ornamental purposes. The conical rootstock, which is fleshy and yellow inside, produces large, cordate, or almost orbicular, 7-lobed leaves on thick petioles that are from 12 to 18 inches long. A hollow flower stem, 5 to 10 feet high, also grows from the rootstock and is topped by a leafy panicle of greenish or whitish flowers.

Properties and Uses: Appetizer, astringent, purgative, tonic. The rootstock of rhubarb has a Janus-like property of being both laxative and astringent, the activity depending on the amount used (see below). However, prolonged use is not advisable, since rhubarb aggravates any tendency toward chronic constipation. Pregnant women and those nursing babies are also cautioned against using it. In small doses, a cold extract of the rootstock is useful to stimulate appetite. The tincture is sometimes added to wines and aperitifs to stimulate appetite and digestion. CAUTION: The leaf blades (although not the stalks) of rhubarb contain enough oxalic acid to cause poisoning.

Preparation and Dosage:

Cold Extract: Soak the rootstock in cold water for 8 to 10 hours. For a laxative, take 1 tbsp. two or three times a day; for an appetizer, take 1 tsp. two or three times a day, shortly before meals.

Rootstock: For a laxative, take 1 tsp. powdered or chopped rootstock in ½ cup water. As an astringent for diarrhea, take ¼ tsp. rootstock in ½ cup water. These are doses for one day.

379   ROCK-ROSE

(Helianthemum canadense)

Common Names: Frost plant, frostwort, sun rose.

Medicinal Part: The herb.

Description: Rock-rose is a native North American perennial plant which grows in dry, sandy soils and in the U.S. can be found as far south as North Carolina and Mississippi and as far west as Indiana and Wisconsin. The unbranched, downy stem bears alternate, linear-oblong leaves which are dark green above and downy white beneath. The plant flowers twice in a season: the first flowers are bright yellow and have large petals that drop a day or so after opening; later another set of inconspicuous flowers develops, growing in axillary clusters.

Properties and Uses: Astringent, tonic. Rock-rose is relatively little used, at least alone. As an astringent, it can be used for diarrhea, mouth and throat irritations, and skin problems. It has also been used at times as an eyewash. In large doses it acts as an emetic.

Preparation and Dosage:

Infusion: Steep 1 tsp. herb in 1 cup water. Take 1 tbsp. three to six times a day.

Tincture: A dose is from 5 to 10 drops.

ROSE

(Rosa spp.)

Common Names: There are over 100 species of rose, and to them and their varieties have been given thousands of names. In the face of such abundance, it may be best to say with Shakespeare's Juliet:

> What's in a name? that which we call a rose
> By any other name would smell as sweet.

Medicinal Parts: Flowers, hips.

Description: The genus *Rosa* consists of prickly shrubs found wild and widely cultivated in the temperate parts of the Northern Hemisphere. Their trailing, climbing, or erect stems bear alternate, odd-pinnate leaves; the familiar white to deep-red flowers are usually single and five-petaled in the wild species, but are often double in cultivated varieties. The fruit consists of hairy achenes that are borne like seeds by the fruitlike, fleshy hip, which is technically a ripened hypanthium.

Properties and Uses: Aperient, astringent, stomachic. The common red garden rose has long been a favorite medicinal plant in the practice of European folk medicine. An infusion of dried rose petals is taken for headache and dizziness and, with honey added, as a heart and nerve tonic and a "blood purifier." A decoction of the petals serves to treat mouth sores; and a decoction made with wine invigorates the tired body and is also useful to ease uterine cramps. As a mouthwash, the wine decoction helps allay toothache; as a cold compress for the forehead, it relieves headache; and as a warm trickle into the ear, it helps earache. Cloths soaked with rose vinegar can also be used as a compress for headache; and rose honey is an ancient remedy for sore throat.

Red roses are considered best for medicinal use. Of the horticultural types, those classified as Hybrid Perpetuals are the most suitable. The following are the species most commonly used medicinally.

380   ROSA CALIFORNICA
Californian rose; found growing in moist places from Oregon to Baja California. West-coast Indians used it to make cold remedies. Spanish-Americans still eat the ripe hips either raw or stewed, collecting them after they have been sweetened by enduring frost.

381   ROSA CENTIFOLIA
Cabbage rose; found wild in eastern Caucasia, cultivated elsewhere and one of the oldest of cultivated roses. Cabbage rose is the source of commercial rose water. The infusion, powder, and tincture are also said to be useful for hemorrhage, and the infusion has aperient properties. Rose water can be made into a good ointment for rough, dry, or chapped skin.

382   ROSA DAMASCENA
Damask rose; found wild in the Balkans and Asia Minor, cultivated on a large scale in Bulgaria, Turkey, and southern France. Steam distillation of damask rose petals produces attar (or otto) of roses, the rose oil used mostly for perfumes and as a flavor-

ing agent. Attar of roses, however, is also used as a rejuvenating agent and is said to be helpful in regulating the menstrual cycle. Inhaled, it helps to induce sleep too.

383   ROSA EGLANTERIA
Eglantine, sweetbriar; found wild in Asia, Europe, and North America, and widely cultivated. In Iran it is used to relieve colic and diarrhea.

384   ROSA GALLICA
French rose; found wild in Europe and West Asia, and elsewhere often escaped from cultivation. Preparations of the dried petals are mildly astringent and tonic; the infusion can be used as a vaginal douche or as an eyewash.

385   ROSA LAEVIGATA
Cherokee rose; an evergreen vine found wild in China and Japan and also as an escaped plant in the southern U.S. In China it is used to treat problems with frequent or excessive involuntary release of semen.

386   ROSA ROXBURGHII
A species found in China. Its hips are used in Chinese medicine to relieve dyspepsia.

Preparation and Dosage: Petals to be dried are collected before the flower unfolds.

Infusion: Use 2 heaping tsp. per cup of water.

Rose Water: Boil fresh petals in water and condense the vapor in another vessel to get rose water. For internal use, a dose is 1 to 2 oz.

Rose Honey (old style): Pound fresh petals in a little boiling water. Filter and boil the remaining liquid with honey.

Rose Honey (new style): Blend clarified honey and fluid extract of roses.

Rose Vinegar: Steep rose petals in distilled vinegar. Do not boil.

Tincture: Add 1 pint boiling-hot water to 1 oz. dried petals; add 15 drops of oil of vitriol and 3 to 4 tsp. white sugar. Strain. Take 3 to 4 tsp., two or three times a day for hemorrhage or as a stomachic. See also Brier hip, no. 66.

ROSEMARY

(Rosmarinus officinalis)

Medicinal Parts: Leaves, flowering tops.

Description: Rosemary is an evergreen shrub which originated in the Mediterranean area and is now widely cultivated for its aromatic leaves and as a kitchen seasoning. The numerous branches have an ash-colored, scaly bark and bear opposite, leathery, thick leaves which are lustrous and dark green above and downy white underneath. They have a prominent vein in the middle and margins which are rolled down. The pale blue (sometimes white) flowers grow in short axillary racemes, blooming during April and May, or later in cooler climates.

Properties and Uses: Antispasmodic, cholagogue, emmenagogue, stimulant, stomachic. The stimulant action of rosemary helps promote liver function, the production of bile, and proper digestion. It also acts to raise blood pressure and improve circulation. Because of the genuine danger of poisoning, however, rosemary is more often used externally. Leaves cooked in wine or salve made from rosemary oil is useful for rheumatism, scrofulous sores, eczema, bruises, and wounds. An infusion of the leaves has also been used, alone or with borax, as a scalp wash to prevent baldness. Rosemary tea makes a good mouthwash for halitosis, too. CAUTION: Excessive amounts of rosemary taken internally can cause fatal poisoning.

Preparation and Dosage:

Infusion: Steep 1 tsp. dried flowering tops or leaves in ½ cup water. Take up to 1 cup a day.

Tincture: A dose is from 5 to 20 drops.

388 ROWAN
(Sorbus aucuparia)

Common Names: European mountain ash, mountain ash, sorb apple.

Medicinal Part: Fruit.

Description: Rowan is a deciduous tree or shrub which grows wild in the deciduous forests and mountains of Europe and Asia. It is often planted for ornament there and elsewhere. Growing up to 50 feet high, the stem has close and smooth gray bark. The leaves are alternate and odd-pinnate, with 9 to 15 oblong-lanceolate, serrate leaflets which are usually finely hairy underneath. Numerous small white flowers appear in compound, terminal, shaggy corymbs during May and June, developing eventually into a berry-like, pea-sized, red pome which ripens in the fall.

Properties and Uses: Aperient, astringent, diuretic. The fresh juice of the fruit is mildly laxative, and it is also useful to soothe inflamed mucous membrane—it makes a good gargle for hoarseness and sore throat. When made into a jam, however, the fruit becomes astringent and useful for mild cases of diarrhea. One of the sugars contained in the fruit is sometimes given intravenously to reduce pressure in the eyeball in cases of glaucoma.

Preparation and Dosage:

Juice: Take 1 tsp. fresh juice at a time, as needed.

Cold Extract: Soak 1 tsp. dried fruit in 1 cup water for 10 hours. Take 1 cup a day.

Jam: Cook fruit with half as much sugar as berries. Take 1 tbsp., three to five times a day for mild diarrhea.

389 AMERICAN MOUNTAIN ASH
(Sorbus americana)

NOTE: American mountain ash (*Sorbus americana*) can also be used in the same way. This shrub or tree grows to 30 feet high and is found from Newfoundland to North Carolina and Michigan.

390 RUE

(Ruta graveolens)

Common Names: Common rue, garden rue, German rue, herb-of-grace.

Medicinal Part: The herb.

Description: Rue is an aromatic perennial plant native to southern Europe and northern Africa and commonly cultivated in Europe and the U.S., sometimes escaping to grow wild locally. The branched, pale green, glabrous stem bears alternate, pinnately decompound, somewhat fleshy leaves with oblong to spatulate leaflets. Small yellow or yellow-green flowers grow in paniculate clusters from June to August.

Properties and Uses: Anthelmintic, carminative, emmenagogue, stimulant, stomachic. The main uses for rue are to relieve gouty and rheumatic pains and to treat nervous heart problems, such as palpitations in women going through menopause. The infusion is also said to be useful in eliminating worms. In European folk medicine, rue serves to relieve gas pains and colic, improve appetite and digestion, and promote the onset of menstruation. Rue can also be made into an ointment for external use against gout, rheumatism, and sciatica. CAUTION: Large doses of rue can cause mild poisoning. Contact with the fresh plant may cause dermatitis in sensitive persons; the juice is a local irritant. Rue is not to be used by pregnant women.

Preparation and Dosage:

Infusion: Steep 1 tsp. dried herb in ½ cup water. Take ½ cup a day.

Cold Extract: Soak 1 tsp. dried herb in ¾ cup cold water for 10 hours and strain. Take ¾ cup a day.

Tincture: A dose is from 5 to 20 drops.

391 SAFFLOWER

(Carthamus tinctorius)

Common Names: American saffron, dyers' saffron, false saffron.

Medicinal Part: Flowers.

Description: Safflower is an annual plant native to the Mediterranean countries and cultivated in Europe and the U.S. Its glabrous, branching stem grows from 1 to 3 feet high and bears alternate, sessile, oblong, or ovate-lanceolate leaves armed with small, spiny teeth. The orange-yellow flowers grow in flower heads about 1 to 1½ inches across.

Properties and Uses: Diaphoretic, diuretic. Taken hot, safflower tea produces strong perspiration and has thus been used for colds and related ailments. It has also been used at times for its soothing effect in cases of hysteria, such as that associated with chlorosis.

Preparation and Dosage:

Infusion: Steep 1 tsp. flowers in 1 cup water. Take 1 to 2 cups a day.

Tincture: A dose is from 20 to 60 drops.

392   SAFFRON

(*Crocus sativus*)

Common Names: Autumn crocus, Spanish saffron..

Medicinal Part: The stigmas.

Description: Saffron is a small perennial plant which is cultivated in many places, but particularly in France, Spain, Sicily, and Iran. In springtime, an onion-like corm produces basal, linear leaves which are surrounded as a group at the bottom by cylindrical sheaths. These gray-green leaves have hairy margins and grow to about 1 or 1½ feet long. About August or September, the corm produces a funnel-shaped, reddish-purple (sometimes lilac or white) flower.

Properties and Uses: Anodyne, antispasmodic, aphrodisiac, appetizer, emmenagogue, expectorant, sedative. Saffron has been used, in small doses only, for coughs, whooping cough, stomach gas, gastrointestinal colic and insomnia. As an ingredient in herb liqueurs, it serves as a stimulant to appetite; and it is sometimes made into a salve for treatment of gout. CAUTION: Saffron contains a poison that acts on the central nervous system and damages the kidneys. Large doses can have severe effects; 10 to 12 grams is a fatal dose for human beings. The high cost of saffron and the availability of synthetic substitutes make its use as medicine rare.

Infusion: Steep 6 to 10 stigmas in ½ cup water. Take ½ to 1 cup a day, unsweetened, a mouthful at a time.

393   SAGE

(*Salvia officinalis*)

Common Name: Garden sage.

Medicinal Part: Leaves.

Description: Sage is a shrubby perennial plant which grows wild in southern Europe and the Mediterranean countries and is commonly cultivated elsewhere as a kitchen spice. A strongly branched root system produces square, finely hairy stems which are woody at the base and bear opposite, downy, oblong leaves which may be entire or finely crenate. The floral leaves are ovate to ovate-lanceolate. Purple, blue, or white two-lipped flowers grow in whorls which form terminal racemes. Flowering time is June and July.

Properties and Uses: Antihydrotic, antispasmodic, astringent. Sage's best-known effect is the reduction of perspiration, which usually begins about two hours after taking sage tea or tincture and may last for several days. This property makes it useful for night sweats, such as those common with tuberculosis. A nursing mother whose child has been weaned can take sage tea for a few days to help stop the flow of milk. The tea has also been prescribed for nervous conditions, trembling, depression, and vertigo. It is said to be helpful too in cases of leucorrhea, dysmenorrhea, and amenorrhea. As an astringent, it can be used for diarrhea, gastritis, and enteritis. As a gargle, the tea is good for sore throat, laryngitis, and tonsillitis. It also helps to eliminate mucous congestion in the respiratory passages and the stomach. Finally, crushed fresh sage leaves can be used as first aid for insect bites. CAUTION: Extended or excessive use of sage can cause symptoms of poisoning.

Preparation and Dosage: Use leaves collected before flowering.

Infusion: Steep 1 tsp. leaves in ½ cup water for 30 minutes. Take 1 cup a day, a tablespoonful at a time.

Powder: Take ¼ to ½ tsp. powdered leaves at a time.

Tincture: Take 15 to 40 drops, three or four times a day.

NOTE: Wild or lyre-leaved sage *(Salvia lyrata)*, found in dry woodlands of the eastern U.S. and characterized by lyre-shaped basal leaves, has properties like those of garden sage; but it also contains acrid substances, and its crushed leaves have been used to remove warts. It is generally used in mixtures rather than alone.

395   ST. BENEDICT THISTLE

(Cnicus benedictus)

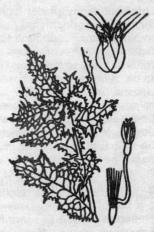

Common Names: Blessed thistle, cardin, holy thistle, spotted thistle.

Medicinal Part: The herb.

Description: St. Benedict thistle is an annual plant which grows wild in southern Europe and western Asia and is cultivated elsewhere. It is occasionally found wild in North America. The pentagonal, branched, bristly stem bears oblong, pinnatifid, spiny leaves with sinuate margins. Yellow, rayless flower heads, surrounded by leathery, spiny bracts, bloom from May to August.

Properties and Uses: Diaphoretic, diuretic, emetic, tonic. In normal dosage, St. Benedict thistle tea can be taken daily for stomach and digestive problems, flatulence, constipation, and liver and gallbladder ailments, chronic headache, and fever. A strong tea acts as an emetic and should be used cautiously. The plant can be made into a poultice or the tea used externally for chilblains, wounds, and sores.

Preparation and Dosage:

Infusion: Steep 1 tsp. dried herb in ½ cup water. Take 1 to 1½ cups a day, unsweetened, a mouthful at a time.

Tincture: A dose is from 5 to 20 drops.

396 ST. JOHNSWORT
(Hypericum perforatum)

Common Names: Amber, goat-weed, Johnswort, Klamath weed, Tipton weed.

Medicinal Part: The herb.

Description: St. Johnswort is a shrubby perennial plant commonly found in dry, gravelly soils, fields, and sunny places in many parts of the world, including eastern North America and the Pacific coast. A woody, branched root produces many round stems which put out runners from the base. The opposite, oblong to linear leaves are covered with transparent oil glands that look like holes. Flat-topped cymes of yellow flowers, whose petals are dotted with black along the margins, appear from June to September. The fruit is a three-celled capsule containing small, dark brown seeds. The whole plant has a turpentine-like odor.

Properties and Uses: Antispasmodic, astringent, expectorant, nervine, vulnerary. The calming properties of St. Johnswort have been useful in treating bedwetting, insomnia, and other nervous conditions, as well as some forms of melancholy. An oil extract of the herb can be taken for stomachache, colic, intestinal problems, and as an expectorant for congestion in the lungs. A tea made from the flowers is good for anemia, headache, insomnia, jaundice, chest congestion, and catarrh. A tea made from the herb has been used for uterine cramping and menstrual difficulties. The oil extract also makes a good external application for burns, wounds, sores, bruises, and other skin problems. CAUTION: St. Johnswort has sometimes poisoned livestock. Its use may also make the skin sensitive to light.

Preparation and Dosage:

Infusion: Steep 1 tsp. dried herb in ½ cup water for 5 minutes, covered. Take warm, ½ cup before breakfast and ½ cup when going to bed.

Oil Extract: Take 10 to 15 drops in water. To make, put fresh flowers and leaves in a jar and fill with olive oil. Close the jar and leave it in a sunny or warm place for 6 to 7 weeks, shaking it often. The oil will turn red. Strain the oil through a cloth. If a watery layer appears when the oil has stood a while, decant or siphon it off. In a dark container the oil will keep for up to two years.

397 SANDALWOOD

(Santalum album)

Common Names: White sandalwood, white saunders, yellow sandalwood.

Medicinal Part: Wood.

Description: Sandalwood is a small tree that grows primarily in India. The wood of its stem, which grows from 20 to 30 feet high, is heavy and straight-grained and varies in color from white when young to yellow or orange when older. Its oval leaves are covered with a whitish bloom; its small flowers, varying in color, grow in numerous cymes.

Properties and Uses: Astringent, disinfectant, diuretic, expectorant, stimulant. The medicinal properties of sandalwood reside in the oil, which can be pressed from the wood or extracted with alcohol or water. The antiseptic and disinfectant properties of this oil are similar to those of cubeb oil. The oil can also be used for bronchitis and for inflammation in mucous tissue. A decoction of the wood may be helpful for indigestion and fever and externally for skin problems, especially those of bacterial origin.

Preparation and Dosage:

Decoction: Boil 1 heaping tsp. wood in 1 cup water. Take 1 to 2 cups a day, a mouthful at a time.

Tincture: A dose is from 20 to 40 drops.

398 SANICLE

(a) (Sanicula marilandica)

Common Names: American sanicle, black sanicle, black snakeroot.

Medicinal Part: Rootstock.

Description: American sanicle is a perennial plant found in rich woods from Newfoundland south to Georgia, and west to Alberta and Colorado. A fibrous rootstock produces a lightgreen, furrowed, hollow stem bearing a few sessile leaves or none at all. Most of the plant's bluish-green, palmately lobed leaves are basal, growing on long petioles. Small umbels of white, greenish-white, or yellowish flowers bloom from May to July.

Properties and Uses: Astringent, expectorant, nervine. The astringent properties of sanicle root make it useful as a gargle for irritations and sores in the mouth and throat and also internally for ulcers, hemorrhage and excessive menstrual flow. The powdered root has been popularly used against intermittent fever and chorea (St. Vitus' dance).

Preparation and Dosage:
Infusion: Steep 1 tsp. rootstock in water. Take 1 cup a day.
Tincture: A dose is from 15 to 30 drops.

399 SANICLE (cont.)

(b) (Sanicula europaea)

Common Names: European sanicle, wood sanicle.

Medicinal Part: Leaves.

Description: European sanicle is a perennial plant commonly found in shady, moist places in the deciduous forests of Europe. The short, woody rootstock produces a naked stem up to 1½ feet high, as well as the basal, palmately divided, serrate leaves. Small, white to reddish flowers grow in compound umbels from May to July. Later the plant produces a globular fruit with hooked prickles.

Properties and Uses: Astringent, expectorant, styptic. European sanicle tea helps to relieve mucous congestion in the chest, stomach, and intestines. As a gargle and mouthwash, it is good for mouth and throat inflammations and sores. It is sometimes used externally to treat skin eruptions, scrofula, and suppurating wounds. The plant also has a mildly styptic action which makes it helpful for internal hemorrhage.

Preparation and Dosage:

Infusion: Steep 2 tsp. in ½ cup water for 10 minutes. Take ½ cup a day.

Powder: Take ¼ to ½ tsp., three times a day.

400 SARSAPARILLA

(Smilax officinalis)

Common Names: Honduras sarsa-parilla, red sarsaparilla, Spanish sarsaparilla.

Medicinal Part: Rootstock.

Description: Sarsaparilla is a tropi-cal American perennial plant. Its long, tuberous rootstock produces a vine which trails on the ground and climbs by means of tendrils growing in pairs from the petioles of the alternate, obicular to ovate, evergreen leaves. The small, greenish flowers grow in axillary umbels.

Properties and Uses: Carminative, diaphoretic, diuretic, tonic. Sarsaparilla root is said to be good for gout, rheumatism, colds, fevers, and catarrhal problems, as well as for relieving flatulence. A tea made from it has also been used externally for skin problems, scrofula, ringworm, and tetters. Sarsaparilla would be classed generally as a "blood purifier." It was once commonly taken as a spring tonic.

Preparation and Dosage:

Infusion: Steep 1 tsp. rootstock in 1 cup water. Take 1 to 2 cups a day.

Tincture: A dose is from 30 to 60 drops.

401   SASSAFRAS

(Sassafras albidum)

Common Names: Ague tree, cinnamon wood, saxifrax.

Medicinal Part: Bark.

Description: Sassafras is a native North American deciduous tree which can be found in woods from Ontario to Michigan, and south to Florida and Texas. In places it is also grown as an ornamental. The stem, which is usually 10 to 40 feet high but sometimes reaches 125 feet, is covered with rough, grayish bark. The leaves are alternate, downy on the lower side, and variable in shape from ovate to elliptic, entire or three-lobed. The small, yellowish-green flowers grow in racemes, blooming before the leaves appear. The fruit is a pea-sized, yellowish-green drupe.

Properties and Uses: Anodyne, antiseptic, diaphoretic, diuretic, stimulant. A hot infusion of sassafras bark makes a good "blood purifier," promoting perspiration and urination. It has therefore been recommended for rheumatism, gout, arthritis, and skin problems. For the latter, as for various ulcers, combined internal and external use is recommended. The bark of the roots contains a volatile oil that has anodyne and antiseptic properties. It has been used in the past as a pain reliever and also to treat venereal disease. American Indians used an infusion of sassafras roots to bring down a fever. Sassafras tea has also had its day as a popular tonic drink.

Preparation and Dosage:

Infusion: Steep 1 tsp. bark in 1 cup water. Take 1 cup a day.

Tincture: A dose is 15 to 30 drops.

402 SAVORY

(Satureja hortensis)

Common Names: Bean herb, summer savory.

Medicinal Part: The herb.

Description: Savory is an annual plant that grows wild in the Mediterranean area and is widely cultivated elsewhere as a kitchen herb. Its branching root produces a bushy, hairy stem which grows from 1 to 1½ feet high, often taking on a purple hue as it matures. The opposite, small, oblong-linear leaves are sessile or nearly so and may have hairy margins. The pink or white, two-lipped flowers grow in whorl-like cymes from July to October. The entire plant is strongly aromatic.

Properties and Uses: Astringent, carminative, expectorant, stimulant, stomachic. Savory tea is a safe remedy for most stomach and intestinal disorders, including cramps, nausea, indigestion and lack of appetite. As an astringent, it makes a good remedy for diarrhea. The tea also serves as a gargle for sore throat. Savory has also been said to have aphrodisiac properties.

Preparation and Dosage:

Infusion: Steep 2 to 4 tsp. dried herb in 1 cup water. Take 1 cup a day, a mouthful at a time.

403 WINTER SAVORY
(Satureja montana)

NOTE: Winter savory *(Satureja montana)* is a perennial species, more woody and bristly than summer savory. It has the same medicinal properties as summer savory.

404 SAW PALMETTO
(Serenoa serrulata)

Medicinal Part: Berries.

Description: Saw palmetto is a low, shrubby plant found growing in dense stands along the Atlantic coast in Georgia and Florida. The trunk or rootstock remains below the ground, producing palmate, green to white-coated leaves on saw-toothed petioles. The olive-like, dark-purple to black berries grow in bunches, ripening from October to December.

Properties and Uses: Diuretic, expectorant, tonic. Saw palmetto berries are particularly useful for conditions associated with colds, asthma, and bronchitis. Catarrhal problems and mucous congestion respond to a tea made from the dried berries. The tea has also been recommended as a general tonic to build strength during convalescence from illness. Saw palmetto is considered by some to have aphrodisiac powers.

Preparation and Dosage:

Infusion: Steep 1 tsp. dried berries in 1 cup water. Take 1 to 2 cups a day.

Tincture: A dose is from 30 to 60 drops.

405 SCOTCH BROOM
(Cytisus scoparius)

Common Names: Broom, link, Irish broom.

Medicinal Parts: Young flowering twigs, seeds.

Description: Scotch broom is a deciduous shrub native to Europe and naturalized in the U.S., particularly in the rural areas of the western states. The angular, slender stems and branches bear alternate leaves consisting of 1 to 3 obovate or oblanceolate, downy leaflets. The solitary, axillary flowers are bright yellow and bloom from April to June. The fruit is a brownish-black, shaggy pod containing 12 to 18 seeds.

Properties and Uses: Cathartic, diuretic, emetic. Scotch broom seeds and twigs are sometimes mixed with equal parts of dandelion root to make a diuretic mixture. The seeds are effective as an emetic. There are some reports of hallucinogenic properties in the flowering tops when they are smoked in cigarettes.

Scotch broom also speeds up the heartbeat. CAUTION: Large doses of scotch broom can cause fatal poisoning.

Preparation and Dosage: Use with caution, preferably under medical direction.

Decoction: Boil 1 tsp. flowering tops or seeds in 1 cup water. Take 1 to 2 cups a day, a mouthful at a time.

406   SCURVY GRASS

(*Cochlearia officinalis*)

Common Names: Scrubby grass, spoonwort.

Medicinal Part: Leaves.

Description: Scurvy grass is a biennial or perennial plant which grows wild in moist places in northern Europe and the northern parts of North America and Asia; it is also found in cultivation. The main root has many fibrous branch roots and produces angular, furrowed stems as well as fleshy basal leaves. The basal leaves are oblong, reniform, or cordate; the scattered stem leaves are obovate to oblong and sessile or nearly so. Small white flowers grow in racemes from April to August. The fruit is a small, almost globose pod containing small, reddish-brown seeds.

Properties and Uses: Diuretic, stomachic, tonic. As a source of vitamin C, scurvy grass has in the past been used to prevent and treat the disease it is named after. It has also been considered a good "blood purifier" and has been recommended for rheumatism, dropsy, and venereal diseases. The juice of scurvy grass can be added to orange juice to make a healthful spring tonic.

Preparation and Dosage: Scurvy grass must be used fresh.

407   SENEGA SNAKEROOT

(*Polygala senega*)

Common Names: Milkwort, mountain flax, Seneca snakeroot.

Medicinal Part: Rootstock.

Description: Senega snakeroot is a perennial plant native to the rocky woods and hills of eastern North America, growing as far south as North Carolina and Arkansas. The hard, crooked, snake-like rootstock produces 15 to 20 or more smooth, erect stems which grow from 6 to 18 inches high. The alternate, lanceolate leaves are sessile or almost so and come to a fairly sharp point. Small white or greenish flowers grow in dense terminal spikes from May to June.

Properties and Uses: Cathartic, diaphoretic, emetic, expectorant, stimulant. Senega snakeroot found its most common application in medicine as an expectorant in respiratory problems. The Seneca Indians, who introduced it to the white man, chewed the rootstock to make a mash which was applied to snakebites (after cutting the bite and sucking out the poison). CAUTION: Large doses causes vomiting and diarrhea; an overdose is poisonous.

Preparation and Dosage: The rootstock is used dried.

Infusion: Steep 1 tsp. rootstock in 1 cup water. Take 1 cup a day, a mouthful at a time.

Tincture: A dose is from 5 to 10 drops.

408 SENNA

(a) (Cassia marilandica)

Common Names: American senna, locust plant, wild senna.

Medicinal Part: Leaves.

Description: American senna is a perennial plant that may reach a height of 4 to 6 feet in the rich soils of the eastern U.S. where it grows. The stems are round and slightly hairy, with even-pinnate leaves on long petioles. Each leaf consists of 8 to 10 narrow, oblong, pointed leaflets. The yellow flowers appear in June to September and are borne in racemes. The seed pod is a legume, about 2 to 4 inches long.

Properties and Uses: Cathartic, diuretic, vermifuge. American senna is an effective laxative and is much used by herbalists for that purpose, but usually in combination with other herbs since it tends to cause griping by itself. It is also often combined with other anthelmintics to get rid of intestinal worms. If your friends are avoiding you lately, try the infusion as a mouthwash for halitosis and that bad taste in your mouth.

Preparation and Dosage: Gather leaves while the plant is in bloom.

Infusion: Use 1 tsp. leaves with 1 cup boiling water; steep for ½ hour. Take hot or cold, a mouthful three times a day or ½ cup before going to bed. Take no more than 2 cups total.

Tincture: The dose is ½ to 1 tsp.

409 SENNA (cont.)
(b) (Cassia acutifolia)

Common Name: Alexandrian senna.

Medicinal Parts: Leaflets, fruit.

Description: Alexandrian senna is a shrub which grows jn northern Africa, its pale green stems and branches reaching up to 2 feet in height. The alternate leaves are even-pinnate, with four or five pairs of lanceolate or obovate leaflets that are brittle and grayish-green in color. The small yellow flowers are characterized by five spreading, clawed petals. The fruit is an oblong pod about 2 inches long.

Properties and Uses: Cathartic, cholagogue. The leaves of Alexandrian senna make a potent cathartic which must be combined with other herbs to reduce its griping tendencies and to make it palatable. The pods are milder in their effects. Senna acts mostly on the lower bowel and is particularly useful for chronic constipation, but it should not be used when hemorrhoids are present or the alimentary canal is inflamed.

Preparation and Dosage:

Infusion: Steep 3½ oz. leaves and ¼ to ½ tsp. coriander, ginger, or cinnamon in 1 qt. water for 15 minutes and strain. Take 1 to 4 tbsp. at a time. This infusion is more palatable cold than hot.

Pods: Steep 6 to 12 pods in 4 to 5 tbsp. cold water to make a gentle but effective laxative. (Use 3 to 6 pods for children or old people.)

410 TINNEVELLY SENNA
(Cassia angustifolia)

NOTE 1: The leaves of Tinnevelly senna (Cassia angustifolia) have similar properties but are somewhat weaker.

411 PURGING CASSIA
(Cassia fistula)

NOTE 2: Commercial cassia pods come from purging cassia (Cassia fistula), also called golden-shower or pudding-pipe tree, which is native to India but is cultivated in other tropical coun-

tries as well. The black, cylindrical pods contain a sweet mucilage which is the main cathartic ingredient. Its bark is said to
be strongly astringent.

412   SEVEN BARKS
(Hydrangea arborescens)

Common Names: Hydrangea, wild hydrangea.

Medicinal Part: Root.

Description: Seven barks is a native North American shrub
found on dry slopes, in shady woods, and on streambanks from
New York to Iowa, Florida, and Louisiana. The stems, growing
from 3 to 10 feet high, are covered with thin layers of different-
colored bark. The opposite, ovate, serrate leaves have hairy
veins on the underside when mature. Rounded or globular
clusters of small, creamy-white flowers appear during June and
July.

Properties and Uses: Antilithic, diuretic. The root of seven barks
has long been used as a mild diuretic. It also has a reputation
for helping to prevent and remove gravel, bladder stones, and
kidney stones.

Preparation and Dosage:

Infusion: Steep 1 tsp. root in 1 cup water. Take 1 cup a day.

Tincture: A dose is from 5 to 20 drops.

413   SHAVE GRASS
(Equisetum arvense)

Common Names: Horsetail grass,
horsetail rush.

Medicinal Part: The plant.

Description: Shave grass is a perennial plant common in moist
loamy or sandy soil all over North
America and Eurasia. A creeping,
stringlike rootstock with roots at
the nodes produces numerous hollow stems, which are of two types.
A fertile, flesh-colored stem grows
first, reaching a height of 4 to 7
inches and bearing on top a conelike spike which contains spores;

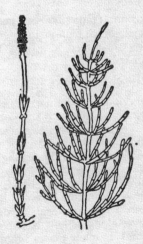

this stem dies quickly. A green, sterile stem grows up to 18
inches high and features whorls of small branches.

Properties and Uses: Diuretic, hemostatic, vulnerary. Shave grass has been praised for its usefulness in lung problems, including mild tuberculosis (its silicic acid content is said to stabilize the scar tissue). The juice of the plant—essentially, the sterile stems —is good for anemia which results from internal bleeding such as stomach ulcers, since it promotes the coagulation of blood. A tea made from shave grass has been recommended for stomach and leg ulcers, urinary tract problems, water retention, excessive menstrual flow and leucorrhea. For the latter two complaints, the tea can also be used as a douche. Externally, the tea makes a good wash for wounds, sores, skin problems, and mouth and gum inflammations. CAUTION: Excessive doses can lead to symptoms of poisoning.

Preparation and Dosage:

Infusion: Steep 2 tsp. dried plant in ½ cup water. Take 1 cup a day.

Decoction: Put 1 heaping tsp. fresh or dried plant in ½ cup cold water. Bring to a boil, boil for one minute, then steep for one minute and strain. Take 1 to 1½ cups a day, a mouthful at a time. For internal bleeding, make 2 cups in the morning and take in the course of the day, 1 tbsp. at a time. For external use, boil and steep for a longer time.

Juice: Take 1 tsp. at a time, with water.

414   SHEPHERD'S
PURSE

(*Capsella bursa-pastoris*)

Common Names: Cocowort, pick-pocket, St. James' weed, shepherd's heart, toywort.

Medicinal Part: The herb.

Description: Shepherd's purse is a ubiquitous annual plant, common in fields and waste places and along roadsides everywhere. Its erect, simple or branching stem grows from 6 to 18 inches high above a rosette of basal, gray-green, pinnatifid leaves. It also bears a few small, sessile, dentate leaves along its length. The small white flowers grow in terminal cymes, in many places blooming all year. The fruit is a flattened, heart-shaped or triangular, notched pod.

Properties and Uses: Diuretic, styptic, vasoconstrictor. An extract of shepherd's purse is an effective blood coagulant which can be used for internal or external bleeding. An infusion of the dried herb can also be used. Shepherd's purse acts to constrict the blood vessels and thus to raise blood pressure, but it has also been said to regularize blood pressure and heart action whether the pressure is high or low. It is effective too for various menstrual problems, including excessive and difficult menstruation. It is sometimes used to promote uterine contractions during childbirth and can promote bowel movements with a similar effect on the intestines.

Preparation and Dosage: Do not keep shepherd's purse longer than a year.

Infusion: Steep 1 tsp. fresh or 2 tsp. dried herb in ½ cup water. Take 1 cup a day, unsweetened, a mouthful at a time.

Cold Extract: Soak 3 tsp. fresh herb in ¾ cup cold water for 8 to 10 hours. Take in the course of a day.

Juice: Take a teaspoon of the juice several times a day.

Tincture: Take 20 to 40 drops, two or three times a day.

415 SHINLEAF

(Pyrola elliptica)

Common Name: Wild lily-of-the-valley.

Medicinal Part: Leaves.

Description: Shinleaf is a perennial, evergreen herb found in rich woods in Canada and in the northern and Rocky Mountain states of the U.S. A slender, branching rootstock sends up a set of basal, dark green, ovate to elliptical leaves with margined petioles and shallow-toothed edges. The naked flower stalk bears from 7 to 15 white, waxy, drooping flowers, which smell like lily-of-the-valley and bloom from June to August.

Properties and Uses: Astringent. Shinleaf has mild astringent properties and can be used as a mouthwash, gargle, and vaginal douche, as well as for any of the other uses that astringents are generally applied to. The leaves also make a good poultice for insect bites, bruises, and other skin problems.

SKULLCAP

(Scutellaria lateriflora)

Common Names: Blue skullcap, blue pimpernel, helmet flower, hoodwort, mad-dog-weed, side-flowering skullcap.

Medicinal Part: The plant.

Description: Skullcap is a North American perennial plant which grows in wet places in Canada and the northern and eastern U.S. The fibrous, yellow rootstock produces a branching stem from 1 to 3 feet high, with opposite, ovate, serrate leaves that come to a point. The axillary, two-lipped flowers are pale purple or blue, blooming from July to September.

Properties and Uses: Antispasmodic, diuretic, sedative, tonic. An infusion of skullcap is good for spasms and convulsions and for nervous conditions, such as excitability, insomnia, and general restlessness. It has also been recommended for rheumatism, neuralgia, and delirium tremens. American Indians used the plant to promote menstruation, and it was reputed to be effective against rabies.

Preparation and Dosage:

Infusion: Steep 1 tsp. dried plant in a teacup of water for 30 minutes. Take three or four times a day.

Tincture: A dose is from 3 to 12 drops, taken in hot water.

417 SKUNK CABBAGE

(Symplocarpus foetidus)

Common Names: Collard, meadow cabbage, polecat weed, skunk weed, swamp cabbage.

Medicinal Parts: Rootstock, roots.

Description: Skunk cabbage is a native American perennial plant, to be found in the swamps of eastern North America, as far west as Manitoba and Iowa. The large, tuberous rootstock produces fleshy roots and heart-shaped, cabbage-like leaves on thick leaf-stalks. Numerous small, purple flowers grow on a small, oval, fleshy spike (or spadix), covered by a purple and yellowish-green, hoodlike bract (or spathe). Flowering time is from February to April, before the leaves appear. The whole plant emits a skunk or garlic odor.

Properties and Uses: Antispasmodic, diuretic, emetic, expectorant, slightly narcotic. The rootstock and roots of skunk cabbage have been used to treat respiratory ailments, including hay fever, asthma, whooping cough, bronchial problems, and mucous congestion. It has also been helpful for nervous disorders, spasmodic problems, rheumatism, and dropsy. Some American Indians boiled the root hairs to make a wash for stopping external bleeding. Those of one tribe inhaled the odor of the crushed leaves to cure headache—which may be a classic case of a cure worse than the disease. CAUTION: The fresh plant has acrid properties.

Preparation and Dosage: Skunk cabbage loses effectiveness with long storage.

Infusion: Steep 1 tsp. rootstock and roots in 1 cup water. Take 1 cup a day, a tablespoon at a time.

Tincture: A dose is from 3 to 15 drops.

418   SOAPWORT

(Saponaria officinalis)

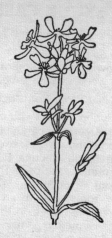

Common Names: Bouncing Bet,
bruisewort, dog cloves, old maids'
pink, soap root.

Medicinal Part: Rootstock.

Description: Soapwort is a widespread perennial plant found in
waste places and along roadsides
and railroad embankments in eastern North America, Asia, and
Europe. The finger-thick creeping
rootstock produces a reddish,
branching stem, which grows from
1 to 3 feet high and bears opposite, ovate, pointed leaves whose
bases clasp the stem. Flat-topped, corymbed clusters of pink
(sometimes white or purple) flowers bloom from June to
August.

Properties and Uses: Cholagogue, diuretic, expectorant, purgative. A decoction of the rootstock is used most commonly as an
expectorant for respiratory congestion. It has also been used for
gout and externally as a wash or fomentation for dermatitis,
itching skin, furuncles, and tumors. Soapwort has mild purgative
action.

Preparation and Dosage:

Decoction: Boil 1 to 2 tbsp. dried rootstock in 1 cup water.
Take 1 tbsp. at a time.

419   SOLOMON'S SEAL

(Polygonatum multiflorum)

Common Names: Dropberry, sealroot, sealwort.

Medicinal Part: Rootstock.

Description: Solomon's seal is a perennial plant which grows in
woods and thickets in eastern North America, Europe, and Asia.
Its thick, horizontal, scarred rootstock produces one or two
erect stems, 1 to 3 feet high, whose lower half is naked and
upper half leafy. The alternate, elliptic to ovate leaves are green
with a whitish bloom underneath. Two to five or more greenish-
white, bell-shaped flowers hang from the leaf axils from April to
August. The fruit is a blue or blue-black berry.

Properties and Uses: Astringent, emetic, tonic. The rootstock of
solomon's seal has found application mainly for external prob-

lems. It makes a good poultice for bruises, inflammations, and wounds and a good wash for skin problems and blemishes. It has also been used as a wash to counteract the effects of poison ivy. American Indians made a tea of the rootstock to take for women's complaints and general internal pains.

420 SOLOMON'S SEAL
(Polygonatum odoratum)

NOTE: Other species of solomon's seal have similar properties. A European variety (*Polygonatum odoratum*) contains a substance that lowers the level of blood sugar. This variety has long been used in the Orient for diabetes and is included in many tea mixtures designed to lower blood sugar.

421 SORREL
(Rumex acetosa)

Common Names: Common sorrel, garden sorrel, meadow sorrel, sourgrass.

Medicinal Part: The plant.

Description: Sorrel is a perennial plant that is very common in damp meadows and along roads and shorelines in Europe and Asia but is found only sparingly in North America. The stem grows from 1 to 3 feet high and bears alternate, light-green leaves that are oblong or oblong-oval in shape and range from long-petioled at the bottom to nearly sessile at the top of the plant. They have two pointed lobes at the base and may be obtuse or pointed at the apex. Small greenish or reddish flowers bloom in panicled racemes from May to August.

Properties and Uses: Astringent, diuretic, laxative. Sorrel root has astringent properties, and a decoction made from it has been used for hemorrhage in the stomach and for excessive menstruation. A tea made from the leaves and stem is diuretic and may be helpful for gravel and stones. For mouth and throat ulcers, a tea made from leaves and flowers and taken with honey has been recommended. Sorrel leaves are sometimes used like spinach, particularly for "spring cures." Externally, a tea made from the herb can be used as a wash or fomentation to treat skin diseases and problems. CAUTION: Consuming large quantities of sorrel can irritate the kidneys and produce mild to severe poisoning.

Preparation and Dosage: Use the fresh plant.

422   SPEEDWELL

(Veronica officinalis)

Common Names: Fluellin, ground-hele, gypsy weed, low speedwell, Paul's betony, upland speedwell, veronica.

Medicinal Part: The flowering herb.

Description: Speedwell is a small perennial plant which grows in dry meadows, fields, and woods over the eastern half of North America, as far south as North Carolina and Tennessee. The creeping, woody, hairy stem sends up branches from 3 to 10 inches high and is rooted at the joints. The opposite, oblong, grayish-green leaves are soft and have finely toothed margins. The light blue flowers have violet streaks and grow in dense, axillary, spikelike racemes from May to August. The fruit is an obovate, compressed, hairy capsule.

Properties and Uses: Diuretic, expectorant, stomachic, tonic. Although speedwell has a reputation, especially in Europe, as a healer of all illnesses, it is used primarily as an expectorant for respiratory problems. It has also been used for stomach ailments, migraine headache, and as a gargle for mouth and throat sores. The fresh juice taken in large quantities is helpful for gout, and it can also be used externally to relieve chronic skin problems.

Preparation and Dosage:

Infusion: Steep 2 tsp. flowering herb in ½ cup water. Take 1 to 1½ cups a day, a mouthful at a time.

Juice: Take 2 tsp. in water or milk, three times a day.

SPIKENARD

(a) (Aralia racemosa)

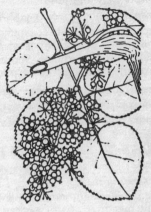

Common Names: American spikenard, Indian root, life-of-man, nard, spignet, spikenard.

Medicinal Parts: Rootstock and roots.

Description: American spikenard is a perennial plant found in rich woodlands in eastern North America, as far south as Georgia and west to South Dakota and Missouri. Its thick, fleshy rootstock features long, thick roots and produces one or more branched stems growing up to 6 feet high. The leaves are alternate and usually ternate, with the parts pinnately divided into 3 to 5 ovate to orbicular, pointed leaflets with doubly serrate margins. Its small, greenish-white flowers grow in panicled umbels during July and August.

Properties and Uses: Diaphoretic, expectorant, stimulant. The powdered root has been used in medicine for rheumatism, asthma and coughs, as well as externally for skin diseases and problems. Taking spikenard tea for sometime before labor is said to make childbirth easier. American Indians used the plant in various ways: internally for backache and externally for wounds, bruises, swellings, inflammations, and chest pains. For external use, the pounded root was generally made into a poultice or dressing.

Preparation and Dosage:
Infusion: Steep 1 to 2 tsp. powdered rootstock and roots in 1 cup water. Take 1 to 2 cups a day.

SPIKENARD (cont.)

(b) (Aralia nudicaulis)

Common Names: Wild sarsaparilla, rabbit's root, small spikenard, wild licorice.

Medicinal Part: Rootstock.

Description: Wild sarsaparilla is a perennial plant inhabiting moist woods in eastern North America, as far south as Georgia and west to Colorado and Manitoba. This essentially stemless plant has a long rootstock which produces one long-stalked, ternate leaf, each part being divided into 3 to 5 ovate to ovate-lanceolate leaflets with finely serrate margins. The small, greenish-white flowers usually grow in three simple umbels during May and June.

Properties and Uses: Diaphoretic, diuretic, stimulant. Wild sarsaparilla can be used much like its close relative, American spikenard. Several tribes of American Indians used the roots to make cough medicine. Some tribes used the root for its diuretic properties, taking it to help kidney and bladder ailments.

Preparation and Dosage:

Infusion: Steep 2 oz. dried rootstock in 1 pint water for an hour. Take 2 to 3 tbsp., three or four times a day.

425 SPOTTED CRANEBILL

(*Geranium maculatum*)

Common Names: Alum root, cranesbill, crowfoot, geranium, spotted geranium, wild cranesbill, wild geranium.

Medicinal Part: Rootstock.

Description: Spotted cranebill is a perennial plant common in woodlands over most of North America, especially the eastern half. The stout, horizontal rootstock produces a hairy stem, growing from 1 to 2 feet high, as well as long-petioled basal leaves. Both basal and stem leaves are deeply 5- to 7-parted, with coarsely toothed, pointed lobes. The rose-purple flowers grow in pairs on axillary peduncles from April to July.

Properties and Uses: Astringent, styptic. Spotted cranebill root is a strong astringent for both internal and external use. Internally, it is helpful against diarrhea and hemorrhage. It also makes a good mouthwash and gargle for sore throat, gum problems, and throat and mouth sores. One tribe of American Indians used a decoction of wild grape and spotted cranebill root as a mouthwash for children who had thrush. The powdered root is an effective blood coagulant and can be used to stop external bleeding.

Preparation and Dosage:

Infusion: Steep 1 tsp. rootstock in 1 cup water. Take 1 to 2 cups a day, a mouthful at a time.

Tincture: Take 10 to 30 drops in water, every one or two hours, as indicated.

426 SPRUCE
(Picea excelsa)

Common Names: Norway pine, Norway spruce.

Medicinal Part: Young shoots.

Description: Norway spruce is an evergreen tree found in central and northern Europe; many varieties of it are cultivated. The stem, covered with scaly, red-brown bark, grows as high as 130 feet. The winter buds are reddish or light brown and produce young shoots at the tips of the branches in May. The dark green, quadrangular needles grow spirally around the branchlets. The catkin-like flowers bloom in May, the male yellow or red, the female bright purple. The light brown cones are cylindric-oblong in shape and from 4 to 7 inches long.

Properties and Uses: Calmative, diaphoretic, expectorant. A tea made from the young shoots of Norway spruce and taken warm is helpful for coughs, catarrh, and influenza. Taken hot, it acts to promote perspiration. For bronchitis, try a vapor bath of the young shoots; and either the shoots or the needles can be used to make a calming bath additive. The Burgundy pitch derived from this tree was once in common use as a base for medicinal plasters.

Preparation and Dosage:

Infusion: Steep 1 to 2 tsp. shoots in ½ cup water for 5 to 10 minutes. Sweeten with honey or raw sugar if desired.

Decoction: Add 2 to 4 oz. shoots to 1 qt. cold water and let stand for several hours. Bring to a boil and boil briefly, then let stand for 15 minutes. Take ½ cup a day, sweetened if desired.

Bath Additive: Add 7 oz. spruce needle extract to a full bath. When fresh shoots are available, a strong decoction made from 1 to 5 lb. shoots can be used in place of the extract.

427 BLACK SPRUCE
(Picea mariana)

NOTE: Black spruce (*Picea mariana*), a North American species found from Alaska as far south as Wisconsin and Virginia, was an important source of vitamin C for Indians and early explorers. A decoction of the bark and needles was used.

SPURGE

(Euphorbia spp.)

Various species of spurge have been used medicinally, mostly as emetics and purgatives. However, the danger of poisoning from an overdose has all but eliminated their use except in homeopathic preparations. The milky sap the spurges contain also causes dermatitis, and the fresh plants must be handled with caution. This sap has sometimes been used against warts. The five species described all have the above mentioned characteristic properties and uses.

428 CYPRESS SPURGE
(Euphorbia cyparissias)

Medicinal Part: Flowering plant.

Description: Cypress spurge is a bushy, perennial plant introduced into the U.S. from Europe as an ornamental and now found as a weed, especially in the northeastern states. Growing from 4 to 20 inches tall, the stems contain a milky, acrid juice and bear alternate, sessile, linear to filiform leaves below and whorled, ovate-cordate leaves near the top. The greenish-yellow "flowers" have neither calyx nor corolla and grow in small, many-rayed umbels from April to July. The fruit is a small, nearly globular capsule.

429 FLOWERING SPURGE
(Euphorbia corollata)

Common Names: Blooming spurge, Bowman's root, emetic root, milk ipecac, milk purslain, milkweed, snake milk, wild hippo.

Medicinal Part: Rootstock.

Description: Flowering spurge is a perennial plant found growing in dry soil from Ontario to Florida and Texas. The yellowish rootstock produces bright green, spotted stems from 1 to 3 feet high. The leaves are thick, oblong to oblong-spatulate or linear, and sessile or short-petioled; the lower leaves are scattered and alternate, the upper whorled. What appear to be flowers are actually greenish-yellow involucral glands subtended by white, petal-like appendages. These appear in terminal umbels from April to October.

430 GARDEN SPURGE
(Euphorbia lathyrus)

Common Names: Caper spurge, mole plant.

Medicinal Parts: Root, seeds.

Description: Garden spurge is an annual or biennial plant introduced from Europe into the U.S., where it has become naturalized in the eastern states and in California. It tends to repel moles and gophers and is sometimes planted for that purpose. Growing from 2 to 3 feet high, the stems have opposite, sessile, lanceolate leaves, each pair growing at right angles to its neighboring pairs. The upper, floral leaves are ovate or ovate-lanceolate. The "flowers" grow in 3- or 4-rayed umbels. The fruit is a nearly globular capsule about ½ inch in diameter; the seeds resemble capers. The plant is covered with a whitish bloom.

431 MILK-PURSLANE
(Euphorbia maculata)

Common Names: Black spurge, dysentery-weed, euphorbia, spreading spurge, spotted spurge.

Medicinal Part: The herb.

Description: Milk-purslane is a low annual plant which is found as a weed in waste places and cultivated soils throughout North America, except in the far north. The hairy, prostrate stems and branches radiate to form spreading mats, from 4 to 30 inches in diameter, on the ground. The small, opposite, finely serrate leaves are oblong-elliptic to oblong-linear in shape and usually have a red blotch in the middle. The tiny "flowers" appear singly or in clusters from April to November. Milk-purslane has astringent properties.

432 PETTY SPURGE
(Euphorbia peplus)

Medicinal Part: Root.

Description: Petty spurge is a small annual plant which is common in moist places as a garden weed in the eastern U.S. and in California. The simple or branched stems, from 4 to 12 inches high, bear alternate, obovate to roundish, petioled leaves; the upper, floral leaves are ovate. The bell-shaped "flowers" feature large yellow glands with spreading, narrow horns.

433 SQUAW VINE
(Mitchella repens)

Common Names: Checkerberry, deerberry, hive vine, one-berry, partridgeberry, twin-berry, squawberry, winter clover.

Medicinal Part: Leaves.

Description: Squaw vine is a perennial, evergreen herb found around the bottoms of trees and stumps in woodlands from Nova Scotia to Ontario and southward to Florida and Texas. Its creeping or trailing stems grow up to a foot long, rooting at various points, and bear opposite, orbicular-ovate leaves that are dark green and shining on top and are often streaked with white. The funnel-shaped white flowers grow in pairs from April to July. The fruit is a scarlet berry-like drupe up to 1/3 inch in diameter.

Properties and Uses: Astringent, diuretic, tonic. Based on American Indian usage, squaw vine tea has been recommended as a drink to take during the last few weeks of pregnancy to make childbirth faster and easier. As a diuretic, it can also be used for gravel and urinary ailments. For external use, the tea makes a good wash for sore eyes and for skin problems. One Indian tribe drank the tea to relieve insomnia.

Preparation and Dosage:

Infusion: Steep 1 tsp. leaves in 1 cup water for 30 minutes. Take 1 to 3 cups a day.

Tincture: As a tonic, take 5 to 15 drops, three times a day.

434 STAR ANISE

(Illicium anisatum or Illicium verum)

Medicinal Part: Seeds.

Description: Star anise is a small tree which grows wild in China, Japan, and Korea and is also grown in the southeastern states of the U.S. Its stem has aromatic white bark and grows from 20 to 35 feet high. The alternate, entire, short-petioled leaves are elliptic and somewhat pointed. The solitary, axillary flowers are greenish-yellow and have many narrow, spreading petals. The fruit is a cluster of dry, woody, gray-brown follicles united in the form of a star.

Properties and Uses: Carminative, stimulant, stomachic. The seed of star anise is used essentially the same way as is anise seed: to promote digestion and appetite and to relieve flatulence. It also makes a good additive to other medicines to improve their taste.

Preparation and Dosage:

Infusion: Steep 1 tsp. crushed seeds in 1 cup water. Take 1 to 2 cups a day.

Tincture: A dose is from 1/4 to 1/2 tsp.

CAUTION: Commercial star anise seeds may be adulterated with a poisonous, similar but slightly smaller and darker, seed of another plant. These have a sharp and bitter odor, resembling cardamom rather than anise.

STAR GRASS

(Aletris farinosa)

Common Names: Ague grass, bitter grass, colic root, mealy star-wort, star root.

Medicinal Part: Rootstock.

Description: Star grass is a native North American perennial plant which grows in grassy or sandy woodlands in the eastern half of North America, from southern Canada to the Gulf of Mexico. Its thick, fibrous rootstock produces a rosette of yellow-green, lanceolate, spreading basal leaves. The numerous white, tubular-oblong, somewhat bell-shaped flowers grow in a terminal spike-like raceme on a flower-stalk that reaches 1½ to 3 feet in height. Flowering time is from May to August. The fruit is an ovoid capsule containing many oblong, ribbed seeds.

Properties and Uses: Bitter tonic, narcotic. A decoction or tincture of star grass root has been used for flatulent colic and for other digestive problems. (American Indians also used the leaves to make a tea for digestive troubles.) It has also been recommended for menstrual problems such as dysmenorrhea and menorrhagia.

Preparation and Dosage: The dried rootstock is used.

Decoction: Boil 1 tsp. dried rootstock in 1 cup water. Take 1 cup a day, a mouthful at a time.

Tincture: A dose is from 15 to 40 drops. For menstrual problems, take in hot water.

CAUTION: Use dried rootstock only. The fresh root causes unpleasant internal effects, including dizziness, intestinal pains, vomiting, and purging.

436 STICKLEWORT

(Agrimonia eupatoria)

Common Names: Agrimony, cockleburr.

Medicinal Part: The plant.

Description: Sticklewort is a perennial plant found all over the world in woods, fields, and waste places and along fences and roadsides. Its reddish, creeping rootstock produces a hairy stem from 1 to 5 feet high. The alternate, pinnate leaves are far apart on the stem and consist of 5 to 9 lanceolate or oblanceolate, crenate-serrate leaflets which are resinous beneath and somewhat hairy along the veins. The small yellow flowers grow in a long raceme at the top of the stem during July and August. The fruiting flower tubes sport hooked bristles that cling to whatever brushes against them.

Properties and Uses: Astringent, vulnerary. Sticklewort makes a good gargle for inflammations in the mouth and throat. Taken internally, a tea made from sticklewort is useful for kidney, liver, and spleen problems and for gallstones. It is sometimes recommended, even in modern medicine, for chronic gallbladder problems which are accompanied by excess acidity in the stomach. In European folk medicine, the root is soaked to make a pleasant-tasting drink that relieves constipation and strengthens the liver. Externally, sticklewort tea or a poultice made from the fresh plant can be used to help heal wounds and to treat varicose veins. Sticklewort can also be made into a salve for external use. For aches and pains due to overexertion, try a footbath containing sticklewort.

Preparation and Dosage:

Infusion: Steep 2 to 4 tsp. dried leaves (or herb) in 1 cup water. Take 1 cup a day, unsweetened, a mouthful at a time.

Decoction: For external use, boil 2 to 4 oz. dried leaves (or herb) in 1 qt. water.

Powder: Take 1 tsp. to 1 tbsp. plant powder a day.

437 STILLINGIA

(Stillingia sylvatica)

Common Names: Cockup hat, marcory, queen's delight, queen's root, silver leaf, yaw root.

Medicinal Part: Rootstock.

Description: Stillingia is a perennial plant which is a native of the pine barrens and sandy soils of the southern states of the U.S. Its stem, growing from 2 to 4 feet high, contains an acrid, milky juice and bears alternate, sessile leaves that have a somewhat leathery texture. The yellow, petalless flowers grow in a terminal spike with the female flowers at the base. The fruit is a three-lobed capsule.

Properties and Uses: Cathartic, diuretic, emetic. A decoction of the rootstock was once used to treat obstinate skin problems and to help clear up continuing pain and ulcerations after a mercurial treatment for syphilis. In large doses, stillingia causes vomiting and diarrhea. CAUTION: Taken internally, the acrid constituents of the fresh plant can cause irritation and symptoms of poisoning.

Preparation and Dosage: Use the dried, but not more than two-year-old, rootstock.

Decoction: Boil 1 tsp. dried rootstock in 1 cup water. Take 1 cup a day, a mouthful at a time.

Tincture: A dose is from 5 to 20 drops.

438   STONE ROOT
(Collinsonia canadensis)

Common Names: Hardhack, horseweed, heal-all, knob grass, knob root, richweed.

Medicinal Parts: Rootstock, leaves.

Description: Stone root is a native North American perennial plant found in damp woods from Quebec to Florida and westward to Wisconsin and Arkansas. The hard, knobby rootstock sends up a quadrangular stem from 1 to 4 feet tall, with opposite, ovate, serrate leaves which are pointed at the apex and narrowed or heart-shaped at the base. The two-lipped, greenish-yellow flowers grow in a loose panicled raceme at the top of the stem from July to October.

Properties and Uses: Diuretic, tonic, vulnerary. An infusion of stone root makes a good diuretic for urinary problems and excessive water retention. Stone root is often included with other plants as part of a mixture. The fresh leaves can be used externally, as poultice or fomentation, to help heal wounds and bruises.

Preparation and Dosage: The fresh rootstock is better than the dried.

Infusion: Steep 1 tsp. rootstock in 1 cup water. Take 1 cup a day, a mouthful at a time.

Tincture: A dose is from 5 to 20 drops.

439 STORKSBILL
(Erodium cicutarium)

Common Names: Alfilaria, heron's bill, pin clover, red-stem filaree.

Medicinal Part: The plant.

Description: Storksbill is an annual plant native to the Mediterranean region and widely naturalized in dry and sandy soils of the eastern, southwestern, and western U.S., where it is often grown for hay. The slender, hairy, reddish, decumbent stem bears pinnate leaves which, like those of the basal rosette, have sessile, oblong or ovate-oblong leaflets which themselves are pinnatifid into narrow, often toothed lobes. The basal leaves survive through the winter. The purple or pink, geranium-like flowers bloom from early spring to late fall. The sepals are terminated by one or two white, bristle-like hairs which give the plant its name.

Properties and Uses: Astringent, hemostatic. Storksbill has been used primarily against bloody discharges from the uterus and to treat difficult or excessive menstruation, particularly when inflammation of the uterus is involved. Small doses are said to raise blood pressure, and larger doses to lower it.

Preparation and Dosage: Storksbill will not keep long in storage. It is generally used in concentrated preparations.

440 SUMAC
(Rhus glabra)

Common Names: Dwarf sumac, mountain sumac, scarlet sumac, smooth sumac.

Medicinal Parts: Bark, leaves, fruit.

Description: Sumac is a North American tree or shrub found growing from 10 to 20 feet high in thickets and waste places. Its branches have smooth, gray bark and bear alternate, pinnate leaves with oblong-lanceolate, serrate leaflets which are green on top and whitish underneath; in fall the leaves turn red. Dense panicles of small, greenish flowers bloom from June to August. The fruit is a small, sticky, finely hairy, bright red erect cluster ripening in the fall.

Properties and Uses: Astringent, diuretic, emmenagogue, febrifuge, refrigerant, tonic. A tea made from sumac bark or leaves is good as a gargle for sore throat and as a remedy for diarrhea and leucorrhea. A tea of leaves and berries can be used for urinary problems, particularly inflammation of the bladder. Berry tea or syrup is useful for fever and also for sores and irritations of mucous membranes. North American Indians chewed the root to cure mouth sores and took a decoction of the root and branches for gonorrhea, reportedly with good results. One tribe made a wet dressing of the fresh leaves and fruit to relieve the irritation of poison ivy, and they used a decoction of the fruit as a wash to stop bleeding after childbirth.

Preparation and Dosage: Take care not to confuse this species of sumac with others, since many are poisonous.

Infusion: Steep 1 tsp. bark, leaves, or fruit in 1 cup water for 30 minutes. Take 1 to 2 cups a day, a mouthful at a time.

Tincture: A dose is from 10 to 20 drops.

441 SUNDEW

(Drosera rotundifolia)

Common Names: Dew plant, lustwort, round-leaved sundew, youthwort.

Medicinal Part: The herb.

Description: Sundew is an insectivorous perennial plant found in wet and moist places in North America, Europe, and Asia. In the U.S., sundew grows in the eastern states, in the Rockies, and in the Sierra Nevada range. The root produces a basal rosette of nearly round, reddish, glandular-hairy leaves which exude a liquid that traps insects. Naked flower stalks, from 2 to 12 inches high, are topped by one-sided racemes of small, white or pinkish flowers which bloom from June to August.

Properties and Uses: Antispasmodic, expectorant. Sundew is an effective remedy for respiratory ailments and chest problems, including coughs, asthma, whooping cough, and bronchitis. It can also be taken to help counteract nausea and upset stomach. The plant contains an antibiotic substance that, in pure form, is effective against streptococcus, staphylococcus, and pneumococcus. In European folk medicine, the fresh juice is used for warts and is taken internally as an aphrodisiac. CAUTION: Sundew contains irritant substances and should be used in small quantities only.

Preparation and Dosage:

Infusion: Steep 1 tsp. herb in 1 pint water. Take 1 to 2 cups a day, a mouthful at a time. For catarrhal problems, sweeten with honey if desired.

Tincture: A dose is from 3 to 6 drops, taken in water.

442   SWEET CICELY

(Osmorhiza longistylis)

Common Names: Anise root, sweet anise, sweet chervil.

Medicinal Part: Root.

Description: Sweet cicely is a perennial plant found growing in the woodlands of Canada, Alaska, and southward to Colorado and Georgia. The thick, bundled roots produce branched stems from 1½ to 3 feet tall. The alternate, ternate-pinnate leaves grow on sheathing petioles and have ovate to oblong-ovate leaf segments. The inconspicuous white flowers grow in loose compound umbels during May and June. The whole plant has an aniselike odor.

Properties and Uses: Carminative, expectorant, stomachic. As indicated by the categories, sweet cicely root is used much like anise. Take it for flatulence, mucous congestion, indigestion, and lack of appetite. See anise for a fuller discussion.

443   SWEET FERN

(Comptonia peregrina)

Common Names: Fern bush, fern gale, meadow fern, sweet bush.

Medicinal Part: The plant.

Description: Sweet fern is a fernlike deciduous shrub which grows on dry hills from Nova Scotia to North Carolina and Maryland. Its slender, reddish-brown branches grow up to 5 feet high and bear alternate, short-petioled, linear-oblong leaves that are deeply pinnatifid with lobes that are broader than they are long. Male flowers grow in cylindrical catkins, female in egg-shaped catkins that develop into clusters of brown, shining, ovoid nutlets.

Properties and Uses: Astringent, tonic. The primary use of sweet fern has been to relieve diarrhea. It can also be used for other complaints where an astringent is called for, including skin problems. American Indians soaked the leaves in water to make a wash for poison ivy irritation.

Preparation and Dosage:

Infusion: Steep 1 tsp. plant in 1 cup water. Take 1 to 2 cups a day, a mouthful at a time.

Tincture: A dose is ½ to 1 tsp.

444   SWEET FERN
(Comptonia peregrina var. asplenifolia)

NOTE: A variety of sweet fern (*Comptonia peregrina* var. *asplenifolia*) with smaller leaves and catkins grows in the pinelands of the northeastern coastal plains. It is medicinally equivalent to *Comptonia peregrina*.

445   SWEET FLAG
(Acorus calamus)

Common Names: Calamus, grass myrtle, myrtle flag, sweet grass, sweet myrtle, sweet rush.

Medicinal Part: Rootstock.

Description: Sweet flag is a perennial plant that grows more or less abundantly throughout the northern hemisphere, inhabiting pond edges, marshes, swamps, and the banks of rivers and streams. Its horizontal, creeping rootstock, which may grow to be 5 feet long, produces sword-shaped leaves from 2 to 6 feet high and also a keeled or ridged flower stalk which bears a cylindrical spadix covered by minute greenish-yellow flowers. The leaf-like spathe covering the stalk continues past the spadix to the same length as the leaves.

Properties and Uses: Carminative, diaphoretic, emmenagogue, febrifuge, sedative, stomachic. Sweet flag is particularly known for its beneficial effects on the stomach. It stimulates appetite and helps to relieve acute and chronic dyspepsia, gastritis, and hyperacidity. Chewing the root is also said to stop pyrosis, the discharge of an acrid liquid from the stomach into the throat. For smokers, however, chewing the dried root tends to cause mild nausea, a property that makes sweet flag useful for breaking the smoking habit. A decoction of the rootstock makes a good bath additive for insomnia and tense nerves; it has also been used in baths for children with scrofula or rickets. Sweet flag is sometimes credited with aphrodisiac powers; for an extended celebration of its properties, see Walt Whitman's poem "Calamus."

Preparation and Dosage:

Infusion: Steep 1 tsp. rootstock in ½ cup water for 5 minutes. Take 1 cup a day.

Decoction: Add 1 tbsp. dried rootstock to 1 cup simmering water and boil briefly. Take 1 cup a day.

Tincture: Take 10 drops, three times a day.

Oil: Take 2 to 3 drops, three times a day.

Bath Additive: Add 1 lb. dried rootstock to 5 qt. water; bring to a boil, then steep for 5 minutes and strain. Add to bath water.

446   SWEET GUM

(Liquidambar styraciflua)

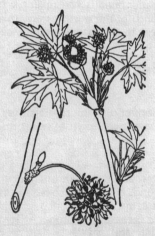

Common Names: Copalm, gum tree, liquidamber, liquid storax, opossum tree, red gum, styrax, white gum.

Medicinal Parts: Balsam, bark.

Description: Sweet gum is a deciduous, forest-dwelling tree native to the eastern and southern areas of the U.S. Growing as high as 150 feet, the tree is covered with rough, gray bark; but the branchlets are reddish-brown and often have corky ridges. When cut, it exudes a sticky, resinous gum or balsam. Its alternate, serrate, palmately lobed leaves are dark green and shiny above and pale green underneath; in fall they turn a deep crimson. The petalless flowers occur in globular heads, the male heads clustered in terminal racemes and the female growing individually on long peduncles. The fruit consists of woody capsules growing in round, spiny heads an inch or more across which stay on the tree through the winter.

Properties and Uses: Antiseptic, astringent, expectorant. The balsam from the sweet gum tree has antiseptic properties which have made it an effective external medication for wounds and for skin problems. For external use, it is usually made into an ointment with lard or oil. American Indians used a decoction of leaves or roots as a wash to treat injuries. For coughs and respiratory congestion due to colds, the gum can be taken to promote expectoration. The bark of sweet gum has been used to relieve diarrhea and dysentery.

Preparation and Dosage:

Decoction: Boil 1 tsp. bark or balsam in 1 cup water. Take 1 cup a day, a mouthful at a time.

Tincture: A dose is from ¼ to ½ tsp.

447, SYCAMORE MAPLE

(Acer pseudo-platanus)

Medicinal Part: Bark.

Description: Sycamore maple is a large deciduous tree found in mountainous and upland areas of Europe and western Asia and cultivated to some extent in the U.S. It grows as high as 100 feet, and its spreading branches bear opposite, five-lobed, coarsely crenate-serrate leaves which resemble those of the sycamore tree. The leaves are dark green on top, pale and whitish beneath. The yellowish-green flowers grow in hanging racemes, producing eventually the winged fruit characteristic of the maples.

Properties and Uses: Astringent, vulnerary. The bark of the sycamore maple has mild astringent properties and has been used to make a wash for skin problems and an eyewash for sore eyes. The inner bark of the tree, containing the sweet sap, can be used as dressing for wounds.

448 TAMARIND

(Tamarindus indica)

Medicinal Parts: Fruit, leaves.

Description: Tamarind is an evergreen tree which grows in tropical climates. It grows up to 80 feet high; and its trunk, covered with shaggy, brownish-gray bark, may reach 25 feet in diameter. The alternate, even-pinnate leaves have from 20 to 40 small, opposite, oblong leaflets. The pale yellow flowers have petals with red veins and grow in racemes at the ends of the branches. Flowering time in the northern hemisphere is during April and May. The fruit is a cinnamon-colored oblong pod, from 3 to 8 inches long, with a thin, brittle shell enclosing a soft, brownish, acidulous pulp.

Properties and Uses: Anthelmintic, laxative, refrigerant. The fruit of tamarind is a mild laxative. In the tropics, it is commonly eaten as food and made into cooling beverages. It makes a refreshing drink for those ill with a fever. The leaves are said to have anthelmintic properties; the natives of the tropics use them externally in the form of a poultice or fomentation.

449   TANSY

(Tanacetum vulgare)

Common Names: Bitter buttons, hindheal, parsley fern.

Medicinal Part: The herb.

Description: Tansy is an aromatic, perennial plant which is cultivated and also found growing wild along ridges and roadsides and in waste places. It grows in Europe, in the U.S. from the Atlantic seaboard westward to Minnesota, and in Oregon and Nevada. The short, creeping rootstock sends an erect, nearly round, often purplish-brown stem to a height of 1 to 5 feet. The alternate, smooth, lanceolate, dark green leaves are pinnately divided, their segments acute and toothed. Blooming from July to September, the golden-yellow flowers grow in terminal, flattened cymes. The fruit is an achene.

Properties and Uses: Anthelmintic, emmenagogue, tonic. A weak anthelmintic and mild irritant, tansy can be poisonous even when applied externally; therefore, it is little used. In Europe tansy has been used to promote suppressed menstruation; American Indians made a tea from the entire plant for the same purpose and to induce abortion. A leaf tea has also been used at times for its bitter tonic properties and recommended for hysteria. An infusion of leaves and flowers makes a good wash for skin problems and blemishes and also for bruises, sprains and rheumatism. CAUTION: An overdose of tansy oil or tea can be fatal.

Preparation and Dosage: Except in emergencies, use tansy only under medical supervision.

450 TARRAGON

(Artemisia dracunculus)

Common Name: Estragon.

Medicinal Part: The flowering plant.

Description: Tarragon is a green, glabrous perennial shrub found in sunny, dry areas in the western U.S., southern Asia, and Siberia. In Europe it is cultivated for its leaves, which are used as a seasoning. Its branched root system with runners produces erect, bushy-branched stems from 2 to 4 feet high. The lower leaves are ternate, the upper leaves lanceolate to linear and small-toothed or entire. The small, drooping, whitish-green or yellow flowers are almost globular and bloom from May to July in terminal panicles.

Properties and Uses: Diuretic, emmenagogue, hypnotic, stomachic. In popular use, tarragon serves to relieve digestive problems and catarrhal difficulties, as a diuretic to stimulate the action of the kidneys, and as an emmenagogue to promote the onset of menstruation. The tea stimulates the appetite, especially when it has been lost because of illness. Taking the tea before going to bed helps to overcome insomnia.

Preparation and Dosage:

Infusion: Steep ½ tsp. dried plant in ½ cup water. Take ½ to 1 cup a day, unsweetened.

451 THUJA

(Thuja occidentalis)

Common Names: Arborvitae, tree of life, white cedar, yellow cedar.

Medicinal Parts: Branchlets, leaves, bark.

Description: Thuja is an evergreen pine tree, which grows in swampy areas and along stream banks from Quebec to Manitoba south to Illinois and North Carolina. It is cultivated in European parks and gardens for hedgerows and windbreaks. The tree reaches a height of 70 feet and is 2 to 4 feet in diameter. The outer bark is light brown and shredded, separating into long, narrow strips with a lighter, reddish-brown wood underneath. The branches are short; the lower ones horizontal, the upper ones crowded and forming a dense, conical head. The opposite pairs of bright green, acute leaves resemble overlapping scales and have an aromatic odor when crushed. The minute, solitary, terminal flowers bloom from April to July and are yellow or greenish in color. The small cone is pale green when young, light reddish-brown with pointless, thin, oblong scales when old.

Properties and Uses: Diaphoretic, emmenagogue. Thuja is useful as a counter-irritant in the relief of muscular aches and pains, including those of rheumatism. It can be applied externally in a salve for warts and other skin problems, as well as for rheumatic pains. American Indians made a tea of the inner bark to promote menstruation, relieve headache and heart pain and reduce swelling. The leaves yield an oil which is used internally to promote menstruation and relieve rheumatism. CAUTION: This volatile oil is toxic: cases of death from overdose are on record.

Preparation and Dosage: Use only under medical supervision.

452 THYME

(a) (Thymus vulgaris)

Common Name: Garden thyme.

Medicinal Part: The herb.

Description: Garden thyme, a small shrubby plant with a strong, spicy taste and odor, is extensively cultivated in Europe and the U.S. for culinary use. The numerous quadrangular, procumbent, woody stems grow from 6 to 10 inches high and are finely hairy. Slightly downy on top and very downy underneath, the opposite, sessile leaves are ovate to lanceolate in shape and have slightly rolled edges. The small bluish-purple, two-lipped flowers are whorled in dense, head-like clusters, blooming from May to September.

Properties and Uses: Anthelmintic, antispasmodic, carminative, diaphoretic, expectorant, sedative. As a tincture, extract, or infusion, thyme is commonly used in throat and bronchial problems, including acute bronchitis, laryngitis, and whooping cough, and also for diarrhea, chronic gastritis, and lack of appetite. For coughs and spasmodic complaints, make the medication from the fresh plant. A warm infusion promotes perspiration and relieves flatulence and colic. Oil of thyme (thymol) has a powerful antiseptic action for which it is used in mouthwashes and toothpastes. Thymol is also effective against ascarids and hookworms. As a local irritant, it can be used externally for warts or to encourage the flow of blood to the surface. Thyme baths are said to be helpful for neurasthenia, rheumatic problems, paralysis, bruises, swellings, and sprains. A salve made from thyme can be used for shingles. CAUTION: Excessive internal use of thyme can lead to symptoms of poisoning and to overstimulation of the thyroid gland.

Preparation and Dosage:

Infusion: Steep ½ tsp. fresh herb or 1 tsp. dried herb in ½ cup water for 3 to 5 minutes. Take 1 to 1½ cups a day, a mouthful at a time.

Oil: Take 2 to 3 drops on a sugar cube, two or three times a day.

Tincture or Extract: Take 10 to 20 drops, three times a day.

Bath Additive: Make a strong decoction and add to bath water.

453 THYME (cont.)

(b) (Thymus serpyllum)

Common Names: Mother of thyme, creeping thyme, mountain thyme, wild thyme.

Medicinal Part: The herb.

Description: Mother of thyme is generally a smaller plant than garden thyme, but the two have characteristics in common, including similar leaves and flowers as well as quadrangular, hairy stems. Mother of thyme, found in thickets and woods and along roadsides, is native to Europe and naturalized in North America. Its creeping stems have erect branches from 2 to 3 inches high, but some varieties under cultivation reach 3 feet in height. Its leaves are similar in shape to those of garden thyme, but they have short petioles and are not downy. The flowers, though smaller, are also similar in shape, color, arrangement on the plant, and time of bloom.

Properties and Uses: Antispasmodic, carminative, expectorant, rubefacient, tonic. Mother of thyme is beneficial for respiratory problems, helping to clear mucous congestion from the lungs and respiratory passages. It makes a good tonic for the stomach and nerves, and is used for gastrointestinal problems such as mild gastritis, enteritis, stomach cramps, and painful menstruation. A bath additive made from the decoction stimulates the flow of blood toward the surface of the body and alleviates nervous exhaustion. An infusion of leaves is said to relieve the headache of a hangover. Used externally, alcoholic extracts are helpful for tumors, stab wounds, bruises, and rheumatism.

Mother of thyme is also reputed to be useful in breaking the alcoholic habit by causing vomiting, diarrhea, sweating, thirst, and hunger, along with a revulsion for alcohol. This "cure" will probably have to be repeated several times, but usually at longer and longer intervals. Mother of thyme has also been recommended for chlorosis, anemia, and insomnia.

Preparation and Dosage:

Infusion: Steep 1 to 2 tsp. herb in 1 cup water. Take 1 to 1½ cups a day. Except when used for gastrointestinal problems, it can be sweetened with honey.

Bath Additive: Add 3 to 4 oz. flowers (or a strong decoction of the herb) to the bath water.

Alcohol Cure: Add a handful herb to 1 qt. boiling-hot water. Steep in a covered pot for 30 minutes. Give (or take) 1 tbsp. every 15 minutes.

454 TORMENTIL

(Tormentilla erecta or Potentilla tormentilla)

Common Names: Shepherd's knot, upright septfoil.

Medicinal Part: The rootstock.

Description: Tormentil is a perennial European plant found in damp meadows, pastures, hills and marshes. The irregular, knobby rootstock is dark brown on the outside, white inside, turning red on exposure to air. The plant has several fine-haired, branched stems from 4 to 16 inches tall. The serrate, fine-haired leaves are palmately 3- to 5-parted; the segments on the stem leaves are oblanceolate, while those on the basal leaves are rounded and wilt soon after developing. The yellow, four-petaled flowers bloom on long stalks from May to August.

Properties and Uses: Antiphlogistic, antiseptic, astringent, hemostatic. The decoction and tincture is used for diarrhea, enteritis, and inflammation of the mucous membranes in the mouth. The tincture is also good for sealing hemorrhages, for leucorrhea, and for fevers. Diluted it makes a good mouthwash and gargle for sore throat. The root, as an excellent astringent, is used for chronic and infectious catarrhal enteritis, dysentery, and jaundice. It is especially beneficial for intestinal problems where diarrhea and constipation alternate.

Preparation and Dosage: Use the fresh or recently dried root-stock.

Infusion or Decoction: Use 1 tbsp. rootstock to 1 cup water. For infusion, steep 30 or more minutes; strain. Take lukewarm in the course of a day in mouthful doses.

Tincture: Take 20 to 30 drops, two or three times a day.

Powder: Use ¼ to ½ tsp., three times a day or as directed by a doctor.

455 TURKEY CORN

(Corydalis formosa)

Common Names: Choice dielytra, stagger weed, wild turkey pea.

Medicinal Part: The root.

Description: Turkey corn is an indigenous perennial plant found in rich soil on hills, among rocks and old, decayed timber in the eastern U.S. from New York to North Carolina. The tuberous root produces a scape 6 to 12 inches high and a set of basal, somewhat triternate leaves, 10 to 15 inches in height. In the early spring, nodding, reddish-purple flowers bloom at the top of the scape. The fruit is a pod-shaped, many-seeded capsule.

Properties and Uses: Bitter tonic, diuretic. Its tonic properties are similar to those of yellow gentian, colombo, and other pure bitters. Specifically, it is beneficial for stomach problems such as indigestion and loss of appetite. It is also used as diuretic for kidney difficulties, and it can be taken for scrofula and all other skin diseases. CAUTION: Turkey corn contains toxic alkaloids and must be used cautiously.

Preparation and Dosage:

Infusion: Steep 1 tsp. root in 1 cup water. Take a mouthful at a time over the course of the day.

Tincture: A dose is from 5 to 20 drops.

456 TURNIP

(*Brassica rapa*)

Medicinal Part: The tuber.

Description: The turnip is a biennial plant cultivated for its flat or globular, white, soft-fleshed tuber. The turnip's roots are located on the slender tap-root beneath the tuber. The erect, branched stem bears alternate, clasping leaves, which are sometimes covered with a whitish bloom. The narrow, basal leaves, 12 to 20 inches in length, are lyrate-pinnatifid. The plant has racemes of small, bright-yellow flowers, and its fruit is a small pod with a slender beak.

Properties and Uses: Ointment and poultice. Applied in a salve, the tuber can be used for chilblains.

Preparation and Dosage:

Salve: Boil finely grated tuber with lard.

457   TURTLEBLOOM

(*Chelone glabra*)

Common Names: Balmony, salt-rheum weed, shell flower, snakehead.

Medicinal Part: Leaves.

Description: Turtlebloom is an herbaceous perennial plant found in wet ground from Newfoundland to Florida and westward to Minnesota, Kansas, and Texas. Its simple, erect, square stem reaches a height of 1 to 3 feet. Opposite and short-petioled, its shining, dark green, pointed leaves are serrate and oblong-lanceolate in shape. Blooming from July to September, the white flowers, often tinged with pink or magenta, grow in dense terminal or axillary spikes. The two-lipped corolla of the flower somewhat resembles a turtle's head. The fruit is an ovoid capsule.

Properties and Uses: Anthelmintic, aperient, cholagogue, stimulant, tonic. Turtlebloom is beneficial for a weak stomach and indigestion, general debility, constipation, and torpid liver. It also stimulates the appetite, and in small doses is a good tonic during convalescence. In addition, turtlebloom is an effective anthelmintic. Externally, it is used for sores and eczema. The ointment is valuable to relieve the itching and irritation of piles.

Preparation and Dosage:

Infusion: Use 1 tsp. leaves to 1 cup water. Take 1 to 2 cups a day.

Tincture: Take 10 to 20 drops in water, three or four times a day.

458   TWIN LEAF

(Jeffersonia diphylla)

Common Names: Ground squirrel pea, helmet pod, rheumatism root, yellowroot.

Medicinal Part: The rootstock.

Description: Twin leaf is a perennial plant found in limestone soils and in woods near rivers from Ontario westward to Wisconsin and southward to Virginia and Tennessee. The horizontal, fleshy rootstock with matted fibrous roots produces a simple, naked scape, 12 to 18 inches tall. Emanating also from the rootstock, the large, smooth basal leaves, 3 to 6 inches long and 2 to 5 inches wide, are divided into two half-ovate leaflets. Blooming from April to May, a large, solitary, white, eight-petaled flower terminates the scape. The fruit is an obovate capsule. The plant is only 6 to 9 inches tall in flower, but is double that height in fruit.

Properties and Uses: Antispasmodic, diuretic, emetic, expectorant, tonic. Twin leaf is beneficial for chronic rheumatism, nervous and spasmodic problems, neuralgia, and cramps. In small doses, it is used as an expectorant and tonic; in large doses, as an emetic. As a gargle, it is useful for throat infections. Applied externally as a poultice or fomentation, it will relieve pain anywhere.

Preparation and Dosage:

Decoction: Steep 1 tsp. root in 1 cup boiling-hot water for thirty minutes, then simmer ten minutes and strain. Take one cup, then follow with small frequent doses.

Tincture: A dose is from 5 to 20 drops.

459 VIRGINIA SNAKEROOT

(Aristolochia serpentaria)

Common Names: Pelican flower, red river snakeroot, sangree root, snakeweed, Texas snakeroot, thick birthwort.

Medicinal Parts: Rootstock and roots.

Description: Virginia snakeroot is a perennial plant indigenous to the rich, dry woods of the eastern U.S. Its fibrous, horizontal rootstock produces many thin roots, as well as a wavy stem that reaches 1 to 3 feet in height. The alternate thin, green leaves are ovate and cordate, tapering gradually to a point at the apex. A few solitary purple flowers, with an S-shaped calyx inflated at both ends, bloom on short, scaly branches near the bottom of the plant during June and July.

Properties and Uses: Bitter tonic, stimulant. Small doses of Virginia snakeroot will stir a languid appetite and promote proper digestion, but large doses will cause vomiting, diarrhea, vertigo, and other unpleasant effects. In proper doses it is also said to stimulate blood circulation. At one time, Virginia snakeroot was perhaps the most highly valued of snakebite remedies, various other species of its genus also being used in different parts of the world for the same purpose. American Indians treated snakebite by cutting into the bite and sucking out the poison, then applying the chewed root of the plant to the wound. CAUTION: Virginia snakeroot contains an alkaloid which, in pure form, can paralyze the respiratory system. Use only small doses of the plant.

Preparation and Dosage:

Infusion: Steep 1 tsp. dried rootstock and roots in 1 cup water. Take 1 tbsp. three to six times a day.

Tincture: A dose is from 1 to 20 drops, taken in cold water. Use with caution.

460 VIRGIN'S BOWER

(Clematis virginiana)

Medicinal Parts: Leaves, flowers.

Description: Virgin's bower is a woody climbing vine found along streambanks, bushes, and fences in the eastern and central states of the U.S. Its opposite, ternate leaves have ovate, acute, serrate leaflets. Its small, petalless flowers have whitish sepals and bloom in leafy, cymose panicles during summer and autumn. The fruit is a feathery achene which grows in prominent heads.

Properties and Uses: Diaphoretic, diuretic, stimulant, vesicant. An infusion of the leaves and flowers of virgin's bower is said to relieve even severe headaches. For external use, virgin's bower is sometimes combined with other plants to make ointments or poultices for sores, skin ulcers and itching skin. CAUTION: Virgin's bower contains acrid substances which can cause severe skin irritation. Sensitive people can get dermatitis from handling the plant.

Preparation and Dosage:

Infusion: Steep 1 heaping tsp. leaves and flowers in 1 cup water for 30 minutes. Take 1 tbsp. four to six times a day.

Inhaling the fumes of the bruised root or leaves is said to relieve headache.

461 WAFER ASH

(Ptelea trifoliata)

Common Names: Pickaway anise, prairie grub, scubby trefoil, stinking prairie bush, swamp dogwood, three-leaved hop tree, wingseed.

Medicinal Part: Root bark.

Description: Wafer ash is a native American shrub found in moist places and along the edges of woods in the eastern states of the U.S. Growing as high as 25 feet, the stems and branches bear alternate leaves, each consisting of three ovate to elliptic-oblong leaflets. The greenish-white, malodorous flowers grow in small, dense corymbs during June. The fruit is an oblong-orbicular samara which is winged all around.

Properties and Uses: Tonic. A tea made from the root bark of the wafer ash has a beneficial effect on the stomach and is often tolerated when other tonic remedies are not. In particular, it helps to arouse a sluggish appetite. The leaves have also sometimes been credited with medicinal properties, as anthelmintics and as applications to wounds.

Preparation and Dosage:

Infusion: Steep 1 tsp. root bark in 1 cup water. Take 1 cup a day, a mouthful at a time.

Tincture: A dose is from 5 to 20 drops.

462 WAHOO

(Euonymus atropurpureus)

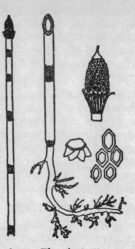

Common Names: Arrow-wood, bitter ash, burning bush, Indian arrow, spindle tree.

Medicinal Part: Bark.

Description: Wahoo is a deciduous shrub or small tree, up to 25 feet high, found in moist woods and along riverbanks in the eastern U.S., as far west as Montana and Texas. Its smooth, somewhat quadrangular branches bear opposite, elliptic, pointed leaves that are finely serrate and fine-haired underneath. Axillary cymes of 7 or more purple flowers appear during June. The fruit is a scarlet, four-lobed capsule containing brown seeds with scarlet arils.

Properties and Uses: Cardiac, diuretic, expectorant, laxative, tonic. Wahoo was a popular diuretic drug during the nineteenth century. It was also recommended for chest and lung congestion, indigestion, and fever. After the discovery early this century that wahoo has a digitalis-like effect on the heart, it also became popular as a cardiac drug. CAUTION: The leaves and fruit of wahoo can cause various symptoms of poisoning, such as nausea, cold sweat, and prostration.

Preparation and Dosage:

Infusion: Steep 1 level tsp. bark in 1 cup water for 30 minutes. Take ½ to 1 cup an hour before meals for indigestion.

463 STRAWBERRY-BUSH

(Euonymus americanus)

NOTE: Strawberry-bush (*Euonymus americanus*) is a related plant, with ovate-lanceolate to lanceolate leaves, reddish-green flowers, and pink fruit. Medicinally it is equivalent to wahoo.

464 WALNUT

(a) (Juglans nigra)

Common Name: Black walnut.

Medicinal Parts: Bark, leaves, rind of the fruit.

Description: Black walnut is a Temperate Zone forest tree

found in the eastern U.S. Its bark is rough and dark; the leaves are pinnately compound, with ovate lanceolate, serrate leaflets. Male and female flowers grow in separate catkins. The fruit is a deeply grooved nut inside a spherical rind.

Properties and Uses: Bark: astringent. Leaves: detergent. Rind: herpatic. An infusion or decoction of the bark can be taken for diarrhea and to stop the production of milk. Use it also as a douche for leucorrhea and as a mouthwash for soreness in the mouth or inflamed tonsils. The leaves can be used to make a cleansing wash, and the green rind of the fruit makes a good poultice to get rid of ringworm.

465 WALNUT (cont.)

(b) (Juglans cinerea)

Common Names: Butternut, lemon walnut, oil nut, white walnut.

Medicinal Part: Bark.

Description: Butternut is a native North American tree that grows to a height of 50 to 75 feet. Its branches spread wide from the trunk and are covered with smooth, gray bark. The leaves are alternate, large, and pinnate, with 7 or 8 pairs of serrate, oblong-lanceolate leaflets. Male and female flowers grow in separate catkins. The fruit is an edible, pleasant-tasting kernel in a hard, dark nutshell.

Properties and Uses: Anthelmintic, cathartic, tonic. Butternut's action as a soothing, tonic laxative has been likened to that of rhubarb and is particularly suitable for chronic constipation. Butternut bark will also expel worms and can be used for feverish colds and flu.

Preparation and Dosage:

Decoction: Use 1 tsp. bark with 1 cup water. Take 1 cup a day, cold, a mouthful at a time.

Syrup: Boil 1 pound of bark in water. Evaporate the solution down to 1 pint. Add a pound of sugar and boil until the desired consistency is reached. Take 1 tbsp. at a time.

Tincture: Take 1 to 15 drops, three times a day.

(c) (Juglans regia)

Common Names: English walnut, caucasion walnut, Circassian walnut, Persian walnut.

Medicinal Part: Leaves.

Description: The English walnut tree is widely cultivated for its fruit. It grows to about 80 feet high and has gray bark and wide-spreading branches. The leaves are odd-pinnate, with oblong-ovate, entire leaflets that are sticky when young but glabrous later. Blooming in May, the male flowers appear in axillary catkins, the female in terminal spikes. The fruit is the common walnut.

Properties and Uses: Astringent. The leaf tea is tonic to the stomach and promotes good appetite; it is also used for catarrhal enteritis. The decoction is more commonly used externally as a wash or bath additive for rheumatism, gout, glandular swelling, gum problems, scrofula, sweaty feet, acne, dandruff, other skin problems and even for excessive milk flow after the child is weaned. A decoction of the green shell surrounding the walnut has been recommended for failing virility.

Preparation and Dosage:

Decoction: Use 4 tsp. leaves or chopped green shells with 1 cup water. Take 1 cup a day, a mouthful at a time.

Bath Additive: Boil 1 lb. dried leaves in 1½ qt. water for 45 minutes, and add the liquid to the bath water. For a footbath, reduce the amounts proportionately.

467. **WATER AVENS**

(Geum rivale)

Common Names: Avens root, cure-all, chocolate root, Indian chocolate, purple avens, throat root.

Medicinal Part: The plant.

Description: Water avens is a hairy perennial plant found mostly in moist and wet places from Colorado and New Mexico northeastward, and in Canada, Europe, and Asia. Its woody rootstock produces a simple, erect stem from 1 to 3 feet high with small, sessile, simple or three-cleft leaves. From the rootstock also grow long-petioled, hairy, pinnate leaves with three large terminal, coarsely double-toothed leaflets and one or two pairs of small lower leaflets. At the top of the stem grow from three to five purplish flowers on short pedicels, blooming from May to July. Some varieties have purplish sepals but rose-colored to yellow petals.

Properties and Uses: Astringent, stomachic, tonic. The rootstock of water avens makes a tasty and effective remedy for diarrhea and dysentery when taken with milk and sugar. It also acts to improve appetite and digestion. An infusion made from the whole plant can be used to clear up respiratory congestion and to counteract nausea. CAUTION: Excessive amounts can produce unpleasant side effects.

Preparation and Dosage:

Infusion: Steep 1 tsp. rootstock in 1 cup water for 30 minutes. Take ½ cup before going to bed, or a mouthful three times a day. Take no more than 2 cups in total consecutive doses.

Infusion: Steep 1 to 2 tsp. fresh plant in 1 cup water. Take 1 cup a day.

Tincture: A dose is from 10 to 20 drops.

468 ROUGH AVENS
(Geum virginianum)

NOTE: Rough avens (*Geum virginianum*) is a related perennial plant found in low places and along the edges of woods northward and eastward from Minnesota and Missouri. Its basal leaves are pinnately 3- to 5-parted, its stem leaves short-petioled and lanceolate. The flowers are creamy white. Rough avens can be used medicinally like water avens.

469 WATERCRESS
(Nasturtium officinale)

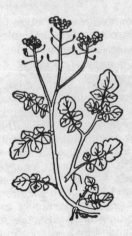

Common Names: Scurvy grass, tall nasturtium.

Medicinal Parts: Leaves, roots, young shoots.

Description: Native to Europe and naturalized in the U.S., watercress is a perennial plant which thrives in clear, cold water and is found in ditches and streams everywhere. It is cultivated for its leaves, which are principally used as salad greens or garnishes. Connected to a creeping rootstock, the hollow, branching stem, 1 to 2 feet in length, generally extends with its leaves above the water. The smooth, somewhat fleshy, dark green leaves are odd-pinnate with one to four pairs of small, oblong or roundish leaflets. The small, white flowers bloom in elongating terminal racemes from May to September. The fruit is a long, curved, linear-cylindric, partitioned pod.

Properties and Uses: Diuretic, expectorant, purgative, stimulant, stomachic. Watercress is recommended for gout, mild digestive disturbances, and catarrh of the upper respiratory tract. Very effective as an expectorant, it is also beneficial for tuberculosis, anemia, and eczema. Its high vitamin C content makes it a good illness preventive. In addition, the richness of its mineral, iron, and iodine content stimulates glandular activity. Limited loss of hair caused by a fungus can be remedied by an application of watercress juice. CAUTION: Excessive or prolonged use can lead to kidney problems. It should not be taken daily and no longer than four weeks even with interruptions. The juice should not be taken undiluted, because it can produce inflammations in the throat and stomach. Some doctors caution against use during pregnancy.

Preparation and Dosage: Watercress must be used fresh.

Infusion: Use 1 tsp. young shoots in ½ cup water. Take ½ cup, freshly made, three times a day. To maintain the greatest possible vitamin content, do not steep a long time or allow to boil.

Juice: Take 1 tsp. in milk or water, three times a day. Fresh watercress juice is easily obtained with an electric vegetable juicer.

470 WATER ERYNGO

(Eryngium aquaticum)

Common Names: Button snakeroot, corn snakeroot, rattlesnake's master, rattlesnake weed.

Medicinal Part: The root.

Description: Water eryngo is a native perennial herb found in swamps and low wetlands from New Jersey to Georgia. This glaucous plant's tuberous root sends up a simple stem, 1 to 5 feet in height. The long, taper-pointed leaves, 1 to 2 feet in length and ½ to 1 inch wide are net-veined and entire or remotely toothed. Blooming in August, the small, whitish flowers grow in spikes subtended by a whorl of bracts.

Properties and Uses: Diaphoretic, diuretic, emetic, expectorant, stimulant. Water eryngo root is very useful when chewed to promote the flow of saliva and thus aid digestion. In large doses, it acts as an emetic. Originally a folk remedy, late-nineteenth-century medical doctors commonly prescribed it as an expectorant, stimulant or diuretic. It has also been applied as a remedy for chronic laryngitis and bronchitis, dropsy, stones, inflammations of the sexual and urinary organs, and impotence. American Indians used it as an emetic and diuretic, and in infusion form as a febrifuge. It is a good substitute for senega snakeroot.

Preparation and Dosage:

Infusion: Use 1 heaping tsp. root to 1 pint boiling-hot water. Take 1 tbsp. two to four times a day.

Tincture: A dose is from 10 to 20 drops.

471 WAX MYRTLE

(Myrica cerifera)

Common Names: Bayberry, candleberry, tallow shrub, vegetable tallow, waxberry, wax myrtle.

Medicinal Parts: Bark, leaves, wax.

Description: Wax myrtle is an evergreen shrub or tree found in woods and fields from New Jersey to Florida and Texas. As a tree it grows as high as 35 feet. Covered with smooth, gray bark, the branches bear alternate, lanceolate to oblong-lanceolate leaves whose downy undersides are dotted with glands. The yellowish flowers grow in scaly catkins, the male catkins elongated, the female tending to globular. The fruit is a grayish-white, round, drupe-like nut covered with a waxy crust.

Properties and Uses: Astringent, tonic. The bark, leaves, and wax from the fruit of the wax myrtle have been made into astringent teas, gargles, and douches for diarrhea, hemorrhages, sore throat, poultices for wounds, cuts, and bruises. wax was said to be highly effective against dysentery. One tribe of American Indians took a decoction of the stems and leaves for fever. Powdered wax myrtle can be used as a snuff for nasal congestion. Wax myrtle tea has also been recommended for jaundice and scrofula.

Preparation and Dosage:

Decoction: Boil 1 tsp. bark, leaves, or wax in 1 cup water. Take 1 to 2 cups a day. (To get the wax, boil the fruit in water; let cool and then skim the wax off the surface.)

Tincture: A dose is from 10 to 30 drops, taken in water.

WHITE PINE
(Pinus strobus)

Common Names: Deal pine, soft pine.

Medicinal Parts: Inner bark, young shoots.

Description: White pine is a large North American evergreen tree found growing from Newfoundland to Georgia and Iowa. Reaching a height of 150 feet or more, the tree is covered with deeply fissured, gray-brown bark. Its branches are arranged in regular whorls. The soft bluish-green, needle-like, linear leaves grow in clusters of five, the clusters spirally arranged on the branches. The male flowers grow in axillary, catkinlike cones, the female in slightly larger lateral or nearly terminal cones. The slender, cylindric seed cones are from 3 to 8 inches long and are often curved. The winged seeds are brown, mottled with black.

Properties and Uses: Expectorant. The inner bark of white pine has long been a standard remedy for coughs and congestion due to colds, as a tea or as an ingredient in cough syrup. This application goes back to the American Indians, some of whom also used the resinous sap and the young leaves as cold remedies. Some tribes used the inner bark or the sap as a poultice or dressing for wounds and sores.

Preparation and Dosage:

Infusion: Steep 1 tsp. inner bark or young shoots in 1 cup water. Take a mouthful at a time, as needed.

Tincture: A dose is from 2 to 10 drops in water.

Mixture: Steep 1 tsp. white pine bark and 1 tbsp. each of wild cherry bark, sassafras bark, and American spikenard root in 1 pint boiling-hot water for 30 minutes. Take 1 tsp. every hour.

WHITE POND LILY
(Nymphaea odorata)

Common Names: Cow cabbage, fragrant water lily, sweet-scented pond lily, sweet-scented water lily, water cabbage, water lily, white water lily.

Medicinal Part: Rootstock.

Description: White pond lily is an aquatic perennial plant commonly found in ponds and slow streams in eastern North America. Its little-branched rootstock produces large orbicular or oblong-orbicular, entire leaves that float on the surface of the water. They are dark green on top and mostly purplish underneath. The fragrant, large, many-petaled white flowers bloom above the water for three days, opening in the forenoon each day. Flowering time is from June to September.

Properties and Uses: Antiseptic, astringent, demulcent. A tea made from white pond lily root makes a good gargle for irritation and inflammation in the mouth and throat. It can also be used as an eyewash and an antiseptic vaginal douche. As a lotion, it helps to heal sores and to make the skin soft and smooth. Both the root and the leaves are sometimes made into poultices for wounds, cuts, and bruises.

474 TUBEROUS WATER LILY
(Nymphaea tuberosa)

CAUTION: Do not mistake the white pond lily for the tuberous water lily (*Nymphaea tuberosa*), which can cause poisoning. The poisonous plant can be distinguished by its tuberous rootstock and odorless (or nearly so) flowers.

475 WHITE WEED
(Chrysanthemum leucanthemum)

Common Names: Golden daisy, herb Margaret, maudlinwort, ox-eye daisy, white daisy.

Medicinal Parts: Leaves, flowers.

Description: White weed is a perennial plant found in fields and waste places over most of North America, Europe, and Asia as a common weed. The furrowed, simple or sparingly branched stem grows from 1 to 3 feet high and bears alternate, toothed, sessile and clasping leaves. Both stem and radical leaves are spatulate or obovate with rounded ends; the radical leaves are more strongly toothed. The stem (and each branch, if any) is topped by a solitary flower head with yellow disk and white rays.

Properties and Uses: Diaphoretic, diuretic, irritant. White weed is very little used today. As indicated by the categories, it can be used to promote sweating and to treat urinary and dropsical disorders. It was also once used to treat pulmonary diseases. As a mild irritant, the fresh leaves and flowers can be applied externally to promote the flow of blood to the surface and possibly to treat warts.

WILD BLACK CHERRY

(Prunus serotina)

Common Names: Black choke, choke cherry, rum cherry, wild cherry.

Medicinal Part: Bark.

Description: Wild black cherry is a large tree which grows from Nova Scotia to Florida and as far west as the Dakotas and Arizona. Growing up to 100 feet high and reaching 4 to 5 feet in diameter, the trunk is covered with rough, black bark. The alternate, stiff, oblong to oval leaves have serrate margins and are shiny green above and lighter underneath. The small white flowers grow in lateral racemes, appearing when the leaves are half or more grown. The fruit is a nearly spherical, purple-black drupe, a half inch or less in diameter, ripening in late summer and autumn.

Properties and Uses: Astringent, sedative, stomachic. The bark of wild black cherry was once a favorite ingredient in cough and cold medicines. Its effectiveness was attributed to a sedative action on the respiratory nerves. American Indians had many uses for wild black cherry: one tribe used a tea made from the inner bark to ease pain during labor; others used a tea of the bark for diarrhea and lung problems. A decoction of the inner bark served one tribe as an enema for hemorrhoids; and another tribe cured dysentery by drinking the juice of the ripe cherries which had been allowed to ferment for a year. CAUTION: The leaves, especially when wilted, have poisoned cattle.

Preparation and Dosage: Use bark collected in the fall. Do not boil wild black cherry bark.

Infusion: Steep 1 tsp. bark in 1 cup hot or warm water. Take 1 to 2 cups a day, a mouthful at a time.

Tincture: A dose is from 10 to 15 drops, taken in water. For digestive problems, fill a quart bottle half full of bark and fill with brandy or whiskey. Let stand for a week, shaking often; then strain. Take a tablespoon or more before meals to stimulate appetite and digestion.

WILD CLOVER

(Trifolium pratense)

Common Name: Red clover.

Medicinal Part: Flowering tops.

Description: Wild clover is a perennial plant common in meadows all over North America and Europe. Its short rootstock produces several reddish stems, 1 to 2 feet high, with close-pressed whitish hairs. The palmate leaves, some basal and some along the stems, have three oval to oblong-oval or obovate leaflets which are minutely toothed and sometimes blotched with white. The rose-purple or magenta (to nearly white in some varieties) flowers grow in a dense, ovoid head subtended by a leaf.

Properties and Uses: Diuretic, expectorant. This common clover has been a popular plant for European folk medicine. A tea made from the flowering tops is believed to stimulate liver and gallbladder activity and is taken for constipation and sluggish appetite. It is sometimes recommended for those convalescing from stomach operations who have no appetite. Externally a fomentation is applied for rheumatic or gouty pains and also to soften hard milk glands. A syrupy extract of the flowers can be used as an external treatment for persistent sores. A poultice of the plant can be tried for athlete's foot and other skin problems.

Preparation and Dosage:

Infusion: Steep 2 tsp. flowering tops in ½ cup water for 10 minutes. Take 1 to 1½ cups a day, with or without honey, a mouthful at a time.

Tincture: A dose is from 5 to 30 drops, taken in water.

478   WILD DAISY

(*Bellis perennis*)

Common Name: English daisy.

Medicinal Parts: Flowers, leaves.

Description: Native to Europe and naturalized in the U.S., the English daisy is cultivated and also grows wild in lawns, meadows, and other grassy places. This fibrous-rooted, perennial plant grows from 3 to 6 inches in height. Finely haired and slightly toothed, its obovate basal leaves are arranged in a rosette close to the ground. Above these leaves arise hairy, scapelike peduncles topped by solitary flower heads with white or rose-colored ray flowers and yellow disk flowers. Blooming from March to September, the flowers close at night and in damp weather.

Properties and Uses: Anodyne, antispasmodic, demulcent, digestive, expectorant, laxative, purgative, tonic. Wild daisy is most often used as a gentle laxative. Its fresh flowers are anodyne and help heal inflamed swellings and burns. It is also beneficial for colds and chest problems, coughs, and mucous congestion. The tea is good for stomach and intestinal problems where some sort of internal fermentation is the source, also for catarrh, colic, and liver, kidney, and bladder problems. The juice can be used externally for injuries and suppuration. As a double treatment to relieve stiffness or soreness, wild daisy can be taken internally as a tea and applied externally in compresses.

Preparation and Dosage:

Infusion: Use 1 tbsp. flowers to 1 cup water. Take 1 cup a day. For soreness, take ½ cup at once, then 1 tbsp. every hour.

Juice: Take 1 tsp. to 1 tbsp. three times a day.

479 WILD GINGER

(*Asarum canadense*)

Common Names: Black snake-weed, Canada snakeroot, coltsfoot snakeroot, false coltsfoot, heart snakeroot, Indian ginger, southern snakeroot, Vermont snakeroot.

Medicinal Part: Rootstock.

Description: Wild ginger is a stemless perennial herb found in rich woods from New Brunswick to North Carolina and Missouri. Its slender, branched rootstock produces two long-petioled, kidney-shaped leaves, from 2 to 7 inches across, which have a deep indentation at the base and are fine-haired on both sides. A solitary purplish-brown flower grows on a short, slender peduncle, blooming during April and May.

Properties and Uses: Carminative, diaphoretic, expectorant, irritant. A tea made from the rootstock of wild ginger has been used to relieve flatulence, colic, and upset stomach. Applied externally, it acts as a local irritant; the powder can be used to induced sneezing. It can substitute for ginger root when the latter is not available. The women of one American Indian tribe drank a strong decoction of the rootstock and roots for contraceptive purposes.

Preparation and Dosage:

Infusion: Steep 1 tsp. rootstock in 1 pint water. Take 2 tbsp. at a time, as required.

Tincture: A dose is from 2 to 5 drops.

480 WILD HYSSOP
(Pycnanthemum virginianum)

Common Names: Prairie hyssop, Virginia mountain mint, Virginia thyme.

Medicinal Part: The plant.

Description: Wild hyssop is a fine-haired perennial plant which grows in dry fields, pastures, and hills from Quebec to North Dakota and southward. The stiff, branching stem grows 1 to 3 feet high and bears whorled sessile, lanceolate or linear leaves. Numerous dense, flat-topped heads of minute white or lilac flowers bloom from July to September. The whole plant has a mintlike odor.

Properties and Uses: Antispasmodic, carminative, diaphoretic, stimulant. A hot infusion of wild hyssop promotes perspiration; a warm infusion helps to dispel flatulent colic; a cold infusion is said to be a useful stimulant and tonic for convalescents. In general, wild hyssop shares the medicinal properties of its relatives, the mints.

Preparation and Dosage:

Infusion: Steep 1 tsp. plant in 1 cup water. Take hot, warm, or cold, 1 to 2 cups a day, a mouthful at a time.

Tincture: A dose is from ½ to 1 tsp.

481 WILD INDIGO
(Baptisia tinctoria)

Common Names: American indigo, horsefly weed, indigo broom, false indigo, yellow broom, yellow indigo.

Medicinal Part: The plant.

Description: Wild indigo is a succulent perennial plant found in dry soil in the eastern and central states of the U.S. Its woody rootstock produces a round, branched stem from 2 to 4 feet high, bearing alternate, gray-green, digitate leaves consisting of three wedge-shaped to obovate leaflets. Bright yellow flowers grow in numerous terminal racemes, blooming from June to September.

Properties and Uses: Antiseptic, astringent, emetic, purgative, stimulant. Wild indigo has found application primarily as an external remedy as an antiseptic wash or lotion for wounds, sores, skin ulcers, and eczema. Strong doses of the root bark taken internally have purgative and emetic action. CAUTION: Large doses of wild indigo tincture have caused poisoning.

Preparation and Dosage:

Infusion: Steep 1 tsp. in 1 pint water. Take 1 tsp. at a time, as required.

Tincture: A dose is from 2 to 20 drops. Use with caution.

482   WILD JALAP

(Ipomoea pandurata)

Common Names: Bindweed, hog potato, man-in-the-earth, man-in-the-ground, man root, scammony root, wild potato, wild scammony, wild sweet-potato vine.

Medicinal Part: Root.

Description: Wild jalap is a native North American perennial plant found in dry soil from Ontario to Florida and as far west as Michigan and Texas. Its large, fleshy, tuberous root, often 2 feet long, produces several round, purplish, trailing or somewhat climbing stems bearing alternate, broad-ovate and cordate or sometimes fiddle-shaped (pandurate) leaves. The large, funnel-shaped, white flowers have dark purple throats and bloom from May to September.

Properties and Uses: Cathartic. Wild jalap root is a strong cathartic which is usually mixed with less drastic herbs in laxative preparations. The root has also been made into preparations for external use against skin diseases, including ringworm. CAUTION: An overdose can cause serious internal effects.

Preparation and Dosage:

Infusion: Steep 1 tsp. root in 1 cup water. Take 1 cup a day, a mouthful at a time.

Tincture: A dose is from 5 to 20 drops.

483 WILD OREGON GRAPE

(Mahonia aquifolium)

Common Names: California barberry, holly mahonia, Oregon grape, Rocky Mountain grape, trailing mahonia.

Medicinal Parts: The rootstock and roots.

Description: Wild Oregon grape is an evergreen shrub found in mountain areas on wooded slopes below 7000 feet from British Columbia to Idaho, southward to Oregon and California. Native to North America, it was introduced into Europe as a cultivated plant and has become naturalized there. Its irregular, knotty rootstock has a brownish bark with yellow wood underneath. It produces branched stems which extend to three feet or more in height and have alternate, pinnate leaves with 5 to 9 leaflets. Ovate- or oblong-lanceolate, the leathery, sessile leaflets have 10 or more spiny teeth on each side and are glossy dark green on top, pale green underneath. The yellow flowers bloom in fascicled racemes from April to May. The globular blue berries resemble bilberry.

Properties and Uses: Diuretic, laxative, tonic. According to European folk medicine, wild Oregon grape is a "blood purifier." It is beneficial for scrofulous and chronic skin conditions, constipation, and rheumatism. In homeopathic practice, the tincture is used for all sorts of skin diseases, including acne, eczema, herpes, and psoriasis.

Preparation and Dosage:

Infusion: Use 1 tsp. rootstock and roots to 1 cup water. Take 1 tbsp. three to six times a day.

Tincture: A dose is from 5 to 10 drops.

WILD STRAWBERRY

(Fragaria vesca)

Common Names: Mountain strawberry, wood strawberry.

Medicinal Part: The plant.

Description: Wild strawberry is a perennial plant found mainly in forests, clearings, and shady roadsides in Europe and northern Asia; but a variety grows also in fields and along roadsides in eastern North America. The leaves and flowers grow on petioles and stalks directly from the rootstock, which also produces long, rooting runners. The thin, light green leaves are divided into three more or less ovate, coarsely toothed leaflets and are lightly hairy on the lower side, at least on the veins. The small white flowers grow in raceme-like clusters during May and June. The familiar red "berry" is actually the enlarged, fleshy receptacle (the flower-bearing tip of the stalk) which holds the seedlike fruits on its surface.

Properties and Uses: Astringent, diuretic, tonic. The leaves and rootstock of wild strawberry are astringent and diuretic. A tea made from them can be used for diarrhea, dysentery, and hematuria, as well as for gravel and other problems in the urinary tract. Used both internally and externally at the same time, such a tea is sometimes effective against eczema and acne. Fresh strawberry juice makes a good refrigerant for feverish illnesses. Leaf tea is said also to be a good tonic for convalescents and for children.

Preparation and Dosage:

Infusion: Steep 2 tsp. leaves or rootstock in ½ cup water. Take as needed.

Juice (of "fruit"): Take 2 tbsp. a day.

Tincture (of leaves): Take 5 to 15 drops in water, three times a day.

NOTE: Cultivated strawberries are of much less medicinal value than wild varieties.

WILD YAM

(Dioscorea villosa)

Common Names: China root, colic root, devil's bones, rheumatism root, yuma.

Medicinal Part: Root.

Description: Wild yam is a perennial vine which grows in the U.S. from Rhode Island to Minnesota, Florida and Texas. Twining in thickets and hedges and over bushes and fences, the thin, woolly, reddish-brown stem grows from 5 to 18 feet long. The slender, tuberous rootstock is crooked and laterally branched. Broadly ovate and cordate, the leaves are from 2 to 6 inches long and about three-fourths as wide, glabrous on top, and finely hairy underneath. They are usually alternate, but the lower leaves sometimes grow in twos and fours. The small, greenish-yellow flowers bloom during June and July, the male flowers in drooping panicles, the female in drooping, spicate racemes. The fruit is a three-winged capsule containing winged seeds.

Properties and Uses: Antispasmodic, diaphoretic, diuretic, expectorant. Wild yam is diuretic, expectorant, and possibly emetic in large doses. It was once commonly prescribed for bilious colic. Wild yam is said to be soothing to the nerves and beneficial for neuralgia and pains in the urinary tract. Some have considered it an antispasmodic and recommended it for cramps. During pregnancy, small frequent doses will help allay nausea.

Preparation and Dosage:

Infusion: Steep 1 tsp. root in 1 cup water for 30 minutes. Take 1 cup in the course of the day, a mouthful at a time.

Tincture: Take 10 to 30 drops in water, three or four times a day as needed.

WILLOW
(a) (Salix alba)

Common Names: White willow, salicin willow, withe, withy.

Medicinal Part: Bark.

Description: White willow is a deciduous tree found in moist places in North Africa, central Asia, and in Europe, from where it was introduced into the northeastern U.S. Covered with rough, gray bark, the tree grows up to 75 feet high; in some parts of the world it grows also as a shrub. Its alternate, lanceolate, serrate leaves are ashygray in color and silky on both sides. Male and female flowers occur on separate trees, appearing in catkins on leafy stalks at the same time as the leaves.

Properties and Uses: Anodyne, antiseptic, astringent, diaphoretic, diuretic, febrifuge, tonic. The ability of willow bark to alleviate pain and reduce fever has been known for at least two thousand years. It contains salicin, a glucoside that is probably converted to salicylic acid in the body. Salicylic acid is closely related to aspirin, the synthetic drug that has displaced willow bark from popular use. Willow bark reduces inflammation and makes an effective treatment for articular rheumatism. As an astringent, it has been recommended for internal bleeding, and as a diuretic for gouty and rheumatic problems. It is even said to be good for heartburn and stomach ailments. A decoction can be used as a gargle for gum and tonsil inflammations; as an external wash for eruptions, sores, burns, and wounds; and as a footbath for sweaty feet. A deodorizing washing liquid can be made from a solution of willow bark mixed with borax.

Preparation and Dosage: Bark is collected in the springtime.

Decoction: Soak 1 to 3 tsp. bark in 1 cup cold water for 2 to 5 hours, then bring to a boil. Take 1 cup a day, unsweetened, a mouthful at a time.

Cold Extract: Soak 1 tbsp. bark in cold water for 8 to 10 hours and strain.

Powder: Take 1 to 1½ tsp., three times a day.

PURPLE WILLOW or PURPLE OSIER
(Salix purpurea)

NOTE: Purple willow or purple osier (Salix purpurea) is a shrub up to 10 feet high, with oblanceolate leaves. Medicinally, it is essentially equivalent to white willow but is most effective against fever.

488   WILLOW (cont.)
(b) (Salix nigra)

Common Names: Black willow, catkins willow, pussywillow.

Medicinal Parts: Bark, buds (catkins).

Description: Black willow is a native of North America. It grows up to 20 feet high and has very dark rough bark and narrow-lanceolate, pointed leaves which often curve at the tip. Varieties of this tree are found in both the eastern and western U.S.

Properties and Uses: Same as white willow. In addition to the uses listed under white willow, the bark and catkins of black willow have seen service as anti-aphrodisiacs and sexual sedatives. An infusion of bark and catkins or a fluid extract of the bark was used.

Preparation and Dosage:

Tincture: Take 10 to 20 drops, as needed.

489   WILLOW (cont.)
(c) (Salix caprea)

Common Names: Sallow, goat willow.

Medicinal Part: Bark.

Description: Sallow is a small tree or tree-like shrub native to Eurasia but sometimes cultivated in the U.S. Its wrinkled, slightly toothed or jagged leaves are broadly ovate to oblong-orbicular and are woolly or felty underneath. The catkins appear well before the leaves.

Properties and Uses: Same as white willow. In addition to the uses described under white willow, sallow bark tea has been recommended for indigestion, whooping cough, and catarrh. As an antiseptic, it can also be used to disinfect bandages.

Preparation and Dosage: Same as white willow.

490 WINTERGREEN
(Gaultheria procumbens)

Common Names: Canada tea, checkerberry, deerberry, ground berry, hillberry, mountain tea, partridge berry, spiceberry, spicy wintergreen, spring wintergreen, wax cluster.

Medicinal Part: Leaves.

Description: Wintergreen is a native North American evergreen shrub which grows in woods and clearings from Newfoundland to Manitoba and south to Georgia, Michigan, and Indiana. The creeping stems send up erect branches,

2 to 6 inches high, which bear alternate, oval, leathery leaves with serrate (and sometimes bristly) margins. Both the leaves and the solitary, nodding, white flowers grow near the tops of the branches. Flowering time is from May to September. The fruit is a scarlet, berrylike capsule about ⅓ inch across.

Properties and Uses: Analgesic, astringent, carminative, diuretic, stimulant. The medicinal virtues of wintergreen leaves reside essentially in the oil of wintergreen which can be obtained by steam distillation. The oil consists mostly of methyl salicylate, a close relative of aspirin. Not surprisingly, then the leaves have long been used for headache and other aches and pains, inflammations, and rheumatism. They have also been recommended for urinary ailments and for colic and flatulence. Externally, a leaf tea can be used as a gargle for sore mouth and throat, as a douche for leucorrhea, and as a compress or poultice for skin diseases and inflammations. A cloth soaked with oil of wintergreen has been applied to relieve pain in joints, but the pure oil can cause irritation and must be used cautiously.

Preparation and Dosage: Collect leaves in the fall.

Infusion: Steep 1 tsp. leaves in 1 cup water. Take 1 cup a day, a mouthful at a time.

Tincture: A dose is from 5 to 15 drops.

491 WITCH GRASS

(Agropyron repens)

Common Names: Couch grass, cutch, dog grass, durfa grass, quack grass, quick grass, triticum.

Medicinal Part: The rootstock.

Description: Witch grass is a perennial grass, 1 to 3 feet high, found as a weed in meadows, fields, and waste places. Native to Europe and naturalized in the U.S., it is more prevalent and troublesome in the eastern states. Its long, pale yellow, creeping, jointed rootstock sends out runners underground. The stem and leaf sheaths are smooth and glabrous; but the thin, flat, linear, bright green leaves are rough and sparsely haired. The yellow to purple flowers grow in spikes from June to August.

Properties and Uses: Aperient, demulcent, diuretic, emollient, tonic. Witch grass may be used freely, and large and frequent doses are considered good tonic or "spring medicine." The infusion was once used to treat cystitis, pyelitis, and gonorrhea. The tea or juice has been used for dropsy, jaundice, and gastrointestinal catarrh, and for bladder, liver, gallbladder, and spleen problems. It has sometimes been recommended for gout and rheumatic problems, diarrhea, the congestion of colds, stomach problems, and as a diaphoretic; but these uses are debatable. A mixture of an infusion and cold extract is sometimes suggested.

Preparation and Dosage:

Infusion: Use 1 tsp. rootstock to 1 cup water. Take in mouthful doses, 1 to 2 cups in the course of the day.

Decoction: Use 1 tsp. rootstock to 1 cup water; boil, then steep a few minutes and strain. Take ½ to 1 cup a day.

Cold Extract: Same amount as decoction, but let stand 10 hours.

Juice: Take 1 tbsp. three times a day.

Tincture: Take 10 to 20 drops in water two or more times a day. To help pass calculi, use a maximum of 40 to 60 drops in hot water.

WITCH HAZEL
(Hamamelis virginiana)

Common Names: Hazel nut, pistachio, snapping hazel, spotted alder, striped alder, tobacco wood, winterbloom.

Medicinal Parts: Bark, leaves.

Description: Witch hazel is a deciduous shrub or small tree which grows in damp woods from Nova Scotia to Georgia and Nebraska; it is also cultivated elsewhere for its autumn-blooming flowers. Growing to a height of up to 15 feet, the stems and branches are covered with scaly gray to brown bark. The alternate, elliptic to obovate leaves are coarsely toothed and often are finely hairy on the veins underneath. The yellow flowers have 4 strap-shaped petals and grow in nodding, axillary clusters, blooming in autumn when the leaves are falling. The fruit is a woody capsule which ejects two shining black seeds when they ripen during the summer or autumn following the flowers.

Properties and Uses: Astringent, hemostatic, sedative, tonic. Witch hazel leaves and bark have served mostly to make astringent preparations, which have been taken internally for diarrhea and used externally as a rinse or gargle for mouth and throat irritations and as a vaginal douche for vaginitis. For skin irritations, bruises, insect bites and stings, minor burns, and poison ivy, an ointment made from the fluid extract or a poultice can be applied. A poultice made from the inner bark is said to be effective for hemorrhoids and for eye inflammation. The inner bark also has sedative and hemostatic properties.

Preparation and Dosage:

Decoction: Boil 1 tsp. bark or leaves in 1 cup water. Take 1 cup a day, a mouthful at a time.

Tincture: A dose is from 5 to 20 drops.

Ointment: Mix one part fluid extract with nine parts lard.

493 WOODRUFF
(Asperula odorata)

Common Names: Master of the wood, sweet woodruff, woodward.

Medicinal Part: The herb.

Description: Woodruff is a perennial plant, 6 to 12 inches high, found in woods and gardens in Europe, Asia, and North Africa; it is cultivated in the U.S. Its thin, creeping rootstock with numerous matted, fibrous roots sends up many slender stems, which are square, shiny, and glabrous. The soft but rough-edged and bristle-tipped, narrow, dark green leaves grow around the stalk in successive whorls with 6 to 8 leaves in each whorl. The lower leaves are oblong-obovate, the middle and upper ones lanceolate. Bell- or funnel-shaped, the small, white, four-petaled flowers bloom in loose branching cymes from May to June, followed by a leathery, bristly fruit.

Properties and Uses: Antispasmodic, calmative, cardiac, diaphoretic, diuretic. Woodruff is beneficial for jaundice and recommended where a tendency toward gravel and bladder stones exists. It also acts as an anodyne for migraine and neuralgia, and as a calmative for nervous conditions such as restlessness, insomnia, and hysteria. The tea relieves stomach pain, regulates heart activity, and is diuretic and lightly diaphoretic. It is sometimes used to improve the taste of mixed herb teas. CAUTION: Consumption of large quantities can produce symptoms of poisoning, including dizziness and vomiting.

Preparation and Dosage:

Infusion: Use 2 tsp. dried herb to 1 cup water; take ½ to 1 cup a day.

Cold Extract: Soak 2 tsp. dried herb in 1 cup cold water for 8 hours. The extract can be warmed as desired after straining.

494 WOOD SORREL
(Oxalis acetosella)

Common Names: Common sorrel, cuckoo bread, green sauce, mountain sorrel, shamrock, sour trefoil, stubwort, white sorrel.

Medicinal Part: The herb.

Description: Wood sorrel is a creeping perennial plant found in cool, shady woods from Nova Scotia to North Carolina and as far west as Saskatchewan, as well as in Europe. The creeping rootstock produces numerous leaves on long, hairy petioles, each leaf digitately divided into three obcordate leaflets. The leaves are sensitive to light changes and fold up at night and often when bad weather is imminent. From 1 to 3 small, white flowers veined with red bloom on scapes 2 to 6 inches high from May to July. In addition, inconspicuous, greenish, self-fertilized flowers (cleistogamous flowers) grow near the ground on very short scapes.

Properties and Uses: Anodyne, diuretic, emmenagogue, irritant, stomachic. A cold infusion of wood sorrel can be helpful for heartburn and for mild liver and digestive problems. It can also be used externally as a wash for skin problems. In spring, the young leaves are sometimes added to soup or eaten with spinach or salad as a "spring cure" to invigorate the organism, arouse appetite, and promote digestion. CAUTION: Wood sorrel leaves contain oxalic acid. Excessive doses can cause internal irritation, resulting in hemorrhage and diarrhea.

Preparation and Dosage: Use the fresh herb.

Infusion: Steep a handful herb in 1 qt. boiling-hot water for 2 to 3 minutes. Take sweetened, if desired.

Tincture: A dose is from 10 to 30 drops.

495 WORMSEED
(*Chenopodium ambrosioides var. anthelminticum*)

Common Names: Chenopodium, feather geranium, goosefoot, Jerusalem oak, Jesuit tea.

Medicinal Parts: Seeds, herb.

Description: Naturalized from Central America, wormseed is an annual or perennial plant found in waste places in almost all parts of the United States. Its erect stem is strongly branched from the base, growing from 1 to 3 feet high. Oblong or lanceolate with lacerate-pinnatifid margins, its alternate, yellowish-green leaves are marked beneath with small resinous particles. Blooming from July to September, the numerous green flowers grow on almost leafless spikes and are followed by small, green, bladdery fruits with solitary, lenticular seeds.

Properties and Uses: Anthelmintic. The oil of chenopodium, derived from the seeds and other overground parts of wormseed, is an excellent anthelmintic for roundworms, hookworms, and other intestinal parasites, though it is not as effective against tapeworms. Either the oil or an infusion of the seeds with milk can be used in treating worms in children. Wormseed is also used as a mild cardiac stimulant and to promote secretions of the skin and kidneys. CAUTION: An overdose of the oil can result in poisoning and death. A one-year-old baby given a dose of four drops three times a day for two days died, and other cases of overdose deaths are on record.

Preparation and Dosage:

Oil: A standard treatment was from 3 to 10 drops of oil taken on sugar three times a day for several days and followed by a strong laxative. Do not fast before using. Do not repeat treatment for at least two weeks.

Seeds: Take 1/3 to 1/2 tsp. seeds mixed with honey two times a day, then follow with a good laxative.

496 CHENOPODIUM AMBROSIOIDES

NOTE: The typical *Chenopodium ambrosioides,* commonly called Mexican tea or American wormseed, is also found as a weed in almost all parts of the U.S., especially in damp waste places. The two plants are very similar except that Mexican tea's leaves are not as strongly toothed and its flower spikes have more leaves. Both plants have the same medicinal uses.

497 WORMWOOD

(*Artemisia absinthium*)

Common Name: Absinthe.

Medicinal Parts: Leaves, flowering tops.

Description: Wormwood is a silky perennial plant found in waste places and along roadsides from Newfoundland to Hudson Bay and south to Montana. It is a native plant in Europe, from where it was introduced into North America. The woody rootstock produces many bushy stems, which grow from 2 to 4 feet high and bear alternate, bi- to tri-pinnate leaves with long, obtuse lobes. Numerous tiny, yellow-green, rayless flower heads grow in leafy panicles from July to October.

Properties and Uses: Anthelmintic, antiseptic, antispasmodic, carminative, cholagogue, febrifuge, stimulant, stomachic. Wormwood is above all a stomach medicine, being useful for indigestion, gastric pain, and lack of appetite, as well as the related problems of heartburn and flatulence. It is also said to be helpful for liver insufficiency by stimulating liver and gallbladder secretions. Wormwood oil is a cardiac stimulant and therefore acts, when taken in proper doses, to improve blood circulation. Wormwood tea has been recommended to help relieve pain during labor. The powdered flowering tops have been used to expel intestinal worms. A fomentation of wormwood tea can be applied externally to irritations, sprains, or bruises. The oil acts as a local anesthetic when applied to relieve pains of rheumatism, neuralgia, and arthritis. CAUTION: Pure wormwood oil is a strong poison, and excessive use of the plant can also cause poisoning. With proper dosage, there is little or no danger.

Preparation and Dosage:

Infusion: Steep 2 tsp. leaves or tops in 1 cup water. Take ½ cup a day, a teaspoonful at a time.

Tincture: Take 8 to 10 drops on a sugar cube, one to three times a day.

Oil: A dose is from 2 to 5 drops, two or three times a day.

Powder: Take ¼ to ½ tsp., one or two times a day.

498   LAD'S LOVE or SOUTHERNWOOD
(Artemisia abronatum)

NOTE: Lad's love or southernwood (*Artemisia abronatum*) is a much safer relative of wormwood which is also native to Europe and has been somewhat naturalized in North America. Its leaves are pinnate to tri-pinnate, the final divisions filiform. The flower heads are yellowish-white. Lad's love can be used like wormwood for stomach problems and fever; in popular use it also serves for coughs, mucous congestion, and bronchial catarrh.

499   WOUNDWORT
(Prunella vulgaris)

Common Names: All-heal, blue curls, brownwort, carpenter's herb, carpenter's weed, Hercules woundwort, hock-heal, selfheal, sicklewort.

Medicinal Part: The herb.

Description: Woundwort is a perennial plant found as a very common weed in open woods, lawns, fields, and waste places in the U.S., Europe and Asia. The slender, creeping rootstock produces ascending or procumbent stems which grow from 1 to 3 feet in height. These slightly hairy, square, grooved stems may be solitary or in clusters. Entire or slightly toothed, the petioled, opposite leaves are ovate to oblong-lanceolate in shape. Tubular and two-lipped, the tiny purple flowers grow in dense terminal spikes, blooming from May to October. The fruit is an ovoid, smooth, angled nutlet.

Properties and Uses: Antispasmodic, astringent, bitter tonic, diuretic, styptic, vermifuge, vulnerary. As a tea, woundwort is beneficial for internal wounds; as a wash, for external wounds. It has also been used as a gargle for throat irritations, including pharyngitis, and for stomatitis and thrush. As an astringent, it is useful for hemorrhage and diarrhea. It is excellent for fits and convulsions, and will expel worms, if not devils.

Preparation and Dosage:

Extract: Soak 1 tsp. herb in 1 pint brandy or whiskey for a few days. Take 2 tbsp. a day or as needed.

500 YELLOW DOCK

(Rumex crispus)

Common Names: Curled dock, garden patience, narrow dock, sour dock, rumex.

Medicinal Part: The root.

Description: Yellow dock is a perennial plant found as a troublesome weed in fields and waste places in Europe, the U.S. and southern Canada. Its spindle-shaped, yellow taproot sends up a smooth, rather slender stem, 1 to 3 feet high. Lanceolate to oblong-lanceolate in shape, the pointed light green leaves have predominantly wavy margins. The lower leaves are larger and longer-petioled than the upper. Blooming from June to July, the numerous pale green, drooping flowers are loosely whorled in panicled racemes. The fruit is a pointed, three-angled and heart-shaped nut.

Properties and Uses: Astringent, cholagogue, tonic. Known as a medicinal plant since ancient times, yellow dock has been used as a laxative or mild astringent tonic. In the nineteenth century, it was considered a "blood purifier" and was prescribed for eruptive diseases, such as scrofula, and skin problems. The ointment is valuable for itching, sores, swellings, and scabby eruptions. American Indians applied crushed yellow dock leaves to boils and the pulverized roots to cuts.

Preparation and Dosage:

Decoction: Boil 1 tsp. root in 1 cup water. Take 1 to 2 cups a day.

Powder: For skin problems the dose is 12 grains.

501

WATER DOCK
(Rumex aquaticus)

NOTE: The root of water dock (*Rumex aquaticus*) has similar medicinal uses except that it is also used for stomach problems. A wineglassful of the decoction (2 oz. of root boiled in 3 pints of water) taken three times a day has been recommended for stomach ailments.

502 YELLOW GENTIAN
(*Gentiana lutea*)

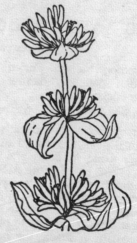

Common Names: Bitter root, bitterwort, gentian root, pale gentian.

Medicinal Parts: Root, leaves.

Description: Yellow gentian is an herbaceous perennial plant found in mountain meadows and pastures in Europe and Asia Minor and under cultivation in the U.S. Ringed and forked, the thick, wrinkled root is brown on the outside and yellow on the inside. The simple, erect, glabrous stem grows to a height of 3 to 4 feet and bears ovate-oblong, bright green leaves that grow up to a foot long and six inches wide. Each pair of opposite leaves is arranged at right angles to its neighboring pairs, the lower ones on short petioles, the upper sessile. The large, bright yellow flowers usually appear for the first time when the root is about 10 years old. Blooming from July to August, the flowers grow in whorls of 3 to 10 axillary blossoms near the top of the stem. The fruit is an oblong, two-valved capsule.

Properties and Uses: Cholagogue, febrifuge, refrigerant, stomachic, tonic. Yellow gentian is excellent for improving appetite and digestion and for strengthening the activity of the stomach. For these uses, take the preparation at least 30 minutes before mealtime, since it takes that long to have any effect. Specific gastrointestinal problems for which yellow gentian is particularly beneficial include stomachache, heartburn, indigestion, catarrhal gastritis with diarrhea, and vomiting. Yellow gentian is useful as a blood-builder during convalescence, since it raises the white blood cell count. It has also been used for podagra, ague, and fainting spells, and externally as a decoction for washing wounds. The fresh leaves placed on open wounds and inflammations act as a refrigerant; and they also make soothing footbaths.

Preparation and Dosage:

Infusion: Put 2 oz. root in 1 pint boiling-hot water and steep until cold. Strain and add ½ pint or more brandy. Take 1 tsp. to 1 tbsp. at a time.

Decoction: Boil 1 tsp. root in 1 cup water. Take 1 tbsp. every two hours or before meals.

Cold Extract: Soak 1 tsp. root in 1 cup cold water for 2 hours. Take 1 cup in the course of the day.

Tincture: Take 10 to 20 drops in water, before each meal.

Powder: Take ¼ to ½ tsp. before each meal.

503	**BLUE or AMERICAN GENTIAN** *(Gentiana catesbaei)*
504	**FRINGED GENTIAN** *(Gentiana crinita)*
505	**STIFF GENTIAN or GALLWEED** *(Gentiana quinquefolia)*

NOTE: Several native North American species of gentian have properties similar to those of yellow gentian. Blue or American gentian (*Gentiana catesbaei*) grows in wet places from Virginia to Florida and features large, blue flowers from September to December. Fringed gentian (*Gentiana crinita*), a biennial species producing solitary blue, fringed flowers during September and October, grows in moist ground from Quebec to Georgia and west as far as Ontario and North Dakota. Stiff gentian or gallweed (*Gentiana quinquefolia*) is an annual species with square stems and purplish-blue, bristly flowers that bloom from August to October. It is found from southeastern Canada to Florida, Michigan, and Missouri. All of these can be used like yellow gentian. American Indians also applied an infusion of blue gentian root to relieve backache.

506 YELLOW GOATSBEARD

(*Tragopogon pratensis*)

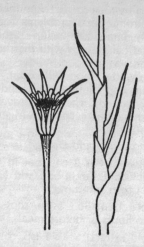

Common Names: Meadow salsify, noonday flower, noon flower, noontide, star of Jerusalem.

Medicinal Part: Root.

Description: Yellow goatsbeard is a biennial or perennial found in pastures, fields, meadows, and waste places of Europe, from where it has come to be naturalized in southern Canada and the northern part of the U.S. The slender, fleshy taproot produces a light green, succulent stem from 1 to 3 feet high, containing a bitter milky juice. The alternate, grasslike, clasping leaves have curled margins and taper to long, pointed, backward-bending tips. The stem bears a solitary yellow flower head with ray flowers that unfold early in the morning and close up at midday.

Properties and Uses: Diuretic, stomachic. Primarily known as a diuretic remedy for urinary and water-retention problems, the root of yellow goatsbeard in decoction has also been used for lack of appetite, heartburn, and digestive difficulties.

507 PURPLE GOATSBEARD or SALSIFY

(*Tragopogon porrifolius*)

NOTE: Purple goatsbeard or salsify (*Tragopogon porrifolius*) is a related larger species with uncurled leaves and purple flowers. It is perhaps more widespread than yellow goatsbeard, since it is often cultivated for its edible, oyster-flavored root. The root also has some diuretic properties, but they are weaker than those of yellow goatsbeard.

508 YELLOW JESSAMINE

(*Gelsemium sempervirens*)

Common Names: Gelsemin, wild jessamine, woodbine.

Medicinal Part: Rootstock.

Description: Yellow jessamine is a perennial evergreen vine found in moist woodlands and thickets from Virginia to Texas and in Mexico and Central America. It is also cultivated elsewhere as an ornamental vine. The slender, woody stems twine about trees and other objects, sometimes reaching a length of 20 feet and climbing from one tree to another. The opposite, lanceolate to ovate leaves are dark green above and pale beneath. The fragrant yellow, funnelform flowers are borne in axillary or terminal cymes from March to May. The fruit is an elliptical capsule containing many seeds.

Properties and Uses: Nervine, sedative. Formerly much used, yellow jessamine has lost much favor because of the danger of poisoning. It has a sedative and soothing effect on the nerves and has been useful for nervous heart conditions, neuralgia, and sciatica. CAUTION: Yellow jessamine may produce a strong reaction, including effects on vision. The flowers, leaves, and roots are poisonous.

Preparation and Dosage: Do not use without medical supervision. Yellow jessamine belongs to the same family from which strychnine and the dreaded arrow poison, curare, are obtained. The toxin from a closely related plant was used in Hong Kong to execute condemned criminals. Two Duke University researchers are studying the vine's active toxins. An overdose of the most active toxin results in death through failure of the respiratory tract, but in therapeutic amounts it stimulates the heart and respiration. Dr. Stephen Baldwin, one of the Duke researchers said, "Almost any substance which affects the heart is a candidate for experimentation in today's research laboratories."

509 YELLOW MELILOT

(Melilotus officinalis)

Common Names: Hay flowers, king's clover, sweet clover, yellow sweet clover.

Medicinal Part: The flowering herb.

Description: Yellow melilot is a biennial plant found along roadsides and in waste places in Eurasia and throughout North America, except in the far north. The slender, branched, hollow stems, from 1½ to 5 feet high, bear pinnate leaves with three obovate or oblanceolate leaflets, which are finely toothed and blunt-tipped.

Blooming from June to November, the fragrant, light golden-yellow flowers grow in axillary racemes.

Properties and Uses: Antispasmodic, diuretic, emollient, expectorant, vulnerary. Yellow melilot is used externally in a salve or as a poultice for swellings, boils and similar skin problems, milk knots, arthritis, rheumatism, and headaches. As an additional treatment for rheumatic pains, headaches, and aching joints, Europeans sew the dried plant into an herb pillow. The decoction can be applied as a wash for wounds. Yellow melilot finds other external application as an astringent and anti-inflammatory eyewash. Internally it has been used for colic, stomach problems, and chronic bronchitis. A concentrated preparation made from the plant is sometimes prescribed by doctors as an anticoagulant to break up blood clots. CAUTION: Large doses can cause vomiting and other symptoms of poisoning.

Preparation and Dosage:

Infusion: Steep 1 tsp. herb in 1 cup water. Take 1 to 1½ cups a day.

Poultice: Put about ½ oz. dried plant into a small cloth bag. Boil briefly in water; let steep a few minutes; then apply as hot as can be tolerated.

510 WHITE MELILOT
(Melilotus alba)

NOTE: White melilot (*Melilotus alba*), a similar but taller, white-flowered species, has the same medicinal uses. Like yellow melilot, it is a very common plant in fields and waste places over most of North America and in Europe and Asia.

511 YELLOW PARILLA
(Menispermum canadense)

Common Names: American sarsaparilla, moonseed, Texas sarsaparilla, vine-maple.

Medicinal Parts: Rootstock and roots.

Description: Yellow parilla is a perennial vine found in moist woods and hedges near streams in eastern North America, from Quebec to Georgia and as far west as Manitoba and Arkansas. The round, woody, twining stem grows from a woody, horizontal, yellow rootstock and sometimes reaches a length of 15 feet. The alternate, roundish leaves are palmately veined and lobed, and may be finely hairy when young. Blooming in July, the small, greenish-white flowers are clustered in loose axillary panicles. The fruit is a globular, bluish-black drupe up to ⅓ inch across.

Properties and Uses: Bitter tonic, diuretic, laxative. Yellow parilla has sometimes been used as a substitute for sarsaparilla. CAUTION: The toxicity of the rootstock is due to its bitter alkaloids; the fruit is probably also poisonous.

Preparation and Dosage: Use only with medical supervision.

512 YELLOW TOADFLAX

(Linaria vulgaris)

Common Names: Butter and eggs, flaxweed, pennywort, wild snapdragon.

Medicinal Part: The plant.

Description: Yellow toadflax is a perennial plant found on sandy soils by roadsides, railroad embankments, ridges, and pastures from Newfoundland southward to Georgia and westward to Manitoba and New Mexico. Its running rootstock produces several smooth, erect stems, 8 to 30 inches tall, with alternate pale green leaves that are narrow, linear and sessile. Blooming from July to September in dense terminal racemes, the yellow flowers resemble an open mouth and throat with an orange-bearded "tongue" or palate.

Properties and Uses: Astringent, cathartic, diuretic. Commonly used as a diuretic or cathartic, yellow toadflax is also recommended for stones and sciatica. It is beneficial for jaundice, cystitis, and gallbladder problems, but it is not a sufficient remedy by itself for these ailments. In European folk medicine, it is used as a "blood purifier." As a bath additive, a salve, a wash, or a fomentation, the tea or juice is used externally for skin problems and hemorrhoids. The ointment from the flowers is also applied to skin irritations. CAUTION: The tincture is not to be self-administered, since even 20 drops can produce serious internal effects.

Preparation and Dosage:

Infusion: Steep 2 tsp. herb in ¾ cup water. Make in the morning are drink in the course of the day.

Salve: Professionally prepared.

Tincture: Only by medical direction.

513 YERBA SANTA

(Eriodictyon californicum)

Common Names: Bearsweed, consumptive's weed, holy herb, mountain balm, tarweed.

Medicinal Part: Leaves.

Description: Native to the western U.S., yerba santa is an aromatic, sticky evergreen shrub, 2 to 7 feet high, found in dry, rocky, mountainous areas below 5,500 feet, mainly in Oregon and California. Its woody, running rootstock sends up a smooth stem with shredding bark and glabrous to sparsely haired branches. Oblong to lanceolate in shape, the alternate, dark green, leathery leaves are pinnately veined and usually serrate. On the upper surface, the leaves are sticky; underneath, they are covered with fine, white, woolly hair and are prominently veined. Blooming from May to July, the tubular-funnelform, lavender to white flowers are clustered at the top of the plant. The fruit is a small oval, grayish-brown seed capsule containing shrivelled, nearly black seeds.

Properties and Uses: Antispasmodic, expectorant, febrifuge, tonic. Yerba santa is an excellent expectorant, valuable for colds, chronic laryngitis, bronchitis, lung problems, and asthma. In the nineteenth century, it was considered a "blood purifier" and a remedy for rheumatism and tuberculosis. It is also useful for reducing fever. Externally, it can be applied as a poultice for bruises, sprains, wounds, and insect bites. American Indians smoked or chewed the leaves as a cure for asthma. They also used the leaves as a tea for colds and for a mouthwash preparation.

Preparation and Dosage:

Infusion: Use 1 tsp. leaves to 1 cup water. Take ½ cup at night or in mouthful doses three times a day. Take only 1 to 2 cups total. It may be taken hot or cold.

Tincture: A dose is from 10 to 30 drops.

514 YEW

(Taxus baccata)

Common Names: Chinwood, English yew, European yew.

Medicinal Parts: Fruit, needles, tips of branches.

Description: The yew is an evergreen tree, which grows to 60 feet in height, and is found in Europe, North Africa, and western Asia. Generally cultivated, it grows wild in small stands in the woods. The tree with its scaly, reddish-brown bark, has a short, thick trunk and spreading branches, which form a broad, low head. Its alternate, linear, pointed leaves or needles are dark green and glossy above and light green below. The male tree has small cones whose scales open at flowering time to expose a globose head of stamens; the female has small, solitary, axillary ovules which later mature into red, berry-like fruit. The flowering time is from April to May. This species of yew is cultivated in many varieties which differ in growth characteristics and leaf color.

Properties and Uses: Expectorant, purgative. Yew is sometimes used for coughs and pulmonary catarrh, for bladder problems, and as a purgative. An extract of its leaves has been prescribed for rheumatism, arthritis, and liver and urinary problems. Its use is probably not necessary, since there are many non-poisonous plants which serve as effective remedies for the same ailments. CAUTION: Except for the fleshy seed covering, all parts of the tree, including the seed itself, are poisonous.

Preparation and Dosage: Take only under medical supervision.

ALPHABETICAL LIST OF HERBS

Proper (Primary) English and Common or Vernacular Names

Aaron's Rod 222, 299
Absinthe 497
Acacia 001
Aconite 292
Acrid Crowfoot 079
Acrid Lettuce 252
Adder's Mouth 096
Adder's Tongue 002
Adder's Violet 372
Africa Lilac 359
Africa Pepper 092
African Ginger 169
Agave 003
Agrimony 436
Ague Grass 435
Ague Tree 401
Ague Weed 063
Alcanna 195
Alder Buckthorn 074
Alder Dogwood 074
Alehoof 179
Alexandrian Senna 409
Alfalfa 004
Alfilaria 439
All-heal 162, 288, 499
Allspice 005
Almond 006
Aloe 007, 008, 009,
                    010, 011
Alpine Cranberry 012
Althea 013
Althea Rose 214
Alum Root 425
Amaranth 014
Amber 396
American Agave 003
American Angelica 020
American Aspen 353
American Centaury 015
American Century 003
American Cowslip 015
American Elder 130
American Elm 136

American Foxglove ..156, 161
American Gentian 503
American Ginseng 171
American Hellebore 016
American Holly 210
American Indigo 481
American Ivy 017
American Linden 256
American Mandrake 267
American Mistletoe 287
American Mountain Ash ..389
American Pennyroyal 330
American Pepper 092
American Saffron 391
American Sanicle 398
American Sarsaparilla 511
American Senna 408
American Spikenard 423
American Valerian 307
American White
  Hellebore 016
American Woodbine 017
American Wormseed 496
Angelica 018, 019, 020
Anise 021
Anise Plant 021
Anise Root 442
Aniseed 021
Anise-scented
  Goldenrod 173
Apple Tree 022
Arberry 033
Arborvitae 451
Archangel 020
Aristolochia Root 047
Arnica 023
Arnica Flowers 023
Arnica Root 023
Arrowwood 074
Arrow-wood 462
Artichoke 024
Arum 025
Asafetida 153

Asarabacca 026
Asarum 026
Asiatic Ginseng 110
Asparagus 027
Aspen Poplar 353
Aspidium 149, 267
August Flower 181
Autumn Crocus 273, 392
Avens Root 467
Azedarach 359

Bachelor's Button 110
Bachelor's Buttons 078
Balm 028
Balm Mint 028
Balm of Gilead 354
Balmony 457
Balsam Poplar 354
Barbados Aloe 007
Barberry 029
Bardana 077
Barley 030
Basil 031
Basswood 256
Bast Tree 256
Bastard Cardamom 086
Bastard Dittany 163
Bastard Hemp 193
Bay 247
Bayberry 471
Bay Laurel 247
Bay Tree 247
Bead Tree 359
Bean 032
Bean Herb 402
Bean Trefoil 073
Bearberry 033
Bearded Darnel 034
Bear's Garlic 035
Bear's Grape 033
Bear's Paw Root 149
Bearsfoot 189
Bearsweed 513
Beaumont Root 054
Beaver Tree 263
Beccabunga 067
Bedstraw 036, 037
Bee Balm 028, 290
Beechdrops 038, 060

Bee-nettle 193
Beesnest Plant 088
Beggarweed 237
Belladonna 039
Bellyache Root 020
Bennet 040
Bethroot 046
Betony 041
Bhang 084
Bilberry 042
Bindweed 482
Birch 043, 044
Bird Knotgrass 237
Bird Pepper 092
Bird's Tongue 045
Birdlime 287, 288
Birdsnest 227
Bird's-nest Root 088
Birdweed 237
Birthroot 046
Birthwort 047
Bistort 048
Bitter Ash 363, 462
Bitter Buttons 449
Bitter Clover 015
Bitter Grass 435
Bitter Herb 140
Bitter Orange 321
Bitter Root 502
Bitter Wintergreen 341
Bitter Wood 363
Bitterbloom 015
Bitterroot 123
Bittersweet 311
Bittersweet Herb 311
Bittersweet Nightshade ...311
Bittersweet Stems 311
Bittersweet Twigs 311
Bitterweed 219
Bitterwort 502
Black Alder 049
Black-alder 212
Black Alder Dogwood 074
Black Alder Tree 074
Black Birch 044
Black Cherry 039
Black Choke 476
Black Cohosh 053
Black Currant 116

Black Dogwood 074
Black Drink Plant 211
Black Elder 130, 131
Black Ginger 169
Black Hellebore 188
Black Henbane 194
Black Mulberry 298
Black Mullein 302
Black Mustard 303
Black Nightshade 312
Black Oak 316
Black Poplar 356
Black Root 054
Black Sanicle 398
Black Snakeroot 053, 398
Black Snakeweed 479
Black Spruce 427
Black Spurge 431
Black Walnut 464
Black Whortleberry 042
Black Willow 488
Blackberried European
    Elder 131
Blackberry 052
Blackthorn 347
Blackwort 107
Bladderpod 258
Blanket-leaf 299
Blazing Star 055, 056, 057
Blazing Star Root 056
Bleeding Heart 307
Blessed Herb 040
Blessed Thistle 395
Blind Nettle 058
Blisterweed 078
Blood Elder 133
Bloodroot 059
Bloodstaunch 219
Blooming Spurge 429
Blowball 119
Blue Balm 028, 290
Blue Blazing Star 057
Blue Centaury 108
Blue Cohosh 060
Blue Curls 499
Blue Flag 061
Blue Gentian 503
Blue Ginseng 060
Blue Gum 139

Blue Mallow 266
Blue Mountain Tea 173
Blue Nightshade 311
Blue Pimpernel 416
Blue Skullcap 416
Blue Vervain 062
Blueberry 042, 060
Bluebonnet 110
Bluebottle 110
Bofareira 089
Bog 089
Bog Myrtle 073
Bogbean 073
Bog-onion 150, 228
Bohea-tea 173
Bombay Aloe 009
Boneset 063
Bookoo 070
Boor Tree 131
Borage 064
Bouncing Bet 417
Bountry 131
Bowman's Root 054, 429
Box 065
Boxwood 065, 127
Brake Fern 148
Brake Rock 148
Brakeroot 148
Bramble 052
Branching Larkspur 246
Brandy Mint 283
Bridewort 274
Brier Hip 066
Brier Rose 066
Brigham Young Weed 120
British Tobacco 105
Broad-leaved Plantain 344
Brook Alder 212
Brook Bean 073
Brooklime 067
Broom 405
Brownwort 499
Bruisewort 107, 418
Bryony 068, 069
Bucco 070
Buchu 070
Buck Bean 073
Buckeye 217
Buckhorn 150, 343

Buckhorn Brake 150
Buckhorn Male Fern 150
Buckthorn 074, 075, 076
Bucku 070
Budwood 127
Buffalo Herb 004
Bugbane 016, 053
Bugloss 064
Bugwort 053
Bulbous Buttercup 079
Bullock's Eye 222
Bullsfoot 105
Burdock 077
Burnet Saxifrage 339
Burning Bush 163, 462
Burr Seed 077
Burrage 064
Burren Myrtle 042
Burrwort 078
Bush Tree 065
Bushy Gerardia 156
Butter and Eggs 512
Butter Rose 360
Butterbur 105
Buttercup 078, 079, 080
Butterfly Weed 346
Butternut 465
Butterweed 219
Button Snakeroot 470

Cabbage Rose 381
Caffeine Nut 241
Calamus 445
Calendula 081
Calico Bush 294
California Barberry 483
California Buckthorn 076
California Rose 380
Calumbo 104
Cammock 376
Camomile 082, 083
Canada Fleabane 219
Canada-pitch Tree 191
Canada Root 345
Canada Snakeroot 479
Canada Tea 490
Cancer Root 038
Candleberry 471
Candlewick 299

Canker Root 257
Cankerroot 177
Cankerweed 257
Cankerwort 119
Cannabis 084
Canoe Birch 043
Cape Gum 001
Caper Spurge 430
Capsicum 092
Caraway 085
Cardamom 086
Cardamom Seed 086
Cardamon 086
Cardin 395
Carline Thistle 087
Carolina Pink 340
Carpenter's Herb 499
Carpenter's Square 158
Carpenter's Weed 499
Carrageen 229
Carrot 088
Cascara 076
Cascara Sagrada 076
Castor Bean 089
Castor-oil Plant 089
Catarrh Root 166
Catchfly 123
Catchweed 036
Catkins Willow 036
Catmint 090
Catnep 090
Catnip 090
Catrup 091
Cat's Foot 091
Cat's-foot 179
Cat's-paw 179
Catswort 090
Caucasian Walnut 466
Cayenne 092
Celandine 093
Celery 094
Celery-leaved Buttercup ..080
Centaury 140
Century Plant 003
Ceylon Cardamom 086
Chafe Weed 143
Chamomile 082
Chamomilla 083
Cheat 034

Checkerberry 433, 490
Cheese Plant 266
Cheese Rennet 037
Cheeseflower 265
Cheeses 266
Chelidonium 093
Chenopodium 495
Cherokee Rose 385
Cherry Birch 044
Chervil 095
Chickentoes 108
Chickweed 096
Chicory 097
Chili Pepper 092
Chimney-sweeps 343
China-berry 359
China Root 485
China-tree 359
Chinese Ginseng 170
Chinese Hibiscus 203
Chinese Rhubarb 378
Chinwood 514
Chive 098
Chocolate Root 467
Choice Dielytra 455
Choke Cherry 476
Christmas Rose 188
Cicuta 350
Cimicifuga 053
Cinchona 335
Cinnamon-colored Fern ..151
Cinnamon Fern 151
Cinnamon Wood 401
Cinquefoil 099, 100, 101
Circassian Walnut 466
Cleavers 036
Cleaverwort 036
Clotbur 077
Cloudberry 052
Clove 102
Clove Garlic 168
Clove Pepper 005
Club Moss 103
Coakum 351
Cocash Weed 367
Cocklebur 077
Cockleburr 436
Cockspur Pepper 092
Cockspur Rye 138

Cockup Hat 437
Cocky Baby 025
Cocowort 414
Colchicum 273
Colic Root 055, 435, 485
Collard 417
Colomba 104
Colomba Root 104
Colombo 104
Colt's Tail 219
Coltsfoot 105
Coltsfoot Snakeroot 479
Columbine 106
Comfrey 107
Common Anise 021
Common Arnica 023
Common Basil 031
Common Bean 032
Common Buckthorn 075
Common Bugloss 064
Common Centaury 140
Common Elder 130
Common Elm 135
Common Evening
  Primrose 142
Common Everlasting 143
Common Fig 157
Common Flax 159
Common Goldenrod 173
Common Groundsel 368
Common Heather 183
Common Knotweed 237
Common Larch 245
Common Lettuce 251
Common Mallow 265
Common Milkweed 280
Common Mugwort 296
Common Mullein 300
Common Nettle 308
Common Parsley 326
Common Peony 332
Common Plantain 344
Common Plum 348
Common Polypody 148
Common Radish 365
Common Rue 390
Common Silkweed 280
Common Sorrel 421, 494

Common Stinging
  Nettle 308
Compass Plant 366
Consumptive's Weed 513
Convulsion-root 227
Copalm 446
Coral Root 108
Coriander 109
Corkwood 207
Corn 226
Corn Snakeroot 470
Cornelian Tree 127
Cornflower 110
Corpse 227
Corydalis 111
Cotton 112
Cottonweed 145, 280
Couch Grass 491
Coughroot 046
Coughweed 367
Coughwort 105
Country Mallow 265
Cow Cabbage 271, 473
Cow Grass 237
Cow Parsnip 271
Cowberry 012
Cowslip 113
Crampweed 099
Cranesbill 425
Crawley 108
Crawlgrass 237
Creeper 017
Creeping Charlie 179
Creeping Thyme 453
Crisped-leaved Mint 285
Cross Mint 285
Crosswort 063
Crowfoot 079, 425
Crowfoot Buttercup ..078, 079
Cuban Bast 207
Cubeb 114
Cuckoo Bread 494
Cuckoo Buds 079
Cuckoopint 025
Cucumber 115
Cudweed 145
Culver's Physic 054
Culver's Root 054
Cup Plant 366

Curacao Aloe 007
Curdwort 037
Cure-all 028, 467
Curled Dock 500
Curled Mint 285
Currant 116, 117
Cursed Crowfoot 080
Custard Apple 325
Cutch 491
Cyani 110
Cypress Powder 025
Cypress Spurge 428

Damask Rose 382
Damiana 276
Dandelion 119
Danewort 133
Daphne 277
Dead Men's Bells 161
Dead Nettle 058
Deadly Nightshade ...039, 312
Deal Pine 472
Deerberry 433, 490
Dense Button-snakeroot ..055
Desert Herb 120
Desert Tea 120
Devil's Apple 233
Devil's Bit 055
Devil's Bite 016, 055
Devil's Bones 485
Devil's Dung 153
Devil's Eye 194
Devil's Fuge 288
Devil's Root 336
Devil's Trumpet 233
Devil's Turnip 069
Devil's Vine 184
Dew Plant 441
Dewberry 052
Digitalis 161
Dill 122
Dilly 122
Diptam 163
Dittany 163
Dog-bur 220
Dog Cloves 418
Dog Grass 491
Dog-nettle 193
Dog Poison 124

Dog Rose 066
Dog-tooth Violet 002
Dogbane 123
Dogberry 066
Dog's Finger 161
Dog's Mercury 125, 126
Dog's Tongue 220
Dogtree 127
Dogwood 127
Dolloff 274
Doorweed 237, 240
Dooryard Plantain 344
Downy Rattlesnake
   Plantain 372
Dragon Root 025
Dragonroot 228
Dragon's Blood 198
Dragon's Claw 108
Dragonwort 048
Dropberry 419
Dropsy Plant 028
Dropwort 275
Duck's Foot 267
Dumpling Cactus 336
Durfa Grass 491
Dwale 039
Dwarf Carline 087
Dwarf Elder 133
Dwarf Mallow 266
Dwarf Milkwort 281
Dwarf Nettle 309
Dwarf Sumac 440
Dyeberry 042
Dyer's Broom 128
Dyer's Greenweed 128
Dyer's Saffron 391
Dyer's Weed 174
Dyer's Whin 128
Dysentery Weed 144
Dysentery-weed 431

Early Fumitory 111
Early-flowering
   Periwinkle 334
Earth Gall 016
Earth Smoke 165
Easter Flower 327
Easter Giant 048
Echinacea 129

Eglantine 383
Eglantine Gall 066
Egyptian Privet 195
Egyptian Thorn 001
Elder 130, 131, 132, 133
Elderberry 130
Elecampane 134
Elfdock 134
Elfwort 134
Ellanwood 131
Ellhorn 131
Elm 135 136
Emetic Herb 258
Emetic Holly 211
Emetic Root 429
Emetic Weed 258
Enchanter's Plant 141
English Cowslip 360
English Daisy 478
English Elm 135
English Hawthorn 182
English Holly 209
English Ivy 137
English Oak 317
English Plantain 343
English Valerian 162
English Walnut 466
English Watercress 187
English Yew 514
Ephedra 120
Ergot 138
Eryngo-leaved Liverwort ..224
Erysimum 187
Erythronium 002
Estragon 450
Eucalyptus 139
Eupatorium 063
Euphorbia 431
Euphrasy 373
European Alder 049
European Angelica 018
European Ash 045
European Aspen 357
European Avens 040
European Barberry 029
European Bitter Polygala ..281
European Black Alder 074
European Buckthorn 074
European Centaury 140

European Elder 131
European Elm 135
European Five-finger
  Grass 101
European Goldenrod 175
European Holly 209
European Larch 245
European Lime Tree 255
European Linden 255
European Lovage 260
European Mandrake 267
European Milkwort 282
European Mistletoe 288
European Mountain Ash ..338
European Pennyroyal 331
European Plum 348
European Ragwort 369
European Red Raspberry ..371
European Sanicle 399
European Senega
  Snakeroot 281
European Seneka 282
European Snakeroot 026
European Vervain 141
European Wild Angelica ..019
European Yew 514
Evening Primrose 142
Evergreen Snakeroot 281
Everlasting 143, 144, 145
Eve's Cup 342
Eye Balm 176
Eye Root 176
Eyebright 015, 373

Fairy Fingers 161
Fairy Flax 160
Fairy Gloves 161
Fairy Smoke 227
False Alder 212
False Box 127
False Coltsfoot 479
False Dittany 163
False Foxglove 156
False Grapes 017
False Indigo 481
False Pimpernel 338
False Saffron 391
False Vervain 062
Feather Geranium 495

Featherfew 155
Febrifuge Plant 155
Felon Herb 295, 296
Felonwort 311
Feltwort 299
Female Fern 148
Fennel 146
Fenugreek 147
Fern 148, 149, 150, 151
Fern Brake 148, 150
Fern Bush 443
Fern Gale 443
Fern Root 148
Fern-leaved False
  Foxglove 156
Ferula 152, 153, 154
Fetid Hellebore 189
Fetid Nightshade 194
Fever Plant 142
Fever Root 108
Fever Twig 311
Feverbush 212
Feverfew 155
Feverweed 156
Feverwort 063
Field Balm 090
Field Balsam 143
Field Goldenrod 174
Field Primrose 142
Field Pumpkin 362
Fig Tree 157
Figwort 158
Figwort Root 158
Finger Flower 161
Finger Leaf 100
Fireweed 337
Fit Plant 227
Five Fingers 100
Five-fingers 171
Five-finger Fern 264
Five-finger Grass 100
Five Leaves 017
Five-leaved Ginseng 171
Flag Lily 061
Flannelflower 299
Flax 159, 160
Flax Seed 159
Flaxweed 512
Fleur-de-lis 061

427

Florentine Iris 323
Florida Cornel 127
Florida Dogwood 127
Flower-de-luce 061
Flower of an Hour 208
Flower Velure 105
Flowering Aloe 003
Flowering Brake 150
Flowering Cornel 127
Flowering Dogwood 127
Flowering Fern 150
Flowering Spurge 429
Flowering Wintergreen ...281
Fluellin 422
Flux Root 346
Flytrap 123, 342
Foal's-foot 105
Folk's Glove 161
Food of the Gods 153
Fool's-cicely 124
Fool's-parsley 124
Foreign Colombo 104
Foxglove 161
Foxtail 103
Fragrant Valerian 162
Fragrant Water Lily 473
Fraxinella 163
French Rose 384
Friar's Cap 292
Fringe Tree 164
Fringed Gentian 504
Fringed Polygala 281
Frogwort 079
Frost Plant 379
Frostwort 379
Fumitory 165
Furze 127

Gaglee 025
Gagroot 258
Galanga 166
Galangal 166
Gall Weed 505
Gang Flower 282
Garden Angelica 018
Garden Artichoke 024
Garden Balm 028
Garden Camomile 082

Garden Celandine 093
Garden Celery 094
Garden Columbine 106
Garden Currant 117
Garden Dill 122
Garden Lettuce 251
Garden Marigold 081
Garden Nightshade ..311, 312
Garden Parsley 326
Garden Patience 500
Garden Radish 365
Garden Raspberry 371
Garden Rue 390
Garden Sage 393
Garden Sorrel 421
Garden Spurge 430
Garden Thyme 452
Garden Violet 167, 324
Garlic 168
Garnetberry 117
Gas Plant 163
Gayfeather 055, 057
Gelsemin 508
Gentian Root 502
Geranium 425
German Camomile 083
German Elder 131
German Rue 390
German Sarsaparilla 375
German Valerian 162
Ghost Flower 227
Gill-over-the-ground 179
Gillrun 179
Ginger 169
Ginseng 170, 171
Globe Amaranth 078
Globe Artichoke 024
Goat Willow 489
Goat's Pepper 092
Goat's Rue 172
Goatsbeard 275
Goatweed 396
Gold Cup 078
Golden Bough 287
Golden Daisy 475
Golden Ragwort 367
Goldenrod 173, 174, 175
Goldenseal 176
Goldthread ....177.

Goose Grass 036
Goosegrass 099
Goose Tansy 099
Goosefoot 495
Gosling Weed 036
Goutberry 052
Goutweed 019
Grain 318
Grass 084
Grass Burdock 077
Grass Myrtle 445
Gravelroot 364
Gray Beard Tree 164
Gray Goldenrod 174
Gray Ribwort 345
Great Bindweed 184
Great Burnet 178
Great Celandine 093
Great Mullein 299
Great Periwinkle 333
Great Stinging Nettle 308
Great Wild Valerian 162
Greater Pimpernel 338
Greater Plantain 344
Grecian Laurel 247
Greek Nuts 006
Green Bean 032
Green Broom 127
Green Hellebore 016, 190
Green Ozier 127
Green Sauce 494
Greenweed 127
Ground Apple 082
Ground Berry 490
Ground-hele 422
Ground Holly 341
Ground Ivy 179
Ground Lemon 267
Ground Lily 046
Ground Raspberry 176
Ground Squirrel Pea 458
Ground Thistle 087
Groundbread 118
Grundy Swallow 367
Guaiac 180
Guayacan 180
Guinea Sorrel 204
Gum Arabic Tree 001
Gum Ivy 137

Gum Myrrh Tree 305
Gum Plant 107, 181
Gum Tree 446
Gumbo 201
Gumweed 181
Guru Nut 241
Gypsy Flower 220
Gypsy Weed 422

Hagbush 359
Hardhack 438
Hardock 077
Hareburr 077
Hartshorn Bush 150
Hawkweed 295
Hawthorn 182
Hay Flower 509
Hay Maids 179
Hazel Alder 051
Hazel Nut 492
Hazelwort 026
Headsman 343
Heal-all 158, 438
Healing Herb 107
Heart Liverleaf 197
Heart Snakeroot 479
Heartease 240
Heartweed 240
Heather 183
Hedge Bindweed 184
Hedge-burs 036
Hedge Fumitory 165
Hedge Garlic 185
Hedge Hyssop 186
Hedge Lily 184
Hedge Maids 179
Hedge Mustard 187
Hedge-taper 299
Heliotrope 162
Hellebore 188, 189, 190
Helmet Flower 416
Helmet Pod 458
Hemlock 350
Hemlock Gum Tree 191
Hemlock Pitch Tree 191
Hemlock Spruce 191
Hemlock Tree 191
Hemp Agrimony 192
Hemp Dead Nettle 192

Hemp Nettle 193
Henbane 194
Henbell 194
Henna 195
Hens and Chickens 222
Hep Tree 066
Hepatica 196, 197
Herb Christopher 150
Herb Margaret 475
Herb-of-grace 390
Herb of the Cross 141
Herb Robert 198
Hercules Woundwort 499
Heron's Bill 439
Hibiscus ...199, 200, 201, 202,
            203, 204, 205,
            206, 207, 208
High Angelica 020
High Balm 290
High Blackberry 052
High Mallow 265
Hillberry 490
Hindheal 449
Hini 054
Hip Fruit 066
Hip Rose 066
Hip Tree 066
Hive Vine 433
Hoarhound 216
Hoary Plantain 345
Hock-heal 499
Hog Apple .....,.......267
Hog Bean 194
Hog Potato 482
Hogseed 066
Hogweed 271
Holigold 081
Holly 209, 210, 211,
            212, 213
Holly Bay 263
Holly Mahonia 483
Hollyhock 214
Holy Herb 141, 513
Holy Thistle 278, 395
Honduras Sarsaparilla 400
Honeybloom 123
Hoodwort 416
Hop Fruit 066
Hops 215

Hoptree 359
Horehound 216
Hornseed 138
Horse Chestnut 217
Horse-elder 134
Horsefly Weed 481
Horsefoot 105
Horseheal 134
Horsehoof 105
Horsemint 289
Horseradish 218
Horsetail Grass 413
Horsetail Rush 413
Horseweed 219, 438
Hound's Tongue 220
Houseleek 222
Huckleberry 042
Huntsman's Cup 342
Hurr-burr 077
Hurtleberry 042
Hydrangea 412
Hyssop 223

Iceland Moss 224
Imperial Masterwort 225
Indian Apple 267
Indian Arrow 462
Indian Balm 046
Indian Bark 263
Indian Bay 247
Indian Black Drink 211
Indian Chocolate 467
Indian Corn 226
Indian Cress 306
Indian Cup 366
Indian Elm 136
Indian Ginger 479
Indian Gum 366
Indian Hemp 084
Indian Hyssop 062
Indian Paint 059
Indian Pink 340
Indian Pipe 227
Indian Plant 059, 176
Indian Posy 143, 145
Indian Red Paint 059
Indian Root 423
Indian Sage 063
Indian Shamrock 046

Indian Tobacco 258
Indian Turnip 228
Indigo Broom 481
Inkberry 351
Iris 061
Irish Broom 405
Irish Moss 229
Ironweed 230
Italian Burnet 178
Italian Pimpernel 178

Jack-by-the-hedge 185
Jack-in-the-pulpit 228
Jacob's Staff 299
Jalap 231
Jamaica Mignonette 195
Jamaica Pepper 005
Jamaica Sarsaparilla 400
Jamaica Sorrel 204
Jamestown Weed 233
Jasmine 232
Jaundice Berry 029
Jaundice Root 176
Java Pepper 114
Jersey Tea 310
Jerusalem Cowslip 261
Jerusalem Oak 495
Jerusalem Sage 261
Jesuit Tea 495
Jesuits' Bark 335
Jew's-harp Plant 046
Jimson Weed 233
Joe-pye Weed 364
Johnny Jumper 324
Johnswort 396
Jordan Almond 006
Juniper 234
Juno's Tears 141
Jupiter's Bean 194
Jupiter's Beard 222
Jupiter's Eye 222

Kalumb 104
Kansas Niggerhead 129
Kernelwort 158
Khus-Khus 235
Kidney Bean 032
Kidney Root 364
Kidney Vetch 236

King's Clover 509
King's Cup 079
King's Cure 341
King's Cureall 142
King's Fern 150
Kinnikinnick 033
Klamath Weed 396
Knight's Spur 246
Knitback 107
Knob Grass 438
Knob Root 438
Knotgrass 237
Knotted Marjoram 269
Knotty Brake 149
Knotty-rooted Figwort ...158
Knotweed ..237, 238, 239, 240
Kola Nut 241
Kola Tree 241
Kousso 242

Ladies' Fingers 236
Ladies' Glove 161
Ladies' Tobacco 145
Lad's Love 498
Lady Bleeding 014
Lady's Bedstraw 037
Lady's Mantle 243, 244
Lady's Nightcap 184
Lady's Slipper 307
Lady's Thumb 240
Ladysmock 025
Lamb Mint 283, 284
Lambkill 294
Lamb's Quarter 046
Lamb's Toes 236
Lamb's Tongue 002
Lance-leaf Plantain 343
Larch 245
Large Button-snakeroot ...057
Large Fennel 146
Large-flowered
  Everlasting 145
Large Galangal 166
Large Indian Cress 306
Lark Heel 246
Lark's Claw 246
Larkspur 246
Laurel 247, 294
Lavender 248

431

Lavose 260
Leek 249
Lemon 250
Lemon Balm 028
Lemon Walnut 465
Leopardsbane 023
Leptandra 054
Lesser Centaury 140
Lesser Periwinkle 334
Lettuce 251
Licorice 253
Licorice Root............253
Life-of-man 423
Life Root 367
Lignum Vitae 180
Lily of the Valley 254
Lime Tree 256
Linden 255, 256
Ling 183
Link 405
Linseed 159
Lint Bells 159
Lion's Ear 293
Lion's Foot 257
Lion's Mouth 161
Lion's Tail 293
Lion's Tooth 119
Liquid Storax 446
Liquidamber 446
Little Pollom 281
Live-forever 222
Liver Lily 061
Liverleaf 196
Liverwort 196
Lobelia 258
Locust Plant 408
Long Buchu 072
Long Purples 259
Loosestrife 259
Lousewort 041, 156
Lovage 260
Loveman 036
Low Balm 290
Low Camomile 082
Low Cudweed 144
Low Mallow 266
Low Speedwell 422
Lucerne 004
Lungwort 261

Lustwort 441
Lycopod 103
Lyre-leaved Sage 394

Mad-apple 233
Madder 262
Mad-dog-weed 416
Madnep 271
Magnolia 263
Mahoe 207
Mahogany Birch 044
Maiden Fern 264
Maidenhair 264
Maid's Hair 037
Maize 226
Malabar Cardamom 086
Male Fern 149
Mallow 265, 266
Malva Flowers 214
Man Root 482
Mandragora 267
Mandrake 267
Man-in-the-ground 482
Man-in-the-earth 482
Maple Lungwort 261
Marcory 437
Mare's Tail 219
Marigold 081
Marihuana 084
Marijuana 084
Marjoram 268, 269
Marrubium 216
Marsh Blazing Star 055
Marsh Cistis 270
Marsh Clover 073
Marsh Crowfoot 080
Marsh Cudweed 144
Marsh Hibiscus 202
Marsh Marigold 113
Marsh Tea 270
Marsh Trefoil 073
Marshmallow 013
Mary Bud 081
Marythistle 279
Master of the Wood 493
Masterwort 020, 225, 271
Maté 213
Matico 272
Maudlinwort 475

May Apple 267
May Bells 254
May Bush 182
May Lily 254
May Tree 182
Maypops 328
Meadow Anemone 327
Meadow Bouts 113
Meadow Cabbage 417
Meadow Crowfoot 078
Meadow Fern 443
Meadow Queen 274
Meadow Saffron 273
Meadow Salsify 506
Meadow Sorrel 421
Meadow-wort 274
Meadowbloom 078, 079
Meadowsweet 274, 275
Meadsweet 274
Mealberry 033
Mealy Starwort 435
Melissa 028
Melon Tree 325
Mercury Herb 126
Mescal Button 336
Mexican Damiana 276
Mexican Tea 496
Mezereon 277
Mignonette Tree 195
Milfoil 278
Milk Ipecac 046, 123, 429
Milk Purslain 429
Milk-purslane 431
Milk Thistle 279
Milk Willow-herb ...123, 280,
                            429
Milkweed 280
Milkwort 281, 282, 407
Mint 283, 284, 285, 286
Mistletoe 287, 288
Moccasin Flower 307
Mock Pennyroyal 330
Mole Plant 430
Monarda 289, 290, 291
Monkey Flower 307
Monkshood 292
Moonseed 511
Moor Grass 099
Moose Elm 136

Mormon Tea 120
Mortification Root 013
Mosquito Plant 330
Moth Herb 270
Mother of Rye 138
Mother of Thyme 453
Motherwort 293
Mountain Arnica 023
Mountain Ash 388
Mountain Balm 290, 513
Mountain Box 033
Mountain Cranberry 033
Mountain Everlasting 091
Mountain Flax 407
Mountain Hemp 123
Mountain Holly 209
Mountain Ivy 294
Mountain Laurel 294
Mountain Mahogany 044
Mountain Mint 268, 290
Mountain Sorrel 494
Mountain Strawberry 484
Mountain Sumac 440
Mountain-sweet 310
Mountain Tea 490
Mountain Thyme 453
Mountain Tobacco 023
Mouse Bloodwort 295
Mouse Ear 144, 295
Mousebane 292
Mouse-ear Hawkweed ...295
Mouthroot 177
Mouth-smart 067
Mugwort 296
Mulberry 297, 298
Mullein 299, 300, 301, 302
Mullein Dock 299
Musk-Mallow 199
Musk Root 152
Musk Seed Plant 199
Mustard 303, 304
Myrrh 305

Naked Ladies 273
Nard 422
Narrow Dock 500
Narrow-leaved Labrador
   Tea 270

433

Narrow-leaved Purple
  Coneflower 129
Nasturtium 306
Navy Bean 032
Neckweed 067
Nerve Root 307
Net-leaf Plantain 372
Nettle 308, 309
Nettle Flowers 058
Networt 372
New Jersey Tea 310
Night Willow-herb 142
Nightshade 233, 311, 312
Nightshade Vine 311
Ninety-knot 237
Noah's Ark 307
Noble Yarrow 278
Nodding Wakerobin 046
Noon Flower 506
Noonday Flower 506
Noontide 506
Norway Pine 426
Norway Spruce 426
Nosebleed 278
Nutmeg 313

Oak 314, 315, 316, 317
Oat 318
Okra 210
Oil Nut 465
Oil Plant 089
Old Field Balsam 143
Old Maids' Pink 418
Old Man's Beard 164
Old Man's Flannel 299
Olive 319
One-berry 433
Onion 320
Opossum Tree 446
Orange 321
Orange Flowers 315
Orange Mullein 301
Orange Swallow-wort 346
Orangeroot 176
Oregano 268
Oregon Alder 050
Oregon Grape 483
Orris Root 323
Our Lady's Mint 284

Oval Buchu 070
Owler 049
Oxadoddy 054
Ox-eye Daisy 475
Oxheal 189

Pale Gentian 502
Palma Christi 089
Palsywort 113
Pansy 324
Papaya 325
Paper Birch 043
Papoose Root 060
Paraguay Tea 213
Pariswort 046
Parsley 326
Parsley Fern 449
Partridge Berry 490
Partridgeberry 433
Pasque Flower 327
Passion Flower 328
Passion Vine 328
Patience Dock 048
Paul's Betony 422
Pauson 059
Pawpaw 325
Peach Tree 329
Pearl Barley 030
Pearl Moss 229
Pearly Everlasting 145
Pelican Flower 459
Pellote 336
Pennyroyal 330, 331
Pennywort 512
Peony 332
Pepperidge 029
Pepperidge Bush 029
Peppermint 283
Perennial Mercury 125
Periwinkle 334, 335
Persian Berries 074
Persian Walnut 466
Peru-apple 233
Peruvian Bark 335
Peruvian Rhatany 377
Petty Spurge 432
Petty Whin 376
Peyote 336
Physic Root 054

Pickaway Anise 461
Pickpocket 414
Pigeonberry 351
Pigeon's Grass 141
Pigeonweed 141
Pigweed 237
Pilewort 014, 079, 337
Pilosella 295
Pimento 005
Pimpernel 338, 339
Pimpinella 338, 339
Pin Clover 439
Pinedrops 038
Pinkroot 340
Pinkweed 240
Pinto Bean 032
Pipe Plant 227
Pipsissewa 341
Pistachio 492
Pitcher Plant 342
Plantain 343, 344, 345
Pleurisy Root 346
Plum 347, 348, 349
Pockwood 180
Pod Pepper 092
Poison Ash 164
Poison Black Cherry 039
Poison Flag 061
Poison Hemlock 350
Poison Lettuce 252
Poison Parsley 350
Poison Root 350
Poison Snakeweed 350
Poison Tobacco 194
Poisonberry 312
Poke 351
Pokeroot 351
Pokeweed 351
Polecat Weed 417
Pomegranate 352
Pond Lily 473
Poor Man's
  Weatherglass 374
Poplar 353, 354, 355,
                356, 357
Portland Arrowroot 025
Pot 084
Pot Marigold 081
Prairie Dock 366

Prairie Grub 461
Prairie Hyssop 480
Prickly Ash 358
Prickly Juniper 234
Prickly Lettuce 252
Pride of China 359
Pride of India 359
Pride-of-the-meadow 274
Pride Tree 359
Priest's Crown 119
Prim 361
Primrose 142, 360
Primwort 361
Prince's Feather 014
Prince's Pine 341
Privet 361
Privy 361
Public House Plant 026
Puffball 119
Pumpkin 362
Purging Buckthorn 075
Purging Cassia 411
Purging Flax 160
Purple Angelica 020
Purple Avens 467
Purple Betony 041
Purple Boneset 364
Purple Foxglove 161
Purple Goatsbeard 507
Purple Leptandra 054
Purple Loosestrife 259
Purple Medic 004
Purple Osier 487
Purple Passion Flower ...328
Purple Willow 487
Purple Willow-herb 259
Purvain 062
Pussywillow 488

Quack Grass 491
Quaking Aspen 353
Quassia 363
Queen Anne's Lace 088
Queen of the Meadow ...364
Queen-of-the-meadow ...274
Queen's Delight 437
Queen's Root 437
Quick Grass 491

Quickset 182
Quinsy Berry 116

Rabbit's Root 424
Raccoon Berry 267
Race Ginger 169
Radish 365
Ragged Cup 366
Ragwort 367, 368, 369
Rainbow Weed 259
Raisin Tree 259
Ramsons 035
Ransoms 035
Raspberry 370, 371
Rattleroot 053
Rattlesnake-Master 056
Rattlesnake Plantain 372
Rattlesnake Root 046, 257
Rattlesnake Violet 002
Rattlesnake's Master 470
Rattleweed 053
Red Alder 050
Red Bay 263
Red Bearberry 033
Red Bryony 069
Red Centaury 015
Red Chickweed 374
Red Clover 477
Red Cockscomb 014
Red Coughgrass 375
Red Elder 132
Red Elm 136
Red Eyebright 373
Red Gum 446
Red Laurel 263
Red Legs 048
Red Mulberry 297
Red Oak 315
Red Pain Root 059
Red Pepper 092
Red Pimpernel 374
Red Puccoon ....059·
Red River Snakeroot 459
Red Root 059, 310
Red Sarsaparilla 400
Red Sedge 375
Red Weed 351
Redberry 171
Redleg 240

Red-stem Filaree 439
Reseda 195
Resin-weed 181
Restharrow 376
Rhatany 377
Rheumatism Root ...458, 485
Rheumatism Weed 341
Rhubarb 378
Ribgrass 343
Ribwort 343
Richweed 053, 438
Ripplegrass 343
Rob Elder 130
Rock Brake 148
Rock Elm 136
Rock Fern 264
Rock Parsley 326
Rock Polypod 148
Rock-Rose 379
Rocky Mountain Grape ...483
Rogation Flower 282
Roman Camomile 082
Roman Laurel 247
Roman Motherwort 293
Rose 380, 381, 382, 383,
                384, 385, 386
Rose Laurel 294
Rose Mallow 199, 214
Rose of China 203
Rose Pink 015
Roselle 204
Rosemary 387
Rosin Weed 366
Rough Avens 468
Round-leaved Plantain ...344
Round-leaved Sundew ...441
Round-lobed Hepatica ...196
Rowan 388, 389
Royal Flowering Fern 150
Rue 390
Rum Cherry 476
Rumex 500
Rutland Beauty 184

Sacred Bark 076
Sacred Mushroom 336
Safflower 391
Saffron 392
Sagackhomi 033

Sage 393, 394
Sage of Bethlehem 284
Sailor's Tobacco 296
St. Anthony's Turnip 079
St. Benedict Thistle 395
St. Christopher's Herb 150
St. James' Weed 414
St. Johnswort 396
St. Josephwort 031
St. Mary's Thistle 279
Salicin Willow 486
Sallow 489
Salsify 107, 507
Salt-rheum Weed 457
Sampson Root 129
Sand Sedge 375
Sandalwood 397
Sandberry 033
Sangree Root 459
Sanguinaria 059
Sanguinary 278
Sanicle 398, 399
Sarsaparilla 400
Sassafras 401
Satan's Apple 267
Satin Flower 096
Savory 402, 403
Saw Palmetto 404
Saxifrage 339
Saxifrax 401
Scabish 142
Scabwort 134
Scaly Blazing Star 056
Scaly Dragon's Claw 108
Scammony Root 482
Scarlet Berry 311
Scarlet Pimpernel 374
Scarlet Sumac 440
Scoke 351
Scotch Barley 030
Scotch Broom 405
Scotch Heather 183
Scrofula Plant 158
Scrofula Weed 372
Scrubby Grass 406
Scrubby Trefoil 461
Scurvish 142
Scurvy Grass 406, 469
Sea Parsley 260

Sea Sedge 375
Sealroot 419
Sealwort 419
Selfheal 499
Seneca Snakeroot 407
Senega Snakeroot ...282, 407
Senna 408, 409, 410, 411
Setwall 162
Seven Barks 412
Seville Orange 321
Shamrock 494
Sharp-lobed Hepatica 197
Shave Grass 413
Sheep Laurel 294
Sheep-lice 220
Shell Flower 457
Shepherd's Club 299
Shepherd's Heart 414
Shepherd's Knot 454
Shepherd's Purse 414
Shinleaf 415
Short Buchu 070, 071
Sicklewort 499
Side-flowering Skullcap ..416
Silkweed 280
Silky Swallow-wort 280
Silver Cinquefoil 099
Silver Leaf 437
Silverweed 099
Silvery Lady's Mantle 244
Simpler's Joy 062, 141
Skullcap 416
Skunk Cabbage 417
Skunk Weed 417
Slipper Root 307
Slippery Elm 136
Slippery Root 107
Sloe 347
Small Hemlock 124
Small Nettle 309
Small Pimpernel 339
Small Spikenard 424
Smallpox Plant 342
Smartweed 238
Smooth Alder 051
Smooth Sumac 440
Smut Rye 138
Snake Leaf 002
Snake Lily 061

437

Snake Milk 429
Snake Plantain 343
Snakebite 046
Snakehead 457
Snakeweed 048, 459
Snap Bean 032
Snapping Hazel 492
Snowflower 164
Soap Root 418
Soapwort 418
Soft Pine 472
Soldiers 259
Soldier's Herb 343
Soldier's Woundwort 278
Solomon's Seal 419, 420
Sorb Apple 388
Sorrel 421
Sour Dock 500
Sour Orange 321
Sour Trefoil 494
Sourgrass 421
Southern Snakeroot 479
Southernwood 498
Southernwood Root 087
Sowberry 029
Sowbread 118
Spanish Chestnut 217
Spanish Pepper 092
Spanish Saffron 392
Spanish Sarsaparilla 400
Sparrow Grass 027
Spearmint 284
Speedwell 067, 422
Spice Birch 044
Spiceberry 490
Spicy Wintergreen 490
Spignet 423
Spiked Aloe 003
Spiked Loosestrife 259
Spiked Willow-herb 259
Spikenard 423, 424
Spindle Tree 462
Spleen Amaranth 014
Spoonwood 256, 294
Spoonwort 406
Spotted Alder 492
Spotted Comfrey 261
Spotted Cowbane 350
Spotted Cranebill 425

Spotted Geranium 425
Spotted Hemlock 350
Spotted Knotweed 240
Spotted Lungwort 261
Spotted Parsley 350
Spotted Plantain 372
Spotted Spurge 431
Spotted Thistle 395
Spreading Dogbane 123
Spreading Spurge 431
Spring Wintergreen 490
Spruce 426, 427
Spurge 428, 429, 430,
                      431, 432
Spurge Flax 277
Spurge Laurel 277
Spurge Olive 277
Spurred Rye 138
Squaw Balm 330
Squaw-Berry 433
Squaw Root 060
Squaw Tea 120
Squaw Vine 433
Squaw Weed 367
Squawmint 330
Squawroot 053
Staff Vine 311
Stagger Weed 455
Staggerweed 246
Staghorn 103
Star Anise 434
Star Bloom 340
Star Grass 435
Star of Jerusalem 506
Star of the Earth 040
Star Root 435
Starchwort 025
Starwort 096
Staunchwort 236
Stavesacre 246
Stayplough 376
Stepmother 323
Stick-a-back 036
Sticklewort 436
Stiff Gentian 505
Stillingia 437
Stinging Nettle 308
Stingless Nettle 058
Stinking Hellebore 189

Stinking Nightshade 194
Stinking Prairie Bush 461
Stinkweed 233
Stinkwort 233
Stitchwort 096
Stone Brake 148
Stone Root 438
Storksbill 198, 439
Stramonium 233
Straw 318
Strawberry-bush 463
String Bean 032
Striped Alder 212, 492
Stubwort 494
Styrax 446
Succory 097
Sumac 440
Sumbul 152
Summer Savory 402
Sun Rose 379
Sundew 441
Swallowwort 280
Swamp Cabbage 417
Swamp Dogwood 461
Swamp Laurel 263
Swamp Sassafras 263
Swamp Tea 270
Sweating Plant 063
Sweet Anise 442
Sweet Balm 028
Sweet Balsam 143
Sweet Basil 031
Sweet Bay 247
Sweet Birch 044
Sweet Brake 149, 267
Sweet Brier 066
Sweet Bush 443
Sweet Chervil 442
Sweet Cicely 442
Sweet Clover 509
Sweet Dock 048
Sweet Elder 130
Sweet Elm 136
Sweet Fennel 146
Sweet Fern 443, 444
Sweet Flag 445
Sweet Goldenrod 173
Sweet Grass 445
Sweet Gum 446

Sweet Licorice 253
Sweet Magnolia 263
Sweet Marjoram 269
Sweet Myrtle 445
Sweet Orange 322
Sweet Rush 445
Sweet Violet 167
Sweet Weed 013
Sweet Wood 253
Sweet Woodruff 493
Sweet-scented Life
   Everlasting 143
Sweet-scented Pond
   Lily 473
Sweet-scented Water
   Lily 473
Sweet-smelling Trefoil ...192
Sweetbriar 383
Sweethearts 036
Swine Snout 119
Swinebread 118
Sycamore Maple 447
Syrian Mallow 199

Tacamahac 355
Tailed Cubebs 114
Tailed Pepper 114
Tall Blazing Star 057
Tall Crowfoot 078
Tall Field Buttercup 078
Tall Nasturtium 469
Tall Speedwell 054
Tall Veronica 054
Tallow Shrub 471
Tamarind 448
Tansy 440
Tare 034
Target-leaved Hibiscus ...199
Tarragon 450
Tarweed 513
Teamster's Tea 120
Teasel 063
Tetterberry 068
Tetterwort 059, 093
Texas Sarsaparilla 511
Texas Snakeroot 459
Thalictroc 187
Thick Birthwort 459
Thimbleberry 052

Thorn-apple 233
Thorn-apple Tree 182
Thoroughwort 063
Thousand-leaf 278
Three-leaved Hop Tree ...461
Three-leaved
  Nightshade 046
Throat Root 467
Throw-wort 293
Thuja 451
Thunder Plant 222
Thyme 452, 453
Tickleweed 016
Tickweed 330
Tinnevelly Senna 410
Tipton Weed 396
Tobacco Wood 492
Tongue-grass 096
Toothache Bush 358
Toothache Tree 358
Tormentil 454
Toywort 414
Trailing Bindweed 184
Trailing Mahonia 483
Traveler's Joy 062
Tree of Life 451
Tree Primrose 142
Trembling Poplar 353
Trillium 046
Triticum 491
True Ivy 137
True Pennyroyal 331
Trumpet Weed 364
Tuber Root 346
Tuberous Water Lily 474
Tumeric Root 176
Turkey Aloe 009
Turkey Burrseed 077
Turkey Claw 108
Turkey Corn 455
Turkey Rhubarb 378
Turnhoof 179
Turnip 456
Turtlebloom 457
Twin-berry 433
Twin Leaf 458

Upland Cranberry 033
Upland Speedwell 422

Upright Birthwort 047
Upright Septfoil 454
Upstart 273
Uva Ursi 033

Valerian 162
Vandal Root 162
Vegetable Antimony 063
Vegetable Sulfur 103
Vegetable Tallow 471
Velvet Dock 299
Velvet Plant 299
Venice Mallow 208
Venus Shoe 307
Vermont Snakeroot 479
Vermont Valerian 162
Veronica 422
Vervain 062, 141
Vetiver 235
Vine-maple 511
Violet Bloom 311
Virginia Creeper 017
Virginia Dogwood 127
Virginia Mountain
  Mint 480
Virginia Mouse-ear 221
Virginia Silk 280
Virginia Snakeroot 459
Virginia Thyme 480
Virgin's Bower 460
Vomitroot 258
Vomitwort 258

Wafer Ash 461
Wahoo 462, 463
Wakerobin 046
Wake-robin 228
Walewort 133
Wallflower 123
Wallwort 107, 133
Walnut 464, 465, 466
Walpole Tea 310
Wandering Milkweed 123
Wartwort 144
Water Avens 467, 478
Water Cabbage 473
Water Crowfoot 080
Water Dock 501
Water Dragon 113

Water Eryngo 470
Water Fern 150
Water Flag 061
Water Hemlock 350
Water Lily 473
Water Mallow 199
Water Maudlin 192
Water Mint 286
Water Parsley 350
Water Pepper 238
Water Pimpernel 067
Water Plantain 372
Water Purslain 067
Water Shamrock 073
Water Smartweed 239
Watercress 469
Watercup 342
Wax Bean 032
Wax Cluster 490
Wax Myrtle 471
Waxberry 471
Waxen Woad 127
Way Bread 344
Waythorn 075
Weed 084
Weeping Spruce 191
Western Wallflower 123
Whig Plant 082
Whinberry 042
White Archangel 058
White Balsam 143
White Bay 263
White Birch 043
White Bryony 068
White Cankerweed 257
White Cedar 451
White Daisy 475
White Endive 119
White Fringe 164
White Gum 446
White Hellebore 016
White Holly 210
White Horehound 216
White Lettuce 257
White Man's Foot 344
White Melilot 510
White Mustard 304
White Nettle 058
White Oak 314

White Pine 472
White Pond Lily 473
White Root 346
White Sandalwood 397
White Saunders 397
White Sorrel 494
White Walnut 465
White Water Lily 473, 474
White Weed 475
White Willow 486
Whitethorn 182
Whorlywort 054
Whortleberry 012, 042
Wild Angelica 019
Wild Archangel 020
Wild Bergamot 291
Wild Black Cherry 476
Wild Brier 066
Wild Bryony 068
Wild Camomile 083
Wild Celery 094
Wild Cherry 476
Wild Chicory 097
Wild Clover 477
Wild Crane's-bill 198
Wild Cranesbill 425
Wild Crocus 327
Wild Daisy 478
Wild Elder 133
Wild Endive 119
Wild Fennel 146
Wild Geranium 425
Wild Ginger 479
Wild Hippo 429
Wild Hops 068, 069
Wild Hydrangea 412
Wild Hyssop 062, 480
Wild Indigo 481
Wild Iris 061
Wild Jalap 482
Wild Jessamine 508
Wild Lemon 267
Wild Lettuce 252
Wild Licorice 424
Wild Lily-of-the-valley ...415
Wild Mandrake 267
Wild Marjoram 268
Wild Nard 026
Wild Oregon Grape 483

Wild Pepper 277
Wild Plum 347, 349
Wild Potato 482
Wild Red Raspberry 370
Wild Rosemary 270
Wild Sage 394
Wild Sarsaparilla 424
Wild Scammony 482
Wild Senna 408
Wild Snapdragon 512
Wild Snowball 310
Wild Strawberry 484
Wild Succory 015, 097
Wild Sweet-potato
  Vine 482
Wild Thyme 453
Wild Tobacco 258
Wild Turkey Pea 455
Wild Turnip 228
Wild Valerian 162
Wild White Vine 069
Wild Woodbine 017
Wild Woodvine 017
Wild Yam 485
Willow 486, 487, 488, 489
Willow Sage 259
Wind Flower 327
Wind Root 346
Wineberry 042, 117
Winged Elm 136
Wingseed 461
Winter Clover 433
Winter Fern 350
Winter Hellebore 190
Winter Marjoram 268
Winter Savory 403
Winterberry 212
Winterbloom 492
Wintergreen 341, 490
Winterlien 159
Wintersweet 268
Winterweed 096
Witch Grass 491
Witch Hazel 492
Witches' Brier 066
Withe 486
Withy 486
Woad Waxen 127
Wolf Claw 103

Wolfsbane 023, 292
Wonder of the World 170
Wood Betony 041
Wood Boneset 063
Wood Sanicle 399
Wood Sorrel 494
Wood Strawberry 484
Wood Vine 068
Wood Waxen 127
Woodbine 017, 508
Woodruff 493
Woodward 493
Woody 311
Woody Climber 017
Woody Nightshade 311
Woolmat 220
Woolly Parsnip 271
Woolly Plantain 345
Worm Grass 340
Wormseed 495, 496
Wormwood 497, 498
Wound Weed 173
Woundwort 236, 499
Wycopy 256
Wymote 013

Yarrow 278
Yaupon Holly 211
Yaw Root 437
Yellow Avens 040
Yellow Bedstraw 037
Yellow Broom 481
Yellow Cedar 451
Yellow Cleavers 037
Yellow Dock 500, 501
Yellow Erythronium 002
Yellow Gentian 502, 503
Yellow Ginseng 060
Yellow Goatsbeard ..506, 507
Yellow Goldenrod 174
Yellow Indigo 481
Yellow Jessamine 508
Yellow Lady's Slipper 307
Yellow Melilot 509, 510
Yellow Parilla 511
Yellow Puccoon 176
Yellow Sandalwood 397
Yellow Snakeleaf 002
Yellow Snowdrop 002

Yellow Sweet Clover 509
Yellow Toadflax 512
Yellow-weed 078
Yellow Wood 358
Yellowroot 176, 177, 458
Yellows 078, 307
Yerba 213
Yerba Maté 213

Yerba Santa 513
Yew 514
Youthwort 271, 441
Yuma 485

Zanzibar Aloe 009
Zanzibar Pepper 092

ALPHABETICAL LIST OF HERBS

Latin Botanical Names

Acacia senegal 001
Acer pseudo-platanus 447
Achillea millefolium 278
Aconitum napellus 292
Acorus calamus 445
Adiantum pedatum 264
Aesculus
   hippocastanum 217
Aethusa cynapium 124
Agave americana 003
Agrimonia eupatoria 436
Agropyron repens 491
Alchemilla alpina 244
Alchemilla vulgaris 243
Aletris farinosa 435
Allium cepa 320
Allium porrum 249
Allium sativum 168
Allium
   schoenopraesum 098
Allium ursinum 035
Alnus glutinosa 049
Alnus rubra 050
Alnus serrulata 051
Aloe latifolia 008
Aloe perryi 009
Aloe saponaria 010
Aloe tenuior 011
Aloe vera 007
Alpinia galanga 166
Althaea officinalis 013
Althaea rosea 214
Amaranthus
   hypochondriacus 014
Anagallis arvensis 374
Anaphalis margaritacea ...145
Anemone patens 327
Anethum graveolens 122
Angelica archangelica 018
Angelica atropurpurea ...020
Angelica sylvestris 019
Antennaria dioica 091
Anthemis nobilis 082
Anthriscus cerefolium 095

Anthyllis vulneraria 236
Apium graveolens 094
Apocynum
   androsaemifolium 123
Aquilegia vulgaris 106
Aralia nudicaulis 424
Aralia racemosa 423
Arctium lappa 077
Arctostaphylos uva-ursi ...033
Arisaema triphyllum 228
Aristolochia clematitis ..047
Aristolochia serpentaria ..459
Armoracia lapathifolia 218
Arnica montana 023
Artemisia abronatum 498
Artemisia absinthium 497
Artemisia dracunculus 450
Artemisia vulgaris 296
Arum maculatum 025
Asarum canadense 479
Asarum europaeum 026
Asclepias syriaca 280
Asclepias tuberosa 346
Asparagus officinalis 027
Asperula odorata 493
Atropa belladonna 039
Avena sativa 318

Baptisia tinctoria 481
Barosma betulina 070
Barosma crenulata 071
Barosma serratifolia 072
Bellis perennis 478
Berberis vulgaris 029
Betula alba 043
Betula lenta 044
Borago officinalis 064
Brassica hirta 304
Brassica nigra 303
Brassica rapa 456
Bryonia alba 068
Bryonia dioica 069
Buxus sempervirens 065

Calendula officinalis 081
Calluna vulgaris 183
Caltha palustris 113
Cannabis sativa 084
Capsella bursa-pastoris ...414
Capsicum frutescens 092
Carduus marianus 279
Carex arenaria 375
Carica papaya 325
Carlina acaulis 087
Carthamus tinctorius 391
Carum carvi 085
Caryophyllus aromaticus ..102
Cassia acutifolia 409
Cassia angustifolia 410
Cassia fistula 411
Cassia marilandica 408
Caulophyllum
   thalictroides 060
Ceanothus americanus ...310
Centaurea cyanus 110
Centaurium
   umbellatum 140
Cetraria islandica 224
Chelidonium majus 093
Chelone glabra 457
Chenopodium
   ambrosioides 496
Chenopodium ambrosioides
   var. anthelminticum 495
Chimaphila umbellata 341
Chionanthus virginicus ...164
Chondrus crispus 229
Chrysanthemum
   leucanthemum 475
Chrysanthemum
   parthenium 155
Cichorium intybus 097
Cimicifuga racemosa 053
Cinchona spp. 335
Citrus aurantium 321
Citrus limon 250
Citrus sinensis 322
Claviceps purpurea 138
Clematis virginiana 460
Cnicus benedictus 395
Cocculus palmatus 104
Cochlearia officinalis 406
Cola acuminata 241

Colchicum autumnale 272
Collinsonia canadensis ...438
Commiphora myrrha 305
Comptonia peregrina 443
Comptonia peregrina
   var. asplenifolia 444
Conium maculatum 350
Convallaria majalis 254
Convolvulus sepium 184
Conyza canadensis 219
Coptis trifolia ....177.
Corallarhiza
   odontorhiza 108
Coriandrum sativum 109
Cornus florida 127
Corydalis cava 111
Corydalis formosa 455
Crataegus oxyacantha 182
Crocus sativus 392
Cucumis sativus 115
Cucurbita pepo 362
Cyclamen europaeum 118
Cynara scolymus 024
Cynoglossum morrisoni ..221
Cynoglossum officinale ...220
Cypripedium pubescens ..307
Cytisus scoparius 405

Daphne mezereum 277
Datura stramonium 233
Daucus carota 088
Delphinium consolida ...246
Dictamnus albus 163
Digitalis purpurea 161
Dioscorea villosa 485
Drosera rotundifolia 441
Dryopteris filixmas 149

Echinacea angustifolia 129
Elettaria cardamomum ...086
Ephedra spp. 120
Ephedra sinica 121
Epifagus virginiana 038
Equisetum arvense 413
Erechtites hieracifolia 337
Erigeron canadensis 219
Eriodictyon
   californicum 513
Erodium cicutarium 439

Eryngium aquaticum 470
Erythraea centaurium 140
Erythronium
  americanum 002
Eucalyptus globulus 139
Euonymus americanus 463
Euonymus
  atropurpureus 462
Eupatorium
  cannabinum 192
Eupatorium perfoliatum ..063
Eupatorium purpureum ..364
Euphorbia corollata 429
Euphorbia cyparissias 428
Euphorbia lathyrus 430
Euphorbia maculata 431
Euphorbia peplus 432
Euphrasia officinalis 373

Ferula assa-foetida 154
Ferula foetida 153
Ferula sumbul 152
Ficus carica 157
Filipendula hexapetala ...275
Filipendula ulmaria 274
Foeniculum vulgare 146
Fragaria vesca 484
Fraxinus excelsior 045
Fumaria officinalis 165

Galega officinalis 172
Galeopsis tetrahit 193
Galium aparine 036
Galium verum 037
Gaultheria procumbens ..490
Gelsemium
  sempervirens 508
Genista tinctoria 128
Gentiana catesbaei 503
Gentiana crinita 504
Gentiana lutea 502
Gentiana quinquefolia ...505
Geranium maculatum 425
Geranium robertianum ...198
Gerardia pedicularia 156
Geum rivale 467
Geum urbanum 040
Geum virginianum 468
Glycyrrhiza glabra 253

Gnaphalium
  polycephalum 143
Gnaphalium uliginosum ..144
Goodyera pubescens 372
Gossypium spp. 112
Gratiola officinalis 186
Grindelia robusta 181
Guaiacum officinale 180

Hagenia abyssinica 242
Hamamelis virginiana 492
Hedeoma pulegioides 330
Hedera helix 137
Helianthemum
  canadense 379
Helleborus foetidus 189
Helleborus niger 188
Helleborus viridis 190
Hepatica acutiloba 197
Hepatica triloba 196
Heracleum lanatum 271
Hibiscus abelmoschus 199
Hibiscus bancroftianus ...200
Hibiscus esculentus 201
Hibiscus palustris 202
Hibiscus rosa-sinensis 203
Hibiscus sabdariffa 204
Hibiscus sagittifolius 205
Hibiscus surattensis 206
Hibiscus tiliaceus 207
Hibiscus trionum 208
Hieracium pilosella 295
Hordeum vulgare 030
Humulus lupulus 215
Hydrangea arborescens ...412
Hydrastis canadensis 176
Hyoscyamus niger 194
Hypericum perforatum ...396
Hyssopus officinalis 223

Ilex aquifolium 209
Ilex opaca 210
Ilex paraguariensis 213
Ilex verticillata 212
Ilex vomitoria 211
Illicium anisatum 434
Illicium verum 434
Imperatoria ostruthium ..225
Inula helenium 134

Ipomoea jalapa 231
Ipomoea pandurata 482
Iris florentina 323
Iris versicolor 061

Jasminum officinale 232
Jeffersonia diphylla 458
Juglans cinerea 465
Juglans nigra 464
Juglans regia 466
Juniperus communis 234
Juniperus oxycedrus 234

Kalmia latifolia 294
Krameria triandra 377

Lactuca sativa 251
Lactuca virosa 252
Lamium album 058
Larix europaea 245
Laurus nobilis 247
Lavandula officinalis 248
Lavandula vera 248
Lawsonia inermis 195
Ledum palustre 270
Leonurus cardiaca 293
Levisticum officinale 260
Liatris scariosa 057
Liatris spicata 055
Liatris squarrosa 056
Ligustrum vulgare 361
Linaria vulgaris 512
Linum catharticum 160
Linum usitatissimum 159
Liquidambar styraciflua ...446
Lobelia inflata 258
Lolium temulentum 034
Lophophora williamsii ...336
Lycopodium clavatum 103
Lythrum salicaria 259

Magnolia glauca 263
Mahonia aquifolium 483
Majorana hortensis 269
Malva rotundifolia 266
Malva sylvestris 265
Mandragora officinarum ..267
Marrubium vulgare 216
Matricaria chamomilla ...083
Medicago sativa 004

Melia azedarach 359
Melilotus alba 510
Melilotus officinalis 509
Melissa officinalis 028
Menispermum
  canadense 511
Mentha aquatica 286
Mentha crispa 285
Mentha piperita 283
Mentha pulegium 331
Mentha spicata 284
Menyanthes trifoliata 073
Mercurialis annua 126
Mercurialis perennis 125
Mitchella repens 433
Monarda didyma 290
Monarda fistulosa 291
Monarda punctata 289
Monotropa uniflora 227
Morus nigra 298
Morus rubra 297
Myrica cerifera 471
Myristica fragrans 313

Nasturtium officinale 469
Nepeta cataria 090
Nepeta hederacea 179
Nymphaea odorata 473
Nymphaea tuberosa 474

Ocimum basilicum 031
Oenothera biennis 142
Olea europaea 319
Ononis spinosa 376
Origanum vulgare 268
Osmorhiza longistylis 442
Osmunda cinnamomea ...151
Osmunda regalis 150
Oxalis acetosella 494

Paeonia officinalis 332
Panax quinquefolius 171
Panax schin-seng 170
Parthenocissus
  quinquefolia 017
Passiflora incarnata 328
Petroselinum sativum 326
Phaseolus vulgaris 032

Phoradendron
flavescens 287
Phytolacca americana 351
Picea excelsa 426
Picea mariana 427
Picraena excelsa 363
Pimenta officinalis 005
Pimpinella anisum 021
Pimpinella magna 338
Pimpinella saxifraga 339
Pinus stobus 472
Piper angustifolium 272
Piper cubeba 114
Plantago lanceolata 343
Plantago major 344
Plantago media 345
Podophyllum peltatum ...267
Polygala amara 281
Polygala senega 407
Polygala vulgaris 282
Polygonatum
multiflorum 419
Polygonatum odoratum ..420
Polygonum aviculare 237
Polygonum bistorta 048
Polygonum hydropiper ...238
Polygonum persicaria 240
Polygonum punctatum ...239
Polypodium vulgare 148
Populus balsamifera 355
Populus candicans 354
Populus nigra 356
Populus tremula 357
Populus tremuloides 353
Potentilla anserina 099
Potentilla canadensis 100
Potentilla reptans 101
Potentilla tormentilla 454
Prenanthes alba 257
Primula officinalis 360
Prunella vulgaris 499
Prunus americana 349
Prunus amygdalus 006
Prunus domestica 348
Prunus persica 329
Prunus serotina 476
Prunus spinosa 347
Ptelea trifoliata 461
Pulmonaria officinalis ...261

Punica granatum 352
Pycnanthemum
virginianum 480
Pyrola elliptica 415
Pyrus malus 022

Quercus alba 314
Quercus robur 317
Quercus rubra 315
Quercus tinctoria 316

Ranunculus acris 078
Ranunculus bulbosus 079
Ranunculus sceleratus 080
Raphanus sativus 365
Rhamnus cathartica 075
Rhamnus frangula 074
Rhamnus purshiana 076
Rheum palmatum 378
Rhus glabra 440
Ribes nigrum 116
Ribes rubrum 117
Ricinus communis 089
Rosa californica 380
Rosa canina 066
Rosa centifolia 381
Rosa damascena 382
Rosa eglanteria 383
Rosa gallica 384
Rosa laevigata 385
Rosa roxburghii 386
Rosmarinus officinalis ...387
Rubia tinctorum 262
Rubus idaeus 371
Rubus strigosus 370
Rubus villosus 052
Rumex acetosa 421
Rumex aquaticus 502
Rumex crispus 500
Ruta graveolens 390

Sabatia angularis 015
Salix alba 486
Salix caprea 489
Salix nigra 488
Salix purpurea 487
Salvia lyrata 394
Salvia officinalis 393
Sambucus canadensis ...130

Sambucus ebulus 133
Sambucus nigra 131
Sambucus racemosa 132
Sanguinaria canadensis ...059
Sanguisorba officinalis 178
Sanicula europaea 399
Sanicula marilandica 398
Santalum album 397
Saponaria officinalis 418
Sarracenia purpurea 342
Sassafras albidum 401
Satureja hortensis 402
Satureja montana 403
Scrophularia nodosa 158
Scutellaria lateriflora 416
Sempervivum tectorum ...222
Senecio aureus 367
Senecio jacoboea 369
Senecio vulgaris 368
Serenoa serrulata 404
Silphium perfoliatum 366
Sisymbrium alliaria 185
Sisymbrium officinale 187
Smilax officinalis 400
Solanum dulcamara 311
Solanum nigrum 312
Solidago nemoralis 174
Solidago odora 173
Solidago virgaurea 175
Sorbus americana 389
Sorbus aucuparia 388
Spigelia marilandica 340
Stachys officinalis 041
Stellaria media 096
Stillingia sylvatica 437
Symphytum officinale 107
Symplocarpus foetidus ...417
Syzygium aromaticum 102

Tamarindus indica 448
Tanacetum vulgare 449
Taraxacum officinale 119
Taxus baccata 514
Thuja occidentalis 451
Thymus serpyllum 453
Thymus vulgaris 452

Tilia americana 256
Tilia europaea 255
Tormentilla erecta 454
Tragopogon porrifolius ...507
Tragopogon pratensis 506
Trifolium pratense 477
Trigonella
    foenum-graecum 147
Trillium pendulum 046
Tropaeolum majus 306
Tsuga canadensis 191
Turnera aphrodisiaca 276
Tussilago farfara 105

Ulmus campestris 135
Ulmus fulva 136
Urtica dioica 308
Urtica urens 309

Vaccinium myrtillus 042
Vaccinium vitis idaea 012
Valeriana officinalis 162
Veratrum viride 016
Verbascum nigrum 302
Verbascum phlomoides ..301
Verbascum thapsiforme ..300
Verbascum thapsus 299
Verbena hastata 062
Verbena officinalis 141
Vernonia fasciculata 230
Veronica beccabunga 067
Veronica officinalis 422
Veronicastrum
    virginicum 054
Vetiveria zizanioides 235
Vinca major 333
Vinca minor 334
Viola odorata 167
Viola tricolor 324
Viscum album 288

Zanthoxylum
    americanum 358
Zea mays 226
Zingiber officinale 169

PART 3

INTRODUCTION

This part of *The Herb Book* presents basic information to help you use the plants of Part 2—and many others—in a variety of ways. Beginning with specific formulas for combined-herb treatments, it then goes beyond purely remedial uses of plants to consider other important applications, from nutrition to woodworking. It ends with an excursion into space and time, through plants in astrology, myth, and history.

Each topic in Part 3 could (and does) fill one or more books by itself, so that much detail must be omitted here. But the core of basic information included will provide a useful starting place and point the direction toward greater possibilities. The Bibliography lists many useful books that deal with these subjects in detail, and new books are joining them all the time. Endless adventures lie behind the door of knowledge, and these pages can be your key.

HERBAL MIXTURES
FORMULAS FOR HEALTH

We use only a limited number of terms to describe the medicinal effects of herbs, but it is rare for any two plants to produce exactly the same results in the body. Among herbs with purgative properties, for example, there will be differences in strength, in the time before taking effect, in the mechanism of action on the bowels, in side effects such as griping, in aftereffects, and in palatability. Often even the same herb will act differently on different persons. Herb mixtures are designed to minimize such variations by combining plant medicines that compensate for one another's undesirable properties. A laxative mixture, to continue the example, may combine a small amount of a strong cathartic with a larger amount of a mild laxative to produce a moderate effect, adding perhaps a carminative to counteract griping and an aromatic herb to improve the taste. Similarly, stimulants are useful additions to some mixtures, either to counteract the depressant side effect of another ingredient or to speed assimilation of the remedy by stimulating metabolic activity.

The mixtures in this section represent balanced formulas to use for the indicated conditions or to produce the indicated results. The general comments about plant treatments in "How to Make and Use Herb Preparations" (Part 1) also apply here. The formulas are organized alphabetically by ailment and effect. Ingredients are specified in terms of proportions rather than amounts, so that you can prepare any amount of mixture you find convenient. The directions indicate the amount of mixtures needed for each preparation.

ANEMIA

European centaury   Wormwood
Nettle leaves   Brier hip

Mix in equal parts. Let 1 tbsp. soak in 1 cup cold water for 3 hours. Then bring quickly to a boil and steep for 10 minutes. Sweeten with honey. Take in the course of a day, in mouthful doses.

℞

Mother of thyme
Nettle

Mix in equal parts. Steep 1 tsp. in ½ cup boiling-hot water. Take 1 to 1½ cups a day, sweetened with honey, in mouthful doses.

℞

European centaury
St. Johnswort

Mix in equal parts. Steep 1 level tsp. in ½ cup boiling-hot water; then add 1 tsp. honey. Take 1 to 1½ cups a day, in mouthful doses.

APHRODISIAC TEA

Mexican damiana leaves
Saw palmetto berries

Powder and mix in equal parts. Take 1 to 2 tsp. a day, in water, wine or gelatin capsules.

℞

Jasmine flowers   Rose hips
Rose buds   Tea leaves

Mix in equal parts. Steep 2 tbsp. mixture in 1 cup boiling-hot water for 10 minutes. Sweeten with honey and add lemon if desired.

APHRODISIAC BATH

Corn poppy   Maidenhair
Early-flowering periwinkle   Male fern
Fragrant valerian   Pansy

Mix in equal parts. Add 1 oz. mixture to 1 qt. cold water and bring to a boil. Simmer briefly, then steep 15 to 30 minutes. Strain and add to bath water.

APPETITE, FOR LACK OF

Juniper berries
Balm leaves

European centaury
Nettle leaves

Mix in equal parts. Steep 1 tsp. in ½ cup boiling-hot water. Take ½ to 1 cup a day, sweetened with honey, in mouthful doses.

℞

Watercress [2 parts]
Fresh horseradish [3 parts]

Soak 3 oz. of the mixture in 2 qt. white wine for several days. Strain. Take ½ cup daily, before breakfast.

ARTERIOSCLEROSIS

Fragrant valerian
   root [1 part]
Shave grass [1 part]

European mistletoe [4 parts]
Hawthorn [4 parts]

Soak 1 tbsp. chopped plant parts in ½ cup cold water for 8 hours. Take ½ cup a day, spaced out in 3 or 4 doses.

ARTHRITIS TEA

Alder buckthorn bark
American angelica root
Black cohosh
Colombo

Fragrant valerian root
Rue
Skullcap
Yellow gentian root

Mix in equal parts. Steep 1 heaping tsp. in 1 cup boiling-hot water until lukewarm. Take 3 cups a day, a half-cup at a time.

℞

Bearberry leaves
Black cohosh
Camomile

Cascara sagrada
Pokeweed root
Sassafras

Mix in equal parts. Steep 1½ tsp. mixture in 1 cup

boiling-hot water for 10 minutes. Take 1 cup morning and evening. Sweeten with honey if desired.

℞

Parsley
Yerba buena
Yerba santa

Mix in equal parts. Steep 1½ tbsp. mixture in 1 cup boiling-hot water until the tea is cold. Take 2 cups a day, in mouthful doses.

ARTHRITIS POULTICE

(for swollen joints)

Mullein leaves [6 parts]	Lobelia [3 parts]
Slippery elm bark [9 parts]	Cayenne [1 part]

Add 3 oz. mixture to boiling-hot water to make a paste. Spread the paste on a cloth and apply to the affected area.

[See also "Poultice, Formula for a" in this section.]

ARTHRITIS LINIMENT

Wintergreen
Yerba santa

Mix in equal parts. Put any amount of mixture in enough olive oil to cover. Simmer for 30 to 60 minutes. Strain, and apply to affected parts when cool.

[See also "Liniment" in this section.]

ASTHMA

Garlic	Ground ivy
Blackthorn	Blue vervain

Mix in equal parts. Simmer 4 tbsp. mixture in 1 qt. water for 20 minutes and strain. Take 3 to 4 tbsp. 3 or 4 times a day.

ASTHMA, FOR RELIEF OF ATTACK

Lobelia	Euphorbia
Garlic	Ground ivy

Yerba santa	Blue vervain
Blackthorn	Cayenne
Gum plant	

Simmer 8 tbsp. mixture in 1 qt. water for 20 minutes and strain. Take 4 tbsp. as a first dose, followed by 2 tbsp. every half hour. When the attack subsides, take 4 tbsp. every 4 hours.

BRONCHIAL ASTHMA

| Sundew | Fennel |
| Thyme | Silverweed |

Mix in equal parts. Steep 1 tsp. in ½ cup boiling-hot water. Take ½ to 1 cup a day, sweetened with honey, in mouthful doses.

BATHS
(an herbal bath)

| Hops [1 lb.] | Sage [1 oz.] |
| Thyme [1 oz.] | Lavender [1 oz.] |

Put mixture into a muslin bag and tie securely. Soak the bag in the bath water for 10 minutes.

[See also "Some Useful Bath Formulas" in Part 1.]

SITZBATH FOR WOMEN'S ABDOMINAL PROBLEMS
(also for wounds and sores)

| Lady's mantle | Shave grass |
| Oak bark | Oat straw |

Mix in equal parts. Boil 8 to 9 oz. in 5 qt. water briefly, then steep for 10 minutes. Use warm for sitzbath.

[See also "The Sitzbath" in Part 1.]

BLOOD BUILDER TEA
(vitamins and minerals)

Spinach [2 parts]
Parsley [1 part]

Put three handsful of this mixture through an electric vegetable juicer. Then add an equal amount of orange juice. Take a cup of this "cocktail" 2 or 3 times a day.

BLOOD PRESSURE, HIGH

Caraway [1 part]   Milfoil [1 part]
Fennel [1 part]   Camomile [2 parts]
Anise [1 part]   Peppermint leaves [2 parts]

Steep 1 tsp. in ½ cup boiling-hot water. Take 1 to 1½ cups a day, in mouthful doses.

BLOOD CLEANSERS
(to purify the blood)

These mixtures are composed of herbs that interact to eliminate toxins and metabolic end products such as uric acid.

Dandelion root [1 part]
Young nettle leaves [1 part]
Elder shoots [2 parts]
Primrose flowers and leaves [2 parts]

Steep 1 to 2 tsp. in ½ cup boiling-hot water. Take 1 cup a day, sweetened with honey, in mouthful doses.

℞

Burdock root [3 parts]   Nettle [5 parts]
Black elder leaves [5 parts] Pansy [10 parts]

Steep 1 heaping tsp. in ½ cup boiling-hot water for a short time. Sweeten with 1 tsp. honey. For a "spring cure" take ½ cup a day for 8 to 14 days.

℞

Blackberry leaves [2 parts]   Black elder leaves [1 part]
Nettle leaves [2 parts]   Dandelion root [1 part]

Steep 1 tsp. in ½ cup boiling-hot water. Take 1 to 1½ cups in the course of a day, in mouthful doses.

℞

Wormwood [1 part]   European centaury [2 parts]
Milfoil [2 parts]   Peppermint leaves [4 parts]
White birch leaves [2 parts] Pansy [4 parts]

Steep 1 tsp. in ½ cup boiling-hot water. Take ½ cup 3 times a day, each time with fresh juice from watercress or nettle.

℞

Alder buckthorn bark [6 parts]
Burdock root [2 parts]
Yellow dock [2 parts]
Sarsaparilla root [2 parts]
Pansy herb [2 parts]
Wild-clover blossoms [2 parts]
Licorice root [3 parts]
Coriander seed [1 part]

Boil 1 tsp. mixture in 2 cups water for 2 to 3 minutes; let stand 10 minutes and strain. Take 1 cup in the morning and 1 cup at night.

℞

Anise [1 part]
German camomile [4 parts]
Caraway [4 parts]
American senna leaves [8 parts]

Steep 2 tsp. in 1 cup boiling-hot water. Take ½ cup, morning and evening.

℞

Dandelion root and leaves
German camomile flowers
American senna leaves

Mix in equal parts. Steep 2 tsp. in ½ cup boiling-hot water. Take ½ cup, morning and evening, freshly made each time.

℞

Witch grass root   Nettle
Ground ivy   Elder leaves

Mix in equal parts. Steep 1 heaping tsp. in ½ cup boiling-hot water. Take 1 to 1½ cups a day, sweetened with 2 tsp. honey per cup, in mouthful doses.

℞

Blackthorn flowers   Milfoil
American senna leaves   Dandelion
Black elder flowers   Buck bean
Watercress

Mix in equal parts. Steep 1 tsp. in ½ cup boiling-hot water for 10 minutes. Take ½ to 1 cup a day.

BLOOD SUGAR, TO LOWER

Bean pods [4 parts]
Fumitory [5 parts]
Eucalyptus leaves [5 parts]
Dyer's broom [5 parts]

Birch leaves [6 parts]
Milk thistle seeds [7 parts]
Bilberry leaves [7 parts]

or

Bean pods [1 part]
Nettle leaves [1 part]

Birch leaves [2 parts]
Bilberry leaves [6 parts]

Steep 1 tbsp. in ½ cup boiling-hot water. Take ½ cup, 3 times a day.

BOILS, CARBUNCLES

Flax seed powder [10 parts]
Althea root powder [5 parts]

Oat powder [5 parts]
Echinacea powder [1 part]

Use the powder mixture to make a poultice for treatment.

[See "Poultices" under *How to Make and Use Herb Preparations* in Part 1.]

BRONCHITIS, HEALING AND SOOTHING TEAS

Althea leaves [1 part]
High mallow [1 part]

Licorice root [1 part]
Flax seed [2 parts]

Bring 1 tsp. in ½ cup water to a boil. Sweeten with honey; take ½ cup, 2 or 3 times a day, as hot as possible.

℞

Anise
Licorice root
Lance-leaf plantain leaves

Fennel seed
Coltsfoot leaves

Mix in equal parts. Bring 1 tsp. in ½ cup water to a boil. Sweeten with honey or brown sugar; take ½ cup, 3 times a day, as hot as possible.

℞

Mallow leaves and flowers
Mullein leaves and flowers
Coltsfoot leaves

Mix in equal parts. Steep 1 tsp. in ½ cup boiling-hot water. Sweeten with honey; take ½ cup, 3 or 4 times a day, hot.

℞

Mullein	Althea herb
Licorice	Coltsfoot leaves
Althea root	

Mix in equal parts. Steep 1 tsp. in ½ cup boiling-hot water. Take ½ cup hot, sweetened with honey, 3 or 4 times a day.

℞

Elecampane root	Nettle leaves
Thyme	Lungwort

Mix in equal parts. Sweeten with honey, as above.

CARMINATIVES
(*for relief of gas and bloat*)

Balm
Camomile
Peppermint

Mix in equal parts. Steep 1 tsp. in ½ cup boiling-hot water. Take unsweetened, in mouthful doses.

℞

Caraway	Peppermint leaves
German camomile	Anise

Mix in equal parts. Steep 1 tbsp. in ½ cup boiling-hot water. Take ½ cup, once or twice a day.

℞

German camomile	Anise
Balm leaves	Caraway
Fennel seed	

Mix in equal parts. Steep 1 tsp. in ½ cup boiling-hot water. Take ½ to 1 cup a day.

CHEST and LUNG PROBLEMS
(*teas to relieve congestion and inflammation*)

Lance-leaf plantain [1 part]	Lungwort [1 part]
Mullein flowers [1 part]	Speedwell [2 parts]

Steep 1 tsp. in ½ cup boiling-hot water. Take 1 to 1½

cups a day, sweetened with raw sugar or honey, in mouthful doses.

℞

Milfoil [1 part]
Coltsfoot leaves and flowers [1 part]
Lungwort [2 parts]
Nettle leaves [2 parts]
Lance-leaf plantain leaves [4 parts]

Steep 2 level tsp. in ½ cup boiling-hot water. Take 1 to 1½ cups a day, sweetened with 2 tsp. honey per cup, in mouthful doses.

℞

Knotgrass   Hemp nettle
Shave grass   Primrose flower

Boil equal parts of knotgrass and shave grass lightly, then steep equal parts of hemp nettle and primrose flowers in the decoction for 5 minutes. Add 1 tsp. honey per cup. Take 1 to 1½ cups a day, in mouthful doses.

℞

Shave grass
Witch grass
Hemp nettle

Mix in equal parts. Add 1 heaping tsp. to ½ cup cold water. Bring to a boil, boil for 1 minute, then steep for 1 minute and strain. Take 1 to 1½ cups a day, in mouthful doses, sweetened with 2 tsp. honey per cup if desired.

℞

Shave grass [1 part]
Nettle leaves [1 part]
Lance-leaf plantain leaves [2 parts]
Lungwort [2 parts]

Steep 3 heaping tsp. in 1½ cups boiling-hot water. Strain and add 3 tsp. honey. Take 1½ cups in the course of a day, in mouthful doses.

FOR CHEST COLDS

Anise seed [1 part]
Coltsfoot leaves [2 parts]
Lungwort [2 parts]

Steep 2 tsp. in ½ cup boiling-hot water. Add this tea to 1½ cups althea tea which has been prepared by soaking 1 tbsp. althea root, leaves and/or flowers in ½ cup cold water for 8 hours. Take the mixture with honey, in mouthful doses.

FOR LUNG HEMORRHAGE

Shepherd's purse   European mistletoe
Knotgrass   Tormentil root

Mix in equal parts. Steep 1 tsp. in ½ cup boiling-hot water. Take every 4 hours. If condition has reached a serious stage, summon physician without delay.

CHOLAGOGUE

(to treat the gall bladder and increase bile flow)

Milfoil   St. Benedict thistle
Pansy   Alder buckthorn bark

Mix in equal parts. Soak 1 tbsp. in ½ cup cold water for 8 hours, then bring to a boil. Take 1 to 1½ cups a day, in mouthful doses.

COLD COMPRESS FORMULA

[See also "How to Make and Use Herb Preparations" in Part 1.]

Horseweed [2 parts]   Henbane leaves [1 part]
Low mallow leaves [2 parts]   Celandine leaves [1 part]
Wild sage leaves [2 parts]

Boil 1 tbsp. mixture in 1 pt. water for 2 to 3 minutes; let stand until lukewarm, then strain.

COLDS

[See "Chest and Lung Problems" in this section.]

COLIC

Camomile   Fragrant valerian
Balm   Buck bean

Mix in equal parts. Steep 1 tbsp. in 1 cup boiling-hot water for 10 minutes. Drink warm.

FOR COLIC IN INFANTS

Fennel seed [4 parts]   Camomile flowers [2 parts]
Water mint leaves [3 parts]   Fragrant valerian [1 part]

Steep ½ tsp. mixture in 1½ cups boiling-hot water for 5 minutes, then strain. Give in 5 or 6 doses during the day, in warm milk or by itself.

COLIC, A TEA FOR RELIEF

Juniper berries Camomile flowers
Wormwood   Milfoil

Mix in equal parts. Steep 1 tsp. in ½ cup boiling-hot water. Take ½ cup, unsweetened.

CONSTIPATION, A GOOD LAXATIVE

Take a drink consisting of 2 parts tomato juice and 1 part of sauerkraut juice.

A GOOD LAXATIVE TEA

Borage leaves and flowers [2 parts]
Dandelion [1 part]
Sticklewort [1 part]
Witch grass [1 part]

Steep 1 tbsp. in 1½ cups boiling-hot water. Take unsweetened, in mouthful doses.

AN HERBAL ENEMA FOR PERSISTENT CONSTIPATION

European centaury [2 oz.]
Dandelion [2 oz.]
Witch grass [2 oz.]

Mix in equal parts. Bring the mixture to a boil, in a qt. of water, then let steep until lukewarm. Use in the evening.

ARNOLD EHRET'S HERBAL INTESTINAL BROOM

Note: All "ground" ingredients should be about as coarse as loose tea, the "powdered" ones about as fine as powdered sugar.

Ground senna leaves [6 parts]
Ground buckthorn bark [3 parts]
Ground psyllium seed husks [1 part]
Powdered sassafras root bark [1/10th part]
Ground dark anise seed [½ part]
Ground buchu leaves [1/10 part]
Ground blonde psyllium seed [½ part]
Powdered Irish moss [1/8th part]
Granulated agar-agar [1/8 part]
Ground dark fennel seed [½ part]

Mix the first three ingredients thoroughly. Then combine the remaining seven real well, and add this to the mixure. If you have a blender, it makes an ideal mixer for preparing the formula. Use low speed.

The "Intestinal Broom" is easy to use. Usually a small amount, about the quantity that fits on half a teaspoon, or less, swallowed with a glassful of water, is sufficient for adults. It may be increased or decreased according to your own reaction.

It may also be used sprinkled over salads, or brewed as a tea: ½ tsp. to a cup of boiling water. Remove from heat and allow to steep for 10 or 15 minutes. Strain and enjoy. It has a fascinating flavor.

MORE GOOD LAXATIVE TEAS

Hedge hyssop leaves
Milfoil

American senna leaves
Caraway

Mix equal parts. Add 1 tsp. to ½ cup simmering water, bring to a boil, and let cool. Take ½ cup, morning and evening.

℞

Alder buckthorn bark
German camomile

Garlic
Milfoil

Mix in equal parts. Steep 1 tbsp. in ½ cup boiling-hot water for 10 minutes. Take ½ cup before eating in the morning. This mixture is a mild laxative.

Alder buckthorn bark   Pansy
American senna leaves   Milfoil

Mix in equal parts. Soak 1 tbsp. in ½ cup cold water for 3 hours, then bring quickly to a boil. Take ½ cup, morning and evening.

℞

Angelica
Alder buckthorn bark

Mix in equal parts. Take ½ to 1 cup a day, unsweetened, in mouthful doses.

COUGHS, A NATURAL COUGH SYRUP

Put 6 cut-up white onions in a double boiler and add ½ cup honey. Cook slowly over low heat for 2 hours and strain. Take at regular intervals, preferably warm.

TO RELIEVE BRONCHIAL COUGH

Licorice [16 parts]   Wild cherry bark [8 parts]
Lungwort [10 parts]   Oswego tea [5 parts]
Spotted cranebill [8 parts]   Irish moss [4 parts]
Aniseed [8 parts]   Lobelia [3 parts]

Boil 1½ tsp. mixture slowly in 2 cups water, in a covered pot, for 2 to 3 minutes; then let stand for 10 minutes. Strain and take 1 cup, morning and evening. Sweeten with honey or raw sugar if desired.

FOR BRONCHIAL COUGH IN SMALL CHILDREN

Coltsfoot [2 parts]
Horehound [2 parts]
Cherry bark [1 part]

Simmer 5 tbsp. mixture in 2½ cups water for 20 minutes and strain. Add honey to sweeten. The dose is from 1 to 4 tbsp. four times a day, depending on age.

FOR RELIEF OF COUGHS

Coltsfoot leaves and flowers
Lungwort

Mullein
Lance-leaf plantain

Mix in equal parts. Steep 2 tsp. in ½ cup boiling-hot water. Take 1½ cups a day, warm, with honey, in mouthful doses.

℞

Lance-leaf plantain [2 parts]
Coltsfoot [2 parts]
Knotgrass [3 parts]

Steep 1 tsp. in ½ cup boiling-hot water. Sweeten with honey. Take 1 to 1½ cups a day, in mouthful doses.

℞

Licorice root
Coltsfoot

Althea root
Lance-leaf plantain

Mix in equal parts. Steep 1 tsp. in ½ cup boiling-hot water. Take 1 to 1½ cups a day, sweetened with honey, in mouthful doses.

℞

Witch grass [12 parts]
Aniseed [12 parts]
Licorice [18 parts]
Elecampane root [11 parts]
Lungwort herb [10 parts]

Thyme leaves [8 parts]
Murillo bark [4 parts]
Irish moss [4 parts]
Lobelia herb [1 part]

Boil 2 tsp. mixture in 3 cups water for 2 to 3 minutes; let stand for 10 minutes and strain. Take 1 cup, morning, noon, and night.

FOR COUGHS, BRONCHITIS, AND OTHER RESPIRATORY PROBLEMS

Sage [1 part]
Althea root [1 part]

Lungwort [2 parts]
Milfoil [4 parts]

Lance-leaf plantain leaves [2 parts]

Steep 1 tsp. in ½ cup boiling-hot water. Take 1½ to 2 cups a day, sweetened with 2 tsp. honey per cup; take warm, in mouthful doses.

Oil of broom pine [80 parts] Camphor [5 parts]
Oil of eucalyptus [5 parts]   Oil of cloves [2 parts]
Oil of pine needles [5 parts]

Mix and shake until the camphor is dissolved. Add 1
tsp. mixture to slowly boiling water and inhale the vapors,
or let evaporate in patient's room.

℞

Sage [5 parts]   Althea root [15 parts]
Anise [8 parts]   Elder flowers [15 parts]
Primrose [10 parts]   Thyme [15 parts]

Soak 1 tbsp. in ½ cup cold water for 3 hours, then bring
to a boil and steep 10 minutes. Take ½ cup a day, in
tablespoon doses.

℞

Elecampane root   Nettle leaves
Thyme   Lungwort

Mix in equal parts. Steep 10 minutes in boiling-hot water.
Strain. Sweeten with honey.

℞

Mother of thyme   Coltsfoot
Mouse ear   Licorice root

Mix in equal parts. Steep 2 tbsp. mixture in 3 cups
boiling-hot water for 30 minutes, covered. Strain and
sweeten with honey. Take 1 to 4 tbsp. 4 times a day
between meals, dose depending on age.

℞

Sundew   Lance-leaf plantain
Elder flowers   Pansy flowers

Mix in equal parts. Steep 1 tsp. in ½ cup boiling-hot
water. Take ½ to 1 cup daily, sweetened with honey, in
mouthful doses.

℞

Sundew   Sage
Horehound   Garden violet flowers
Black currant leaves

Preparation and dosage same as preceding formula.

℞

Sundew [1 part]   Primrose flowers [3 parts]
Fennel [1 part]   Thyme [5 parts]

Steep 1 tsp. in ½ cup boiling-hot water for 3 to 5 minutes, then add 1 tsp. honey. Take 1 to 1½ cups a day, in mouthful doses.

℞

Licorice root [2 parts]   Lance-leaf plantain [2 parts]
Sundew leaves [2 parts]   Mother of thyme [5 parts]

Steep 1 tsp. in ½ cup boiling-hot water. Take 1 cup a day, sweetened with honey, in mouthful doses. Good for children.

℞

European mistletoe
Sage

Soak 2 tsp. mistletoe in ½ cup cold water for 6 to 8 hours. Then steep 2 tsp. sage in 1 cup boiling-hot water, strain, and let cool to drinking temperature. Add to mistletoe tea. Take the mixed tea, unsweetened, in mouthful doses as needed.

CRAMPS AND SPASMS, TO RELIEVE

Silverweed
Balm leaves
Camomile flowers

Mix in equal parts. Steep 1 tsp. in ½ cup boiling-hot water. Take 1 to 1½ cups a day, sweetened with honey, in mouthful doses.

CYSTITIS

[See "Urinary Problems" in this section.]

DEBILITY, TO IMPROVE GENERAL VITALITY

Balm
St. Johnswort

Mix in equal parts. Steep 1 tsp. in ½ cup boiling-hot water. Take 1 to 1½ cups a day, sweetened with honey, in mouthful doses. Take daily doses for an extended period.

DIABETES, TEA TO IMPROVE SUGAR TOLERANCE

Pumpkin seeds, peeled
Fragrant valerian root
Bilberry leaves

Mix in equal parts. Steep 1 tbsp. in 1 cup boiling-hot water. Take 1 cup in the course of a day, unsweetened, in mouthful doses.

℞

Mix bilberry leaves in equal parts with 1 or 2 of the following:

Bean pods   European centaury
Nettle   Dandelion
Milfoil   Blackberry leaves

Parboil 1 tbsp. in ½ cup water for 10 minutes. Take 1 to 1½ cups a day, unsweetened, in mouthful doses, but not within an hour of meals (before or after).

DIARRHEA, TEAS TO CONTROL IT

Pomegranate [8 parts]   Black birch bark [4 parts]
Spotted cranebill [4 parts] Ginger [3 parts]
Colombo root [4 parts]   Wild sage [3 parts]
White oak bark [4 parts]

Boil 1½ tsp. mixture in 2 cups water for 2 to 3 minutes, covered; let stand for 10 minutes and strain. Take 1 cup, morning and evening. Sweeten with honey if desired.

℞

Milfoil herb   German camomile flowers
Pansy herb   American senna leaves
St. Benedict thistle   Peppermint leaves

Mix in equal parts. Steep 1 tbsp. in ½ cup boiling-hot water for 10 minutes. Take warm.

℞

Oak bark
Horse chestnut bark

Mix in equal parts. Boil 2 tsp. in ½ cup water for a short time. Take unsweetened, in mouthful doses.

℞

Tormentil root
European mistletoe
Shave grass

Boil 1 tsp. tormentil root briefly in ½ cup water and steep for 1 to 2 minutes. In this tea, parboil 1 tsp. each of the other plants.

DIURETIC, TEAS TO IMPROVE THE EXCRETION OF FLUIDS

Asparagus root	Celery root
Fennel root	Parsley root

Mix in equal parts. Steep 1 tsp. in ½ cup boiling-hot water. Take ½ to 1 cup a day, unsweetened, in mouthful doses.

℞

Lovage root	Licorice root
Restharrow root	Juniper berries (crushed)

Mix in equal parts. Steep 1 tsp. in ½ cup boiling-hot water. Daily dose should be medically determined.

DOUCHES, HERBAL VAGINAL DOUCHES FOR FEMININE HYGIENE

Red oak bark [4 parts]	Wild sage [1 part]
Murillo bark* [2 parts]	Lance-leaf plantain [1 part]
Black birch leaves [1 part]	Horseweed [1 part]

Boil ½ tsp. mixture in 1 qt. water for 5 minutes; let stand until lukewarm and strain. Use to soothe and heal, and also for abnormal discharges.

* Bark of Quillai (*Quillaja saponaria*), an evergreen tree

found in Chile. The inner bark is used for colds and fevers and as a soap substitute.

℞

| Comfrey | Spearmint |
| Peppermint | Wax myrtle |

Mix leaves in equal parts. Steep ½ cup mixture in 2 cups boiling-hot water for 15 to 20 minutes and strain. Add warm water to make up the full amount needed.

℞

Rosemary
Wax myrtle

Mix leaves in equal parts, add a pinch of alum. Steep 4 tbsp. mixture in 2 cups boiling-hot water for 10 minutes and strain. Add warm water to make up the full amount needed.

℞

Camomile
Sage
Wintergreen

Mix in equal parts. Steep ½ cup mixture in 2 cups boiling-hot water for 10 to 20 minutes and strain. Add warm water to make up the full amount needed.

℞

Alum [1 part]	Rosemary [4 parts]
Myrrh [2 parts]	Wax myrtle leaves [4 parts]
Milfoil [4 parts]	

Bring ⅓ cup mixture to a boil in 2 cups water; simmer for 10 minutes and strain. Add warm water to make up the full amount needed.

DROPSY

Birch leaves [1 part]	Nettle leaves [1 part]
Rosemary [1 part]	Shave grass [2 parts]
Brier hips [1 part]	Juniper berries [2 parts]

Steep 1 tsp. in ½ cup boiling-hot water. Take ⅓ to 1 cup a day, sweetened with honey, in mouthful doses.

DYSENTERY, A TEA FOR RELIEF

Black pepper [1 part]
Coriander [2 parts]
Sweet flag root (powdered) [30 parts]

Boil 2 oz. of the mixture in 1 pt. water until 1 cup liquid remains. Strain immediately. Take 1 tsp. 3 times a day.

EPILEPSY

European mistletoe
Peony root
Orange flowers

Soak 1 tbsp. mistletoe leaves and 1 tsp. berries in ½ cup cold water for 6 to 8 hours. Steep 1 tsp. each of peony root and orange flowers in 1 cup boiling-hot water. When ready to drink, mix the two teas. Administer in mouthful doses.

ERYSIPELAS, HERBAL DRESSINGS

Crush raw cranberries and add buttermilk to produce a paste. Put directly on the skin and cover with cloth to keep it on.

℞

Witch hazel powder [50 parts]
Wild indigo powder [5 parts]
Myrrh powder [2 parts]
Boric acid powder [20 parts]
Echinacea powder [2 parts]

Blend thoroughly. Use as a dusting powder, particularly where inflammation becomes septic.

FEET, A TEA TO REDUCE SWELLING

Oak bark
Wormwood
Shave grass

Mix in equal parts. Steep 1 tbsp. in ½ cup boiling-hot water. Take in tablespoon doses.

[See also "The Foot Bath" in Part 1.]

FEVER, TEA TO COMFORT AND REDUCE THE FEVER

Sallow bark
Yellow gentian root

Mix in equal parts. Steep 1 tsp. in ½ cup boiling-hot water for at least 5 minutes. Take ½ to 1 cup, in mouthful doses, as needed.

GALACTAGOGUE, A TEA FOR NURSING MOTHERS

Anise seed
Dill seed
Sweet marjoram

Mix in equal parts. Steep 1 tsp. in ½ cup boiling-hot water. Take 1 to 1½ cups a day, sweetened with honey, in mouthful doses.

On the subject of successful nursing: Antiseptics should not be used for either mother's breast or for baby's mouth. Ordinary cleanliness is all that is essential. It has been conclusively proven that baby consumes two-thirds of his entire nursing during the first five minutes. It is then that he suckles hard and quickly. It is then also that he takes in considerable quantities of air which often cause distress.

When baby has nursed four or five minutes he should be taken from the breast and placed over mother's shoulder, abdomen down, then gently patted for a few moments in order that he may bring up whatever gas is within. This should be repeated two or three times during a twenty-minute nursing.

GALL BLADDER PROBLEMS

Alder buckthorn bark [1 part]
Restharrow root [5 parts]
Yellow gentian root [5 parts]
Peppermint leaves [10 parts]

Steep 1 tsp. in ½ cup boiling-hot water. Take 1 to 1½ cups a day, in mouthful doses.

[See also "Cholagogue" in this section.]

GALL STONES, TEA TO ASSIST IN PASSING

St. Benedict thistle   Pansy
Mallow flowers   Alder buckthorn bark
Calendula   Milfoil

Steep 1 to 2 tsp. in ½ cup boiling-hot water. Take ½ to 1½ cups a day.

[See also "Gravel and Stones" in this section.]

GAS AND BLOAT

[See "Carminatives" in this section.]

GASTROINTESTINAL PROBLEMS

Juniper berries
Wormwood
Camomile

Mix in equal parts. Steep 1 tsp. in ½ cup boiling-hot water. Take ½ to 1 cup a day, in mouthful doses.

TO STRENGTHEN THE GASTROINTESTINAL SYSTEM

Peppermint leaves [2 parts]
Lavender flowers [4 parts]
Thyme [5 parts]

Steep 1 tsp. in ½ cup boiling-hot water for 3 to 5 minutes. Take 1 to 1½ cups a day, in mouthful doses.

GOUT AND RHEUMATISM, TEAS FOR RELIEF

Sallow bark
Birch leaves

Mix in equal parts. Steep 1 tsp. in ½ cup boiling-hot water for 5 minutes. Take 1 to 1½ cups a day, in mouthful doses, as needed. Sweeten with honey if desired.

℞

Birch leaves
Alder buckthorn bark
Nettle leaves

Mix in equal parts. Steep 1 tsp. in ½ cup boiling-hot water. Take ½ to 1½ cups a day, sweetened with honey, in mouthful doses.

GRAVEL AND STONES, A TEA TO HELP PASS THEM

Birch leaves   Speedwell
Witch grass   Chicory

Mix in equal parts. Steep 1 tsp. in ½ cup boiling-hot water. Take 1 to 1½ cups a day, unsweetened, in mouthful doses.

HAIR, LOSS OF

(a scalp massage mixture)

Nettle leaves [1 part]
Onion [1 part]
70% alcohol [100 parts]

Soak the leaves and onion in the alcohol for several days. Use to massage the scalp daily.

HALLUCINOGENS

These are not generally used as mixtures. See the glossary in Part 1 for list of herbs with this property.

HEART, TEAS FOR A NERVOUS HEART

Fragrant valerian root   Camomile
Lavender flowers   Fennel

Mix in equal parts. Steep 2 tsp. in ½ cup boiling-hot water. Take 1 to 1½ cups a day, in mouthful doses.

℞

Arnica flowers [1 part]   Borage herbs and flowers [1 part]
Rue leaves [2 parts]   Great burnet root [3 parts]
Balm leaves [3 parts]

Steep 1 tsp. in ½ cup boiling-hot water. Take 1 cup a day in mouthful doses.

HEMORRHOIDS, A HEALING HERBAL ENEMA

Willow bark [8 parts]   Pilewort [3 parts]
Red oak bark [8 parts]   Horseweed [3 parts]
Wild sage leaves [3 parts]

Boil 1½ tsp. mixture slowly in 1 pt. water. Let stand until cold, then strain. Use as a rectal enema before going to bed.

TWO TEA MIXTURES TO RELIEVE HEMORRHOIDS INTERNALLY

Alder buckthorn bark   Licorice root
Milfoil   Fennel seed

Mix in equal parts. Steep 1 tbsp. in ½ cup boiling-hot water for 10 minutes. Drink hot.

℞

Balm [3 parts]   Milfoil [3 parts]
Blackthorn flowers [3 parts] Arnica flowers [5 parts]
            Alder buckthorn bark [15 parts]

Soak 1 tbsp. of mixture in ½ cup cold water for 6 hours, then bring to a boil and simmer for 10 minutes. Take 1 cup a day.

HOARSENESS

[See "Laryngitis and Hoarseness" in this section.]

INFLUENZA, A REMEDY TEA MIXTURE

Juniper berries   Black elder flowers
Coltsfoot   Sallow bark
Lance-leaf plantain

Mix in equal parts. Steep 1 tsp. in ½ cup boiling-hot water. Take ½ to 1 cup a day, sweetened with honey, in mouthful doses.

INSOMNIA, TEAS TO HELP YOU SLEEP

Fragrant valerian [1 part]   Lavender flowers [5 parts]
St. Johnswort [2 parts]   Primrose flowers [10 parts]
Hops [3 parts]

Steep 1½ tsp. in ½ cup boiling-hot water for 10 minutes. When cool enough to drink, add 1 tsp. honey. Take before going to bed.

℞

Hops [3 parts]
Fragrant valerian root [2 parts]

Steep 1 tsp. in ½ cup boiling-hot water. Take ½ to 1 cup a day, unsweetened, in mouthful doses. Do not take for more than 2 or 3 weeks without interruption.

℞

Lavender flowers   St. Johnswort
Primrose flowers   Fragrant valerian root

Mix in equal parts. Steep 1 heaping tsp. in ½ cup boiling-hot water. Take shortly before going to bed, a mouthful at a time.

FOR INSOMNIA DUE TO OVEREXHAUSTION OR NEURASTHENIA

Balm
Hops
Fragrant valerian root

Mix in equal parts. Steep 1 tsp. in ½ cup boiling-hot water.

℞

This mixture is especially good for nervous insomnia;

Dill seed [2 parts]   Camomile [1 part]
Anise seed [2 parts]   Hops [1 part]

Steep 1 tsp. in ½ cup boiling-hot water. When lukewarm, add 1 tsp. honey. Sip just before retiring.

℞

Dill seed
Fennel seed
Peppermint leaves

Mix in equal parts. Steep 1 tsp. in ½ cup boiling-hot water. Take ½ cup warm, sweetened with raw sugar or honey, before going to bed.

℞

Fragrant valerian	Lavender
Balm	Milfoil

Mix in equal parts. Steep 1 to 2 tsp. in ½ cup boiling-hot water for a short time. Take warm.

KIDNEY PROBLEMS

[See also "Gravel and Stones" in this section.]

Rhubarb root [1 part]
Restharrow [1 part]
Sticklewort [2 parts]

Steep 1½ tsp. in ½ cup boiling-hot water. Take ½ cup before breakfast, and 1 cup more during the rest of the day.

℞

This tea is helpful when the kidneys show signs of bleeding:

Shepherd's purse
Shave grass

Mix in equal parts. Steep 1 tsp. in ½ cup boiling-hot water. Take unsweetened.

℞

Bearberry leaves [8 parts]	Pipsissewa herb [3 parts]
Witch grass [6 parts]	Juniper berries [3 parts]
Buchu [5 parts]	Celery seed [1 part]
Button snakeroot [3 parts]	Lovage root [1 part]

Boil 1½ tsp. mixture in 2 cups water for 2 to 3 minutes; let stand for 10 minutes and strain. Take 1 cup, morning and evening. Sweeten if desired.

LARYNGITIS AND HOARSENESS

Mallow flowers	Mullein
Althea root	Coltsfoot
Licorice root	Pimpernel

Mix in equal parts. Steep 1 tsp. in ½ cup boiling-hot water; sweeten with honey and take hot.

or

Soak 1 tsp. in ½ cup of cold water for 6 hours, then bring to a boil and steep for 5 minutes. Take hot.

℞

Burnet saxifrage root [6 parts] Elecampane root [2 parts]
Licorice [6 parts] Althea root [2 parts]
Fennel seed [2 parts] Wild sage [2 parts]

Boil 1 tsp. mixture in 3 cups water for 2 to 3 minutes; let stand for 10 minutes and strain. Take 1 cup, morning, noon, and night.

LAXATIVES

[See "Constipation" in this section.]

LEUCORRHEA

Shepherd's purse
Blind nettle

Mix in equal parts. Steep 1 tsp. in ½ cup boiling-hot water. Take 1 to 1½ cups a day, unsweetened, in mouthful doses.

LINIMENT

Oil of camphor [7 parts] Oil of eucalyptus [3 parts]
Oil of cloves [2 parts] Oil of origanum [3 parts]
Oil of wintergreen [3 parts]

Mix thoroughly. Use for soreness, swelling, pain, stiffness, colds, etc. Shake the bottle well before using each time.

LIVER PROBLEMS

Chicory flowers [1 part] Dandelion root [2 parts]
Woodruff [1 part] Speedwell [2 parts]

Steep 1 tsp. in ½ cup boiling-hot water. Take 1 cup a day, unsweetened, in mouthful doses.

℞

Alder buckthorn bark [1 part] Yellow gentian root [5 parts]
Restharrow root [5 parts] Peppermint leaves [10 parts]

Steep 1 tsp. in ½ cup of boiling-hot water. Take 1 to 1½ cups a day, in mouthful doses.

℞

Alder buckthorn bark [2 parts]   Rosemary flowers [3 parts]
Woodruff [2 parts]   Celandine [6 parts]

Steep 2 tsp. in ½ cup boiling-hot water. Take ½ cup before breakfast and ½ cup before going to bed, a mouthful at a time.

℞

Sticklewort
Cleavers
Woodruff

Mix in equal parts. Steep 1 tsp. in ½ cup boiling-hot water. Take 1½ cups a day.

MEASLES

Safflower [4 parts]   Licorice [2 parts]
Balm [4 parts]   Elder blossoms [2 parts]
            Wild violet leaves [1 part]

Boil 1⅓ tsp. mixture in 3 cups of water for 2 to 3 minutes, covered; let stand for 10 minutes and strain. Take 1 cup morning, noon, and night. Sweeten if desired.

MENSTRUAL PROBLEMS

Blind nettle
Lady's mantle
Milfoil

Mix in equal parts. Steep 1 tsp. in ½ cup boiling-hot water. Take 1 to 1½ cups a day, unsweetened, in mouthful doses.

℞

Rosemary [1 part]   Shepherd's purse [2 parts]
Shave grass [1 part]   Milfoil [2 parts]

Add 1 tbsp. to ½ cup cold water. Bring to boil and steep briefly. Take ½ to 1½ cups a day, by medical direction.

℞

Goldthread [8 parts]   Rosemary leaves [2 parts]
Tansy [8 parts]   Rue herb [2 parts]
Fragrant valerian root [4 parts]

Boil 1½ tsp. mixture slowly in 2 cups of water, covered,
for 2 to 3 minutes. Let stand for 10 minutes and strain.
Take 1 cup morning and night. Sweeten if desired.

℞

St. Johnswort
European mistletoe

Mix in equal parts. Parboil 1 tsp. in ½ cup of water, then
steep covered for 5 minutes. Take warm in mouthful
doses.

℞

Mexican damiana leaves [4 parts]
Quaking aspen bark [3 parts] Cassia bark [3 parts]
Birthroot [3 parts]   Squaw vine [2 parts]
Cramp bark [3 parts]   Blazing star root [2 parts]

Boil 1 tsp. mixture in 2 cups water for 2 to 3 minutes; let
stand for 10 minutes and strain. Take 1 cup morning and
evening. Sweeten if desired.

METABOLISM, TO STIMULATE

Juniper berries
Milfoil
Nettle

or

Juniper berries
Birch leaves
Camomile

Mix in equal parts. Steep 1 tsp. in ½ cup boiling-hot
water. Take ½ to 1 cup a day, sweeten with honey, in
mouthful doses.

℞

Alder buckthorn bark [2 parts]
Licorice root [2 parts]
Dandelion root and leaves [3 parts]
Pansy leaves [3 parts]

Soak 1 tbsp. in ½ qt. cold water for 3 hours. Bring to
boil and steep for 15 minutes. Take in tablespoon doses.

MOUTHWASH OR GARGLE

Wild sage leaves [10 parts] Goldthread root [2 parts]
Marsh rosemary [10 parts] Rhatany root [2 parts]
Spotted cranebill root Cassia bark [2 parts]
   [6 parts] Cloves [2 parts]
Red oak bark [6 parts]

Boil 4 tsp. mixture in 1 pt. water for 5 minutes; let stand
for 10 minutes and strain. Add 1 tbsp. table salt. For inflammation and swelling, use every 2 to 3 hours. Dilute
with water if too astringent.

NERVES, TO CALM

Hops Balm leaves
Lavender flowers Primrose

Mix in equal parts. Steep 1 tsp. in ½ cup boiling-hot
water. Take ½ to 1 cup a day, unsweetened, in mouthful
doses, as needed.

℞

Camomile [1 part] Fragrant valerian root
Lavender flowers [1 part]   [2 parts]
Peppermint leaves [1 part] Fennel seed [3 parts]
   Milfoil [3 parts]

Steep 1 tsp. in ½ cup boiling-hot water. Take ½ cup
warm a day.

℞

Fragrant valerian root [3 parts]
Peppermint leaves [3 parts]
Buck bean [4 parts]

Steep 1 tsp. in ½ cup boiling-hot water. Take ½ to 1 cup
a day.

℞

Fragrant valerian Balm
Hops Camomile
Lavender flowers Anise

Mix in equal parts. Steep 1 tbsp. in ½ cup boiling-hot
water. Take 1 cup a day.

NIGHTMARE, PREVENTION OF

Anise
Fragrant valerian root

Mix in equal parts. Simmer 1 tsp. mixture in ½ cup water for 15 minutes; let cool and strain. Add enough water to restore the volume lost in simmering. Take before going to bed.

OBESITY

Dandelion root and leaves [7 parts]
Peppermint leaves [7 parts]
Alder buckthorn bark [15 parts]
American senna leaves [15 parts]

Steep 1 tbsp. in 1 cup boiling-hot water for 30 minutes. Take ½ cup several times a day. Medical supervision suggested.

PERSPIRATION, TO PREVENT
(*antihydrotic*)

Sage leaves
Hyssop leaves
Walnut (rind of the fruit)

Mix in equal parts. Steep 2 tbsp. in ½ cup boiling-hot water for 10 minutes. Take ½ cup 2 hours before going to bed.

FOR NIGHT SWEATS

Wild sage leaves [12 parts]   Boneset [2 parts]
Buck bean [4 parts]   Rosemary leaves [2 parts]

Steep 1 tsp. mixture in 1 cup boiling-hot water for 5 minutes, then strain. Take before going to bed.

PERSPIRATION, TO PROMOTE
(*diaphoretic*)

Linden flowers   Mullein flowers
Elder flowers   Camomile

Mix in equal parts. Steep 1 to 2 tsp. in ½ cup boiling-hot water. Take hot.

℞

Elder flowers [4 parts]	Black birch leaves [2 parts]
Boneset [2 parts]	Water mint [2 parts]

Steep ½ tsp. mixture in 2 cups boiling-hot water for 3 to 5 minutes and strain. Drink hot before going to bed. For children amounts may be decreased and sweetened.

PILES

[See "Hemorrhoids" in this section.]

PLEURISY

Pleurisy root [4 parts]	Elder flowers [2 parts]
Spotted cranebill [3 parts]	Boneset [2 parts]
Licorice [3 parts]	Irish moss [1 part]

Boil ¾ tsp. mixture slowly in 3 cups water, covered; let stand for 10 minutes, and strain. Take 1 cup, morning, noon, and night. Sweeten if desired.

℞

Anise seed [2 parts]
Camomile flowers [3 parts]
Nettle [5 parts]
Coltsfoot leaves and flowers [5 parts]

Steep 4 tsp. in 1½ cups boiling-hot water. Take 1½ cups a day sweetened with honey, warm, in mouthful doses.

POULTICE, FORMULA FOR A

Flax seed powder [8 parts]
Slippery elm bark powder [4 parts]
Fenugreek seed powder [4 parts]

Mix 1 lb. mixture with hot water or milk to make a thick, smooth paste. Apply to inflammations, swellings, painful areas, etc.

PREGNANT WOMEN

*(prevents nausea, miscarriage, reduces labor pains
and increases milk production in)*

Cinnamon [1 part]   Milfoil [5 parts]
Blackberry leaves [5 parts] Raspberry leaves [10 parts]

Steep 1 tsp. in ½ cup boiling water. Take ½ to 1 cup a day, in mouthful doses.

RHEUMATISM

Take a combination of cucumber juice, carrot juice, and beet juice for rheumatic problems resulting from the retention of uric acid in the body.

SKIN TROUBLES, ACNE, ECZEMA, BAD COMPLEXION

Mix 2 oz. each of beet juice, celery juice and tomato juice. Take 2 or 3 times a day. As a general blood purifier, take several times a week.

℞

Witch grass root   Ground ivy
Elecampane root   Elder leaves and flowers
Juniper berries

Mix in equal parts. Steep in 1 tsp. in ½ cup boiling-hot water. Take ½ to 1 cup a day, unsweetened in mouthful doses. Take daily over an extended period.

℞

Black elder leaves   English walnut leaves [1 part]
  [1 part]   Speedwell [2 parts]
Pansy [1 part]

Steep 1 tsp. in ½ cup boiling water. Take 1 to 1½ cups a day, unsweetened in mouthful doses.

STIMULANTS, BEVERAGE TEAS

Blackberry leaves [1 part] Primrose [1 part]
Blackthorn leaves [1 part] Raspberry leaves [1 part]
Wild strawberry leaves [2 parts]

Steep 1 tsp. in ½ cup hot water for 5 to 10 minutes. Sweeten to taste, if desired.

℞

Juniper berries [1 part]	Milfoil [6 parts]
Woodruff [2 parts]	Primrose [8 parts]
Blackberry leaves [4 parts]	Raspberry leaves [10 parts]

Same as the preceding directions.

℞

Juniper berries (dried) [1 part]
Blackberry leaves [2 parts]
Wild strawberry leaves [5 parts]
Raspberry leaves [10 parts]

Same as the preceding directions.

℞

Woodruff	Thyme
Wild strawberry leaves	Blackberry leaves
Raspberry leaves	

Mix in equal parts. Steep 1 heaping tsp. in ½ cup boiling-hot water. Take as desired.

STOMACH PROBLEMS, TEAS TO AID DIGESTION, REDUCE FEVER AND COUNTERACT CRAMPS

A STOMACH STIMULANT

Sweet flag root [1 part]	Wormwood [1 part]
Milfoil [1 part]	European centaury [2 parts]

Steep 1 tsp. in ½ cup boiling-hot water. Take ½ cup, 30 to 60 minutes before eating.

TO CALM THE STOMACH

Hops [3 parts]	European centaury [1 part]
Balm leaves [1 part]	Camomile flowers [1 part]

Steep 1 tsp. in ½ cup boiling-hot water. Take ½ to 1 cup a day, unsweetened, in mouthful doses as needed.

FOR A WEAK STOMACH

Sweet flag root
Wormwood

Mix in equal parts. Steep 1 heaping tsp. in 1 cup boiling-hot water. Take in the course of a day.

FOR STOMACH ULCERS

Calendula flowers   Nettle
Speedwell   Oak bark
Celandine

Mix in equal parts. Steep 2 tsp. in 1 cup boiling-hot water. Take 1 cup a day, unsweetened, in mouthful doses.

℞

Comfrey [2 parts]
Calendula [1 part]
Knotgrass [1 part]

Steep 1 tsp. in ½ cup boiling-hot water. Take 1½ to 2 cups a day, unsweetened, in mouthful doses.

TO STRENGTHEN THE STOMACH

Angelica
Wormwood or yellow gentian

Mix in equal parts. Steep 1 tsp. in ½ cup boiling-hot water. Take 1 to 1½ cups a day.

℞

European centaury   Sweet flag
Yellow gentian root   Camomile

Mix in equal parts. Steep 1 tsp. in ½ cup boiling-hot water. Take 1 to 1½ cups a day, in mouthful doses.
Mix buck bean in equal parts with sage, European centaury, or wormwood. Steep 1 tsp. in ½ cup boiling-hot water. Take 1 to 1½ cups a day, unsweetened, in mouthful doses.

℞

Anise seed	Caraway seed
Dill seed	Peppermint leaves (dried)
Fennel seed	

Crush the 4 varieties of seeds together and mix in equal parts with the peppermint. Steep 1 tsp. of the mixture in ½ cup boiling-hot water. Take ½ cup, 30 minutes before eating; or take at mealtime, in mouthful doses.

TONIC

(teas that provide a good tonic any time)

Arnica	Buck bean
Balm	Imperial masterwort

Mix in equal parts. Steep 1 tsp. in 1 cup boiling-hot water. Take ½ cup, twice a day.

℞

Yellow gentian	Colombo root
Camomile herb	Quaking aspen bark
Peruvian bark	

Mix in equal parts. Steep 5 tbsp. mixture in 1 qt. boiling-hot water for 2 hours, covered; then strain. Take 3 to 4 tbsp. 30 minutes before each meal and before going to bed.

℞

Woodruff	Blackberry leaves
Thyme	Raspberry leaves
Wild strawberry leaves	

Mix in equal parts. Steep 1 heaping tsp. in ½ cup boiling-hot water. Take as desired.

SALAD FOR A SPRING TONIC

Mix the fresh, young leaves of:

Brooklime	Nettle
Watercress	Ground ivy
Black elder	Dandelion

TONSILS

Tea for inflamed tonsils and mucous membranes:

Mallow leaves
Mullein
Black elder leaves

Use equal amounts. Soak mallow leaves in cold water for 8 hours. Steep the others in boiling-hot water. Mix the two teas and use as a gargle.

URINARY PROBLEMS

(teas to help urination and to soothe burning or painful urination)

Rowan berries
Club moss
Barberry bark

Mix in equal parts. Steep 1 tsp. in ½ cup boiling-hot water for 10 minutes. Take ½ to 1 cup a day, unsweetened or sweetened with honey, in mouthful doses.

℞

Juniper berries [1 part]   Shave grass [1 part]
Parsley root [1 part]   Restharrow root [2 parts]

Steep 1 tsp. in ½ cup boiling-hot water. Take 1½ cups a day.

℞

Yellow toadflax
Sage
Shave grass

Mix in equal parts. Steep 1 to 1½ tsp. in ½ cup boiling-hot water. Take 1½ cups a day.

CYSTITIS

Lovage root [1 part]
Parsley seed [1 part]
Bearberry leaves [2 parts]

Bring 1½ tsp. in 1 cup water quickly to a boil. Take ½ cup, twice a day.

VARICOSE VEINS
(*an herbal wash that relieves*)

Sweet flag root
Nettle leaves

Horse chestnut leaves and fruit
Thyme leaves

Mix in equal parts. Add 3 tbsp. to 1 qt. cold water, bring to a boil. Add ½ tbsp. salt and use to bathe the legs.

EAT, DRINK,
AND BE HEALTHY

Next to water and air, food is the most important requirement for the maintenance of human life. Unlike plants, we cannot use the energy of the sun to combine simple constituents from the air and soil into the complex substances that make up living matter. We must rely on food to supply us with the nutrients we need: proteins, vitamins, minerals, fats, and carbohydrates. Good health requires that all these be provided in sufficient quantities and in proper proportions. Many authorities attribute such "modern" diseases as high blood pressure, arteriosclerosis, ulcers, and heart disease—which are practically epidemic in the United States—at least partially to dietary abuse: eating too much of an unbalanced diet of overprocessed foods. There is more than a little truth in the saying "You are what you eat."

The vegetable world has much to offer for practically every dietary requirement. This section presents an overview of the nutritive potential (and limitations) of many common and some uncommon food plants. Nutritional data are sadly lacking for most wild edible plants, but books by Euell Gibbons, Alan Hall, Bradford Angier, and others contain much practical information on their uses (see the Bibliography). Data have been published for most of the plants named in this section, but it is important to remember that these are only averages. The amount of a given nutrient in a given plant depends on the conditions under which the plant grew, as well as on methods and time of storage and preparation.

The lists of plants following the nutrient descriptions are of two kinds: quantitative (the first list where two appear) and alphabetical. The quantitative list presents plants and plant products containing significant amounts of the nutrient involved, in approximate order from highest to lowest content for a given weight. Plants marked with an asterisk (*) contain significantly more of the nutrient than do the unmarked plants. Those marked with a double asterisk (**) contain considerably more than those with a single asterisk. Unless otherwise noted, all items are fresh and unprocessed. Dried fruits are often included without their fresh equivalents because the dried versions weigh considerably less and therefore contain more nutrients than the same weight of fresh fruit.

Each alphabetical list includes plants and plant products that contain smaller amounts of the nutrient than do those in the quantitative list, or that have been mentioned as sources of the nutrient but for which no quantitative information is available.

A note on "greens": The term "plant greens" generally refers to the young, tender leaves of the plant. Some are eaten as cooked vegetables, others as fresh salad greens, and some as both.

PROTEIN

Protein makes up 15 to 20 percent of the human body, about half of it being concentrated in muscles and bone cartilage. The other half is dispersed throughout the body as an essential part of cell and connective tissues, enzymes, hormones, antibodies, hereditary material, and other body elements.

Protein molecules consist of smaller units called amino acids; and for nutritional purposes these are the important items, since the body does not assimilate protein directly. The digestive process breaks down food proteins into their constituent amino acids, which are then absorbed and recombined into the proteins the body needs. Twenty amino acids are considered necessary for human nutrition. Of these, eight (for infants, nine) "essential" amino acids must be supplied in food; the body can synthesize the rest, assuming the needed materials are provided in the diet.

Since to make protein the body needs to have all the

amino acids available at the same time, the protein value of food is measured in terms of both quantity and quality. Quality is judged by the content levels of all eight essential amino acids. Protein sources that provide all the essential amino acids in proper proportions and adequate amounts to support life and growth are classified as *complete proteins*. Those that contain essential amino acids in unbalanced proportions or in amounts adequate to support life but not growth are classified as *partially incomplete proteins*. Finally, foods whose essential amino acid content cannot support either life or growth are classified as *incomplete proteins*.

On the whole, eggs, dairy products, fish, poultry, and meat provide more concentrated, higher quality protein than do vegetable sources. Most plants and plant products, used individually, fall in the partially incomplete protein classification. However, there are innumerable combinations of plant foods in which the amino acid deficiencies of one can be supplied by others to make a complete protein meal. This is a desirable alternative to relying on meat for protein. An adequate discussion of this subject is far beyond the scope of this book; two helpful references are Lappé's *Diet for a Small Planet* and Altschul's *Proteins: Their Chemistry and Politics* (see the Bibliography).

The following plants are good sources of protein when properly supplemented to provide complete protein value. In terms of average servings, dried legumes (beans, lentils, peas) have the highest protein content, followed by nuts and seeds, grains, and then vegetables.

Artichoke, asparagus, barley, black walnuts, Brazil nuts, brewer's yeast, broad beans (dried), broccoli, brussels sprouts, cashews, cauliflower, chard, collards, cottonseed, garbanzo beans (dried), Indian corn, kale, kidney beans (dried, all kinds), lentils (dried), lima beans (dried or cooked fresh), millet, mushrooms, mustard greens, oats, okra, peanuts, peas (dried or fresh), pistachio nuts, rice, rye (whole), sesame seeds, soybeans (dried), soybean sprouts, spinach, sunflower seeds, turnip greens, wheat (whole), wheat germ.

Vegetable sources of protein are best to avoid the high uric acid residue found in the blood composition of heavy meat-eaters.

VITAMINS

Vitamins are organic compounds that are necessary in small quantities to prevent disease and to participate in regulating the biochemical processes of the body. Some vitamins dissolve in water; these are easily lost when cooking water is discarded. Some are destroyed or impaired by heat; cooking times for foods containing these should be as short as possible. Some are affected by light or oxygen; these must be protected during storage. Prolonged excessive doses of three vitamins—A, D, and K—can have toxic effects. Overdoses are unlikely to occur if you rely upon natural sources of these vitamins.

In addition to the vitamins listed here, four vitamins of the B complex are considered essential nutrients for man: biotin, choline, folic acid, and pantothenic acid. At least two others—inositol and para-aminobenzoic acid (PABA) —are also known to be important. Foods containing the other B vitamins also contain these.

Vitamin A

Vitamin A as such is not found in plants: it is manufactured by the human and animal body from pigment substances called carotenes, which are quite common in plants. Carrots and apricots advertise their carotene content by their color, but green plants can be just as rich in these vital pigments.

Vitamin A is essential for night vision, and it promotes healthy skin and mucous membrane. It is important for good bones and teeth, for growth and proper digestion, for the production of red and white corpuscles in the blood, and for lactation. Vitamin A is fat-soluble and is sensitive to oxygen, especially with heat.

1. *Dandelion greens, *yellow dock, *carrots, *lamb's-quarters, *apricots (dried), *turnip greens, pokeweed (young shoots), spearmint, parsley, blue violet (leaves), spinach, sweet potatoes, collards, kale, mustard greens, nettle (young leaves), chard, green amaranth, beet tops, winter cress, watercress, chicory greens, broccoli, elderberries, apricots (fresh), winter cress (buds), papaya, cantaloupe.
2. Alfalfa, Alpine cranberry, artichoke, bilberries, brier

hips, buckwheat, calendula, cannabis, cowslip (flowers), elecampane (flowers), garlic, Iceland moss, Indian corn, lettuce, lily of the valley (fruit), okra, red currants, rowan (fruit), saffron.

Vitamin B₁ (Thiamine)

Vitamin B_1 occurs in both plant and animal tissues. It is a vital element in the body's production of energy through the breakdown of carbohydrates, and it takes part in other metabolic reactions. It also appears to be necessary for normal functioning of the nervous system and is involved in the action of the heart. Beriberi is a thiamine deficiency disease. Vitamin B_1 is water-soluble and is sensitive to heat.

1. **Brewer's yeast, *sunflower seeds, *wheat germ, *rice polish, English walnuts, rice (brown), peas, almonds (dried), black walnuts, soybeans, lima beans, kale, turnip greens, collards, barley, dandelion greens, avocados, raisins, figs (dried), potatoes (baked), watercress, broccoli, cauliflower, dates (dried), pineapple, sweet potatoes (baked), mustard greens, oats, lamb's-quarters, oranges, parsnips, spinach, green beans, leaf lettuce.
2. Most plants contains trace amounts of vitamin B_1.

Vitamin B₂ (Riboflavin)

Vitamin B_2 occurs generally in the same foods as vitamin B_1. Riboflavin is essential for cell growth and for enzymatic reactions by which the body metabolizes proteins, fats, and carbohydrates. It also helps to maintain healthy skin, eyes, and mucous membranes. Vitamin B_2 is water-soluble and is sensitive to light but not heat.

1. **Brewer's yeast, *almonds (dried), *wheat germ, *rice polish, *sunflower seeds, lamb's-quarters, turnip greens, watercress, avocados, broccoli, collards, kale, dandelion greens, apricots (dried), mustard greens, spinach, English walnuts, black walnuts, peas, beet tops, dates (dried), figs (dried), lima beans, green beans, raspberries, barley, cauliflower, leaf lettuce, parsnips, raisins, chard, prunes, rice (brown), sweet potatoes (baked), soybeans.
2. Most plants contain trace amounts of vitamin B_2.

Vitamin B₆ (Pyridoxine)

Although small amounts occur in most plant and animal tissues, vitamin B_6 is still a relatively little-known vitamin, perhaps because recognized deficiency problems are rare. Vitamin B_6 takes part in many enzyme reactions and is particularly important for brain and nervous system functions. Vitamin B_6 is water-soluble and is sensitive to oxygen and ultraviolet light.

1. Yeast, blackstrap molasses, wheat bran, wheat germ, soybeans, Indian corn, barley, rice, peanuts, peas (dry), cabbage, potatoes, carrots.
2. Many other foods contain vitamin B_6, but definitive information is not yet available.

Vitamin B₁₂ (Cyanocobalamin)

There is little or no vitamin B_{12} in plants. That's why strict vegetarians sometimes suffer from pernicious anemia, a disease associated with a deficiency of this vitamin. Vitamin B_{12} is necessary for proper functioning of body cells, particularly in the nervous system, the bone marrow, and the gastrointestinal tract. It is also involved in the metabolism of fats, proteins, and carbohydrates. Vitamin B_{12} is water-soluble and is sensitive to light, acids, and alkalis.

Vitamin C (Ascorbic Acid)

Vitamin C is a plant vitamin, occurring to some degree in almost all plants. The body neither makes nor stores vitamin C; a continuous supply must be provided in the food we eat. Normal body cell functioning requires ascorbic acid, as does the formation of healthy collagen (the basic protein of connective tissue), bones, teeth, cartilage, skin, and capillary walls. Vitamin C also promotes the body's effective use of other nutrients, such as iron, B vitamins, vitamins A and E, calcium, and certain amino acids. By promoting the formation of strong connective tissue, it helps to heal wounds and burns. Stress, fever, and infection increase the body's need for vitamin C. Scurvy is a vitamin C deficiency disease. Ascorbic acid is water-soluble and is sensitive to air, heat, light, alkalis, and copperware.

1. **Acerola (fruit), *rose hips, *wild strawberry (leaves), *blue violet (leaves), *parsley, winter cress (buds), winter cress (leaves), blue violet (flowers), pokeweed

(young shoots), green pepper, yellow dock, catnip, green amaranth, lamb's-quarters, watercress, nettle (young leaves), broccoli, spearmint, boneset, wild persimmons, turnip greens, kohlrabi, papaya, ground ivy, kale, collards, mustard green, oranges, strawberries, lemons.

2. Alfalfa, Alpine cranberries, barberries, bear's garlic (leaves), bilberries (also leaves), blackberry (leaves), black currants, elderberries, brooklime, cantaloupe, carrot, cayenne, celery, chickweed, coltsfoot, common buckthorn (fruit), coriander, English walnuts, garlic, garden raspberries, horseradish, knotgrass, lance-leaf plantain, lettuce, nasturtium (leaves), onions, oregano, primrose (leaves), radishes, rowan (fruit), scurvy grass, sorrel, spinach, spruce (young tips), sundew, wormwood.

Vitamin D

Vitamin D does not occur in plants, but some plants do contain compounds called sterols, which can be irradiated with ultraviolet light to make vitamin D. Yeast and fungi, for example, are major sources of ergosterol, which is irradiated artificially to make commercial vitamin D. The human skin contains another sterol, which is converted to vitamin D by the ultraviolet part of sunlight; unfortunately, modern life means relatively little exposure to sunlight for most people, besides daily bathing with soap which removes the skin's oil. Other natural sources are fish liver oils, milk, and egg yolk. Processed milk is generally fortified with additional vitamin D.

Vitamin D is necessary for healthy bones and teeth, for proper assimilation and body balances of calcium and phosphorus, and for preventing rickets. It is fat-soluble and is not sensitive to heat, light, or oxygen.

Vitamin E (Tocopherol)

Vitamin E occurs in both plant and animal tissue, more abundantly in the former. As an antioxidant, it acts in the body to protect red blood cells, vitamin A, and unsaturated fatty acids from oxidation damage. It also appears to help maintain healthy membrane tissue. In experiments with rats, vitamin E was found necessary for fertility. Vitamin

E is fat-soluble and is sensitive to oxygen, alkalis, and ultraviolet light.

1. Sunflower oil, cottonseed oil, wheat germ oil, walnuts, corn oil, wheat germ, peanuts, olive oil, Brazil nuts, soybean oil, broccoli, spinach, asparagus, dandelion greens, oatmeal, pecans, apples.
2. Much research is needed to determine the vitamin E content of plants other than the usual foods. Generally, it is found in whole grains and their oils, green leaves, and seeds.

Vitamin K

Vitamin K occurs primarily in plants; it is also synthesized by intestinal bacteria in the small intestine. Vitamin K is necessary for the synthesis by the liver of the blood-clotting enzyme prothrombin. It is fat-soluble and is sensitive to light, oxygen, strong acids, and alcoholic alkalis.

1. Alfalfa, green leafy vegetables, soybean oil, cauliflower, tomatoes.

Niacin (Nicotinic Acid)

Niacin, a vitamin of the B complex, occurs in both plant and animal tissue, but in different forms. The body changes the niacin from plant foods to niacinamide for use; animal foods contain niacinamide ready-made. Niacin takes part in enzyme reactions involved in the production of body energy and in tissue respiration. Pellagra is a niacin deficiency disease. Niacin is water-soluble and is not sensitive to heat, acids, or alkalis.

1. **Torula or primary yeast, *brewer's yeast, *rice polish, *sunflower seeds, *peanuts, sesame seeds, wheat germ, rice (brown), wheat (whole), rice (converted), apricots (dried), almonds (dried), parsley, peas, dates (dried), figs (dried), cashews, avocados, Brazil nuts, potatoes (baked), chard, Indian corn.
2. Alfalfa, artichoke, asparagus, barley, beans (green), broccoli, burdock (seed), carrots, cauliflower, celery, dandelion greens, fenugreek (seed), kale, lamb's-quarters, lentils, lima beans, mustard greens, oats, okra, peaches, prunes, raisins, rutabagas, sage, soybeans, sticklewort, sweet potatoes, tomatoes, turnip greens, watercress.

MINERALS

In nutrition, the term "minerals" refers to chemical elements that are necessary for proper functioning of the body. Our supply of minerals comes almost exclusively through the food chain—plants take them from the ground and incorporate them into organic compounds that we consume by eating either the plants or the animals that ate the plants. The main exception is table salt, which provides sodium and chlorine (and iodine if iodized) in inorganic form. Minerals are grouped into two types: *macrominerals* are found in relatively large amounts in the body; *microminerals* are found in smaller amounts (less than .005 percent of body weight). The minerals in this list are known to be necessary in human nutrition, as are three other microminerals: cobalt, molybdenum, and selenium. Trace amounts of other minerals also appear in the body, but their functions have not been determined.

MACROMINERALS

Calcium

Calcium is the most abundant mineral element in the body. It occurs primarily in plants, dairy products, and seafoods. Calcium is necessary for healthy bones and teeth, for clotting of the blood, for the functioning of nerve tissue and muscles (including the heart), for enzymatic processes, and for controllling the movement of fluids through cell walls. It also acts to balance the amounts of other minerals and promotes better use of iron by the body. Calcium dissolves in acid but is not affected by heat or light.

1. **Kelp (edible), **Irish moss, **blackstrap molasses, *lamb's quarters, *dulse, *green amaranth, *turnip greens, *almonds (dried), *mustard greens, *parsley, figs (dried), collards, dandelion greens, watercress, broccoli, beet tops, kale, purslane, maple syrup, chard, spinach, chicory greens, elderberries, endive, yellow dock, pokeweed (young shoots).
2. Cabbage, cauliflower, celery, chives, cleavers, coltsfoot, kidney beans (dried), lance-leaf plantain, leeks, lentils, lettuce, nettle (young leaves), okra, oranges, peas, radishes, restharrow, rose hips, shave grass, shepherd's purse, silverweed, turnips, yellow toadflax.

Chlorine

Chlorine is a poisonous gas, but in the form of chloride compounds it is an essential mineral nutrient. Chloride acts with sodium to maintain the balance between fluids inside and outside cells. Gastric juice contains hydrochloric acid, the production of which requires chloride. Table salt (sodium chloride) is our main source, but generally used to excess with harmful results.

1. Blackstrap molasses, coconut (dried), parsley, celery, bananas, coconut (fresh), kale, watercress, leaf cabbage, barley (pearled), dandelion greens, turnip greens, sweet potatoes, leaf lettuce, endive, hazelnuts, spinach, head lettuce, beets, Brazil nuts, carrots, rhubarb, kohlrabi, turnips (white), pecans, wheat (whole).
2. Other plants contain trace amounts, but many have not been analyzed.

Magnesium

Magnesium occurs in both plant and animal tissue. It is essential as an enzyme activator and is probably involved in the formation and maintenance of body protein.

1. *Cashews, *soybeans (dried), *almonds, *Brazil nuts, lima beans (dried), barley (whole), peanuts, kidney beans (dried), rye (whole), pecans, wheat (whole), oats, hazelnuts, peas (dried), English walnuts, Indian corn, beet tops, rice (brown), figs (dried), coconut (dried), apricots (dried), dates, collards, chard, spinach, prunes (dried), okra (without seeds), chestnuts, avocados, parsley.
2. Apples, asparagus, bananas, beets, blackberries, black pepper, black willow (bark), buckwheat, cabbage, carrots, cayenne, celery, cherries, cocoa, coffee, cucumbers, dandelion greens, dulse, grapes, kelp (edible), lemons, lettuce, limes, oranges, parsnips, peaches, peppermint, potatoes, primrose (leaves), radishes, raspberries, restharrow, silverweed, tea, tomatoes, watercress, wintergreen, yellow toadflax.

Phosphorus

Phosphorus occurs widely in both plant and animal tissue. It takes part in the production of energy for the body, and it is second only to calcium as a constituent of bones and teeth. Phosphorus is necessary for metabolic functions relating to the brain and the nerves, as well as for muscle action and enzyme formation.

1. **Rice polish, **wheat germ, *sunflower seeds, *sesame seeds, *almonds (dried), English walnuts, rice (brown), dulse, kelp (edible), wheat (whole), soybeans, Irish moss, raisins, figs (dried), peas, lima beans, Indian corn, lentils, radishes, apricots (dried), parsley, parsnips, dates (dried), lamb's-quarters, blackstrap molasses, cauliflower, artichokes, green amaranth, broccoli, dandelion greens, potatoes (baked), okra, oats, elderberries, endive, watercress, sweet potatoes (baked), kale, spinach, collards, asparagus, beet tops, celery, turnip greens, pokeweed (young shoots), mustard greens, onions, yellow dock, chicory greens, chard, purslane, avocados, prunes.

2. Apple, barley (whole), buckwheat, cabbage, calendula, caraway, chickweed, cucumbers, garlic, kidney beans (dry), lemons, lettuce, licorice, nuts, oranges, pumpkins, rose hips, rye (whole), sweet flag, tomatoes.

Potassium

Potassium is abundant in both plant and animal tissue. It promotes certain enzyme reactions in the body, and it acts with sodium to maintain normal pH levels and balance between fluids inside and outside cells.

1. **Dulse, **kelp (edible), **blackstrap molasses, **Irish moss, *parsley, *apricots (dried), *figs (dried), *sunflower seeds, *wheat germ, *almonds (dried), *dates (dried), *raisins, *rice polish, bananas, soybeans, avocados, chard, potatoes (baked), spinach, English walnuts, chicory greens, green amaranth, dandelion greens, carrots, kohlrabi, okra, parsnips, mustard greens, celery, beet tops, wild persimmons, artichokes, Indian corn, prunes, elderberries, endive, watercress, broccoli, leaf lettuce, collards, sweet potatoes (baked), radishes, lentils, apricots (fresh), cantaloupe, tomatoes, cherries, papaya.

2. American centaury, American sanicle, beans, bilberries, birch, blackberries, borage, cauliflower, coltsfoot, comfrey, eggplant, fennel, German camomile, lance-leaf plantain, milfoil, mullein, nettle (young leaves), nuts, oats, onions, peaches, peppermint, primrose (leaves),

red eyebright, rhubarb, rye, savory, shepherd's purse, sweet flag, turnips, watermelon, wintergreen.

Sodium

Sodium is a common mineral in both plant and animal tissues, the latter generally having a higher content. The use of salt in treating foods and preparing meals adds considerable sodium (as sodium chloride) to our diet. Sodium regulates the volume of body fluids and, balanced with potassium, maintains pressure equilibrium between fluids outside cells and those inside. Sodium is also necessary for nerve and muscle functioning. The results of almost 40 years of research by Dr. Walter Kempner indicate that it is unnatural and harmful to use the amount of salt to which we have become accustomed. Man is the only animal to salt his food. The ideal amount is obtained through our diet when we include the vegetables listed below.

1. **Kelp (edible), **Irish moss, **dulse, blackstrap molasses, chard, celery, spinach, dandelion greens, kale, turnips, watercress, mustard greens, carrots.
2. Plant foods especially low in sodium (all unsalted): apples, apricots, bananas, blackberries, cherries, coconut, dates, eggplant, green peppers, Indian corn, lima beans, okra, oranges, peas, pecans, pineapple, plums, raspberries, rice polish, watermelon, wheat (whole).

Sulfur

The body's supply of sulfur comes from sulfur-containing amino acids and from the B vitamins thiamine and biotin. The main sources are dairy products, meats, nuts, legumes, and grains. Sulfur is involved in bone growth, blood clotting, and muscle metabolism. It also helps to counteract toxic substances in the body by combining with them to form harmless compounds.

1. Soybeans (dried), kidney beans (dried), peanuts, oats, Brazil nuts, hazelnuts, peas (dried), parsley, lima beans (dried), wheat (whole), Indian corn, almonds, watercress, black walnuts, English walnuts, rye (whole), barley (whole), broccoli, chard, kale, barley (pearled), pecans, rice (white), cauliflower, coconut (dried), figs (dried), onions, cabbage, dates, turnips, turnip greens, peas (fresh), chestnuts, asparagus, avocados. (See also the plants listed for vitamin B_1.)

2. Asafetida, cabbage, chervil, coltsfoot, dill, endive, fennel, garlic, Irish moss, lance-leaf plantain, mullein, nasturtium (leaves), nettle (young leaves), okra, onions, radishes, red eyebright, restharrow, sage, sesame seeds, shave grass, shepherd's purse, silverweed, sunflower seeds, sweet flag, thyme.

MICROMINERALS

Copper

Copper occurs in both plant and animal tissue. It is essential (with iron) for the formation of hemoglobin in red blood cells; and it is important for protein and enzyme formation, as well as for the nervous and reproductive systems, bones, hair, and pigmentation.
1. The richest plant sources are: currants, legumes, mushrooms, nuts, raisins.

Iodine

Iodine occurs dependably only in seafood and seaweeds. Plants contain iodine if they are grown on iodine-rich soil; dairy products contain it if the cows were fed with such plants. Iodine is necessary for normal physical and mental growth and development, as well as for lactation and reproduction. An iodine deficiency causes goiter.
1. Dulse, Irish moss, kelp (edible), laver. The ashes of burned inedible kelp can also be used as a source of iodine.

Iron

Iron occurs in both plant and animal tissue. Because the body tends to retain iron very effectively, only trace amounts are needed in the diet. But iron is essential to form the oxygen-carrying hemoglobin in red blood cells, and it is also involved in muscle functioning and in enzyme reactions for producing energy.
1. **Rice polish, **blackstrap molasses, *kelp (edible), *wheat germ, *sunflower seeds, *parsley, *black walnuts, *apricots (dried), almonds (dried), figs (dried), green amaranth, cashews (roasted), purslane, raisins, Brazil nuts, beet tops, chard, dates (dried), dandelion greens, spinach, English walnuts, mustard greens, soy-

beans, wild persimmons, pecans, turnip greens, peanuts (roasted), barley, lentils, leaf lettuce, peas, rice (brown), olives (canned), elderberries, asparagus, endive, poke-weed (young shoots), prunes, watercress, lima beans, yellow dock, maple syrup, broccoli, artichokes, kale, lamb's-quarters, cauliflower, radishes, blackberries, chicory greens.

2. Apples, beans, beets, blueberries, burdock (root), cabbage, carrots, celery, cherries, collards, cucumbers, currants, grapes, leeks, mullein, nettle (young leaves), oats, onions, oranges, parsnips, pears, potatoes, restharrow, rhubarb, rose hips, shave grass, silverweed, sorrel, strawberries, tomatoes, turnips, wheat (whole), witch grass (rootstock), yellow toadflax.

Manganese

Plants are the best sources of manganese. Traces of this metal are necessary in the body for healthy bones and for enzyme reactions involved in the production of energy.

1. The plant foods highest in manganese content are: bran, whole grains, nuts, green leafy vegetables, wheat germ.

Zinc

Zinc occurs in animal tissue, and in plants when they grow on good soil. It is important for various enzyme reactions, for the reproduction system, and for the manufacture of body protein.

1. The plant foods highest in zinc content are: bran, nuts, green leafy vegetables.

FATS AND CARBOHYDRATES

Fats and carbohydrates share the primary function of being energy sources for the body, but they also perform various other functions. (Fats, for example, are needed for the absorption of fat-soluble vitamins.) Fats consist of fatty acids and glycerol, the fatty acids being either "saturated" or "unsaturated." Unsaturated fatty acids are more readily "burned" for energy than saturated ones, and they appear also to be connected with lower blood cholesterol levels. Animal fats are generally high in saturated fatty acids, and vegetable fats in unsaturated fatty acids.

Carbohydrates—which comprise the bulk of most of the world's diet—are sugars or compounds that break down into sugars in the digestive process. Starch is a common form of carbohydrate found in grains, bulbs, roots, and tubers; the various sugars are common especially in fruits, sugar cane, sugar beets, and milk. (The structural plant material cellulose is also a carbohydrate, but we can't eat trees because our bodies have no digestive enzymes to break cellulose down into usable sugars.) Meats may provide small amounts of stored carbohydrates in a form called glycogen.

Sources of Vegetable Fats: avocados, nuts, olives, seeds, soybeans, vegetable oils (e.g., corn, cottonseed, peanut, soybean, safflower seed, sunflower seed, walnut), wheat germ.

Sources of Carbohydrates: apples, apricots, bananas, beets, blackberries, blackstrap molasses, blueberries, brussels sprouts, carrots, cherries, dates, figs, grapes, Indian corn, kidney beans (dried, all kinds), lentils, lima beans, nuts, oats, parsnips, peas, potatoes, prunes, raisins, raspberries, rice, sesame seeds, soybeans, sunflower seeds, sweet potatoes, wheat, yams, yeasts (edible).

ENZYMES

All living tissue contains enzymes—special protein molecules that act as biological catalysts to promote the innumerable chemical reactions necessary for life. Basically, the enzymes speed up these chemical reactions to the rates necessary for the body's metabolism. The body produces its own enzymes, and they function everywhere in it, each enzyme performing a highly specialized task. Digestive enzymes act in the mouth, stomach, and intestines to break down food into simpler compounds usable for producing energy or for building various body substances. In case of enzyme deficiency, digestive enzymes, unlike other kinds, can readily be used by the body when provided by an external source. The following plants contain enzymes, many of them useful in the digestive process:

Alfalfa, apple, artichoke (leaves and root), barley

(malt), carline thistle, cascara sagrada (bark), castor bean (oil), dandelion (root), papaya, peppermint, soybeans, wood sorrel, yellow bedstraw.

HORMONES

Hormones are substances manufactured by the glands of the body. They stimulate the body's metabolic processes, each hormone having a specific effect on the functioning of a particular organ. Plants contain "phytohormones" that regulate their own growth processes, but some plants contain also steroid substances that form the basis of hormones found in the human body. Among the hormones derivable from plant steroids are cortisone (used for rheumatoid arthritis), corticosterone (used in carbohydrate and protein metabolism, also for Addison's disease), and several sex hormones (used in oral contraceptives, also to treat irregularities in menstruation and pregnancy). The following plants contain steroid substances (usually in the roots or rootstocks) or exhibit hormone-like activity:

Agave (juice), black cohosh, chaste tree (fruit), ginseng, hops, licorice, Mexican yam, purple trillium, sage, sarsaparilla, star grass, stoneseed.

NOTES:

1. The collard plant is a type of kale, hence the same botanical name.
2. Mustard greens (referred to in these sections) are the basal leaves of various wild mustards.
3. Elderberries (referred to in these sections) are the fruit of American elder (*Sambuscus canadensis*).

HERBS AND SPICES:
THE ART OF SEASONING

Developing skill in seasoning takes a certain amount of time and effort, but its rewards in enjoyable eating make it well worthwhile. It involves familiarizing yourself with the different herbs and spices and conscientiously working on your ability to season all your dishes to a "just right" taste. After some experimentation and practice you will find yourself developing a feel for seasonings that will enable you to produce more consistently good flavor in your meals.

Fortunately, there are some general guidelines in using seasonings. One basic principle is that herbs and spices should be used sparingly—to enhance the natural flavor of foods, rather than to dominate them. (Certain exceptions exist in some heavily spiced but delicious exotic dishes.) On the average, in a dish with 4 to 6 servings, use ½ teaspoon or less of any spice; and for herbs, use one of these equivalents: ⅛ teaspoon powdered, ½ teaspoon dried coarsely chopped, or 1 tablespoon fresh chopped. (Dried herbs require less because of their more concentrated form and less delicate flavor.) Some herbs and spices are stronger than others and should be used in smaller amounts (see individual listings).

In understanding seasoning, it is also essential to know that much of the best flavor and aroma of herbs and spices comes from aromatic oils contained within them and that ingredients in these oils dissipate with time. Leaf herbs have the most aromatic oil and the best flavor when fresh. In their dried, whole form, the more delicate and refined qualities in the flavor have been lost; and the dried, finely chopped or powdered forms have the least refined flavor of all because more surfaces are available from which the volatile elements of the oil can escape. Some herbs lose flavor more rapidly than others; for example, chervil, borage, burnet, and summer savory must be used fresh, because most of their flavor is lost in drying. You can, however, get more flavor out of many dried herbs if you reconstitute them in some liquid to be used in your recipe (water, wine, stock, melted butter, or oil), letting them stand for ten minutes or longer before using. Spices and herb seeds are generally used in their dried form (except ginger), but even here it is preferable to purchase them whole and grind, powder, or mash them when needed instead of buying the ground form (black and white peppercorns, nutmeg kernels, cardamom seed pods, and mace pieces are available in better stores). Ground spices and herbs are likely to deteriorate in flavor and should be replaced at least once a year. In spite of the decorative spice racks available, spices and dried herbs retain their flavor best when stored in a cool, dark place. For the most dependable and flavorful results in your recipes, always buy the best quality of commercial herbs and spices available.

In increasing your seasoning repertoire, you will find that the listings in this section will give you a broad range from which to choose. Quite a few of the herbs must be used fresh, and because they are generally not available have to be home grown. This is not difficult, requires only limited space, and is well worth the effort. Your garden might include a number of the more common herbs which are really best fresh—like basil, chives, marjoram, rosemary, tarragon, and thyme—as well as some of the herbs that *must* be used fresh, which include anise leaves, borage, burnet, chervil, cilantro, scented geraniums, lemon balm, lemon verbena, nasturtium, savory, sorrel, and violets. The following listings will also give you general information about the foods used with the various herbs and spices. To find more specific information on this subject, get some good herb and spice cookbooks from the library. Try some of the recipes, and then begin improvising on your own.

LISTING OF HERBS AND SPICES

Allspice (Pimenta officinalis). Tastes like a blend of cloves, cinnamon, and nutmeg, but is actually a single spice ground from the under-ripe dried berry of a tropical, ever-green myrtle tree, native to the West Indies and Central America. Uses: cakes, cookies, pies, puddings, fruit desserts, pickling liquids, spiced syrups, spiced beef, stews, pot roasts, red cabbage, and sweet potatoes.

Anise (Pimpinella anisum). Leaves and seeds have a licorice flavor. Uses: 1) fresh leaves in salads; 2) whole or crushed seeds added to cookies, cakes, sweet rolls, court bouillon for fish, various fish sauces.

Balm or Lemon Balm (Melissa officinalis). Fresh leaves have a refreshing lemon flavor and aroma. Uses: fruit or vegetable salads, drinks (such as tea, fruit punches, and wine punches), sauces, egg dishes, chicken, and fish.

Basil (Ocimum basilicum). Used fresh or dried, flavor reminiscent of mint and cloves combined. Seems to sweeten tomatoes, thus very good in all tomato dishes (including tomato juice, soup, and even spaghetti sauce). Other uses: eggs and cheese dishes, especially scrambled eggs, salads, meats, chicken, fish, sausage mixtures, soups, salad dressings, bland vegetables like eggplant. Use with care; a dominant herb whose flavor gets stronger with cooking.

Bay Leaf or Laurel Leaf (Laurus nobilis). Aromatic and slightly bitter flavor. Well known for its uses in meats, game, fish, poultry, stuffings, soups, sauces, and marinades for game (especially venison). To add subtle flavor to bland vegetables such as eggplant, potatoes, and carrots, put some bay leaf in their cooking water. Fresh or dried, use bay leaf sparingly, for it is strong (1 leaf or less for 6 to 8 servings).

Borage (Borago officinalis). Only usable fresh because its refreshing cucumber-like flavor is not retained after drying. Uses: 1) tender young leaves in salads, cold drinks, fish sauces, or cooked as a vegetable like spinach; 2) the beautiful, peacock-blue flowers as a garnish in punches and other iced drinks, and in salads, or in candied form as decoration on cakes. Since it is not generally available, this herb must be home grown.

Burnet or Salad Burnet (Sanguisorba minor). Has a nutty flavor that hints of cucumber, and is similar to borage in its taste and uses. Add the fresh, tender young leaves to cold drinks, salads, soups, cream cheese, vinegar; or use as a garnish like parsley. Fresh leaves essential; must be home grown.

Capers (Capparis spinosa). The pickled unopened flower buds of the caper bush, a spiny Mediterranean shrub. They taste like tiny, sharp pickles and add piquancy to salads, canapes, meat gravies, and fish sauces.

Caraway (Carum carvi). Seeds have a characteristic, pungent flavor. Uses: breads, rolls, cheeses, sauerkraut, cabbage dishes including cole slaw, soups, goulashes, and stews. The crushed seeds can enhance the flavor of salads or vegetables. Use cautiously because the flavor is strong and turns bitter with long cooking (add to stews for the last half hour of cooking).

Cardamom (Elettaria cardamomum). Seeds come from the dried fruit of the cardamom plant, found in India and other tropical areas. Their flavor is slightly gingerish, leaving a medicinal aftertaste. Uses: 1) whole seed pod added to hot punches, spiced wines, marinades, pickling liquids, demitasse or regular coffee (1-2 pods per cup); 2) ground seeds in bread, pastries, cookies, fruit salads; Mexican, Spanish, and East Indian dishes.

Cassia or Chinese Cinnamon (Cinnamomum cassia). Related to cinnamon and closely resembles it in taste and appearance (though its flavor is stronger and not as sweet as cinnamon's). Most of the cinnamon sold in the U.S. is cassia, rather than the more expensive true cinnamon. Uses: the same as cinnamon. (The spice cassia is unrelated to the cassias described in Part 2 under Senna.)

Cayenne Pepper (Capsicum frutescens var. longum). Comes from the ground, dried ripe red pepper pods of a small tropical shrub of the Capsicum family. This ground red pepper, combined with yeast and flour, is baked into a hard cake, which is then ground into the finished spice. Uses: in curries and chili powders; in small amounts added to bland foods like eggs and cream sauce.

Celery (Apium graveolens). Its leaves and stalks are well-known additions to soups, stocks, stews, and many other savory dishes.

Chervil (Anthriscus cerefolium). Has a delicate, subtle flavor with a slight hint of anise. Must be used fresh; requires home growing. Uses: soups, salads, sauces, omelets, souffles, chicken, veal, fish, and shellfish dishes. Continental recipes for chervil soup and various chervil sauces are said to be delicious. Flavor does not withstand long cooking.

Chili Powder (Capsicum frutescens). A blend of dried powdered Mexican chili peppers from several varieties of capsicum. Other spices such as coriander, cumin, and oregano are added to most chili powders.

Chives (Allium schoenoprasum). The dark green tubular chive leaves with their mild onion flavor are an attractive, flavorful seasoning in salads, baked potatoes, omelets, and sauces.

Cinnamon (Cinnamomum zeylanicum). The dried inner bark of the branches of a small, tropical, evergreen laurel tree. The bark is peeled off and as the pieces are dried, they curl up into quills. Uses: 1) quills in spiced punches, teas, cooked fruit, pickling liquids; 2) ground spice in sweet baked goods, cooked fruit, and some meat and fish dishes.

Cloves (Syzygium aromaticum or Caryophyllus aromaticus). The spicy, dried, unopened flower buds of the beautiful tropical evergreen clove tree. Uses: 1) whole cloves in stewed fruit, hot spiced drinks, pickling liquids, marinades; 2) ground spice in breads, cookies, spice cakes, pies, fruit dishes, curries, and some meat dishes.

Coriander (Coriandrum sativum). Seeds when dried have a sweet taste reminiscent of lemon peel and sage. Fresh coriander leaves with their slightly bitter taste are known as Chinese parsley or cilantro and are featured in Mediterranean, Latin American, Spanish, and oriental cooking. Uses: 1) whole seed in hot spiced drinks, marinades, pickling liquids; 2) ground seed in breads, pastries, puddings, cream sauces, fruit sauces, chili sauce, curries, and other exotic dishes; 3) fresh leaves in meat and poultry dishes, chicken or pea soups, and as a garnish like parsley.

Cumin (Cuminum cyminum). Seed is similar to that of caraway in appearance and flavor; however it is lighter in color and its flavor is stronger and less refined. Uses of whole and ground seed: cheeses, sauerkraut and cabbage dishes, barbecue and spaghetti sauces, chili and curry powders, and in bland dishes like scrambled eggs, egg salad, and potato salad.

Curry Powder. Not derived from a single plant; it is the blended mixture of various spices such as cardamom, cayenne, cloves, coriander, cumin, dill, fenugreek, ginger, mace, pepper, and turmeric. Because there is no standard recipe for curry powder, the number of spices included and the amounts used vary with each spice manufacturer.

Dill (Anethum graveolens). Both seeds and leaves are used. Dill's pungent, characteristic flavor comes through in both forms, but is less pronounced and more delicate in the leaves. Uses of both seeds and leaves: cream cheese, sour cream dips, sauces, soups, salads, salad dressings, eggs, cheese, pickles, sauerkraut, poultry, and especially fish. The leaves, also known as dill weed, add an attractive green accent to light-colored foods.

Fennel (Foeniculum vulgare). Has a licorice flavor like that of anise but weaker. Uses: 1) whole seed added to bread, rolls, cakes, cookies, and even apple pie; 2) fresh leaves in salads, soups, sauces. Fennel is excellent with fish, for it aids digestion of oily fish like mackerel or eel; and if used in fish poaching liquid, it helps to keep fish firm. Fresh leaves have to be home grown.

Fenugreek (Trigonella foenum-graecum). Seed smells like celery but has a more bitter taste. Ground seed's primary use is as an ingredient in curries.

Filé (Sassafras variifolium). Made from young powdered sassafras leaves, filé or filet powder is used in thickening and flavoring creole gumbos.

Garlic (Allium sativum). Its discreet use enhances many foods. Best known as a meat seasoning—fresh-cut clove rubbed on or inserted in meats (especially delicious with lamb). Mediterranean cooking goes far in exploiting the culinary possibilities of garlic.

Geraniums (Pelargonium species). There are about 75 species of scented-leaf geraniums with different fragrances. Those best for culinary purposes are the almond, apple, apricot, coconut, lemon, licorice, lime, nutmeg, orange, peach, peppermint, and rose-scented ones. Uses of leaves: in poundcakes, jellies, compotes, custards, and even salad dressing.

Ginger (Zingiber officinale). Comes from the root of the ginger plant, a beautiful tropical lily. Fresh ginger is best peeled and sliced thin or grated and added to stews, sauces, salad dressings, and oriental dishes. Fresh-cut ginger rubbed on fish removes fishy odors. Ground ginger finds use in gingerbread, cakes, cookies, pies, sausages, curries, and various exotic dishes.

Horseradish (Armoracia lapathifolia). The freshly grated root, combined with vinegar or lemon juice, is used as a condiment with meat. It is also an ingredient in many sauces. Fresh root will not keep more than three months.

Hyssop (Hyssopus officinalis). Fresh or dried, hyssop leaves with their bitter, slightly minty flavor add interest to fruit cocktails, salads, soups, meats (especially stews), poultry, and rich, fatty fish.

Juniper (Juniperus communis). Dried juniper berries with their spicy, somewhat bittersweet flavor find use in marinades, sauerkraut, cabbage, and bean dishes, and in seasoning wild game and other meats.

Leek (Allium porrum). Leeks with their mild, sweet onion flavor are excellent in soups, salads, and stews or cooked as a vegetable. They provide the base for the French soup vichyssoise.

Lemon Verbena (Aloysia triphylla). Its fresh lemon-flavored leaves are used in fruit salads, jellies, and custards, and as a garnish in iced drinks. Since its leaves are best used fresh, it requires home growing.

Lovage (Levisticum officinale). Flavor similar to celery's but stronger. Uses: 1) tender young leaves, fresh or dried, in soups, salads, sauces, stews; 2) seeds, crushed or whole in cakes, candies, soups, salads, stews, and roasts; 3) stems, when blanched, can be eaten raw like celery or sliced into soups or stews. Use carefully since lovage is somewhat stronger than other herbs.

Mace (Nutmeg tree-Myristica fragrans). Is the lacy dried aril or outer covering of the seed of the tropical nutmeg tree. The kernel inside the seed is the spice nutmeg. Mace's flavor is somewhat like nutmeg's but is stronger. Uses in whole or powdered form: cakes, cookies, cooked fruit, chocolate puddings, and other desserts. It is often combined with bay leaf, cloves, and onions in seasoning savory dishes.

Marigold (Calendula officinalis). Often used as a less-expensive substitute for saffron, fresh or dried petals give subtle flavor and golden color to seafood, soups, stews, puddings, rice, and omelets. The dried petals, softened in hot milk, can be added to the batters of cakes, breads, and cookies. The fresh, tender young leaves are good in salads.

Marjoram (Majorana hortensis). Strong, sweet, sage-like flavor. Used to season meats (makes duck, pork, and goose seem less heavy), poultry, salad dressings, vegetables, and legumes. The fresh, finely chopped leaves are nice in salads. Use this dominant herb sparingly.

Mints (Mentha species). Fresh or dried mint leaves find use with lamb, veal, coleslaw, salads, peas, zucchini, cream cheese, in mint sauce, and as a garnish for cold drinks. Besides peppermint and spearmint, there are also pineapple, apple, and orange mints which can be used in fruit dishes and drinks.

Mustard (Brassica nigra and B. hirta). The appetite-stimulating mustard preparations used as a condiment with meat are all made from the dry powdered seeds of black or white mustard plus a liquid medium like water, vinegar, or wine. Dry mustard powder can also be used as a spice to flavor all types of savory dishes. Whole mustard seeds of the white variety serve as seasoners too in pickles, sausages, salads, and vegetables. White mustard leaves are used in salads and cooked as a vegetable.

Nasturtium (Tropaeolum majus). Fresh leaves and flowers, with their peppery flavor similar to watercress, are good in salads or chopped and combined with cream cheese or butter in canapes and sandwiches. The unripe seed pods can be pickled and used as a substitute for capers.

Nutmeg (Myristica fragrans). The dried kernel from inside the seed of the beautiful, tropical evergreen nutmeg tree. Best freshly grated. Uses: spice cakes, cookies, fruit pies, desserts, stewed fruits, milk drinks, spice blends, and in discreet amounts in some savory dishes.

Oregano (Origanum vulgare). Is a wild marjoram whose taste is sharper and spicier than marjoram's. It is a common ingredient in Spanish, Mexican, and Italian dishes; may also be used in the same foods as marjoram.

Paprika (Capsicum frutescens). Comes from the dried ripe pods of the largest and mildest varieties of capsicum shrubs (see also cayenne and chili powder). Different varieties of paprika vary in quality and pungency; some of the best come from Hungary. Uses: in goulashes, and to add color and flavor to many bland, savory dishes.

Parsley (Petroselinum sativum). Well known as a garnish and seasoning, parsley underlines the flavor of foods without being dominant and it tones down the odor of strong vegetables like onions. Combines well with other herbs.

Pepper (Piper nigrum). Both black and white peppercorns are the dried berries of the tropical pepper vine. The black comes from underripe berries which have been dried and cured; the white, from dried ripe berries whose dark outer shell has been removed. White pepper is not as strong as black, but its flavor is finer and more aromatic. Best freshly ground, both black and white pepper enhance all savory foods. White is often used in light-colored sauces.

Poppy Seed (Papaver rhoeas). These little dark seeds come from the corn poppy, not the opium poppy. Uses: as a topping on cookies, breads, rolls; in cake fillings, fruit salads, canapes, and sweet vegetables.

Rose (Rosa species). The delicate, fruity flavor of rose hips can enhance fruit dishes and drinks. Both the hips and the petals are made into jellies. Do not use roses that have been treated with pesticides or pesticide-containing fertilizers.

Rosemary (Rosmarinus officinalis). Fresh or dried, rosemary has a pungent, pine-like, sweet but savory taste. It is excellent in flavoring meats, fish, and chicken dishes (especially good with lamb), and some vegetables like peas and spinach. Use sparingly, because it is a dominant herb.

Rue (Ruta graveolens). A favorite Balkan seasoning, rue's bitter, fresh, chopped leaves are used sparingly in cheeses, salads, sauces, stews, and vegetables. Rue can produce allergic reactions similar to poison ivy in some individuals, so it is best not to season dishes with it for company.

Safflower or Mexican Saffron (Carthamus tinctorius). Unrelated to saffron, but the dried and powdered orange-red florets are used as a saffron substitute.

Saffron (Crocus sativus). The most delicately flavored of all spices. Imparts golden color and a beautiful flavor to rice dishes, fish and shellfish soups (such as bouillabaisse), poultry, bread, cakes, and cookies. It aids the digestion of rich meats like pork, duck, and goose. The most expensive of all spices, saffron fortunately needs to be used only in very small quantities in order to work its magic.

Sage (Salvia officinalis). Pungent, aromatic flavor when dried, but delicate and somewhat minty in the fresh leaves. Best known for its use with meats, poultry, fish, and in stuffings, omelets, and cheese. Makes fatty meats and fish (like pork, goose, duck, eel, mackerel) seem less heavy— for this purpose, place sage leaves directly on top of meat or fish, or in cooking liquid or sauce, or in accompanying stuffing. A strong herb, use with care; also tends to be bitter with long cooking. Clary sage and pineapple sage varieties are also used in cooking for similar purposes.

Savory (Summer savory—Satureja hortensis; Winter savory —S. montana). Both summer and winter savory have a pleasant, piquant flavor, though winter savory is stronger and more resinous. Used similarly, both are best known for their use with vegetables and all types of beans. Known as "bean herb" in Germany, the savories not only give flavor but cut down on the gas produced by beans. They also eliminate the strong odors in cabbage and turnips if you put 2 to 3 leaves in the cooking water. Best used fresh; must be home grown.

Sesame Seeds (Sesamum orientale). Have a sweet nutty flavor and are used as a topping for breads, cookies, vegetables, and casseroles.

Shallots (Allium ascalonicum). Have a subtle, delicate onion flavor. Used in many French sauce recipes and as a meat or poultry accompaniment. Expensive and not generally available, they can be easily grown at home.

Sorrel (Garden sorrel—Rumex acetosa and French sorrel— R. scutatus). The fresh, slightly acid leaves of both species can be used for culinary purposes, but French sorrel is preferable. Their sour-flavored leaves add a desirable tartness to salads, vegetables (particularly cabbage, lettuce, and spinach), and soups, especially cream soups.

Sweet Cicely or European Sweet Cicely (Myrrhis odorata). Has a sweet, anise-like flavor. Fresh or dried leaves enhance the flavor of desserts, fruit salads, fruit juices, salads, delicate soups, all root vegetables, and cabbage. Should be more widely used as a healthful sugar substitute. If 2 to 4 teaspoons of dried herb or the fresh leaves and stalks are added in cooking stewed fruit or fruit for pies, only half the normal amount of sugar will be needed. Dry seeds used in cakes and cookies. Note: This plant is unrelated to the sweet cicely described in Part 2.

Tarragon (Artemisia dracunculus). Has a licorice flavor that is both sweet and slightly bitter. One of the important herbs in French cooking—indispensable in béarnaise sauce. Uses: eggs, salads, sauces, fish, meat, poultry, and excellent in vinegars for salads. Fresh leaves are best and can be preserved by holding them in vinegar until needed.

Thyme or Garden Thyme (Thymus vulgaris). One of the strongest herbs with its pungent, clove-like flavor; use with care. An essential herb in French cooking. Principally used in meats, poultry, fish, stuffings, egg and cheese dishes, salads, vegetables, and vegetable juices. Helps in the digestion of fatty foods (including pork, goose, duck, sausage, and fatty fish) and stimulates the appetite. Fresh leaves of lemon thyme (*Thymus citriodorus*), another species of thyme, find use in fruit drinks, salads, and desserts.

Turmeric (Curcuma longa). Has a bitter, somewhat gingery taste; use with care. Comes from the dried root of a plant in the ginger family. Principally used in small quantities to give golden color to foods such as curries, mustards, mayonnaise, pickles, and sauces. Sometimes substituted for saffron.

Vanilla (Vanilla planifolia). Comes from the long pod of a tropical vine. To develop flavor, the pods (usually called vanilla beans) are fermented and cured for six months before marketing. Extract is prepared by macerating beans in alcohol solution. Make your own extract simply by keeping a vanilla bean in a little brandy—flavor will improve with age.

Violets (Sweet violet—Viola odorata; Blue violet—V. papilionacea). Leaves used in puddings, jellies, and salads; flowers in salads or in candied form as a decorative garnish for desserts.

Watercress (Nasturtium officinale). Fresh leaves may be used in salads or as a garnish, raw or deepfried. Also in chopped form, added to appetizers, eggs, cheese, and fish.

PLANTS
ARE FOR DRINKING

Plants are the souce of practically all the beverages—alcoholic or non-alcoholic—consumed by mankind, milk and water being the main exceptions. They provide flavor, color, and aroma for endless variety and pleasure; they provide nutrients for health; and they provide fermentable materials for alcoholic drinks that have been the delight and despair of mankind for thousands of years. Our synthetic era manages to produce drinks with artificial chemical flavors, colors, and aromas; but even these break no new ground and merely imitate the real thing.

Here, then, *is* the real thing: teas, juices, and alcoholic beverages you can make and experiment with for your health and pleasure.

HERB TEAS

This section describes a number of herbal teas which can be enjoyed as beverages, taken either hot or iced If you are not familiar with herbal teas, you may wan to try some of the best-known ones first—teas which have long been used in Europe and other places, such as camomile, peppermint, linden or lime flower, elder flower, hibiscus, rose hip, balm, oswego tea, and sage. After trying these, you can experiment with some of the others.

Most herbal teas are infusions made by pouring boiling water over herb leaves or flowers and steeping them for 5 to 10 minutes to release the herb's aromatic oils. The general rule is one teaspoon of dried herb, or 3 teaspoons fresh crushed herb, per cup boiling water. (Crush fresh herbs in a clean cloth immediately before using.) Some herbs may require larger or smaller amounts to give a desirable flavor. If stronger flavor is desired, it is generally better to use more of the herb rather than to steep the tea longer; long steeping often makes the tea bitter. For best results with hot tea, warm the teapot first by rinsing it with boiling water. For iced tea, strain after steeping to the desired flavor; then cool in the refrigerator before serving. Iced teas can be brewed stronger than hot teas because the ice will dilute their flavor after serving. Some herb leaf or flower teas, such as clover blossom, horehound, lemon verbena, and oswego tea, and all root and seed teas are prepared as decoctions—that is, simmered in water, usually for 10 to 20 minutes—to bring out their full flavor. To avoid a metallic taste, make your teas in glass, porcelain, or enamelled containers. Most herb teas can be sweetened with honey or sugar, but milk or cream is not recommended because it tends to cover up the desirable delicate flavors. You might also experiment with combining various herb teas for interesting flavor results. For example, equal amounts of peppermint leaves and elder flowers make a good tea; costmary and orange mint combine well also.

Today most health food stores offer a wide variety of herbal teas, including many that do not appear in this section because they are basically medicinal teas rather than beverages for regular use. Herb teas taken for medicinal purposes are described under the individual herb listings in Part 2.

Alfalfa Tea (Medicago sativa). Suitable for daily use, this brisk, appetite-stimulating tea is improved by the addition of peppermint or some other botanical flavoring. Rich in vitamins and minerals.

Balm, Lemon Balm, or Melissa Tea (Melissa officinalis). Tasty, lemon-scented tea. Can be used daily. Very soothing to the nervous system. Must be steeped 10 minutes or longer (flavor does not get bitter with long steeping). Served hot or iced and sweetened.

Basil Tea (Ocimum basilicum). Subtle flavor and aroma.

Betony Tea (Stachys officinalis). A good substitute for oriental black tea because it is similar in flavor. Can be used daily.

Birch Bark Tea (Betula alba and B. lenta). The inner bark of both these trees contains an oil which is identical in flavor with that of the wintergreen plant (*Gaultheria procumbens*). Euell Gibbons prepares a wholesome wintergreen-flavored tea by pouring boiling water or boiling birch sap over diced pieces of the inner birch bark or birch twigs and letting it steep a few minutes.

Blackberry Leaf Tea (See Strawberry Leaf).

Borage Tea (Borago officinalis). Mild, refreshing, cucumber-like flavor. Made from fresh or dried leaves; some flowers can be added also. Served hot or iced. High in organic calcium and potassium. Gives a feeling of exhilaration and well-being, but not recommended for extended daily use.

Burnet or Salad Burnet Tea (Sanguisorba minor). Attractive tea. Made from fresh or dried leaves. Served hot or iced. Herb has a cucumber-like flavor and was at one time used to flavor wine.

Camomile Tea (Matricaria chamomilla). Delicate flavor with fruity aroma reminiscent of apples. Long has been one of the most popular herb teas in Europe. Taken hot or cold, aids digestion after heavy meals. An excellent nightcap—reputed to prevent nightmares. Steep only 3 to 5 minutes. Fresh grated ginger makes a nice addition to it.

Cassina or Cassene (Ilex vomitoria). Pleasant tea whose caffeine content is mildly stimulating. Originated by the Indians of the southeastern United States and adopted by early white settlers. During certain tribal ceremonies, these Indians used a much stronger version of this tea, called Indian black drink, a brew which was both emetic and narcotic.

Catnip Tea (Nepeta cataria). Good-tasting, aromatic tea. Old country favorite in England even before oriental tea was introduced there. High in vitamin C. Stimulates the appetite if served cold before meals; aids digestion if served hot after meals. Hot tea also makes a soothing nightcap.

Clover Blossom Tea (Trifolium pratense). Delicate flavor. Must be simmered for a short time to bring out full flavor. Very good if peppermint or spearmint leaves are added to it. Suitable for daily use.

Costmary or Sweet Mary Tea (Chrysanthemum balsamita). Used by American colonists. Minty taste. Do not steep too long.

Damiana Tea (Turnera aphrodisiaca). Fragrant golden tea from Mexico. Agreeable, slightly bitter flavor.

Desert or Mormon Tea (Ephedra spp.). Used by Indians

and early white settlers in southwestern United States. Delicious and unusual flavor, good aroma.

Elder Flower Tea (Sambucus nigra and S. canadensis). Pleasant tea. An English favorite. Good with the addition of mint. Helps induce sleep.

Fenugreek Tea (Trigonella foenum-graecum). Smooth flavor, soothing. Used in Mediterranean countries.

Fraxinella, Dictamnus, or Gas Plant Tea (Dictamnus albus). Strong lemon scent. Used by American colonists.

Goldenrod or Blue Mountain Tea (Solidago odora). Fragrant, golden tea; delicious, sweet, anise-like flavor.

Ground Ivy or Gill Tea (Nepeta hederacea). English country tea. Keep in closed container while brewing and do not steep too long. Improved by the addition of one of the following: licorice, a few leaves of rosemary, balm, sage, or lavender. Served cold and unsweetened, it makes an appetite-stimulating bitter tonic.

Hawthorn Leaf Tea (Crataegus oxyacantha). Germans use it as a substitute for oriental green tea.

Hibiscus Tea (Various Hibiscus spp.). Rose-colored tea with lemony flavor. Served hot or iced. Delightful summer drink in its cold form. Commercial hibiscus teas are made either from the flowers or from the calyces of the flowers.

Horehound Tea (Marrubium vulgare). Mild pleasant flavor, suitable for children. Must be simmered for about 20 minutes. A favorite cough remedy. Used by American pioneers and soldiers.

Labrador or Swamp Tea (Ledum latifolium). Originally used by American Indians and adopted by frontiersmen and pioneers. Fragrant, soothing, rose-colored tea with mellow flavor.

Lemongrass Tea (Cymbopogon citratus). Delightful lemony tea originating in the West Indies.

Lemon Verbena Tea (Aloysia triphylla). Lemony taste and scent. Served hot or iced. The Spanish prepare it as a decoction and serve it cold and sweetened. Good with the addition of mint.

Licorice Root Tea (Glycyrrhiza glabra). Roots contain glycyrrhizin, a substance many times sweeter than sugar; but the tea is an excellent thirst quencher. Cold licorice tea is good for hot summer days.

Linden or *Lime Flower Tea (Tilia europaea and T. americana)*. One of the most popular continental herb teas. Fragrant jasmine-like aroma and sweet, pleasant flavor. Soothes the nerves and aids digestion.

Lovage Tea (Levisticum officinale). Flavor similar to celery's—thus more like a broth than a tea. Season with herb salt.

Marjoram Tea (Majorana hortensis). A good tea can be made from the fresh leaves. Served hot or iced. Mint leaves make a nice addition to it.

Mint Teas. For tea made from fresh mint leaves, use ½ cup chopped herb to 1 cup boiling water; of the dried herb, use 1 to 2 tsp. per cup water. For all mint teas, steep only 5 minutes. Mint teas aid the digestion and are suitable for children. Each of the different mint varies slightly in flavor. Peppermint tea (*Mentha piperita*) is the most popular of all the mint teas. Spearmint (*M. spicata*) is milder and more fragrant than peppermint. The apple mints (*M. rotundifolia* and *M. gentilis*), and orange or bergamot mint (*M. citrata*), as well as the wild mints such as watermint (*M. aquatica*) and field mint (*M. arvensis*), make very palatable teas.

Nettle Tea (Urtica dioica). English country tea. Thought to have been introduced by the Romans to Britain. Tea made from fresh or dried young shoots. Boiling water removes the herb's sting; drying does also. Served hot it is a warming tea on a wintry day. Also can be served cold.

New Jersey Tea or *Liberty Tea (Ceanothus americanus)*. The nearest American plant equivalent in flavor to oriental tea. Contains no harmful stimulants, thus an excellent tea substitute. Used during the American Revolution for this purpose.

Oswego Tea or *Bee Balm Tea (Monarda didyma)*. Delightful, fragrant tea. Used by American Indians and also by American colonists during the Revolution. Sleep-inducing. Must be simmered 10 minutes to bring out full flavor.

Parsley Tea (Petroselinum sativum). Good aromatic tea, rich in vitamin C.

Pennyroyal Tea (Hedeoma pulegioides). Flavorful and fragrant tea with a somewhat minty taste. Another of the teas used as an oriental tea substitute during the American Revolution. Caution: Should not be used during pregnancy.

Peppermint Tea (See Mint).

Persimmon Leaf Tea (Diospyros virginiana). Has very pleasant flavor somewhat similar to sassafras. Very high in vitamin C. Dried leaves produce a better tea than the fresh leaves.

Raspberry Leaf Tea (See Strawberry Leaf Tea).

Rose Geranium Tea (Pelargonium graveolens). Delicate, slightly spicy rose flavor. Serve hot or iced. Mint leaves make a nice addition.

Rose Hip Tea (Rosa spp.). Long served in northern Europe. Very high in vitamin C. Good for daily use. The dried, finely chopped rose hips must be soaked in a small amount of water for 12 hours before using. The tea is made by simmering 1 tbsp. rosehips in 3 cups of water for 30 to 40 minutes. A small amount of dried hibiscus flowers makes a nice addition to this tea, giving it a lemony flavor and a very attractive burgundy color.

Rosemary Tea (Rosmarinus officinalis). A fragrant tea. Lavender flowers are often added to it. Serve hot or iced.

Sage Tea (Salvia officinalis). A very good tea when made from fresh chopped green leaves. Aids the digestion. Serve hot or cold.

Sassafras Tea (Sassafras albidum). A rose-colored tea made by simmering the fresh or dried bark of the roots. Long considered a spring tonic.

Spearmint Tea (See Mint).

Speedwell Tea (Veronica officinalis). Similar in flavor to Chinese green tea. A common tea in Europe and is, in fact, known there as *Thé de l'Europe.*

Strawberry Leaf Tea (Fragaria vesca). A pleasant and fragrant tea. Very high in vitamin C. Considered a good substitute for coffee or oriental tea (contains tannin as does oriental tea). Made from dried leaves, which must be thoroughly dried before using because the wilting process produces a toxic substance in the leaves that disappears on drying.

Other berry leaf teas, such as raspberry and blackberry (*Rubus* spp.), are similar to strawberry, but each kind yields a slightly different flavor.

Sweet Cicely Tea (Myrrhis odorata). An anise-like sweet tea. Aids digestion.

Tea or Oriental Tea (Thea sinensis). Tea is processed in three forms: black tea, whose color is the result of its leaves being fermented; oolong tea, which is made from partially fermented leaves; and green tea, made from unfermented leaves. Tea leaves are graded into different qualities, depending on their position on the plant, with the leaf buds and youngest leaves being the highest grades. Flowery pekoe or pekoe tip is the top grade, containing only the leaf buds; next is orange pekoe, the first open leaf on the stem; then pekoe, the second leaf; and so on.

The following herbs make good additions to oriental tea: balm, basil, camomile, costmary, elder flowers, lemon thyme, lemon verbena, any of the mints, nettle leaves, oswego tea, wintergreen, and woodruff.

Thyme Teas (Garden Thyme—Thymus vulgaris; Lemon Thyme—T. citriodorus; Mother of Thyme or Wild Thyme —T. serpyllum). Aromatic, tonic teas. Lemon thyme is the most fragrant. In spite of its name, wild thyme tea is good for recovering from a hangover.

Wintergreen Tea (Gaultheria procumbens). The fresh leaves make a sweet, mild tea with the familiar wintergreen flavor. Euell Gibbons suggests, for better flavor, making the tea by adding boiling water to the leaves, covering the container and letting the leaves soak for a couple of days, then reheating the tea for drinking. The fermenting of the leaves while they soak stimulates the production of wintergreen's flavoring oils.

Woodruff Tea (Asperula odorata). A very delightful, fragrant tea. Made from green dried leaves. Can be steeped up to an hour.

Yerba Maté, or Paraguay Tea (Ilex paraguariensis). A favorite beverage tea in South America. Contains caffeine, but in smaller amounts than coffee or oriental tea. Like oriental tea, it comes in a green and a black variety.

COFFEE SUBSTITUTES

For those whose diets don't permit coffee, or those whose coffee nerves are getting out of hand, or those who just like a change of pace—the following plant parts can be roasted and used in place of coffee beans:

Asparagus seeds, carrots, chicory root, cleavers fruit, dandelion root, English oak acorns, figs, hawthorn seeds, milk thistle seeds, rowan fruit, soybeans, witch grass rootstock.

JUICES

Another way to turn a plant into a drink is to juice it. Like cooking and chewing, juicing is a way to release the liquid contents of plant cells by breaking their indigestible cellulose walls. The beneficial elements are then readily available for digestion and assimilation by the body.

You can get juice from plant greens or fruit by squeezing them, but the most effective way is to use a juicer or a blender. Take the stones out of fruits and cut or chop relatively hard or dry plant parts into small pieces before juicing them. Celery and carrots can be juiced raw if cut into enough pieces. When using a blender, unless the material is itself very juicy, add a little liquid to reduce the load on the motor. Finally, strain the blended liquid through a sieve or a cloth, depending on how much pulp you want to remove. If necessary, dilute with water to get the right taste and consistency.

The problem with juices is that in releasing the cell contents you expose them to air, with two undesirable results: 1) oxygen-sensitive elements (like vitamins A and C) begin to deteriorate; 2) the juice may lose its natural color and turn gray. The easiest solution is to drink your juice as soon as it is made. But if you want to keep juices for short periods, you can minimize the detrimental effects of oxygen by keeping them refrigerated in a closed container. Stirring in a little lemon juice before drinking will help eliminate the gray color, at least temporarily.

Taken regularly, vegetable and fruit juices can make important contributions to your general well-being. And many taste good enough, singly or in various combinations, to make "getting juiced" a pleasure. You can improve the flavor of others by adding carrot or fruit juices, herbs, spices, or honey. There's lots of opportunity for experimenting with the following listing to please your palate, revive jaded taste buds, and do the rest of you some good too:

Alfalfa, American mandrake fruit (May apples), apples, apricots, barberries, beets, bilberries, blackberries, black currants, buffalo berries, cabbage, cantaloupes, carrots, celery, chard, chives, chufa tubers, coconuts, cranberries, cucumbers (including skin), dandelion, elderberries, endive, garden rhubarb, garlic, grapefruit, grapes, green peppers, guava, kale, kohlrabi, lance-leaf plantain (young leaves), lemons, lettuce, milfoil (young leaves), mulberries, okra, onions, oranges, papaya, parsley, peaches, pears, pineapples, plums, potatoes (including skin), prickly pear fruit, radishes, raspberries, red currants, sorrel leaves, spinach, strawberries, sumac fruit, tamarind fruit, tangerines, tomatoes, turnip greens, watercress, wild clover.

ALCOHOLIC BEVERAGES

For some a curse, for others a crutch, for still others one of the last vestiges of a dying gentility—alcoholic beverages are, and for thousands of years have been, all things to mankind. For that you can blame or give praise to the plant kingdom, since all alcoholic drinks come from plant products. But "natural" alcoholic beverages, produced by fermentation only, are never stronger than wine, since the yeasts that convert sugars to alcohol cannot function when the alcohol content goes over about 14 percent. It takes distillation to make the "hard liquor" that consists of 50 to 80 percent alcohol.

Almost anything that contains sugars or starches (or to which sugar has been added) can be fermented to produce an alcoholic liquid—whether it is drinkable or not is another question. But again, plants come to the rescue, providing or improving flavor, color, and aroma where they may be less than enticing in the original product. Or they can change a perfectly good product into something altogether different and delectable in its own way: as, for example, brandy into liqueur or wine into vermouth.

The following plants are or have been used in making various kinds of alcoholic beverages. If you want to try making wine or beer, home winemaking and brewing kits and books with directions are readily available. If you just want to try flavoring some wine or brandy, the simplest way is to soak the plant parts in it. For wine, use one to two ounces of plant parts per gallon of wine, soaking them for a few days. Making your own "liqueur" from brandy is a little harder, if only because the required soaking time is a year or two (to extract all the flavor from the plant and "marry" it to the alcohol). Commercial liqueurs are made by soaking secret combinations of herbs and plant parts in alcohol, distilling it to concentrate the flavor, and then sweetening and perhaps coloring the flavored product. Don't expect to create Benedictine or Grand Marnier at home; then again, you may come up with something you like even better!

Beer Makings and Flavorings: Barley malt, black birch sap (in springtime), buck bean, ginger, ground ivy, hops, Indian corn, oats, quassia wood, rice, Scotch broom twigs, sweet flag root, wafer ash fruit (substitute for hops), wheat.

To Make Wine: Apples, bilberries, blackberries, cherries, dandelion flowers, elderberries (American elder and black elder), European cranberry, figs, garden rhubarb juice, ginger, grapes, hybrid rhubarb juice, red currants, rose hips, white birch sap (in springtime).

To Flavor Wine: Balm, basil, burnet saxifrage, camomile, cinnamon, cloves, galangal root, ginger, hyssop, rosemary, sage, wintergreen, woodruff.

Vermouth Flavorings: Balm, camomile, caraway, celery seed, cinnamon, cloves, dill seed, elecampane root, European angelica root, fennel seed, ginger, lemon rind, milfoil flowers, nutmeg, orange rind, peppermint, rosemary, sage, spearmint, star anise, sweet flag root, thyme, wintergreen, wormwood, yellow gentian root.

To Flavor Liqueurs and Cordials: Aloes, American spikenard berries, aniseed oil, apples, arnica flowers, balm, bennet root, blackberries, black currants, blackthorn fruit, cacao, caraway, cardamom seed, carrot seed oil, cinnamon, coffee beans, coriander seed, damask roses, elecampane root, European angelica root oil, fennel seed, garden violet flowers, German camomile flowers, ginger root, ginseng root, grapes, heather flower honey, horehound oil, hyssop oil, juniper berries, lemon oil, lovage seeds, mace, maidenhair, Mexican damiana leaves, myrrh, nutmeg, orange peel, orris root, peaches, peppermint oil, plums, pomegranates, potatoes, raspberries, Roman camomile oil, rowan fruit, saffron, strawberries, sweet flag root oil, wild black cherries, woodruff, wormwood, yellow gentian root.

BEAUTY FROM PLANTS: SOME NATURAL COSMETICS

The newest trend in the cosmetic industry is toward natural cosmetics. Made from natural plant and animal substances with few or no chemical additives, these cosmetics are more beneficial for your skin and hair than most ordinary commercial preparations, which are almost totally composed of chemical ingredients. Even the big-name cosmetic companies have started to offer some natural items, but the best selection of natural cosmetics can generally be found in health food stores. All commercial natural cosmetics tend to be expensive; fortunately, you can make many natural beauty preparations yourself at a much lower cost. To get you started, this section presents a listing of natural, plant-derived beauty preparations—all of which you can easily make yourself. Many of these are based on home beauty recipes that have been used successfully for centuries. The listing also includes general descriptive material on some important cosmetic herbs. Most of these herbs are used medicinally to treat skin disorders, and they have also been found to be beneficial to the skin for cosmetic purposes.

If you want to progress to making more elaborate natural cosmetic preparations than are presented here, such as various creams, you will find excellent recipes in Alexandra York's *The Natural Skin Care and Beauty Cookbook* and Beatrice Travern's *Here's Egg on Your Face*. For a very good discussion of total natural beauty care, see Linda Clark's *Secrets of Health and Beauty*.

Almond Facial Mask. Pulverized almonds made into a paste with a small amount of liquid. Best for oily skin, almonds soften the skin, cleanse it with their abrasive action, and nourish it with protein. Note: Most facial masks are applied to the skin, left on 15 to 20 minutes and washed off with warm water followed by a cold rinse. Do not apply masks to the eye area. Your face should be washed or cleansed with cream before using any mask.

Apricot Facial Mask. Fresh or dried mashed apricots mixed with warm olive oil to form a spreadable paste. Dry skin moisturizer, and vitamin A source.

Avocado Facial Mask. Mashed avocado heated over a double boiler until just warm. Dry skin moisturizer, provides protein and vitamins.

Banana Facial Mask. Made like apricot mask. Another dry skin moisturizer.

Barley Water Skin Freshener. Astringent; cleanses and softens skin. Made by simmering 3 tbsp. barley in 3 cups water for an hour. Strain and cool. Rinse off face after using. Must be refrigerated. Best for normal skin. Drinking barley water is also reputed to clear and beautify your skin (sweeten with honey and orange juice).

Beer Hair Rinse. Let a can of beer go flat and use as an after-shampoo hair rinse. Do not rinse out. Provides body to the hair. The beer smell goes away by the time the hair is dry.

Brewer's Yeast Facial Mask. Mix into a paste using a small amount of water. Its abrasive action cleanses pores and stimulates skin. Best for oily skin.

Camomile Flower Hair Rinse for Blondes. Gives blond highlights. Infuse ⅓ cup flowers in 1 qt. water. Steep until tepid. Pour repeatedly over hair. Leave on 15 minutes and then rinse out. Camomile flower infusion also has a soothing, healing, disinfectant effect on the skin and eyes; used in skin lotions and eye preparations.

Carrot Facial. Astringent, provides vitamin A. Carrot shavings with a little lemon juice can be applied directly to the face like a facial mask. Best for oily skin.

Cocoa Butter and Coconut Oil. Both make very good wrinkle removers.

Cucumber Facial. Astringent, cleansing, bleaching (for freckles and discolored skin); also used for sunburn and rough skin. Cucumber slices or juice applied to face (and hands, if desired) and left on 10 to 15 minutes, then rinsed off. Best for normal or oily skin.

Elder Flower Facial Mask. Tonic, clears and softens skin. Made by adding flowers or their infusion to commercial clay packs, or by mixing them into a paste with yogurt. Lactic bacteria in yogurt increases elder flowers' effectiveness. Elder flowers are one of the best plant cosmetics. Their mildly astringent infusion smoothes skin and removes wrinkles, bleaches freckles, helps relieve sunburn, and is good in eye preparations.

Fennel Facial Mask for Wrinkles. Strong infusion of fennel herb or seed, a liberal amount of honey, and some fennel herb added to commercial clay pack or yogurt; antiseptic, soothing, tones skin as well as removes wrinkles. Fennel infusion is also good for eye baths and compresses.

Flax Seed Hair Set. 1 cup of flax seed simmered with 3 cups of water. Strain and thin to the desired consistency. Flax seed available in health food stores.

Herbal Beauty Baths. 1) *Method:* tie ½ cup or more of a mixture of any of the herbs listed below into a wash cloth or small muslin bag and fasten this herb bag to the spout of your tub so that the hot water runs directly through it. When the bath is drawn, place the bag in the water. For a stronger effect, first simmer herbs 10 to 20 minutes in 1 qt. water. Then place both the resulting decoction and the herbs (in a bag or washcloth) in the bath water. 2) *Listing of some herbs according to their effects as a bath addition:* any of these can be combined into a bath mixture of several herbs.

Antiseptic—lavender, thyme, peppermint, eucalyptus, wintergreen.

Astringent—sage, milfoil, comfrey root, strawberry leaves or root, nettle.

Calming—fragrant valerian, balm, marjoram, hops, passion flower.

Cleansing (especially for oily skin)—lovage, milfoil, lemongrass, geranium leaves.

Healing—peppermint, milfoil, camomile flowers, elder flowers, linden flowers, rosemary, lovage.

Moisturizing—orange blossoms, camomile flowers, rose leaves, rose petals, rose hips, white willow bark.

Softening, wrinkle-removers—fennel, rose petals, elder flowers, linden flowers.

Stimulating circulation—thyme, mother of thyme, rosemary, lavender.

Toning the skin—thyme, lavender, milfoil, peppermint, nettle.

The "Glossary of Plant Categories and Properties" in Part 1 will help you find more plants to use in herbal baths for these and other effects.

Herbal Facial Steam. Cleans pores, softens, refines, and moisturizes the skin. Pour 1 qt. boiling water over ⅔ to 1 cup herbs in a large bowl. A mixture of sage, peppermint, and linden flowers is good, or make up your own mixture from the bath herbs listed in the last entry. Holding your head about 3 inches over bowl, cover both your head and the bowl with a towel to make a tent to retain steam. Steam face 10 minutes or less. You can also use a vaporizer or electric skillet to provide more constant steam and do away with the towel.

Honey Facial Mask. Massage a small amount of slightly heated honey over face. Leave on 15 minutes. Honey is antiseptic, cleanses pores, and tones skin. Good for oily and blemished skin. Wheat germ is often added to a honey mask (provides abrasive action, protein, and vitamins).

Hot Oil Facial for Dry Skin. Cleanse face and if possible steam it for 5 to 10 minutes to open pores. Apply warm olive oil or any other vegetable oil to face and throat. Put a warm, wet washcloth over face and lie down for 10 minutes. Remove oil with another warm, wet washcloth and a liberal application of witch hazel or any other skin freshener. The vegetable oil not only supplements the skin's natural oil supply, but the act of absorbing it stimulates the skin's own oil production. Note: The skin can absorb all vegetable and animal oils, but mineral oil—which forms the base of most ordinary commercial cosmetic creams— cannot penetrate the skin; it merely lubricates the surface. Natural commercial cosmetic creams, however, generally have a vegetable oil base.

Hot Oil Treatment for Dry Hair. Using cotton pads, apply warm olive oil or any vegetable oil to your scalp. Working with your fingers, distribute oil throughout hair, taking care that the ends are covered. Take a towel that has been dipped in hot water and wrung out and wrap it on your head. Reheat towel when it cools. After 20 minutes to an hour, shampoo hair thoroughly. For an easier oil treatment, apply oil to hair before retiring. Wrap head in a dry towel and leaves on all night, shampooing in the morning.

Hot Oil Treatment for Weak and Brittle Fingernails. See wheat germ oil fingernail treatment.

Lady's Mantle Acne Remedy. Infusion of this herb is tonic, soothing, and healing to skin.

Lemon Bleacher for Freckles and Discolored Skin. Apply lemon juice or cut lemon slice directly to skin. Wash off after 15 minutes. If your skin is the dry type, use a skin conditioning cream afterwards.

Lemon Hair Rinse for Blondes. Gives blond highlights. Use the strained juice of 2 lemons in an equal amount of warm water. Leave on 15 minutes and sit in the sun if possible. Then rinse out. The juices of lemons and other citrus fruits are often added to cosmetic preparations because of their astringent and acidic qualities.

Linden or Lime Flowers. Excellent cosmetic herb, antiseptic, mildly bleaching, good against wrinkles, stimulates circulation and hair growth, lovely fragrance. Can be used in skin lotions and other cosmetic preparations.

Lovage. One of the best bath herbs; good used by itself. Cleanses, deodorizes, heals.

Milfoil (Yarrow) Facial for Oily, Troubled Skin. Apply infusion directly to skin twice daily and rinse off. Good for blackheads. Herb or its infusion can be added to facial masks, facial steams, and hair preparations. It is astringent, healing, and tonic.

Nettle. Astringent, tonic, stimualtes hair growth, and improves skin. Dried or slightly cooked fresh young leaves are used in facial masks, bath mixtures, and hair preparations.

Oatmeal Facial Mask. Paste of dry regular oatmeal and a little warm water. Good for oily skin. Dry oatmeal rubbed directly on skin will remove flaky, peeling skin.

Papaya Skin Treatment. A fresh, mashed papaya applied as a face mask will remove dead, flaky skin.

Peach Facial Mask. Made like apricot mask. Peach kernel oil or almond oil can be substituted for olive oil. Serves as a dry skin moisturizer.

Peppermint. Antiseptic; contains menthol, thus cools and stimulates the skin. Good in facial steams and as a bath addition. Keep all preparations containing menthol away from the eyes.

Rosemary. Healing; stimulates hair growth. Used in hair rinses for thinning hair; also good as a bath addition.

Rosewater and Glycerin Skin Softener. An old-fashioned cosmetic, but really very effective. Use a rosewater-to-glycerin ratio between 50-50 and 75-25. Available from your druggist.

Sage Hair Rinse to Darken Hair. Make an infusion of ⅓ cup sage leaves in 1 qt. water. Steep 2 hours; strain. Pour over hair and leave on for ½ hour, then rinse out. Because of its astringent properties, sage is also used in facial steams and facial masks.

Strawberry. Astringent, very good skin cleaner. Used in facial packs and other cosmetic preparations. Best for oily skin.

Tomato Facial. Astringent, good against blackheads. Apply tomato slices or mashed tomato directly to face. Leave on 15 minutes and rinse off.

Vinegar Skin Freshener. One part apple cider or distilled white vinegar to eight parts water. Apply after each face washing. Restores the skin's natural acidity, and really does clear and refine rough, blemished skin. Can be made more aesthetic by the addition of fragrant ingredients. You can also use the same ratio for a vinegar hair rinse; blondes should use the white vinegar on their hair. Note: According to recent research, the skin and hair have a natural acid surface that affords protection against harmful bacterial action. It is essential to the health (and beauty) of your skin and hair to restore their acid balance after washing. This can be done with the above vinegar solution or any preparation with an acidity similar to the skin's (pH 4.2 to 5.6).

Wheat Germ Oil Fingernail Treatment. Place fingernails in warmed oil for 3 to 4 minutes. Wipe off oil and massage nails. Strengthens weak and brittle nails. Other vegetable oils can be substituted but they may not be as efficacious.

Witch Hazel Astringent. Excellent used alone or in combination with other ingredients.

Other Natural Beauty Aids. Though these are not made from plants, they are too good not to at least mention.

Egg-white mask, used as is or beaten, tightens and tones skin; mayonnaise as a marvelous skin softener, wrinkle remover, and hair conditioner; yogurt, sour cream, or buttermilk mask for oily, sallow skin; milk bath (1 qt. made from powdered skim milk and added to your bath), whitens and softens skin.

SCENTS—COMMON & UNCOMMON

Although all the five senses can appreciate beauty, sight and smell respond most universally to the aesthetic qualities of plants. The beauty of nature at its best is a blend of color, fragrance, and design, creating a single impression in the mind of the beholder. But you don't have to rough it in the woods or get up before dawn to enjoy nature's sensory delights: you can bring them into your own home whenever you want—in the form of a potpourri.

A potpourri is a mixture of flowers, other aromatic plant parts, and oils kept in a decorative covered container. When you want the fragrance of the mixture to scent the air, you remove the lid for as long as it takes to achieve the desired effect. At other times you keep the container closed to conserve the fragrance. But potpourris can please the eye as well. Those made of colorful dried flowers and plant parts show off to good advantage in a glass container; those made by the wet method (see below) can be kept in an attractive opaque container.

Although rose petals are the traditional main ingredient of a potpourri, any number of other flowers, plant parts, and oils can be combined to make for unlimited variety of scent and appearance. Roses have the advantage—shared by only a few other flowers, including lavender, lemon verbena, rose geranium, and tuberose—of not losing their fragrance with drying. Other flowers can be dried and then scented with their own volatile oils, or they can be used in the potpourri for color and bulk. Other plant parts —leaves, roots, fruit rinds, etc.—can also contribute fragrance or add interest by providing variety of color and form.

You can make potpourris by either the dry or the wet method. The dry method is easier and more common, and it has the visual advantage of preserving the ingredients in something like their live state. The older wet method—often called "sweet jar"—actually accounts for the name *potpourri*, which comes from the French term *pot pourri*, meaning "rotten pot." Perhaps you'd rather not have been told that little tidbit, but it's true: the ingredients, mixed with salt, do actually rot into an aromatic caked mass. Some claim that the fragrances are extracted and retained better in this method; but the wet potpourri is also more likely to take on a stale or musty odor with time. The dry potpourri tends to have a lighter, more subtle scent.

If you gather your own potpourri ingredients, following a few rules will help produce better results. Collect roses and other flowers on a dry, sunny day, preferably no less than two days after the last rainfall. The best time of day is in the morning, just after the dew has dried. Pick flowers that are nearly or recently opened; never use damaged flowers or those that have passed their peak, since the latter will have little volatile oil left. Pick other decorative plant parts (leaves, buds, etc.) at the same time.

The next step is to dry your collection. Use the standard methods described in "Getting and Keeping Herbs" (Part 1), being especially careful not to bruise delicate petals and leaves. Drying the parts on a raised window screen is very effective because it allows air to circulate on all sides. Turn them every few days. If the parts tend to blow away, cover them with cheesecloth or nylon netting. Keep them out of sunlight while drying; otherwise their colors will fade. For a dry potpourri, let the parts dry thoroughly; for a wet one, use them after one or two days, when they have become limp.

Unless you have a very large garden and lots of room to dry flowers, it will take time to accumulate enough materials for one or more potpourris. Keep your dried materials in large, well-sealed jars, protecting them as much as possible from light. If you have enough containers, you can store the different colors separately and then blend them in any proportions you like when making the potpourri mixture.

To make a dry potpourri, begin by mixing your flower petals to achieve the desired color effect. Put the mixture in a large bowl and for each quart of petals add about a tablespoon of fixative material (in crushed or ground form), which helps to keep the potpourri fragrant longer by retarding the evaporation of volatile oils. Then, carefully stir in a like amount of crushed or ground spices, and add any miscellaneous decorative or aromatic items your sense of artistry or of smell may suggest. Finally, stir a few drops of one or more aromatic oils into the mixture, but don't overdo it: too much oil or too many kinds of oil can unbalance the fragrance enough to ruin a good potpourri. To determine your own preferences, experiment by dividing your mixed petals into small batches and adding the rest of the ingredients (reduced proportionately, of course) in various combinations. When doing this, keep a good record of each experiment so that you can duplicate the most successful ones.

When the potpourri mixture is complete, store it in a sealed container for about six weeks to let the various fragrances meld into a smooth, harmonious blend. Fill the container only half to two-thirds full, so that you can stir the mixture every few days by turning and shaking the container. After six weeks, divide the mixture into as many portions as you plan to make up into individual potpourris, making sure that all ingredients are equally well balanced in each portion. For the longest-lasting fragrance, put up each potpourri in a decorative glass jar that can be tightly stoppered. If you open it sparingly, the fragrance can last for years. Potpourris made up in baskets or otherwise continuously exposed to the air will fade much sooner. Adding a little flower oil or brandy can revive a potpourri when its scent begins to weaken.

Dry potpourri mixtures can also be made into sachets and bath potpourris. To make a sachet, put an ounce or so of mixture into a small bag and keep it in a closet or drawer to perfume clothing, linens, etc. For a bath potpourri, crush or powder all the dry ingredients, then mix with an equal amount of borax crystals. Age the mixture in a sealed jar for a week or two. For each bath, put a teaspoon of the aged mixture into a small bag, and hang the bag where the steam from the incoming hot water will pass over it to release the scent.

For the wet method of making potpourris, put a layer of partly dried petals in the bottom of a large, wide-mouth jar; then add a layer of un-iodized salt (or even better, bay salt—salt from evaporated sea water). Add alternate layers of petals and salt until you run out of petals. Stir the mixture with a wooden spoon and compress it by putting a weighted plate on it (you see why you need a wide-mouth jar). Repeat the stirring daily, adding layers of salt and petals as more become available. Keep the weight on between stirrings. Eventually, fermentation will produce a broth at the top of the mixture. When this happens, stir the mixture—broth and all—thoroughly, replace the weight, and let everything sit undisturbed for one to two weeks. The result should be a caked mass that you can remove and break up into small bits. To complete the potpourri, combine the crushed cake with spices, oils, and fixatives as in the dry method. Because its appearance is not one of its appealing qualities, keep this potpourri in an opaque container. The best ones have two lids, a solid one to retain the scent and underneath it another with holes to release the fragrance when the solid lid is removed.

There are innumerable recipes for potpourris, but ultimately your own nose and eyes are the best guides. Keep in mind the general proportions of one tablespoon each of spices and fixatives per quart of petals. Add flower oils a few drops at a time until the fragrance is what you want. Whatever you add, always err on the side of caution: you can always add more.

The most common ingredients for potpourris are listed below. Some you can grow and prepare yourself; the others are available at drug stores, herb stores, or perfume supply houses. Experiment with these ingredients to get used to the processes involved; then you can strike out confidently in new directions to produce your own unique fragrances and effects.

Flowers

Aster, baby's breath, calendula, camomile, cardinal flower, carnation, common mullein, cornflower, elder, elecampane, European linden, garden violet, heliotrope, hollyhock, hyacinth, jasmine, jonquil, larkspur, lavender, lemon verbena, lily of the valley, mignonette, monkshood, narcissus, nasturtium, orange, Oswego tea, pansy, peppermint, rose, rose geranium, safflower, sweet acacia, tiger lily, tuberose, white melilot, wild daisy, woad, ylang-ylang.

Leaves

Balm, basil, bay, cinnamon, garden violet, lad's love, lavender, lemon thyme, lemon verbena, life everlasting, lovage, mint, Oswego tea, patchouli, rose, rose geranium, rosemary, sage, sweet cicely, sweet fern, sweet marjoram, sweet vernal grass, tarragon, thyme, wild vanilla, woodruff.

Spices

Allspice, caraway, cardamom, cinnamon, cloves, cubebs, ginger, mace, nutmeg.

Fixatives

Ambrette, asafetida, balsam of Peru, balsam of Tolu, clary sage oil, gum benzoin, gum mastic, khus-khus root, labdanum, myrrh, oakmoss, orris root, patchouli oil, reindeer moss, sandalwood, storax, sumbul, sweet flag root.

Oils

To make your own, soak at least ten successive batches of fresh petals in olive, safflower, or ben oil, leaving each batch in the oil for a day or two. When finished, strain and keep in a tightly closed container.

Bergamot, bitter almond, caraway, dill, eucalyptus, fennel, gardenia, heliotrope, honeysuckle, jasmine, lavender, lemon, lemon verbena, lilac, lime, meadowsweet, narcissus, orange flower (neroli oil), peppermint, rose (attar), rosemary, rosewood, sandalwood, tonka bean, vanilla, wallflower.

Miscellaneous Additions

Aniseed, cedar wood, coriander seed, European angelica root, lemon peel, linaloe wood, orange peel, rose buds, sandalwood, sassafras root, tonka bean, vanilla bean.

NOTES:

Ambrette comes from abelmosk (*Hibiscus moschatus*).
Balsam of Peru comes from the Peruvian balsam tree (*Myroxylon pereirae*).
Balsam of Tolu comes from the balsam tree (*Myroxylon balsamum*).
Ben oil comes from the horseradish tree (*Moringa oleifera*).
Gum mastic comes from the mastic tree (*Pistacia lentiscus*).
Labdanum comes from rock-rose (*Cistus ladaniferus*).
Oakmoss is a general term for various lichens that grow on oak trees.
Rosewood oil comes from rhodium shrubs (*Convolvulus scoparius* and *Convolvulus virgatus*).
Storax comes from the oriental sweet gum (*Liquidambar orientalis*).

DYES IN
LIVING COLOR

In dyeing, as in medicine, the once nearly universal use of plants has given way to the use of synthetic replacements (derived from coal-tar products), at least in the developed countries of the world. There is little point in disputing that, on the whole, synthetic dyes produce a wider range of colors, are more resistant to change or fading, and are simpler to use than natural dyes. And, unlike most plant dyes, they come in packages with plain instructions. So why bother?

Why, indeed? Why walk when you can ride? Why barbecue when you can cook in the kitchen? Why camp out when you can tour in your motor home? Why watch a sunset when you can watch television? Because—unless you are that modern marvel, the instant human being, as thoroughly boxed in and labeled by modern life as that synthetic dye—you still feel some kinship with the greatest synthesizer on earth: Nature. For uncounted ages, Nature provided man with color in his surroundings; and over the last 5,000 years or so man learned to transfer some of her colors to cloth, paper, wood, leather, etc. If this heritage means anything to you, then you will know why to "bother."

The vegetable dye known to have been in use the longest is indigo. An indigo-dyed garment dating from about 3000 B.C. was found in the ancient Egyptian city of Thebes; and references to blue in the biblical book of Exodus (25:4 and 35:25) undoubtedly mean also that indigo was used, although by this time purple and red had joined the company. Indigo dye happens to be naturally resistant to fading, but most vegetable dyes are "fugitive" and need added treatment to become color-fast. The process called *mordanting*—treating the material to be dyed with other substances that serve to fix the color—was discovered, probably in India, about 2000 B.C. Mordanting made it possible to get long-lasting colors from other plants as well: another blue came from woad, red from madder, yellow from weld, and brown from certain species of acacia. All these have been used for thousands of years to brighten man's life, and many others were added through the centuries.

The discovery of aniline dyes in the middle of the nineteenth century changed all that, until today only natives in primitive cultures, some rural people in developed countries, and a few persistent traditionalists practice the ancient arts of natural dyeing. There are, however, signs of reviving interest as man relearns something he apparently forgot in the heady rush of technological achievement: that as a being he is a part of, not apart from, Nature.

But renewed interest faces two obstacles: lack of knowledge about dyeing methods and limited availability of plants or plant dyes. The public library and personal experimentation can help overcome the first; the second may be a little harder. Many species of wild plants are protected by state law, and much of the land they grow on is privately owned. One answer is to grow them yourself (here again the library can be helpful). But if you are not the green-thumb type, or if your climate makes it difficult to grow the plants you want, you should be able to get much of what you need from commercial sources. Some dyes are available in ready-to-use forms, such as powders or extracts (e.g., indigo, catechu, fustic). Try botanical or dye supply houses for these. Dried plant parts for many others should be available through herb dealers. Four sources (with catalogs available) are:

Skilbeck Brothers Limited Bagnall House 55 & 57 Glengall Road London, S.E. 15, England	(Mordants, brazilwood, catechu, fustic, galls, logwood, madder, turmeric)

Dominion Herb
  Distributors, Inc.
61 St. Catherine Street
  West
Montreal 129, Quebec,
  Canada
	(Claim to have all herbs
	used for dyeing)

Comak Chemicals Ltd.
Swinton Works
Moon Street
London N1, England

C. D. Fitz Harding-Bailey
15 Dutton Street
Bankstown, NSW 2200
Australia

General Information about Dyeing

First of all, here are the things you need for dyeing:

1. Scales to weigh plant parts, material to be dyed, mordants, etc. Large postal scales (reading up to 5 pounds) are good for this purpose.

2. A copper, stainless steel, or enamelware kettle or pot large enough comfortably to hold 4 to 5 gallons of liquid and the material to be dyed. An iron pot can be used for dark colors.

3. Measuring cups and utensils for measuring from ½ oz. to 1 qt. of liquid.

4. A cooking thermometer.

5. Glass or wooden stirring rods (wooden ones can be used for only one color each).

6. Plastic spoons for handling mordants.

7. Soft water (rain water is best). Hard water can be softened by adding acetic acid or vinegar; a neutral reaction on litmus paper indicates softness.

8. Rinse buckets.

As for mordants, these are the most common ones, which are usually available at drug stores or even grocery stores:

Acetic acid (or vinegar, which contains acetic acid)
Alum (potassium aluminum sulfate). The most commonly used mordant
Ammonia (ammonium hydroxide)
Blue vitriol (copper sulfate)

Caustic soda (sodium hydroxide)
Chrome, in two main forms:
  Bichromate of potash (potassium dichromate)
  Bichromate of soda (sodium dichromate)
Copperas, or green vitriol (ferrous sulfate)
Cream of tartar, or potassium acid tartrate (potassium bitartrate)
Lime (calcium oxide)
Tannic acid
Tartaric acid
Tin (stannous chloride)

Directions for mordanting and dyeing vary considerably, depending on the dye source, the material to be dyed, the mordant involved, and the shade or color desired. Detailed instructions and recipes are available in books on dyeing (see the Bibliography and check your library). Only a general description and typical directions will be given here.

The raw animal fibers wool and silk have a greasy or waxy coating which must first be removed—the wool by washing (perhaps repeatedly) with a mild soap and rinsing; the silk by boiling with soap. The vegetables fibers cotton and flax do not need washing (unless, or course, they have accumulated greases), but their mordanting is longer and more complicated. In mordanting, the clean material is simmered (wool), boiled (cotton, linen), or soaked in hot water (silk) in which the mordanting agents have been dissolved. After a prescribed time, the material is rinsed and allowed to dry (chrome mordanting, however, is usually followed immediately by dyeing). The dye bath is prepared by soaking the chopped or crushed plant material in water overnight and then boiling until sufficient color is extracted. The plant material is then strained out and water added to make 4 to 4½ gal. of lukewarm dye bath, to which a pound (dry weight) of wet yarn or fabric is added. Wool, cotton, and linen are usually simmered in the dye bath; for silk the temperature must be kept at 160°F or less. After dyeing and stirring as long as necessary to get the desired color, the operator passes the dyed material through a series of rinses, each a little cooler than the previous one, until the rinse water remains clear. After drying, the dyed material is ready to use.

Typical mordanting instructions for one pound of wool (dry weight):

Heat 4 to 4½ gal. of soft water until it is lukewarm. Add 3 oz. alum and 1 oz. cream of tartar which have first been dissolved in a little hot water. Immerse wet (but not dripping wet) wool in the water; spread and stir to ensure even coverage. Heat gradually to boiling and then simmer for an hour, turning the wool occasionally. When the bath is cool enough to let the wool be handled, remove the wool and squeeze (don't wring) out the excess liquid. Place loosely in a bag or towel and let dry slowly in a cool place.

Typical dyeing instructions for one pound of wool (dry weight):

Crush or chop about 1 peck of leaves, soft stems, or flowers, or about 1 lb. of hard materials such as bark or wood; soak overnight in enough soft water to cover. The next day, boil for 30 minutes to 2 hours, depending on how readily the color is extracted. Strain out the plant matter and add water to make 4 to 4½ gal. of dye. After heating the dye bath to lukewarm, add the mordanted wool, which has first been wetted in lukewarm water. Move the wool back and forth and lift it in and out of the dye for even coverage. Heat the dye to boiling and simmer for 30 minutes or more. When the color is right, rinse the wool in buckets of successively cooler water until the rinse water remains clear. Squeeze out the excess water, roll the wool in absorbent cloth, and hang it up in a shady place to dry.

LIST OF PLANT DYES BY COLOR

This list gives only plant names applicable to each color. For details on the use of each plant, consult the following list which is organized alphabetically by plant name. The asterisk (*) in this list indicates that the plant so marked gives a dye which is not a simple color but a mixture; e.g., bloodroot, which gives a reddish-orange dye, is listed with an asterisk under both red and orange. Some plants give both a simple color and a mixed color which includes the simple one; these are not asterisked under the simple color but are under the color found only in the mixture. For example, logwood yields both a gray and a blue-gray dye; it is asterisked under blue but not under gray.

BLACK
Barberry
Black alder
Blackthorn
Common plum
English oak
Flowering ash
Logwood
Meadowsweet
Valley oak
Yellow dock

BLUE
*Bearberry
Cornflower
Dog's mercury
Elecampane
Hollyhock
Indigo
*Logwood
Meadowsweet
Mesquite
*Pomegranate
Privet
*Sweet potato
Woad

BROWN
*Alder buckthorn
Bird's tongue
*Black alder
*Black birch
Black gum
*Black oak
*Blackthorn
Black walnut
Canoe birch
Cascara sagrada
Catechu
Cotton
*Dyer's camomile
English walnut
*Ginkgo
Heather
Hemlock spruce
Iceland moss
*Indigo bush
Juniper

BROWN (cont.)
Larch
*Logwood
*Lombardy poplar
Osage-orange
Pomegranate
Rooibos
Rose of China
Sumac
*Sweet potato
*Turmeric
White oak

GOLD
Black oak
Dyer's camomile
Fustic
Goldenrod
Lily of the valley
Osage-orange
Privet
Smartweed
*Turmeric

GRAY
Bearberry
*Black alder
Blackberry
Bracken
Butternut
Logwood
Red maple
Rhododendron
*Rose of China
Rowan
St. Johnswort
*Shave grass
Sumac
*Wax myrtle

GREEN
Bearberry
Beard grass
Bird's tongue
*Black alder
*Black oak
*Bracken
Canoe birch

GREEN (cont.)
Coltsfoot
*Dog's mercury
Dyer's broom
Fumitory
Heather
Lady's mantle
Larkspur
*Lily of the valley
*Lombardy poplar
*Meadowsweet
Motherwort
*Nettle
Onion
*Red maple
*Rose of China
Scotch broom
Shave grass
*Sorrel
*Tansy
*Wax myrtle
White birch

ORANGE
Annatto
Black oak
*Bloodroot
Calliopsis
*Henna
Onion
Sumac

PURPLE
Black elder
*Dandelion
Heather
*Pomegranate
*Rose of China
Tall field buttercup
*Yellow bedstraw

RED
Alkanet
Alpine cranberry
*American ivy
Annatto
*Barberry
*Black birch

RED (cont.)
*Blackthorn
*Bloodroot
Calliopsis
*Dandelion
Dye bedstraw
*Henna
Madder
Poinsettia
Pokeweed
Red alder
Rue
Safflower
White birch
Wild marjoram
*Yellow bedstraw

TAN
*Apple
Butternut
*Fustic
*Goldenrod
*Osage-orange
Sumac
*Tea

YELLOW
Almond
Alpine cranberry
Apple
Barberry

YELLOW (cont.)
*Bearberry
Beard grass
Big-bud hickory
*Black alder
Black elder
Black oak
Bracken
Broad-leaved dock
Calliopsis
Chinese arborvitae
*Coltsfoot
Cotton
*Dog's mercury
Dyer's broom
Dyer's camomile
European ragwort
Flowering ash
Fumitory
*Fustic
Goldenrod
Hackberry
Heather
*Indigo bush
Jewelweed
Lily of the valley
*Lombardy poplar
Marigold
*Meadowsweet
*Nettle

YELLOW (cont.)
*Osage-orange
Peach
Pomegranate
Privet
*Red maple
*Rooibos
Rose of China
Safflower
Saffron
St. Johnswort
Sassafras
Scotch broom
Shave grass
Smartweed
*Sorrel
Sticklewort
Sumac
Sundew
Sunflower
*Sweet potato
*Tansy
Turmeric
Virgin's bower
Weld
White birch
White mulberry
Wild crab apple
Yellow bedstraw
Yellow root

LIST OF PLANT DYES BY PLANT

The following listing includes many of the plants that have been used for dyeing from antiquity to the present. Colors are given, but it is important to remember that in practice colors will vary, depending on where the plant grew, whether it is used fresh or dried, which mordant is used, what material is being dyed, and the strength of the dye bath. Mordants are indicated in many cases; where they are not, use alum to be safe unless you are sure none is needed. Above all, feel free to experiment—with different plants, different mordants, different techniques. It helps to keep records of all your attempts; that way there are no experiments that fail—only experiments that teach.

LIST OF PLANT DYES BY PLANT

Plant	Plant Part	Color	Material	Mordants/Additives
Alder buckthorn (Rhamnus frangula)	Bark (after drying for a year)	Bronze-brown	Wool	
Alkanet (Alkanna tinctoria)	Roots	Red	Wool	
Almond (Prunus amygdalus)	Leaves	Yellow	Wool	Alum
Alpine cranberry (Vaccinium vitis idaea)	Stems and leaves	Yellow to red	Cotton, linen, wool	Alum
American ivy (Parthenocissus quinquefolia)	Fruit	Pink	Wool	
Annatto (Bixa orellana)	Fruit pulp Seeds	Red Orange	Wool Wool	
Apple tree (Pyrus malus)	Bark	Yellow to yellow-tan	Wool	

Plant	Part used	Color	Material	Mordant
Barberry (Berberis vulgaris)	Leaves	Black	Wool	Copperas
	Roots	Yellow	Wool	
	Twigs and young leaves	Red-yellow	Wool	
Bearberry (Arctostaphylos uva-ursi)	Plant without roots	Yellow-green to gray	Wool	
		Green	Wool	Alum and copperas
		Blue-green	Wool	Blue vitriol
Beard grass (Andropogon virginicus)	Stalks and leaves	Greenish-yellow	Wool	Alum
		Brass	Wool	Chrome
		Green	Wool	Dye over indigo
		Henna	Wool	Dye over madder
		Yellow	Cotton	Alum-tannic acid-alum
Big-bud hickory (Carya tomentosa)	Bark	Yellow	Wool	
Bird's tongue (Fraxinus excelsior)	Bark and wood	Green, brown	Wool	
Black alder (Alnus glutinosa)	Bark	Gray-brown to black	Wool, cotton	Copperas
	Leaves	Brownish-yellow	Wool, cotton	Alum
		Greenish-yellow	Wool, cotton	Alum

551

Plant	Plant Part	Color	Material	Mordants/Additives
Blackberry (Rubus spp.)	Young shoots	Light gray	Wool	Alum
Black birch (Betula lenta)	Roots	Red-brown	Wool	
Black elder (Sambucus nigra)	Fruit	Violet	Wool	Alum
		Lilac	Wool	Alum and salt
	Leaves	Lemon-yellow	Wool	Alum
Black gum (Nyssa sylvatica)	Bark	Brown	Wool	
Black oak (Quercus velutina)	Inner bark (quercitron is commercial extract)	Yellow to buff	Wool, cotton	Alum
		Gold	Wool, cotton	Chrome
		Olive-green	Wool, cotton	Copperas
		Orange	Silk	Tin
Blackthorn (Prunus spinosa)	Bark	Reddish-brown	Wool	
		Black	Wool	Copperas
Black walnut (Juglans nigra)	Green hulls of nuts	Dark brown	Wool	Alum (or none)
		Drab	Cotton.	Alum-tannic acid-alum
Bloodroot (Sanguinaria canadensis)	Rootstock	Reddish-orange	Wool	Alum

552

Name	Part used	Color	Fiber	Mordant
Bracken (Pteridium aquilinum vars.)	Roots / Young shoots	Yellow / Yellowish-green / Gray	Wool / Wool, silk / Silk	Chrome / Alum, chrome / Copperas
Broad-leaved dock (Rumex obtusifolius)	Roots	Dark yellow	Wool	Alum
Butternut (Juglans cinerea)	Green hulls of nuts	Tan / Gray	Wool / Cotton	Alum / Alum-tannic acid-alum
Calliopsis (Coreopsis tinctoria)	Flowers	Orange to red / Yellow	Wool / Wool	Chrome / Tin and cream of tartar
Canoe birch (Betula papyrifera)	Inner bark	Light brown / Green	Wool / Wool	None / Blue vitriol
Cascara sagrada (Rhamnus purshiana)	Bark	Brown	Wool	
Catechu, or cutch (Acacia catechu)	Resin from heart-wood (extract available)	Brown	Wool, cotton	Chrome
Chinese arborvitae (Thuja orientalis)	Leaves	Yellow	Wool	
Coltsfoot (Tussilago farfara)	Herb	Yellow-green / Green	Wool / Wool	Alum / Copperas

Plant	Plant Part	Color	Material	Mordants/Additives
Common plum (Prunus domestica)	Bark	Black	Wool	Copperas
Cornflower (Centaurea cyanus)	Flowers	Blue	Wool	
Cotton (Gossypium spp.)	Petals	Yellow, brown	Wool, cotton	
Dandelion (Taraxacum officinale)	Plant	Magenta	Wool	
Dog's mercury (Mercurialis perennis)	Herb	Greenish-yellow to blue (with long boiling)	Wool	
Dye bedstraw (Galium tinctorium)	Roots	Red	Wool	
Dyer's broom (Genista tinctoria)	Flowering tops	Yellow Green	Wool, linen Wool, linen	Alum, chrome Dye over indigo
Dyer's camomile (Anthemis tinctoria)	Flowers	Yellow Khaki Gold	Wool Wool Wool	Alum Alum plus second dyeing Chrome

Plant	Part used	Color	Fiber	Mordant
Elecampane (Inula helenium)	Roots	Blue	Wool	
English oak (Quercus robur)	Bark	Black	Wool	Copperas
English walnut (Juglans regia)	Green hulls of nuts	Light brown Medium brown Dark brown	Wool Wool Wool	Chrome Copperas Tin
European ragwort (Senecio jacoboea)	Plant	Yellow	Wool	Alum
Flowering ash (Fraxinus ornus)	Bark and leaves	Yellow Black	Wool Wool	Alum Copperas
Fumitory (Fumaria officinalis)	Herb	Yellow, green	Wool	
Fustic (Chlorophora tinctoria)	Wood (extract available)	Yellowish-tan Gold Yellowish-tan	Wool Wool Cotton	Alum Chrome Alum
Ginkgo (Ginkgo biloba)	Inner bark	Whitish-brown	Cloth	Lime, potassium carbonate
Goldenrod (Solidago spp.)	Flowers	Yellow to yellowish-tan Gold	Wool Wool	Alum Chrome

Plant	Plant Part	Color	Material	Mordants/Additives
Hackberry (Celtis occidentalis)	Roots	Yellow	Wool	
Heather (Calluna vulgaris)	Young tips Flowering plant Tops Plant after flowering	Green Yellow Purple Brown	Wool Wool Wool Wool	Alum None Alum None
Hemlock spruce (Tsuga canadensis)	Bark	Brown	Wool	Alum (or none)
Henna (Lawsonia inermis)	Dried leaves	Orange-red	Wool	
Hollyhock (Althaea rosea)	Flowers	Blue	Wool	
Iceland moss (Cetraria islandica)	Plant	Brown	Wool	
Indigo (Indigofera tinctoria)	Leafy branches (powder available)	Blue	Wool	Caustic soda and sodium hydrosulfite

Plant	Part used	Color	Fiber	Mordant
Indigo bush (Dalea emoryi)	Small branches	Yellowish-brown	Wool	
Jewelweed (Impatiens biflora)	Plant	Yellow	Wool	
Juniper (Juniperus communis)	Fruit	Brown	Wool	
Lady's mantle (Alchemilla vulgaris)	Green parts	Green	Wool	
Larch (Larix europaea)	Needles (picked in autumn)	Brown	Wool	
Larkspur (Delphinium consolida)	Flowers	Green	Wool	Alum
Lily of the valley (Convallaria majalis)	Young leaves	Yellow to greenish-yellow	Wool	Chrome
	Autumn leaves	Gold	Wool	Chrome
Logwood (Haematoxylon campechianum)	Wood	Black	Wool	Alum and copperas
		Brown	Wool	Chrome
		Gray	Wool	Chrome and cream of tartar
		Gray-brown	Wool	Tin
		Gray-blue	Wool	Alum and cream of tartar

Plant	Plant Part	Color	Material	Mordants/Additives
Lombardy poplar (Populus nigra var. italica)	Leaves	Lime-yellow Golden brown	Wool Wool	Alum Chrome
Madder (Rubia tinctorum)	Roots	Lacquer red Garnet red Red Red Red	Wool Wool Cotton, linen Silk Leather	Alum Chrome Alum-tannic acid-alum Alum
Marigold (Tagetes spp.)	Flowers	Yellow	Wool, silk	Alum
Meadowsweet (Filipendula ulmaria)	Tops Roots Stems and leaves	Greenish-yellow Black Blue	Wool Wool Wool	Alum None Boil with sorrel root to fix color after dyeing
Mesquite (Prosopis juliflora var. Torreyana)	Leaves and fruit	Blue	Wool	
Motherwort (Leonurus cardiaca)	Herb	Dark green	Wool	

Nettle (Urtica dioica)	Herb	Greenish-yellow	Wool	Alum
Onion (Allium cepa)	Outside skins	Burnt orange Brass Green	Wool Wool Wool	Alum Chrome Copperas and blue vitriol
Osage-orange (Maclura pomifera)	Bark (extract available)	Yellowish-tan Gold Yellowish-tan	Wool Wool Cotton	Alum Chrome Alum-tannic acid-alum
Peach tree (Prunus persica)	Leaves	Yellow	Wool	Alum
Poinsettia (Euphorbia pulcherrima)	Flower bracts	Red	Wool	
Pokeweed (Phytolacca americana)	Fruit	Red	Wool	
Pomegranate (Punica granatum)	Skin of fruit	Yellow Brown Violet-blue	Cloth Cloth Cloth	Alum Iron water* Iron water followed by potassium carbonate

* Made by boiling rusty iron in vinegar and water.

Plant	Plant Part	Color	Material	Mordants/Additives
Privet (Ligustrum vulgare)	Branch tips	Yellow	Wool	Alum
		Gold	Wool	Chrome
	Fruit	Blue	Wool	
Red alder (Alnus rubra)	Bark	Red	Wool	
Red maple (Acer rubrum)	Bark	Olive	Wool	Alum
		Gray	Wool	Copperas
Rooibos (Combretum apiculatum)	Bark	Brown	Wool	Copperas
		Brownish-yellow	Wool	Alum, chrome, tin
Rose of China (Hibiscus Rosa-sinensis)	Flowers	Yellow	Wool	Alum, chrome
		Brown	Wool	Tin
		Lavender to purplish-gray	Wool	Copperas
	Stalks and flowers with calyx	Olive-green	Wool	Alum, chrome
Rowan (Sorbus aucuparia)	Bark	Gray	Wool	
Safflower (Carthamus tinctorius)	Flowers	Yellow	Wool, silk	Alum
		Yellow	Leather	
		Scarlet	Cloth	Dye over turmeric

Saffron (Crocus sativus)	Stigmas	Yellow	Wool, silk	Alum
St. Johnswort (Hypericum perforatum)	Tops	Yellow	Wool	Alum
Sassafras (Sassafras albidum)	Flowers	Yellow	Wool	Alum
Scotch broom (Cytisus scoparius)	Flowers	Light green	Wool	Alum
	Flowering branches	Yellow	Wool	Alum, chrome
		Green	Wool	Dye over indigo
Shave grass (Equisetum arvense)	Sterile stalks	Yellow	Wool, cotton, linen	Alum
		Gray-green	Wool, cotton, linen	Copperas
		Grass-green	Wool, cotton, linen	Blue vitriol
Smartweed (Polygonum hydropiper)	Herb	Yellow	Wool, cotton, linen	Alum
		Gold	Wool, cotton, linen	Chrome
Sorrel (Rumex acetosa)	Leaves	Greenish-yellow	Wool	

Plant	Plant Part	Color	Material	Mordants/Additives
Sticklewort (Agrimonia eupatoria)	Stalks and leaves	Yellow	Wool	Alum, chrome
Sumac (Rhus glabra)	Ripe fruit	Yellowish-tan	Wool, cotton	Alum
	Dry leaves and shoots	Gray	Wool, cotton	Copperas
		Tan to dark brown	Wool, cotton	None
	Roots	Yellow to orange	Wool, cotton	
Sundew (Drosera rotundifolia)	Plant	Yellow	Wool	Boil in ammonia to make dye bath
Sunflower (Helianthus annuus)	Ray flowers	Yellow	Wool	
Sweet potato (Ipomoea batatas)	Dried leaves	Yellowish blue-brown	Wool	Iron water
Tall field buttercup (Ranunculus acris)	Tops	Purple	Wool	Baking soda
Tansy (Tanacetum vulgare)	Leaves	Yellow-green	Wool	

Plant	Part Used	Color	Material	Mordant
Tea (Thea sinensis)	Leaves	Rose-tan	Wool	
Turmeric (Curcuma longa)	Rootstock	Yellow	Cloth	Potassium carbonate, citric acid
		Gold-brown	Cloth	Iron water followed by slaked lime (calcium hydroxide)
Valley oak (Quercus lobata)	Bark	Black	Wool	Iron water
Virgin's bower (Clematis virginiana)	Twigs and leaves	Yellow	Wool	
Wax myrtle (Myrica cerifera)	Leaves	Gray-green	Wool	Alum
Weld (Reseda luteola)	Herb	Lemon-yellow	Wool	Alum
		Golden-yellow	Wool	Chrome
		Yellow	Silk	Chrome
White birch (Betula alba)	Young leaves	Green	Wool	Alum
		Yellow	Wool	Chalk
White mulberry (Morus alba)	Bark and wood	Yellow	Wool	Alum

Plant	Plant Part	Color	Material	Mordants/Additives
White oak (Quercus alba)	Bark	Brown	Wool	
Wild crab apple (Malus baccata)	Bark	Yellow	Wool	
Wild marjoram (Origanum vulgare)	Herb	Reddish	Wool	Alum
Woad (Isatis tinctoria)	Leaves	Blue	Wool	Alum, potash (potassium carbonate)
Yellow bedstraw (Galium verum)	Roots	Light red	Wool	Alum
		Purplish-red	Wool	Chrome
	Flowering tops	Yellow	Wool	Alum, chrome
Yellow dock (Rumex crispus)	Roots	Black	Wool	Chrome
Yellow root (Xanthorhiza simplicissima)	Roots	Yellow	Wool	

A PLANT
MISCELLANY

The usefulness of plants is unending, and a single book can hardly pay sufficient tribute to the diversity of their worth. This section briefly describes some of the more important remaining uses of plants, from sweetening your breath to building your house. For greater detail, consult some of the very helpful books listed in the Bibliography.

Breath Sweeteners and Mouthwashes

Most of these have been chewed to freshen the breath. Made into tea, or soaked in 75% alcohol for a week and then diluted, they become mouthwashes:

Aniseed, cardamom seeds, cloves, European angelica root, gum mastic, mint leaves, orris root, parsley, peppermint oil (additive), sweet flag root, tarragon tea.

Dentifrice Ingredients

Dried and powdered plant parts can be used as tooth powders. Mix them with plant extracts or oils to make a toothpaste.

Alder bark (vinegar decoction), charcoal, clove oil, lemon oil, mint, myrrh, nutmeg oil, orris root, Peruvian bark, rhatany root, rose oil, sage, sassafras oil, soapwort (decoction of root as additive), sweet flag root, thyme oil. wintergreen.

Deodorants

These liquid plant preparations can be used as deodorizing washes:

Creosote bush (leaf decoction), lovage (infusion), thyme oil (disinfectant additive), white willow bark (infusion) with borax, witch hazel extract.

Fibers

Stems, twigs, and inner bark are the usual sources of plant fibers. Soaking or beating or both are often necessary before the fibers can be extracted. After drying, they can be worked into such things as rope, twine, cloth, netting, stuffings, baskets, blankets, and mats:

Agave leaves, baobab, basswood, bear-grass, buckhorn brake (leaf hairs), cannabis, carnauba leaves, coconut husks, corkwood, cotton, date palm leaves, dwarf nettle, flax, giant arbor vitae, Guinea sorrel, hemp dogbane, *Hibiscus surattensis*, hops, iris leaves, Joshua tree (root bark), jute, kapok tree seeds, maidenhair, milkweed, musk-mallow, nettle, ramie, Scotch broom, Spanish bayonet leaves, squaw bush, yucca leaves.

Honey

These plants are preferred by bees. The color and to some extent the flavor of the honey depend on the plant contributing the bulk of the nectar.

Alfalfa, balm, basil, basswood, black sage, blind nettle, borage, buckwheat, camomile, catnip, chicory, cotton, dropwort, European linden, European sweet cicely, fennel, ground ivy, heather, hyssop, inkberry, lavender, marjoram, meadowsweet, mezereon, Oswego tea, partridge pea, rosemary, saw palmetto, Scotch broom, sugar bush, sweet orange, thyme, tulip tree, white clover, white melilot, winter savory, yellow melilot.

Insect Repellents

Either the plant parts or various extracts and other preparations made from them can be used. Those marked with * are good for moths, those with † for fleas:

Aspic oil, †black alder leaves, black birch bark, chili pepper, columbine seeds (crushed), English walnut leaves, †eucalyptus leaves, European pennyroyal oil, garlic, khus-khus root, *†laurel leaves, mugwort, onion, patchouli, pine needles, *red cedar wood, true, *sweet flag root, *tansy, wild marjoram (for ants), †winter savory, *wormwood, *yellow melilot, yew leaves.

Insecticides and Parasiticides

These plants are usually made into a spray or dusting powder to kill insects and parasitic vermin. Those marked with * are for lice:

*Alder bark (vinegar decoction), American hellebore root, *aniseed (salve), *columbine seeds (crushed), cube plant root (source of rotenone), derris root (source of rotenone), dittany, *European pennyroyal oil, feverfew flowers, green hellebore root, *larkspur seed (tincture), mayweed, *parsley fruit, prickly juniper (oil of cade), pride of China fruit, pyrethrum flowers, red cedar wood oil, sweet flag root, tansy, thyme oil, *wild angelica fruit, wild tobacco leaves (decoction).

Livestock Feed

These plants are used to provide forage, fodder, and silage. The pulp remaining after extracting the oil from the seeds of plants is called oil cake; the plants marked with * provide an oil cake that makes a high-protein food for livestock:

Acorns (hogs), alfalfa, barley, carrots, chicory, *coconut, *cotton, dropwort (hogs), fenugreek, foxtail millet, goat's rue (dried), *Indian corn (oil cake or whole), *jojoba, kidney bean plants, kidney vetch (sheep and goats), oats (horses), *opium poppy, rape (sheep and hogs), rice hulls and straw, rye, *safflower, *St. Benedict thistle, *sesame, sorghum, velvet bean, white melilot, wild clover.

Oils

Drying oils react with oxygen to form a tough elastic film. Semidrying oils react slowly with oxygen to form a soft film. Nondrying oils remain liquid at normal temperatures and form no film when exposed to air.

Oils for Edible Uses. Mostly semidrying and nondrying oils and plant fats (oils that are solid at ordinary temperatures) are used for cooking and salad oils. Some drying oils are used in making cooking fats and other food products:

Avocado, black mustard seed, Brazil nut, celery seed, cocoa bean (cocoa butter), coconut, cottonseed, cucumber seed, English walnut, horseradish tree seed (ben oil), Indian corn, linseed, oil palm fruit, olive, opium poppy seed, peanut, pumpkin seed, rapeseed, safflower, sesame seed, shea tree seed, sour cherry kernel, soybean, sunflower seed.

Oils for Illumination. Semidrying oils are most commonly used for burning in lamps:

Cannabis seed, coconut, olive, pumpkin seed, rapeseed, soybean, sunflower seed, white mustard seed.

Oils for Lubricants. These are generally nondrying oils that remain liquid and retain their properties over a certain range of conditions:

Black mustard seed, cashew nut, castor bean, jojoba seed, oil palm fruit, olive, rapeseed, white mustard seed.

Oils for Making and Scenting Soap. Soap consists of a mixture of various oils and fats with lye. Semidrying oils are the most important for this use. Aromatic oils provide the scent.

Baobab seed, black mustard seed, Brazil nut, cannabis seed, castor bean, clary sage, coconut, coriander seed, cottonseed, English walnut, European pennyroyal, Indian corn, laurel seed (bay fat), lavender, lemon grass, lemon seed, linseed, oil palm fruit, olive, opium poppy seed, orange seed, peanut, red cedar wood, sesame seed, shea tree seed, soybean, thuja leaf, rapeseed, ylang-ylang flower.

Poison Ivy (Oak) Remedies

Decoctions or liquid extracts of these plants can be used as a wash for poison ivy irritation, or the fresh plant can be made into a dressing for small areas. Euell Gibbons has had excellent results with a jewelweed decoction, which can be preserved by freezing.

Gum plant, jewelweed, lobelia, mugwort, Solomon's seal, sumac, sweet fern, witch hazel.

Soap Substitutes

These plants contain compounds called saponins in sufficient quantities to produce lather when the mashed plant parts are beaten up in water. They can also be used to make shampoos:

Amole root, California soap plant root, California soaproot bulb, guaiac leaves, papaya leaves, quillai bark, red campion root and leaves, saltbush root, soapberry fruit, soap pod fruit, soap tree yucca root, soapwort root, Spanish bayonet root, wild gourd fruit.

Tanning

Hot water extracts the tannic acid (or tannin) from plant materials—usually bark or wood. When a prepared animal skin or hide is soaked in a tannic acid solution, the tannin combines with the protein of the hide to form decay-resistant leather. Samples of Egyptian leather over 3000 years old have been found in nearly perfect condition.

American chestnut wood, baobab bark, bearberry leaves, black alder bark, black wattle bark, catechu wood, divi-divi pods, Douglas fir bark, dwarf sumac leaves, heather bark, hemlock spruce bark, Iceland moss, mangrove bark, myrobalan fruit, oak galls and bark, pomegranate rind, quebracho wood, red pine bark, rhatany root, tanbark oak wood, tanner's dock root.

Tobacco Substitutes and Additives

These are most commonly mixed with regular smoking tobacco (*Nicotiana tabacum*), but the leaves of most of them can be smoked alone as a nicotine-free tobacco substitute. Those marked with * are additives for flavor or aroma:

*Bearberry, buck bean, chervil, coltsfoot, *corn silk, *cubebs, dittany, evergreen sumac, *field mint, hawthorn (young leaves), *licorice, life everlasting, manzanita, milfoil, mugwort, pearly everlasting, rock-rose, rosemary, sage, sumac, *sweet flag root, *sweet gum balsam, *wild marjoram, *wild vanilla, *woodruff, *yellow melilot, yerba santa.

Waxes

Natural plant waxes usually occur as external coatings on various plant parts. The jojoba plant is a notable exception, its wax occurring in liquid form in the seeds. Carnauba is the hardest wax known.

Candelilla, carnauba, jojoba, sugar cane, wax myrtle, wax tree.

Wood—Small Objects

These woods are made into such items as tools and implements, decorative artifacts, gunstocks, and inlay or mosaic work:

Alder buckthorn, apple, barberry, basswood, bird's tongue, black alder, black birch, black poplar, blackthorn, black walnut, black willow, boxwood, California laurel, common buckthorn, common plum, dogwood, English elm, English ivy, English walnut, eucalyptus, European aspen, European linden, guaiac, hawthorn, horse chestnut, Joshua tree, magnolia, maple, mountain holly, mountain laurel, olive, pear, privet, quaking aspen, red ash, redwood, rowan, sandalwood, shagbark hickory, sour cherry, spruce, sweet cherry, teak, white ash, white birch, white holly, white pine, white willow, yew.

Wood—Interior Uses

These woods are made into larger interior items such as furniture, cabinets, and paneling:

American chestnut, basswood, bird's tongue, black ash, black birch, black walnut, boxwood, butternut, English elm, English oak, English walnut, European linden, giant arbor vitae, horse chestnut, larch, longleaf pine, mahogany, manzanita, maple, mountain holly, Oregon ash, pride of China, quaking aspen, red alder, red ash, red gum, rosewood, sour cherry, sweet cherry, sweet gum, sycamore maple, teak, tulip tree, white ash, white holly, white oak, white pine, wild black cherry.

Wood—Exterior Uses

These woods provide materials for such heavy-duty applications as building, marine uses, agricultural implements, and fence posts:

American chestnut, bald cypress, black birch, black walnut, blue ash, coconut palm, Douglas fir, English elm, English oak, eucalyptus, giant arbor vitae, guaiac, hemlock spruce, larch, longleaf pine, mangrove, maple, mesquite, mulberry, Oregon ash, pecan, ponderosa pine, quaking aspen, red alder, red ash, red oak, red pine, redwood, rowan, sallow, sassafras, shagbark hickory, slippery elm, spruce, sweet gum, teak, thuja, white ash, white oak, white pine.

PLANTS
AND ASTROLOGY

Astrology had its beginnings with the ancient Sumerians and Babylonians, but it was the Greeks who started the development of an elaborate system of correspondences linking plants (as well as animals, metals, stones, colors, parts of the body, and other qualities and things) with the sun, the moon, the known planets, and the twelve constellations of the zodiac. But through the ages, no single authoritative system of classification for these correspondences was ever established. In fact, when you compare several sources on this subject, you will find a staggering amount of disagreement on which individual plants relate to the various astrological signs. In this section, we will not try to give a full presentation of the subject with its many discrepancies. Instead you will find a listing of some of the better-established correspondences (generally those upheld by two or more sources) and whenever possible a description of the reasoning used by ancient and medieval peoples in classifying these correspondences.

There were many different reasons for relating plants to certain signs, but the main idea behind most of the correspondences is simply making connections on the basis of similar qualities: it was believed that a plant's physical appearance or various other attributes would in some way resemble the sign which governed it. (Often the connections required considerable ingenuity to "discover.") Another means of classifying plant correspondences was by their use as medicines. Because each astrological sign governed a particular part or function of the body, a plant used as medicine for some part of the body could be linked to the sign ruling that part. For example, the planet Jupiter ruled the blood functions, so a plant known as a blood purifier could very well be assigned to Jupiter.

In the medical practices of the late Middle Ages, doctors actually based prescriptions on reference lists of such plant-astrological sign correspondences. Through a very complicated system, they used not only those plant medicines that related to certain affected parts of the body, but also those which were ruled by favorable signs in the sick person's horoscope.

We who have seen men walk on the moon are not likely to recover such faith in the stars that we would entrust our health to them, yet we still can find fascination and significance in astrology, even in this skeptical, scientific age.

ASTROLOGICAL SIGNS AND SOME OF THE PLANTS THEY RULE

THE SUN, THE MOON, AND THE PLANETS. The correspondences of plants to the sun, the moon, and the planets come first in this list, because they are historically more important and better defined than those relating to the signs of the zodiac.

The Sun. Rules 1) plants with parts resembling it in shape and/or color, as the orange, the reddish-orange spice saffron, and the following yellow flowers: camomile, celandine, marigold, sunflower; 2) medicinal plants affecting the heart, a part of the body ruled by the sun: European angelica, lovage, rosemary, rue (all stimulate circulation); 3) others: centaury, eyebright, storax, walnuts.

The Moon. Rules 1) plants with parts similar in shape and/or color, as banana, gourds, mango, melons, pumpkin, and the following white or yellow flowers: opium poppy, orris root, sweet flag, water lilies; 2) plants with high water content, often with soft, juicy leaves: cabbage, cucumber, lettuce, and other leafy vegetables; 3) plants that live in or near water: seaweed, watercress, willow, wintergreen.

Mercury. Rules 1) plants with fine or highly divided leaves (because of the planet's supposed airy nature): caraway, carrots, dill, fennel, parsley; 2) medicinal plants affecting the brain, nervous system, or speech: lavender, lily of the valley, marjoram, parsnips; 3) others: elecampane, horehound, mandrake.

Venus. Rules 1) plants with particularly pretty flowers (relate to Venus as goddess of love and beauty): columbine, daisy, periwinkle, primrose, some roses, violet; 2) red fruits (Venus' favorites): apple, blackberry, plum, raspberry, red cherries, red elderberry, strawberry, tomato; 3) others: birch, burdock, elder, feverfew, mother of thyme, sorrel, tansy, thyme, vervain.

Mars. Rules 1) plants with thorns or prickles (thorns represent weapons and relate to Mars as the god of war): barberry, cacti, hawthorn, nettle; 2) plants with a strong acrid taste: capers, coriander, garlic, gentian, hops, horseradish, mustards, onion, peppers, radish, tobacco, wormwood; 3) others: basil, sarsaparilla, tarragon.

Jupiter. Rules 1) certain nutritious fruits and nuts: almond, chestnut, currant, fig, olive, rose hip; 2) plants with a pleasant odor: anise, balm, cloves, English myrrh, jasmine, linden, meadowsweet, nutmeg; 3) the oak tree, which is associated with the god Jupiter in mythology; 4) medicinal plants affecting the arterial system or liver, parts of the body ruled by Jupiter: chervil, cinquefoil, dandelion, docks, sage; 5) others; fir tree, mulberry.

Saturn. Rules 1) plants with cooling qualities: barley, comfrey root, tamarind; 2) woody shrubs or trees that show annual rings (like Saturn's rings): elm, cypress, pine; 3) poisonous or narcotic plants: hellebore, hemlock, marijuana, mezereon, monkshood, yew; 4) others: quince, red beet, sloes, Solomon's seal.

The outer planets—Uranus, Neptune, and Pluto—were discovered after the seventeenth century, so that no comparably long-established plant associations exist for them.

SIGNS OF THE ZODIAC. A plant can be ruled by both a planet or the sun or moon and a sign of the zodiac. Some items here are not upheld by two sources because of the small amount of material available on them.

Aries. Rules 1) many of the plants also governed by Mars, including cacti, garlic, hops, mustard, nettle, onion, peppers, radish; 2) others: betony, lichens, rosemary.

Taurus. Rules lovage, and plants of the earth like mushrooms.

Gemini. Rules 1) mosses because it is an airy sign; 2) others: tansy, vervain.

Cancer. Rules 1) many plants governed by the moon (both Cancer and the moon relate to water): cucumber, lettuce, melons, rushes, water plants including water lilies; 2) others: agrimony, alder, lemon balm, honeysuckle, hyssop, and jasmine.

Leo. Rules 1) many plants also governed by the sun: camomile, celandine, European angelica, eyebright, marigold, orange, rue, saffron; 2) others: borage, bugloss, peony, poppy.

Virgo. Dedicated to Ceres, the Roman goddess of agriculture, and thus rules the cereal plants—barley, oats, rye, wheat—and grasses and sedges.

Libra. Rules 1) many of the plants also governed by Venus: apple, cherry, primrose, strawberry, white rose, violet.

Scorpio. 1) As the ruler of the sex organs, governs plants that could be considered phallic symbols, such as palms, flowers like calla lilies; 2) others: basil, bramble, wormwood—all plants that are also ruled by Mars.

Sagittarius. 1) As the centaur and ruler of the forests, rules forest trees with catkins: oak, beech, elm; 2) others: mallows, feverfew.

Capricorn. Rules comfrey, cypress, hemlock, nightshades, yew—plants that are also governed by Saturn.

Aquarius. Rules frankincense, myrrh.

Pisces. As the fishes, rules algae, seaweed, and water mosses.

LEGEND
AND LORE

Many plants have a rich history of fact, folklore, symbolism, and mythology that often dates back thousands of years. Generally, the plants that have the most lore connected with them are those which were most useful to man as food, medicine, or commercial products or those which impressed him with special characteristics such as striking size, beauty, or longevity. But plant folklore, symbols, and myths also represent men's efforts—ranging from naive to sophisticated—to fulfill basic human psychological needs, especially the need to explain the unknown. Thus gods, devils, witches, and magic make up much of the body of world plant lore. As modern, twentieth-century folk we may be tempted to react with amused condescension toward these stories, but in the wholesale discarding of old beliefs we may also run the risk of losing more than we gain. Both the tenacity and the symbolic richness of legendary stories suggest that they have a psychological validity that survives even when we can no longer believe them literally. With so much still left to discover about the mind and world of man, we can hardly afford to throw away anything we may already have learned.

But even aside from such weighty considerations, both fact and fiction in plant history make interesting reading in themselves. By providing a glimpse into the past, they let us see even the most familiar plants around us in a new light. The dandelion in your lawn or the parsley on your plate may never be the same again.

ACACIA

Acacia was a sacred wood for the ancient Hebrews. According to God's instructions, Moses used acacia wood

575

in the building of the Ark of the Covenant and the sacred Tabernacle (Exodus, chapters 25-40).

According to Near-Eastern Christian legend, a thorny species of acacia was used for Christ's crown of thorns.

AGAVE

The agave is considered the Mexican Tree of Life and Abundance, probably because the people of that region have had so many uses for it. It provides them with food, fodder, paper, twine, soap, roofing, dye, and alcoholic drinks. Its popular name century plant comes from the mistaken notion that it blooms only once in a hundred years. Actually, it flowers after eight or ten years and then dies.

ALMOND

Because the almond tree blossoms in the early spring, it is an emblem of hope. In Greek legend, the almond is associated with Phyllis, a Thracian princess who was abandoned on her wedding day by the Greek prince Demophon. She eventually died of a broken heart, after waiting many years for him to return from Greece. In sympathy, the gods transformed her into an almond tree, the symbol of hope.

In Christian medieval art, the almond is a symbol of divine approval. This symbolism is based on a biblical passage (Numbers 17:1-8) in which the rod of Aaron (presumably made from an almond tree) grew buds, flowers, and ripe almonds as a sign that God had chosen Aaron and his tribe of Levi to be the priests of Israel. (See the poplar entry for another biblical passage referring to the almond.)

AMARANTH

The name amaranth is derived from the Greek word for *unfading* or *unwithering* and was given to this plant because its flowers retain their color and appearance when dried. The Greeks considered the unfading amaranth a symbol of immortality, using it to embellish the images of their gods and tombs. Amaranth is frequently used in poetic literature as a symbol of constancy, fidelity, and immortality.

ANGELICA

Whenever the plague swept over Europe in the Middle Ages, angelica was a first line of medical defense. An old legend tells how an angel had appeared to a monk in a dream, revealing to him that this herb was a cure for pestilence. From then on, it was called angelica and was considered the most effective of all plants against witchcraft—the only plant no respectable witch would ever include in her brews.

APPLE

Apples are thought to have originated in Southwest Asia, in the region between the Black Sea and the Caspian Sea. From earliest times, the apple has been a popular and important fruit, partly because of its hardiness and the fact that it can be grown in a wide variety of climatic conditions. The diggings of Stone Age lake dwellers in central Europe show that these people used apples long before recorded history began.

Because of the apple's widespread use, it appears in many myths and stories; the most famous is the one based on the biblical account of Adam and Eve. The Bible does not identify the fruit from the tree of knowledge of good and evil, but popular tradition most often names the apple as the devil's lure. Symbolically, Eve's apple represents enticing temptation, indulgence in earthly desires, disobedience, and loss of innocence. It has appeared frequently with these and other connotations in literature through the ages.

The Greeks also had some famous apple stories. The origin of the Trojan War, for example, was attributed to the Apple of Discord, a golden apple thrown down in front of an assembly of the gods by the goddess of hate, Eris. It was inscribed, "For the Fairest." Naturally, the three most eminent goddesses—Hera, wife of Zeus and queen of the gods; Athene, goddess of wisdom; and Aphrodite, goddess of love—all wanted the apple. Paris, the handsome son of the king of Troy, was appointed to choose the most beautiful of the three. Hera offered him power and riches; Athene offered wisdom and fame; but he yielded to Aphrodite, who promised to give him the most beautiful woman in the world—Helen, the wife of a Greek king. With Aphrodite's help, Paris abducted Helen and took her to Troy. His refusal to return her to her husband started the Trojan War, which resulted finally in the destruction of Troy.

Another Greek story involves the golden apples of the Gardens of the Hesperides. One of the twelve heroic labors performed by Herakles (or Hercules) in his pursuit of virtue and immortality was to obtain these apples. He succeeded only after slaying a hundred-headed serpent that guarded them.

There is also the Greek story of Hippomenes, a young man who was able to win the hand of the beautiful and swift-footed Atalanta by beating her in a footrace. Aphrodite had helped Hippomenes by giving him three golden apples, which he threw down during the race to distract Atalanta's attention.

Apples also appear in many folk tales. Grimm's Fairy Tales, which are all taken from old folk tales, have at least four stories involving apples, including the famous Snow White. Two of these use the theme of the young man securing a golden apple to obtain the hand of a princess. The accounts of the lives of William Tell and Johnny Appleseed could also be considered in the folk tradition even though they involved real persons.

ASAFETIDA

As its name suggests, asafetida has a fetid smell and a nauseating taste—characteristics that also burdened it with the name devil's dung. In the Middle Ages, a small piece of the gum was worn around the neck to ward off disease. Whatever effectiveness it had was probably due to the antisocial properties of the amulet rather than any medicinal virtue.

Surprisingly, in Persia asafetida was used as a condiment and called the "food of the gods."

BALM

The name balm comes from the Greek *balsamon* meaning "balsam," an oily, fragrant resin. Since balm does not actually exude a balsam, it probably received its name from its fragrant aroma and its ability to soothe and calm the nerves. Balm has been known since antiquity for its medicinal qualities and for its use in bee-keeping (bees are particularly attracted to its pollen). Balm's genus name *Melissa* is the Greek word for bee.

The balm of Gilead mentioned in the Bible (Genesis 37:25 and Jeremiah 8:22) is a different plant, *Commiphora meccanensis*. Furthermore, the balm of Gilead described in Part 2 of this book is not the biblical plant; it is a North American tree, *Populus candicans*, a member of the poplar family. This North American poplar, because of its medicinal properties, was probably named after its biblical counterpart. Both of these plants exude balsam.

BASIL

Basil is reputed to stimulate sensuality. In Haiti the herb is associated with the pagan goddess of love, Erzulie. Haitian store-owners sprinkle basil water over their places of business to chase away evil spirits and to bring buyers and prosperity.

In rural New Mexico, carrying basil in your pockets is supposed to attract money into them. In the same region, a wife who wishes to cure her husband's wandering eye is told to go through a ritual of dusting basil powder over various parts of her upper body, especially over the heart. Her husband will then become a faithful and loving spouse.

BEAN

The species of bean described in Part 2 of this book, *Phaseolus vulgaris*, is indigenous to the Americas, being unknown to the rest of the world before Columbus. (This species includes the common green bean as well as wax beans, and various dried beans such as red kidney, pinto, and navy.) These beans were extensively cultivated by Indian tribes from Canada to South America, with each tribe having its own names and folklore for the beans.

Before the discovery of the New World, Europeans did have other bean species with various traditions associated with them. On three days of the year, the Roman head of the household went through a ritual ceremony of spitting beans out of his mouth to rid his home of evil spirits. This custom carried over to the Middle Ages, where spitting a mouthful of beans in a witch's face was considered to negate her powers. Perhaps beans were thought to be a potent deterrent against evil because as a seed they have stored within them the positive life force of all living and growing things.

BELLADONNA

Of the three Greek goddesses of fate, Clotho was said to have spun life's thread for men at their birth; her sister Lachesis to have determined its length; and the third sister, Atropos, to have cut the thread off. Atropos was said to have used poisonous belladonna berries in carrying out her duties.

In the Middle Ages belladonna was considered to be the favorite plant of the devil, who supposedly watched over it night and day. The name is derived from the two Italian words, *bella* and *donna*, which together mean "beautiful lady." To make themselves more beautiful, Italian ladies used the juice of the berries for a cosmetic coloring agent and to dilate their pupils to give themselves mysterious, appealing eyes (an effect due to the alkaloid atropine).

BIRCH

The source of the name birch has not been definitely established. According to one authority the name goes back to the ancient Indian word *bharg*, meaning "shining." Another less poetic theory imputes its origin to the Latin word *batuere*, to strike. Possibly the Latin word may be the true source, for birch rods have been used since ancient times to punish children and others. According to legend, Christ was beaten with birch rods. The fasces, a bound bundle of birch sticks enclosing an axe with the blade projecting, were carried by Roman soldiers in advance of emperors or important officials. These fasces symbolized the state's power to punish by flogging (the birch sticks) or by putting to death (the axe).

Birch wood has also been used for furniture, wooden spoons, tool handles, and broomsticks. (Witches on Walpurgis Night were said to have ridden on broomsticks made of birch.) American Indians used the water-resistant birch bark for their canoes and wigwams.

To the peoples of northern Europe, the birch was a sacred tree. In the *Kalevala*, a Finnish epic, the birch is designated as a holy tree of great use to mankind. The Germanic peoples dedicated it to their god of thunder, Thor.

BIRD'S TONGUE (EUROPEAN ASH)

The ash was a sacred tree to the Scandinavian and Germanic tribes of northern Europe. In their mythology a mighty ash tree called Yggdrasill served as a representation of the cosmos. The tree's roots were the underworld. The earth or Midgard (meaning "middle land") where people lived was a disk surrounded by a ring of water. This disk and its circular ocean covered the tree's lower branches, supported by the trunk. In the upper branches, Valhalla, the heaven of the gods, was located, along with the land of the giants and the land of the frozen north.

According to this same mythology, the universe, the gods, and the giants came into being first. After that, vegetation sprouted forth; then the gods created the first human couple out of two trees. The first man, who was called *Ask,* sprang from an ash tree; and the woman, *Embla,* was thought to have come from the elm or alder tree. The name ash is derived from *Ask.*

BLACK HELLEBORE

Black hellebore's pearly white flowers, which suggest purity and innocence, provide a dramatic contrast to its black root. The flower is also called the Christmas rose, because it blooms from December through March—one of the few flowers that bloom in the winter. A medieval nativity play contains a charming story about the origin of this flower. In the play, a country girl named Madelon, who has come with the shepherds to Bethlehem, is very sad because she has no gift for the Christ child. Since it is winter, there are not even flowers to pick. An angel, seeing her plight, leads her outside and touches the ground, from which springs the first Christmas rose.

Even though black hellebore is poisonous, it was highly regarded by the Egyptians, Greeks, Romans, and medieval Europeans for its beneficial medicinal effects in treating mental illness. Already in the time of Moses, an Egyptian physician was advocating it for this purpose. That the Greeks valued it for the same use is evident in their legend of Melampus (or Mecampe) and the daughters of the King of Argos. Melampus was the first Greek seer, who was able to understand the secrets of Nature because he had shown kindness to some snakes. After Melampus' reputation as a seer and healer was established, Proetus, the king of Argos, begged him to cure his mad daughters. This Melampus was able to do because the goats in his pastures had revealed the black hellebore to him. This use is still mentioned in the writings of the sixteenth-century herbalist Gerard.

Another belief that survived through the Middle Ages was that the Christmas rose was useful to ward off evil spirits. The flower was used to bless animals and homes and was even strewn on the floors of houses to drive out evil influences. Naturally, it was used to ward off the power of witches and to break spells and enchantments. However, witches were also said to have used it for their own purposes.

BORAGE

In ancient times and in the Middle Ages, borage was known for its cooling quality and refreshing flavor and was said to make men merry. Thus, it was put into drinks and salads.

BRYONY

Bryony was considered a wicked plant in the Middle Ages. Medieval con men passed off carved bryony roots as mandrakes, making great profits and deceiving many people, including childless women who bought the root as a fertility drug or charm.

CARLINE THISTLE

In the Middle Ages an angel is supposed to have shown Charlemagne how to use the carline thistle against an epidemic of the plague which was killing his soldiers. Consequently this plant was named after Charlemagne, whose name in German was Karl der Grosse, or Carl the Great.

Some of the other medieval beliefs about the carline thistle are quite intriguing. One was that a person carrying this thistle could draw strength into himself from other people and animals. Related to this is another belief that by eating a cooked carline thistle root a man could gain the sexual strength and potency of a stallion. For this to be effective, the root had to be grown and prepared according to a prescribed ritual which included planting and harvesting it only under a new moon at the stroke of midnight and fertilizing it with the sperm of a black stallion.

Even today some people in rural Germany believe that carrying a carline thistle will protect a person from harm. In the same area, the people regard the carline thistle as a weather predicter. The flower closes when the air becomes more humid, which is usually the indication of rain and bad weather.

CLOVER

Clover, one of the first plants cultivated by man, has been highly regarded since ancient times. The three-leaf clover was associated with the Christian Trinity, and in pre-Christian times with the triad goddesses of the Greeks and the Romans and the sacred sun wheel of the Celts. In the Middle Ages it was considered a charm against witches. The national flower of Ireland, the three-leaf clover was said to have been planted there by St. Patrick because of its Christian symbolism. (Wood sorrel, *Oxalis acetosella*, is considered by some authorities to be the true shamrock, rather than the clover.)

The rare four-leaf clover, also a Christian symbol with its four leaves representing the form of the cross, was said to enable its wearer to ward off evil (including witches), to see fairies and various spirits, to heal illnesses, to have good fortune, and to escape military service. According to an old medieval folk rhyme, each leaf of a four-leaf clover represents a different aspect of happiness. One leaf stood for fame; the second, wealth; the third for a faithful lover; and fourth for excellent health. Together these qualities could be said to represent the epitome of good fortune, a completely happy life. The five-leaf clover was said to be unlucky and the two-leaf clover was supposed to enable a maid to see her future lover.

DAISY

According to Roman myth, the daisy originated when the meadow nymph Belides changed herself into a daisy to avoid the amorous attentions of Vertumnus, the god of the orchards. The English name daisy comes from the Anglo-Saxon *daeges eage*, meaning "day's eye," referring to the flower's characteristic of opening its petals in the daytime and closing them at night. The genus name for the daisy, *Bellis*, is from the Latin *bellus*, for "pretty."

The daisy has always been associated with purity, innocence, and loyal love. It was dedicated to Aphrodite, Venus, and the Northern goddess of love and spring, Freyja. Chaucer in his *Legende of Goode Women* has Queen Alceste transformed into a daisy because her virtues were as numerous as the daisy's florets. According to Christian legend the daisy sprung from Mary's tears during the flight into Egypt. In Christian medieval art, the flower was used as a symbol of the innocence of the Christ child.

The daisy was once named *measure of love* after the well-known custom of using the flower as a love oracle by pulling off its petals and reciting, "he loves me, he loves me not." Because the daisy's petals are usually odd-numbered, if you start with "he loves me," you will end up the "right" way. According to a German folk belief, daisies picked between 12 noon and 1 p.m. have magical qualities. They should be dried and then carried as a good luck charm that will bring a successful result in any new undertaking.

DANDELION

The name dandelion comes from the French term for "lion's tooth," *dent-de-lion*, and was given to the plant because its jagged, irregularly toothed leaves resembled a row of teeth in a lion's jaw as shown in early medieval woodcuts. To carry your thoughts to your sweetheart, blow the feathered seeds off the puffball of a dandelion (if the wind is blowing in the right direction). To dream of a dandelion is suppposed to be bad luck.

DILL

The common name dill probably comes from the Saxon word *dillan*, meaning "to dull," referring to the practice of giving dill to restless babies to make them sleep. Dill was supposed to be effective against witches in the Middle Ages.

ELDER

Elder seeds and branches found in Stone and Bronze Age diggings show that this plant has been used by man since before recorded history. The elder's Latin genus name

Sambucus is derived from the Greek word *sambuke*, a musical wind instrument made from elder wood. The pith can be easily removed from elder sticks, leaving a hollow pipe suitable for making music. The Roman writer Pliny (23 to 79 A.D.) tells us that shepherds in his day made trumpets and flutes from the elder.

In the mythology of the early northern European tribes, the goddess Freyja chose the black elder as her abode because of its beneficial medicinal qualities. In contrast, in medieval Europe the elder had a very bad reputation, being associated with evil and witches. It was considered dangerous to sleep in the shade of an elder or to plant one near a house because of its supposed evil, narcotic effects. Cradles were never made of elder wood for the same reason. The elder and the hawthorn were the favorite plants of witches. A witch who wanted to hide in a hurry could always transform herself into a branch on the nearest elder tree. Witches were also said to live in elder trees, so people were loath to chop them down for fear of what the tree's witch might do to them. One belief held that a person would die within three days after chopping down an elder; another claimed that it was all right if you apologized aloud to the witch first. One reason for the elder's tainted image is that the berries and most other parts of the plant are poisonous when eaten raw. In the Middle Ages, poisonous plants were usually the province of the Devil and of witches.

ELECAMPANE

Its species name *helenium* is a reference to Helen of Troy, who is said to have been carrying this plant when Paris abducted her. The common name elecampane is a corruption of the plant's former botanical name *Inula campana*.

ENGLISH IVY

Ivy was dedicated to the Greek god of wine, Dionysus, who is often pictured crowned with an ivy wreath. According to one myth, Dionysus when a youth used ivy to foil some sailors who abducted him in hopes of selling him as a slave in Egypt. But their ship would not proceed toward Egypt, for Dionysus caused the ship to be bound and fastened with ivy and grape vines. In Greece ivy is called *cissos*, after the nymph Cissos, who is said to have joyously danced herself to fatal exhaustion before Dionysus. Feeling pity, he turned her to ivy.

EUROPEAN VERVAIN

In ancient Egypt vervain was said to have originated from the tears of Isis, who wept for her murdered husband Osiris. In Rome, heralds sent to other countries with messages of war or peace wore wreaths of vervain as magical protection against enemies. For the Druids, vervain was a holy food used in their ritual ceremonies to produce magic spells. The Druid ritual specified that the plant could be collected only when neither the sun nor the moon was in the sky and that honeycombs were to be put on the ground as recompense for depriving the earth of such a sacred herb. The Druids also used vervain as a protection against evil; it was used similarly in the Middle Ages to make one immune against the powers of witches.

FENNEL

Fennel has been used as a condiment since the times of the Romans and Anglo-Saxons. In the Middle Ages people ate fennel seeds to stave off hunger during Church fasts. This custom was still going strong in the time of the American Puritans, who took fennel and dill seeds to church in handkerchiefs to eat discreetly during long services.

In sixteenth-century Europe, the expression "to give fennel" meant to flatter or give false compliments. Possibly this expression was derived from fennel's use during fasting. Just as fennel allayed hunger for a while, bringing no lasting nourishment, a false compliment flatters temporarily but brings no real satisfaction to its recipient. For some unknown reason fennel is also connected with sorrow as in the old proverb, "to sow fennel is to sow sorrow."

FIG TREE

From the Far East to Africa and the Mediterranean, the fig was an important food and a sacred tree to many ancient peoples. The tree is still sacred in India, China, and Japan because under it the monk Gautama received his divine illumination and thus became the Buddha. The Moslems call the fig "Tree of Heaven" and revere it because Mohammed swore by it. And the fig, of course, played a significant part in the life of the early Hebrew people, as many biblical references show, including the Garden of Eden story. The discovery of a fig-harvesting scene on the wall of an Egyptian tomb dated about 1900 to 1700 B.C. indicates that the fruit was also important to the ancient Egyptians. Sacred to the Greeks and Romans, the fig was said to be a gift to the people from the Greek god of wine and agriculture, Dionysus, and Bacchus, his Roman counterpart. In festivals of Dionysus, the fig was included along with the phallus as a fertility symbol. This association is the origin of its sexual symbolism, which survives even today in certain vulgar expressions and gestures.

The fig tree also had a part in the founding of Rome. According to legend, Rome was built at the spot where a fig tree caught Romulus and Remus as they floated down the river Tiber in a basket.

GARDEN VIOLET

According to Greek legend, the violet originated from the tears of Io, a beautiful nymph whom Zeus loved. To hide Io from Hera, his jealous wife, Zeus changed her into a white heifer. When Io cried because the field grasses were too coarse and bitter for her taste, Zeus transformed her tears into violets to provide her a more delicate food. In Greek burials it was the custom to cover the dead person with violets as a symbol of both the beauty and the transitory quality of life.

Because of his fondness for the flower, Napoleon was sometimes known as Corporal Violet. When he was exiled on Elba, the violet became his symbol for his supporters.

Violets were strewn along the parade route when he returned to power in Paris, after escaping from the island.

In literature, violets are often associated with modesty and simplicity. In Shakespeare's play *Hamlet*, Laertes says of his sister Ophelia at her funeral:

> *Lay her in the earth:*
> *And from her fair and unpolluted flesh*
> *May violets spring!*

GARLIC

Garlic has a long history as a food plant. In Egypt several thousand years before Christ, garlic was given for strength and nourishment to the laborers who built the pyramids. The Bible records that the Israelites who lived in Egypt at the time of Moses also ate garlic before their exodus out of that country (see Numbers 11:4-6). Like the Egyptians, the Romans gave garlic to their laborers; and their soldiers ate it in the belief that it inspired courage. Thus it was dedicated to Mars, the Roman god of war.

Garlic has also been valued for its medicinal and antiseptic qualities. It has seen use since ancient times in the West and the Orient as an antiseptic medicine against the plague and for many other ailments besides. Even today in rural New Mexico, garlic is worn strung on a necklace to preserve against infection from diphtheria. Because of its strong odor and antiseptic properties, seventeenth-century sailors used it in cooking their stale and rotting food supplies, especially their meats.

Since the ancients believed that many diseases were the result of evil spells, garlic with its effective medicinal qualities was thought to possess magical power against evil; thus it was used in many charms or countercharms. In Greek legend, Odysseus used moly, a wild garlic, as a charm to keep the sorceress Circe from turning him into a pig. In the Middle Ages, garlic was considered strong against the evil eye, witches, and demons. Another tradition still held in rural New Mexico is the use of garlic as a charm to help a young girl rid herself of an unwanted boyfriend. She first puts a piece of garlic and two crossed pins in a spot where two roads intersect, and then she must get the boy to walk over the charm without noticing it. If the task is accomplished successfully, the boy will miraculously lose all interest in her.

GENTIAN

The gentians take their name from Gentius (second century B.C.), the king of Illyria, who was said to have first discovered the medicinal value in these plants. Actually an Egyptian papyrus, found in a tomb at Thebes and dated about 1,000 years before Gentius, describes medicines containing plants of the gentian family.

GINSENG

The name ginseng is derived from the Chinese words for "likeness of man" because its roots sometimes resemble a human figure. (The Chinese consider such roots to be the most efficacious medicinally and will pay high prices for them.) Ginseng's genus name *Panax*, like the word *panacea*, comes from the Greek word *panakeia*, meaning "all-healing." This refers to the plant's reputation as a Chinese cureall—a reputation it has enjoyed for thousands of years.

To the Chinese, ginseng is a tangible link between man and the unseen spiritual reality on which existence is based: they believe that the ginseng plant contains an embodiment of the great spirit of the universe. When a ginseng hunter finds the plant growing wild, he will first kneel in prayer, claiming that his soul is pure and asking that the great spirit remain in the plant. Its efficacy thus assured, he digs up the root and takes it home—probably for his own use rather than for the herb market, since wild specimens are very rare.

Most ginseng used for medicinal purposes is cultivated, some of it here in the United States. In the early 1900's, ginseng was one of the nation's chief moneymaking export crops; and most of the ginseng grown in the U.S. today is still exported.

HAWTHORN

In ancient Greece and Rome, the hawthorn had happy associations, being linked with sweet hope, marriage, and babies. Dedicated to Hymen, the god of marriage, the hawthorn was used as a symbol of hope at weddings in Greece; bridal attendants wore its blossoms while the bride carried an entire bough. Also, in both Greece and Rome, torches carried in wedding processions were made of hawthorn. The Romans put hawthorn leaves in the cradles of newborn babies to ward off evil spirits.

In medieval Europe, hawthorn had an entirely different image. Generally regarded as an unlucky plant, it was thought that bringing its branches inside would portend the death of one of the household's members. Hawthorn was also one of the witch's favorite plants and was especially to be avoided on Walpurgis Night, when witches turned themselves into hawthorns. With a little superstitious imagination, the hawthorn's writhing, thorny branches at night probably do look enough like a witch to have instilled fear in medieval folk.

HEMP (CANNABIS)

Thought to have originated in the area just north of tne Himalaya mountains, the hemp plant was used by the Chinese to produce fiber as early as 2800 B.C. By 500 A.D. the plant had spread to Europe, and eventually it was brought to the New World by the explorers. Now it is a common plant found wild or cultivated over much of the world.

The mind-affecting properties of hemp have also been known since antiquity. According to the Greek historian Heroditus (fifth century B.C.), the ancient Scythians and Thracians got high on the fumes of the roasted seeds. Because of their effects on the mind, hemp drugs are outlawed or restricted in most countries of the world; but the demand for them is more than sufficient to maintain considerable illegal world traffic.

Hemp drugs are prepared in three main grades: bhang, ganja, and charras. Bhang, the least potent and cheapest form, consists basically of the dried leaves and flowering tops of male and female hemp plants. The marijuana used in the United States is comparable to bhang in quality and potency. Ganja, a more potent preparation, consists of a mixture of resin and plant parts from the flowering tops of female plants. Charras, the most potent and expensive grade, consists of pure resin from the female flowers of plants grown at high altitudes. Within the three main grades are further graduations of quality, depending on the actual method of preparation. Hashish, for example, is an inferior grade of charras.

The word *assassin* is generally linked with hashish through the Arabic word *hashshashin* or *hashishin* (meaning "hashish eaters"), a term applied to a class of followers of a Persian secret society active from the eleventh to the thirteenth century A.D. Assassination of enemies, the predominant feature of the sect, was carried out by the *hashishin* under the influence of a drug, presumably hashish. However, both the identification of hashish with the drug involved and the validity of the etymology of *assassin* have been challenged as inaccurate. A definitive resolution of the question is of some importance, since the story of the Persian assassins provides one of the main arguments for those who associate marijuana with crime.

HOREHOUND

Horehound was dedicated by the ancient Egyptians to Horus, their god of the sky and light. It was also one of the bitter herbs taken by the Jews at their celebration of the Passover.

HOUSELEEK

In the Middle Ages the houseleek was grown on housetops as an especially potent charm against lightning and evil spirits—a sort of medieval lightning rod. Under Charlemagne's edict, all landlords in his empire were required to plant houseleeks on their rooftops for this purpose. The Romans and the early Scandinavians also associated the houseleek with thunder and lightning; it was dedicated to the Roman god Jupiter with his thunderbolts, and to the Scandinavian thunder-god Thor. There may, in fact, be some validity in the houseleek's use as a natural lightning rod; its pointed leaves apparently do tend to dissipate atmospheric electric charge, reducing perhaps the probability that lightning will strike where it grows.

IMPERIAL MASTERWORT

During the Middle Ages imperial masterwort was a panacea—good for everything that ailed a person. For this reason it was considered the king or emperor of all the roots, and that is how it got its name.

INDIAN CORN

Like the kidney bean, Indian corn was a contribution from the Americas to world agriculture. Before Columbus this food was unknown in the Old World. Grown on a wide scale by the Indians of the Americas, corn, as the sustainer of life, provided a major symbol in the rituals and mythologies of many tribes. One of the best-known Indian myths of the origin of corn is the one recounted in Longfellow's poem *Hiawatha*. Longfellow's source was a contemporary account written by a U.S. government agent, Henry Schoolcraft, who had married an Indian girl of the Ojibwa tribe from the Great Lakes region. According to Schoolcraft's account, the Ojibwa myth has as its protagonist an Indian youth named Wunzh, who had reached the proper age to undertake a ceremony of ritual fasting. According to the custom of his tribe, he fasted for seven days alone in a little hut in the forest to receive communication from his guardian spirit. During his fast a handsome young god wearing green and yellow garments and a plumed, feathered headdress came to him out of the sky. The god told Wunzh that he had information for him that would be of great benefit to his tribe, but that Wunzh must wrestle with him first. After three wrestling matches on three separate days, the god declared himself subdued and gave Wunzh instructions. He told him that they would wrestle again on the following day and that the match would result in the god's death. He directed Wunzh to bury him and to water and cultivate the burial spot at certain intervals so that a corn plant would grow up there. The god told Wunzh how to harvest and cook the corn and described the process of growing it again from the kernels. Naturally, all these things came to pass, and the tribe had a great feast of celebration at their first corn harvest.

The corn harvest also provided a central focus for the religious ceremonies of the Aztecs, Incas, and Mayas, whose high levels of civilization were made possible by their well-developed systems of agriculture, with corn as the major crop. The Aztecs held a yearly pre-harvest corn festival in which a beautiful young girl representing the corn goddess was sacrificed in an elaborate ritual lasting several days. A grisly eye-witness account of this festival, written by a Spanish priest, is given in James G. Frazer's *The Golden Bough*.

IRIS

The name iris is the Greek word for the rainbow. To the Greeks the rainbow was personified in the beautiful, swift-footed goddess Iris, Zeus and Hera's messenger, whose path between heaven and earth was the rainbow. The Greeks planted irises on women's graves, for Iris was said to lead the souls of women to the Elysian Fields.

The iris, prized for its medicinal value in antiquity and the Middle Ages, was used medicinally as early as about 1540 B.C. during the reign of the Egyptian pharaoh Thutmosis I, who had the iris depicted on the walls of the Temple of Theban Ammon at Karnak. To the ancient Egyptians the iris was also a symbol of life and resurrection, and was associated with their god Osiris and his son Horus. Osiris was the first legendary pharaoh, who was killed and was then made immortal. After his death, his earthly duties were transferred to Horus, who later also acquired powers of regeneration. A stylized iris appears on the brows of Egyptian sphinx statues, which are said to be representations of Horus.

The iris is thought to be the source of the fleur-de-lis

symbol, which has been used since antiquity but is best known for its associations with French kings. (Since the words *fleur-de-lis* in French mean "flower of lily," the lily also has been named as the model for this symbol; but the iris in its actual appearance and its history has a better claim to this title.) Tradition has it that the first French ruler linked with the fleur-de-lis symbol was Clovis I (466-511 A.D.), who founded the Merovingian dynasty of Frankish kings. There are at least five different legends that purport to explain why Clovis chose the symbol. One is that he wished to commemorate the iris because his men had fashioned victory wreaths for themselves out of irises after the Battle of Tolbiac (496 A.D.).

The first historically documented use of the fleur-de-lis by a French king was when Louis VII chose it for his banner in the Second Crusade in 1150. After that time both the symbol and the iris flower were called *fleur de Louis* (flower of Louis) which eventually was modified to *fleur de luce*, then *fleur de lis*. Until the eighteenth century the iris had this name in France. In 1376 Charles V of France adopted three golden fleurs-de-lis on a blue field as the official coat of arms of France. This design remained the emblem of the monarchy until the French Revolution.

The sweet-smelling orris root, a white iris (described in Part 2 of this book), was used in the Middle Ages and antiquity in making cosmetics and perfumes. Because many iris roots resemble a seated figure, they have been used for voodoo dolls in the West Indies.

JASMINE

Jasmine, which originated in the Near East, takes its name from the Persian word *jasemin*. Its beautiful white flower is most famous for the perfumes made from its oil. In the first century A.D., Dioscorides, a Greek physician and author of the famous book on medical herbs *De Materia Medica*, tells us that the Persians used jasmine oil to perfume the air at their banquets. To the Chinese the jasmine symbolizes womanly sweetness. In medieval Christian art, jasmine was associated with the Virgin Mary. Dreaming of jasmine is supposed to portend good fortune, especially in love.

JIMSON WEED

Found in Europe, Asia, and North and South America, jimson weed has been used for hallucinogenic and medicinal purposes since ancient times. The Greek priests of Apollo used it to produce prophecies. In 38 B.C. Antony's soldiers ate some of the plant while retreating and became ridiculously incoherent. The plant's name is derived from a similar incident involving soldiers who were sent to put down some rebellious colonists in Jamestown in 1676. They too ate the plant and were good for little but clowning for eleven days. As a result, the plant came to be called Jamestown weed, which evolved into jimson weed.

Its use was supposedly introduced to medieval Europe by gypsies who brought it from India. The gypsies smoked it to experience hallucinations. Because it also gives the sensation of flying and releases inhibitions, especially in women, jimson weed was associated in the Middle Ages with witchcraft. Witches inhaled its vapors while casting their spells.

Jimson weed has been taken for its narcotic and hallucinogenic effects by Indian tribes from the southwestern United States to South America. Many tribes used it to induce visions in priests, medicine men, and others, including initiates in puberty rites. The Zuni and many California Indian tribes set broken bones after administering jimson weed as an anesthetic. The Mariposa tribe gave it to its women as an aphrodisiac.

For some first-hand experiences with jimson weed, read anthropologist Carlos Castaneda's book *The Teachings of Don Juan: A Yaqui Way of Knowledge*.

LAD'S LOVE

It takes its name from the fact that young boys in Europe once made an ointment from olive oil, rosemary, and the ashes of this plant and applied it to their faces to promote the growth of their beards.

LARCH

In European folklore the larch was said to be a preventative against enchantment. The smoke from burning larch bark was thought to drive away evil spirits, and parents had children wear collars of larch bark as a protection against the evil eye.

In Siberia the larch is associated with the primitive shamanistic religion of the native Tungus tribe. According to a shaman interview in 1925,* larch poles are used in sacred rites as an earthly representation of a mythical tree called Tuuru, where the souls of all shamans are said to develop before coming to earth. When a Tungus shaman practices his art, his soul is symbolically climbing up the Tuuru tree's larch pole representation, which is said to extend itself invisibly to heaven during the rite. In addition the shaman's drum, which he uses to induce his trance, has a rim of larch bark. The actual tree from which this bark is taken is always left standing in honor of the tree Tuuru.

* See Joseph Campbell's *The Masks of God: Primitive Mythology,* pp. 251-257.

LAUREL

According to Greek and Roman myth, the nymph Daphne was changed at her own wish into a laurel tree by her father, the river god Peneus, to keep her from being attacked by the love-smitten god Apollo. Eros (or Cupid) had played a trick on the self-righteous Apollo by shooting arrows with opposite effects into him and Daphne: Apollo's arrow stimulated love for Daphne, but hers caused her to hate Apollo. Apollo, amazed by Daphne's transformation, made the tree sacred to himself and declared that he would wear a crown of its leaves, as would triumphant men of war. Thus associated with fame and achievement, the laurel wreath was conferred also on poets, athletes, statesmen, and other notables.

The Romans believed that a person standing under a laurel tree would be shielded from infection by the plague and also from lightning. In the Middle Ages, laurel would shield you from lightning and from witches too.

LAVENDER

The name lavender is derived from the Latin *lavandus*, "to be washed," probably because it was used in ancient times to perfume bath water. Lavender has long had a reputation as an anaphrodisiac. One old belief advocates sprinkling lavender on your head as an aid in maintaining chastity (if that's what you want).

LEEK

The word *leek* comes from the Anglo-Saxon name for the plant, *leac*. The leek, like its relatives the onion and garlic, has been known as a food plant for thousands of years. Over 1,200 years before Christ, the Israelites in the Sinai wilderness longed for the leeks, onions, garlic, meat, and other foods they had known in Egypt (see Numbers 11:4-6). The emperor Nero ate great quantities of leeks under the delusion that they improved his voice.

Beginning in antiquity, soldiers of many centuries believed that carrying a leek in battle would assure safety and victory. In the sixth century, St. David, the patron saint of Wales, directed the Welshmen to wear leeks in their caps to identify themselves in their successful battle against the Saxon invaders. To commemorate the victory, the leek was made the national emblem of Wales.

LINDEN

The name linden comes from the Latin word *lentus*, meaning "flexible," for its pliable, fibrous inner bark has been used since ancient times for binding vines and other creeping plants to supports without damaging them.

In Greece and Rome, the linden was associated with the mythical story of Baucis and Philemon, a humble, elderly married couple who extended kindly hospitality to the disguised gods Zeus and Hermes after all their richer neighbors had refused to do so. The two gods punished the inhospitable neighbors by covering all the homes in the area with a lake except the small cottage of Baucis and Philemon, which was transformed into a beautiful temple.

The couple held priestly office there until the end of their lives, when the gods granted their request that they would die at the same time so as not to be separated by death. At their death, the loving couple was transformed into two trees growing side by side; Baucis was turned into the linden tree, the symbol of conjugal love and the qualities of a good wife, Philemon into an oak tree, the symbol of hospitality.

In old Germany the linden was a sacred and symbolic tree. There it was often associated with the fates of individuals and groups. When a male heir was born into a family, a linden tree was often planted and the growth of the tree was supposed to parallel the growth of the child. The analogy extended to families also. It was said that in the eighteenth century, a linden tree with three distinct stems representing three separate families, had each of the three sections of the tree die out as the last member of each family died, leaving no heirs. One of the families involved was that of Linnaeus, the famous naturalist who originated the systems of botanical and zoological classification. Since every town in Germany has its official town linden in the main square, with some over 1,000 years old, it could be presumed that each of these trees serves as an indicator of its town's fate.

The linden also had its effect on the fate of Siegfried, the famous mythological German hero. He was dipped into a magical river by his mother to make him invulnerable, but during this process a linden leaf clung to his back, giving him one vulnerable spot which later proved to be his undoing.

LUNGWORT

In the Middle Ages it was commonly believed that the outward appearance of a plant was a God-given sign of the medicinal value contained within. Under this concept, called the Doctrine of Signatures, lungwort received its name: its lung-shaped leaves were considered a sign of its ability to treat lung diseases. Based on folklore, this doctrine was formally stated by the sixteenth-century physician Philippus Aureolus Theophrastus Bombastus Paracelsus von Hohenheim. Interestingly, American Indians had the same idea in their herb lore, even before they were exposed to white men. The problem with the concept is that, although it works well for some plants, it generally takes a great deal of creative imagination to match the outward appearance of most plants to the "appropriate" medicinal use.

MAIDENHAIR FERN

The Romans were fascinated by the unusual qualities of the delicate maidenhair fern when it is immersed in water: under water it glistens with a silvery sheen; but when removed, it is perfectly dry for water will not cling to it. Because of these seemingly magic qualities, the maidenhair fern in Roman mythology was said to represent the hair of Venus when she arose from the foam of the sea, thus the name maidenhair. The plant's Latin genus name *Adiantum* comes from the Greek words *Adian-tum*, meaning "unwetted."

MALE FERN

In the Middle Ages people made a good luck charm out of the rootstock of this plant. They cut off all but five of the curved finger-like fronds from the rootstock, so that it resembled a hand. Called Lucky Hand, Dead Man's Hand, or St. John's Hand, this charm was considered to be very strong against bad luck, devils, and witches. It was usually fashioned on June 23rd, St. John's Eve, so that it would gain extra potency by being fumigated in the fires set that night (see St. Johnswort for an explanation of St. John's Eve). Genghis Khan is supposed to have carried one of these charms.

MANDRAKE (MANDRAGORA)

Native to the Near East, the European mandrake, whose narcotic roots often fork and branch to resemble a human figure, has been considered a mystic plant since primitive times. The name mandrake is thought to be a corruption of the Greek and Latin name for the plant, *mandragorus*, which in turn comes from the Sanskrit words *mangros* and *agora*, meaning together "sleep substance." An alternative English name for mandrake is mandragora.

Our earliest record of mandrake's use is found in Genesis 30:14-16, where Rachel agrees to let Leah sleep with Jacob one night in exchange for some mandrake plants. Biblical scholars believe that Rachel desired the plant because of its reputed properties as an aphrodisiac and fertility drug. Jacob and his wives lived about 4000 B.C. Descriptions of mandrakes have also been found written on Assyrian clay tablets dating around 800 B.C. Well known in ancient Greece for its narcotic medicinal qualities, the mandrake was described by Hippocrates, Aristotle, and other writers. The Greeks also considered it a love plant, associating it with Aphrodite, the goddess of love. The Romans used it as an anesthetic in surgery.

A belief dating from the second century A.D. held that pulling a mandrake root out of the ground would cause death, because the root was or contained a demon whose shrieks would kill his uprooter. The recommended method for extracting the root was to tie the plant to a dog, who when whipped would pull the plant out. The dog would then die, of course. Anyone witnessing this event was to have his ears stopped with wax to keep from hearing the fatal screams.

In the Middle Ages the mandrake's use as a medicinal narcotic and an aphrodisiac continued, and the superstitious lore surrounding it proliferated. Medieval people believed that mandrakes grew up under the gallows, having received their seed from the blood (or other remains) of hanged murderers. Mandrake roots carved with human features were sold at high prices as charms with supposed miraculous powers. Many different regional folk beliefs grew up about these mannikins and their efficacy as charms. For example, in Germany, they were considered all-purpose good luck charms and were called *alrauns*, after a legendary Teutonic sorceress, the Alrauna maiden, who first used such charms. In France the figures, as representations of an elf named Mandegloire, were thought to bring wealth. Possessing one of these mannikins could be risky, however, because if the owner did not keep the charm in secret, he could be accused of practicing witchcraft. Indeed, the mandrake was the medieval witch's most potent plant, capable of working every spell.

MARJORAM

Sweet marjoram was one of the Greeks' favorite herbs. According to Greek legend, Aphrodite first cultivated the marjoram, and its sweet scent came from her gentle touch. Because of its association with Aphrodite, the ancient Greeks wore wreaths of it as wedding flowers. They also considered it an antidote for snakebite. And if it failed in that use, they planted it on the grave in the belief that it would help the dead to sleep in peace.

MILFOIL (YARROW)

Milfoil's genus name *Achillea* is taken from Achilles, the Greek hero in the Trojan War. During this war, a plant related to milfoil was used to heal the wounds of Achilles' soldiers. The Ute Indians employed milfoil for similar purposes; the Ute name for milfoil means "wound medicine."

In ancient China milfoil or yarrow was considered a sacred plant with spiritual qualities. Thus it was an appropriate medium for use in the ancient system of divination called the I Ching or Oracle of Change. In the oldest, most complex, and therefore most accurate method of consulting the I Ching, fifty dried yarrow stalks are manipulated to provide answers to the questions given.

MINT

According to classical legend, mint originated from the nymph Menthe, the daughter of the river god Cocyte. Because Pluto loved her, his jealous wife Proserpine changed Menthe into a mint plant.

MISTLETOE

The mistletoe was considered sacred by the early Teutonic and Celtic tribes of Northern Europe. To the Celtic Druids, the gathering of mistletoe was a religious act, involving a prescribed ritual in which a white-robed priest climbed the tree and cut off the mistletoe with a golden sickle, catching it in a white mantle. Afterwards, two oxen were sacrificed under the tree, while prayers were said in thanks for the gift of the sacred mistletoe. The Druids used mistletoe in their fertility rites and as a medicine, calling it "all-heal" because it was thought a remedy for all diseases. The Druids also originated the practice of hanging branches of mistletoe from the ceiling in order to ward off evil spirits in their homes. Whom we have to thank for the practice of kissing under the mistletoe is not known, but it has been a popular custom from the Middle Ages on to the present day.

In Northern European mythology the kindly and just god Baldur was killed by an arrow made from a mistletoe twig. Baldur had received premonitions of his death in his dreams and had related this to his parents, Odin (or Wotan) and Frigga, the king and queen of the gods. Frigga then exacted an oath from fire and water, and all the metals, plants, animals, poisons, and diseases on the whole earth that they would not harm Baldur, but she left out the mistletoe plant because it seemed too young and feeble to hurt anyone. Obviously mistletoe is not a plant to be dismissed so lightly.

A yellow-colored withered mistletoe branch was thought to be the "golden bough" described in Virgil's *Aeneid*. This was the branch that Aeneas had to remove from a specific tree in order to visit the underworld.

MONKSHOOD

Used as a poison in hunting and war in Europe and Asia since ancient times, monkshood has acquired an extremely bad image through the ages. Its juice was used by soldiers to poison water supplies in the path of advancing enemies, and by hunters to poison spears, arrowheads, and bait.

In Greek legend, monkshood originated from the foam dripping from the fangs of the three-headed dog Cerberus that Herakles (Hercules) brought up from the underworld. Also Hecate—the Greek goddess of the moon, ghosts, witches, and magic—poisoned her father with monkshood.

Not surprisingly, then, in the Middle Ages witches were associated with monkshood. Since it numbs the senses and gives a sensation of flying, they are said to have smeared it on their bodies and broomsticks.

The name monkshood comes from its hood-shaped flowers.

MOTHERWORT

Orientals ascribe to motherwort the power of prolonged life. According to Chinese legend, an emperor who at age seven assumed the throne was alarmed by predictions that he would not live to double that age. After an extensive search for a remedy to prolong life, he chose a brew made from motherwort. Drinking this every day, he lived past age 70. Another legend tells of a youth banished for a minor crime to a valley where the only water supply was in contact with a large amount of motherwort plants. Because he drank this water daily, the youth lived three centuries.

This herb probably derived its name from the fact that it has been used medicinally to prevent miscarriage.

MUGWORT

The name mugwort comes from the old Germanic *muggiwurti*, meaning "fly or gnat plant," and refers to the plant's use since the time of Dioscorides (first century A.D.) to repel moths and other insects.

In the Middle Ages mugwort was considered a magical protective herb. It was very strong against witches and a branch of it kept in the house would scare off the Devil. Hanging mugwort above your door was a protection against lightning; best of all, putting it under the doorstep ensured that no annoying person would come to your door. (Try it if you are plagued by solicitors.) Mugwort also afforded its protection to the traveler, guarding him against fatigue, sunstrokes, wild beasts, and the evil eye. If a foot traveler put mugwort in his shoes, he would not become weary on his journey. Medieval legend held that John the Baptist wore a girdle of mugwort to help sustain him in the wilderness.

It was believed that sleeping on a pillow filled with mugwort would cause a person to see his entire future in his dreams.

MULBERRY

About 2700 B.C. the Chinese began cultivating the white mulberry tree as food for silkworms to produce silk. The secret of the art of silk production was kept in China for about 2,000 years, but around 700 B.C. the practice spread to other peoples, including the Babylonians, the Greeks, and the Romans.

According to Chinese legend, the silk industry was started by the beautiful Chinese empress Si Ling-Shi, who, watching a silkworm spin his gossamer cocoon on a mulberry tree in her garden, desired a gown made from the threads of many such cocoons. She accidentally dropped the cocoon in her tea and it softened, allowing the empress to unwind its threads. Si Ling-Shi got her husband to give her a whole grove of mulberry trees, so that she could get enough threads to weave her gown. Though it took her several years of working long hours with the worms and the cocoons, she finally unwound enough thread to weave the material for the dress. The Chinese named the material *Si* for their empress, and silk is still known by that name today in China. Because the prosperous silk industry was so important to the early Chinese people, the mulberry was revered in ancient China as a sacred tree. Some scholars connect it with the *fu-sang* tree, a symbolic tree of life that appears in the mythology and art of the Han Dynasty (202 B.C.-220 A.D.).

In classical legend the red berries of the mulberry tree acquired their color only after two young Babylonian lovers, Pyramus and Thisbe, bled and died under a white-berried mulberry tree. The Pyramus and Thisbe legend is the source of the story of Romeo and Juliet.

MULLEIN

According to Agrippa, a general and minister under Caesar Augustus, mullein leaves because of their fragrance had an overpowering effect on demons. More mundanely, the plant was also used by the Greeks and the Romans to make torches or lampwicks by dipping its dried flower-stalks in tallow.

In the Middle Ages people deprecatingly called the mullein "hag taper," because witches used it in their incantations and as an important ingredient in their brews and love potions.

MYRRH

The clear, fragrant gum resin of this tree has been used since ancient times as an incense, as an ingredient in cosmetics and perfumes, as a fumigant, and in embalming. One of the earliest records of man's use of myrrh is found in an Egyptian papyrus dated about 2000 B.C. Moses (about 1400-1200 B.C.) was instructed by God to use myrrh as one of the main ingredients in a holy oil for anointing the priests (Exodus 30:22-33). There are many references in the Bible to myrrh, the most famous of which is Matthew 2:11, describing the wise men's gifts to the infant Jesus. Perhaps the most interesting biblical passages about myrrh are found in Song of Solomon, where myrrh is compared to the joys of sexual love (Song of Solomon 1:13 and 4:6). The name myrrh is derived from the Arabic word *mur* meaning "bitter," referring to the spice's bitter taste.

A legendary account of the origin of myrrh is found in a Syrian myth, which was later adopted by the Greeks. According to this legend, Myrrha, the daughter of the king of Syria, Thesis, refused to worship Aphrodite and was cruelly punished by the goddess, who caused her to commit incest with her father. With the help of her nurse, Myrrha disguised herself and deceived her father for eleven nights, but on the twelfth night Thesis realized who she was. Furious at her, he threatened to kill Myrrha and began chasing her with a knife. To save her, the gods transformed her into a myrrh tree. The clear gum resin exuded by the tree is said to represent Myrrha's tears.

OAK

The majestic oak, with its impressive size and longevity (some trees have lived well over a thousand years), has been revered as a sacred tree by a remarkable number of different peoples. To the ancient Hebrews, it was sacred because under it Abraham gave hospitality to God and two of his angels, who were disguised as three travelers. (See Genesis 18; this is only one of nearly 60 references to oak in the Bible.) The early Gauls worshipped it as a symbol of their supreme god. Both the oak and the mistletoe were involved in almost all of the Celtic-Druid ritual ceremonies, for the oak was considered their sacred celestial tree (see also Mistletoe entry).

One of the most interesting aspects in the oak's history as a sacred tree is its widespread association with thunder gods in various European cultures. To the Northern Europeans, it was the tree of life sacred to the thunder god, Thor. The oak was also sacred to the principal Greek god Zeus with his thunderbolts, and to his Roman counterpart, Jupiter. The oracle of Zeus at Dodona, Greece, mentioned by Homer, was situated in a sacred grove of oak trees. Predictions were made at this oracle by interpreting the rustling of oak leaves. The Slavic countries had their own versions of a thunder god associated with oak. In Russia, his name was Perun, which was derived from the word for thunderbolt. In Lithuania the god was called Perkunas, a name thought to be taken from an Indo-European name for oak. This widespread association of oak with thunder gods is probably due to the fact that oak seems to attract more lightning than any other tree.

To the Northern European peoples, the oak leaf cluster was a token of heroism and victory—a symbolism that survives in American military decorations. In Rome the oak wreath crown was a prize for saving a citizen's life in battle.

In Greece and Rome, the oak is associated with the legend of Baucis and Philemon in which Philemon is turned into an oak tree (see Linden entry for more details).

In literature, the oak often connotes strength, masculinity, stability, and longevity.

OLIVE

In the prehistoric Neolithic period, men in the Near East and the eastern Mediterranean area were already cultivating the olive tree, mainly for its oil. Since then, olive oil has served primarily as a food, but also as a fuel for lamps, as medicine, as an emollient for dry skin, and as an anointing oil for religious purposes. In many countries, from the Orient to the Mediterranean, the olive has been a symbol of peace and wealth. It is also regarded as a sign of safe travel, from the biblical accounts of the dove's bringing back an olive leaf to Noah on Mount Ararat to indicate that the waters of the flood had nearly subsided.

According to Greek myth, the goddess of wisdom, Athene, taught men the use of the olive tree. Both Athene and Poseidon, the god of the sea, wanted to be the patron of Attica, the section of Greece that includes the city of Athens. The other gods on Mount Olympus devised a contest for them, specifying that the winner would be the one who could provide the best gift to the people of Attica. Poseidon struck the ground with his trident, and a horse sprang forth; Athene did likewise with her spear, and an olive tree grew up. The gods decided that the olive, as a symbol of peace and agriculture, was a much better gift than Poseidon's horse, a symbol of war. So Athene became the patron of Attica, and its principal city was named after her. Hardly by coincidence, Attica was the number one producer of olives in all of Greece.

Olive trees are known to live a long time, some well over a thousand years. It is claimed that some olive trees growing in the garden of Gethsemane date back to the time of Christ.

ORANGE

Originating in Southeast Asia or India, oranges are described in Chinese writings as early as 2200 B.C., though their use is thought to date back much farther. The name orange is derived from the Sanskrit word for the fruit, *narange*. The bitter orange was introduced to Europe by the Crusaders; the sweet orange was not known in Europe until the fifteenth century, probably brought there from the Orient by Genoese merchants.

The Crusaders observed that Saracen brides wore orange blossom wreaths at their weddings. To the Saracens, the orange was a symbol of fecundity, because the tree bears fruit and blossoms at the same time. After the Crusaders' return, the custom of using orange blossoms as bridal flowers was adopted in Europe; but it did not become widespread until the seventeenth century, probably because the blossoms were very rare and expensive until then.

The orange, as a traditional Chinese symbol of good luck and prosperity, is still used today in Chinese New Year's celebrations.

PARSLEY

Sprightly, nutritious parsley, known since very early times as a widely cultivated food plant, has had some surprising associations in its past, namely with death and the Devil.

Used as a grave decoration, parsley was symbolic of death in ancient Greece and Rome. In Greek legendary history, parsley is associated with the ominous story of the death of Opheltes, the infant son of King Lycurgus of Nemea. According to the legend, the baby's nurse had left him for a short time on the grass while she pointed out the location of a spring to some thirsty soldiers. When she returned, the child had been killed by a snake. One of the soldiers, the seer Amphiarus, saw the child's death as a bad omen predicting his own death in an upcoming battle; so he gave Opheltes the surname Archemorus, meaning "first to die." Thus the child became a symbol of impending death, and from his blood were said to have sprung the first parsley plants.

The psychological effect of parsley on the Greek mind is shown in one historical incident recorded by Plutarch, in which a group of soldiers on their way to a battle, on seeing a mule loaded with parsley, panicked and fled. On the other hand, garlands of parsley were used as prizes in both Greek and Roman public games. But even here, it was connected indirectly with death, for this custom survived from funeral games that were held in connection with the deaths of important persons in very early Grecian times.

Perhaps because of its earlier ominous associations, parsley in the Middle Ages became one of the Devil's favorite plants. Its wickedness, in fact, could be nullified only by sowing it on Good Friday under a rising moon. Because the germination of the seed is slow and incomplete, it was said that parsley went nine times to the Devil and back before germinating and that the Devil kept some of it for himself. Also, parsley was never to be transplanted, because doing so would surely bring a disaster to the household. One late medieval belief advocated sprinkling your head with parsley seeds three nights a year as a cure for baldness.

PASSION FLOWER

The priests who accompanied the conquistadors to the New World in the sixteenth century considered the discovery of this beautiful flowering vine in South America to be a propitious, God-given sign that Christianity would be well received in the new land. They gave the plant its name because the various parts of the flower appeared to them to be symbolic of Christ's passion: the ten petals represent the faithful apostles, excluding the traitor Judas and also Peter for his denial; the corolla symbolizes the crown of thorns; the five stamens stand for the five wounds; the ovary suggests the hammer with which Christ was nailed to the cross; and the styles with their rounded heads provide the nails. Because the natives relished the yellow fruit of the plant, the priests were encouraged in their mission, interpreting the eating of the fruit as symbolic of the Indians' hunger for Christianity.

PEACH

The ancient Greeks thought the peach had originated in Persia, but China is its true home. We find records of peaches in China before 2000 B.C., but in the Near East not until 1500 B.C. As the most important sacred plant in the Chinese Taoist religion, the peach was considered a symbol of immortality and of the Tao, the way of attaining this immortality. In Taoist writings, the tree of life in a mythical garden paradise is a peach tree which bears fruits that ripen once in 3,000 years. Whoever eats of these fruits becomes immortal. Even today the Chinese consider the peach a symbol of longevity. Peach blossoms are also associated in the Orient with marriage.

PEONY

According to the Roman writer Pliny the Elder (23-79 A.D.), the peony was the oldest of all cultivated flowers. Modern botanists have no way of authenticating Pliny's statement, but we do know that the Chinese emperor Chin Ming (2737-2697 B.C.) cultivated these flowers. The peony takes its name from the Greek legendary physician Paeon who first learned of the plant's important medicinal use of lessening the pains of childbirth. Paeon was said to have been eventually transformed into a peony by Zeus. In the Middle Ages ground peony seeds were taken as a preventative against bad and melancholy dreams.

PEYOTE

The hallucinogenic peyote plant has been incorporated into the religious practices of more than thirty Indian tribes from northern Mexico to Saskatchewan. From accounts of Spanish missionaries, we know that this cactus was used by the Indians of northern Mexico as early as the sixteenth century; but Indian myths contain evidence of its use much earlier. One of peyote's names, "the Devil's root," was coined by the missionaries, who condemned the plant and zealously attempted to suppress its use. The Indians believed then and still believe today that peyote is a god or a messenger of the gods sent to communicate directly with an individual without the medium of a priest or minister. The Indians also used peyote not only to induce visions but also to bolster courage in warfare, to give stamina in dancing, and to relieve pain and promote healing.

According to Indian myth, peyote's properties were discovered by an Indian lost in the desert and dying of hunger and thirst. Prompted by an inner voice and his own desperation, he decided to eat the tough and unpalatable peyote cactus. When he did, his strength was miraculously revived and he found his way back to his people to tell them of this new god of healing. The god Peyote is also said to have revealed his ritual to the people in a vision.

In the 1880's the use of peyote spread rapidly to the Indian tribes of North America after the Comanches and Kiowas discovered it in their raids across the Mexican border. A contemporary account of the peyote cult is found in anthropologist Carlos Castaneda's book *The Teachings of Don Juan: A Yaqui Way of Knowledge*. Castaneda describes his own experiences with peyote and its role in the education of a sorcerer in the old Mexican Indian tradition.

PLANTAIN

According to legend, plantain originated from a maiden who spent so much time by the roadside watching for her absent lover that she eventually turned into this common roadside plant. In medieval Christian art, plantain symbolizes the well-trodden path of the multitude that sought Christ.

POMEGRANATE

The pomegranate, along with the peach and the citron, was one of China's three blessed fruits. To the Chinese, it was a symbol of fecundity and a prosperous future. The many seeds represented numerous male offspring earning fame and glory.

Peoples of the Near East and the Greeks and Romans also associated the pomegranate with fecundity. In Greece it was involved in the story of the goddess of agriculture, Demeter, and her daughter Persephone. When Hades, the god of the underworld, kidnapped Persephone, Zeus promised to retrieve her if Persephone had not eaten anything in the underworld. When it was discovered that she had eaten a few seeds of a pomegranate given to her by Hades, a compromise settlement was made: Persephone was allowed to stay with her mother nine months of the year but was required to spend the remaining three with Hades. The story can be seen as an allegory representing the cycle of growth, decay, and regeneration of vegetation, the time in the underworld representing the resting period of the seed during the winter. The story of Persephone was reenacted every year at the temple of Demeter at Eleusis near Athens. In these rites, called the Eleusinian mysteries, the pomegranate was considered the mystic fruit. These ceremonies were the most important and impressive of all Greek religious celebrations and were later adopted by the Romans.

The pomegranate is compared to the joys of a beguiling lover in the Song of Solomon (4:3, 13; 6:11).

POPLAR

Known and used since antiquity, the poplar finds a unique application in the biblical account (Genesis 30:37-43) of Jacob as a breeder of goats. Jacob's father-in-law had promised him all the mottled and striped goats and sheep born to his herd, thinking the promise would cost him little since such animals were rare. But the clever Jacob placed before the breeding animals an arrangement of striped rods made from the poplar, almond, and plane trees. Presumably with God's help, such visual aids produced the desired offspring; and Jacob was able to outsmart his crafty father-in-law.

The Greeks and Romans used the poplar as an ornamental shade tree. In Greek legend, the origin of the poplar is attributed to the Heliades, the three grief-stricken sisters of Phaeton, who saw their brother fall from the sky into the river Eridanus after his unsuccessful attempt to drive the chariot of the sun. They wept unceasingly by the river and eventually were turned into poplar trees. It was said that their tears continued to ooze out of the trees and were turned into amber by the sun god Helios. (Actually, amber is fossilized pine tree sap used today and in ancient times in making jewelry.)

The Greeks also dedicated the poplar to the hero Herakles (or Hercules), who wore a crown of its leaves when he retrieved the three-headed dog Cerberus from Hades. The poplar leaves became darker green on the top side, the Greeks said, from their exposure to the smoky fumes of Hades during Herakles' efforts.

The leaves of the quaking aspen "quake" in the wind because they grow on very thin stalks. Legend has it that the tree quakes because it was used to make Christ's cross, and it trembles whenever it remembers this fact.

ROSE

The rose, cultivated for well over 3,000 years and known from time immemorial as the queen of the flowers, is thought to have originated in Asia Minor. The genus name *Rosa* is derived from the Greek word *rodon*, meaning "red." The ancient Persians, Egyptians, Greeks, and Romans used the rose not only as a garden ornamental but also as the main ingredient in various perfumes and cosmetics.

In Greece and Rome, the rose was the favorite flower of the goddess of the flowers, the Greek Chloris and her Roman counterpart Flora. In festivals for these goddesses, people bedecked themselves and their animals with flowers, using mostly roses. At Roman banquets roses were used lavishly for decoration and were even strewn on the floor. At these same banquets, the diners often wore rose garlands as a preventative against drunkenness.

In Greek myth, Chloris was said to have created the rose from the dead body of a beautiful nymph that she came upon in the woods. Chloris called on the other gods to help her transform the nymph's body into a flower that would surpass all others in beauty. Aphrodite bestowed upon it beauty; the three Graces—Aglaia, Euphrosyne, and Thalia —donated their respective qualities of brilliance, joy, and youthful bloom; Dionysus gave it nectar and fragrance. When the flower was finished and its perfection was apparent to all, Chloris crowned it with a diadem of dewdrops, proclaiming it the queen of the flowers.

Probably the most frequently used flower in all literature, the beautiful rose with its forbidding thorns has been an arresting symbol for writers through the ages. The rose's perfect blossom is associated with love, beauty, youth, perfection, and even immortality; its thorns with the pain of love and guilt; its withering blossom with the ephemeral nature of beauty and youth. According to Christian legend, the rose grew in the Garden of Eden without thorns; but after the fall, thorns sprouted to remind man of his sinful and imperfect nature.

Roses of different colors often have special connotations: the pink rose represents simplicity or happy love; the white rose stands for purity and innocence, often being associated with the Virgin Mary; the yellow rose means perfect achievement, and sometimes jealousy; and the red rose signifies passion and sensual desire, shame, and occasionally blood and sacrifice.

Many legends purport to explain how the red rose acquired its color. Assuming that the rose was originally white, the Greeks held that it became red from the blood of Aphrodite, who had pricked her foot on a thorn while trying to aid her beloved, dying Adonis. The Turks claim the white rose was stained red by the blood of Mohammed. Christian legend has the red rose resulting from the blood of martyrs.

From the time of the ancient Egyptians, the rose has been a token of silence. The Greeks gave it this meaning in a legend in which Cupid bribes Harpocrates, the god of silence, with a rose to induce him to conceal the amorous affairs of his mother, Aphrodite. For Teutonic peoples, the rose was the flower of the northern goddess of love, Freyja, who was known for her ability to keep secrets. The expression *sub rosa*, literally "under the rose," means that a matter is to be kept in strict confidence. It stems from an old custom of attaching a rose to the ceiling (or having one sculptured there) to remind revelers that anything said under the influence of wine was not to be repeated to others afterwards.

The rose has also been a popular heraldic flower for soldiers' shields since Roman times. The most famous example is that of the English rose which came out of the War of the Roses (1455-1485), in which the House of York with the white rose as its heraldic emblem fought the House of Lancaster, whose symbol was the red rose. At the war's end, the two houses were joined by the marriage of Henry VII of Lancaster to Elizabeth of York. Henry became the first Tudor king, his symbol being a red and white Tudor rose, which is now the national flower of England.

ROSEMARY

Rosemary's name is derived from its Latin name, *Rosmarinus*, meaning "dew of the sea" and referring to its blue flowers or to the fact that this herb thrives by the seashore, especially in Spain where its thick growth covers the cliffs. To explain the range in the color of rosemary's flowers from a pale bluish-white to a deep blue, Christian legend claims the flowers were originally white but were turned varying shades of blue when Mary hung her blue cloak over a rosemary bush. Since the rosemary plant seldom grows higher than a man's height, it was believed that rosemary grew to the height of Christ in 33 years, and after that it grew thicker but not higher.

Rosemary, one of the most beloved of all herbs, has been associated with remembrance from the time of the ancient Greeks when students studying for examinations wore garlands of rosemary to strengthen their memories. It was also linked with happy memories, fidelity, and love; and thus it became a wedding flower in Europe from the time of Charlemagne. Members of the wedding party carried sprigs or small branches of rosemary, which were often gilded, while the bride wore a garland fashioned from it. It is still worn by some brides today in Europe. Rosemary became a funeral flower too in seventeenth- and eighteenth-century Europe because it symbolized the memories of loved ones. Mourners brought sprigs of it to the funeral and dropped them into the grave. Robert Herrick, a seventeenth-century English poet, in his poem *The Garden* said of rosemary:

Grow it for two ends, it matters not at all
Be't for my bridall or my buriall . . .

Many folk beliefs endowed rosemary with magical qualities. In the Middle Ages, it was placed under the pillow to repel evil spirits and bad dreams. It was also good against witches and the plague. As a love charm, it was said if a young man tapped a girl (or vice-versa) on the finger with a blooming sprig of rosemary, this action would make the couple fall in love with a wedding soon to follow. In England, a rosemary plant flourishing outside a house was a sign that the wife was the boss of the household. Because of this belief, some men were known to sneak out at night and cut off the plant's roots to hide the truth from their neighbors. Another belief held that a man indifferent to rosemary's perfume would be incapable of giving true love to a woman. In Belgium children were told that babies came from rosemary plants.

The versatile rosemary has had still other intriguing uses. Applying rosemary powder to the body has been credited with putting a person in a merry frame of mind. In contrast, in France at one time, combing the hair daily with a comb made out of rosemary wood was a preventative against giddiness. And perhaps best of all, Banke's *Herbal* of 1525 claims that smelling rosemary often will keep a person young.

RUE

The bitter herb rue traces its name to the Greek word *ruta*, meaning "repentance." It has long been a symbol of sorrow and repentance and was called in Christian times the "herb of grace," after the God-given grace that usually follows true repentance.

Rue was well known to the ancients. Hippocrates (about 460-377 B.C.) commended rue for its medicinal qualities. Aristotle (384-322 B.C.) recorded that, because rue was considered good against evil and witches, the Greeks used it to combat the nervousness they experienced when they had to eat with foreigners, who were often suspected of having evil powers. According to the Roman writer and naturalist Pliny (23-79 A.D.), painters, carvers, and engravers of his day ate rue to improve their eyesight.

The plant was also well known in ancient times as an antidote against poisons. In the first century B.C., the cunning and cultured King Mithridates VI of Pontus (an ancient country in northeastern Asia Minor) immunized himself against poison by taking rue in gradually increasing doses over an extended time.

In the Middle Ages, rue was considered a good defense against the plague and witches, though many witches made use of it themselves in their enchantments. In the sixteenth and seventeenth centuries, rue was scattered on the floors of law courts as a fumigant, and judges carried branches of it to guard against jail fever.

Rue's gray leaves served as the model for the suit of clubs in playing cards.

SAFFRON

The early Greeks used saffron to produce a royal dye color. Both the Greeks and the Romans used the expensive saffron to perfume their streets, homes, public buildings, theaters, and baths. Evidently saffron's use in Europe declined during the Dark Ages; but it was reintroduced, probably by the Crusaders, in the fourteenth century. From the fourteenth to the eighteenth century, saffron enjoyed wide use in Europe both as a spice and as a medicine in women's diseases. An indication of its importance is the fact that during those times spice dealers were generally called "saffron grocers." Saffron is very expensive, because the only portions of the plant used are the flower's dried stigmas and part of the style; thus to produce one pound of the spice, some 35,000 to 40,000 flowers are required.

SAGE

Sage has been used as a medicine and a flavoring since prehistoric times. Its genus name *Salvia* is derived from the Latin *salvus,* meaning "safe" or "well," and was given to the plant because it was so highly regarded medicinally as a safeguard to health. The word *sage* comes to us from the French name for the plant, *sauge.*

Because of its medicinal and healthful qualities, sage has since ancient times had a reputation for promoting longevity. An ancient Arabian proverb asks, "How shall a man die who has sage in his garden?" Even as late as the seventeenth century, John Evelyn, an English writer of diaries and author of several books on botanical subjects, claimed that an assiduous use of sage would render a man immortal.

Like rosemary, sage was said to flourish in the garden only when the woman dominated the house. But another folk belief held that sage plants reflected the fortunes of the man of the house, flourishing when he prospered and withering when he did not.

ST. JOHNSWORT

St. Johnswort is one of the best known of a whole group of herbs which were smoked in fires set on St. John's Eve (June 23) during medieval times. The purpose of the fires, which were lit on hills and other high places, was to purify the air of evil spirits to ensure the protection of the people, their animals, and their crops. The herbs, when properly smoked, could be hung in houses and barns to make further assault on the powers of evil. The herbs could also be worn around the neck as protective amulets. Some other herbs smoked during St. John's Eve were ivy, mugwort, milfoil, vervain, elder, figwort, fennel, melilot, camomile, plantain, hawthorn, lavender, and male fern. This custom of burning fires at the beginning of summer is thought to have originated with the ancient Gauls.

SANDALWOOD

Since ancient times in India, Burma, and China, the aromatic sandalwood tree has played an important part in the religious rituals of Hindus and Buddhists, providing them incense, embalming ingredients, and wood for funeral pyres and temples. The Buddhists continue to use it today in their funeral rites and other religious ceremonies. Its oil is a famous and expensive ingredient in perfumes. The age-old process of the harvesting of sandalwood is interesting, because termites play an important role in it. First the trees are cut down or uprooted, and the branches and roots are removed. The remaining tree trunks are left on the ground for several months so that termites can eat away the worthless outer layer of sapwood, exposing the fragrant heartwood, the only commercially usable part of the tree.

SOLOMON'S SEAL

Several explanations have been given of the origin of Solomon's seal's name. It has been ascribed to round scars on the rootstock which resemble an impression of a seal, or to the fact that the cross-section of a cut rootstock has markings that look like Hebrew characters. The sixteenth-century herbalist Gerard claimed that its name was also due in part to the plant's medicinal virtue of sealing up wounds and broken bones. But the most plausible explanation is that the flower when lightly dipped in ink and pressed on a paper like a seal produces a six-pointed star made up of two superimposed triangles like the Jewish Star of David, also known as the Seal of Solomon. This star is also an ancient Hindu symbol of supreme power.

According to one legend, when workmen were unable to quarry the extremely hard rock needed for Solomon's temple, King Solomon himself, armed with this plant as a tool, ripped the necessary blocks of stone from the cliffs. In German folklore, Solomon's seal is considered to be a key to subterranean treasure chambers.

STRAWBERRY

Strawberries have been known since antiquity and are mentioned in the writings of the Roman authors Virgil (70-19 B.C.) and Pliny the Elder (23-79 A.D.). The name strawberry was originally strewberry because the berries appear to be strewn or scattered among the leaves of the plant. In art and literature the strawberry is usually a symbol of sensuality and earthly desire. For example, giant strawberries are featured as delicacies savored by some of the multitudinous pallid, naked revelers in the late medieval painting titled *The Garden of Delights* (dated about 1500) by the Dutch artist Hieronymus Bosch. In contrast, medieval artists sometimes portrayed the Virgin Mary with strawberries; in such painting the fruit symbolized perfection and righteousness.

TANSY

Tansy's name originally came from the Greek word for immortality, probably because its flowers do not wither easily. In classical legend, a drink made from tansy was used to make the beautiful young man Ganymede immortal, so that he could serve as Zeus' cup-bearer.

THUJA (ARBORVITAE)

The American species of this strongly scented coniferous tree was introduced into Europe in the sixteenth century by explorers who brought it back from the New World. In 1576 the Flemish botanist Jules Charles de L'Ecluse (or Clusius) named this tree arborvitae, meaning "tree of life" in Latin. We really do not know his reason for doing so since there seems to be no established association of the thuja with any of the tree of life symbols found in various cultures.* Possibly the name was given because of the tree's medicinal qualities, which had impressed the explorers. The most plausible explanation is that the tree's structure resembles the tree-like form of the white matter seen in a cross-section of the cerebellum of the brain, known since ancient times as the arborvitae.

In the seventeenth century the French botanist Tournefort gave the present thuja tree the name *Thuya*, which was changed to *Thuja*, the present generic name, by Linnaeus in the eighteenth century. Tournefort apparently thought the modern thuja was the same tree that the ancient Greeks called *thyia* or *thuia*, whose scented wood or resin was burned in sacrificial ceremonies. The Greek *thyia* tree may in fact have been a species of thuja (possibly *Thuja orientalis*), but modern botanists are not sure of this because the Greeks never identified their tree specifically as a conifer.

*The tree of life symbol appears in the cultures of the Hebrews, Persians, Egyptians, Phoenicians, Hindus, Chinese, Japanese, Druids, early Germans and Scandinavians, Aztecs, Mayas, Incas, and the Maoris of New Zealand. Some of these symbolic trees are related to actual trees such as the oak, palm, or pine; sometimes they are undefined, like the tree of life in the biblical account of the Garden of Eden.

THYME

Thyme's Greek name *thymon* is thought to be derived from either a Greek verb meaning "to fumigate" or a noun meaning "courage." The Roman writers Virgil (70-19 B.C.) and Pliny (23-79 A.D.) described thyme as a fumigant. On the other hand, in both ancient and medieval times, the invigorating qualities of the plant were thought to inspire courage. In the Middle Ages, sleeping on a pillow stuffed with thyme was recommended for people afflicted with melancholy or epilepsy. According to legend, at midnight on Midsummer Night the king of the fairies and his followers dance in beds of wild thyme. (For one Midsummer Night where everyone has a wild time, see Shakespeare's *A Midsummer Night's Dream*.)

WATER LILY

The water lily takes its genus name, *Nymphaea,* from the Greek *numphe,* meaning "water nymph" or "virgin." The Greeks are said to have given the flower this name because of its reputed anti-aphrodisiac qualities. Poets and artists through the ages have also associated a virginal aloofness with water lilies (especially the white-flowered ones). The plant has often been used as a symbol of purity and chastity, for the water lily flower holds itself erect as if disdaining to touch the murky water surrounding it.

As long as 5,000 years ago, the lotus flower (whose different varieties are members of the water lily family) was one of the most important symbolic and religious plants in both the Near East and the Orient. In Egypt the lotus symbolized the fertility of the rich soil of the Nile's yearly inundation on which the prosperity of Egypt depended. Lotus blossoms were often placed on statues of Osiris, the god of vegetation and regeneration. The lotus was also a symbol of immortality, an attribute of both Osiris and his son Horus, god of light and the sun. Horus is sometimes pictured in Egyptian art sitting on a lotus blossom. In Persia the lotus also symbolized the sun and light.

The lotus has similarly been a major symbol in the culture of India. Brahma, the Hindu god who created the universe, issued forth out of a lotus blossom and, like the Egyptian Horus, is often pictured sitting on the flower. Many of India's spiritual ideas are linked with the lotus. For example, the state of *samadhi*, or spiritual ecstasy, in yoga is represented by a thousand-petaled lotus flower. Indian Buddhists claim the lotus for a symbol of Buddha also, because the flower is supposed to have sprung up to announce his birth. Chinese Buddhists consider the lotus as Buddha's footprint, and their concept of heaven features a sacred lake of lotuses.

The Mayas of Central America and Mexico revered the water lily growing in their region as the sacred symbol of the earth.

WEEPING WILLOW

The weeping willow (*Salix babylonica*) is a well-known symbol of unlucky love and mourning in the Western world. In the Orient, it has been associated with the springtime regeneration of nature, eternal friendship, patience, perseverance, and meekness.

WITCH HAZEL

Witch hazel's name is thought to be derived from early American settlers who used this plant's forked branches as a divining rod in their searches for water or gold, just as the hazel's branches were used in England. However, it is also possible that the name was transferred from the English wych-hazel, or wych-elm, with its ultimate origin in the Old English word *wican,* meaning "to yield." The reference, of course, would be to the springiness of the wood.

WOODRUFF

Teutonic warriors wore a sprig of woodruff in their helmets in the belief that it promoted success in battle. In the Middle Ages garlands of woodruff were hung in houses as air fresheners. It is said that Queen Elizabeth I, when she wished to honor an individual with temporary favor, gave him a sprig of woodruff. Today in Germany woodruff is used to flavor May wine.

WORMWOOD

Wormwood's name is obviously derived from its medicinal property of expelling intestinal worms, for which it has been well known since ancient times. An Egyptian papyrus dated 1,600 years before Christ describes this bitter herb.

Legend has it that wormwood first sprang up on the impressions marking the serpent's trail as he slithered his way out of Eden. According to old folk beliefs, wormwood was reputed to deprive a man of his courage, but a salve made from it was supposed to be effective in driving away goblins who came at night.

Wormwood is a principal ingredient in the dangerous alcoholic drink absinthe, which has been made illegal all over the world because it deteriorates the nervous system, causing attacks similar to epileptic seizures.

BIBLIOGRAPHY AND REFERENCES

BOOKS ON HERBS AND THEIR USES

Angier, Bradford. *Free for the Eating.* Harrisburg, Pennsylvania: Stackpole Books, 1966.

Baker, H. G. *Plants and Civilization.* Second edition. Belmont, California: Wadsworth Publishing Company, 1970.

Balls, Edward K. *Early Uses of California Plants.* Berkeley and Los Angeles, California: University of California Press, 1965.

Boros, Georges, *Unsere Küchen- und Gewürzkräuter.* Stuttgart, West Germany: Verlag Eugen Ulmer, 1966.

Brauchle, Alfred. *Das Grosse Buch der Naturheilkunde.* Gütersloh, West Germany: C. Bertelsmann Verlag, 1957.

Clarkson, Rosetta E. *Herbs, Their Culture and Uses.* New York: The Macmillan Company, 1942.

Clymer, R. Swinburne. *Nature's Healing Agents.* Fourth edition. Philadelphia: Dorrance and Company, 1963.

Curtin, L. S. M. *Healing Herbs of the Upper Rio Grande.* Los Angeles: Southwest Museum, 1965.

Dunglison, Robley. *Dunglison's Medical Dictionary.* Twenty-third edition, revised by Thomas L. Stedman. Philadelphia and New York: Lea Brothers and Co., 1903.

Dye Plants and Dyeing. A special printing of *Plants & Gardens,* vol. 20, no. 3. Brooklyn, New York: Brooklyn Botanic Garden, 1964.

Fitzpatrick, Frederick L. *Our Plant Resources.* New York: Holt, Rinehart and Winston, Inc., 1964.

Fox, Helen M. *The Years in My Herb Garden.* New York: The Macmillan Company, 1953.

Gäbler, Hartwig. *Aus dem Heilschatz der Natur.* Stuttgart, West Germany: Paracelsus-Verlag, 1965.

Gibbons, Euell. "Going Wild in San Francisco," *Organic Garden-*

ing and Farming. Emmaus, Pennsylvania: Rodale Press, Inc., January 1973.

———. *Stalking the Good Life*. New York: David McKay Company, Inc., 1971.

———. *Stalking the Healthful Herbs*. New York: David McKay Company, Inc., 1966.

———. *Stalking the Wild Asparagus*. New York: David McKay Company, Inc., 1962.

Gordon, Jean. *Rose Recipes*. Woodstock, Vermont: Red Rose Publications, 1958.

Grieve, Maud. *A Modern Herbal*. Third printing. New York and London: Hafner Publishing Co., 1967. First published 1931.

Grigson, Geoffrey. *A Herbal of All Sorts*. London: Phoenix House, 1959.

Grinspoon, Lester. *Marihuana Reconsidered*. Cambridge, Massachusetts: Harvard University Press, 1971.

Hall, Alan. *The Wild Food Trail Guide*. New York: Holt, Rinehart and Winston, 1973.

Harper-Shove, F. *Prescriber and Clinical Repertory of Medicinal Herbs*. Revised edition. Bognor Regis, Sussex, England: Health Science Press, 1938.

Harris, Ben Charles. *Eat the Weeds*. Barre, Massachusetts: Barre Publishers, 1968.

———. *Kitchen Medicines*. Barre, Massachusetts: Barre Publishers, 1968.

Holthausen, Henriette. *Chicken Cookery Round the World*. New York: Paperback Library, Inc., 1964.

Hooker, Alan. *Herb Cookery and Other Recipes*. San Francisco: 101 Productions, 1971.

Karl, Josef. *Phytotherapie*. Munich, West Germany: Verlag Tibor Marczell, 1970.

Kirk, Donald. *Wild Edible Plants of the Western United States*. Healdsburg, California: Naturegraph Publishers, 1970.

Kloss, Jethro A. *Back to Eden*. New York: Beneficial Books, Benedict Lust Publications, 1971.

Kneipp, Sebastian. *My Water Cure*. New York: Benedict Lust Publications, 1974.

Knutson, Gunilla. *Beauty and Health the Scandinavian Way*. New York: Hawthorn Books, Inc., 1969.

Kroeber, Ludwig. *Das Neuzeitliche Kräuterbuch*. Stuttgart, Germany: Hippokrates-Verlag G.m.b.H., 1934.

Landry, Robert. *The Gentle Art of Flavoring: A Guide to Good*

Cooking. Translated by Bruce H. Axler. London, New York, Toronto: Abelard-Schuman, 1970.

Loewenfeld, Claire and Philippa Back. *Herbs, Health and Cookery.* New York: Hawthorn Books, Inc., 1967.

Lust, Benedict. *About Herbs.* New York: Benedict Lust Publications, 1961.

———. *Nature's Path Magazine.* Bound volumes 1935, 1936, 1937, 1938, 1939, 1940. New York, Benedict Lust Publications.

———. *Only Nature Cures.* New York: Benedict Lust Publications, 1974.

———. *Kneipp Herbs.* New York: Benedict Lust Publications, 1968.

Meyer, Joseph E. *The Herbalist.* Revised and enlarged edition by Clarence Meyer. (No publisher) 1960.

Miloradovich, Milo. *Home Garden Book of Herbs and Spices.* Garden City, New York: Country Life Press, 1952.

Neuthaler, Heinrich. *Das Kräuterbuch.* Salzburg, West Germany: Andreas & Andreas, Verlagsbuchhandel, 1962.

Newman, Laura. *Make Your Juicer Your Drugstore.* New York: Benedict Lust Publications, 1970.

Null, Gary. *The Natural Organic Beauty Book.* New York: Dell Publishing Company, 1972.

Osborne, Richard. *How to Grow Herbs.* Menlo Park, California: Sunset Books, Lane Magazine and Book Company, 1972.

Rose, Jeanne. *Herbs and Things.* New York: Grosset and Dunlap, Workman Publishing Company, 1972.

Schafer, Violet. *Herbcraft.* San Francisco: Yerba Buena Press, 1971.

Scully, Virginia. *A Treasury of American Indian Herbs.* New York: Crown Publishers, Inc., 1970.

Simmonite, W. J. and Nicholas Culpeper. *The Simmonite-Culpeper Herbal Remedies.* New York: Award Books, 1957.

Spice Islands Home Economics Staff. *The Spice Islands Cookbook.* Menlo Park, California: Lane Book Company, 1961.

Stecher, Paul G. (ed.). *The Merck Index.* Eighth edition. Rahway, New Jersey: Merck and Co., Inc., 1968.

Taylor, Walter S. and Richard P. Vine. *Home Winemaker's Handbook.* New York: Harper and Row, Publishers, 1968.

Travern, Beatrice. *Here's Egg on Your Face.* New York: Pocket Books, 1970.

Tucker, Ann. *Potpourri, Incense and Other Fragrant Concoctions.* New York: Workman Publishing Company, 1972.

Vogel, Virgil J. *American Indian Medicine*. Norman, Oklahoma: University of Oklahoma Press, 1970.

Wagner, Frederick. *Popular Methods of Natural Healing*. Translated by H. K. Carroll. Mexico City: El Sobre Azul, 1940.

Weiner, Michael A. *Earth Medicine—Earth Foods*. New York: Collier Books, 1972.

Weiss, R. F. *Moderne Pflanzenheilkunde*. Bad Worishofen, West Germany: Sanitas Verlag, 1966.

Willfort, R. *Gesundheit durch Heilkräuter*. Linz, Austria: Rudolf Trauner Verlag, 1969.

York, Alexandra. *The Natural Skin Care and Beauty Cookbook*. New York: Ballantine Books, 1973.

BOTANICAL REFERENCE BOOKS

Bailey, L. H. *Manual of Cultivated Plants*. Revised edition. New York: The Macmillan Company, 1968.

Britton, N. L. and J. N. Rose. *The Cactaceae*. New York: Dover Publications, Inc., 1963.

Coulter, Merle C. *The Story of the Plant Kingdom*. Third edition. Chicago: The University of Chicago Press, 1964.

Cronquist, Arthur. *Introductory Botany*. New York: Harper & Row, Publishers, 1961.

Fernald, Merritt Lyndon. *Gray's Manual of Botany*. Eighth edition. New York: American Book Company, 1950.

Fernald, Merritt Lyndon and Alfred Charles Kinsey. *Edible Wild Plants of Eastern North America*. Revised by Reed C. Rollins. New York: Harper & Brothers, Publishers, 1958.

Hardin, James W. and Jay M. Arena. *Human Poisoning from Native and Cultivated Plants*. Durham, North Carolina: Duke University Press, 1969.

Hausman, Ethel H. *The Illustrated Encyclopedia of American Wild Flowers*. Garden City, New York: Garden City Publishing Company, 1947.

Jepson, Willis Linn. *A Manual of the Flowering Plants of California*. Berkeley and Los Angeles, California: University of California Press, 1960.

Kingsbury, John M. *Deadly Harvest: A Guide to Common Poisonous Plants*. New York: Holt, Rinehart and Winston, 1965.

———. *Poisonous Plants of the United States and Canada*. Englewood Cliffs, New Jersey: Prentice-Hall, Inc., 1964.

Mathews, Ferdinand. *Field Book of American Wild Flowers.* Revised edition. New York: G. P. Putnam's Sons, 1955.

Muenscher, Walter Conrad. *Poisonous Plants of the United States.* New York: The Macmillan Company, 1961.

Munz, Philip A. *A California Flora.* Fourth edition. Berkeley and Los Angeles, California: University of California Press, 1968.

Nickell, J. M. *J. M. Nickell's Botanical Ready Reference.* New edition. Los Angeles: M. L. Baker, 1972.

U. S. Department of Agriculture. *Selected Weeds of the United States.* Agricultural Handbook No. 366, Agricultural Research Service, U. S. Department of Agriculture. Washington, D.C.: U. S. Government Printing Office, 1970.

Uphoff, J. C. Th. *Dictionary of Economic Plants.* Second edition. Würzburg, West Germany: Verlag von J. Cramer, 1968.

REFERENCE BOOKS ON NUTRITION

Altschul, Aaron M. *Proteins: Their Chemistry and Politics.* New York: Basic Books, Inc., 1965.

Davis, Adelle. *Let's Eat Right to Keep Fit.* Revised edition. New York: Harcourt Brace Jovanovich, 1970.

Dixon, Malcolm. *Enzymes.* Second edition. New York: Academic Press Inc., Publishers, 1964.

Fleck, Henrietta. *Introduction to Nutrition.* Second edition. New York: The Macmillan Company, 1971.

Lappé, Frances Moore. *Diet for a Small Planet.* New York: Ballantine Books, Inc., 1971.

Locke, David M. *Enzymes—The Agents of Life.* New York: Crown Publishers, Inc., 1969.

National Research Council Food and Nutrition Board. *Recommended Dietary Allowances.* Seventh revised edition. Washington, D.C.: National Academy of Sciences, 1968.

Sherman, Henry. *Chemistry of Food and Nutrition.* Eighth edition. New York: The Macmillan Company, 1952.

HISTORICAL REFERENCE BOOKS

Buck, Albert H. *The Growth of Medicine.* New Haven, Connecticut: Yale University Press, 1917.

Inglis, Brian. *The Case for Unorthodox Medicine.* New York: G. P. Putnam's Sons, 1965.

———. *A History of Medicine*. Cleveland and New York: The World Publishing Company, 1965.

Kett, Joseph F. *The Formation of the American Medical Profession*. New Haven, Connecticut: Yale University Press, 1968.

Lees, Carlton B. *Gardens, Plants and Man*. Englewood Cliffs, New Jersey: Prentice-Hall, Inc., 1970.

Maple, Eric. *Magic, Medicine and Quackery*. Cranbury, New Jersey: A. S. Barnes and Company, Inc., 1968.

Taylor, Norman. *Plant Drugs that Changed the World*. New York: Dodd, Mead and Company, 1965.

REFERENCE BOOKS FOR "LEGEND AND LORE" AND "ASTROLOGY"

Barnard, Mary. *The Mythmakers*. Athens, Ohio: Ohio University Press, 1966.

Boom, B. K. and H. Kleijn. *The Glory of the Tree*. Garden City, New York: Doubleday and Company, Inc., 1966.

Bulfinch, Thomas. *Bulfinch's Mythology*. London: Spring Books, 1964.

Camp, Wendell H. *The World in Your Garden*. Washington, D.C.: National Geographic Society, 1957.

Campbell, Joseph. *The Masks of God: Primitive Mythology*. New York: Viking Press, 1959.

Castaneda, Carlos. *The Teachings of Don Juan: A Yaqui Way of Knowledge*. New York: Ballantine Books, 1968.

Cirlot, J. E. *A Dictionary of Symbols*. Translated by Jack Sage. New York: Philosophical Library, Inc., 1962.

Coats, Alice F. *Flowers and Their Histories*. London: Pitman Publishing Corporation, 1956.

———. *Garden Shrubs and Their Histories*. New York: E. P. Dutton and Company, Inc., 1965.

Coats, Peter. *Flowers in History*. New York: Viking Press, 1970.

Crow, W. B. *The Occult Properties of Herbs*. New York: Samuel Weiser, Inc., 1969.

Douglas, Alfred. *How to Consult the I Ching*. New York: Berkley Medallion Books, 1972.

Ferguson, George. *Signs and Symbols in Christian Art*. Second edition. New York: Oxford University Press, 1955.

Grimal, Pierre (ed.). *Larousse World Mythology*. Translated by Patricia Beardsworth. New York: Prometheus Press, 1965.

Jacob, Dorothy. *A Witch's Guide to Gardening*. New York: Taplinger Publishing Company, 1965.

Leek, Sybil. *Astrological Guide to Successful Everyday Living*. Englewood Cliffs, New Jersey: Prentice-Hall, Inc., 1970.

Lehner, Ernst and Johanna. *Folklore and Odysseys of Food and Medicinal Plants*. New York: Tudor Publishing Company, 1962.

———. *Folklore and Symbolism of Flowers, Plants and Trees*. New York: Tudor Publishing Company, 1960.

McCarthy, Frank J. *Herbs of the Zodiac*. New York: Dell Publishing Company, 1971.

Payne, Robert. *The Horizon Book of Ancient Rome*. New York: American Heritage Publishing Co., Inc., 1966.

Seyffert, Oskar. *Dictionary of Classical Antiquities*. Revised edition. Cleveland and New York: Meridian Books, World Publishing Company, 1956.

Speiser, E. A. (trans.). *The Anchor Bible: Genesis*. Garden City, New York: Doubleday & Company, Inc., 1964.

Sullivan, Michael. *The Birth of Landscape Painting in China*. Berkeley and Los Angeles, California: University of California Press, 1962.

Tergit, Gabriele. *Flowers Through the Ages*. Philadelphia: Dufour Editions, 1962.

Thompson, C. J. *The Mystic Mandrake*. New Hyde Park, New York: University Books, 1968.

Walsh, William S. *Handy-Book of Literary Curiosities*. Philadelphia: J. B. Lippincott Company, 1892. Republished by Gale Research Company, Detroit, 1966.

GENERAL REFERENCE

The Organic Directory. Emmaus, Pennsylvania: Rodale Press, 1971.

Also, standard encyclopedias and dictionaries.

INDEX

This index consists of two main parts: "Comprehensive Botanical Index" and "General Index." The "Comprehensive Botanical Index" is subdivided into a "Plant Index" and a "List of Plants by Botanical Name."

The "Plant Index" lists alphabetically the English names of all the plants mentioned in the book, with their page numbers. For the plants in Part 2, it includes only the primary name; consult the indexes at the end of Part 2 for the various other common names of those plants. Similarly, the Part 2 plant numbers are not shown in the "Plant Index," only page numbers. The page numbers in bold indicate major listings in the "Compendium of Botanical Medicine" (Part 2).

"List of Plants by Botanical Name" is a supplementary reference list to help you find a plant for which you know only the botanical name.

The "General Index" is the kind of index normally found in a book, listing the page numbers of the significant subjects appearing in the text.

COMPREHENSIVE BOTANICAL INDEX

PLANT INDEX

NOTE: spp. means "species"

var. means "variety"

vars. means "varieties"

Abelmosk (Hibiscus moschatus), 541

Acacia (Acacia spp.), 543, 575-76

Acacia (Acacia senegal), 87

Acerola (Malpighia punicifolia), 498

Adder's-tongue (Erythronium americanum), 88

Agave (Agave spp.), 576

Agave (Agave americana), 89

Agave (Agave sisalana), 508, 566

Agrimony (Agrimonia spp.), 574

Alder (Alnus spp.), 122-23

Alder Buckthorn (Rhamnus frangula), 138-140, 456, 460, 464, 466, 467, 475, 476, 478, 481, 482, 483, 485, 550, 570

Alexandrian Senna (Cassia acutifolia), 352

Alfalfa (Medicago sativa), 89-90, 496, 500, 507, 521, 528, 566, 567

Alkanet (Alkanna tinctoria), 550

Allspice (Pimenta officinalis), 90, 510-11, 541

Almond (Prunus amygdalus), 15, 91, 241, 497, 500, 502, 503, 504, 505, 530-31, 534, 541, 550, 573, 576, 613

Aloe (Aloe latifolia), 92

Aloe (Aloe saponaria), 92

Aloe (Aloe tenuior), 92

Aloe (Aloe vera), 45, 91-92, 529

Alpine Cranberry (Vaccinium vitis idaea), 93, 496, 499, 550

Althea (Althaea officinalis), 93-94, 226, 461, 462, 468, 469, 480, 481

Amaranth (Amaranthus hypochondriacus), 95, 576-77. See also Green Amaranth.

American Angelica (Angelica atropurpurea), 99, 456, 467, 489

American Centaury (Sabatia angularis), 95, 503

American Chestnut (Castanea dentata), 502, 504, 569, 570, 573

American Elder (Sambucus canadensis), 178, 459, 460, 469, 482, 485, 486, 496, 499, 501, 503, 506, 520, 521, 523, 526, 528, 529, 532, 540

American Ginseng (Panax quinquefolius), 17, 207, 508, 529, 590

American Hellebore (Veratrum viride, 96, 567

American Ivy (Parthenocissus quinquefolia), 96-97, 550

American Mistletoe (Phoradendron flavescens), 278

American Mountain Ash (Sorbus americana), 339

American Sanicle (Sanicula marilandica), 345-46, 503

American Senna (Cassia marilandica), 351-52, 460, 466, 467, 471, 485

American Spikenard (Aralia racemosa), 361, 362, 392, 529

Amole (Agave schottii), 568

Angelica (Angelica spp.), 97-99

Anise (Pimpinella anisum), 99-100, 173, 309, 316, 366, 372, 459, 460, 461, 462, 463, 466, 467, 468, 469, 475, 484, 485, 486, 490, 510, 511, 529, 541, 565, 567, 573

Annatto (Bixa orellana), 550

Apple Mint (Mentha gentilis), 516, 524

Apple Mint (Mentha rotundifolia), 516, 524

Apple Tree (Pyrus malus), 100-01, 117, 154, 168, 500, 502, 503, 504, 506, 507, 528, 529, 535, 550, 570, 573, 574, 577-78

Apricot (Prunus armeniaca), 496, 497, 500, 502, 503, 504, 505, 507, 528, 531

Arnica (Arnica montana), 101-02, 477, 478, 490, 529

Artichoke (Cynara scolymus), 102, 495, 496, 500, 503, 506, 507

Arum (Arum maculatum), 103

Asafetida (Ferula assa-foetida), 195, 505, 541, 578-79

Asafetida (Ferula foetida), 194-95, 505, 541, 578-79

Asarum (Asarum europaeum), 104

Asiatic Ginseng (Panax schin-seng), 206-07, 508, 529, 590

Asparagus (Asparagus officinalis), 104-05, 472, 495, 500, 502, 503, 504, 506, 527

Aspic (Lavandula spica), 566

Aster (Aster spp.), 540

Avens (Geum spp.), 115, 388-89

Avocado (Persea americana), 497, 500, 502, 503, 504, 507, 531, 567

Baby's Breath (Gypsophila paniculata), 540

Bald Cypress (Taxodium distichum), 570, 573

Balm (Melissa officinalis), 45, 105-06, 157, 456, 462, 464, 470, 477, 478, 479, 480, 482, 484, 488, 490, 510, 511, 520, 521, 523, 526, 529, 532, 540, 566, 573, 574, 579

Balm of Gilead (Commiphora meccanensis), 579

Balm of Gilead (Populus candicans), 319, 579

Balsam Tree (Myroxylon balsamum), 541

Banana (Musa paradisiaca var.

634

sapientum), 502, 503, 504, 507, 531, 572

Baobab *(Adansonia digitata)*, 566, 568

Barberry *(Berberis vulgaris)*, **106-07**, 491, 499, 528, 551, 570, 573

Barley *(Hordeum vulgare)*, 4, **107**, 190, 495, 497, 498, 500, 502, 503, 504, 506, 507, 529, 531, 567, 573, 574

Basil *(Ocimum basilicum)*, **108**, 510, 511, 521, 526, 529, 540, 566, 573, 574, 579

Basswood *(Tilia americana)*, **256**, 485, 524, 332, 533, 534, 566, 570

Bayleaf. *See* Laurel.

Bean. *See* Broad Bean, Kidney Bean, Lima Bean, Velvet Bean.

Bearberry *(Arctostaphylos uva-ursi)*, 93, **110**, 456, 480, 491, 551, 569

Bearded Darnel *(Lolium temulentum)*, 111

Beard Grass *(Andropogon virginicus)*, 551

Bear-grass *(Xerophyllum tenax)*, 566

Bearsfoot *(Helleborus foetidus)*, 219

Bear's Garlic *(Allium ursinum)*, 111, 499

Bedstraw *(Galium spp.)*, **112-13**

Beech *(Fagus spp.)*, 574

Beechdrops *(Epifagus virginiana)*, 114

Beet *(Beta vulgaris)*, 487, 496, 497, 501, 502, 503, 505, 506, 507, 528, 573

Belladonna *(Atropa belladonna)*, 114, 580

Bennet *(Geum urbanus)*, **115**, 529

Bergamot *(Citrus bergamia)*, 541

Betony *(Stachys officinalis)*, **116**, 521, 573

Big-bud Hickory *(Carya tomentosa)*, 551

Bilberry *(Vaccinium myrtillus)*, 109, **116-17**, 461, 471, 496, 499, 503, 528, 529

Birch *(Betula spp.)*, **117-19**, 461, 473, 476, 477, 483, 503, 521-22, 573, 581

Bird's Tongue *(Fraxinus excelsior)*, 119, 551, 570, 581-82

Birthroot *(Trillium pendulum)*, **120**, 483

Birthwort *(Aristolochia clematitis)*, **120-21**

Bistort *(Polygonum bistorta)*, **121-22**

Bitter Milkwort *(Polygala amara)*, 274

Bitter Orange. *See* Orange.

Bittersweet Nightshade *(Solanum dulcamara)*, 293, 574

Black Alder *(Alnus glutinosa)*, **122**, 123, 551, 565, 566, 567, 569, 570, 574

Black Ash *(Fraxinus nigra)*, 570

Blackberry *(Rubus villosus)*, **123-24**, 459, 471, 487, 488, 490, 499, 502, 503, 504, 506, 507, 525, 528, 529, 552, 573

Black Birch *(Betula lenta)*, **118-19**, 471, 472, 486, 521-22, 529, 552, 566, 570

Black Cohosh *(Cimicifuga racemosa)*, **124-25**, 456, 508

Black Currant *(Ribes nigrum)*, **168-69**, 469, 499, 528, 529

Black Elder *(Sambucus nigra)*, **179-80**, 459, 460, 478,, 487, 490, 491, 520, 521, 523, 526, 528, 529, 552, 573, 585-86

Black Gum *(Nyssa sylvatica)*, 552

Black Hellebore *(Helleborus niger)*, **219**, 220, 582

Black Mulberry *(Morus nigra)*, 285

Black Mullein *(Verbascum nigrum)*, 286-87

Black Mustard *(Brassica nigra)*, **287-88**, 516, 567, 568, 573

Black Nightshade *(Solanum nigrum)*, 293, 574

Black Oak *(Quercus tinctoria* or *Quercus velutina)*, **295**, 552

Black Pepper *(Piper nigrum)*, 474, 502, 510, 514, 517

Black Poplar *(Populus nigra)*, **320**, 570

Black Root *(Veronicastrum virginicum)*, **125**

Black Sage *(Salvia mellifera)*, 566

Black Spruce *(Picea mariana)*, 363

Blackthorn *(Prunus spinosa)*, **314**, 457, 460, 478, 487, 529, 552, 570, 573

Black Walnut *(Juglans nigra)*, **386-87**, 495, 497, 504, 505, 552, 570

Black Wattle *(Acacia mollissima* and other *Acacia* spp.*)*, 569

Black Willow *(Salix nigra)*, **403**, 502, 570

Blazing Star *(Liatris spp.)*, **126-27**, 483

Blind Nettle *(Lamium album)*, **127-28**, 481, 482, 566

Bloodroot *(Sanguinaria canadensis)*, **128**, 552

Blue Ash *(Fraximus quadrangulata)*, 570

Blueberry *(Vaccinium angustifolium)*, 15, 506, 507

Blueberry *(Vaccinium corymbosum)*, 15, 506, 507

Blue Cohosh *(Caulophyllum thalictroides)*, 129

Blue Flag *(Iris versicolor)*, **129-30**

Blue Gentian *(Gentiana catesbaei)*, 413

Blue Vervain *(Verbena hastata)*, **130-31**, 457, 458

Blue Violet *(Viola papilionacea)*, 482, 496, 498, 519

Bombay Aloe *(Aloe perryi)*, **92**

Boneset *(Eupatorium perfoliatum)*, **131**, 485, 486, 499

Borage *(Borage officinalis)*, **132**, 465, 477, 503, 510, 511, 522, 566, 574, 583

Boxwood *(Buxus sempervirens)*, **133**, 570

Bracken *(Pteridium aquilinum* vars.*)*, 553

Bramble *(Rubus* spp.*)*, 574

Brazil Nut *(Bertholletia excelsa)*, 495, 500, 502, 504, 505, 567, 568

Brewer's Yeast *(Saccharomyces*

635

cerevisiae), 304, 495, 497, 500, 507, 531,

Brier Hip *(Rosa canina)*, 85, **133-34**, 455, 473, 496-97

Broad Bean *(Vicia faba)*, 495

Broad-leaved Dock *(Rumex obstusifolius)*, 553

Broccoli *(Brassica oleracea* var. *italica)*, 495, 496, 497, 499, 500, 501, 503, 504, 506

Brooklime *(Veronica beccabunga)*, 134, 490, 499

Broom Pine. *See* Longleaf Pine.

Brussels Sprout *(Brassica oleracea* var. *gemmifera)*, 495, 507

Bryony *(Bryonia* spp.), **135-36**, 583

Buchu *(Barosma betulina)*, 136, 466, 480

Buck Bean *(Menyanthes trifoliata)*, 137, 460, 464, 484, 485, 490, 529, 569

Buckhorn Brake *(Osmunda regalis)*, 193, 566

Buckthorn *(Rhamnus* spp.), 138

Buckwheat *(Fagopyrum esculentum)*, 497, 502, 503, 566

Buffalo Berry *(Shepherdia argentea)*, 528

Buffalo Berry *(Shepherdia canadensis)*, 528

Bugloss *(Anchusa officinalis)*, 574

Bulbous Buttercup *(Ranunculus bulbosus)*, 142

Burdock *(Arctium lappa)*, **140-41**, 459, 460, 500, 506, 573

Burnet *(Sanguisorba minor)*, 510, 511-12, 522

Burnet Saxifrage *(Pimpinella saxifraga)*, **308-09**, 481, 529

Buttercup *(Ranunculus* spp.), **141-43**

Butternut *(Juglans cinerea)*, 387, 553, 570

Button Snakeroot. *See* Water Eryngo.

Cabbage *(Brassica oleracea* var. *capitata)*, 465, 498, 501, 502, 503, 504, 505, 506, 512, 514, 515, 518, 528, 572

Cabbage Rose *(Rosa centifolia)*, 336

Cacao. *See* Cocoa.

Calendula *(Calendula officinalis)*, 143, 476, 489, 497, 503, 515-16, 540, 572, 574

California Laurel *(Umbellularia californica)*, 570

Californian Rose *(Rosa californica)*, 336

California Soap Plant *(Chenopodium californicum)*, 568

California Soaproot *(Chlorogalum pomeridianum)*, 568

Calliopsis *(Coreopsis tinctoria)*, 553

Calla Lily *(Zantedeschia aethiopica)*, 574

Camomile. *See* Dyer's Camomile, German Camomile, Roman Camomile.

Camphor Tree *(Cinnamomum camphora)*, 469, 481

Candelilla *(Euphorbia antisyphilitica)*, 569

Cannabis *(Cannabis sativa)*, **145-46**, 294, 497, 566, 568, 573, 591-92

Canoe Birch *(Betula papyrifera)*, 553

Cantaloupe *(Cucumis melo* var. *cantalupensis)*, 496, 499, 503, 528

Capers *(Capparis spinosa)*, 512, 516, 573

Caraway *(Carum carvi)*, 4, 100, **146-47**, 173, 459, 460, 462, 466, 490, 503, 512, 529, 541, 572

Cardamom *(Elettaria cardamomum)*, 147, 366, 510, 512, 513, 529, 541, 565

Cardinal Flower *(Lobelia cardinalis)*, 540

Carline Thistle *(Carlina acaulis)*, 148, 508, 583

Carnation *(Dianthus caryophyllus)*, 540

Carnauba *(Copernicia cerifera)*, 566, 569

Carrot *(Daucus carota)*, 149, 154, 168, 487, 496, 498-499, 500, 502, 503, 504, 506, 507, 511, 527, 528, 529, 531, 567, 572

Cascara Sagrada *(Rhamnus purshiana)*, **139-40**, 456, 508, 553

Cashew *(Anacardium occidentale)*, 495, 500, 502, 505, 568

Cassia *(Cinnamomum cassia)*, 483, 484, 512

Cassina. *See* Indian Black Drink.

Castor Bean *(Ricinus communis)*, 4, 150, 324, 508, 568

Catechu *(Acacia catechu)*, 543, 553, 569

Catnip *(Nepeta cataria)*, 150, 499, 522, 566

Cat's Foot *(Antennaria dioica)*, 151

Cauliflower *(Brassica oleracea* var. *botrytis)*, 495, 497, 500, 501, 503, 504, 506

Cayenne *(Capsicum frutescens)*, **151-52**, 313, 457, 458, 499, 502, 512, 514, 516, 574

Cedar *(Cedrus* spp.), 541

Cedar Apple. *See* Red Cedar.

Celandine *(Chelidonium majus)*, **152-53**, 464, 482, 572, 574

Celery *(Apium graveolens)*, **153-54**, 168, 472, 480, 487, 499, 500, 501, 502, 503, 504, 506, 512, 528, 529, 567

Chard *(Beta vulgaris* var. *cicla)*, 495, 496, 497, 500, 501, 502, 503, 504, 505, 528

Chaste Tree *(Vitex agnus-castus)*, 508

Cherokee Rose *(Rosa laevigata)*, 337

Cherry *(Prunus* spp.), 15, 502, 503, 504, 506, 507, 529, 573, 574. *See also* Sour Cherry, Sweet Cherry, Wild Black Cherry.

Chervil *(Anthriscus cerefolium)*, 154, 505, 510, 512-13, 569, 573

Chestnut. *See* American Chestnut.

Chickweed *(Stellaria media)*, 155, 499, 503

Chicory *(Cichorium intybus)*, **155-56**, 477, 481, 496, 501, 503, 506, 527, 566, 567

Chinese Arborvitae. *See* Oriental Arborvitae.

Chinese Cinnamon. *See* Cassia.

Chinese Parsley. *See* Coriander.

Chive (Allium schoenoprasum), 156,
501, 510, 513, 528
Chufa (Cyperus esculentus), 528
Cilantro. See Coriander.
Cinnamon (Cinnamomum zeylani-
cum), 352, 487, 512, 513, 529, 541
Cinnamon Fern (Osmunda cinna-
momea), 193-94
Cinquefoil (Potentilla spp.), 157-58,
573
Clary Sage (Salvia sclarea), 518, 541,
568
Cleavers (Galium aparine), 112-13,
482, 501, 527
Clove (Caryophyllus aromaticus or
Syzygium aromaticum), 159, 469,
481, 484, 513, 515, 529, 541, 565,
573
Clover. See Wild Clover.
Club Moss (Lycopodium clavatum),
11, 159-60, 491
Cocoa (Theobroma cacao), 502, 529,
531, 567
Coconut (Cocos nucifera), 502, 504,
528, 531, 566, 567, 568, 570
Coffee (Coffea arabica), 229, 247,
275, 296, 502, 512, 529
Collard (Brassica oleracea var.
acephala), 495, 496, 497, 499, 501,
502, 503, 506
Colombo (Cocculus palmatus), 160,
381, 456, 471, 490
Coltsfoot (Tussilago farfara), 160-61,
461, 462, 463, 467, 468, 469, 478,
480, 486, 499, 501, 503, 505, 553,
569
Columbine (Aquilegia vulgaris), 161-
62, 566, 567, 573
Comfrey (Symphytum officinale),
162-63, 473, 489, 503, 532, 573,
574
Common Buckthorn (Rhamnus
cathartica), 139, 499, 570
Common Groundsel (Senecio vulgaris), 328
Common Lettuce (Lactuca sativa),
253, 494, 497, 499, 501, 502, 503,
506, 518, 528, 572, 574
Common Mullein (Verbascum thapsiforme), 286, 540
Common Plantain (Plantago major),
312
Common Plum (Prunus domestica),
314-15, 497, 500, 502, 503, 504,
506, 507, 528, 529, 554, 570, 573
Coral Root (Corallohiza odontorhiza), 163
Coriander (Coriandrum sativum), 4,
164, 173, 352, 460, 474, 499, 513,
514, 529, 541, 568, 573
Corkwood (Hibiscus tiliaceus), 226,
566
Cornflower (Centaurea cyanus), 165,
540, 554
Corn Poppy (Papaver rhoeas), 455,
517
Corydalis (Corydalis cava), 165-66
Costmary (Chrysanthemum balsamita), 521, 522, 526
Cotton (Gossypium spp.), 166, 288,
495, 500, 507, 554, 566, 567, 568
Cowslip (Caltha palustris), 166-67,
497

Cramp Bank. See Highbush Cran-
berry.
Cranberry (Vaccinium macrocar-
pon), 474, 528
Cranberry (Vaccinium oxycoccus),
474, 528
Creosote Bush (Covillea mexicana),
565
Cubeb (Piper cubeba), 167, 345, 541,
569
Cube Plant (Lonchocarpus spp.), 567
Cucumber (Cucumis sativus), 15,
168, 487, 502, 503, 506, 528, 531,
567, 572, 574
Cumin (Cuminum cyminum), 103,
513, 514
Curled Mint (Mentha crispa), 277
Currant (Ribes spp.), 168-69, 505,
506, 573
Cyclamen (Cyclamen europaeum),
170
Cypress (Cupressus spp.), 573, 574
Cypress Spurge (Euphorbia cyparissias), 364
Daffodil (Narcissus spp.), 12
Daisy. See Wild Daisy.
Damask Rose (Rosa damascena),
336-37, 529, 541
Dandelion (Taraxacum officinale),
15, 17, 109, 170-71, 349, 459, 460,
465, 471, 481, 483, 485, 490, 496,
497, 500, 501, 502, 503, 504, 505,
508, 527, 528, 529, 554, 573, 585
Date Palm (Phoenix dactylifera),
497, 500, 502, 503, 505, 507, 566
Derris Plant (Derris spp.), 567
Desert Tea (Ephedra spp.), 172, 522-
23
Dill (Anethum graveolens), 173, 475,
479, 490, 505, 514, 529, 541, 572,
585, 587
Dittany (Cunila origanoides), 567,
569
Divi-Divi (Caesalpinia coriaria), 569
Dock (Rumex spp.), 359-60, 411-12
Dogbane (Apocynum androsaemi-
folium), 173-74
Dog Poison (Aethusa cynapium),
174
Dog's Mercury (Mercurialis peren-
nis), 175, 554
Dogwood (Cornus florida), 175-76,
570
Double Coconut (Lodoicea seychel-
larum), 16
Douglas Fir (Pseudotsuga taxifolia),
569, 570
Dropwort (Filipendula hexapetala),
270, 567
Dulse (Rhodymenia palmata), 501,
502, 503, 504, 505
Dwarf Elder (Sambucus ebulus),
180-81
Dwarf Nettle (Urtica urens), 292,
566
Dwarf Sumac (Rhus copallina), 569
Dye Bedstraw Galium tinctorium),
554
Dyer's Broom (Genista tinctoria),
176, 461, 554
Dyer's Camomile (Anthemis tinctoria), 554

Early-flowering Periwinkle *(Vinca minor)*, 305, 455, 573

Echinacea *(Echinacea angustifolia)*, 177, 461, 474

Eggplant *(Solanum melongena* var. *esculentum)*, 503, 504, 511

Eglantine *(Rosa eglanteria)*, 337

Elder *(Sambucus* spp.), 178-81, 585-86, 619

Elecampane *(Inula helenium)*, 181-82, 462, 468, 469, 481, 487, 497, 529, 540, 555, 573, 586

Elm Tree *(Ulmus* spp.), 182-83, 573, 574

Endive *(Cichorium endivia)*, 501, 502, 503, 505, 506, 528

English Elm *(Ulmus campestris)*, 182, 570

English Ivy *(Hedera helix)*, 183, 570, 586-87, 619

English Myrrh. *See* European Sweet Cicely.

English Oak *(Quercus robur)*, 295-96, 527, 555, 570

English Walnut *(Juglans regia)*, 45, 388, 485, 487, 497, 499, 500, 502, 503, 504, 505, 507, 555, 566, 567, 568, 570

Ergot *(Claviceps purpurea)*, 11, 184

Eucalyptus *(Eucalyptus globulus)*, 184-85, 461, 469, 481, 532, 541, 566, 570

Euphorbia. *See* Candelilla, Poinsettia, Spurge.

European Angelica *(Angelica archangelica)*, 45, 97-98, 467, 489, 529, 541, 565, 572, 574, 577

European Aspen *(Populus tremula)*, 320, 570

European Centaury *(Centaurium umbellatum* or *Erythraea centaurium)*, 185-86, 455, 456, 459, 471, 488, 489, 572

European Cranberry *(Viburnum opulus)*, 529

European Five-finger Grass *(Potentilla reptans)*, 158

European Goldenrod *(Solidago virgaurea)*, 209-10

European Linden *(Tilia europaea)*, 255-56, 485, 520, 524, 532, 533, 534, 540, 566, 570, 573, 598-99

European Mandrake *(Mandragora officinarum)*, 4, 264-65, 573, 583, 600-02

European Mistletoe *(Viscum album)*, 278-79, 456, 464, 470, 472, 474, 483, 603, 607

European Pennyroyal *(Mentha pulegium)*, 304, 566, 567, 568

European Ragwort *(Senecio jacoboea)*, 328, 555

European Sanicle *(Sanicula europaea)*, 346

European Seneka *(Polygala vulgaris)*, 274-75

European Solomon's Seal *(Polygonatum odoratum)*, 359

European Sweet Cicely *(Myrrhis odorata)*, 518, 525, 540, 566

European Vervain *(Verbena officinalis)*, 186, 573, 587, 619

European Water Hemlock *(Cicuta virosa)*, 98

Evening Primrose *(Oenothera biennis)*, 187

Evergreen Sumac *(Rhus sempervirens)*, 569

Everlasting. *See* Life Everlasting, Low Cudweed, Pearly Everlasting.

Eyebright. *See* Red Eyebright.

Female Fern *(Polypodium vulgare)*, 191

Fennel *(Foeniculum vulgare)*, 100, 173, 189-90, 239, 458, 459, 461, 462, 465, 470, 472, 477, 478, 479, 481, 484, 490, 503, 505, 514, 529, 532, 541, 566, 572, 587, 619

Fenugreek *(Trigonella joenumgraecum)*, 190-91, 486, 500, 514, 523, 567

Fern. *See* Bracken, Buckhorn Brake, Cinnamon Fern, Female Fern, Male Fern, Maidenhair.

Ferula *(Ferula* spp.), 194-95

Feverfew *(Chrysanthemum parthenium)*, 195-96, 567, 573, 574

Feverweed *(Gerardia pedicularia)*, 196

Field Mint *(Mentha arvensis)*, 524, 569

Fig Tree *(Ficus carica)*, 196-97, 497, 500, 502, 503, 504, 505, 507, 527, 529, 573, 588

Figwort *(Scrophularia nodosa)*, 197, 619

Fir Tree *(Abies* spp.), 573

Five-finger Grass *(Potentilla canadensis)*, 158

Flax *(Linum usitatissimum)*, 198-99, 461, 486, 532, 566, 567, 568

Flowering Ash *(Fraxinus ornus)*, 555

Flowering Spurge *(Euphorbia corollata)*, 364

Flower-of-an-hour *(Hibiscus trionum)*, 227

Foxglove *(Digitalis purpurea)*, 8, 199

Foxtail Millet *(Setaria italica)*, 567

Fragrant Valerian *(Valeriana officinalis)*, 45, 199-200, 231, 282, 455, 456, 464, 465, 471, 477, 478, 479, 480, 483, 484, 485, 532

Frankincense Tree *(Boswellia* spp.), 574

Fraxinella *(Dictamnus albus)*, 200-01, 523

French Rose *(Rosa gallica)*, 337

French Sorrel *(Rumex scutatus)*, 510, 518

Fringed Gentian *(Gentiana crinita)*, 413

Fringe Tree *(Chionanthus virginicus)*, 202

Fumitory *(Fumaria officinalis)*, 202, 461, 555

Fustic *(Chlorophora tinctoria)*, 543, 555

Galangel *(Alpinia galanga)*, 203, 529

Garbanzo Bean *(Cicer arietinum)*, 495

Gardenia *(Gardenia* spp.), 541

Garden Raspberry *(Rubus idaeus)*, 329, 487, 488, 490, 497, 499, 502, 504, 507, 525, 528, 529, 573

Garden Rhubarb *(Rheum rhaponticum)*, 502, 504, 506, 528, 529
Garden Spurge *(Euphorbia lathyrus)*, **364-65**
Garden Thyme *(Thymus vulgaris)*, 4, 47, **378-80**, 458, 462, 468, 469, 470, 476, 488, 490, 492, 505, 510, 519, 526, 529, 532, 533, 540, 565, 566, 567, 573, 622
Garden Violet *(Viola odorata)*, **203-04**, 469, 510, 519, 529, 540, 573, 588-89
Garlic *(Allium sativum)*, 4, 111-12, **204-05**, 217, 252, 457, 466, 497, 499, 503, 505, 514, 528, 566, 573, 589-90, 598
Gentian *(Gentiana* spp.), **412-13**, 590
Geranium *(Pelargonium* spp.), 510, 514, 532
German Camomile *(Matricaria chamomilla)*, 40, 45-46, 109, 141, **144-45**, 157, 293, 456, 459, 460, 462, 464, 465, 466, 470, 471, 473, 476, 477, 483, 484, 485, 486, 488, 489, 490, 503, 520, 522, 526, 529, 531, 532, 540, 566, 572, 574, 619
Giant Arbor Vitae *(Thuja plicata)*, 566, 570
Ginger *(Zingiber officinale)*, 203, **205-06**, 352, 396, 471, 510, 514-15, 529, 541
Ginkgo *(Ginkgo biloba)*, 555
Ginseng *(Panax* spp.), **206-07**, 590
Gladiolus *(Gladiolus* spp.), 12
Goatsbeard *(Tragopogon* spp.), 414
Goat's Rue *(Galega officinalis)*, 208, 567
Goldenrod *(Solidago* spp.), **208-10**, 555
Goldenseal *(Hydrastic canadensis)*, 46, **210-11**, 229, 289
Goldthread *(Coptis trifolia)*, 211, 483, 484
Grape *(Vitis vinifera)*, 15, 497, 500, 502, 503, 505, 506, 507, 528, 529. Wild Grape.
Grapefruit *(Citrus paradisi)*, 528
Gray Goldenrod *(Solidago nemoralis)*, 209
Great Burnet *(Sanguisorba officinalis)*, **211-12**, 477
Greater Pimpernel *(Pimpinella magna)*, **307-08**, 309, 480
Great Periwinkle *(Vinca major)*, 305, 573
Green Amaranth *(Amaranthus retroflexus)*, 16, 496, 499, 501, 503, 505
Green Hellebore *(Helleborus viridis)*, 220, 567
Green Pepper *(Capsicum frutescens* var. *grossum)*, 499, 504, 528
Ground Ivy *(Nepeta hederacea)*, **212-13**, 457, 460, 487, 490, 499, 523, 529, 566
Guaiac *(Guaiacum officinale)*, 213, 568, 570
Guava *(Psidium guajava)*, 528
Guinea Sorrel *(Hibiscus sabdariffa)*, 226, 566
Gum Plant *(Grindelia robusta)*, 214, 458, 568
Hackberry *(Celtis occidentalis)*, 556

Hawthorn *(Crataegus oxyacantha)*, **214-15**, 456, 523, 527, 569, 570, 573, 586, 591, 619
Hazelnut *(Corylus americana)*, 502, 504
Heather *(Calluna vulgaris)*, **215-16**, 529, 556, 566, 569
Hedge Bindweed *(Convolvulus sepium)*, 216
Hedge Garlic *(Sisymbrium alliaria)*, 217
Hedge Hyssop *(Gratiola officinalis)*, **217-18**, 466
Hedge Mustard *(Sisymbrium officinale,)* 218
Heliotrope *(Heliotropium arborescens)*, 540, 541
Hellebore *(Helleborus* spp.), **219-20**, 573. *See also* American Hellebore.
Hemlock Spruce *(Tsuga canadensis)*, **220-21**, 556, 569, 570
Hemp Agrimony *(Eupatorium cannabinum)*, 221
Hemp Dogbane *(Apocynum cannabinum)*, 566
Hemp Nettle *(Galeopsis tetrahit)*, **221-22**, 463
Henbane *(Hyoscyamus niger)*, **222-23**, 464
Henna *(Lawsonia inermis)*, **223**, 556
Hepatica *(Hepatica triloba)*, **223-24**
Herb Robert *(Geranium robertianum)*, **224-25**
Hibiscus *(Hibiscus* spp.), **225-27**, 520, 523, 525
Hibiscus *(Hibiscus bancroftianus)*, 226
Hibiscus *(Hibiscus sagittifolius)*, 226
Hibiscus *(Hibiscus surattensis)*, 226, 566
High Mallow *(Malva sylvestris)*, **262-63**, 461, 476, 480, 491
Hoary Plantain *(Plantago media)*, 313
Holly *(Ilex* spp.), **227-28**
Hollyhock *(Althaea rosea)*, 230, 540, 556
Honeysuckle *(Lonicera fragrantissima)*, 541, 574
Hops *(Humulus lupulus)*, **230-31**, 458, 478, 479, 484, 488, 508, 529, 532, 566, 573
Horehound *(Marrubium vulgare)*, **231-32**, 276, 467, 469, 521, 523, 529, 573, 592
Horse Chestnut *(Aesculus hippocastanum)*, 46, 232, 472, 492, 570
Horsemint *(Monarda punctata)*, **279**, 280, 281
Horseradish *(Armoracia lapathifolia)*, 233, 456, 499, 515, 573
Horseradish Tree *(Moringa oleifera)*, 541, 567
Horseweed *(Conyza canadensis* or *Erigeron canadensis)*, **234**, 464, 472, 478
Hound's-tongue *(Cynoglossum officinale)*, **234-35**
Houseleek *(Sempervivum tectorum)*, 17, **235-36**, 592-93

Hyacinth *(Hyacinthus orientalis)*, 540

Hybrid Rhubarb *(Rheum hybridum)*, 529

Hyssop *(Hyssopus-officinalis)*, **236-37**, 485, 515, 529, 566, 574

Iceland Moss *(Cetraria islandica)*, 237, 497, 556 569

Imperial Masterwort *(Imperatoria ostruthium)*, **237-38** 490, 593

Indian Black Drink *(Ilex vomitoria)*, **228**, 522

Indian Corn *(Zea mays)*, 15, **238-39**, 495, 497, 498, 500, 502, 503, 504, 507, 529, 567, 568, 569, 593-94

Indian Pipe *(Monotropa uniflora)*, 239

Indian Turnip *(Arisaema triphyllum)*, **239-40**

Indigo *(Indigofera tinctoria)*, 4, 542, 543, 556

Indigo Bush *(Dalea emoryi)*, 557

Inkberry *(Ilex glabra)*, 566

Iris *(Iris* spp.), **129-30** 299, 594-95

Iris *(Iris douglasiana)*, 566

Iris *(Iris macrosiphon)*, 566

Irish Moss *(Chondrus crispus)*, 11, **240**, 466, 467, 468, 501, 503, 504, 505

Ironweed *(Vernonia fasciculata)*, **240-41**

Jalap *(Ipomoea jalapa)*, **241.** *See also* Wild Jalap.

Jasmine *(Jasminum officinale)*, **241-42**, 455, 540, 541, 573, 574, 595

Jewelweed *(Impatiens biflora)*, 557, 568

Jimson Weed *(Datura stramonium)*, **242**, 596

Jojoba *(Simmondsis chinensis)*, 567, 568, 569

Jonquil *(Narcissus jonquilla)*, 540

Joshua Tree *(Yucca arborescens)*, 566, 570

Juniper *(Juniperus communis)*, 46, 109, **243-44**, 456, 465, 472, 473, 476, 478, 480, 483, 487, 488, 491, 515, 529, 557

Jute *(Cochorus capsularis* and other *Corchorus* spp.), 566

Kale *(Brassica oleracea* var. *acephala)*, 495, 496, 497, 499, 500, 501, 502, 503, 504, 506, 528

Kapok Tree *(Eriodendron anfractuosum)*, 566

Kelp *(Alaria esculenta)*, 501, 502, 503, 504, 505

Khus-Khus *(Vetiveria zizanioides)*, 244, 551, 566

Kidney Bean *(Phaseolus vulgaris)*, 15, **109**, 461, 471, 495, 497, 500, 501, 502, 503, 504, 506, 507, 515, 518, 567, 580, 593

Kidney Vetch *(Anthyllis vulneraria)*, **244-45**, 567

Knotgrass *(Polygonum aviculare)*, **245**, 463, 464, 468, 489, 499

Knotweed *(Polygonum* spp.), 245-47

Kohlrabi *(Brassica caulorapa)*, 499, 502, 503, 528

Kola Tree *(Cola acuminata)*, **247-48**

Kousso *(Hagenia abyssinica)*, 248

Labrador Tea *(Ledum latifolium)*, 523

Lad's Love *(Artemisia abronatum)*, 410, 540, 596

Lady's Mantle *(Alchemilla vulgaris)*, **248-49**, 458, 482, 534, 557

Lady's Thumb *(Polygonum persicaria)*, **247**

Lamb's-quarters *(Chenopodium album)*, 496, 497, 499, 500, 501, 503, 506

Lance-leaf Plantain *(Plantago lanceolata)*, 104, **311-12**, 313, 461, 462, 463, 468, 469, 470, 472, 478, 499, 501, 503, 505, 528

Larch *(Larix europaea)*, **249-50**, 557, 570, 597

Larkspur *(Delphinium consolida)*, **250**, 540, 557, 567

Laurel *(Laurus nobilis)*, 4, **251**, 511, 515, 540, 566, 568, 597

Lavender *(Lavandula officinalis* or *Lavandula vera.)*, **251-52**, 458, 476, 477, 478, 479, 480, 484, 523, 525, 532, 533, 537, 540, 541, 566, 568, 572, 598, 619

Laver *(Porphyra* spp.), 505

Leaf Lettuce. *See* Common Lettuce.

Leek *(Allium porrum)*, **252**, 501, 506, 515, 598

Lemon *(Citrus limon)*, 100, 191, **252-53**, 499, 502, 503, 514, 515, 528, 529, 534, 541, 565, 568

Lemon Balm. *See* Balm.

Lemongrass *(Cymbopogon citratus)*, 523, 532, 568

Lemon Thyme *(Thymus citriodorus)*, 519, 526, 540

Lemon Verbena *(Aloysia triphylla)*, 510, 515, 521, 523, 526, 537, 540, 541

Lentil *(Lens culinaris)*, 495, 500, 501, 503, 506, 507

Lettuce *(Lactuca* spp.), **253-54**

Licorice *(Glycyrrhiza glabra)*, **254-55**, 460, 461, 462, 467, 468, 469, 470, 472, 478, 480, 481, 482, 483, 486, 503, 508, 523, 569

Life Everlasting *(Gnaphalium polycephalum)*, **187-88**, 189, 540, 569

Lilac *(Syringia vulgaris)*, 541

Lily of the Valley *(Convallaria majalis)*, **255**, 497, 540, 557, 573

Lima Bean *(Phaseolus limensis)*, 495, 497, 500, 502, 503, 504, 506, 507

Lime *(Citrus aurantifolia)*, 502, 541

Linaloe *(Bursera aloexylon)*, 541

Linden *(Tilla* spp.), **255-56**

Linseed. *See* Flax.

Lion's Foot *(Prenanthes alba)*, **257**

Lobelia *(Lobelia inflata)*, 17, **257-58**, 457, 467, 468, 568

Logwood *(Haematoxylon campechianum)*, 557

Lombardy Poplar *(Populus nigra* var. *italica)*, 558

Long Buchu *(Barosma serratifolia)*, 137, 466, 480

Longleaf Pine *(Pinus palustris)*, 469, 570

Loosestrife *(Lythrum salicaria)*, **258**

Lotus. *See* Water Lily.

Lovage *(Levisticum officinale)*, **259**,

472, 480, 491, 515, 524, 529, 532, 534, 540, 565, 572, 573

Low Cudweed (Gnaphalium uliginosum), 188

Low Mallow (Malva rotundifolia), 263, 461, 464, 476, 480

Lungwort (Pulmonaria officinalis), 260, 462, 463, 467, 468, 469, 599-600

Madder (Rubia tinctorum), 260-61, 543, 558

Magnolia (Magnolia glauca), 261, 570

Mahogany (Swietania mahogani), 570

Ma-huang (Ephedra sinica), 4, 8, 172

Maidenhair (Adiantum pedatum), 262, 455, 529, 566, 600

Male Fern (Dryopteris filixmas), 46, 192, 309, 455, 600, 619

Mallow (Malva spp.), 263-64, 574

Mandrake (Podophyllum peltatum), 264-65, 528

Mango (Mangifera indica), 572

Mangrove (Rhizophora spp.), 569, 570

Manzanita (Arctostaphylos tomentosa), 569, 570

Maple (Acer saccharum and other Acer spp.), 501, 506, 570

Marigold (Tagetes spp.), 558. See also Calendula.

Marijunana. See Cannabis.

Marjoram. See Sweet Marjoram, Wild Marjoram.

Marsh Blazing Star (Liatris spicata), 126, 127

Marsh Crowfoot (Ranunculus sceleratus), 142-43

Marsh Hibiscus (Hibiscus palustris), 226

Marsh Rosemary (Limonium spp.), 484

Marsh Tea (Ledum palustre), 267

Masterwort (Heracleum lanatum), 268

Mastic Tree (Pistacia lentiscus), 541

Matico (Piper angustifolium), 268

Mayweed (Anthemis cotula), 567

Meadow Saffron (Colchicum autumnale), 269

Meadowsweet (Filipendula ulmaria), 269-70, 541, 558, 566, 573

Melilot (Melilotus spp.), 415-16

Mercury Herb (Mercurialis annua), 175

Mesquite (Prosopis juliflora var. torreyana), 558, 570

Mexican Damiana (Turnera aphrodisiaca), 270, 455, 483, 522, 529

Mexican Saffron. See Safflower.

Mexican Tea (Chenopodium ambrosioides), 409

Mexican Yam (Dioscorea spp.), 507-508

Mezereon (Daphne mezereum), 271, 566, 573

Mignonette (Reseda odorata), 540

Milfoil (Achillea millefolium), 109, 138, 271-72, 459, 460, 463, 464, 465, 466, 467, 468, 471, 473, 476, 478, 480, 482, 483, 484, 487, 488,

503, 528, 529, 532, 533, 534, 569, 602, 619

Milk purslane (Euphorbia maculata), 365

Milk Thistle (Carduus marianus), 272-73, 461, 527

Milkweed (Asclepias syriaca), 273, 566

Milkwort (Polygala spp.), 274-75, 350-51

Millet (Pucium miliaceum), 495

Mint (Mentha spp.), 14, 275-77, 397, 524, 526, 540, 565, 602

Mistletoe. See American Mistletoe, European Mistletoe.

Monarda (Monarda spp.), 279-81

Monkshood (Aconitum napellus), 281, 540, 573, 603-04

Mother of Thyme (Thymus serpyllum), 46, 379-80, 455, 469, 470, 526, 532, 573, 622

Motherwort (Leonurus cardiaca), 282, 558, 604

Mountain Ash (Sorbus spp.), 339

Mountain Holly (Ilex aquifolium), 227, 570

Mountain Laurel (Kalmia latifolia), 282-83, 570

Mouse Ear (Hieracium pilosella), 283-84, 469

Mugwort (Artemisia vulgaris), 40, 284, 566, 568, 569, 604-05, 619

Mulberry (Morus rubra), 285, 528, 570, 573, 605-06

Mullein (Verbascum spp.), 285-87

Mullein (Verbascum thapsus), 285-86, 457, 461, 462, 468, 480, 485, 491, 503, 505, 506, 606

Murillo. See Quillai.

Musk-mallow (Hibiscus abelmoschus), 225, 566

Mustard (Brassica spp.), 46, 217, 246, 287-88, 495, 496, 497, 499, 500, 501, 503, 504, 505, 516

Myrobalan (Terminalia bellerica), 569

Myrobalan (Terminalia chebula), 569

Myrrh (Commiphora myrrha), 46, 177, 288-89, 473, 474, 529, 541, 565, 574, 606-07

Narcissus (Narcissus tazetta), 540, 541

Nasturtium (Tropaeolum majus), 289, 499, 505, 510, 516, 540

Nerve Root (Cypripedium pubescens), 290

Nettle (Urtica dioica), 291-92, 455, 456, 459, 460, 461, 462, 463, 469, 471, 473, 476, 477, 483, 486, 489, 490, 492, 496, 499, 501, 503, 505, 506, 524, 526, 532, 533, 534, 559, 566, 573

New Jersey Tea (Ceanothus americanus), 292, 524

Nightshade (Solanum spp.), 293-94

Norway Spruce. See Spruce.

Nutmeg (Myristica fragrans), 294, 510, 515, 516, 529, 541, 565, 573

Oak (Quercus spp.), 46, 295-96, 458, 472, 474, 489, 541, 569, 573, 574, 599, 607-08, 622

Oakmoss, 541

Oat (Avena sativa), 46, 296-97, 458,

461, 495, 497, 500, 502, 503, 504, 506, 507, 529, 534, 567, 574

Oil Palm *(Elaeis guineensis)*, 567, 568

Okra *(Hibiscus esculentus)*, 226, 495, 497, 500, 501, 502, 503, 504, 505, 528

Olive *(Olea europaea)*, 102, 297, 318, 344, 500, 506, 507, 533, 541, 567, 568, 570, 573, 596, 608

Onion *(Allium cepa)*, 12, 298, 467, 477, 499, 503, 504, 505, 506, 515, 517, 528, 559, 566, 573, 598

Opium Poppy *(Papaver somniferum)*, 4, 8, 254, 567, 568, 572

Orange *(Citrus aurantium)*, 15, 298-99, 474, 529, 540, 541, 574, 609. *See also* Sweet Orange.

Orange Mint *(Mentha citrata)*, 516, 521, 524

Orange Mullein *(Verbascum phlomoides)*, 286

Oregano. *See* Wild Marjoram.

Oregon Ash *(Fraxinus oregona)*, 570

Oriental Arborvitae *(Thuja orientalis)*, 553, 621-22

Oriental Sweet Gum *(Liquidambar orientalis)*, 541

Origanum. *See* Wild Marjoram.

Orris Root *(Iris florentina)*, 299, 529, 541, 565, 572

Osage-orange *(Maclura pomifera)*, 559

Oswego Tea *(Monarda didyma)*, 280, 467, 520, 521, 524, 526, 540, 566

Pansy *(Viola tricolor)*, 300, 455, 459, 460, 464, 467, 469, 471, 476, 487, 540

Papaya *(Carica papaya)*, 300-01, 496, 503, 508, 528, 534, 568

Paprika *(Capsicum frutescens* varieties), 516

Parsley *(Petroselinum sativum)*, 174, 301-02, 316, 457, 458, 472, 491, 496, 498, 500, 501, 502, 503, 504, 505, 517, 524, 528, 565, 567, 609-10

Parsnip *(Pastinaca sativa)*, 316, 497, 502, 503, 506, 507, 573

Partridge Pea *(Cassia fasciculata)*, 566

Pasque Flower *(Anemone patens)*, 141, 166, 302

Passion Flower *(Passiflora incarnata)*, 303, 532, 610

Patchouli *(Pogostemon cablin)*, 540, 541, 566

Pea *(Pisum sativum)*, 15, 495, 497, 498, 500, 501, 502, 503, 504, 506, 507, 513, 516, 517

Peach Tree *(Prunus persica)*, 15, 303-04, 500, 502, 503, 528, 529, 534, 559, 611

Peanut *(Arachia hypogaea)*, 15, 91, 312, 495, 498, 500, 502, 504, 506, 507, 567, 568

Pearly Everlasting *(Anaphalis margaritacea)*, 189, 569

Pear Tree *(Pyrus communis)*, 506, 528, 570

Pecan *(Carya illinoensis)*, 500, 502, 504, 506, 570

Pennyroyal *Hedeoma pulegioides)*, 304, 524. *See also* European Pennyroyal.

Peony *(Paeonia officinalis)*, 303, 474, 574, 611

Pepper. *See* Cayenne.

Peppermint *(Mentha piperita)*, 119, 191, 275, 277, 459, 459, 462, 471, 473, 475, 476, 479, 481, 484, 485, 490, 502, 503, 508, 516, 520, 521, 522, 524, 525, 529, 532, 533, 534-35, 540, 541, 565

Periwinkle *(Vinca* spp.), 305

Peruvian Balsam Tree *(Myroxylon pereirae.)*, 541

Peruvian Bark *(Cinchona* spp.), 8, 176, 261, 306, 490, 565

Petty Spurge *(Euphorbia peplus)*, 365

Peyote *(Lophophora williamsii)*, 306-07, 611-12

Pilewort *(Erechtites hieracifolia)*, 307, 478

Pimpernel *(Pimpinella* spp.), 307-09. *See also* Anise.

Pine *(Pinus* spp.), 566, 573, 622

Pineapple *(Ananas comosus)*, 15, 497, 504, 528

Pinkroot *(Spigelia marilandica)*, 309

Pipsissewa *(Chimaphila umbellata)*, 310, 480

Pistachio *(Pistacia vera)*, 495

Pitcher Plant *(Scarracenia purpurea)*, 310-11

Plane Tree *(Platanus* spp.), 613

Plantain *(Plantago* spp.), 311-12, 612, 619

Pleurisy Root *(Asclepias tuberosa)*, 313, 486

Plum *(Prunas* spp.), 314-15

Poinsettia *(Euphorbia pulcherrima)*, 559

Poison Hemlock *(Conium maculatum)*, 316, 573, 574

Pokeweed *(Phytolacca americana)*, 317, 456, 496, 498, 503, 506, 559

Pomegranate *(Punica granatum)*, 317-18, 471, 529, 559, 569, 612-13

Ponderosa Pine *(Pinus ponderosa)*, 570

Poplar *(Populus* spp.), 318-20, 613-14

Poppy *(Papaver* spp.), 574. *See also* Corn Poppy, Opium Poppy.

Potato *(Solanum tuberosum)*, 12, 497, 498, 500, 502, 503, 506, 507, 511, 513, 528, 529

Prickly Ash *(Zanthoxylum americanum)*, 321

Prickly Juniper *(Juniperus oxycedrus)*, 243-44, 567

Prickly Lettuce *(Lactuca virosa)*, 254

Prickly Pear *(Opuntia* spp.), 528

Pride of China *(Melia azedarach)*, 322, 567, 570

Primrose *(Primula officinalis)*, 322-23, 459, 463, 469, 470, 478, 479, 484, 487, 488, 499, 502, 503, 573, 574

Privet *(Ligustrum vulgare)*, 323, 560, 570

Prune. *See* Common Plum.

Psyllium *(Plantago psyllium)*, 466

Pumpkin (*Cucurbita pepo*), 325, 471, 503, 567, 568, 572
Purging Cassia (*Cassia fistula*), 352-53
Purging Flax (*Linum catharticum*), 198-99
Purple Goatsbeard (*Tragopogon porrifolius*), 414
Purple Trillium (*Trillium erectum*), 508
Purple Willow (*Salix purpurea*), 403
Purslane (*Portulaca oleracea*), 501, 503, 505
Pyrethrum (*Chrysanthemum cinerariaefolium*), 567
Pyrethrum (*Chrysanthemum coccineum*), 567
Quaking Aspen (*Populus tremuloides*), 318, 319, 320, 483, 490, 570, 614
Quassia (*Picraena excelsa*), 324-25, 529
Quebracho (*Schinopsis lorentzii*), 569
Queen of the Meadow *Eupatorium purpureum*), 325
Quillai (*Quillaja saponaria*), 468, 472-73, 568
Quince (*Cydonia oblonga*), 573
Radish (*Raphanus sativus*), 174, 326, 499, 501, 502, 503, 505, 506, 528
Ragged Cup (*Silphium perfoliatum*), 326-27
Ragwort (*Senecio aureus*), 327-28
Raisin. See Grape.
Ramie (*Boehmeria nivea*), 566
Rape (*Brassica napus*), 567-68
Raspberry (*Rubus* spp.), 328-29
Rattlesnake Plantain (*Goodyera pubescens*), 329-30
Rauwolfia (*Rauwolfia serpentina*), 8
Red Alder (*Alnus rubra*), 123, 560, 570
Red Ash (*Fraxinus pubescens*), 570
Red Bryony (*Bryonia dioica*), 136
Red Campion (*Lychnis dioica*), 568
Red Cedar (*Juniperus virginiana*), 229, 566, 567, 568
Red Currant (*Ribes rubrum*), 169, 497, 528, 529
Red Elder (*Sambucus racemosa*), 180, 573
Red Eyebright (*Euphrasia officinalis*), 330, 504, 505, 572, 574
Red Gum (*Eucalyptus calophylla* and other *Eucalyptus* spp.), 570
Red Maple (*Acer rubrum*), 560
Red Oak (*Quercus rubra*), 295, 472, 478, 484, 570
Red Pimpernel (*Anagallis arvensis*), 331
Red Pine (*Pinus resinosa*), 569, 570
Red Sedge (*Carex arenaria*), 332
Redwood (*Sequoia sempervirens*), 10, 570
Reindeer Moss (*Cladonia rangiferina*), 541
Restharrow (*Ononis spinosa*), 333, 472, 475, 480, 481, 491, 501, 502, 505, 506
Rhatany (*Krameria triandra*), 333-34, 484, 565, 569

Rhodium (*Convolvulus scoparius*), 541
Rhodium (*Convolvulus virgatus*), 541
Rhubarb (*Rheum palmatum*), 138, 334-35, 387, 480. See also Garden Rhubarb.
Rice (*Oryza sativa*), 288, 495, 497, 500, 502, 503, 504, 506, 507, 529, 567
Rock-rose (*Helianthemum canadense*), 335
Rockrose (*Cistus landaniferus*), 541
Rockrose (*Cistus villosus* var. *undulatus*), 569
Roman Camomile (*Anthemis nobilis*), 40, 141, 144, 293, 456, 459, 462, 464, 465, 470, 473, 476, 477, 479, 483, 484, 485, 486, 488, 489, 490, 529, 540, 566, 572, 574, 619
Rooibos (*Combretum apiculatum*), 560
Rose (*Rosa* spp.), 15, 133-34, 335-37, 455, 498, 501, 503, 506, 517, 520, 525, 529, 532, 535, 537, 540, 541, 565, 573, 574, 614-16
Rose (*Rosa roxburghii*), 337
Rose Geranium (*Pelargonium graveolens*), 514, 525, 537, 540
Rosemary (*Rosmarinus officinalis*), 46, 297, 338, 473, 482, 483, 485, 510, 517, 523, 525, 529, 532, 535, 540, 541, 566, 569, 572, 573, 596, 616-17, 619
Rose of China (*Hibiscus rosa-sinensis*), 226, 560
Rosewood (*Dahlbergia nigra* and other *Dahlbergia* spp.), 570
Rough Avens (*Geum virginianum*), 389
Rowan (*Sorbus aucuparia*), 339, 491, 497, 499, 527, 529, 560, 570
Rue (*Ruta graveolens*), 340, 456, 477, 483, 517, 566, 572, 574, 617-18
Rutabaga (*Brassica napobrassica*), 500
Rye (*Secale cereale* or *Secale cornatum*), 4, 47, 184, 288, 495, 502, 503, 504, 567, 574
Safflower (*Carthamus tinctorius*), 340-41, 482, 507, 517, 540, 541, 560, 567, 568
Saffron (*Crocus sativus*), 341-42, 497, 515, 517, 519, 529, 561, 572, 574, 618
Sage (*Salvia officinalis*), 27, 236, 342-43, 458, 468, 469, 470, 473, 485, 491, 500, 505 508, 518, 520, 523, 525, 529, 532, 533, 535, 540, 565, 569, 573, 618-19
St. Benedict Thistle (*Cnicus benedictus*), 343, 464, 471, 476, 567
St. Johnswort (*Hypericum perforatum*,) 344, 455, 470, 478, 479, 483, 561, 619
Salad Burnet. See Burnet.
Sallow (*Salix caprea*), 403, 475, 476, 478
Saltbush (*Atriplex californica*), 568
Sandalwood (*Santalum album*), 345, 541, 570, 619-20

Sanicle *(Sanicula* spp.), **345-46**
Sarsaparilla *(Smilax officinalis)*, **346-47**, 417, 460, 573
Sarsaparilla *(Smilax ornata)*, 508, 573
Sassafras *(Sassafras albidum)*, **347-48**, 392, 456, 466, 525, 541, 561, 565, 570
Sassafras *(Sassafras variifolium)*, 514
Savory *(Satureja hortensis)*, **348**, 504, 510, 518. *See also* Winter Savory.
Saw Palmetto *(Serenoa serrulata)*, 270, **349**, 455, 566
Scaly Blazing Star *(Liatris squarrosa)*, **126-27**
Scotch Broom *(Cytisus scoparius)*, **349-50**, 529, 561, 566
Scurvy Grass *(Cochlearia officinalis)*, **350**, 499
Seaweed. *See* Dulse, Irish Moss, Kelp, Laver.
Senega Snakeroot *(Polygala senega)*, **350-51**, 391
Senna *(Cassia* spp.), 138, 197, 309, **351-52**, 466
Sesame *(Sesamum indicum* or *Sesamum orientale)*, 495, 500, 503, 505, 507, 518, 567, 568
Seven Barks *(Hydrangea arborescens)*, **353**
Shagbark Hickory *(Carya ovata)*, 570
Shallot *(Allium ascalonicum)*, 518
Sharp-lobed Hepatica *(Hepatica acutiloba)*, **224**
Shave Grass *(Equisetum arvense)*, 46, **353-54**, 456, 458, 463, 472, 473, 474, 480, 482, 491, 501, 505, 506, 561
Shea Tree *(Butyrospermum parkii)*, 567, 568
Shepherd's Purse *(Capsella bursapastoris)*, **354-55**, 464, 480, 481, 482, 501, 504, 505
Shinleaf *(Pyrola elliptica)*, **355**
Short Buchu *(Barosma crenulata)*, 137, 466, 480
Silverweed *(Potentilla anserina)*, 157, 158, 458, 470, 501, 502, 505, 506
Silvery Lady's Mantle *(Alchemilla alpina)*, 249
Skullcap *(Scutellaria lateriflora)*, **356**, 456
Skunk Cabbage *(Symplocarpus foetidus)*, **357**
Slippery Elm *(Ulmus fulva)*, **182-83**, 457, 486, 570
Sloe. *See* Blackthorn.
Smartweed *(Polygonum hydropiper)*, 246, 561
Smooth Alder *(Alnus serrulata)*, **123**
Soapberry *(Sapindus saponaria)*, 568
Soap Pod *(Acacia concinna)*, 568
Soap Tree Yucca *(Yucca elata)*, 568
Soapwort *(Saponaria officinalis)*, **358**, 565, 568
Solomon's Seal *(Polygonatum multiflorum)*, **358-59**, 568, 573, 620,
Sorghum *(Sorghum vulgare* varieties), 567

Sorrel *(Rumex acetosa)*, **359-60**, 499, 506, 510, 518, 528, 561, 573
Sour Cherry *(Prunus cerasus)*, 567, 570
Soybean *(Glycine max)*, 312, 495, 497, 498, 500, 502, 503, 504, 505-06, 507, 508, 527, 567, 568
Spanish Bayonet *(Yucca baccata)*, 566, 568
Spearmint *(Mentha spicata)*, **276**, 473, 496, 499, 516, 522, 524, 529
Speedwell *(Veronica officinalis)*, 360, 462, 477, 481, 487, 489, 525
Spikenard *(Aralia* spp.), **361-62**
Spinach *(Spinacea oleracea)*, 155, 359, 408, 458, 495, 496, 497, 499, 500, 501, 502, 503, 504, 505, 517, 518, 528
Spotted Cranebill *(Geranium maculatum)*, **362**, 467, 471, 484, 486
Spruce *(Picea excelsa)*, 46-47, **363**, 499, 570
Spurge *(Euphorbia* spp.), **364-65**
Squaw Bush *(Rhus trilobata* var. *malacophylla)*, 566
Squaw Vine *(Mitchella repens)*, **365-66**, 483
Star Anise *(Illicium anisatum* or *Illicium verum)*, 366, 529
Star Grass *(Aletris farinosa)*, **367**, 508
Sticklewort *(Agrimonia eupatoria)*, **368**, 465, 480, 482, 500, 562
Stiff Gentian *(Gentiana quinquefolia)*, **413**
Stillingia *(Stillingia sylvatica)*, **368-69**
Stone Root *(Collinsonia canadensis)*, **369**
Stoneseed *(Lithospermum ruderale)*, 508
Storksbill *(Erodium cicutarium)*, **370**
Strawberry. *See* Wild Strawberry.
Strawberry-bush *(Euonymus americanus)*, **386**
Sugar Bush *(Rhus ovata)*, 566
Sugar Cane *(Saccharum officinarum)* 569
Sumac *(Rhus glabra)*, **370-71**, 528, 562, 568, 569
Sumbul *(Ferula sumbul)*, **194**, 541
Summer Savory. *See* Savory.
Sundew. *(Drosera rotundifolia)*, **371-72**, 458, 469, 470, 499, 562
Sunflower *(Helianthus annuus)*, 495, 497, 500, 503, 505, 507, 562, 567, 568, 572
Sweet Acacia *(Acacia farnesiana)*, 540
Sweet Cherry *(Prunus avium)*, 570
Sweet Cicely *(Osmorhiza longistylis)*, 372. *See also* European Sweet Cicely.
Sweet Fern *(Comptonia peregrina)*, **372-73**, 540, 568
Sweet Fern *(Comptonia peregrina)*, (var. *asplenifolia)*, 17, **373**
Sweet Flag *(Acorus calamus)*, 47, 103, **373-74**, 474, 488, 489, 492, 503, 504, 505, 529, 541, 565, 566, 567, 569, 572

Sweet Goldenrod (Solidago odora), 208-09, 523
Sweet Gum (Liquidambar styraciflua), 374-75, 569, 570
Sweet Marjoram (Marjorana hortensis), 119, 266, 475, 510, 516, 524, 532, 540, 566, 573, 602
Sweet Orange (Citrus sinensis), 15, 299, 350, 497, 499, 501, 502, 503, 506, 528, 532, 540, 541, 566, 568, 574, 609
Sweet Potato (Ipomoea batatas), 496, 497, 500, 502, 503, 507, 562
Sweet Vernal Grass (Anthoxanthum odoratum), 540
Sweet Violet. See Garden Violet.
Sycamore Maple (Acer pseudoplatanus), 375, 570
Tacamahac (Populus balsamifera), 319
Tall Blazing Star (Liatris scariosa), 127
Tall Field Buttercup (Ranunculus acris), 141, 142, 143, 562
Tamarind (Tamarindus indica), 375-76, 528, 573
Tanbark Oak (Lithocarpus densiflora), 569
Tangerine (Citrus reticulata), 528
Tanner's Dock (Rumex hymenosepalus), 569
Tansy (Tanacetum vulgare), 376, 483, 562, 566, 567, 573, 574, 621
Tarragon (Artemisia dracunculus), 377, 510, 519, 540, 565, 573
Tea (Thea sinensis), 141, 229, 275, 455, 502, 526, 563
Teak (Tectona grandis), 570
Thuja (Thuja occidentalis), 377-78, 568, 570, 621-22
Thyme (Thymus spp.), 378-79. See also Lemon Thyme.
Tiger Lily (Lilium tigrinum), 540
Tinnevelly Senna (Cassia angustifolia), 352
Tobacco (Nicotiana tabacum), 188, 189, 261, 569, 573. See also Wild Tobacco.
Tomato (Lycopersicon esculentum), 15, 465, 487, 500, 502, 503, 506, 511, 528, 535, 573
Tonka Bean (Dipteryx odorata), 541
Tormentil (Potentilla tormentilla or Tormentilla erecta), 380-81, 464, 472
Tuberose (Polianthes tuberosa), 537, 540
Tuberous Water Lily (Nymphaea tuberosa), 393
Tulip Tree (Liriodendron tulipifera), 566, 570
Turkey Corn (Corydalis formosa), 381
Turmeric (Curcuma longa), 514, 519, 563
Turnip (Brassica rapa), 382, 495, 496, 497, 499, 500, 501, 502, 503, 504, 506, 518, 528
Turtlebloom (Chelone glabra), 309, 382-83
Twin Leaf (Jeffersonia diphylla), 383

Valley Oak (Quercus lobata), 563
Vanilla (Vanilla planifolia), 519, 541
Velvet Bean (Stizolobium deeringianum), 567
Vetch (Vicia spp.), 4
Violet. See Garden Violet, Blue Violet.
Virginia Mouse-ear (Cynoglossum morrisoni), 235
Virginia Snakeroot (Aristolochia serpentaria), 384
Virgin's Bower (Clematis virginiana), 384-85, 563
Wafer Ash (Ptelea trifoliata), 385, 529
Wahoo (Euonymous atropurpureus), 386
Wallflower (Cheiranthus cheiri), 541
Walnut (Juglans spp.), 15, 386-87, 572
Water Avens (Geum rivale), 388-89
Watercress (Nasturtium officinale), 389-90, 456, 460, 490, 496, 497, 499, 500, 501, 502, 503, 504, 506, 519, 528, 572
Water Dock (Rumex aquaticus), 412, 573
Water Eryngo (Eryngium aquaticum), 390-91
Water Lily (Nymphaea spp.), 392-93, 572, 574, 622-23
Watermelon (Citrullus vulgaris), 504
Water Mint (Mentha aquatica), 277, 465, 486, 524
Water Smartweed (Polygonum punctatum), 246
Wax Myrtle (Myrica cerifera), 391, 473, 563, 569
Wax Tree (Rhus succedanea), 569
Weeping Willow (Salix babylonica), 623
Weld (Reseda luteola, 543, 563
Wheat (Triticum aestivum), 4, 47, 495, 497, 498, 500, 502, 503, 504, 505, 506, 507, 529, 533, 535, 574
White Ash (Fraxinus americana), 570
White Birch (Betula alba), 117-18, 459, 521-22, 529, 563, 570
White Bryony (Bryonia alba), 135, 136
White Clover (Trifolium repens), 566
White Holly (Ilex opaca), 227-28, 570
White Melilot (Melilotus alba), 416, 540, 566, 567
White Mulberry (Morus alba), 563, 605-06
White Mustard (Brassica hirta), 288, 516, 568, 573
White Oak (Quercus alba), 295, 296, 471, 564, 570
White Pepper. See Black Pepper.
White Pine (Pinus strobus), 392, 570
White Pond Lily (Nymphaea odorata), 392-93
White Weed (Chrysanthemum leucanthemum), 393
White Willow (Salix alba), 402, 403, 532, 565, 570

Wild Angelica (*Angelica sylvestris*), 98, 467, 489, 567

Wild Bergamot (*Monarda fistulosa*), 280-81

Wild Black Cherry (*Prunus serotina*), 28, 392, 394, 467, 529, 570

Wild Clover (*Trifolium pratense*), 394-95, 460, 521, 522, 528, 567, 584

Wild Crabapple (*Malus baccata*), 564

Wild Daisy (*Bellis perennis*), 17, 395-96, 540, 573, 584-85

Wild Ginger (*Asarum canadense*), 396-97

Wild Gourd (*Cucurbita foetidissima*), 568, 572

Wild Grape (*Vitis* spp.), 362

Wild Hyssop (*Pycnanthemum virginianum*), 397

Wild Indigo (*Baptisia tinctoria*), 397-98, 474

Wild Jalap (*Ipomoea pandurata*), 398

Wild Marjoram (*Origanum vulgare*), 265, 266, 499, 513, 516, 564, 566, 569

Wild Oregon Grape (*Mahonia aquifolium*), 399

Wild Persimmon (*Diospyros virginiana*), 499, 503, 506, 525

Wild Plum (*Prunus americana*), 315

Wild Red Raspberry (*Rubus strigosus*), 328, 487, 488, 490, 497, 499, 502, 504, 507, 525, 528, 529, 573

Wild Sage (*Salvia lyrata*), 343, 464, 471, 472, 478, 481, 484, 485

Wild Sarsaparilla (*Aralia nudicaulis*), 361-62

Wild Strawberry (*Fragaria vesca*), 12, 15, 400, 488, 490, 498, 506, 525, 528, 529, 532, 535, 573, 574, 620-21

Wild Tobacco (*Nicotiana rustica*), 567, 573

Wild Vanilla (*Trilisa odoratissima*), 540, 569

Wild Violet. *See* Blue Violet.

Wild Yam (*Dioscorea villosa*), 401, 507

Willow (*Salix* spp.), 402-03, 478, 572

Winterberry (*Hex verticillata*), 228-29

Winter Cress (*Barbarea vulgaris*), 496, 498

Wintergreen (*Gaultheria procumbens*), 404, 457, 473, 481, 502, 504, 521, 526, 529, 532, 565, 572

Winter Savory (*Satureja montana*), 348, 518, 566

Witch Grass (*Agropyron repens*), 138, 405, 460, 463, 465, 468, 477, 480, 487, 506, 527

Witch Hazel (*Hamamelis virginiana*), 406, 474, 533, 535, 565, 568, 623-24

Woad (*Isatis tinctoria*), 540, 543, 564

Woodruff (*Asperula odorata*), 407, 481, 482, 488, 490, 526, 529, 540, 569, 624

Wood Sorrel (*Oxalis acetosella*), 407-08, 508, 584

Wormseed (*Chenopodium ambrosioides* var. *anthelminticum*), 408-09

Wormwood (*Artemisia absinthium*), 27, 409-10, 455, 459, 465, 474, 476, 488, 489, 499, 529, 566, 573, 574, 624

Woundwort (*Prunella vulgaris*), 410-11

Yellow Bedstraw (*Galium verum*), 113, 508, 564

Yellow Dock (*Rumex crispus*), 293, 411-12, 460, 496, 499, 501, 503, 506, 564, 573

Yellow Gentian (*Gentiana lutea*), 27, 381, 412-13, 456, 475, 481, 489, 490, 529, 573

Yellow Goatsbeard (*Tragopogon pratensis*), 414

Yellow Jessamine (*Gelsemium sempervirens*), 414-15

Yellow Melilot (*Melilotus officinalis*), 415-16, 566, 569, 619

Yellow Parilla (*Menispermum canadense*), 416-17

Yellow Root (*Xanthorhiza simplicissima*), 564

Yellow Toadflax (*Linaria vulgaris*), 417, 491, 501, 502, 506

Yerba Buena (*Satureja douglasii*), 457

Yerba Maté (*Ilex paraguariensis*), 229, 526

Yerba Santa (*Eriodictyon californicum*), 418, 457, 458, 569

Yew (*Taxus baccata*), 419, 566, 570, 573, 574

Ylang-Ylang (*Cananglum odoratum*), 540, 568

Yucca (*Yucca* spp.), 566

Zucchini (*Cucurbita pepo* var. *melopepo*), 516

GENERAL INDEX

See the "Comprehensive Botanical Index" beginning on page 634 for listings of individual plants.

Abdominal problems: bath 43; mixtures for, 458

Abortion, plants causing, 48

Aches, footbath for, 368

Acne: mixtures for, 487; plants for, 59, 534

Acupuncture, 8, 9

Alcoholic beverages, 528-29

Alcoholism, plants for, 59

Allergy, plants for, 59

Alum: in douche, 473; in dye, 544, 546, 549

Ambrette, 541

American School of Naturopathy, 7

Anaphrodisiac plants, 49, 66 (under "Erotomania")

Anemia: mixtures for, 455; plants for 59-60
Anesthetic: bath, 90; plants, 49
Antibiotic plants, 49
Antihydrotics: mixtures, 485; plant, 49. See also Night sweats.
Antiseptic plants, 50
Aphrodisiac: mixtures, 455-56; plants, 50
Appetite, lack of: mixtures for, 456; plants for, 50-51 (under "Appetizer," "Bitter," and "Bitter Tonic"), 60
Aromatic plants, 51
Arteriosclerosis: mixture for, 456; plants for, 60
Arthritis: liniment for, 457; mixtures for, 456-57; plants for, 60-61; poultice for, 457
Ascorbic acid. See Vitamin C.
Asthma: bath for, 47; mixture for, 457-58; plants for, 61; 145, 185
Astringent plants, 51
Astrology, 571-74
Athlete's foot, 395
Aztec Indians, 594, 622, 623
  Babylonians, 571, 605-06
Backache, plants for, 61
Balsams, 51
Balsam of Peru, 541
Balsam of Tolu, 541
Baths, 41-47; aphrodisiac bath, 455-56; beauty baths, 532-33; eyebath, 44; footbath, 43; formulas (single herbs) 45-47; full bath, 42; half bath, 42; herbal mixtures for, 458, 532-33; oat baths, 296; potpourri for, 539; sitzbath, 43, 458; thyme baths, 379, 380; vapor bath, 44-45; 533. See also specific ailments.
Bedwetting, plants for, 61
Beer, 529, 531
Ben oil, 541, 567
Beverages, 520-29
Beverage teas, 520-26; mixtures 487-88
Bible, plants in, 4, 542, 575-76, 577, 579, 582, 588, 598, 606, 607, 608, 613
Bile, to increase: mixture for, 464; plants for, 52 (under "Cholagogue")
Binomial system, 16
Blackheads, 534, 535
Bleeding. See Hemorrhage, Wounds.
Blood builder, mixture for, 458-59
Blood cleansers: mixtures for, 459-60, 487; plants for, 53 (under "Depurative")
Blood clots, preventatives, 49 (under "Anticoagulant")
Blood pressure, high: footbath for, 43; mixture for, 459; plants for, 58 (under "Vasodilator") 61
Blood pressure, low: bath for, 42, 47; plants for, 58, (under "Vasoconstrictor"), 62
Blood purifiers. See Blood cleansers.
Blood sugar, to lower, mixtures for, 461
Boils, 92, 94, 119, 128, 143, 177, 197, 412, 416, 461
Boredom, plants for, 62

Botanical terms 18-24
Botany, 10-24
Breath, bad. See Halitosis.
Breath Sweeteners, 565
Bronchial asthma, mixture for, 458. See also Asthma.
Bronchitis: bath for, 47; mixtures for 461-62, 468; plants for, 62; vapor baths for, 243, 363
Bruises, plants for, 62-63
Buddhism, 588, 619, 623
Bulb, defined, 12
Burns, plants for, 63
Buttermilk, cosmetics use, 536
Cade, oil of, 243
Calcium, 501
Calculi. See Stones.
Callouses, plants for, 64
Calming baths, 265, 363, 373-74, 413
Cannabis, 591-92
Carbohydrates, 506-07
Carbuncles, mixtures for, 461
Carminatives. See Gas, intestinal
Carotenes, 496
Castenada, Carlos, 596, 612
Charlemagne, 583, 592, 616
Chemotherapy, 6, 7, 9
Chest problems: mixtures for, 462-64; plants for, 54, (under 'Expectorant"), 56 (under "Pectoral")
Chilblains: baths for, 46, 47, 233; plants for, 63
Childbirth, plants to ease, 56 (under "Oxytocic"), 63
Chinese beliefs and practices. See Oriental beliefs and practices.
Chinese plant myths: motherwort, 604; peach, 611; silk, 605
Chiropractic, 8
Chlorine, 502
Chlorophyll, 13
Cholagogue. See Bible.
Christian legends and symbolism, 575-76, 581, 584, 585, 595, 605, 610, 612, 614, 615, 620, 621, 624
Circulation, to stimulate. See Stimulant.
Coffee substitutes, 526-27
Cold compress: described, 41; mixture for, 464
Cold extract, described, 38
Colds: baths for, 43, 44, 46; mixtures for, 392, 463-64; plants for, 63-64; vapor baths for, 145, 286, 319. See also Chest problems.
Colic mixtures, 464-65
Commercial sources of herbs. See Herb dealers.
Complexion; mixture, 487. See also Cosmetics.
Compress, cold. See Cold compress.
Constipation: baths for, 42, 43; mixtures for, 465-67; plants for, 50, (under "Aperient"), 50, (under "Cathartic"), 55, (under "Laxative"), 56, (under "Purgative"), 64
Copper, 505
Corm, defined, 12
Corns, plants for, 64
Cosmetics, natural, 530-36
Cough: mixtures for, 467-69; plants for, 54, (under "Expectorant"), 64-65; syrups, 467-69

647

Cramps: baths for, 43, 47; mixtures for 470, 488; plants for, 50, (under "Antispasmodic"), 65
Culpeper, Nicholas, 5-6
Cuts. See Wounds.
Cyanocobalamin. See Vitamin B₁₂.
Cystitis: mixture for, 491. See also Genitourinary problems.
Dandruff, plants for, 65
Debility, mixture for, 470-71
Decoction, described, 38
Definitions: botanical terms, 18-24; medicinal effects, 48-58; medicinal preparations, 37-45
Demulcents, 52
Dentifrices, 565
Deodorants, 52, 565
Depression, 187, 219, 342
Devil, the 580, 586, 604, 609, 610
Diabetes: mixture for 471; plants for, 65-66
Diaphoretic: mixtures, 485-86; plants, 53
Diarrhea: mixtures for, 471-72; plants for, 66
Diet, 4, 7, 9, 37
Digestion: baths to aid, 46, 47; mixtures for, 488, 489, 490; plants for, 51 (under "Bitter" and "Bitter Tonic"), 53 (under "Digestive"). See also Indigestion.
Digitalis, 8, 199, 219, 255, 386
Dioscorides, 4, 595
Diuretic: mixtures, 472; plants, 53-54
Dizziness, plants for, 66
Doctrine of Signatures, 599
Douche, vaginal. See Vaginal douche.
Dropsy, mixture for, 473
Druids, 584, 587, 603, 607, 622
Dry skin. See Skin.
Dyes, plant, 542-64; list by color, 546-48; list by plant, 549-64
Dysentery, mixture for, 474
Dyspepsia, plants for, 71-72
Earache, 222-23, 230, 336
Eczema: mixture for, 487; plants for, 109, 128, 153, 154, 177, 186, 197, 209, 218, 247, 333, 338, 383, 390, 398, 399, 400
Egyptian beliefs or practices, 4, 121, 190, 225, 542, 582, 587, 588, 589, 590, 592, 594, 606, 614, 615, 622, 623, 624
Emollients, 54
Emphysema. See Lungs.
Enema, mixtures for, 465, 478
Enzymes, 507-08
Ephedrine, 4, 8, 172
Epilepsy, mixture for, 474
Erotomania, plants for, 66
Erysipelas, 210, 225, 261; mixture for, 474
Essence, described, 40
Euphoriant, euphorigen, 54. See also Boredom.
Expectorant, 54
Extract, cold. See Cold extract.
Eyes, plants for, 67
Eyewash: described, 44; plants for, 45, 46, 92, 100, 132, 190, 210, 225,

226, 239, 270, 296, 330, 335, 337, 366, 375, 393, 416
Facial masks. See Skin, cosmetics for.
Facial steam, herbal, 533
Fatigue. See Tiredness.
Fats, nutritional, 506-07
Feet: baths for, 43; cold feet, 43, 287; odor, 220; sweaty feet, baths for, 45, 145, 388, 402; swollen feet, mixture for, 474; tired feet, 43
Fever: bath for, 42; mixture for, 475; plants for, 54-55 (under "Febrifuge"), 56 (under "Refrigerant"), 67
Fibers, sources of, 566
Fingernails, weak, 535
Flatulence. See Gas, intestinal.
Fleur-de-lis, 594-95
Flower, 13-15; inflorescences, 14; parts of, 13-15; pollination of, 15; types of, 15
Flu. See Influenza.
Folk medicine. See Medicine.
Fomentation, described, 41
Foot. See Feet.
Frigidity, plants for, 71
Fruit, 15-16; functions of, 16; types of, 15-16
Galactagogue: mixtures, 475, 487; plants, 55
Galen, 4, 5, 100
Gall bladder: mixture for, 475; plants for, 67-68
Gallstones: mixture for, 476; plants for, 68
Gargle: mixture for, 484; plants for, 78-79, 80
Gas, intestinal: bath for, 42; mixtures for, 462; plants for, 52 (under "Carminative"), 68
Gastroenteritis, plants for, 68
Gastrointestinal system, mixtures for, 476
Genito-urinary ailments, plants for, 68-69
Genus, defined, 16-17
Gerard, John, 5-6
German folk beliefs, 583, 585, 599, 601, 620
Germanic Tribes, plant myths: Baldur, 603 (mistletoe); "fate tree," 599 (linden); Freyja, 584 (daisy), 586 (elder), 615 rose; Siegfried, 599 (linden); Thor, 593 (houseleek), 607 (oak); Yggdrasill, 581 (European ash)
Gibbons, Euell, 25, 493, 568
Gout: mixture for, 476-77; plants for, 69
Gravel, mixture for, 477. See also Stones.
Greek beliefs or practices, 4, 5, 192, 318, 571, 576, 577-78, 579, 580, 582, 584, 586-87, 588, 589, 591, 594, 595, 597, 598, 601, 602, 604, 606, 607, 608, 609-10, 611, 613-15, 616, 617, 618, 621, 622
Greek plant myths: Aphrodite-Adonis, 615 (rose); Aphrodite's plants, 584 (daisy), 602 (mandrake, marjoram); Apollo-Daphne, 597 laurel); Apple of

Greek plant myths *(Continued)*
Discord, 577-78; Apples of Hesperides, 578; Archemorus, 609-
10 (parsley); Athena-Poseidon,
608 (olive); Baucus-Philemon,
598-99, 608 (oak and linden);
Cerberus-Herakles, 604 (monkshood), 613-14 (poplar); Chloris,
rose, 614-15; Cupid-Harpocrates,
615 (rose); Dionysus, 586-87
(English ivy), 588 (fig); Gany-
mede, 621 (tansy); Heliades-
Phaeton, 613-14 (poplar); Hippo-
menes-Atalanta, 578 (apple); Iris,
594; Melampus, 582 (black hel-
lebore); Myrrha, 606-07 (myrrh);
Odysseus-Circe, 589-90 (garlic);
Paeon, 611 (peony); Persephone,
613 (pomegranate); Pyramus-
Thisbe, 605-06 (mulberry); three
sisters of fate, 580 (belladonna);
Zeus and Io, 588 (garden violet);
Zeus, the thundergod, 607 (oak)
Grimm's Fairy Tales, 578
Grippe. *See* Iufluenza.
Gum benzoin, 37, 40, 541
Gum mastic, 541, 565
Gums, plants for, 69
Hahnemann, Samuel, 6
Hair: blonde, 531, 534; dry, 533-34;
loss of, 69, 477; rinses, 531, 534,
535; setting preparations, 531, 532;
to darken, 535; to stimulate
growth, 535
Half bath, 42
Halitosis, plants for, 69. *See also*
Breath sweeteners.
Hashishin, 592
Hay Fever. *See* Allergy.
Headache: baths for, 42, 43; plants
for, 69-70
Heart: nervous, mixture for, 477;
plants for, 51-52 (under "Cardi-
ac"), 70
Hemorrhage, to stop; mixture for
lung hemorrhage, 464; plants for,
52 (under "Coagulant"), 55
(under "Hemostatic"), 57 under
"Styptic"), 70-71
Hemorrhoids: baths for, 43, 46, 145,
417; mixtures for 478; plants for,
71
Hemp. *See* Cannabis.
Herb, definitions of, 3, 21, 86
Herbalism: definition, 3, history,
3-9; modern, 8-9
Herbals: age of herbals, 5, Bankes',
617; Chinese, 4, *De Materia
Medica*, 4, 595; *The English
Physician Enlarged*, 5; *Grete
Herball*, 5; *The Herball or General Historie of Plants*, 5
Herb dealers, 27-28, 543-44; list of,
30-35
Herb garden, 26-27, 510
Herb preparations, defined: baths,
41-47; cold compress, 41; cold
extract, 38, decoction, 38, essence,
40; fomentation, 41; juice, 38-39;
infusion, 37-38; ointment, 40;
poultice, 40-41; powder, 39; syrup,
39; tincture, 39

Herbs: buying, 27-28, 543-44; col-
lecting, 25-26; drying, 28; grow-
ing, 26-27, 510; identifying, 26;
storing, 29
Herpes, 111, 137, 153, 176, 182, 293,
399
Hippocrates, 4, 190, 617
Hoarseness: mixtures for, 480-81;
plants for, 71
Homeopathy, 6-7, 8, 9
Honey plants, 566
Hormones, 508
Hydrotherapy, 41-47. *See also*
Baths.
I-Ching, 602
Impotence, plants for, 71
India, 543, 588, 619, 620, 622, 623
Indians, American: herbs in medicine, 6, 125, 129, 130, 159, 172,
178, 188, 207, 209, 228, 234, 240,
254, 264, 273, 278, 279, 281, 283,
285, 292, 304, 306, 307, 309, 311,
313, 315, 321, 325, 327, 347, 351,
356, 357, 359, 361, 362, 366, 367,
371, 373, 375, 376, 378, 384, 391,
392, 394, 396, 412, 418; beverages,
522, 523, 524; plant legends, 581,
593-94, 596, 599-600, 602, 610, 611-
12
Indigestion, plants for, 71-72. *See
also* Digestion.
Inflammation: baths for, 43; plants
for, 50 (under "Antiphlogistic"),
72
Influenza: mixture for, 478; plants
for, 72
Infusion, described, 37-38
Insect bites, plants for, 72
Insecticides, 566-67
Insect repellents, 566
Insomnia: baths for, 42, 43, 45;
mixtures for, 478-79; plants for,
55 (under "Hypnotic"), 55 (under
"Narcotic"), 72-73
Iodine, 505
Iron, 505-06
Irritation, skin, 92, 94, 101, 114,
155, 183, 187, 190, 201, 214, 229,
235-36, 256, 258, 263, 275, 295,
371, 373, 406, 410, 417
Itching: bath for, 275; plants for,
98, 109, 181, 182, 218, 225, 284,
297, 304, 321, 333, 358, 383, 385,
411
Jaundice. *See* Liver.
Juice: beverages, 527-28; described,
38-39; mixtures, 350, 459, 465, 487
Kidney: mixtures for, 480; plants
for, 73; stones (*see* Stones)
Kneipp, Sebastian, 7, 27
Labdanum, 541
Lactation: mixtures for, 475, 487;
plants for, 73
Laryngitis, mixture for, 480-81
Laxative. *See* Constipation.
Leaf, 12-13; arrangement of, 12-13;
illustrations of, 14, parts of, 13;
types of, 13
Legends, 575-624. *See also names of
various peoples (Greeks, Chinese,
etc.).*
Leucorrhea: mixture for, 481; plants
for, 73

Liniment, mixture for, 481
Liqueurs, plants used in, 528-29
Liver: mixtures for, 481-82; plants for, 55 (under "Hepatic"), 73-74
Livestock feed, plants for, 567
Lumbago. See Backache.
Lungs: mixtures for, 462-63; plants for, 56 (under "Pectoral"), 74
Lust, Dr. Benedict, 7
Mace, 294, 510, 514, 515, 529, 541
Magnesium, 502
Manganese, 506
Marijuana, 592
Mayonnaise, cosmetic use, 536
Measles: mixture for, 482; plants for, 281, 308
Medicinal effects, defined, 48-58
Medicine: folk, 4, 5, 6, 192, 218, 222, 232, 247, 249, 326, 336, 340, 368, 372, 395, 399, 417; Greek, 4, 192, 318, 582, 601, 602; historical, 3-7; medieval, 5, 572, 577, 578-79, 582, 583, 593, 600, 618, 622; modern, 8-9, 84; historic 4; Roman, 4, 192, 582, 601, 617, 618; U.S. 6-7
Medieval beliefs and practices, 5, 203, 571, 572, 576, 577, 578-79, 580, 582, 583, 584, 585, 586, 587, 589, 591, 592, 593, 594, 595, 596, 597, 599, 600, 601, 603, 604, 605, 606, 609, 610, 612, 617, 618, 619, 620, 621, 622, 624
Menopause: bath for, 42; plants for, 74
Menstrual problems: bath for, 43; mixtures for, 482-83; plants for, 54, under "Emmenagogues"), 74-75
Metabolism, mixtures to stimulate, 483
Middle Ages. See Medieval beliefs and practices.
Migraine. See Headache.
Milk bath, 536
Milk, mother's. See Lactation.
Minerals, 501-06
Mixtures, herbal, 454-92
Mohammedans, 588, 615
Moisturizers. See Skin, cosmetics for.
Molasses, blackstrap, 498, 501, 502, 503, 504, 505, 507
Mordants, for dyeing, 544-45
Morning sickness. See Nausea.
Morphine, 8
Mouthwash: mixture for, 484; plants for, 565. See also Halitosis.
Mushrooms, 495
Mustard plaster, 40, 287-88
Names of plants. See Plant names.
Napoleon, 588
Natural healing, 7-8
Naturopathy, 7, 8, 9
Nausea, plants for, 49 (under "Antiemetic"), 75
Nervous conditions: baths for, 42, 45, 46, 47, 98; mixtures for, 484; plants for, 51 (under "Calmative"), 52 (under "Depressant"), 56 (under "Nervine"), 56 (under "Sedative"), 75-76

Neuralgia: bath for, 46; plants for, 76
New Mexican folk beliefs, 579, 589
Niacin, 500
Nicotinic acid. See Niacin.
Nightmare, mixture for, 485
Night sweats: mixture for, 485; plants for, 76
Nosebleed: footbath for, 43; plants for, 70-71
Nutrition, 493-508
Obesity: mixture for, 485; plants for, 76
Oils: edible, 567; flower oils, 541; hot oil treatments for skin and hair, 533; illuminating, 568; lubricating, 568; used in soap, 568; vegetable and animal oils vs. mineral oils, 533
Oily skin. See Skin.
Ointment, described, 40
Oriental beliefs and practices, 4, 8, 206, 337, 588, 589, 590, 591, 595, 602, 604, 605, 608, 609, 611, 612-13, 619, 622, 623
Osteopathy, 8
Pain, analgesic plants, 49; anodyne bath for, 145; anodynes, 49; narcotic plants, 55
Paracelsus 6, 599
Parasiticides, 566-67
Persian beliefs and practices, 579, 592, 595, 623
Perspiration: antihydrotic plants, 49; diaphoretic plants, 53; mixtures to prevent, 485; mixtures to promote, 485-86; night sweats, 76, 485
Phosphorus, 502-03
Photosynthesis, 13
Piles. See Hemorrhoids.
Pimples. See Acne.
Plant names, 16-17, 84-85
Plant parts, described, 11-16
Pleurisy, mixtures for, 486
Pliny the Elder, 170, 611, 617, 620, 622
Poison ivy (oak), remedies for, 568
Potassium, 503-04
Potpourri, 537-41; described, 537-40; ingredients for, 540-41
Poultice: described, 40-41; mixture for, 486
Powder, described, 39
Pregnancy, mixture to ease, 487. See also Childbirth.
Prostate: plants for, 76; vapor bath for, 45
Protein, 494-95
Psychic healings, 8, 9
Pyridoxine. See Vitamin B6.
Quinine, 8, 306
Reserpine, 8
Respiratory problems: baths for, 45, 46; mixture for, 468; plants for, 54 (under "Expectorant"). See also Colds, Coughs.
Rheumatism: baths for 45, 46, 47; mixtures for, 476-77, 487; plants for, 77
Rhizome. See Rootstock.
Riboflavin. See Vitamin B2.

Ringworm, 92, 103, 153, 210, 258, 285, 312, 347, 387, 398
Roman beliefs and practices, 4, 5, 170, 192, 524, 580, 581, 584, 587, 588, 589, 591, 592-93, 597, 598, 600, 601, 606, 607-08, 609-10, 611, 613, 614 617-18, 620, 622
Roman plant myths: Bacchus, 588 (fig); Belides-Vertumnus, 584 (daisy); Flora, 614 (rose); Jupiter, 592-93 (houseleek), 607 (oak); Menthe-Pluto, 602 (mint); Romulus-Remus, 588 (fig); Venus, 584 (daisy), 600 (maidenhair fern)
Roots, described, 11
Rootstock, described, 11-12
Roses, War of the, 616
Rosewood oil, 541
Runner, defined, 12
Sachet, 539
St. John's Eve, 600, 619
Scabies, 98, 100, 122, 181, 197, 202, 246
Scalp: mixture for, 477. See also Hair.
Scents, herbal, 537-41
Sciatica, plants for, 77
Scrofula, plants for, 50 (under "Antiscrofulous")
Seasickness, 265. See also Nausea.
Seasoning, food, 509-10.
Sexual desire, 77
Shampoos, plants for, 568
Sinus problems: plants for, 77; vapor bath for, 44
Sitzbath, described, 43; mixture for, 458
Skin, cosmetics for: dry skin, 531, 533, 534, 535; fresheners, 531, 535; moisturizers, 531, 532, 533, 534; oily skin, 530-31, 534, 535, 536; to remove flaky skin, 534; wrinkled skin, 531, 532.
Skin, medicinal treatment: baths for, 45, 46, 47, 118, 162, 163, 259, 417; mixtures for, 487; plants for, 54 (under "Exanthematous"), 77-78, 534. See also Acne, Boils, Burns, Eczema, Herpes, Irritation, Itching, Ringworm, Scabies, Sunburn.
Sleep, mixtures to promote, 478-80. See also Insomnia.
Smallpox, 311
Smoking: plants to help stop, 78; tobacco substitutes, 569
Snakebite, 121, 126-27, 241, 257, 351, 384
Soap: oils for, 568; substitutes for, 568
Sodium, 504
Sore throat, plants for, 78-79
Sour cream, cosmetic use, 536
Spasms: mixture for, 470; plants for, 50 (under "Antispasmodic"). See also Cramps.
Species, defined, 16-17
Spices, 509-19
Sprains, bath for, 47
Stem, described, 11-12
Stimulant: baths, 43, 46, 47, 249,

287, 379; mixtures, 487-88; plants, 57
Stomach: mixtures for, 488-90; plants for, 57 (under "stomachic"), 79-80
Stomach, upset. See Indigestion.
Stomatitis, plants for, 80
Stones: mixture for, 477; plants for, 49 (under "Antilithic"). See also Gallstones.
Storax, 541, 572
Sulfur, 504-05
Sumerians, 4, 571
Sunburn: bath for, 46; plants for, 92, 232, 252
Swelling, to reduce: baths for, 45, 47; mixture for, 474
Syrup, described, 39
Tanning, plants for, 569
Teas, beverage, 520-26
Tension. See Nervous conditions.
Theophrastus, 5
Thiamine. See Vitamine B1.
Throat, sore. See Sore throat.
Thundergod legends, 592-93 (houseleek), 607 (oak)
Tincture, described, 39
Tiredness, bath for, 47. See also Stimulant.
Tobacco: additives to, 569; substitutes for, 569. See also Smoking.
Tocopherol. See Vitamin E.
Tonic: mixtures, 490; plants, 57-58
Tonsillitis: mixture for, 490-91; plants for, 80
Toothache, plants for, 80
Torula yeast, 500
Tree of Life, 621-22
Tuberculosis. See Lungs.
Tungus tribe, 597
Ulcers, stomach: mixtures, 489; plants for, 79-80
Urinary problems: diuretic plants, 53-54; genito-urinary ailments, plants for, 68-69; incomplete urination, plants for, 80-81; mixture, 491. See also Cystitis, Kidney, Stones.
Vaginal douche: mixtures for, 472-73; plants for, 81
Vapor bath, described, 44-45. See also Facial steam.
Varicose veins: baths for 43, 46, 192; mixture for, 492; plants for, 81
Venereal disease. See Genito-urinary ailments.
Vermouth, plants for flavoring, 529
Vertigo, 342
Virgil, 620, 622
Vitamins, 496-500
Vitamin A, 496-97
Vitamin B1, 497
Vitamin B2, 497
Vitamin B6, 498
Vitamin B12, 498
Vitamin C, 498-99
Vitamin D, 496, 499
Vitamin E, 499-500
Vitamin K, 496, 500

Vomiting: to induce, 54 (under "Emetic") to relieve, 49 (under "Antiemetic"), 75
Wales and the leek, 598
Warts, plants for, 81
Water cure. See Hydrotherapy.
Waxes, plant sources of, 569
Wheat germ, 495, 497, 498, 500, 503, 535
Whooping cough, mixtures for, 469-70
Wine, plants to make and flavor, 529
Wise-women, 5
Witchcraft, 577, 580, 581, 582, 583, 584, 585, 586, 587, 589, 591, 596, 597, 600, 601-02, 604, 606, 617, 618
Woods: for exterior use, 570; for interior use, 570; for small objects, 569-70
Worms: plants for, 49 (under "Anthelmintic"), 58 (under "Vermifuge"), 81; mixture for, 309
Wounds: bath for, 46; plants for, 58 (under "Vulnerary"), 81-82. See also Hemorrhage.
Wrinkles. See Skin, cosmetics for.
Yogurt, cosmetic use, 536
Yggdrasill, 581
Zinc, 506
Zodiac, 571, 573-74

LIST OF PLANTS BY BOTANICAL NAME

Abies spp. .... Fir Tree
Acacia spp. .... Acacia
Acacia catechu .... Catechu
Acacia concinna .... Soap Pod
Acacia farnesiana ... Sweet Acacia
Acacia mollissima
    and other spp. .... Black Wattle
Acacia senegal ... . Acacia
Acer pseudo-
    platanus .... Sycamore Maple
Acer rubrum .... Red Maple
Acer saccharum
    and other spp. .... Maple
Achillea millefolium ...... Milfoil
Aconitum napellus ... Monkshood
Acorus calamus ...... Sweet Flag
Adansonia digitata .... Baobab
Adiantum pedatum ... Maidenhair
Aesculus
    hippocastanum .. Horse Chestnut
Aethusa cynapium .... Dog Poison
Agave spp. .... Agave
Agave americana .... Agave
Agave schottii .... Amole
Agave sisalana .... Agave
Agrimonia spp. .... Agrimony
Agrimonia
    eupatoria .... Sticklewort
Agropyron repens .... Witch Grass
Alaria esculenta .... Kelp
Alchemilla
    alpina ... Silvery Lady's Mantle
Alchemilla
    vulgaris .... Lady's Mantle
Aletris farinosa ...... Star Grass
Alkanna tinctoria .... Alkanet
Allium ascalonicum ...... Shallot
Allium cepa .... Onion
Allium porrum .... Leek
Allium sativum .... Garlic
Allium schoenoprasum ...... Chive
Allium ursinum ..... Bear's Garlic
Alnus spp. .... Alder
Alnus glutinosa ...... Black Alder
Alnus rubra .... Red Alder
Alnus serrulata.. .. Smooth Alder
Aloe latifolia .... Aloe
Aloe perryi .... Bombay Aloe
Aloe saponaria .... Aloe
Aloe tenuior .... Aloe
Aloe vera .... Aloe

Aloysia
    triphylla ...... Lemon Verbena
Alpinia galanga .... Galangal
Althaea officinalis .... Althea
Althaea rosea .... Hollyhock
Amaranthus
    hypochondriacus ..... Amaranth
Amaranthus
    retroflexus .... Green Amaranth
Anacardium occidentale .. Cashew
Anagallis
    arvensis .... Red Pimpernel
Ananas comosus .... Pineapple
Anaphalis
    margaritacea . Pearly Everlasting
Anchusa officinalis ...... Bugloss
Andropogon
    virginicus .... Beard Grass
Anemone patens ... Pasque Flower
Anethum graveolens .... Dill
Angelica spp. .... Angelica
Angelica
    archangelica . European Angelica
Angelica atropurpurea
                    American Angelica
Angelica
    sylvestris .... Wild Angelica
Antennaria dioica ..... Cat's Foot
Anthemis cotula .... Mayweed
Anthemis
    nobilis .... Roman Camomile
Anthemis
    tinctoria ..... Dyer's Camomile
Anthoxanthum
    odoratum .. Sweet Vernal Grass
Anthriscus cerefolium .... Chervil
Anthyllis vulneraria . Kidney Vetch
Apium graveolens .... Celery
Apocynum
    androsaemifolium .... Dogbane
Apocynum
    cannabinum .... Hemp Dogbane
Aquilegia vulgaris ..... Columbine
Arachis hypogaea .... Peanut
Aralia spp. .... Spikenard
Aralia
    nudicaulis .... Wild Sarsaparilla
Aralia
    racemosa .. American Spikenard
Arctium lappa .... Burdock
Arctostaphylos
    tomentosa .... Manzanita

Arctostaphylos
uva-ursi .... Bearberry
Arisaema
triphyllum ...... Indian Turnip
Aristolochia clematitis .. Birchwort
Aristolochia
serpentaria .. Virginia Snakeroot
Armoracia
lapathifolia .... Horseradish
Arnica montana .... Arnica
Artemisia abronatum .. Lad's Love
Artemisia
absinthium .... Wormwood
Artemisia dracunculus .. Tarragon
Artemisia vulgaris ...... Mugwort
Arum maculatum .... Arum
Asarum canadense ... Wild Ginger
Asarum europaeum ...... Asarum
Asclepias syriaca ...... Milkweed
Asclepias tuberosa .. Pleurisy Root
Asparagus
officinalis .... Asparagus
Asperula odorata ...... Woodruff
Aster spp. .... Aster
Atriplex californica ...... Saltbush
Atropa belladonna .... Belladonna
Avena sativa .... Oat
Baptisia tinctoria .... Wild Indigo
Barbarea vulgaris .... Winter Cress
Barosma betulina .... Buchu
Barosma crenulata .. Short Buchu
Barosma serratifolia .. Long Buchu
Bellis perennis .... Wild Daisy
Berberis vulgaris .... Barberry
Bertholletia excelsa .... Brazil Nut
Beta vulgaris .... Beet
Beta vulgaris var. cicla ..... Chard
Betula spp. .... Birch
Betula alba .... White Birch
Betula lenta .... Black Birch
Betula papyrifera .... Canoe Birch
Bixa orellana .... Annatto
Boehmeria nivea .... Ramie
Borago officinalis .... Borage
Boswellia spp. .. Frankincense Tree
Brassica spp. .... Mustard
Brassica caulorapa ...... Kohlrabi
Brassica hirta .... White Mustard
Brassica napobrassica ... Rutabaga
Brassica napus .... Rape
Brassica nigra .... Black Mustard
Brassica oleracea
var. *acephala* .... Collard
Brassica oleracea
var. *acephala* .... Kale
Brassica oleracea
var. *botrytis* .... Cauliflower
Brassica oleracea
var. *capitata* .... Cabbage
Brassica oleracea
var. *gemmifera* . Brussels Sprouts
Brassica oleracea
var. *italica* .... Broccoli
Brassica rapa .... Turnip
Bryonia spp. .... Bryony
Bryonia alba .... White Bryony
Bryonia dioica .... Red Bryony
Bursera aloexylon .... Linaloe
Butyrospermum
parkii .... Shea Tree
Buxus sempervirens ..... Boxwood
Caesalpinia coriaria ..... Divi-Divi

Calendula officinalis .... Calendula
Calluna vulgaris .... Heather
Caltha palustris .... Cowslip
Canangium
odoratum .... Ylang-Ylang
Cannabis sativus .... Cannabis
Capparis spinosa .... Capers
Capsella bursa-
pastoris .... ..Shepherd's Purse
Capsicum frutescens ..... Cayenne
Capsicum frutescens
vars. .... Paprika
Capsicum frutenscens var.
grossum .... Green Pepper
Carduus marianus .... Milk Thistle
Carex arenaria .... Red Sedge
Carica papaya .... Papaya
Carlina acaulis .... Carline Thistle
Carthamus tinctorius .... Safflower
Carum carvi .... Caraway
Carya illinoensis .... Pecan
Carya ovata .... Shagbark Hickory
Carya tomentosa . Big-bud Hickory
Caryophyllus aromaticus .... Clove
Cassia spp. .... Senna
Cassia
acutifolia .... Alexandrian Senna
Cassia
angustifolia ... Tinnevelly Senna
Cassia fasciculata ... Partridge Pea
Cassia fistula ..... Purging Cassia
Cassia
marilandica .... American Senna
Castanea
dentata ..... American Chestnut
Caulophyllum
thalictroides ...... Blue Cohosh
Ceanothus
americanus ..... New Jersey Tea
Cedrus spp. .... Cedar
Celtis occidentalis ..... Hackberry
Centaurea cyanus ..... Cornflower
Centaurium
umbellatum . European Centaury
Certraria islandica .. Iceland Moss
Cheiranthus cheiri ..... Wallflower
Chelidonum majus ..... Celandine
Chelone glabra ...... Turtlebloom
Chenopodium
album .... Lamb's-quarters
Chenopodium
ambrosioides ...... Mexican Tea
Chenopodium ambrosioides
var. *anthelminticum* ... Wormseed
Chenopodium californicum
                    California Soap Plant
Chimaphila
umbellata .... Pipsissewa
Chionanthus virginicus . Fringe Tree
Chlorogalum pomeridianum
                    California Soaproot
Chlorophora tinctoria ...... Fustic
Chondrus crispus ...... Irish Moss
Chrysanthemum
balsamita .... Costmary
Chrysanthemum
cinerariaefolium ..... Pyrethrum
Chrysanthemum
coccineum .... Pyrethrum
Chrysanthemum
leucanthemum ..... White Weed

Chrysanthemum
parthenium .... Feverfew
Cicer arietinum .... Garbanzo Bean
Cichorium endivia .... Endive
Cichorium intybus .... Chicory
Cicuta
virosa . European Water Hemlock
Cimicifuga
racemosa .... Black Cohosh
Cinchona spp. ..... Peruvian Bark
Cinnamomum
camphora .... Camphor Tree
Cinnamomum cassia ...... Cassia
Cinnamomum
zeylanicum .... Cinnamon
Cistus ladaniferus .... Rockrose
Cistus villosus var.
undulatus .... Rockrose
Citrullus vulgaris .... Watermelon
Citrus aurantifolia .... Lime
Citrus aurantium.. .. Bitter-Orange
Citrus bergamia .... Bergamot
Citrus limon .... Lemon
Citrus paradisi .... Grapefruit
Citrus reticulata .... Tangerine
Citrus sinensis ...... Sweet Orange
Cladonia
rangiferina ...... Reindeer Moss
Claviceps purpurea .... Ergot
Clematis
virginiana ...... Virgin's Bower
Cnicus
benedictus .. St. Benedict Thistle
Cocculus palmatus ...... Colombo
Cochlearia officinalis . Scurvy Grass
Cocos nucifera .... Coconut
Coffea arabica .... Coffee
Cola acuminata .... Kola Tree
Colchicum
autumnale ..... Meadow Saffron
Collinsonia
canadensis .... Stone Root
Combretum apiculatum .. Rooibos
Commiphora
meccanensis .... Balm of Gilead
Commiphora myrrha ...... Myrrh
Comptonia peregrina .. Sweet Fern
Comptonia peregrina
var. asplenifolia ..... Sweet Fern
Conium
maculatum .... Poison Hemlock
Convallaria
majalis ...... Lily of the Valley
Convolvulus scoparius ... Rhodium
Convolvulus
sepium .... Hedge Bindweed
Convolvulus virgatus .... Rhodium
Conyza canadensis ..... Horseweed
Copernicia cerifera .... Carnauba
Coptis trifolia .... Goldthread
Corallorhiza
odontorhiza .... Coral Root
Corchorus capsularis
and other spp. .... Jute
Coreopsis tinctoria ..... Calliopsis
Coriandrum sativum .... Coriander
Cornus florida .... Dogwood
Corydalis cava .... Corydalis
Corydalis formosa .. Turkey Corn
Corylus americana ...... Hazelnut
Covillea mexicana .. Creosote Bush

Crataegus
oxyacantha .... Hawthorn
Crocus sativus .... Saffron
Cucumis melo var.
cantalupensis .... Cantaloupe
Cucumis sativus .... Cucumber
Cucurbita
foetidissima .... Wild Gourd
Cucurbita pepo .... Pumpkin
Cucurbita pepo var.
melopepo .... Zucchini
Cuminum cyminum .... Cumin
Cunila origanoides .... Dittany
Cupressus spp. .... Cypress
Curcuma longa .... Turmeric
Cyclamen europaeum ... Cyclamen
Cydonia oblonga .... Quince
Cymbopogon
citratus .... Lemongrass
Cynara scolymus .... Artichoke
Cynoglossum
morrisoni .. Virginia Mouse-ear
Cynoglossum
officinale .... Hound's-tongue
Cyperus esculentus .... Chufa
Cypripedium
pubescens .... Nerve Root
Cytisus scoparius ... Scotch Broom
Dahlbergia nigra
and other spp. .... Rosewood
Dalea emoryi .... Indigo Bush
Daphne mezereum ...... Mezereon
Datura
stramonium ...... Jimson Weed
Daucus carota .... Carrot
Delphinium
consolida .... Larkspur
Derris spp. .... Derris Plant
Dianthus
caryophyllus .... Carnation
Dictamus albus .... Fraxinella
Digitalis purpurea ...... Foxglove
Dioscorea spp. ...... Mexican Yam
Dioscorea villosa ...... Wild Yam
Diospyros
virginiana ..... Wild Persimmon
Dipteryx odorata ..... Tonka Bean
Drosera rotundifolia ...... Sundew
Dryopteris filixmas ..... Male Fern
Echinacea angustifolia .. Echinacea
Elaeis guineensis .... Oil Palm
Elettaria
cardamomum .... Cardamom
Ephedra spp. .... Desert Tea
Ephedra sinica .... Ma-huang
Epifagus virginiana .... Beechdrops
Equisetum arvense ... Shave Grass
Erechtites, hieracifolia ... Pilewort
Erigeron canadensis ... Horseweed
Eriodendron
anfractuosum ...... Kapok Tree
Erodium cicutarium ..... Storkbill
Eryngium
aquaticum .... Water Eryngo
Eriodictyon
californicum .... Yerba Santa
Erythraea
centaurium .. European Centaury
Erythronium
americanum .... Adder's Tongue
Eucalyptus calophylla
and other spp. .... Red Gum

Eucalyptus globulus ... Eucalyptus
Euonymus
   americanus .... Strawberry bush
Euonymus
   atropurpureus .... Wahoo
Eupatorium
   cannabinum .... Hemp Agrimony
Eupatorium
   perfoliatum .... Boneset
Eupatorium purpureum
           Queen of the Meadow
Euphorba spp. .... Spurge
Euphorbia
   antisyphilitica .... Candelilla
Euphorbia
   corollata ...... Flowering Spurge
Euphorbia
   cyparissias ...... Cypress Spurge
Euphorbia
   lathyrus .... Garden Spurge
Euphorbia
   maculata ...... Milk-purslane
Euphorbia peplus .... Petty Spurge
Euphorbia pulcherrima .. Poinsettia
Euphrasia
   officinalis .... Red Eyebright
Fagopyrum
   esculentum .... Buckwheat
Fagus spp. .... Beech
Ferula spp. .... Ferula
Ferula assa-foetida ..... Asafetida
Ferula foetida .... Asafetida
Ferula sumbul .... Sumbul
Ficus carica .... Fig Tree
Filipendula
   hexapetala .... Dropwort
Filipendula
   ulmaria .... Meadowsweet
Foeniculum vulgare .... Fennel
Fragaria vesca ... Wild Strawberry
Fraxinus americana .... White Ash
Fraxinus excelsior .. Bird's Tongue
Fraxinum nigra .... Black Ash
Fraxinum oregona .... Oregon Ash
Fraxinum ornus ... Flowering Ash
Fraxinus pubescens ...... Red Ash
Fraxinus
   quadrangulata .... Blue Ash
Fumaria officinalis ...... Fumitory
Galega officinalis ...... Goat's Rue
Galeopsis tetrahit ... Hemp Nettle
Galium spp. .... Bedstraw
Galium aparine .... Cleavers
Galium tinctorium .. Dye Bedstraw
Galium verum ... Yellow Bedstraw
Gardenia spp. .... Gardenia
Gaultheria
   procumbens .... Wintergreen
Gelsemium
   sempervirens .. Yellow Jessamine
Genista tinctoria .... Dyer's Broom
Gentiana spp. .... Gentian
Gentiana catesbaei ... Blue Gentian
Gentiana crinita .. Fringed Gentian
Gentiana lutea .... Yellow Gentian
Gentiana
   quinquefolia ...... Stiff Gentian
Geranium
   maculatum .... Spotted Cranebill
Geranium
   robertianum .... Herb Robert
Gerardia pedicularia ... Feverweed

Geum spp. .... Avens
Geum rivale .... Water Avens
Geum urbanum .... Bennet
Geum virginianum .. Rough Avens
Ginkgo biloba .... Ginkgo
Gladiolus spp. .... Gladiolus
Glycine max .... Soybean
Glycyrrhiza glabra ...... Licorice
Gnaphalium
   polycephalum ... Life Everlasting
Gnaphalium
   uliginosum .... Low Cudweed
Goodyera
   pubescens .. Rattlesnake Plantain
Gossypium spp. .... Cotton
Gratiola officinalis .. Hedge Hyssop
Grindelia robusta ...... Gum Plant
Guaiacum officinale .... Guaiac
Gypsophila
   paniculata .... Baby's Breath
Haematoxylon
   campechianum .... Logwood
Hagenia abyssinica .... Kousso
Hamamelis virginiana . Witch Hazel
Hedeoma pulegioides .. Pennyroyal
Hedera helix .... English Ivy
Helianthemum
   canadense .... Rock-rose
Helianthus annuus ...... Sunflower
Heliotropium
   arborescens .... Heliotrope
Helleborus spp. .... Hellebore
Helleborus foetidus ..... Bearsfoot
Helleborus niger .. Black Hellebore
Helleborus viridis . Green Hellebore
Hepatica
   acutiloba .. Sharp-lobed Hepatica
Hepatica triloba .... Hepatica
Heracleum lanatum ... Masterwort
Hibiscus spp. .... Hibiscus
Hibiscus esculentus .... Okra
Hibiscus moschatus .... Abelmosk
Hibiscus palustris .. Marsh Hibiscus
Hibiscus rosa-
   sinensis .... Rose of China
Hibiscus sabdariffa .. Guinea Sorrel
Hibiscus sagittifolius ..... Hibiscus
Hibiscus surattensis ...... Hibiscus
Hibiscus tiliaceus ...... Corkwood
Hibiscus
   trionum ...... Flower-of-an-hour
Hieracium pilosella .... Mouse Ear
Hordeum vulgare .... Barley
Humulus lupulus .... Hops
Hyacinthus orientalis .... Hyacinth
Hydrangea
   arborescens .... Seven Barks
Hydrastis canadensis .. Goldenseal
Hyoscyamus niger .... Henbane
Hypericum
   perforatum .... St. Johnswort
Hyssopus officinalis .... Hyssop
Ilex spp. .... Holly
Ilex aquifolium .. Mountain Holly
Ilex glabra .... Inkberry
Ilex opaca .... White Holly
Ilex paraguariensis ... Yerba Maté
Ilex verticillata ...... Winterberry
Ilex vomitoria . Indian Black Drink
Illicium anisatum ...... Star Anise
Illicium verum .... Star Anise
Impatiens biflora ...... Jewelweed

Imperatoria
  ostruthium . Imperial Masterwort
Indigofera tinctoria .... Indigo
Inula helentum .... Elecampane
Ipomoea batatas .... Sweet Potato
Ipomoea Jalapa .... Jalap
Ipomoea pandurata .... Wild Jalap
Iris spp. .... Iris
Iris douglasiana .... Iris
Iris florentina .... Orris Root
Iris macrosiphon .... Iris
Iris versicolor .... Blue Flag
Isatis tinctoria .... Woad
Jasminum officinale ...... Jasmine
Jeffersonia diphylla .... Twin Leaf
Juglans spp. .... Walnut
Juglans cinerea .... Butternut
Juglans nigra ...... Black Walnut
Julgans regia ...... English Walnut
Juniperus communis ...... Juniper
Juniperus
  oxycedrus ...... Prickly Juniper
Juniperus virginiana ... Red Cedar
Kalmia latifolia .. Mountain Laurel
Krameria triandra .... Rhatany
Lactuca spp. .... Lettuce
Lactuca sativa ... Common Lettuce
Lactuca virosa .... Prickly Lettuce
Lamium album ...... Blind Nettle
Larix europaea .... Larch
Laurus nobilis .... Laurel
Lavandula officinalis .... Lavender
Lavandula spica .... Aspic
Lavandula vera .... Lavender
Lawsonia inermis .... Henna
Ledum latifolium ... Labrador Tea
Ledum palustre .... Marsh Tea
Lens culinaris .... Lentil
Leonurus cardiaca .... Motherwort
Levisticum officinale ...... Lovage
Liatris spp. .... Blazing Star
Liatris scariosa .. Tall Blazing Star
Liatris spicata . Marsh Blazing Star
Liatris
  squarrosa .... Scaly Blazing Star
Lingustrum vulgare .... Privet
Lilium tigrinum .... Tiger Lily
Limonium spp. .. Marsh Rosemary
Linaria vulgaris .. Yellow Toadflax
Linum catharticum ... Purging Flax
Linum usitatissimum .... Flax
Liquidambar
  orientalis ... Oriental Sweet Gum
Liquidambar
  styraciflua .... Sweet Gum
Liriodendron
  tulipifera .... Tulip Tree
Lithocarpus
  densiflora .... Tanbark Oak
Lithospermum
  ruderale .... Stoneseed
Lobelia cardinalis . Cardinal Flower
Lobelia inflata .... Lobelia
Lodoicea
  seychellarum .. Double Coconut
Lolium
  temulentum .... Bearded Darnel
Lonchocarpus spp. .... Cube Plant
Lonicera
  fragrantissima ..... Honeysuckle
Lophorphora williamsii ... Peyote
Lychnis dioica ...... Red Campion

Lycopersicon esculentum .. Tomato
Lycopodium clavatum .. Club Moss
Lythrum salicaria ..... Loosestrife
Maclura pomifera ... Osage-orange
Magnolia glauca .... Magnolia
Mahonia
  aquifolium .. Wild Oregon Grape
Majorana
  hortensis ...... Sweet Marjoram
Malpighia punicifolia ..... Acerola
Malus bracata .... Wild Crabapple
Malva spp. .... Mallow
Malva rotundifolia .... Low Mallow
Malva sylvestris ..... High Mallow
Mandragora
  officinarum . European Mandrake
Mangifera indica .... Mango
Marrubium vulgare .... Horehound
Matricaria
  chamomilla .. German Camomile
Medicago sativa .... Alfalfa
Melia azedarach ... Pride of China
Melilotus spp. .... Melilot
Melilotus alba ...... White Melilot
Melilotus
  officinalis .... Yellow Melilot
Melissa officinalis .... Balm
Menispermum
  canadense ...... Yellow Parilla
Mentha spp. .... Mint
Mentha aquatica ...... Water Mint
Mentha arvensis .... Field Mint
Mentha citrata .... Orange Mint
Mentha crispa .... Curled Mint
Mentha gentilis .... Apple Mint
Mentha piperita ...... Peppermint
Mentha
  pulegium .. European Pennyroyal
Mentha
  rotundifolia .... Apple Mint
Mentha spicata .... Spearmint
Menyanthes
  trifoliata .... Buck Bean
Mercurialis annua .. Mercury Herb
Mercurialis
  perennis .... Dog's Mercury
Mitchella repens ...... Squaw Vine
Monarda spp. .... Monarda
Monarda didyma ..... Oswego Tea
Monarda fistulosa .. Wild Bergamot
Monarda punctata ..... Horsemint
Monotropa uniflora ... Indian Pipe
Moringa
  oleifera ...... Horseradish Tree
Morus alba .... White Mulberry
Morus nigra ...... Black Mulberry
Morus rubra .... Mulberry
Musa paradisiaca
  var. *sapientum* .... Banana
Myrica cerifera ...... Wax Myrtle
Myristica fragrans .... Nutmeg
Myroxylon balsamum . Balsam Tree
Myroxylon
  pereirae .. Peruvian Balsam Tree
Myrrhis
  odorata .. European Sweet Cicely
Narcissus spp. .... Daffodil
Narcissus jonquilla ...... Jonquill
Narcissus fazetta .... Narcissus
Nasturtium officinale .. Watercress
Nepeta cataria .... Catnip
Nepeta hederacea ..... Ground Ivy

Nicotiana rustica ... Wild Tobacco
Nicotiana tabacum ..... Tobacco
Nymphaea spp. ...... Water Lilly
Nymphaea
    odorata .... White Pond Lily
Nymphaea
    tuberosa .. Tuberous Water Lily
Nyssa sylvatica .... Black Gum
Ocimum basilicum .... Basil
Oenothera
    biennis .... Evening Primrose
Olea europaea .... Olive
Ononis spinosa .... Restharrow
Opuntia spp. .... Prickly Pear
Origanum
    vulgare .... Wild Marjoram
Oryza sativa .... Rice
Osmorhiza longistylis . Sweet Cicely
Osmunda
    cinnamomea .... Cinnamon Fern
Oxalis acetosella ..... Wood Sorrel
Paeonia officinalis .... Peony
Panax spp. .... Ginseng
Panax
    quinquefolius . American Ginseng
Panax schin-seng .. Asiatic Ginseng
Panicum miliaceum .... Millet
Papaver spp. .... Poppy
Papaver rhoeas .... Corn Poppy
Papaver somniferum . Opium Poppy
Parthenocissus
    quinquefolia ...... American Ivy
Passiflora
    incarnata .... Passion Flower
Pastinaca sativa .... Parsnip
Pelargonium spp. ...... Geranium
Pelargonium
    graveolens ..... Rose Geranium
Persea americana .... Avocado
Petroselinum sativum ...... Parsley
Phaseolus limensis ..... Lime Bean
Phaseolus vulgaris ... Kidney Bean
Phoenix dactylifera .... Date Palm
Phoradendron
    flavescens .. American Mistletoe
Phytolacca americana ... Pokeweed
Picea excelsa .... Spruce
Picea mariana ...... Black Spruce
Picraena excelsa .... Quassia
Pimenta officinalis .... Allspice
Pimpinella spp. .... Pimpernel
Pimpinella anisum .... Anise
Pimpinella
    magna .... Greater Pimpernel
Pimpinella
    saxifraga ...... Burnet Saxifrage
Pinus spp. .... Pine
Pinus palustris ..... Longleaf Pine
Pinus ponderosa .. Ponderosa Pine
Pinus resinosa .... Red Pine
Pinus strobus .... White Pine
Piper angustifolium .... Matico
Piper cubeba .... Cubeb
Piper nigrum .... Black Pepper
Piper nigrum .... White Pepper
Pistacia lentiscus ..... Mastic Tree
Pistacia vera .... Pistachio
Pisum sativum .... Pea
Plantago spp. .... Plantain
Plantago
    lanceolata .. Lance-leaf Plantain
Plantago major . Common Plantain
Plantago media .... Hoary Plantain

Plantago psyllium .... Psyllium
Platanus spp. .... Plane Tree
Podophyllum peltatum .. Mandrake
Pogostemon cablin ...... Patchouli
Polianthes tuberosa ..... Tuberose
Polygala spp. .... Milkwort
Polygala amara ... Bitter Milkwort
Polygala senega . Senega Snakeroot
Polygala
    vulgaris ...... European Seneka
Polygonatum
    multiflorum ..... Solomon's Seal
Polygonatum odoratum
                European Solomon's Seal
Polygonum spp. .... Knotweed
Polygonum aviculare ... Knotgrass
Polygonum bistorta ...... Bistort
Polygonum hydropiper . Smartweed
Polygonum
    persicaria .... Lady's Thumb
Polygonum
    punctatum .... Water Smartweed
Polypodium vulgare .. Female Fern
Populus spp. .... Poplar
Populus
    balsamifera .... Tacamahac
Populus
    candicans ...... Balm of Gilead
Populus nigra ...... Black Poplar
Populus nigra var.
    italica ...... Lombardy Poplar
Populus tremula .. European Aspen
Populus
    tremuloides ..... Quaking Aspen
Porphyra spp. .... Laver
Portulaca oleracea ...... Purslane
Potentilla spp. .... Cinquefoil
Potentilla anserina ..... Silverweed
Potentilla
    canadensis .... Five-finger Grass
Potentilla reptans
                European Five-finger Grass
Potentilla
    tormentilla .... Tormentil
Prenanthes alba ...... Lion's Foot
Primula officinalis ...... Primrose
Prosopis juliflora
    var. torreyana .... Mesquite
Prunella vulgaris ...... Woundwort
Prunus spp. .... Cherry
Prunus spp. .... Plum
Prunus americana ...... Wild Plum
Prunus amygdalus .... Almond
Prunus armeniaca .... Apricot
Prunus avium .... Sweet Cherry
Prunus cerasus .... Sour Cherry
Prunus domestica .. Common Plum
Prunus persica .... Peach Tree
Prunus
    serotina ..... Wild Black Cherry
Prunus spinosa .... Blackthorn
Pseudotsuga taxifolia .. Douglas Fir
Psidium guajava .... Guava
Ptelea trifoliata .... Wafer Ash
Pteridium aquilinum
    vars. .... Bracken
Pulmonaria officinalis ... Lungwort
Punica granatum .... Pomegranate
Pycnanthemum
    virginianum .... Wild Hyssop
Pyrola elliptica .... Shinleaf
Pyrus communis .... Pear Tree
Pyrus malus .... Apple Tree

Quercus spp. .... Oak
Quercus alba .... White Oak
Quercus lobata .... Valley Oak
Quercus robur .... English Oak
Quercus rubra .... Red Oak
Quercus tinctoria ...... Black Oak
Quercus velutina ...... Black Oak
Quillaja saponaria .... Quillai
Ranunculus spp. .... Buttercup
Ranunculus
  acris ...... Tall Field Buttercup
Ranunculus
  bulbosus ..... Bulbous Buttercup
Ranunculus
  sceleratus ..... Marsh Crowfoot
Raphanus sativus .... Radish
Rauwolfia serpentina ... Rauwolfia
Reseda luteola .... Weld
Reseda odorata .... Mignonette
Rhamnus spp. .... Buckthorn
Rhamnus
  cathartica .. Common Buckthorn
Rhamnus
  frangula ...... Alder Buckthorn
Rhamnus
  purshiana .... Cascara Sagrada
Rheum
  hybridum ..... Hybrid Rhubarb
Rheum palmatum .... Rhubarb
Rheum
  rhaponticum ... Garden Rhubarb
Rhizophora spp. ...... Mangrove
Rhodymenia
  palmata .... Dulse
Rhus copallina ..... Dwarf Sumac
Rhus glabra .... Sumac
Rhus ovata .... Sugar Bush
Rhus
  sempervirens .. Evergreen Sumac
Rhus succedanea .... Wax Tree
Rhus trilobata var.
  malacophylla ...... Squaw Bush
Ribes spp. .... Currant
Ribes nigrum ...... Black Currant
Ribes rubrum .... Red Currant
Ricinus communis ... Castor Bean
Rosa spp. .... Rose
Rosa Californica . Californian Rose
Rosa canina .... Brier Hip
Rosa centifolia ..... Cabbage Rose
Rosa damascena ... Damask Rose
Rosa eglanteria .... Eglantine
Rosa gallica .... French Rose
Rosa laevigata .... Cherokee Rose
Rosa roxburghii .... Rose
Rosmarinus
  officinalis .... Rosemary
Rubia tinctorum .... Madder
Rubus spp. .... Bramble
Rubus spp. .... Raspberry
Rubus idaeus ... Garden Raspberry
Rubus
  strigosus ... Wild Red Raspberry
Rubus villosus .... Blackberry
Rumex spp. .... Dock
Rumex acetosa .... Sorrel
Rumex aquaticus .... Water Dock
Rumex crispus ...... Yellow Dock
Rumex
  hymenosepalus ... Tanner's Dock
Rumex
  obstusifolius . Broad-leaved Dock
Rumex scutatus .... French Sorrel

Ruta graveolens .... Rue
Sabatia
  angularis ... American Centaury
Saccharomyces
  cerevisiae .... Brewer's Yeast
Saccharum
  officinarum .... Sugar Cane
Salix spp. .... Willow
Salix alba .... White Willow
Salix
  babylonica .... Weeping Willow
Salix caprea .... Sallow
Salix nigra .... Black Willow
Salix purpurea .... Purple Willow
Salvia lyrata .... Wild Sage
Salvia mellifera .... Black Sage
Salvia officinalis .... Sage
Salvia sclarea .... Clary Sage
Sambucus spp. .... Elder
Sambucus
  canadensis ..... American Elder
Sambucus ebulus .... Dwarf Elder
Sambucus nigra ...... Black Elder
Sambucus racemosa .... Red Elder
Sanguinaria canadensis .. Bloodroot
Sanguisorba minor .... Burnet
Sanguisorba
  officinalis .... Great Burnet
Sanicula spp. .... Sanicle
Sanicula
  europaea ..... European Sanicle
Sanicula
  marilandica ... American Sanicle
Santalum album ...... Sandalwood
Sapindus saponaria .... Soapberry
Saponaria officinalis .... Soapwort
Sarracenia purpurea .. Pitcher Plant
Sassafras albidum .... Sassafras
Sassafras variifolium .... Sassafras
Satureja douglasii .... Yerba Buena
Satureja hortensis .... Savory
Satureja montana .. Winter Savory
Schinopsis lorentzii .... Quebracho
Scrophularia nodosa ...... Figwort
Scutellaria lateriflora .... Skullcap
Secale cereale .... Rye
Secale cornatum .... Rye
Sempervivum
  tectorum .... Houseleek
Senecio aureus .... Ragwort
Senecio
  jacoboea .... European Ragwort
Senecio
  vulgaris .... Common Groundsel
Sequoia sempervirens .... Redwood
Serenoa serrulata .... Saw Palmetto
Sesamum indicum .... Sesame
Sesamum orientale .... Sesame
Setaria italica ...... Foxtail Millet
Shepherdia
  argentea .... Buffalo Berry
Shepherdia
  canadensis .... Buffalo Berry
Silphium perfoliatum .. Ragged Cup
Simmondsis chinensis ...... Jojoba
Sisymbrium alliaria .. Hedge Garlic
Sisymbrium
  officinale .... Hedge Mustard
Smilax officinalis ..... Sarsaparilla
Smilax ornata .... Sarsparilla
Solanum spp. .... Nightshade
Solanum dulcamara
              Bittersweet Nightshade

Solanum melongena var.
  esculentum .... Eggplant
Solanum nigrum . Black Nightshade
Solanum tuberosum .... Potato
Solidago spp. .... Goldenrod
Solidago
  nemoralis ...... Gray Goldenrod
Solidago
  odora .... Sweet Goldenrod
Solidago
  virgaurea .. European Goldenrod
Sorbus spp. .... Mountain Ash
Sorbus americana
        American Mountain Ash
Sorbus aucuparia .... Rowan
Sorghum vulgare vars. ... Sorghum
Spigelia marilandica .... Pinkroot
Spinacea oleracea .... Spinach
Stachys officinalis .... Betony
Stellaria media .... Chickweed
Stillingia sylvatica .... Stillingia
Stizolobium
  deeringianum ..... Velvet Bean
Swietania mahogani ... Mahogany
Symphytum officinale .... Comfrey
Symplocarpus
  foetidus .... Skunk Cabbage
Syringia vulgaris .... Lilac
Syzygium aromaticum ...... Clove
Tagetes spp. .... Marigold
Tamarindus indica ...... Tararind
Tanacetum vulgare .... Tansy
Taraxacum officinale .. Dandelion
Taxodium distichum .. Bald Cyress
Taxus baccata .... Yew
Tectona grandis .... Teak
Terminalia bellerica ... Myrobalan
Terminalia chebula .... Myrobalan
Thea sinensis .... Tea
Theobroma cacao .... Cocoa
Thuja occidentalis .... Thuja
Thuja
  orientalis ... Oriental Arborvitae
Thuja plicata .. Giant Arbor Vitae
Thymus spp. .... Thyme
Thymus citrodorus .. Lemon Thyme
Thymus
  serpyllum .... Mother of Thyme
Thymus vulgaris ... Garden Thyme
Tilia spp. .... Linden
Tilia americana .... Basswood
Tilia europaea .. European Linden
Tormentilla erecta ...... Tormentil
Tragopogon spp. .... Goatsbeard
Tragopogon
  porrifolius ... Purple Goatsbeard
Tragopogon
  pratensis .... Yellow Goatsbeard
Trifolium pratense .... Wild Clover
Trifolium repens .... White Clover
Trigonella foenum-
  graecum .... Fenugreek
Trilisa
  odoratissima ...... Wild Vanilla
Trillium erectum .. Purple Trillium
Trillium pendulum ...... Birthroot
Triticum aestivum .... Wheat
Tropaeolum majus .... Nasturtium
Tsuga
  canadensis ..... Hemlock Spruce
Turnera
  aphrodisiaca .. Mexican Damiana

Tussilago farfara .... Coltsfoot
Ulmus spp. .... Elm Tree
Ulmus campestris ... English Elm
Ulmus fulva .... Slippery Elm
Umbellularia
  californica .... California Laurel
Urtica dioica .... Nettle
Urtica urens .... Dwarf Nettle
Vaccinium
  angustifolium .... Blueberry
Vaccinium
  corymbosum .... Blueberry
Vaccinium
  macrocarpon .... Cranberry
Vaccinium myrtillus ..... Bilberry
Vaccinium oxycoccus .. Cranberry
Vaccinium vitis
  idaea .... Alpine Cranberry
Valeriana
  officinalis .... Fragrant Valerian
Vanilla planifolia .... Vanilla
Veratrum
  viride ...... American Hellebore
Verbascum spp. .... Mullein
Verbascum
  nigrum .... Black Mullein
Verbascum
  phlomoides ..... Orange Mullein
Verbascum
  thapsiforme ... Common Mullein
Verbascum thapsus ...... Mullein
Verbena Hastata .... Blue Vervain
Verbena
  officinalis .... European Vervain
Vernonia fasciculata .... Ironweed
Veronica beccabunga .. Brooklime
Veronica officinalis ..... Speedwell
Veronicastrum
  virginicum .... Black Root
Vetiveria
  zizanioides .... Khus-Khus
Viburnum
  opulus .... European Cranberry
Viburnum
  trilobum ... Highbush Cranberry
Vicia spp. .... Vetch
Vicia faba .... Broad Bean
Vinca spp. .... Periwinkle
Vinca major .... Great Periwinkle
Vinca minor
        Early-flowering Periwinkle
Viola odorata ..... Garden Violet
Viola papilionacea .... Blue Violet
Viola tricolor .... Pansy
Viscum
  album ...... European Mistletoe
Vitex agnus-castus .... Chaste Tree
Vitis spp. .... Wild Grape
Vitis vinifera .... Grape
Xanthorhiza
  simplicissima ...... Yellow Root
Xerophyllum tenax ... Bear-grease
Yucca spp. .... Yucca
Yucca arborescens .... Joshua Tree
Yucca baccata ... Spanish Bayonet
Yucca elata .... Soap Tree Yucca
Zanthoxylum
  americanum .... Prickly Ash
Zantedeschia
  aethiopica .... Cally Lily
Zea mays .... Indian Corn
Zingiber officinale .... Ginger

ABOUT THE AUTHOR

JOHN B. LUST (N.D., American School of Naturopathy) is the editor and publisher of *Nature's Path* magazine. A fellow of the Naturopathic Forest University (in Ceylon) and a Permanent Member of the British Guild of Drugless Practitioners, he also holds a degree in Botanical Medicine from the Universidad Naturista Internacional. He is prominent for his thesis which demonstrates the effectiveness of a natural power inherent in everyone. His books reveal how this power can be suitably applied so that man can build and enjoy better physical and mental health. To consolidate the knowledge he gained in the area of botanical medicine (nature's medicine), he has written *THE HERB BOOK*. His other books include: *Lust for Living, Raw Juice Therapy, About Raw Juices, About Diabetes and the Diet, The Massage Manual, Drink Your Troubles Away* and *Ehret's Instructions for Fasting and Dieting*. John B. Lust also edited and translated *My Water Cure* by Father Sebastian Kneipp.